INTRODUCTION

It did not rise mysteriously from a dark peat bog out of the mists. Nor did it emerge from the Gothic imagination of Edgar Allan Poe. It came in a more straightforward fashion from those of us who decided "Batman" should have the charm and wit that was first witnessed in DC comics well before the 1990s.

DC gave us our cue. The magazines were enabling in the sense that we could use them as a touchstone or blueprint. What a gift that was.

When I was a child, my favorite superhero was Batman. He encouraged me to live my life with a certain dedication to moral values. And I found him just human enough to be encouraging to mere mortals. I also got a great laugh as I got older. So it wasn't such a stretch when, in early 1966, I walked nervously into the office of our executive producer, the late Bill Dozier, and listened to his pitch about the way we might create a Batman for the screen. I laughed again. I read the pilot script and laughed louder. Here was something fresh and innovative that I could really cook with. Bob Kane had given all of us an AAA road map to an explosive pop culture phenomenon. Twice a week in color, "Batman" the television show captured a late '60s audience in the same fashion as had Bond and the Beatles. It became a classic that has endeared itself to three generations and still counting.

Some of the biggest stars in entertainment appeared on "Batman," over 200 of them. The entire star firmament of Hollywood wanted to be a part of this extraordinary new vision. Who can forget Burgess Meredith's elegant waddle as The Penguin, the maniacal laugh of Frank Gorshin as Riddler, the chalk-white and frightening face of Cesar Romero as Joker and, of course, the sexy purr and audacious curves of Julie Newmar as Catwoman? From Vincent Price to Milton Berle to Zsa Zsa Gabor to Eartha Kitt to Cliff Robertson to Jerry Lewis to Bruce Lee, our show was a directory of Hollywood elite.

Every day was a fun day full of surprises, regardless of the long hours in and out of costume. When I pulled my cowl over my head I became a child again, playing the same games I had all those years ago reading the *Batman* comic books in a barn on a wheat ranch in Washington State.

I feel especially close to the *Batman* stories of the '60s. They were the cornerstone of our wondrous film experience. It is a pleasure to continue as a party to this exciting adventure that came to life from the pages of DC Comics' *Batman*.

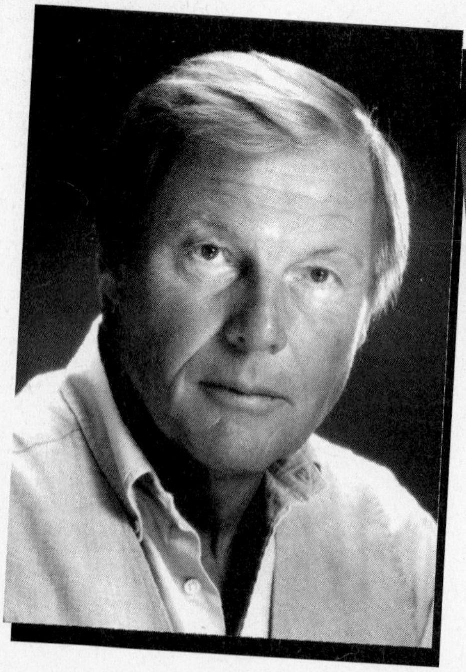

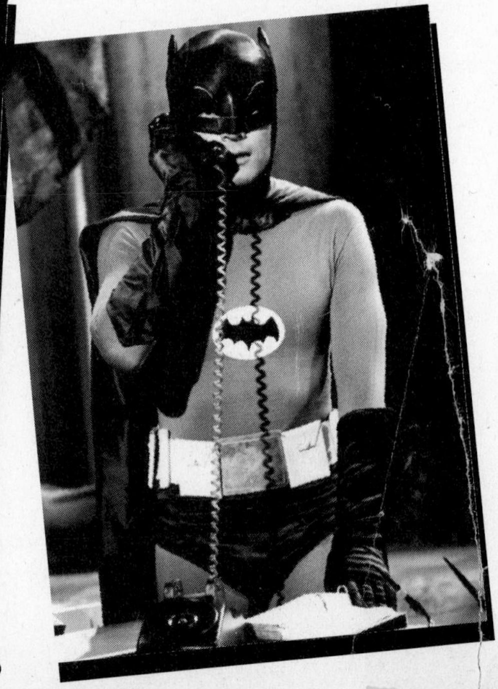

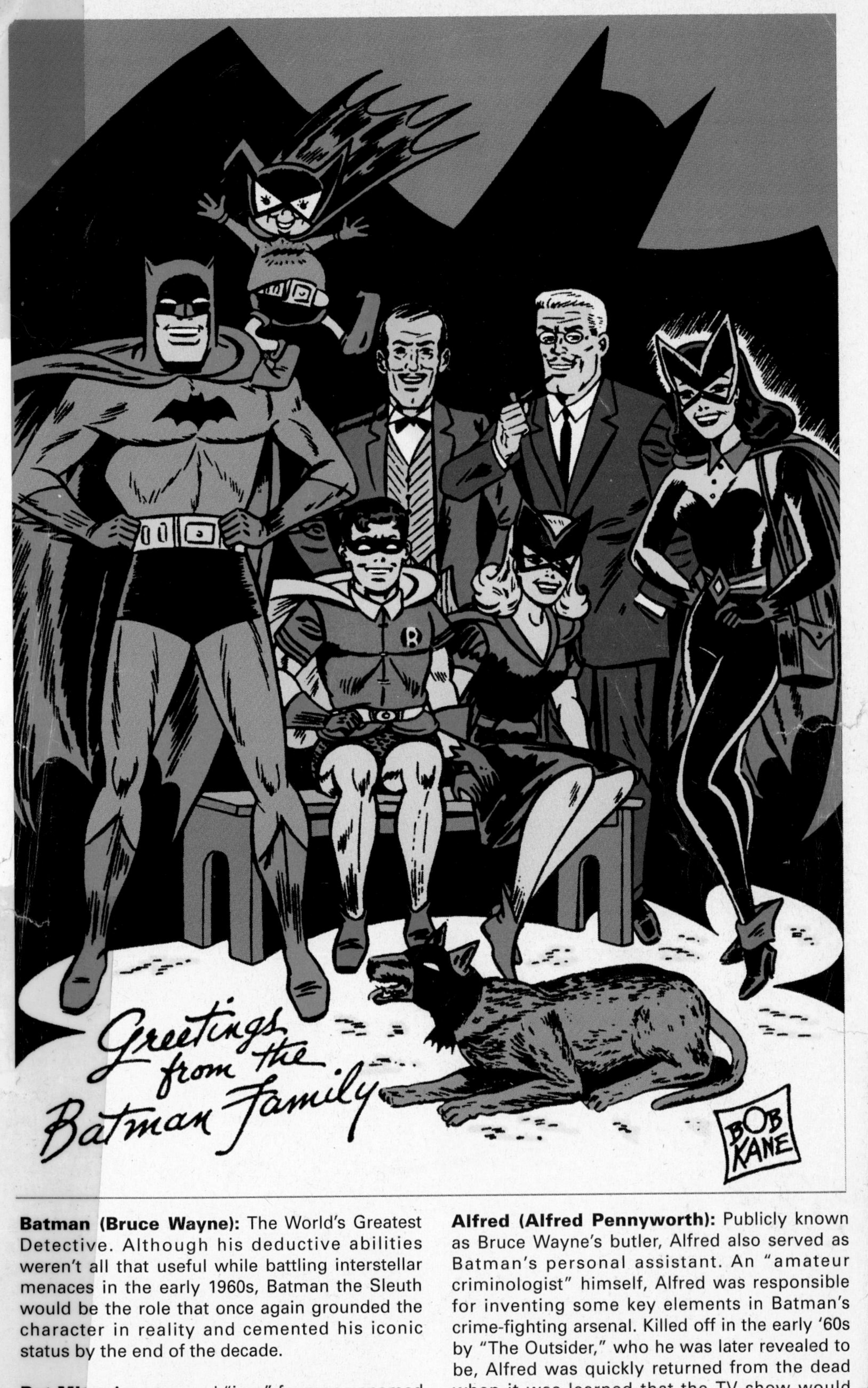
Greetings from the Batman Family
BOB KANE

Batman (Bruce Wayne): The World's Greatest Detective. Although his deductive abilities weren't all that useful while battling interstellar menaces in the early 1960s, Batman the Sleuth would be the role that once again grounded the character in reality and cemented his iconic status by the end of the decade.

Bat-Mite: An unnamed "imp" from an unnamed dimension, Bat-Mite used his magical powers to wreak humorous havoc upon the Batman Family, all the while claiming to be "Batman's biggest fan."

Alfred (Alfred Pennyworth): Publicly known as Bruce Wayne's butler, Alfred also served as Batman's personal assistant. An "amateur criminologist" himself, Alfred was responsible for inventing some key elements in Batman's crime-fighting arsenal. Killed off in the early '60s by "The Outsider," who he was later revealed to be, Alfred was quickly returned from the dead when it was learned that the TV show would prominently feature him.

Continued on page 24

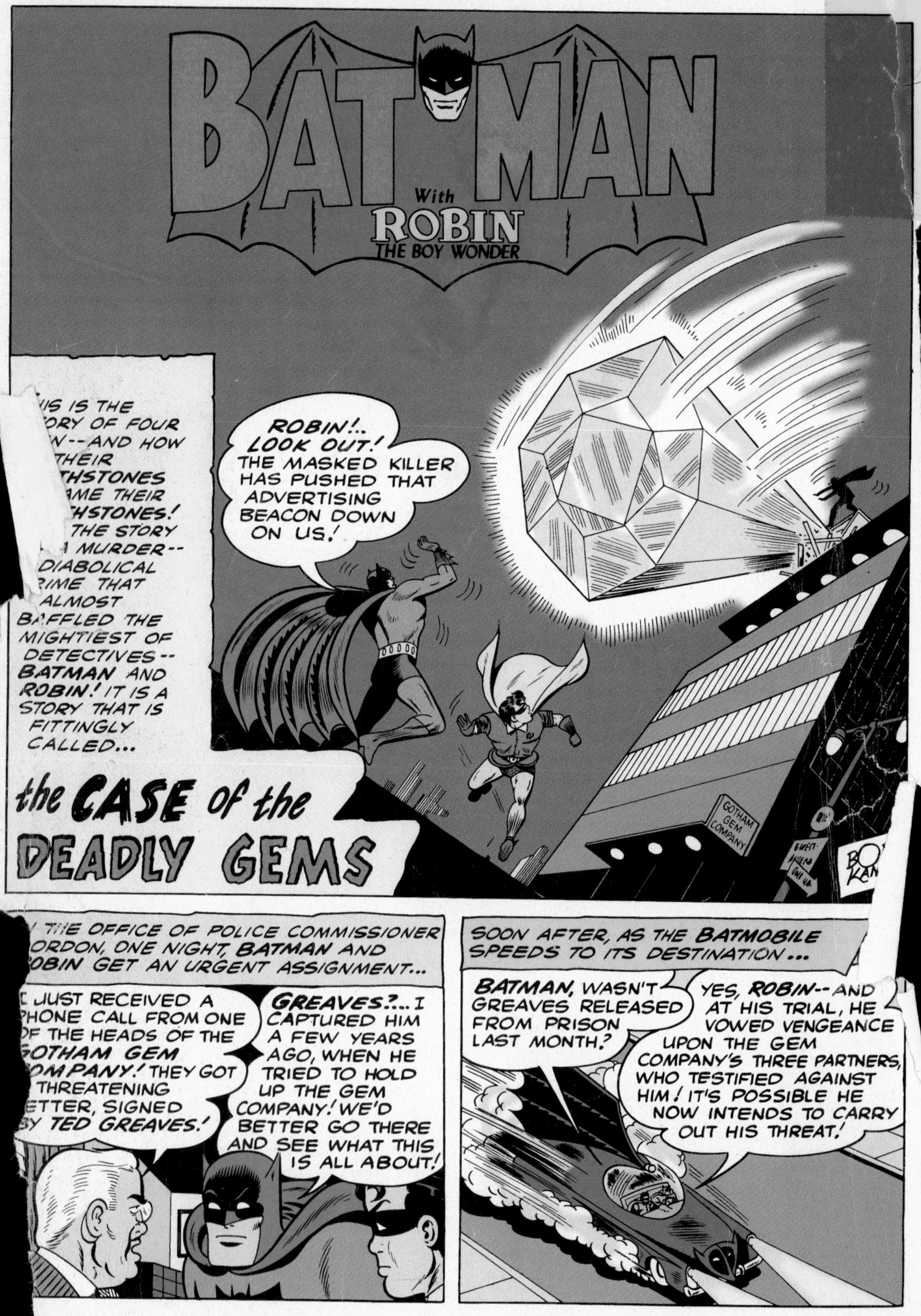
BATMAN
With ROBIN THE BOY WONDER
IS IS THE ORY OF FOUR N--AND HOW THEIR THSTONES AME THEIR THSTONES! THE STORY MURDER-- DIABOLICAL RIME THAT ALMOST BAFFLED THE MIGHTIEST OF DETECTIVES--BATMAN AND ROBIN! IT IS A STORY THAT IS FITTINGLY CALLED...
ROBIN!.. LOOK OUT! THE MASKED KILLER HAS PUSHED THAT ADVERTISING BEACON DOWN ON US!
the CASE of the DEADLY GEMS
GOTHAM GEM COMPANY
THE OFFICE OF POLICE COMMISSIONER ORDON, ONE NIGHT, BATMAN AND OBIN GET AN URGENT ASSIGNMENT...
JUST RECEIVED A PHONE CALL FROM ONE OF THE HEADS OF THE GOTHAM GEM OMPANY! THEY GOT THREATENING ETTER, SIGNED BY TED GREAVES!
GREAVES?... I CAPTURED HIM A FEW YEARS AGO, WHEN HE TRIED TO HOLD UP THE GEM COMPANY! WE'D BETTER GO THERE AND SEE WHAT THIS IS ALL ABOUT!
SOON AFTER, AS THE BATMOBILE SPEEDS TO ITS DESTINATION...
BATMAN, WASN'T GREAVES RELEASED FROM PRISON LAST MONTH?
YES, ROBIN--AND AT HIS TRIAL, HE VOWED VENGEANCE UPON THE GEM COMPANY'S THREE PARTNERS, WHO TESTIFIED AGAINST HIM! IT'S POSSIBLE HE NOW INTENDS TO CARRY OUT HIS THREAT!

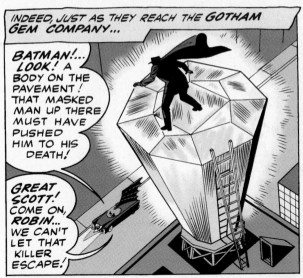

INDEED, JUST AS THEY REACH THE *GOTHAM GEM COMPANY*...

BATMAN!... LOOK! A BODY ON THE PAVEMENT! THAT MASKED MAN UP THERE MUST HAVE PUSHED HIM TO HIS DEATH!

GREAT SCOTT! COME ON, ROBIN... WE CAN'T LET THAT KILLER ESCAPE!

BUT AS THE CRIME-FIGHTERS DASH ACROSS THE STREET...

LOOK OUT! HE'S LOOSENED THAT GEM ADVERTISING BEACON, AND PUSHED IT OVER!

CRASH

BY THE TIME *BATMAN* AND *ROBIN* RECOVER AND REACH THE ROOF...

HE'S GONE-- PROBABLY OVER ANOTHER ROOFTOP!

HMM-- THIS BIT OF BLACK CLOTH, CAUGHT ON THE SIGN'S SUPPORT... LOOKS LIKE IT WAS TORN AWAY FROM THE KILLER'S CAPE!

RETURNING TO THE STREET, THEY FIND THREE FRIGHTENED MEN GATHERED AROUND THE VICTIM...

THE THREE COMPANY PARTNERS! THEN... WHO'S THE MURDERED MAN?

CLAYBER-- OUR *NEW* PARTNER...HE JOINED OUR FIRM JUST A FEW DAYS AGO! HERE, *BATMAN*-- THIS LETTER SHOULD EXPLAIN EVERYTHING!

your company sent me to prison--so now I'll destroy it, by wiping out its owners! Clayber is the youngest, so he goes first. superstition says the turquoise protects one from falling-- but it won't protect Clayber! greaves

SO!... TED GREAVES SEEMS TO BE CARRYING OUT HIS THREAT!

2

9

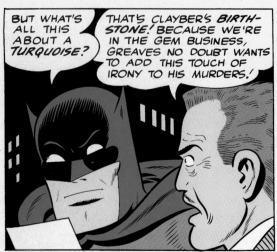

BUT WHAT'S ALL THIS ABOUT A *TURQUOISE?*

THAT'S CLAYBER'S *BIRTH-STONE!* BECAUSE WE'RE IN THE GEM BUSINESS, GREAVES NO DOUBT WANTS TO ADD THIS TOUCH OF IRONY TO HIS MURDERS!

IN OTHER WORDS, GREAVES SEEMS INTENT ON METING OUT DEATHS BEFITTING YOUR BIRTHSTONES -- AND HE PLANS TO DO IT FROM THE YOUNGEST TO THE OLDEST!

GULP! THAT MAKES *ME* HIS NEXT VICTIM!

THREE PARTNERS IN BUSINESS... WILL THEY NOW BE THREE PARTNERS IN *DEATH?*

JOHN WILCOX AGED 35

HENRY STUBBS AGED 40

ED CARDER AGED 44

I WAS BORN IN JUNE -- THE MONTH OF THE *MOON-STONE!* WHAT CAN GREAVES BE PLANNING FOR *ME?*

THERE'S NO WAY OF TELLING, WILCOX! I SUGGEST YOU STAY AT HOME, WHERE *ROBIN* AND I WILL BE KEEPING WATCH!

THUS, SOME HOURS LATER, AS THE WORRIED WILCOX TRIES TO CALM HIS FEARS BY WALKING ABOUT HIS ESTATE...

RROAR

WHAT'S THAT? *BATMAN! ROBIN!* COME QUICKLY!

WE'RE RIGHT HERE, WILCOX!

3

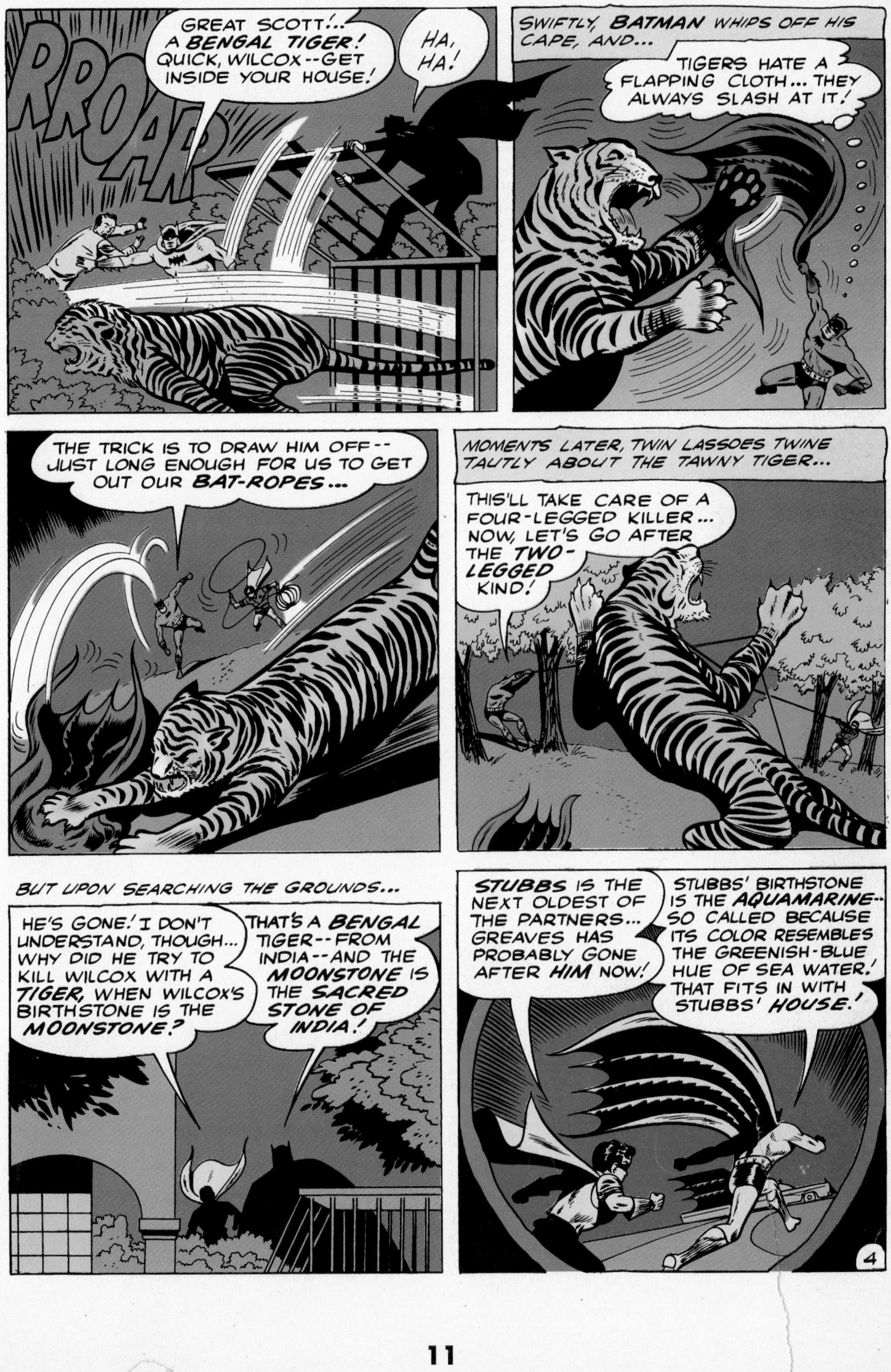
RROAR
GREAT SCOTT!.. A BENGAL TIGER! QUICK, WILCOX--GET INSIDE YOUR HOUSE!
HA, HA!
SWIFTLY, BATMAN WHIPS OFF HIS CAPE, AND...
TIGERS HATE A FLAPPING CLOTH... THEY ALWAYS SLASH AT IT!
THE TRICK IS TO DRAW HIM OFF-- JUST LONG ENOUGH FOR US TO GET OUT OUR BAT-ROPES...
MOMENTS LATER, TWIN LASSOES TWINE TAUTLY ABOUT THE TAWNY TIGER...
THIS'LL TAKE CARE OF A FOUR-LEGGED KILLER... NOW, LET'S GO AFTER THE TWO-LEGGED KIND!
BUT UPON SEARCHING THE GROUNDS...
HE'S GONE! I DON'T UNDERSTAND, THOUGH... WHY DID HE TRY TO KILL WILCOX WITH A TIGER, WHEN WILCOX'S BIRTHSTONE IS THE MOONSTONE?
THAT'S A BENGAL TIGER--FROM INDIA--AND THE MOONSTONE IS THE SACRED STONE OF INDIA!
STUBBS IS THE NEXT OLDEST OF THE PARTNERS... GREAVES HAS PROBABLY GONE AFTER HIM NOW!
STUBBS' BIRTHSTONE IS THE AQUAMARINE-- SO CALLED BECAUSE ITS COLOR RESEMBLES THE GREENISH-BLUE HUE OF SEA WATER! THAT FITS IN WITH STUBBS' HOUSE!
4

UPON REACHING STUBBS' UNIQUE DWELLING...

WHY... IT'S A YACHT-- ON LAND!

YES-- STUBBS LOVES BOATS SO MUCH, HE LIVES ON A YACHT TRANSPLANTED TO HIS ESTATE! IT'S A FIT SETTING FOR A POSSIBLE AQUAMARINE MURDER!

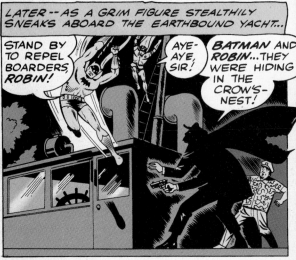

LATER -- AS A GRIM FIGURE STEALTHILY SNEAKS ABOARD THE EARTHBOUND YACHT...

STAND BY TO REPEL BOARDERS, ROBIN!

AYE-AYE, SIR!

BATMAN AND ROBIN...THEY WERE HIDING IN THE CROW'S-NEST!

YOU'RE GOING INTO THE BRIG, GREAVES!

BANG!

BUT RECOVERING QUICKLY, THE KILLER GRABS THE UNWARY STUBBS, AND...

OOOF!

A GREEN KEROSENE LAMP -- THE COLOR OF AQUAMARINE...

5

... A FITTING LAMP TO HELP ME MAKE MY ESCAPE! HA, HA!

STUBBS! LOOK OUT FOR THE SPLASHES OF FLAME!

CRASH!

OHHH... MY YACHT! IT'LL BE BURNED TO THE GROUND!

WE'LL HAVE TO LET THE KILLER ESCAPE AGAIN!

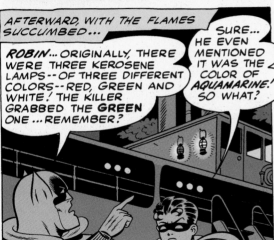

AFTERWARD, WITH THE FLAMES SUCCUMBED...

ROBIN... ORIGINALLY, THERE WERE THREE KEROSENE LAMPS -- OF THREE DIFFERENT COLORS -- RED, GREEN AND WHITE! THE KILLER GRABBED THE GREEN ONE ...REMEMBER?

SURE... HE EVEN MENTIONED IT WAS THE COLOR OF AQUAMARINE! SO WHAT?

SO THIS!... HOW COULD GREAVES KNOW WHAT COLOR THE LAMP WAS, WHEN THE POLICE FILES SHOW HE'S COLOR-BLIND?

GOLLY... THAT MEANS GREAVES CAN'T BE THE KILLER! SOMEBODY IS IMPERSONATING HIM... MOST LIKELY ONE OF THE THREE PARTNERS!

YET, IT CAN'T BE WILCOX OR STUBBS, BECAUSE THE KILLER TRIED TO GET THEM, TOO! THAT LEAVES ONLY CARDER!

LET'S GO TO CARDER'S PLACE FIRST, AND CHECK ON HIS ACTIVITIES TONIGHT!

BUT AT CARDER'S HOME, BATMAN RECEIVES A SURPRISE...

WILCOX! YOU'RE HERE, TOO?

YES...WE GOT TOGETHER A COUPLE OF HOURS AGO TO PLAY SOME CARDS! WE FIGURED IF GREAVES SHOULD ATTACK HERE, THE TWO OF US STOOD A BETTER CHANCE OF CAPTURING HIM!

6

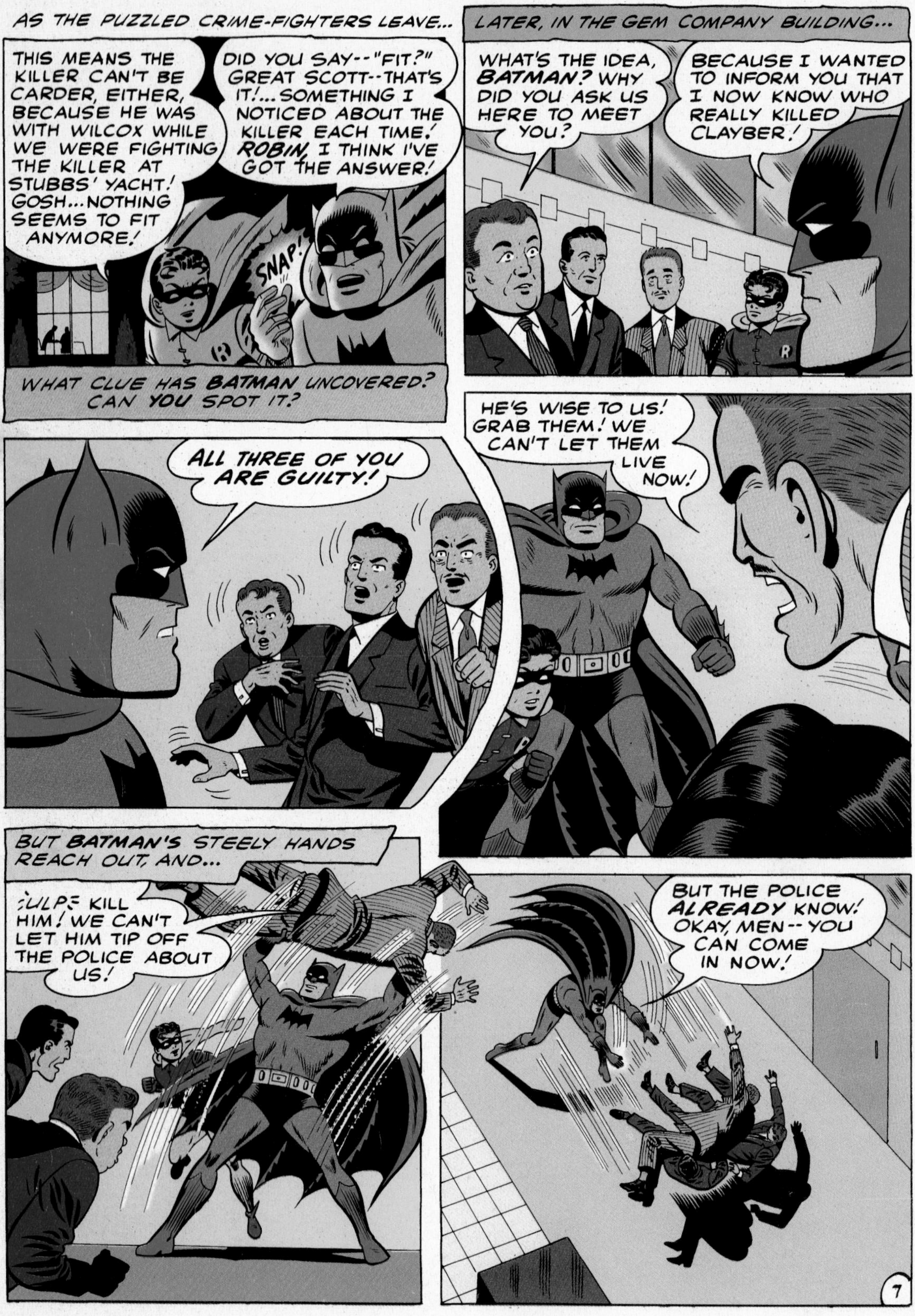
AS THE PUZZLED CRIME-FIGHTERS LEAVE...
THIS MEANS THE KILLER CAN'T BE CARDER, EITHER, BECAUSE HE WAS WITH WILCOX WHILE WE WERE FIGHTING THE KILLER AT STUBBS' YACHT! GOSH...NOTHING SEEMS TO FIT ANYMORE!
DID YOU SAY--"FIT?" GREAT SCOTT--THAT'S IT!...SOMETHING I NOTICED ABOUT THE KILLER EACH TIME! ROBIN, I THINK I'VE GOT THE ANSWER!
SNAP!
WHAT CLUE HAS BATMAN UNCOVERED? CAN YOU SPOT IT?
LATER, IN THE GEM COMPANY BUILDING...
WHAT'S THE IDEA, BATMAN? WHY DID YOU ASK US HERE TO MEET YOU?
BECAUSE I WANTED TO INFORM YOU THAT I NOW KNOW WHO REALLY KILLED CLAYBER!
ALL THREE OF YOU ARE GUILTY!
HE'S WISE TO US! GRAB THEM! WE CAN'T LET THEM LIVE NOW!
BUT BATMAN'S STEELY HANDS REACH OUT, AND...
GULP! KILL HIM! WE CAN'T LET HIM TIP OFF THE POLICE ABOUT US!
BUT THE POLICE ALREADY KNOW! OKAY, MEN--YOU CAN COME IN NOW!
7

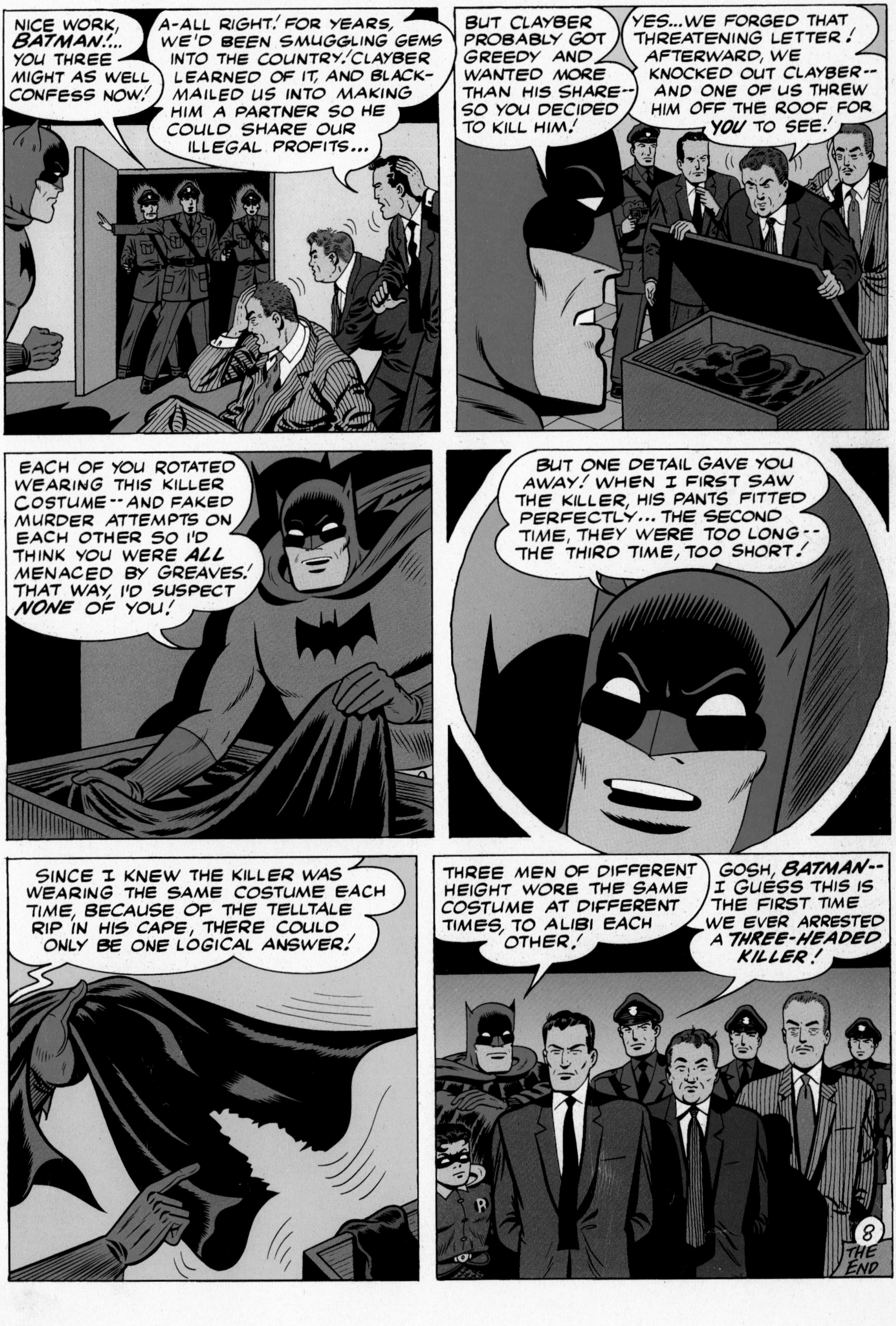
NICE WORK, BATMAN!... YOU THREE MIGHT AS WELL CONFESS NOW!
A-ALL RIGHT! FOR YEARS, WE'D BEEN SMUGGLING GEMS INTO THE COUNTRY! CLAYBER LEARNED OF IT, AND BLACK-MAILED US INTO MAKING HIM A PARTNER SO HE COULD SHARE OUR ILLEGAL PROFITS...
BUT CLAYBER PROBABLY GOT GREEDY AND WANTED MORE THAN HIS SHARE-- SO YOU DECIDED TO KILL HIM!
YES...WE FORGED THAT THREATENING LETTER! AFTERWARD, WE KNOCKED OUT CLAYBER-- AND ONE OF US THREW HIM OFF THE ROOF FOR YOU TO SEE!
EACH OF YOU ROTATED WEARING THIS KILLER COSTUME--AND FAKED MURDER ATTEMPTS ON EACH OTHER SO I'D THINK YOU WERE ALL MENACED BY GREAVES! THAT WAY, I'D SUSPECT NONE OF YOU!
BUT ONE DETAIL GAVE YOU AWAY! WHEN I FIRST SAW THE KILLER, HIS PANTS FITTED PERFECTLY... THE SECOND TIME, THEY WERE TOO LONG-- THE THIRD TIME, TOO SHORT!
SINCE I KNEW THE KILLER WAS WEARING THE SAME COSTUME EACH TIME, BECAUSE OF THE TELLTALE RIP IN HIS CAPE, THERE COULD ONLY BE ONE LOGICAL ANSWER!
THREE MEN OF DIFFERENT HEIGHT WORE THE SAME COSTUME AT DIFFERENT TIMES, TO ALIBI EACH OTHER!
GOSH, BATMAN-- I GUESS THIS IS THE FIRST TIME WE EVER ARRESTED A THREE-HEADED KILLER!
8
THE END

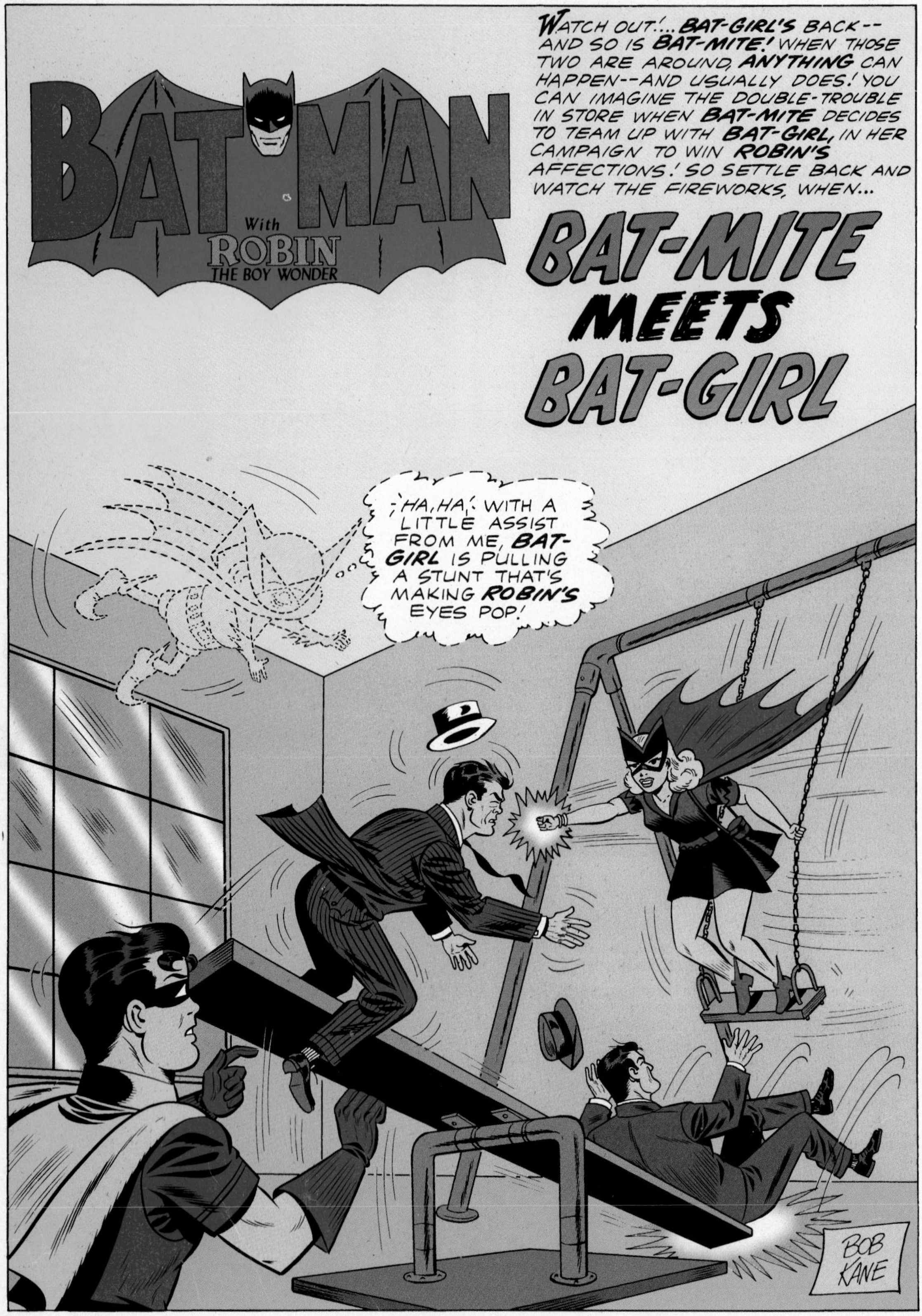
BATMAN
With ROBIN THE BOY WONDER
WATCH OUT!... BAT-GIRL'S BACK-- AND SO IS BAT-MITE! WHEN THOSE TWO ARE AROUND, ANYTHING CAN HAPPEN--AND USUALLY DOES! YOU CAN IMAGINE THE DOUBLE-TROUBLE IN STORE WHEN BAT-MITE DECIDES TO TEAM UP WITH BAT-GIRL, IN HER CAMPAIGN TO WIN ROBIN'S AFFECTIONS! SO SETTLE BACK AND WATCH THE FIREWORKS, WHEN...
BAT-MITE MEETS BAT-GIRL
HA,HA! WITH A LITTLE ASSIST FROM ME, BAT-GIRL IS PULLING A STUNT THAT'S MAKING ROBIN'S EYES POP!
BOB KANE

SUMMONED TO COMMISSIONER GORDON'S OFFICE, BATMAN AND ROBIN FIND A SURPRISE AWAITING THEM...

BATWOMAN!...AND WITH HER IS HER NIECE, BETTY-- WEARING HER BAT-GIRL COSTUME!

BATMAN, IT WAS I WHO ASKED BATWOMAN TO GET BAT-GIRL HERE-- TO HELP OUT!

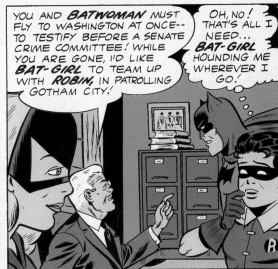

YOU AND BATWOMAN MUST FLY TO WASHINGTON AT ONCE-- TO TESTIFY BEFORE A SENATE CRIME COMMITTEE! WHILE YOU ARE GONE, I'D LIKE BAT-GIRL TO TEAM UP WITH ROBIN, IN PATROLLING GOTHAM CITY!

OH, NO! THAT'S ALL I NEED... BAT-GIRL HOUNDING ME WHEREVER I GO!

INDEED, NO SOONER IS THE YOUNG COUPLE ALONE THAN...

-SIGH!- WORKING WITH YOU IS WHAT I'VE ALWAYS DREAMED OF! OH, ROBIN-- I THINK YOU'RE JUST ADORABLE!

B-BAT-GIRL... PLEASE...

Y-YOU'VE JUST GOT TO STOP DOING THAT! IT--IT ISN'T RIGHT, ESPECIALLY SINCE I'M ... ER... DEVOTED TO ANOTHER WOMAN!

ANOTHER WOMAN? OH, ROBIN... -SOB!- Y-YOU CAN'T MEAN THAT!

HEARTBROKEN, THE LOVESTRUCK LASS RETURNS TO BATWOMAN'S UNDERGROUND LAIR, WHERE SUDDENLY...

WHAT--? OH, DEAR!... YOU MUST BE BAT-MITE! MY AUNT TOLD ME ALL ABOUT YOU!

AND I'VE HEARD ABOUT YOU, TOO, BAT-GIRL! SAY-- HOW COME A CUTE KID LIKE YOU IS CRYING?

POP!

AFTER BAT-GIRL TELLS HER UNHAPPY TALE...

IF ONLY ROBIN WOULD FORGET THE OTHER WOMAN -SOB!- AND FALL IN LOVE WITH ME!

IS THAT ALL? WHY, WITH MY POWERS, IT'LL BE A CINCH... AND BOYOBOYOBOY- WILL I HAVE FUN DOING IT!

ROBIN, BETTER WATCH OUT! WHEN BAT-MITE STARTS PLAYING CUPID-- ANYTHING CAN HAPPEN!

2

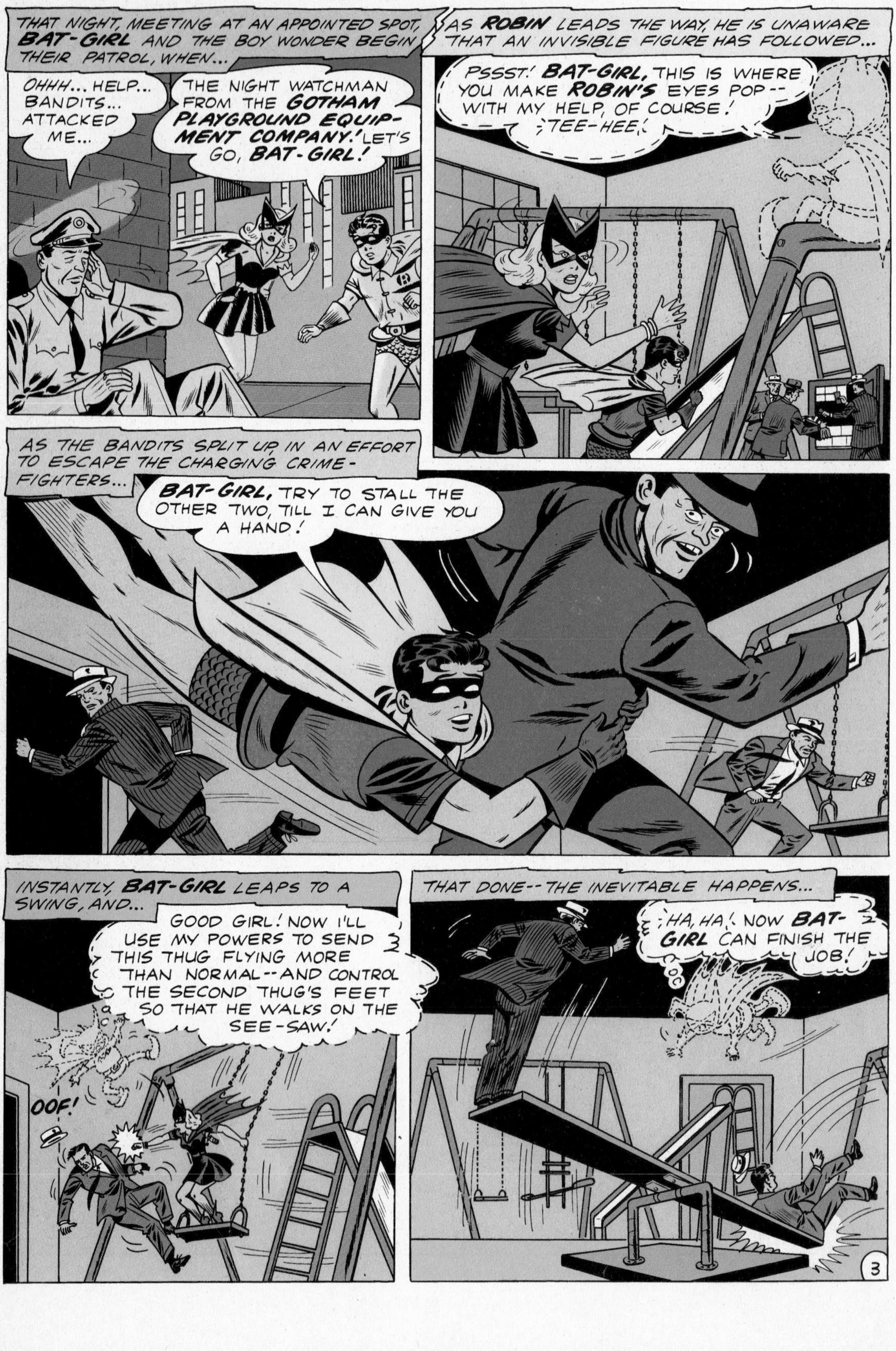
THAT NIGHT, MEETING AT AN APPOINTED SPOT, BAT-GIRL AND THE BOY WONDER BEGIN THEIR PATROL, WHEN...
OHHH... HELP... BANDITS... ATTACKED ME...
THE NIGHT WATCHMAN FROM THE GOTHAM PLAYGROUND EQUIPMENT COMPANY! LET'S GO, BAT-GIRL!
AS ROBIN LEADS THE WAY, HE IS UNAWARE THAT AN INVISIBLE FIGURE HAS FOLLOWED...
PSSST! BAT-GIRL, THIS IS WHERE YOU MAKE ROBIN'S EYES POP -- WITH MY HELP, OF COURSE! TEE-HEE!
AS THE BANDITS SPLIT UP IN AN EFFORT TO ESCAPE THE CHARGING CRIME-FIGHTERS...
BAT-GIRL, TRY TO STALL THE OTHER TWO, TILL I CAN GIVE YOU A HAND!
INSTANTLY, BAT-GIRL LEAPS TO A SWING, AND...
GOOD GIRL! NOW I'LL USE MY POWERS TO SEND THIS THUG FLYING MORE THAN NORMAL -- AND CONTROL THE SECOND THUG'S FEET SO THAT HE WALKS ON THE SEE-SAW!
OOF!
THAT DONE -- THE INEVITABLE HAPPENS...
HA, HA! NOW BAT-GIRL CAN FINISH THE JOB!
3

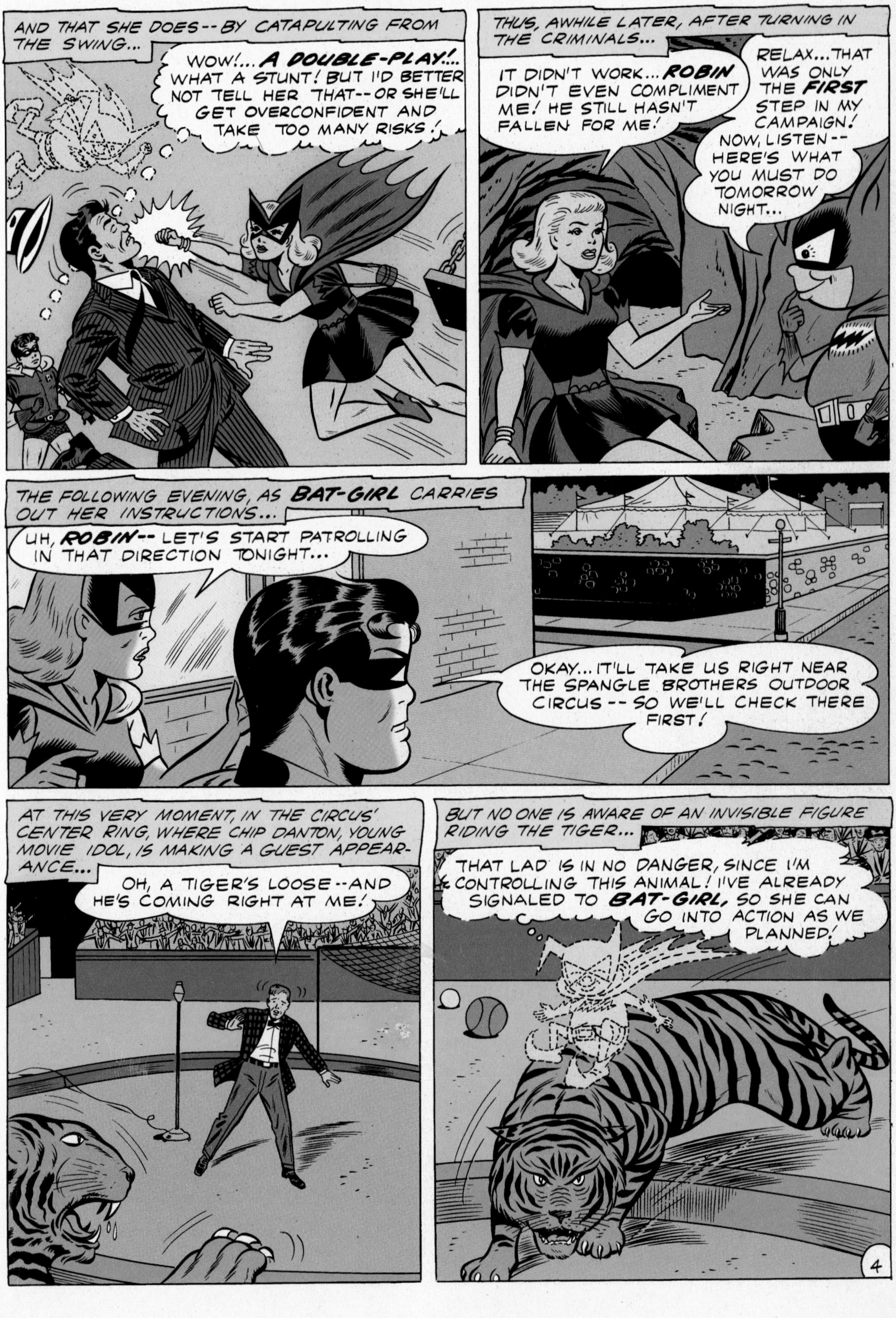
AND THAT SHE DOES--BY CATAPULTING FROM THE SWING...
WOW!... A DOUBLE-PLAY!... WHAT A STUNT! BUT I'D BETTER NOT TELL HER THAT--OR SHE'LL GET OVERCONFIDENT AND TAKE TOO MANY RISKS!
THUS, AWHILE LATER, AFTER TURNING IN THE CRIMINALS...
IT DIDN'T WORK... ROBIN DIDN'T EVEN COMPLIMENT ME! HE STILL HASN'T FALLEN FOR ME!
RELAX...THAT WAS ONLY THE FIRST STEP IN MY CAMPAIGN! NOW, LISTEN--HERE'S WHAT YOU MUST DO TOMORROW NIGHT...
THE FOLLOWING EVENING, AS BAT-GIRL CARRIES OUT HER INSTRUCTIONS...
UH, ROBIN--LET'S START PATROLLING IN THAT DIRECTION TONIGHT...
OKAY...IT'LL TAKE US RIGHT NEAR THE SPANGLE BROTHERS OUTDOOR CIRCUS--SO WE'LL CHECK THERE FIRST!
AT THIS VERY MOMENT, IN THE CIRCUS' CENTER RING, WHERE CHIP DANTON, YOUNG MOVIE IDOL, IS MAKING A GUEST APPEARANCE...
OH, A TIGER'S LOOSE--AND HE'S COMING RIGHT AT ME!
BUT NO ONE IS AWARE OF AN INVISIBLE FIGURE RIDING THE TIGER...
THAT LAD IS IN NO DANGER, SINCE I'M CONTROLLING THIS ANIMAL! I'VE ALREADY SIGNALED TO BAT-GIRL, SO SHE CAN GO INTO ACTION AS WE PLANNED!
4

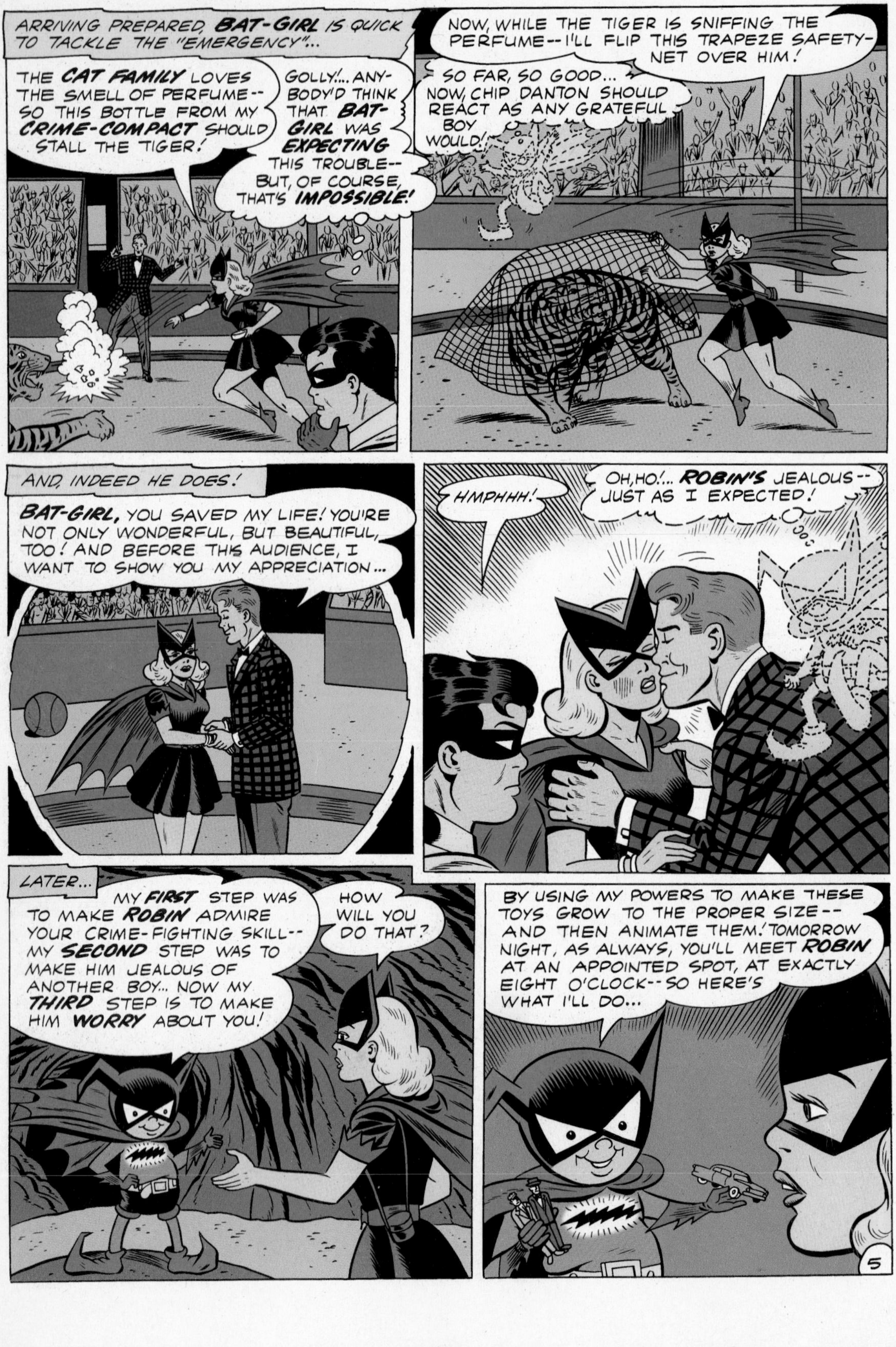

ARRIVING PREPARED, BAT-GIRL IS QUICK TO TACKLE THE "EMERGENCY"...
THE CAT FAMILY LOVES THE SMELL OF PERFUME-- SO THIS BOTTLE FROM MY CRIME-COMPACT SHOULD STALL THE TIGER!
GOLLY!... ANY-BODY'D THINK THAT BAT-GIRL WAS EXPECTING THIS TROUBLE-- BUT, OF COURSE, THAT'S IMPOSSIBLE!
NOW, WHILE THE TIGER IS SNIFFING THE PERFUME--I'LL FLIP THIS TRAPEZE SAFETY-NET OVER HIM!
SO FAR, SO GOOD... NOW, CHIP DANTON SHOULD REACT AS ANY GRATEFUL BOY WOULD!
AND, INDEED HE DOES!
BAT-GIRL, YOU SAVED MY LIFE! YOU'RE NOT ONLY WONDERFUL, BUT BEAUTIFUL, TOO! AND BEFORE THIS AUDIENCE, I WANT TO SHOW YOU MY APPRECIATION...
HMPHHH!
OH,HO!... ROBIN'S JEALOUS-- JUST AS I EXPECTED!
LATER...
MY FIRST STEP WAS TO MAKE ROBIN ADMIRE YOUR CRIME-FIGHTING SKILL-- MY SECOND STEP WAS TO MAKE HIM JEALOUS OF ANOTHER BOY... NOW MY THIRD STEP IS TO MAKE HIM WORRY ABOUT YOU!
HOW WILL YOU DO THAT?
BY USING MY POWERS TO MAKE THESE TOYS GROW TO THE PROPER SIZE-- AND THEN ANIMATE THEM! TOMORROW NIGHT, AS ALWAYS, YOU'LL MEET ROBIN AT AN APPOINTED SPOT, AT EXACTLY EIGHT O'CLOCK-- SO HERE'S WHAT I'LL DO...
5

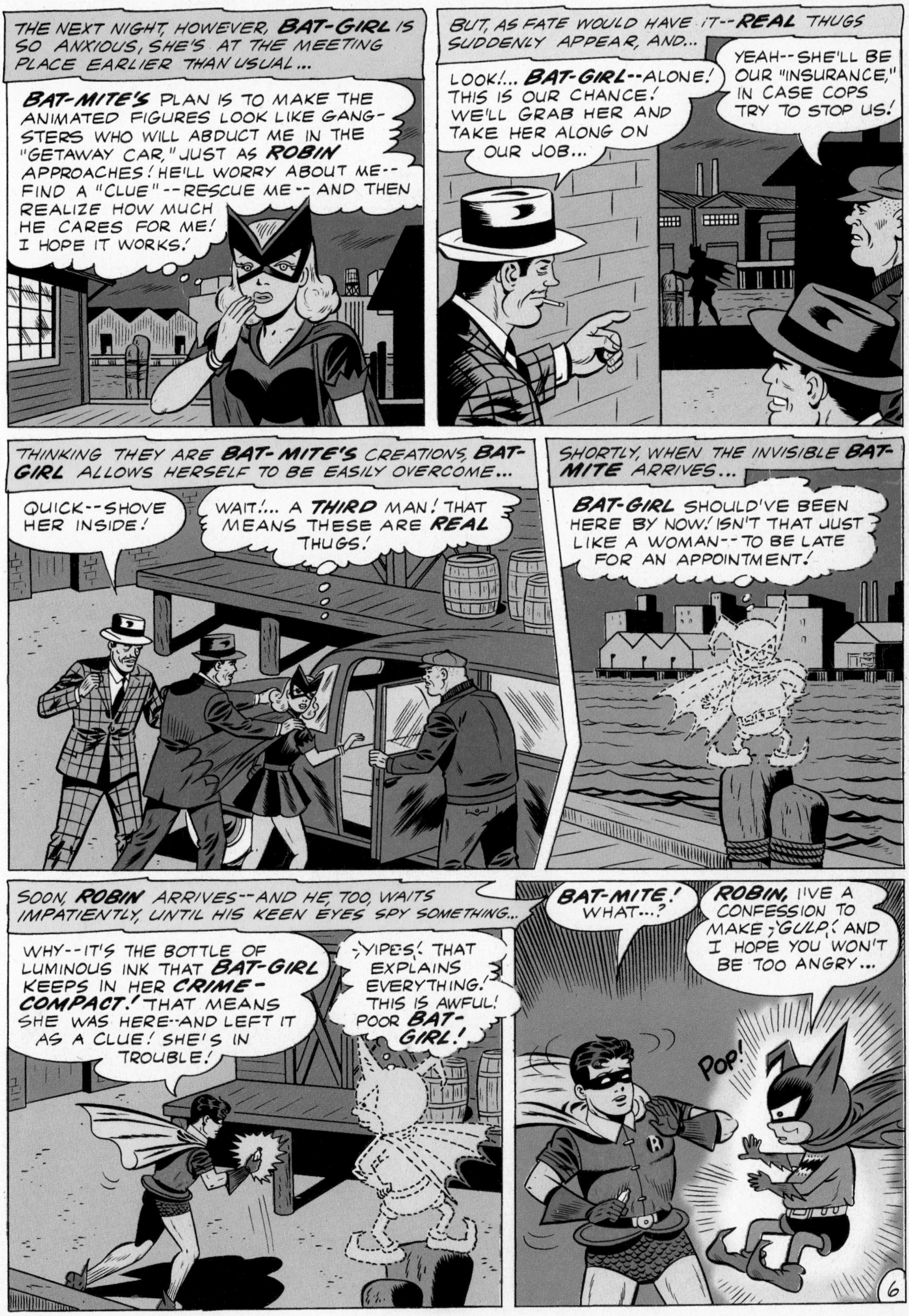
THE NEXT NIGHT, HOWEVER, BAT-GIRL IS SO ANXIOUS, SHE'S AT THE MEETING PLACE EARLIER THAN USUAL...
BAT-MITE'S PLAN IS TO MAKE THE ANIMATED FIGURES LOOK LIKE GANGSTERS WHO WILL ABDUCT ME IN THE "GETAWAY CAR," JUST AS ROBIN APPROACHES! HE'LL WORRY ABOUT ME--FIND A "CLUE"--RESCUE ME--AND THEN REALIZE HOW MUCH HE CARES FOR ME! I HOPE IT WORKS!
BUT, AS FATE WOULD HAVE IT--REAL THUGS SUDDENLY APPEAR, AND...
LOOK!... BAT-GIRL--ALONE! THIS IS OUR CHANCE! WE'LL GRAB HER AND TAKE HER ALONG ON OUR JOB...
YEAH--SHE'LL BE OUR "INSURANCE," IN CASE COPS TRY TO STOP US!
THINKING THEY ARE BAT-MITE'S CREATIONS, BAT-GIRL ALLOWS HERSELF TO BE EASILY OVERCOME...
QUICK--SHOVE HER INSIDE!
WAIT!... A THIRD MAN! THAT MEANS THESE ARE REAL THUGS!
SHORTLY, WHEN THE INVISIBLE BAT-MITE ARRIVES...
BAT-GIRL SHOULD'VE BEEN HERE BY NOW! ISN'T THAT JUST LIKE A WOMAN--TO BE LATE FOR AN APPOINTMENT!
SOON, ROBIN ARRIVES--AND HE, TOO, WAITS IMPATIENTLY, UNTIL HIS KEEN EYES SPY SOMETHING...
WHY--IT'S THE BOTTLE OF LUMINOUS INK THAT BAT-GIRL KEEPS IN HER CRIME-COMPACT! THAT MEANS SHE WAS HERE--AND LEFT IT AS A CLUE! SHE'S IN TROUBLE!
YIPES! THAT EXPLAINS EVERYTHING! THIS IS AWFUL! POOR BAT-GIRL!
BAT-MITE! WHAT...?
ROBIN, I'VE A CONFESSION TO MAKE -GULP!- AND I HOPE YOU WON'T BE TOO ANGRY...
POP!
6

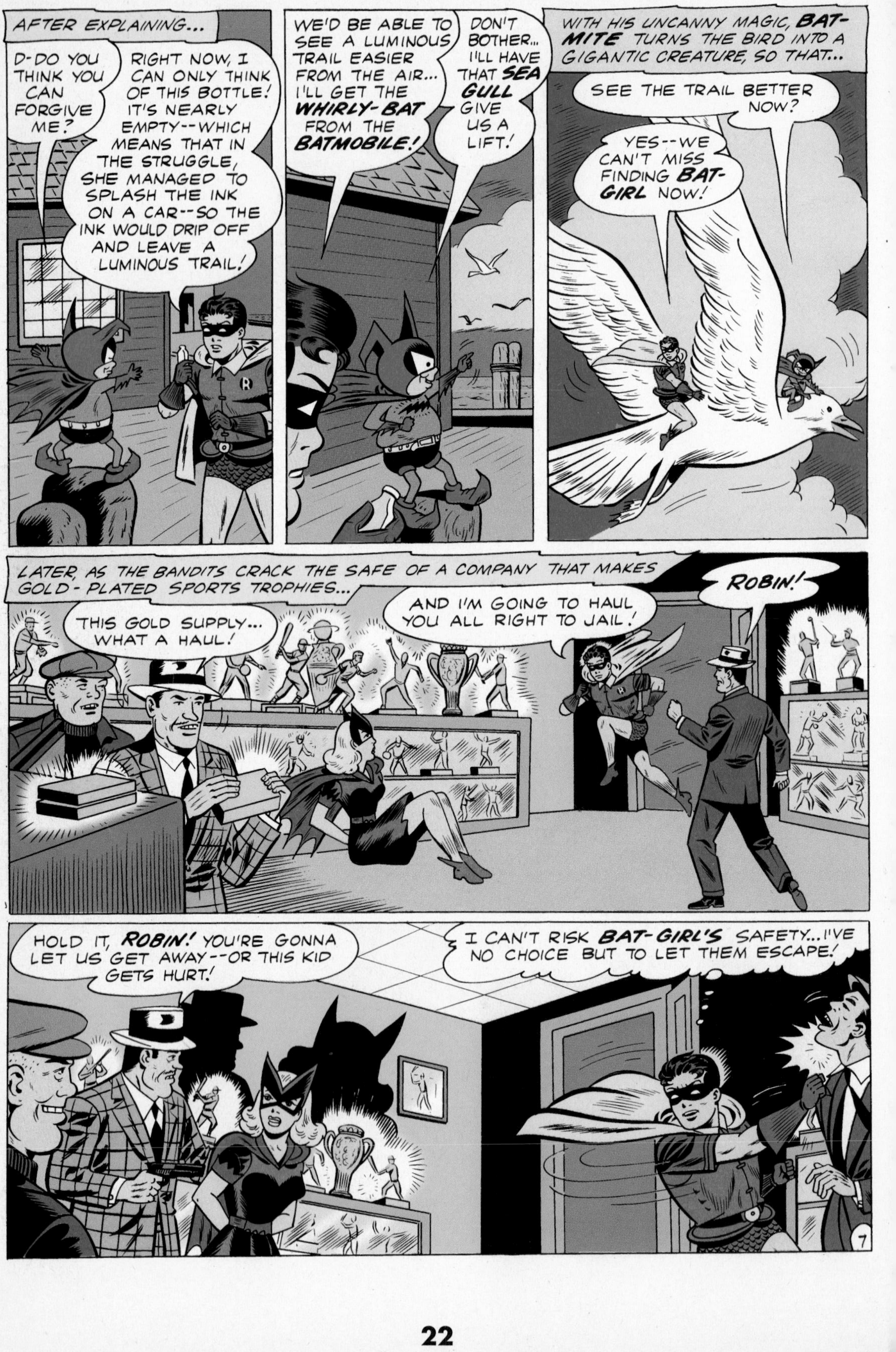
AFTER EXPLAINING...
D-DO YOU THINK YOU CAN FORGIVE ME?
RIGHT NOW, I CAN ONLY THINK OF THIS BOTTLE! IT'S NEARLY EMPTY--WHICH MEANS THAT IN THE STRUGGLE, SHE MANAGED TO SPLASH THE INK ON A CAR--SO THE INK WOULD DRIP OFF AND LEAVE A LUMINOUS TRAIL!
WE'D BE ABLE TO SEE A LUMINOUS TRAIL EASIER FROM THE AIR... I'LL GET THE WHIRLY-BAT FROM THE BATMOBILE!
DON'T BOTHER... I'LL HAVE THAT SEA GULL GIVE US A LIFT!
WITH HIS UNCANNY MAGIC, BAT-MITE TURNS THE BIRD INTO A GIGANTIC CREATURE, SO THAT...
SEE THE TRAIL BETTER NOW?
YES--WE CAN'T MISS FINDING BAT-GIRL NOW!
LATER, AS THE BANDITS CRACK THE SAFE OF A COMPANY THAT MAKES GOLD-PLATED SPORTS TROPHIES...
THIS GOLD SUPPLY... WHAT A HAUL!
AND I'M GOING TO HAUL YOU ALL RIGHT TO JAIL!
ROBIN!
HOLD IT, ROBIN! YOU'RE GONNA LET US GET AWAY--OR THIS KID GETS HURT!
I CAN'T RISK BAT-GIRL'S SAFETY... I'VE NO CHOICE BUT TO LET THEM ESCAPE!
7

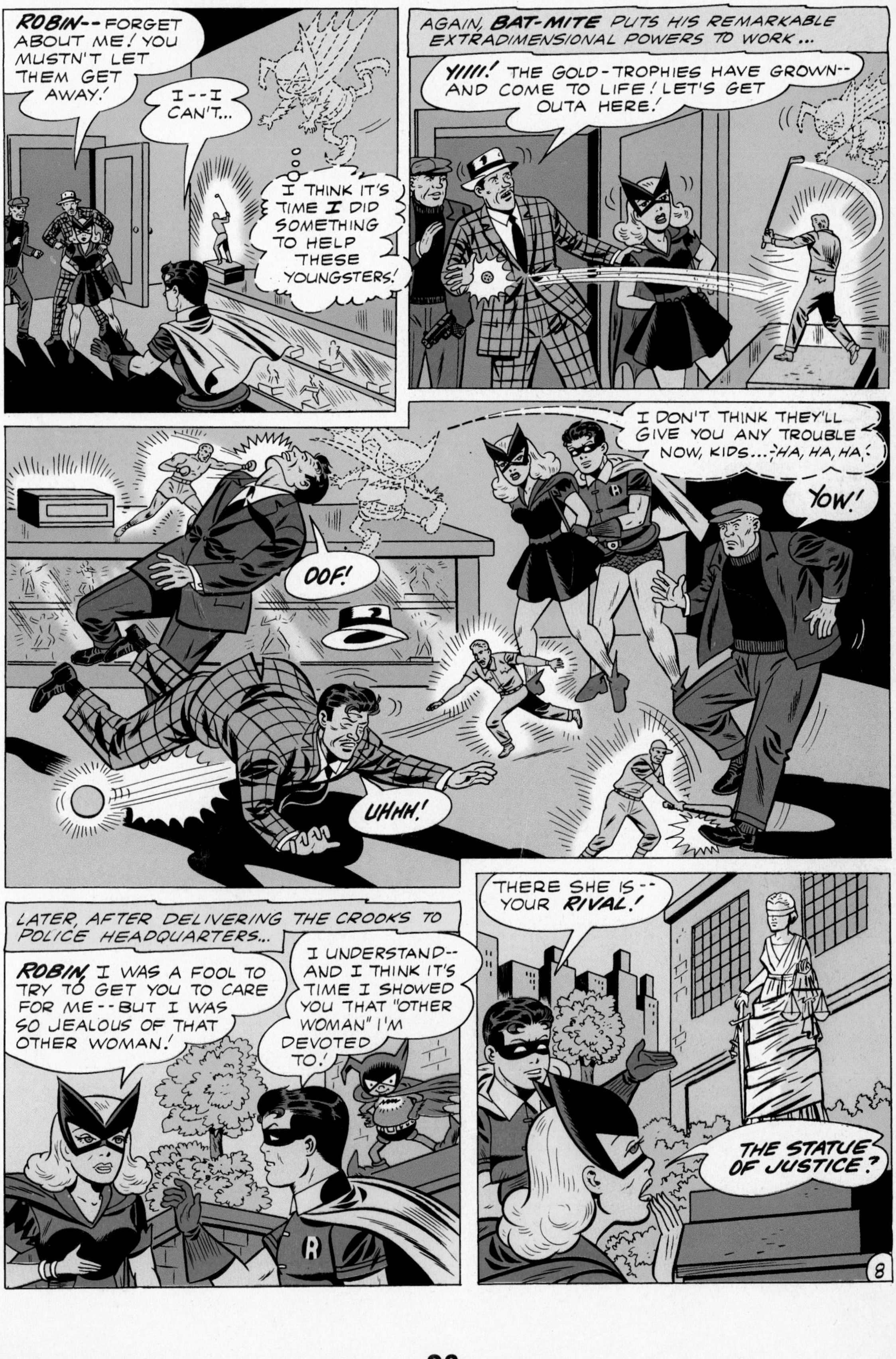
ROBIN-- FORGET ABOUT ME! YOU MUSTN'T LET THEM GET AWAY!
I--I CAN'T...
I THINK IT'S TIME I DID SOMETHING TO HELP THESE YOUNGSTERS!
AGAIN, BAT-MITE PUTS HIS REMARKABLE EXTRADIMENSIONAL POWERS TO WORK...
YIIII! THE GOLD-TROPHIES HAVE GROWN-- AND COME TO LIFE! LET'S GET OUTA HERE!
I DON'T THINK THEY'LL GIVE YOU ANY TROUBLE NOW, KIDS... HA, HA, HA!
YOW!
OOF!
UHHH!
LATER, AFTER DELIVERING THE CROOKS TO POLICE HEADQUARTERS...
ROBIN, I WAS A FOOL TO TRY TO GET YOU TO CARE FOR ME--BUT I WAS SO JEALOUS OF THAT OTHER WOMAN!
I UNDERSTAND-- AND I THINK IT'S TIME I SHOWED YOU THAT "OTHER WOMAN" I'M DEVOTED TO!
THERE SHE IS-- YOUR RIVAL!
THE STATUE OF JUSTICE?
8

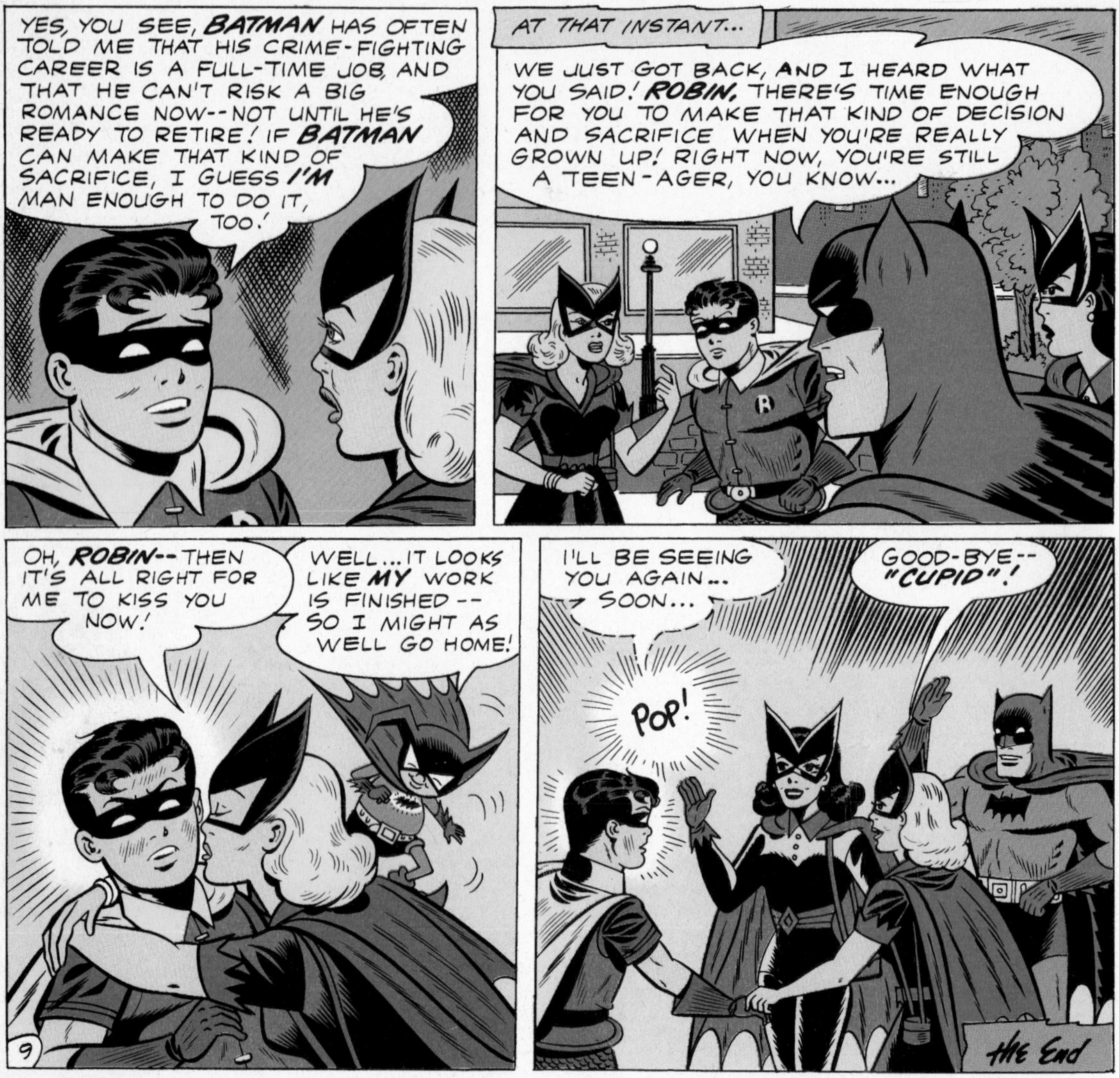
YES, YOU SEE, BATMAN HAS OFTEN TOLD ME THAT HIS CRIME-FIGHTING CAREER IS A FULL-TIME JOB, AND THAT HE CAN'T RISK A BIG ROMANCE NOW--NOT UNTIL HE'S READY TO RETIRE! IF BATMAN CAN MAKE THAT KIND OF SACRIFICE, I GUESS I'M MAN ENOUGH TO DO IT, TOO!
AT THAT INSTANT...
WE JUST GOT BACK, AND I HEARD WHAT YOU SAID! ROBIN, THERE'S TIME ENOUGH FOR YOU TO MAKE THAT KIND OF DECISION AND SACRIFICE WHEN YOU'RE REALLY GROWN UP! RIGHT NOW, YOU'RE STILL A TEEN-AGER, YOU KNOW...
OH, ROBIN--THEN IT'S ALL RIGHT FOR ME TO KISS YOU NOW!
WELL... IT LOOKS LIKE MY WORK IS FINISHED -- SO I MIGHT AS WELL GO HOME!
9
I'LL BE SEEING YOU AGAIN... SOON...
GOOD-BYE-- "CUPID"!
POP!
THE END

Continued from page 7

Commissioner Gordon (James W. Gordon): Although he was seen in more stories than any other *Batman* supporting character, Gordon's personality and background were largely underdeveloped until the 1980s. Most of his showcase roles revolved around trying to deduce Batman's secret identity. Gordon's character became more fully developed when we learned in 1967 that his daughter, Barbara, was secretly Batgirl.

Batwoman (Kathy Kane): A wealthy heiress and one-time "circus daredevil performer," Batwoman used crime-fighting skills such as motorcycle stunt riding (she had her own stylized Bat-cycle) and acrobatics. She operated independently of Batman, having her own Bat-Cave headquarters with crime lab and crime files, but was always shown working with Batman on cases. Tellingly, Batman and Robin knew her secret identity, but the boys did not trust her with theirs. Batwoman's appearances ceased in the mid-sixties.

Robin (Dick Grayson): Dubbed the "Boy Wonder," Robin was the uncrowned prince of comic book sidekicks and the perfect, colorful match to Batman's grim and straitlaced countenance. Throughout the '50s and early '60s, we had no doubt that Robin would grow up to take over the family business. But as the turmoil of the times led to the fracturing of the nuclear family concept, Robin became the character to reflect these changes in society, splitting with Batman to go to college in 1969.

Bat-Girl (Betty Kane): The forgotten Batgirl, Betty was the niece of Kathy Kane and only became Bat-Girl on the occasions that she visited Gotham. Her crime-fighting career coincided with her (mostly unsuccessful) efforts to attract the Boy Wonder. Although fondly remembered, this Bat-Girl only made six appearances in the *Batman* titles of the '60s.

Ace, the Bat-Hound: Ace is his real name, despite the fact that he wore a tight-fitting black mask to conceal his secret identity. The courageous Ace assisted the Batman Family in a remarkable 15 cases before retiring in 1964.

BATMAN'S ROGUES GALLERY

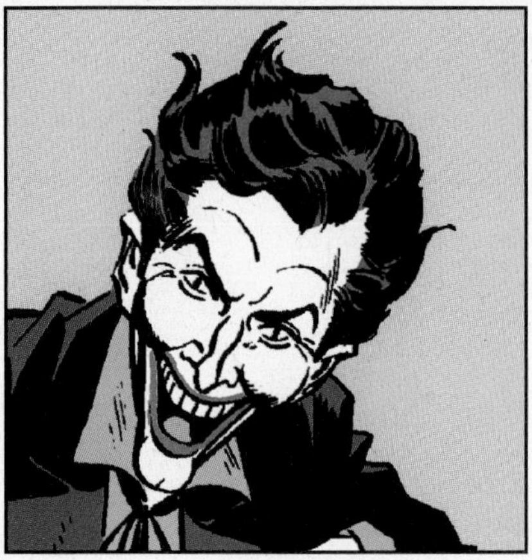

The Joker (real name unknown):
Batman's archfoe, the Clown Prince of Crime is the most unpredictable and dangerous villain in Gotham. His crimes frequently revolve around practical jokes or playing cards, but not as a rule. Reportedly, his grip on sanity was lost when a freak chemical accident disfigured him, permanently dyeing his hair green and his skin chalk-white. He's extremely dangerous and would kill without a second thought.

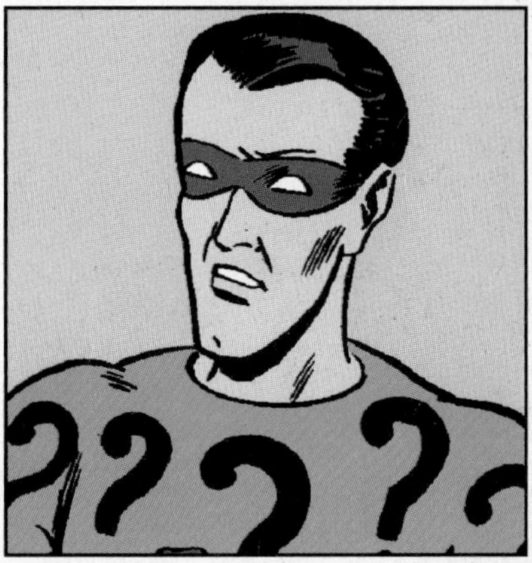

The Riddler (Edward Nigma):
Preoccupied with riddles, puzzles and enigmas of all kinds, Nigma's crimes are intricate, multifaceted affairs. His plans are usually thwarted due to a psychological quirk that forces him to provide clues — usually in the form of riddles — before committing the crime.

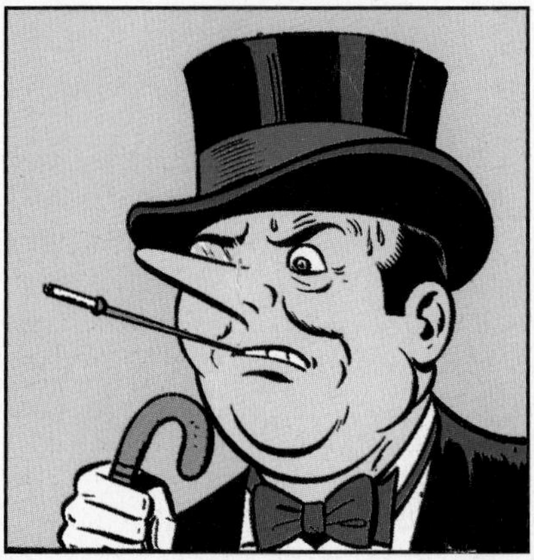

The Penguin (Oswald Cobblepot):
He is a deceptive threat, whose humorous appearance masks his true evil. Obsessed with birds and umbrellas, his crimes usually revolve around one or the other. His ubiquitous umbrellas are usually loaded with deadly gimmicks. A scholar of Shakespeare and Keats, Cobblepot would probably prefer to continue his studies, but his diabolical mind continually leads him back to crime.

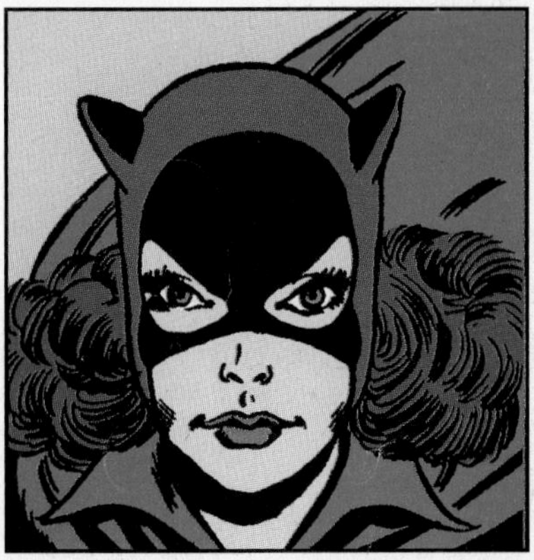

The Catwoman (Selina Kyle):
A brazen criminal whose crimes revolve around feline themes. Romantically attracted to Batman, she cannot make the psychological leap from bad to good. She is extremely schizophrenic and occasionally suffers from amnesia.

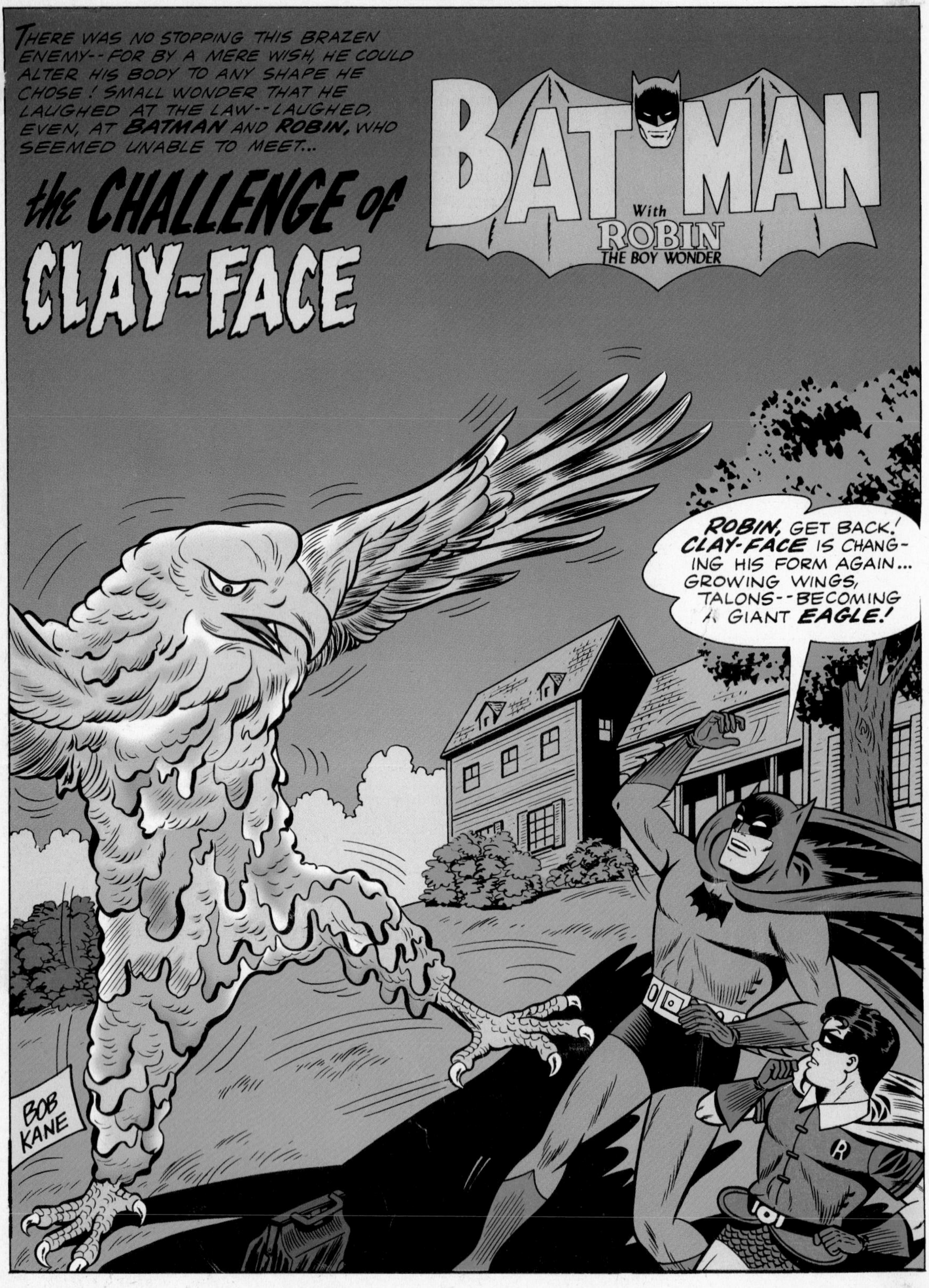
THERE WAS NO STOPPING THIS BRAZEN ENEMY--FOR BY A MERE WISH, HE COULD ALTER HIS BODY TO ANY SHAPE HE CHOSE! SMALL WONDER THAT HE LAUGHED AT THE LAW--LAUGHED, EVEN, AT BATMAN AND ROBIN, WHO SEEMED UNABLE TO MEET...
the CHALLENGE of CLAY-FACE
BATMAN
With ROBIN THE BOY WONDER
ROBIN, GET BACK! CLAY-FACE IS CHANGING HIS FORM AGAIN... GROWING WINGS, TALONS--BECOMING A GIANT EAGLE!
BOB KANE

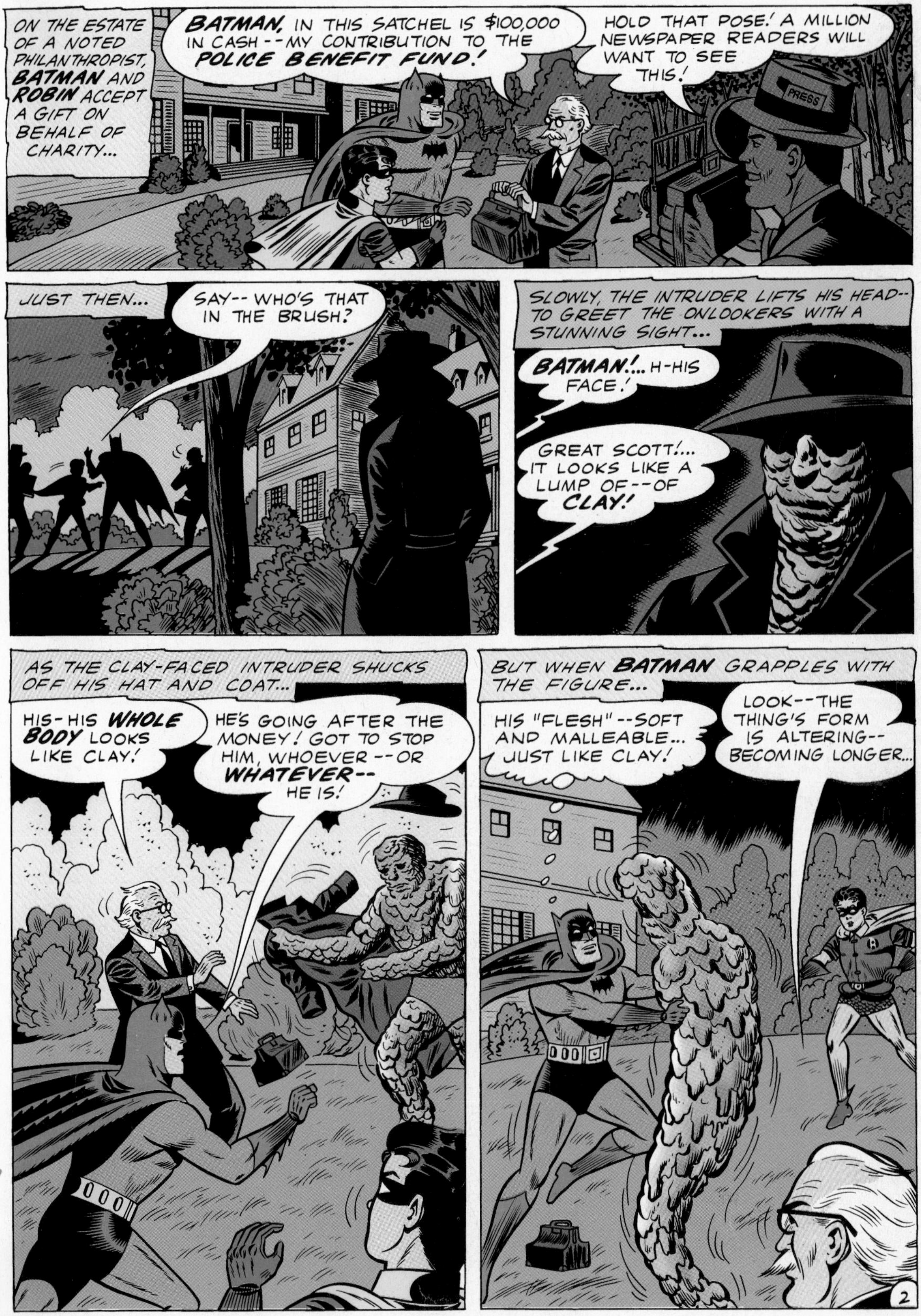
ON THE ESTATE OF A NOTED PHILANTHROPIST, BATMAN AND ROBIN ACCEPT A GIFT ON BEHALF OF CHARITY...
BATMAN, IN THIS SATCHEL IS $100,000 IN CASH--MY CONTRIBUTION TO THE POLICE BENEFIT FUND!
HOLD THAT POSE! A MILLION NEWSPAPER READERS WILL WANT TO SEE THIS!
PRESS
JUST THEN...
SAY--WHO'S THAT IN THE BRUSH?
SLOWLY, THE INTRUDER LIFTS HIS HEAD--TO GREET THE ONLOOKERS WITH A STUNNING SIGHT...
BATMAN!... H-HIS FACE!
GREAT SCOTT!... IT LOOKS LIKE A LUMP OF--OF CLAY!
AS THE CLAY-FACED INTRUDER SHUCKS OFF HIS HAT AND COAT...
HIS-HIS WHOLE BODY LOOKS LIKE CLAY!
HE'S GOING AFTER THE MONEY! GOT TO STOP HIM, WHOEVER--OR WHATEVER--HE IS!
BUT WHEN BATMAN GRAPPLES WITH THE FIGURE...
HIS "FLESH"--SOFT AND MALLEABLE... JUST LIKE CLAY!
LOOK--THE THING'S FORM IS ALTERING--BECOMING LONGER...
2

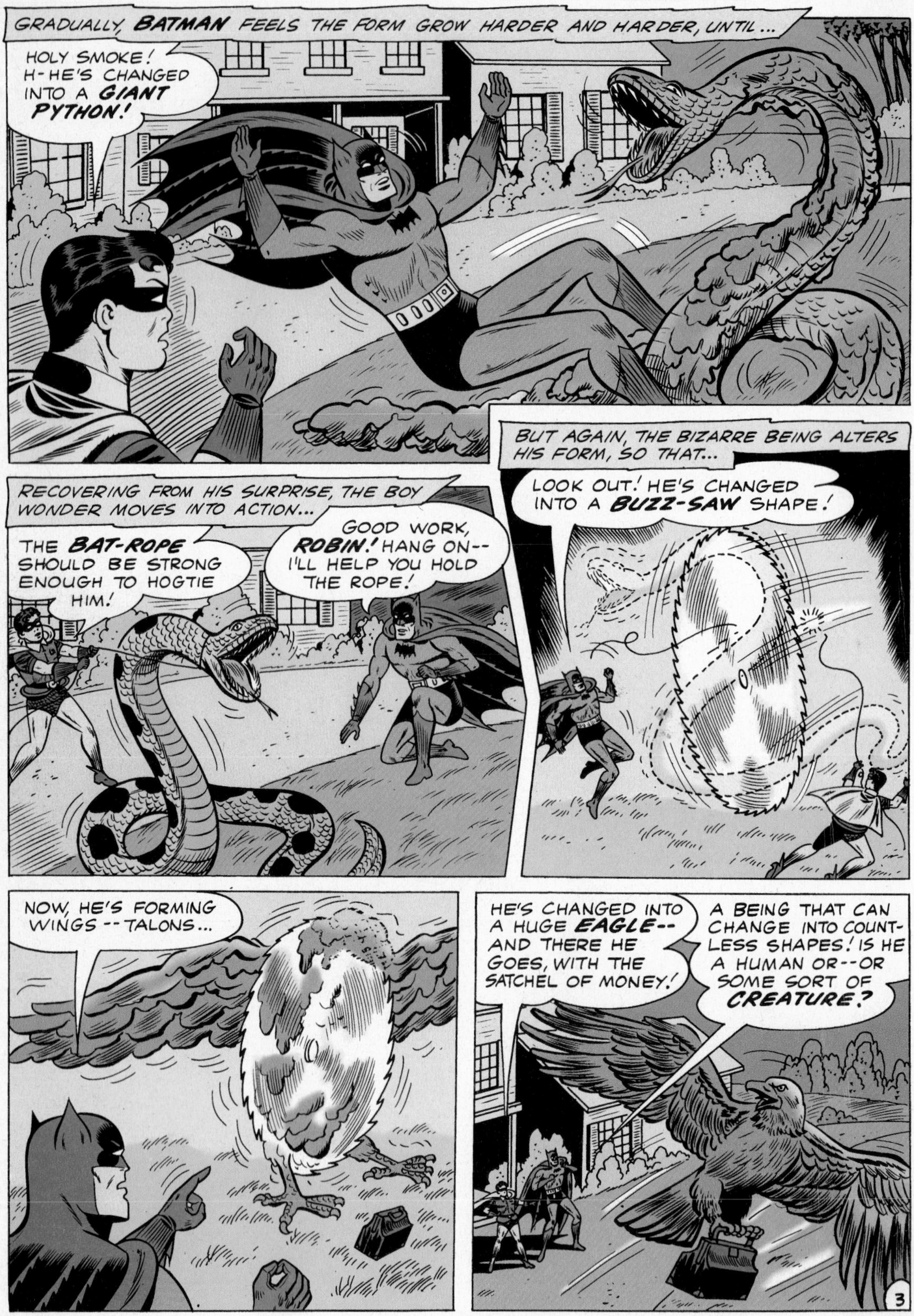
GRADUALLY, BATMAN FEELS THE FORM GROW HARDER AND HARDER, UNTIL...
HOLY SMOKE! H-HE'S CHANGED INTO A GIANT PYTHON!
RECOVERING FROM HIS SURPRISE, THE BOY WONDER MOVES INTO ACTION...
THE BAT-ROPE SHOULD BE STRONG ENOUGH TO HOGTIE HIM!
GOOD WORK, ROBIN! HANG ON-- I'LL HELP YOU HOLD THE ROPE!
BUT AGAIN, THE BIZARRE BEING ALTERS HIS FORM, SO THAT...
LOOK OUT! HE'S CHANGED INTO A BUZZ-SAW SHAPE!
NOW, HE'S FORMING WINGS -- TALONS...
HE'S CHANGED INTO A HUGE EAGLE-- AND THERE HE GOES, WITH THE SATCHEL OF MONEY!
A BEING THAT CAN CHANGE INTO COUNTLESS SHAPES! IS HE A HUMAN OR--OR SOME SORT OF CREATURE?
3

SOON AFTER, THE "EAGLE" ALIGHTS ON A TENEMENT ROOF, AND WALKS ON TALONED FEET...

...FEET THAT CHANGE INTO CLAY-LIKE SHAPES...

...AND, FINALLY, INTO THOSE OF A *MAN!*

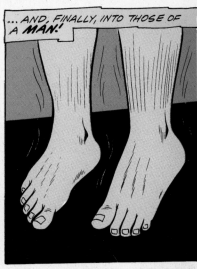

DOWN HE DESCENDS, INTO A SHABBY ATTIC, WHERE...

HA, HA! $100,000! MATT HAGEN -- YOU'RE RICH... RICH!

HOW DID THIS MAN ACQUIRE HIS UNIQUE POWERS? TO LEARN THE ANSWER, WE MUST TURN THE CLOCK BACK TO EARLY MORNING...

... WHEN MATT HAGEN WENT SKIN-DIVING IN SEARCH OF HIDDEN WEALTH...

ONLY CHUMPS WORK AT JOBS... NOT ME! ONE OF THESE DAYS, I'LL FIND A SUNKEN FRIGATE LOADED WITH TREASURE! I'LL BE RICH!

LATER, SURFACING TO REST, HAGEN FOUND HIMSELF IN AN UNDISCOVERED GROTTO...

HMM... A NATURAL POOL! STRANGE -- IT SEEMS TO BUBBLE UP COLORS OF EVERY SHADE! THIS RATES A CLOSER LOOK ...

BUT A STONE, SLIDING UNDERFOOT, SENT HIM PLUNGING *INTO* THE POOL ...

THIS ISN'T WATER! IT'S A KIND OF PROTOPLASM -- CLINGING TO ME... SENDING SOME STRANGE ENERGY THROUGH MY BODY!

4

CLIMBING OUT, HAGEN REELED WITH SHOCK AND TERROR...

AGHH-- THAT POOL DID SOMETHING TO MY BODY! IT'S LIKE SOME KIND OF CLAY... HARD CLAY!

AND NOW, HIS MIND COULD ONLY CONCENTRATE ON ONE SINGLE THOUGHT...

;SOB;! IF ONLY I COULD BE AS I USED TO BE-- IF ONLY I COULD LOOK AS I DID BEFORE...

STRANGE-- I FELT AS IF MY BRAIN WERE SENDING ENERGY THROUGH MY BODY... COMMANDING MY BODY... MAKING IT CHANGE!

IT IS CHANGING! MY BODY'S SOFT AND PLIABLE NOW! IT'S AS IF MY MIND IS MOLDING MY BODY LIKE SOFT CLAY...

I'M MYSELF AGAIN! MY BODY IS HARD AGAIN-- BECAUSE THE CHANGE IS NOW COMPLETE!

THAT STRANGE PROTOPLASM... A FREAK OF NATURE-- OR MAYBE IT DRIFTED HERE FROM OUTER SPACE! I WONDER IF THE POWER IT GAVE ME IS GONE? I'LL TRY ANOTHER MENTAL COMMAND...

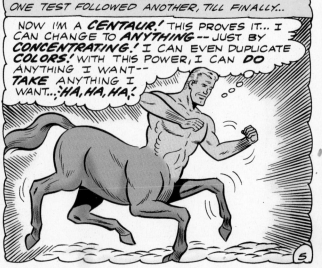

ONE TEST FOLLOWED ANOTHER, TILL FINALLY...

NOW I'M A CENTAUR! THIS PROVES IT... I CAN CHANGE TO ANYTHING-- JUST BY CONCENTRATING! I CAN EVEN DUPLICATE COLORS! WITH THIS POWER, I CAN DO ANYTHING I WANT-- TAKE ANYTHING I WANT...;HA,HA,HA!

5

30

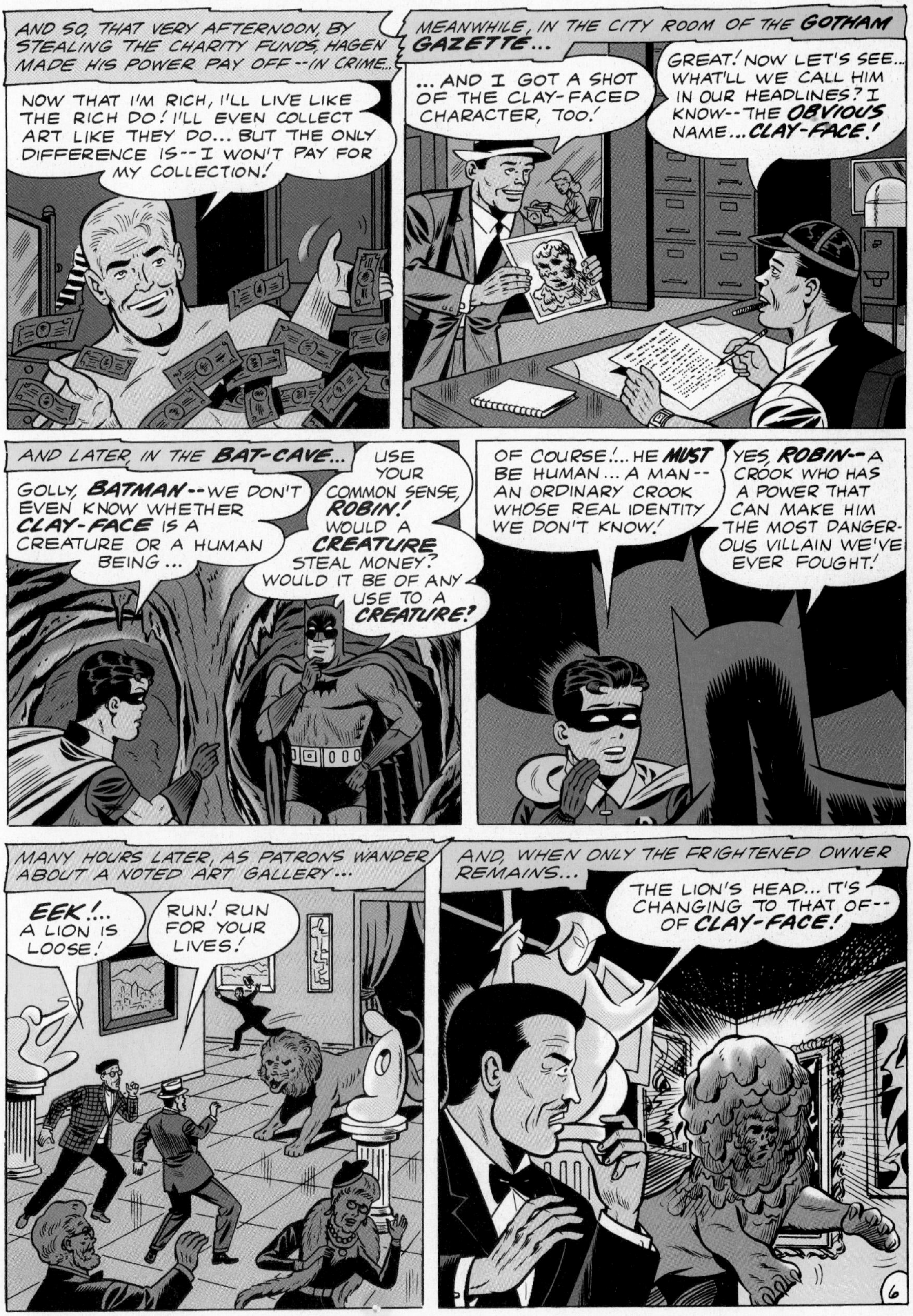
AND SO, THAT VERY AFTERNOON, BY STEALING THE CHARITY FUNDS, HAGEN MADE HIS POWER PAY OFF--IN CRIME...
NOW THAT I'M RICH, I'LL LIVE LIKE THE RICH DO! I'LL EVEN COLLECT ART LIKE THEY DO... BUT THE ONLY DIFFERENCE IS--I WON'T PAY FOR MY COLLECTION!
MEANWHILE, IN THE CITY ROOM OF THE GOTHAM GAZETTE...
...AND I GOT A SHOT OF THE CLAY-FACED CHARACTER, TOO!
GREAT! NOW LET'S SEE... WHAT'LL WE CALL HIM IN OUR HEADLINES? I KNOW--THE OBVIOUS NAME...CLAY-FACE!
AND LATER, IN THE BAT-CAVE...
GOLLY, BATMAN--WE DON'T EVEN KNOW WHETHER CLAY-FACE IS A CREATURE OR A HUMAN BEING...
USE YOUR COMMON SENSE, ROBIN! WOULD A CREATURE STEAL MONEY? WOULD IT BE OF ANY USE TO A CREATURE?
OF COURSE!... HE MUST BE HUMAN... A MAN--AN ORDINARY CROOK WHOSE REAL IDENTITY WE DON'T KNOW!
YES, ROBIN--A CROOK WHO HAS A POWER THAT CAN MAKE HIM THE MOST DANGEROUS VILLAIN WE'VE EVER FOUGHT!
MANY HOURS LATER, AS PATRONS WANDER ABOUT A NOTED ART GALLERY...
EEK!... A LION IS LOOSE!
RUN! RUN FOR YOUR LIVES!
AND, WHEN ONLY THE FRIGHTENED OWNER REMAINS...
THE LION'S HEAD... IT'S CHANGING TO THAT OF--OF CLAY-FACE!
6

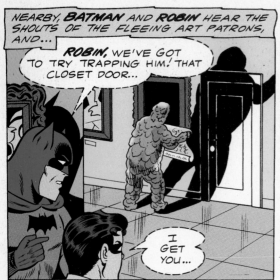

NEARBY, **BATMAN** AND **ROBIN** HEAR THE SHOUTS OF THE FLEEING ART PATRONS, AND...

ROBIN, WE'VE GOT TO TRY TRAPPING HIM! THAT CLOSET DOOR...

I GET YOU...

ON SIGNAL, **BATMAN** CATAPULTS FORWARD... AS **ROBIN** WHIPS OPEN THE CLOSET DOOR, AND...

NOW!

OOF!

DID IT! WE'VE GOT HIM TRAPPED INSIDE!

SLAM

BUT NEXT INSTANT...

GREAT SCOTT! HE CAN MAKE HIS BODY SMALL ENOUGH TO SLIP OUT THROUGH THE KEYHOLE!

NOW I'LL GRAB THAT ROLLED-UP PAINTING, CHANGE INTO A GIANT BIRD AGAIN-- AND FLY OUT OF HERE WITH MY LOOT!

A MOMENT LATER, HOWEVER...

SOMETHING'S WRONG! MY BODY WON'T CHANGE! MY POWER...IT'S EBBING!

7

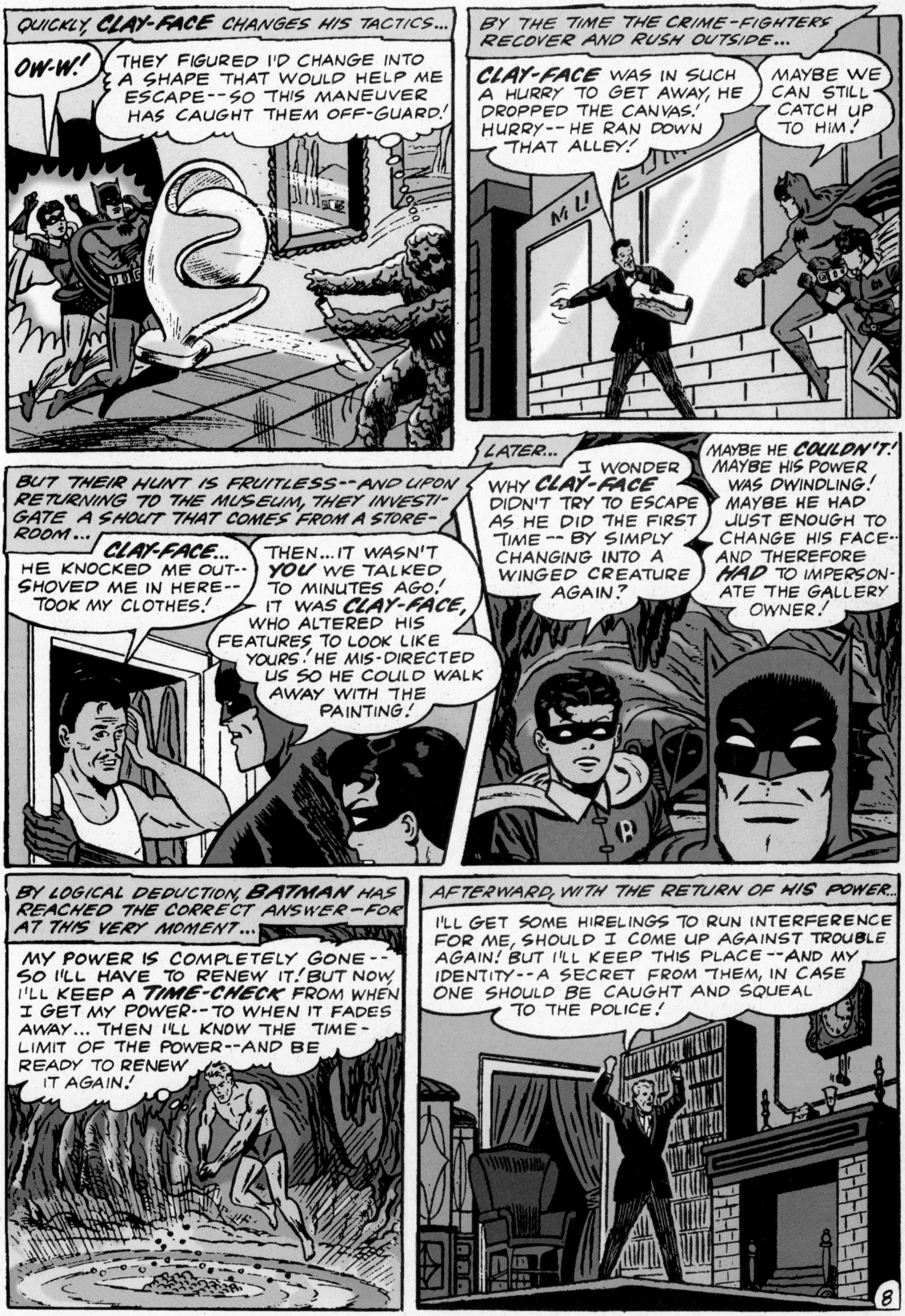
QUICKLY, CLAY-FACE CHANGES HIS TACTICS...
OW-W!
THEY FIGURED I'D CHANGE INTO A SHAPE THAT WOULD HELP ME ESCAPE--SO THIS MANEUVER HAS CAUGHT THEM OFF-GUARD!
BY THE TIME THE CRIME-FIGHTERS RECOVER AND RUSH OUTSIDE...
CLAY-FACE WAS IN SUCH A HURRY TO GET AWAY, HE DROPPED THE CANVAS! HURRY--HE RAN DOWN THAT ALLEY!
MAYBE WE CAN STILL CATCH UP TO HIM!
BUT THEIR HUNT IS FRUITLESS--AND UPON RETURNING TO THE MUSEUM, THEY INVESTIGATE A SHOUT THAT COMES FROM A STOREROOM...
CLAY-FACE... HE KNOCKED ME OUT--SHOVED ME IN HERE--TOOK MY CLOTHES!
THEN...IT WASN'T YOU WE TALKED TO MINUTES AGO! IT WAS CLAY-FACE, WHO ALTERED HIS FEATURES TO LOOK LIKE YOURS! HE MIS-DIRECTED US SO HE COULD WALK AWAY WITH THE PAINTING!
LATER...
I WONDER WHY CLAY-FACE DIDN'T TRY TO ESCAPE AS HE DID THE FIRST TIME -- BY SIMPLY CHANGING INTO A WINGED CREATURE AGAIN?
MAYBE HE COULDN'T! MAYBE HIS POWER WAS DWINDLING! MAYBE HE HAD JUST ENOUGH TO CHANGE HIS FACE--AND THEREFORE HAD TO IMPERSONATE THE GALLERY OWNER!
BY LOGICAL DEDUCTION, BATMAN HAS REACHED THE CORRECT ANSWER--FOR AT THIS VERY MOMENT...
MY POWER IS COMPLETELY GONE--SO I'LL HAVE TO RENEW IT! BUT NOW, I'LL KEEP A TIME-CHECK FROM WHEN I GET MY POWER--TO WHEN IT FADES AWAY... THEN I'LL KNOW THE TIME-LIMIT OF THE POWER--AND BE READY TO RENEW IT AGAIN!
AFTERWARD, WITH THE RETURN OF HIS POWER...
I'LL GET SOME HIRELINGS TO RUN INTERFERENCE FOR ME, SHOULD I COME UP AGAINST TROUBLE AGAIN! BUT I'LL KEEP THIS PLACE--AND MY IDENTITY--A SECRET FROM THEM, IN CASE ONE SHOULD BE CAUGHT AND SQUEAL TO THE POLICE!
8

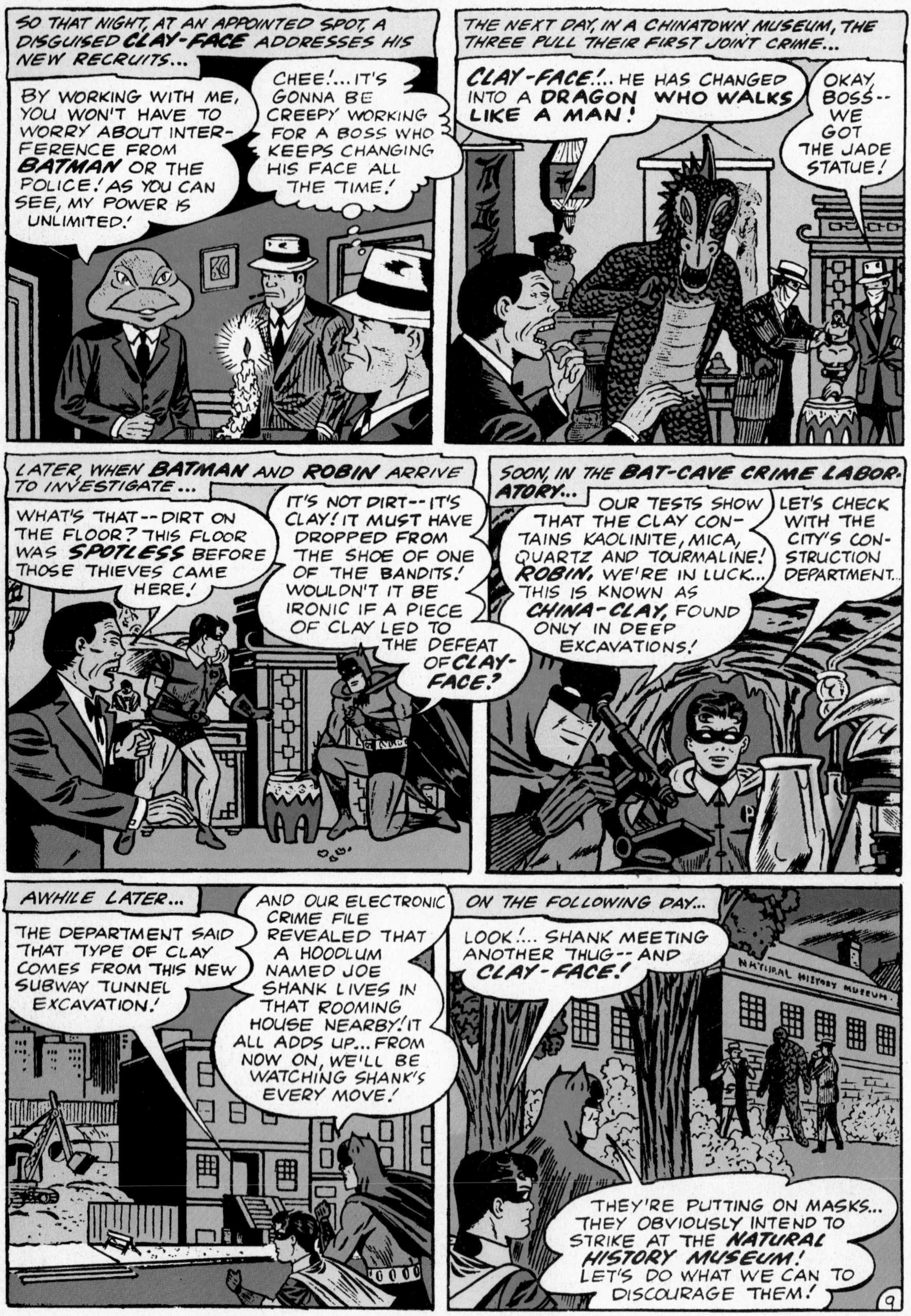

SO THAT NIGHT, AT AN APPOINTED SPOT, A DISGUISED CLAY-FACE ADDRESSES HIS NEW RECRUITS...
BY WORKING WITH ME, YOU WON'T HAVE TO WORRY ABOUT INTERFERENCE FROM BATMAN OR THE POLICE! AS YOU CAN SEE, MY POWER IS UNLIMITED!
CHEE!... IT'S GONNA BE CREEPY WORKING FOR A BOSS WHO KEEPS CHANGING HIS FACE ALL THE TIME!
THE NEXT DAY, IN A CHINATOWN MUSEUM, THE THREE PULL THEIR FIRST JOINT CRIME...
CLAY-FACE!... HE HAS CHANGED INTO A DRAGON WHO WALKS LIKE A MAN!
OKAY, BOSS-- WE GOT THE JADE STATUE!
LATER, WHEN BATMAN AND ROBIN ARRIVE TO INVESTIGATE...
WHAT'S THAT--DIRT ON THE FLOOR? THIS FLOOR WAS SPOTLESS BEFORE THOSE THIEVES CAME HERE!
IT'S NOT DIRT--IT'S CLAY! IT MUST HAVE DROPPED FROM THE SHOE OF ONE OF THE BANDITS! WOULDN'T IT BE IRONIC IF A PIECE OF CLAY LED TO THE DEFEAT OF CLAY-FACE?
SOON, IN THE BAT-CAVE CRIME LABORATORY...
OUR TESTS SHOW THAT THE CLAY CONTAINS KAOLINITE, MICA, QUARTZ AND TOURMALINE! ROBIN, WE'RE IN LUCK... THIS IS KNOWN AS CHINA-CLAY, FOUND ONLY IN DEEP EXCAVATIONS!
LET'S CHECK WITH THE CITY'S CONSTRUCTION DEPARTMENT...
AWHILE LATER...
THE DEPARTMENT SAID THAT TYPE OF CLAY COMES FROM THIS NEW SUBWAY TUNNEL EXCAVATION!
AND OUR ELECTRONIC CRIME FILE REVEALED THAT A HOODLUM NAMED JOE SHANK LIVES IN THAT ROOMING HOUSE NEARBY! IT ALL ADDS UP... FROM NOW ON, WE'LL BE WATCHING SHANK'S EVERY MOVE!
ON THE FOLLOWING DAY...
LOOK!... SHANK MEETING ANOTHER THUG--AND CLAY-FACE!
NATURAL HISTORY MUSEUM
THEY'RE PUTTING ON MASKS... THEY OBVIOUSLY INTEND TO STRIKE AT THE NATURAL HISTORY MUSEUM! LET'S DO WHAT WE CAN TO DISCOURAGE THEM!
9

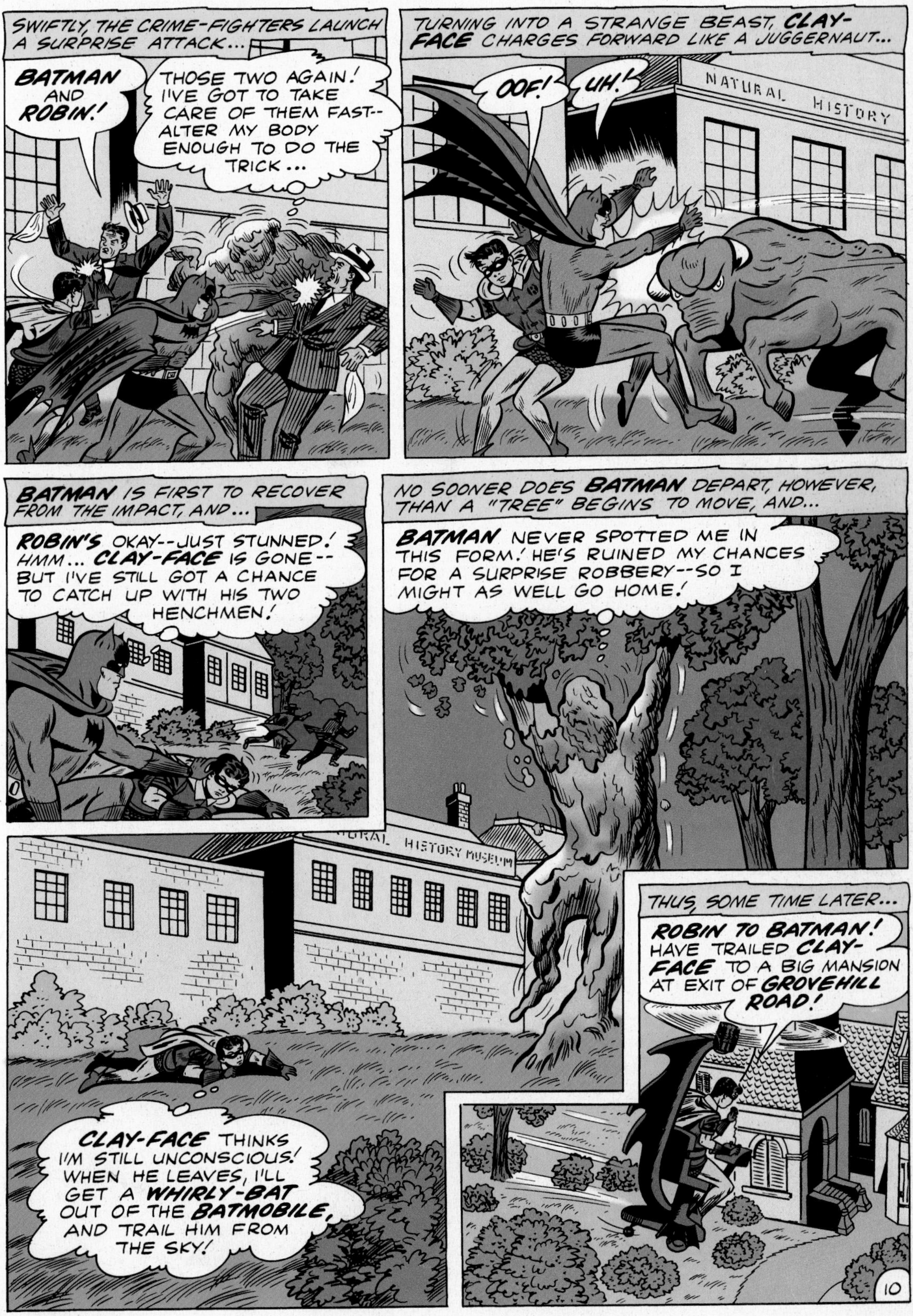
SWIFTLY, THE CRIME-FIGHTERS LAUNCH A SURPRISE ATTACK...
BATMAN AND ROBIN!
THOSE TWO AGAIN! I'VE GOT TO TAKE CARE OF THEM FAST-- ALTER MY BODY ENOUGH TO DO THE TRICK...
TURNING INTO A STRANGE BEAST, CLAY-FACE CHARGES FORWARD LIKE A JUGGERNAUT...
OOF!
UH!
NATURAL HISTORY
BATMAN IS FIRST TO RECOVER FROM THE IMPACT, AND...
ROBIN'S OKAY--JUST STUNNED! HMM... CLAY-FACE IS GONE-- BUT I'VE STILL GOT A CHANCE TO CATCH UP WITH HIS TWO HENCHMEN!
NO SOONER DOES BATMAN DEPART, HOWEVER, THAN A "TREE" BEGINS TO MOVE, AND...
BATMAN NEVER SPOTTED ME IN THIS FORM! HE'S RUINED MY CHANCES FOR A SURPRISE ROBBERY--SO I MIGHT AS WELL GO HOME!
URAL HISTORY MUSEUM
CLAY-FACE THINKS I'M STILL UNCONSCIOUS! WHEN HE LEAVES, I'LL GET A WHIRLY-BAT OUT OF THE BATMOBILE, AND TRAIL HIM FROM THE SKY!
THUS, SOME TIME LATER...
ROBIN TO BATMAN! HAVE TRAILED CLAY-FACE TO A BIG MANSION AT EXIT OF GROVEHILL ROAD!
10

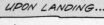

UPON LANDING...

ALL THE WINDOWS ARE SHUTTERED--I CAN'T SEE INTO THE PLACE! BUT I CAN GET INSIDE VIA THAT WIDE CHIMNEY-- AND MAYBE SEE *CLAY-FACE* RESUME HIS REAL IDENTITY!

MEANWHILE, UNAWARE THAT *ROBIN* IS DESCENDING THE CHIMNEY, *CLAY-FACE* HAS ASSUMED HIS HUMAN FORM...

HMM...SO FAR, I STILL HAVE MY POWER--AND IT'S BEEN NEARLY 48 HOURS SINCE I LAST RENEWED IT! I WONDER WHAT THE TIME-LIMIT IS?

WITHOUT WARNING, A LOOSE RUNG IN THE OLD CHIMNEY GIVES WAY UNDER *ROBIN'S* WEIGHT, AND...

ROBIN! HE'S FOUND OUT WHERE I LIVE!

AND WHILE THE BOY WONDER SCRAMBLES OUT OF THE FIREPLACE, *CLAY-FACE* ASSUMES A MENACING FORM...

HE'LL NEVER LIVE TO TELL MY SECRET TO ANYONE!

GOSH... NOW HE'S PART LION -- PART DINOSAUR -- PART UNICORN!

ONLY *ROBIN'S* AGILITY SAVES HIM FROM INSTANT DEATH...

THOUN-NK

11

36

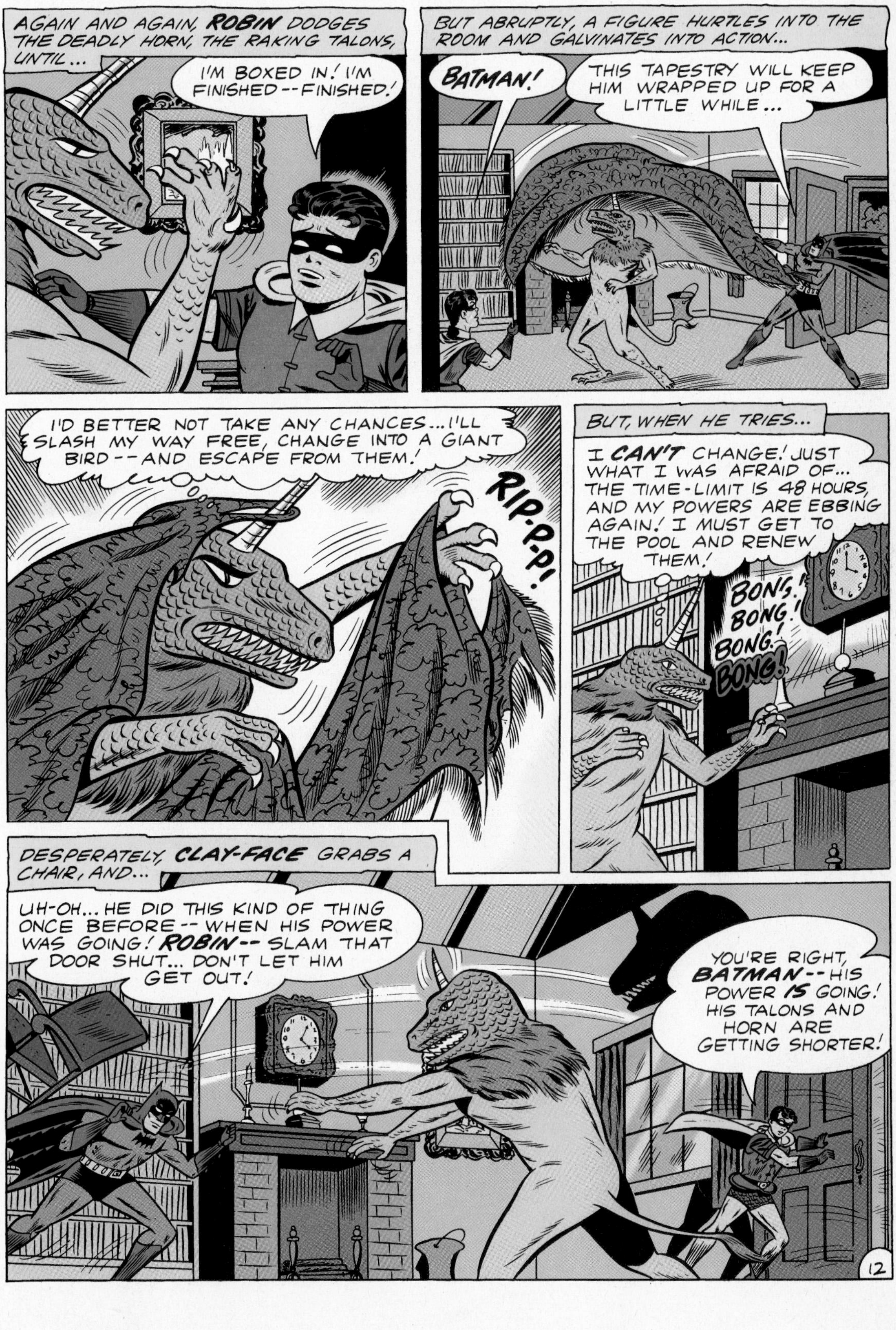
AGAIN AND AGAIN, ROBIN DODGES THE DEADLY HORN, THE RAKING TALONS, UNTIL...
I'M BOXED IN! I'M FINISHED--FINISHED!
BUT ABRUPTLY, A FIGURE HURTLES INTO THE ROOM AND GALVINATES INTO ACTION...
BATMAN!
THIS TAPESTRY WILL KEEP HIM WRAPPED UP FOR A LITTLE WHILE...
I'D BETTER NOT TAKE ANY CHANCES...I'LL SLASH MY WAY FREE, CHANGE INTO A GIANT BIRD--AND ESCAPE FROM THEM!
RIP-P-P!
BUT, WHEN HE TRIES...
I CAN'T CHANGE! JUST WHAT I WAS AFRAID OF... THE TIME-LIMIT IS 48 HOURS, AND MY POWERS ARE EBBING AGAIN! I MUST GET TO THE POOL AND RENEW THEM!
BONG! BONG! BONG! BONG!
DESPERATELY, CLAY-FACE GRABS A CHAIR, AND...
UH-OH... HE DID THIS KIND OF THING ONCE BEFORE--WHEN HIS POWER WAS GOING! ROBIN--SLAM THAT DOOR SHUT... DON'T LET HIM GET OUT!
YOU'RE RIGHT, BATMAN--HIS POWER IS GOING! HIS TALONS AND HORN ARE GETTING SHORTER!
12

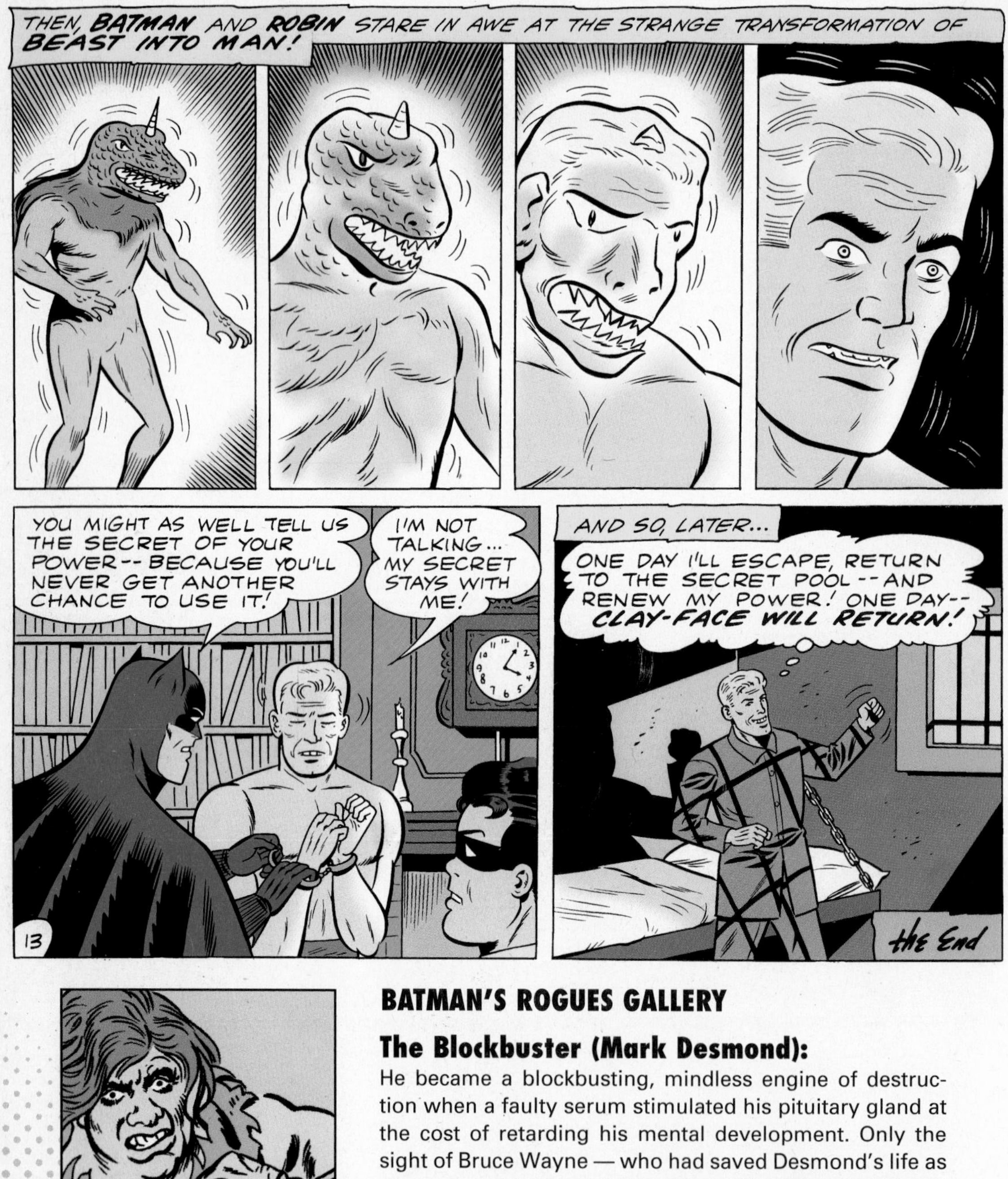
THEN, BATMAN AND ROBIN STARE IN AWE AT THE STRANGE TRANSFORMATION OF BEAST INTO MAN!
YOU MIGHT AS WELL TELL US THE SECRET OF YOUR POWER -- BECAUSE YOU'LL NEVER GET ANOTHER CHANCE TO USE IT!
I'M NOT TALKING... MY SECRET STAYS WITH ME!
13
AND SO, LATER...
ONE DAY I'LL ESCAPE, RETURN TO THE SECRET POOL -- AND RENEW MY POWER! ONE DAY-- CLAY-FACE WILL RETURN!
the End

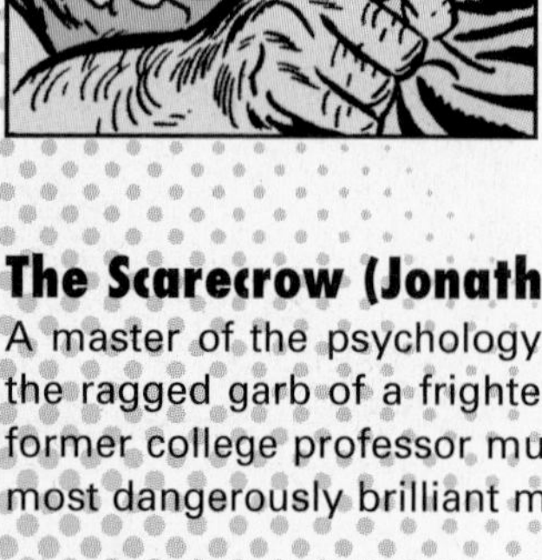

BATMAN'S ROGUES GALLERY

The Blockbuster (Mark Desmond):

He became a blockbusting, mindless engine of destruction when a faulty serum stimulated his pituitary gland at the cost of retarding his mental development. Only the sight of Bruce Wayne — who had saved Desmond's life as a boy — could calm the Blockbuster, forcing a situation in which Batman would have to reveal his secret identity to subdue his threat.

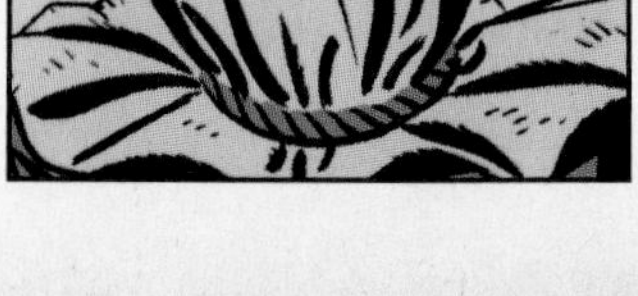

The Scarecrow (Jonathan Crane):

A master of the psychology of terror, Crane dresses in the ragged garb of a frightening, living scarecrow. This former college professor must be considered one of the most dangerously brilliant men in the world.

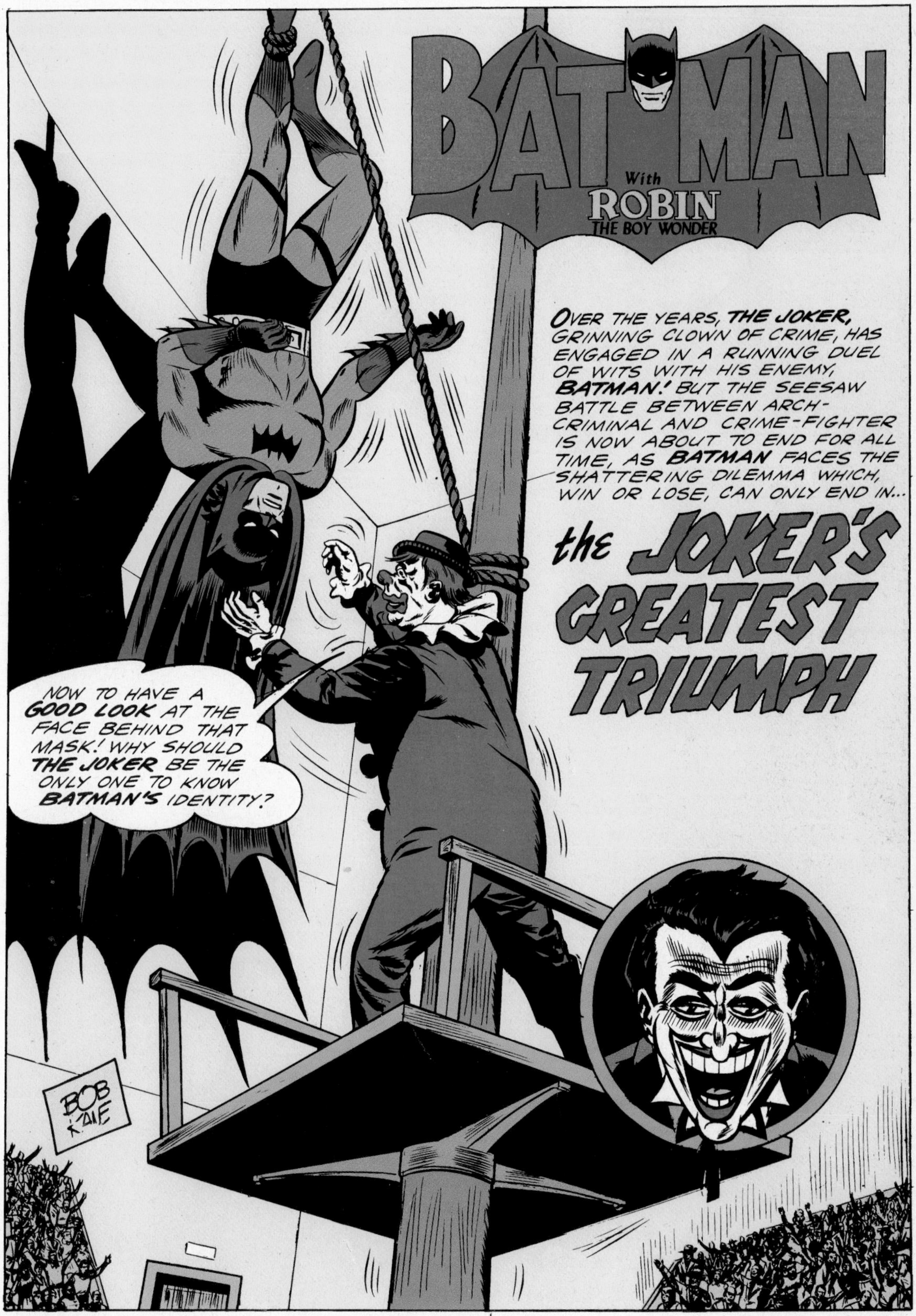
BATMAN
With ROBIN THE BOY WONDER
OVER THE YEARS, THE JOKER, GRINNING CLOWN OF CRIME, HAS ENGAGED IN A RUNNING DUEL OF WITS WITH HIS ENEMY, BATMAN! BUT THE SEESAW BATTLE BETWEEN ARCH-CRIMINAL AND CRIME-FIGHTER IS NOW ABOUT TO END FOR ALL TIME, AS BATMAN FACES THE SHATTERING DILEMMA WHICH, WIN OR LOSE, CAN ONLY END IN...
the JOKER'S GREATEST TRIUMPH
NOW TO HAVE A GOOD LOOK AT THE FACE BEHIND THAT MASK! WHY SHOULD THE JOKER BE THE ONLY ONE TO KNOW BATMAN'S IDENTITY?
BOB KANE

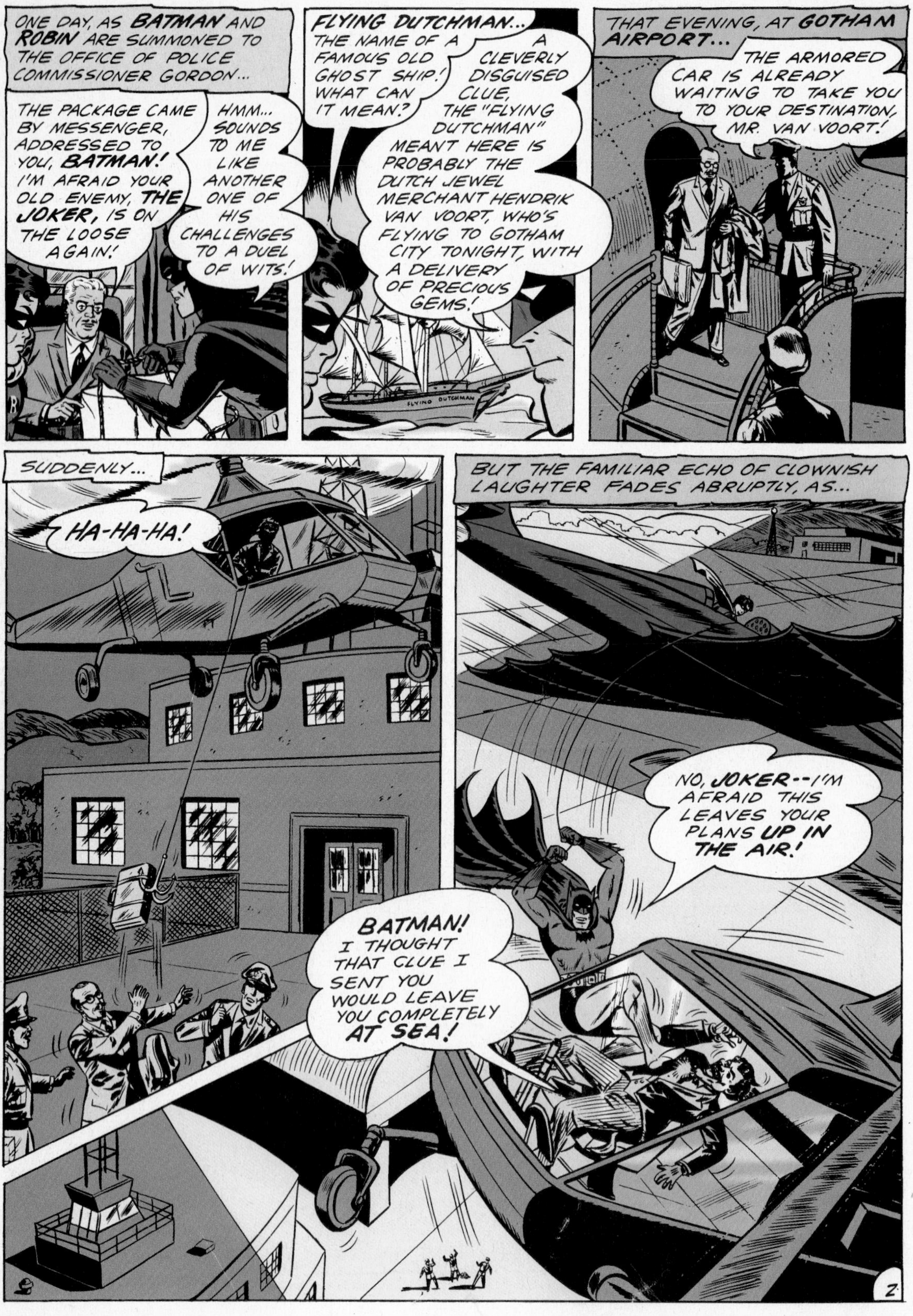
ONE DAY, AS BATMAN AND ROBIN ARE SUMMONED TO THE OFFICE OF POLICE COMMISSIONER GORDON...
THE PACKAGE CAME BY MESSENGER, ADDRESSED TO YOU, BATMAN! I'M AFRAID YOUR OLD ENEMY, THE JOKER, IS ON THE LOOSE AGAIN!
HMM... SOUNDS TO ME LIKE ANOTHER ONE OF HIS CHALLENGES TO A DUEL OF WITS!
FLYING DUTCHMAN... THE NAME OF A FAMOUS OLD GHOST SHIP! WHAT CAN IT MEAN?
A CLEVERLY DISGUISED CLUE, THE "FLYING DUTCHMAN" MEANT HERE IS PROBABLY THE DUTCH JEWEL MERCHANT HENDRIK VAN VOORT, WHO'S FLYING TO GOTHAM CITY TONIGHT, WITH A DELIVERY OF PRECIOUS GEMS!
FLYING DUTCHMAN
THAT EVENING, AT GOTHAM AIRPORT...
THE ARMORED CAR IS ALREADY WAITING TO TAKE YOU TO YOUR DESTINATION, MR. VAN VOORT!
SUDDENLY...
HA-HA-HA!
BUT THE FAMILIAR ECHO OF CLOWNISH LAUGHTER FADES ABRUPTLY, AS...
NO, JOKER--I'M AFRAID THIS LEAVES YOUR PLANS UP IN THE AIR!
BATMAN! I THOUGHT THAT CLUE I SENT YOU WOULD LEAVE YOU COMPLETELY AT SEA!
2

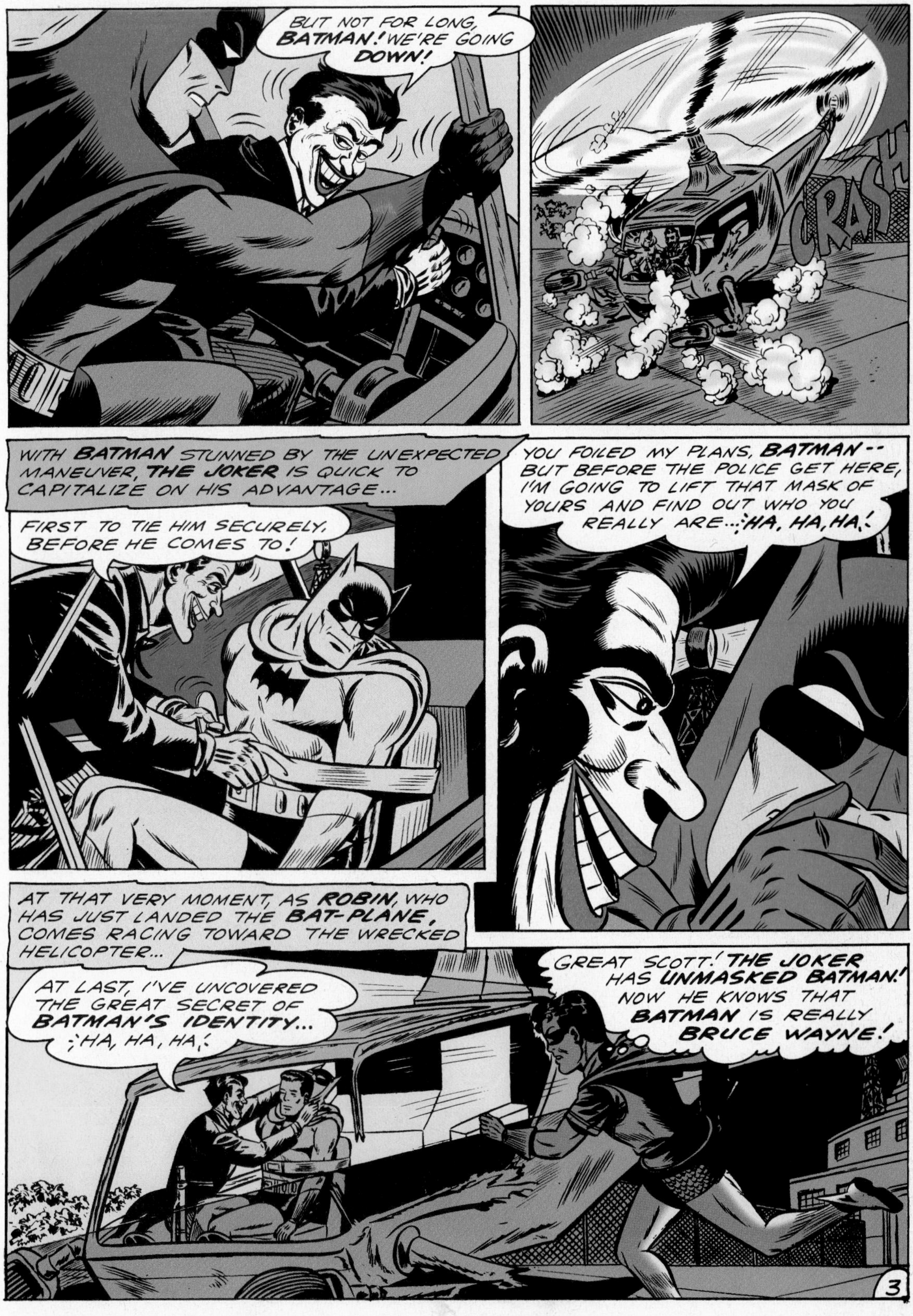
BUT NOT FOR LONG, BATMAN! WE'RE GOING DOWN!
CRASH
WITH BATMAN STUNNED BY THE UNEXPECTED MANEUVER, THE JOKER IS QUICK TO CAPITALIZE ON HIS ADVANTAGE...
FIRST TO TIE HIM SECURELY, BEFORE HE COMES TO!
YOU FOILED MY PLANS, BATMAN-- BUT BEFORE THE POLICE GET HERE, I'M GOING TO LIFT THAT MASK OF YOURS AND FIND OUT WHO YOU REALLY ARE... HA, HA, HA!
AT THAT VERY MOMENT, AS ROBIN, WHO HAS JUST LANDED THE BAT-PLANE, COMES RACING TOWARD THE WRECKED HELICOPTER...
AT LAST, I'VE UNCOVERED THE GREAT SECRET OF BATMAN'S IDENTITY... HA, HA, HA!
GREAT SCOTT! THE JOKER HAS UNMASKED BATMAN! NOW HE KNOWS THAT BATMAN IS REALLY BRUCE WAYNE!
3

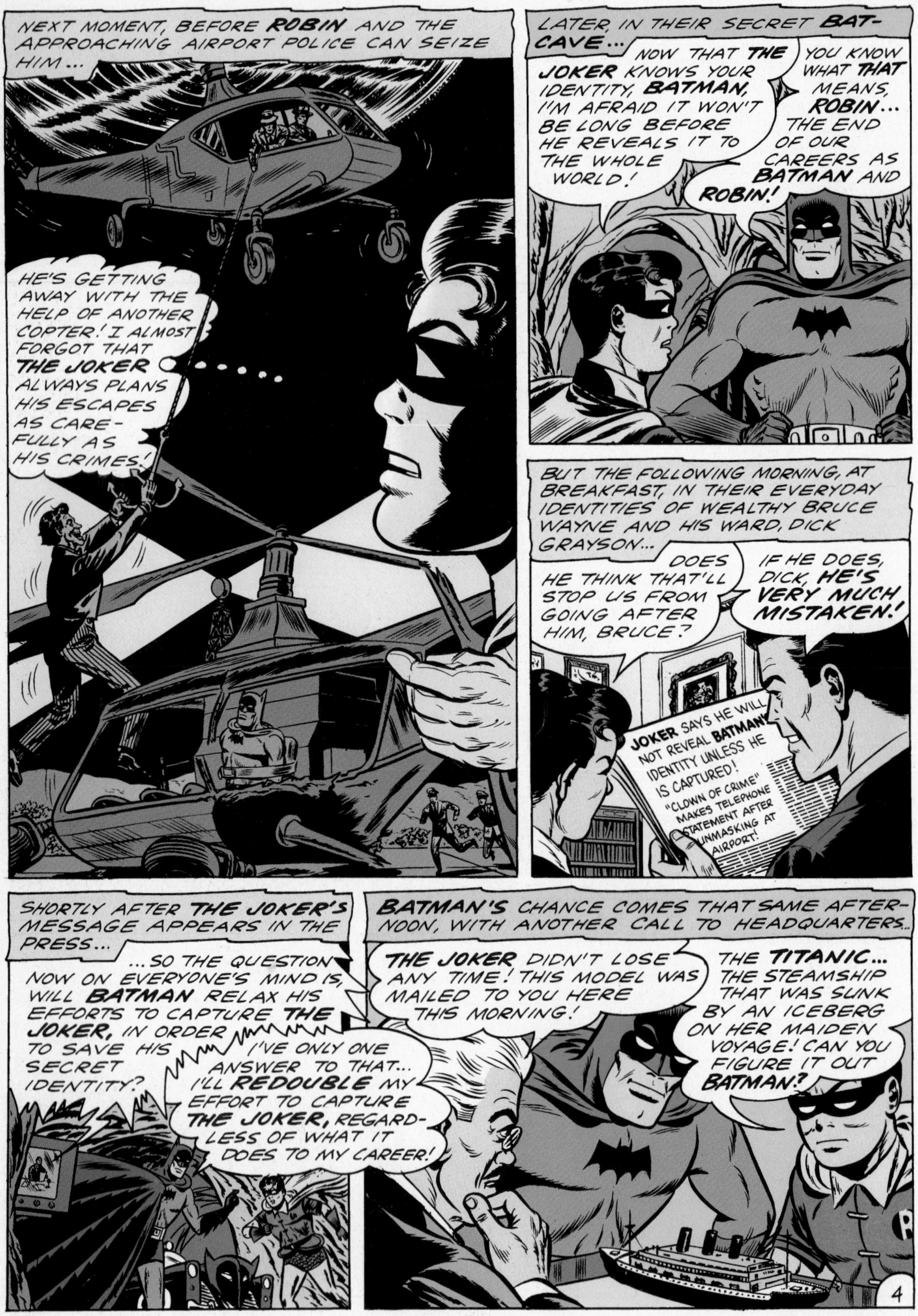
NEXT MOMENT, BEFORE ROBIN AND THE APPROACHING AIRPORT POLICE CAN SEIZE HIM...
HE'S GETTING AWAY WITH THE HELP OF ANOTHER COPTER! I ALMOST FORGOT THAT THE JOKER ALWAYS PLANS HIS ESCAPES AS CARE-FULLY AS HIS CRIMES!
LATER, IN THEIR SECRET BAT-CAVE...
NOW THAT THE JOKER KNOWS YOUR IDENTITY, BATMAN, I'M AFRAID IT WON'T BE LONG BEFORE HE REVEALS IT TO THE WHOLE WORLD!
YOU KNOW WHAT THAT MEANS, ROBIN... THE END OF OUR CAREERS AS BATMAN AND ROBIN!
BUT THE FOLLOWING MORNING, AT BREAKFAST, IN THEIR EVERYDAY IDENTITIES OF WEALTHY BRUCE WAYNE AND HIS WARD, DICK GRAYSON...
DOES HE THINK THAT'LL STOP US FROM GOING AFTER HIM, BRUCE?
IF HE DOES, DICK, HE'S VERY MUCH MISTAKEN!
JOKER SAYS HE WILL NOT REVEAL BATMAN'S IDENTITY UNLESS HE IS CAPTURED!
"CLOWN OF CRIME" MAKES TELEPHONE STATEMENT AFTER UNMASKING AT AIRPORT!
SHORTLY AFTER THE JOKER'S MESSAGE APPEARS IN THE PRESS...
...SO THE QUESTION NOW ON EVERYONE'S MIND IS, WILL BATMAN RELAX HIS EFFORTS TO CAPTURE THE JOKER, IN ORDER TO SAVE HIS SECRET IDENTITY?
I'VE ONLY ONE ANSWER TO THAT... I'LL REDOUBLE MY EFFORT TO CAPTURE THE JOKER, REGARD-LESS OF WHAT IT DOES TO MY CAREER!
BATMAN'S CHANCE COMES THAT SAME AFTER-NOON, WITH ANOTHER CALL TO HEADQUARTERS...
THE JOKER DIDN'T LOSE ANY TIME! THIS MODEL WAS MAILED TO YOU HERE THIS MORNING!
THE TITANIC... THE STEAMSHIP THAT WAS SUNK BY AN ICEBERG ON HER MAIDEN VOYAGE! CAN YOU FIGURE IT OUT BATMAN?
4

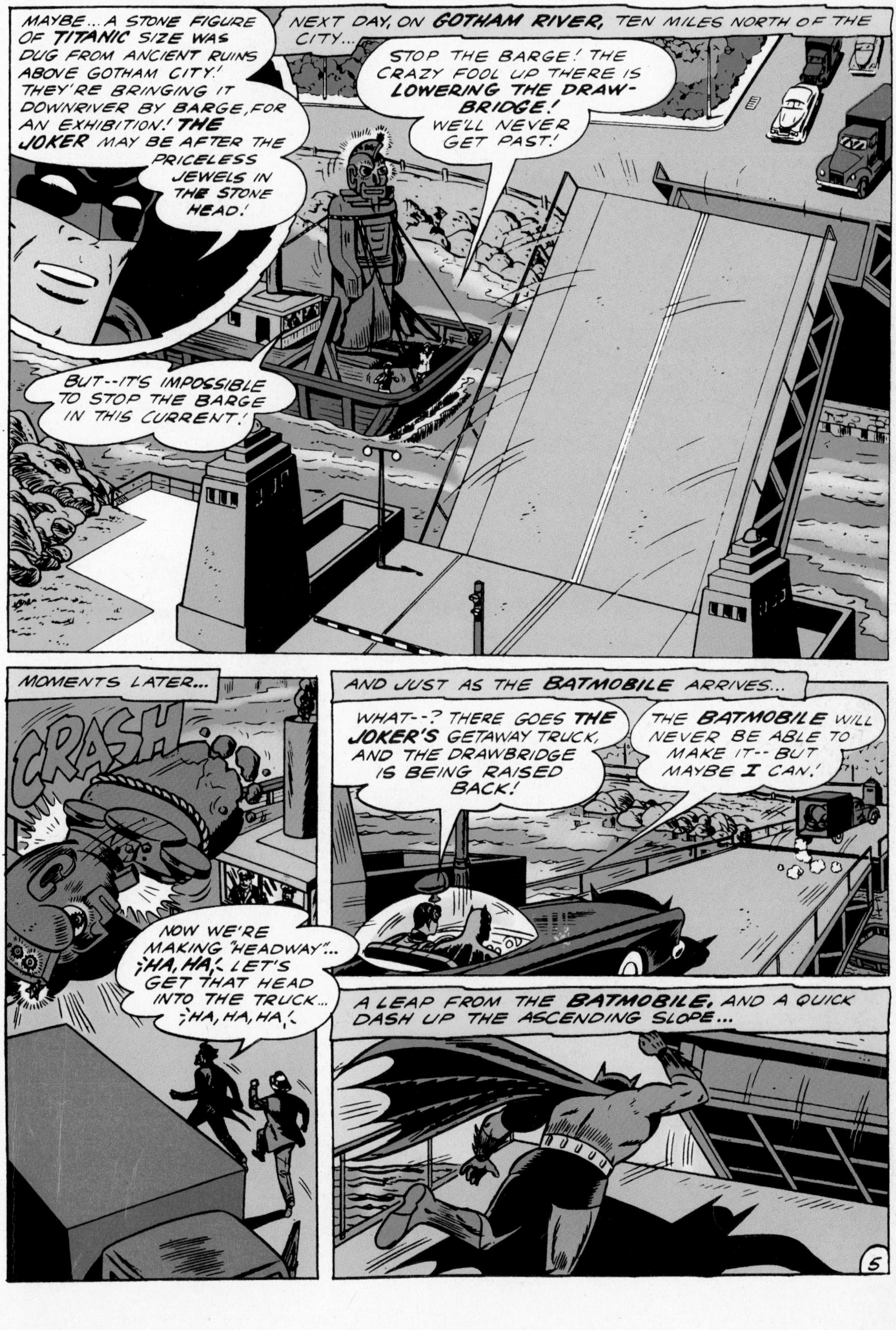

MAYBE... A STONE FIGURE OF TITANIC SIZE WAS DUG FROM ANCIENT RUINS ABOVE GOTHAM CITY! THEY'RE BRINGING IT DOWNRIVER BY BARGE, FOR AN EXHIBITION! THE JOKER MAY BE AFTER THE PRICELESS JEWELS IN THE STONE HEAD!
NEXT DAY, ON GOTHAM RIVER, TEN MILES NORTH OF THE CITY...
STOP THE BARGE! THE CRAZY FOOL UP THERE IS LOWERING THE DRAW-BRIDGE! WE'LL NEVER GET PAST!
BUT--IT'S IMPOSSIBLE TO STOP THE BARGE IN THIS CURRENT!
MOMENTS LATER...
CRASH
NOW WE'RE MAKING "HEADWAY"... ¡HA, HA! LET'S GET THAT HEAD INTO THE TRUCK... ¡HA, HA, HA!
AND JUST AS THE BATMOBILE ARRIVES...
WHAT--? THERE GOES THE JOKER'S GETAWAY TRUCK, AND THE DRAWBRIDGE IS BEING RAISED BACK!
THE BATMOBILE WILL NEVER BE ABLE TO MAKE IT-- BUT MAYBE I CAN!
A LEAP FROM THE BATMOBILE, AND A QUICK DASH UP THE ASCENDING SLOPE...
5

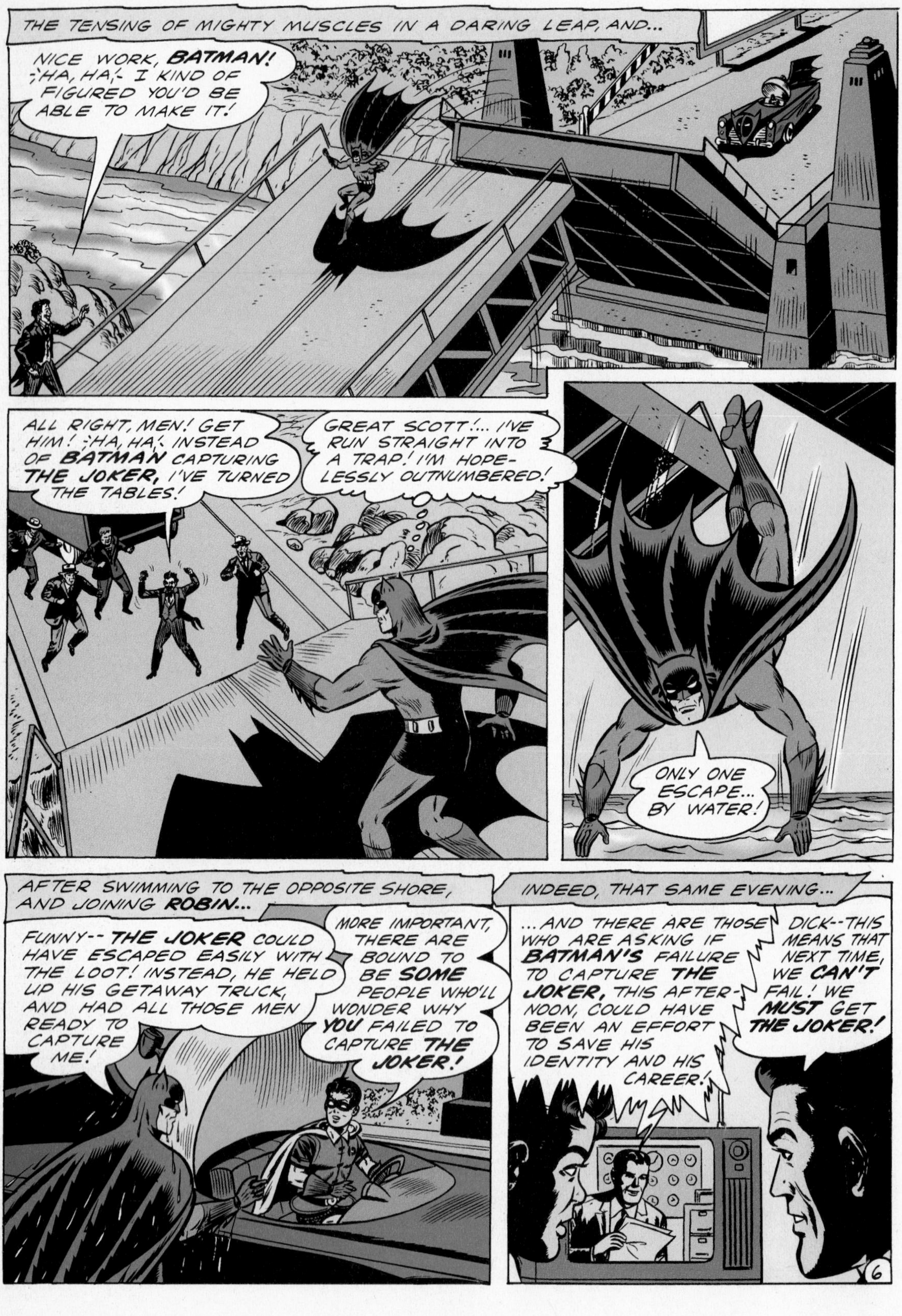
THE TENSING OF MIGHTY MUSCLES IN A DARING LEAP, AND...
NICE WORK, BATMAN! -HA, HA- I KIND OF FIGURED YOU'D BE ABLE TO MAKE IT!
ALL RIGHT, MEN! GET HIM! -HA, HA- INSTEAD OF BATMAN CAPTURING THE JOKER, I'VE TURNED THE TABLES!
GREAT SCOTT!... I'VE RUN STRAIGHT INTO A TRAP! I'M HOPELESSLY OUTNUMBERED!
ONLY ONE ESCAPE... BY WATER!
AFTER SWIMMING TO THE OPPOSITE SHORE, AND JOINING ROBIN...
FUNNY-- THE JOKER COULD HAVE ESCAPED EASILY WITH THE LOOT! INSTEAD, HE HELD UP HIS GETAWAY TRUCK, AND HAD ALL THOSE MEN READY TO CAPTURE ME!
MORE IMPORTANT, THERE ARE BOUND TO BE SOME PEOPLE WHO'LL WONDER WHY YOU FAILED TO CAPTURE THE JOKER!
INDEED, THAT SAME EVENING...
...AND THERE ARE THOSE WHO ARE ASKING IF BATMAN'S FAILURE TO CAPTURE THE JOKER, THIS AFTERNOON, COULD HAVE BEEN AN EFFORT TO SAVE HIS IDENTITY AND HIS CAREER!
DICK--THIS MEANS THAT NEXT TIME, WE CAN'T FAIL! WE MUST GET THE JOKER!
6

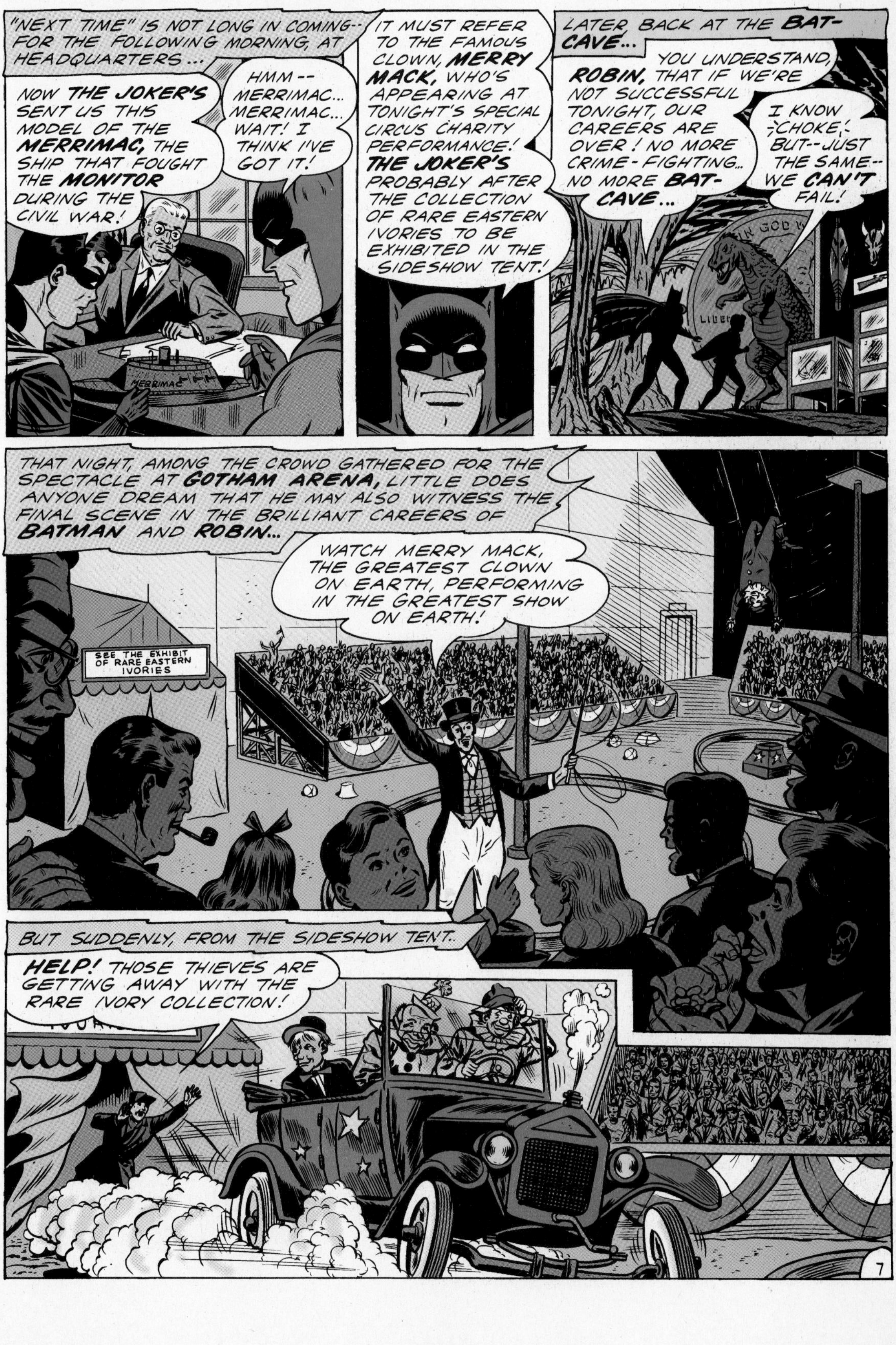
"NEXT TIME" IS NOT LONG IN COMING-- FOR THE FOLLOWING MORNING, AT HEADQUARTERS...
NOW THE JOKER'S SENT US THIS MODEL OF THE MERRIMAC, THE SHIP THAT FOUGHT THE MONITOR DURING THE CIVIL WAR!
HMM -- MERRIMAC... MERRIMAC... WAIT! I THINK I'VE GOT IT!
MERRIMAC
IT MUST REFER TO THE FAMOUS CLOWN, MERRY MACK, WHO'S APPEARING AT TONIGHT'S SPECIAL CIRCUS CHARITY PERFORMANCE! THE JOKER'S PROBABLY AFTER THE COLLECTION OF RARE EASTERN IVORIES TO BE EXHIBITED IN THE SIDESHOW TENT!
LATER BACK AT THE BAT-CAVE...
YOU UNDERSTAND, ROBIN, THAT IF WE'RE NOT SUCCESSFUL TONIGHT, OUR CAREERS ARE OVER! NO MORE CRIME-FIGHTING... NO MORE BAT-CAVE...
I KNOW -CHOKE- BUT--JUST THE SAME-- WE CAN'T FAIL!
THAT NIGHT, AMONG THE CROWD GATHERED FOR THE SPECTACLE AT GOTHAM ARENA, LITTLE DOES ANYONE DREAM THAT HE MAY ALSO WITNESS THE FINAL SCENE IN THE BRILLIANT CAREERS OF BATMAN AND ROBIN...
WATCH MERRY MACK, THE GREATEST CLOWN ON EARTH, PERFORMING IN THE GREATEST SHOW ON EARTH!
SEE THE EXHIBIT OF RARE EASTERN IVORIES
BUT SUDDENLY, FROM THE SIDESHOW TENT..
HELP! THOSE THIEVES ARE GETTING AWAY WITH THE RARE IVORY COLLECTION!
7

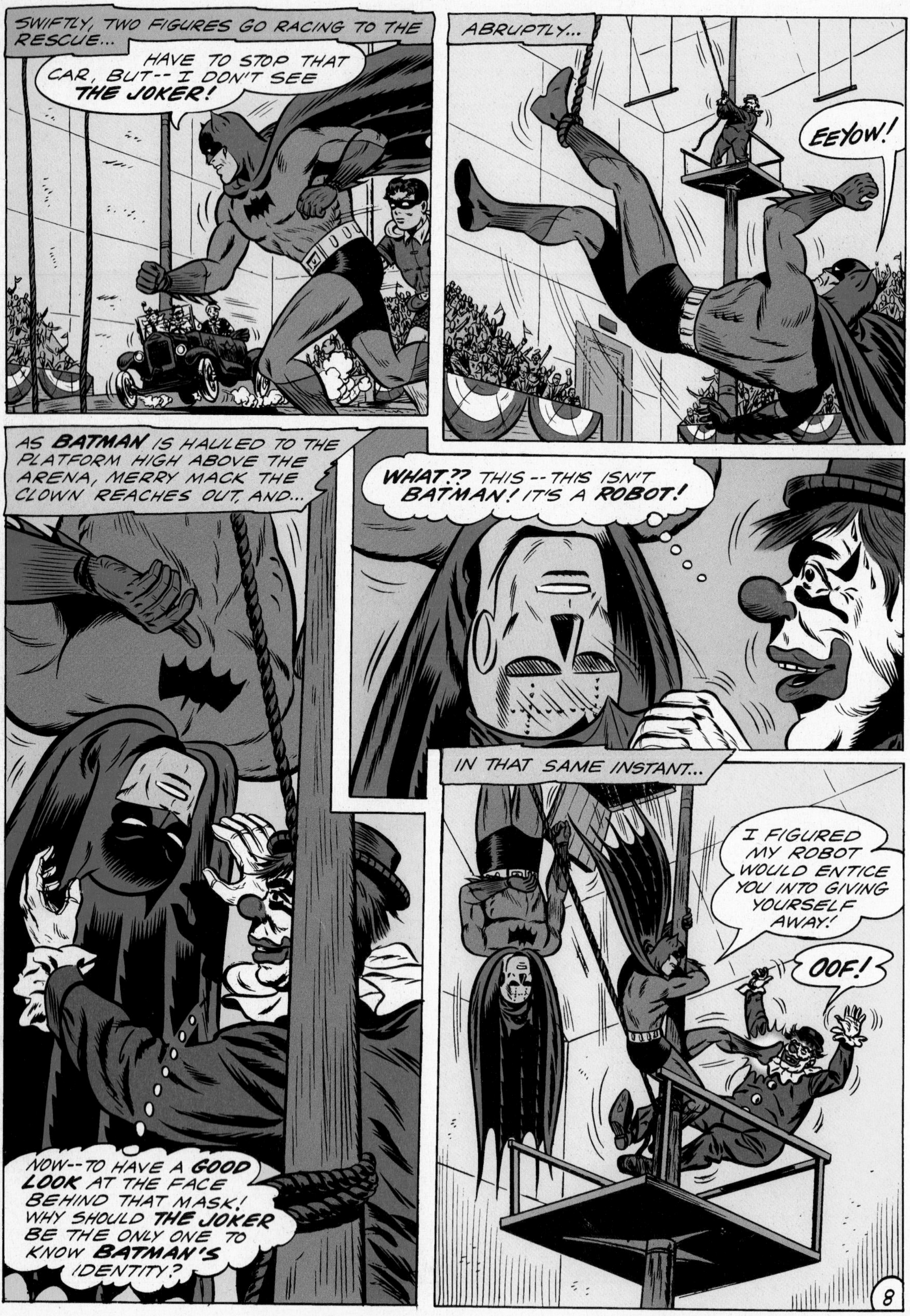
SWIFTLY, TWO FIGURES GO RACING TO THE RESCUE...
HAVE TO STOP THAT CAR, BUT-- I DON'T SEE THE JOKER!
ABRUPTLY...
EEYOW!
AS BATMAN IS HAULED TO THE PLATFORM HIGH ABOVE THE ARENA, MERRY MACK THE CLOWN REACHES OUT, AND...
NOW--TO HAVE A GOOD LOOK AT THE FACE BEHIND THAT MASK! WHY SHOULD THE JOKER BE THE ONLY ONE TO KNOW BATMAN'S IDENTITY?
WHAT?? THIS--THIS ISN'T BATMAN! IT'S A ROBOT!
IN THAT SAME INSTANT...
I FIGURED MY ROBOT WOULD ENTICE YOU INTO GIVING YOURSELF AWAY!
OOF!
8

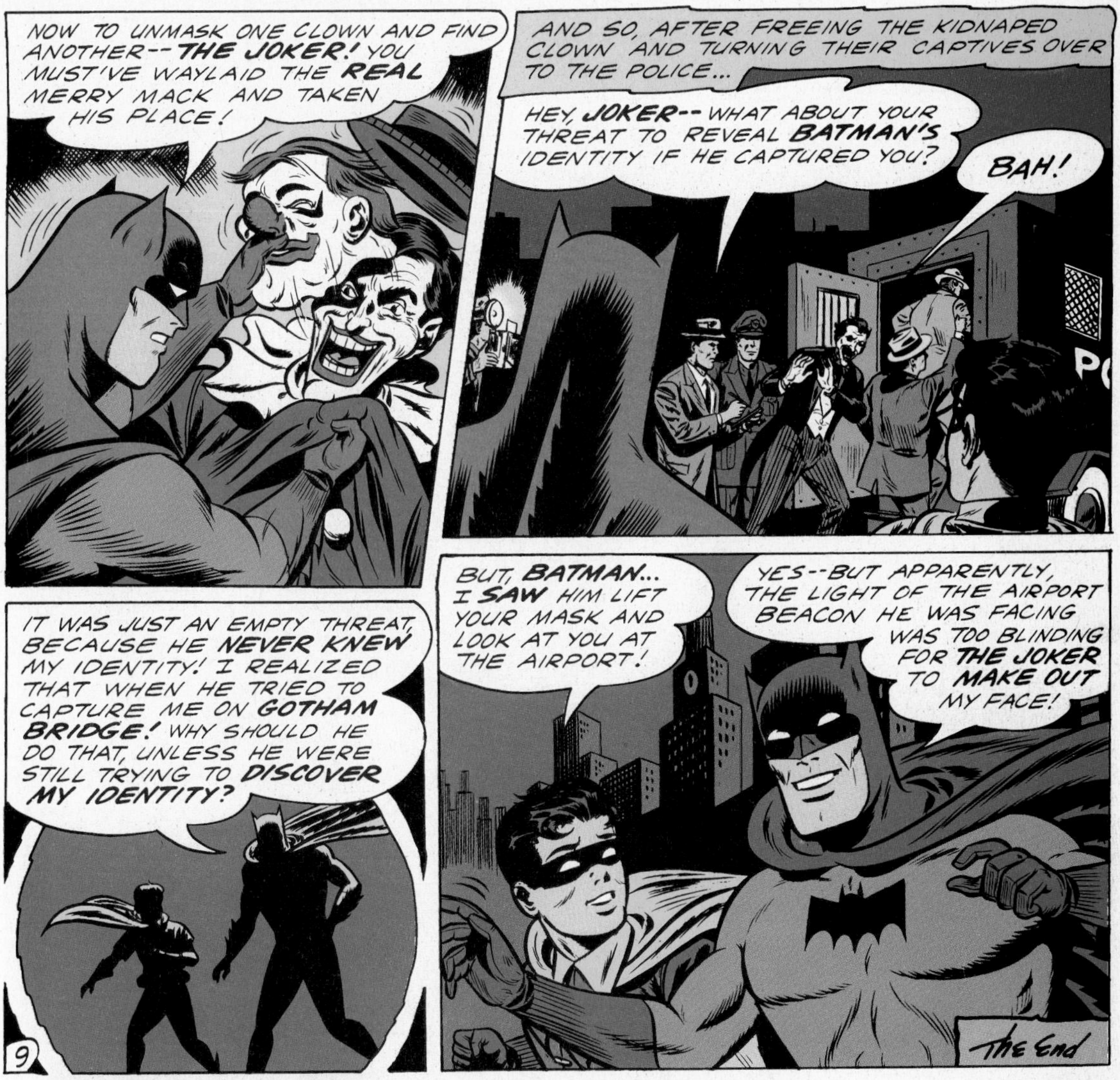
NOW TO UNMASK ONE CLOWN AND FIND ANOTHER-- THE JOKER! YOU MUST'VE WAYLAID THE REAL MERRY MACK AND TAKEN HIS PLACE!
AND SO, AFTER FREEING THE KIDNAPED CLOWN AND TURNING THEIR CAPTIVES OVER TO THE POLICE...
HEY, JOKER-- WHAT ABOUT YOUR THREAT TO REVEAL BATMAN'S IDENTITY IF HE CAPTURED YOU?
BAH!
IT WAS JUST AN EMPTY THREAT, BECAUSE HE NEVER KNEW MY IDENTITY! I REALIZED THAT WHEN HE TRIED TO CAPTURE ME ON GOTHAM BRIDGE! WHY SHOULD HE DO THAT, UNLESS HE WERE STILL TRYING TO DISCOVER MY IDENTITY?
9
BUT, BATMAN... I SAW HIM LIFT YOUR MASK AND LOOK AT YOU AT THE AIRPORT!
YES--BUT APPARENTLY, THE LIGHT OF THE AIRPORT BEACON HE WAS FACING WAS TOO BLINDING FOR THE JOKER TO MAKE OUT MY FACE!
The End

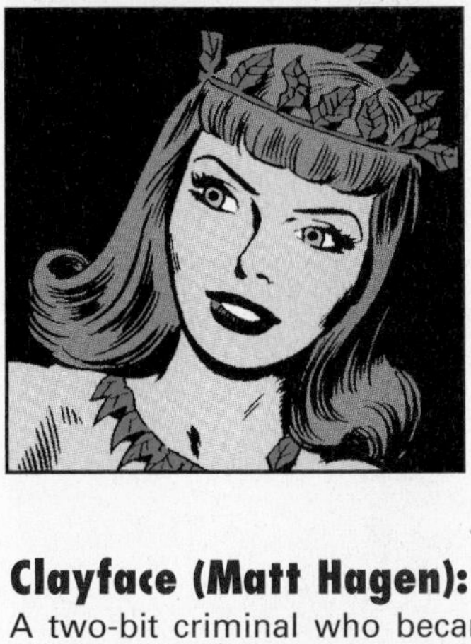

BATMAN'S ROGUES GALLERY

Poison Ivy (Pamela Isley):

Beautiful and brilliant, but deadly, Isley uses her skills in horticulture, preparing deadly plants for her crimes. But her real power lies in her ability to seduce men who succumb to the poison in her kiss — a toxin to which she herself is immune.

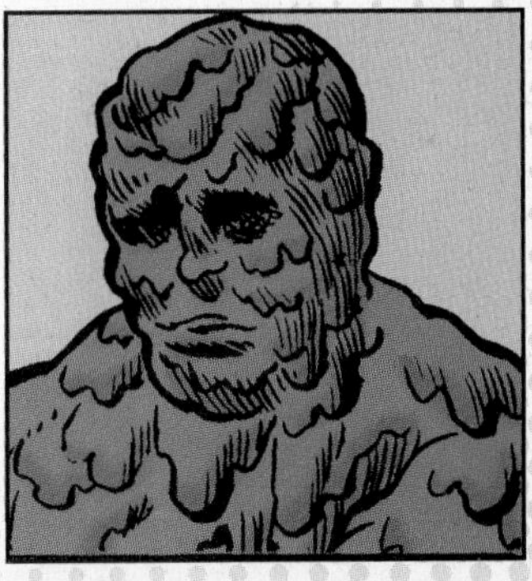

Clayface (Matt Hagen):

A two-bit criminal who became a major threat when he gained fantastic powers after being immersed in a pool of strange, liquid protoplasm. He can transform his body into any form at will, and suffers delusions of grandeur.

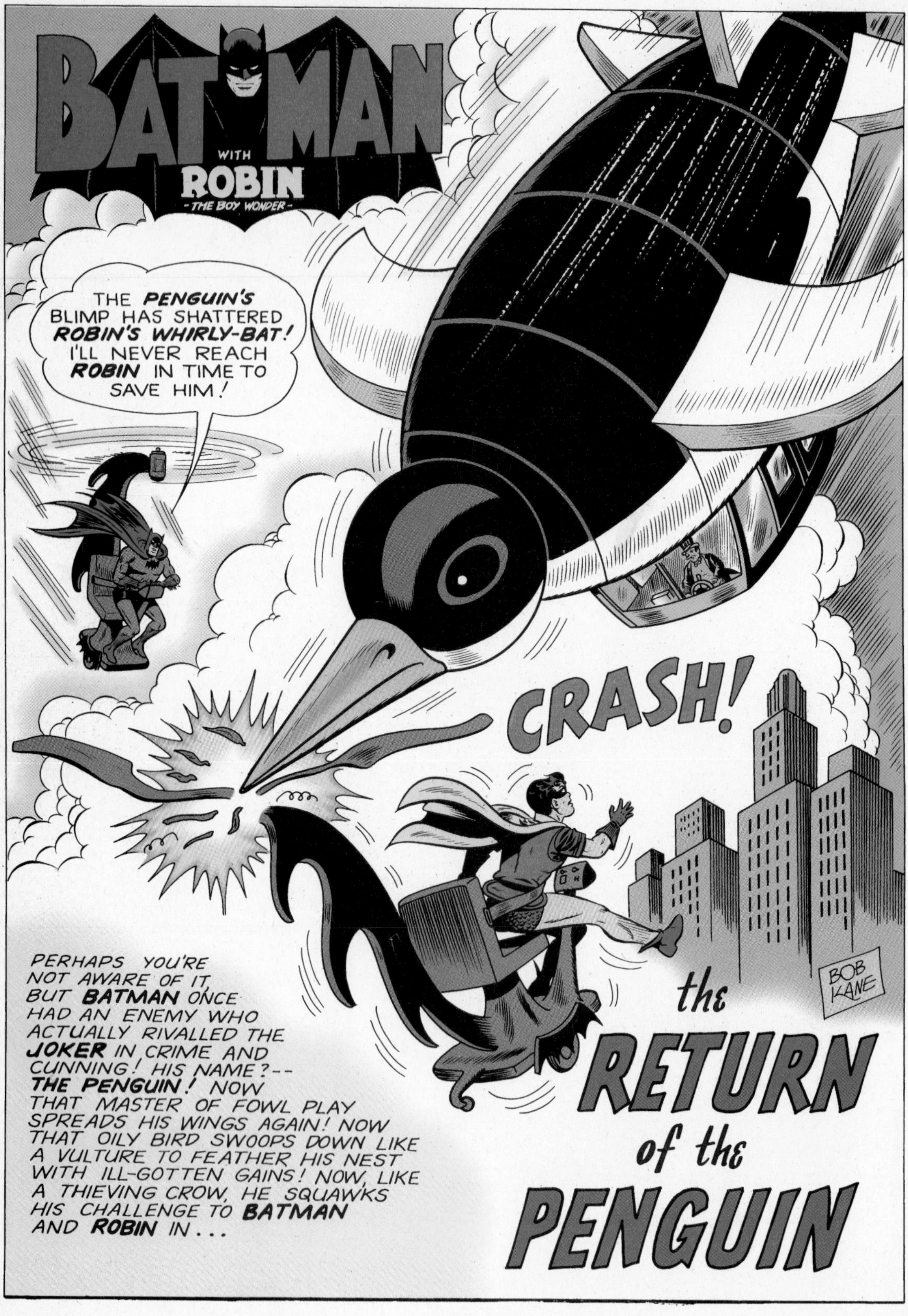

BATMAN WITH ROBIN -THE BOY WONDER-
THE PENGUIN'S BLIMP HAS SHATTERED ROBIN'S WHIRLY-BAT! I'LL NEVER REACH ROBIN IN TIME TO SAVE HIM!
CRASH!
BOB KANE
PERHAPS YOU'RE NOT AWARE OF IT, BUT BATMAN ONCE HAD AN ENEMY WHO ACTUALLY RIVALLED THE JOKER IN CRIME AND CUNNING! HIS NAME?-- THE PENGUIN! NOW THAT MASTER OF FOWL PLAY SPREADS HIS WINGS AGAIN! NOW THAT OILY BIRD SWOOPS DOWN LIKE A VULTURE TO FEATHER HIS NEST WITH ILL-GOTTEN GAINS! NOW, LIKE A THIEVING CROW, HE SQUAWKS HIS CHALLENGE TO BATMAN AND ROBIN IN...
the RETURN of the PENGUIN

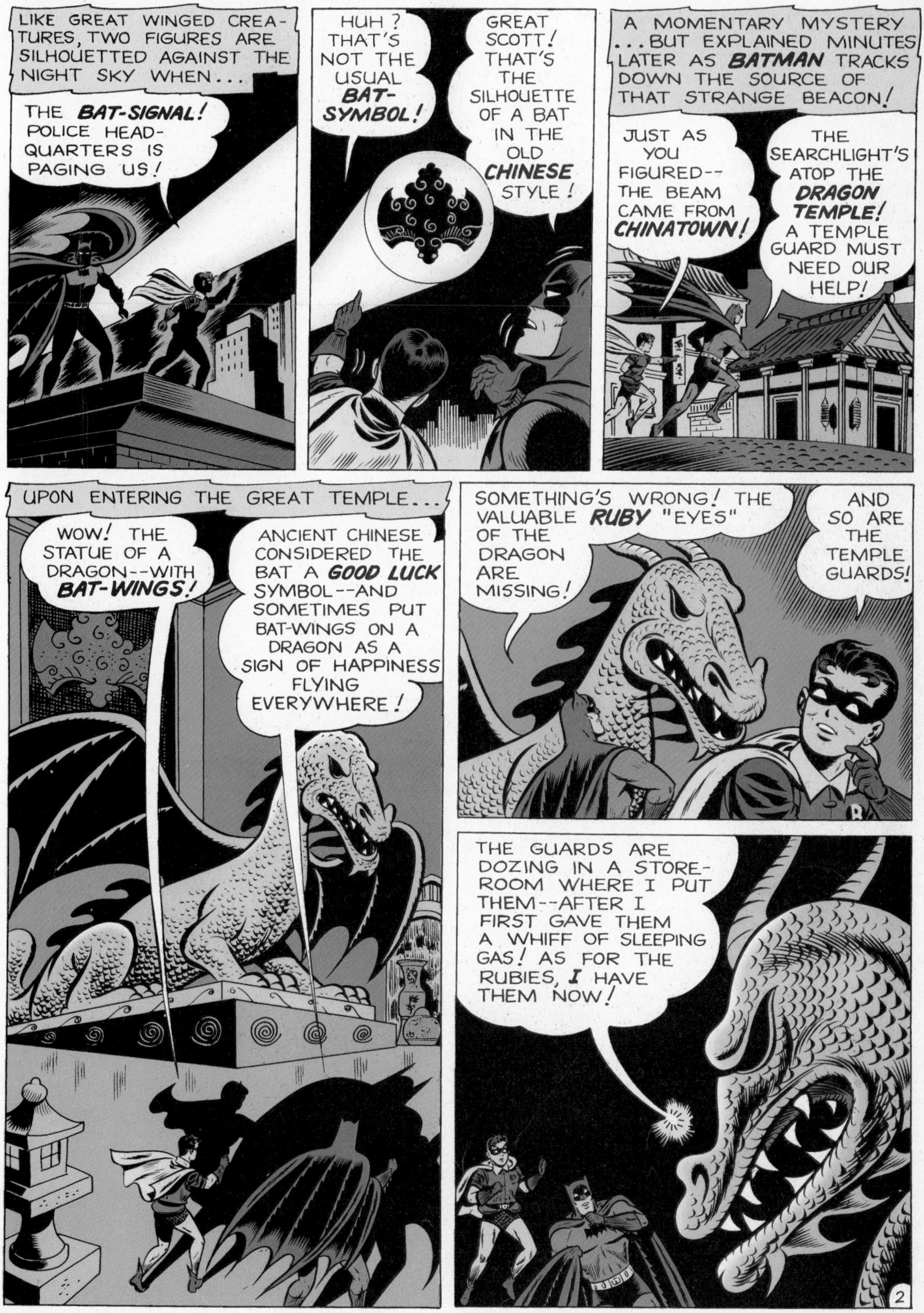
LIKE GREAT WINGED CREATURES, TWO FIGURES ARE SILHOUETTED AGAINST THE NIGHT SKY WHEN...
THE BAT-SIGNAL! POLICE HEADQUARTERS IS PAGING US!
HUH? THAT'S NOT THE USUAL BAT-SYMBOL!
GREAT SCOTT! THAT'S THE SILHOUETTE OF A BAT IN THE OLD CHINESE STYLE!
A MOMENTARY MYSTERY ...BUT EXPLAINED MINUTES LATER AS BATMAN TRACKS DOWN THE SOURCE OF THAT STRANGE BEACON!
JUST AS YOU FIGURED-- THE BEAM CAME FROM CHINATOWN!
THE SEARCHLIGHT'S ATOP THE DRAGON TEMPLE! A TEMPLE GUARD MUST NEED OUR HELP!
UPON ENTERING THE GREAT TEMPLE...
WOW! THE STATUE OF A DRAGON--WITH BAT-WINGS!
ANCIENT CHINESE CONSIDERED THE BAT A GOOD LUCK SYMBOL--AND SOMETIMES PUT BAT-WINGS ON A DRAGON AS A SIGN OF HAPPINESS FLYING EVERYWHERE!
SOMETHING'S WRONG! THE VALUABLE RUBY "EYES" OF THE DRAGON ARE MISSING!
AND SO ARE THE TEMPLE GUARDS!
THE GUARDS ARE DOZING IN A STORE-ROOM WHERE I PUT THEM--AFTER I FIRST GAVE THEM A WHIFF OF SLEEPING GAS! AS FOR THE RUBIES, I HAVE THEM NOW!
2

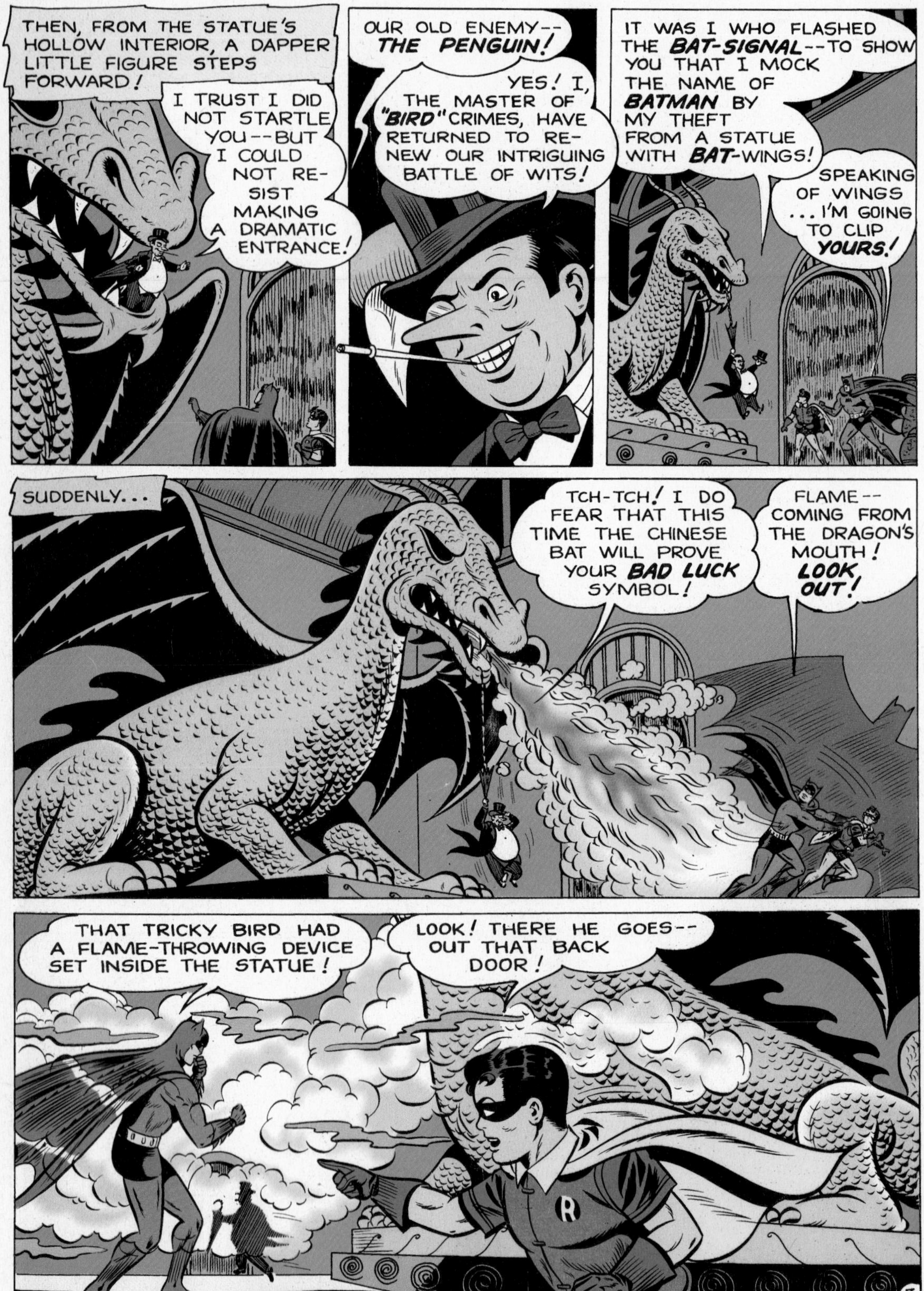
THEN, FROM THE STATUE'S HOLLOW INTERIOR, A DAPPER LITTLE FIGURE STEPS FORWARD!
I TRUST I DID NOT STARTLE YOU--BUT I COULD NOT RESIST MAKING A DRAMATIC ENTRANCE!
OUR OLD ENEMY-- THE PENGUIN!
YES! I, THE MASTER OF "BIRD" CRIMES, HAVE RETURNED TO RENEW OUR INTRIGUING BATTLE OF WITS!
IT WAS I WHO FLASHED THE BAT-SIGNAL--TO SHOW YOU THAT I MOCK THE NAME OF BATMAN BY MY THEFT FROM A STATUE WITH BAT-WINGS!
SPEAKING OF WINGS ...I'M GOING TO CLIP YOURS!
SUDDENLY...
TCH-TCH! I DO FEAR THAT THIS TIME THE CHINESE BAT WILL PROVE YOUR BAD LUCK SYMBOL!
FLAME-- COMING FROM THE DRAGON'S MOUTH! LOOK OUT!
THAT TRICKY BIRD HAD A FLAME-THROWING DEVICE SET INSIDE THE STATUE!
LOOK! THERE HE GOES-- OUT THAT BACK DOOR!
3

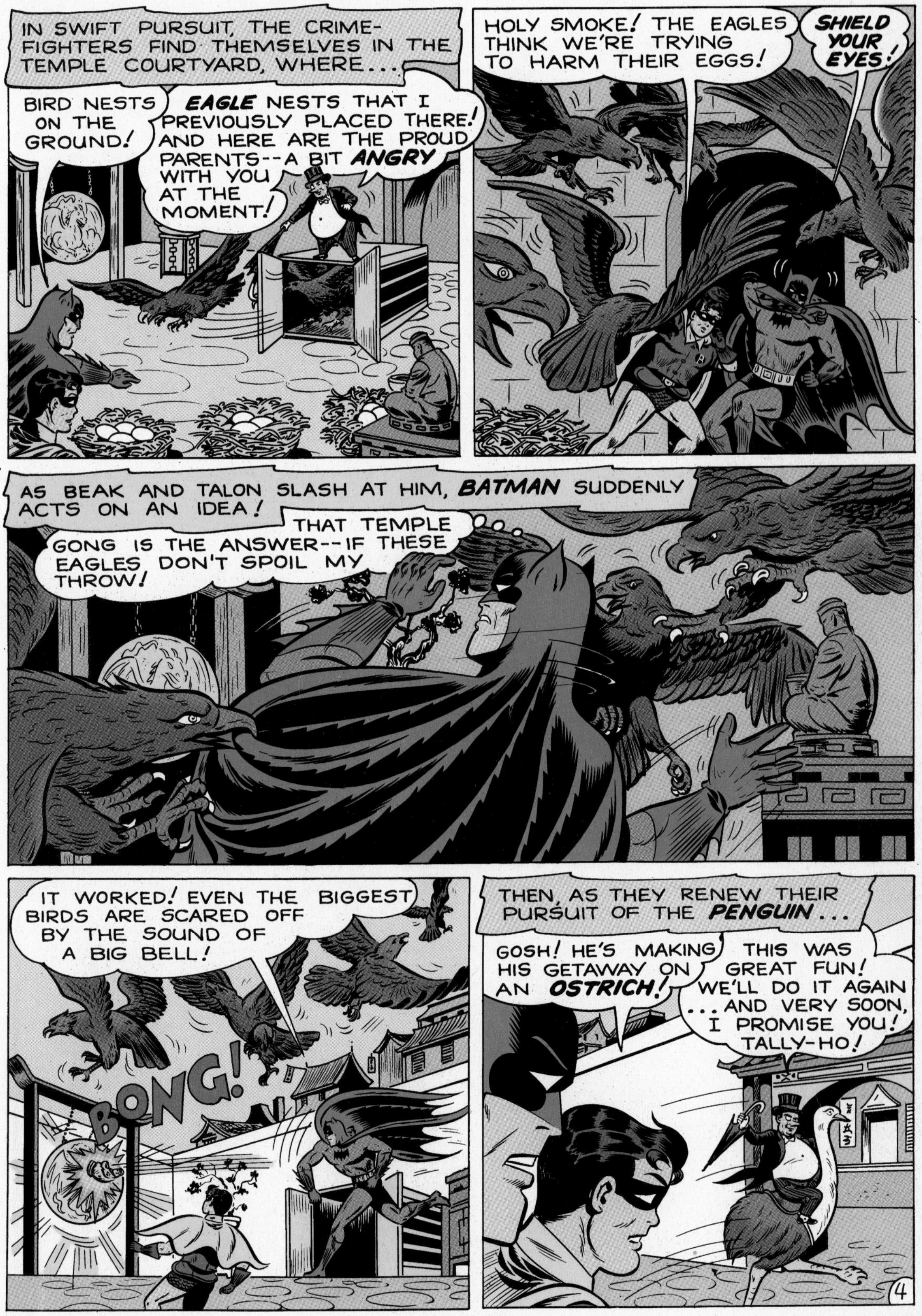
IN SWIFT PURSUIT, THE CRIME-FIGHTERS FIND THEMSELVES IN THE TEMPLE COURTYARD, WHERE...
BIRD NESTS ON THE GROUND!
EAGLE NESTS THAT I PREVIOUSLY PLACED THERE! AND HERE ARE THE PROUD PARENTS--A BIT ANGRY WITH YOU AT THE MOMENT!
HOLY SMOKE! THE EAGLES THINK WE'RE TRYING TO HARM THEIR EGGS!
SHIELD YOUR EYES!
AS BEAK AND TALON SLASH AT HIM, BATMAN SUDDENLY ACTS ON AN IDEA!
THAT TEMPLE GONG IS THE ANSWER--IF THESE EAGLES DON'T SPOIL MY THROW!
IT WORKED! EVEN THE BIGGEST BIRDS ARE SCARED OFF BY THE SOUND OF A BIG BELL!
BONG!
THEN, AS THEY RENEW THEIR PURSUIT OF THE PENGUIN...
GOSH! HE'S MAKING HIS GETAWAY ON AN OSTRICH!
THIS WAS GREAT FUN! WE'LL DO IT AGAIN ... AND VERY SOON, I PROMISE YOU! TALLY-HO!
4

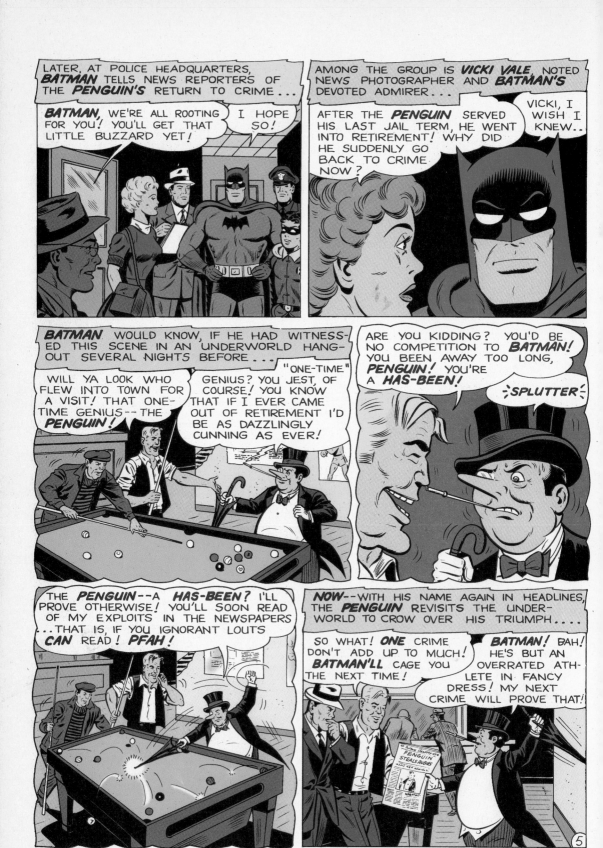

LATER, AT POLICE HEADQUARTERS, **BATMAN** TELLS NEWS REPORTERS OF THE **PENGUIN'S** RETURN TO CRIME...

BATMAN, WE'RE ALL ROOTING FOR YOU! YOU'LL GET THAT LITTLE BUZZARD YET!

I HOPE SO!

AMONG THE GROUP IS **VICKI VALE**, NOTED NEWS PHOTOGRAPHER AND **BATMAN'S** DEVOTED ADMIRER...

AFTER THE **PENGUIN** SERVED HIS LAST JAIL TERM, HE WENT INTO RETIREMENT! WHY DID HE SUDDENLY GO BACK TO CRIME NOW?

VICKI, I WISH I KNEW...

BATMAN WOULD KNOW, IF HE HAD WITNESSED THIS SCENE IN AN UNDERWORLD HANGOUT SEVERAL NIGHTS BEFORE...

WILL YA LOOK WHO FLEW INTO TOWN FOR A VISIT! THAT ONE-TIME GENIUS-- THE **PENGUIN**!

"ONE-TIME" GENIUS? YOU JEST, OF COURSE! YOU KNOW THAT IF I EVER CAME OUT OF RETIREMENT I'D BE AS DAZZLINGLY CUNNING AS EVER!

ARE YOU KIDDING? YOU'D BE NO COMPETITION TO **BATMAN**! YOU BEEN AWAY TOO LONG, **PENGUIN**! YOU'RE A **HAS-BEEN**!

SPLUTTER

THE **PENGUIN**--A **HAS-BEEN**? I'LL PROVE OTHERWISE! YOU'LL SOON READ OF MY EXPLOITS IN THE NEWSPAPERS ...THAT IS, IF YOU IGNORANT LOUTS **CAN** READ! PFAH!

NOW--WITH HIS NAME AGAIN IN HEADLINES, THE **PENGUIN** REVISITS THE UNDERWORLD TO CROW OVER HIS TRIUMPH....

SO WHAT! **ONE** CRIME DON'T ADD UP TO MUCH! **BATMAN'LL** CAGE YOU THE NEXT TIME!

BATMAN! BAH! HE'S BUT AN OVERRATED ATHLETE IN FANCY DRESS! MY NEXT CRIME WILL PROVE THAT!

PENGUIN STEALS RUBIES

5

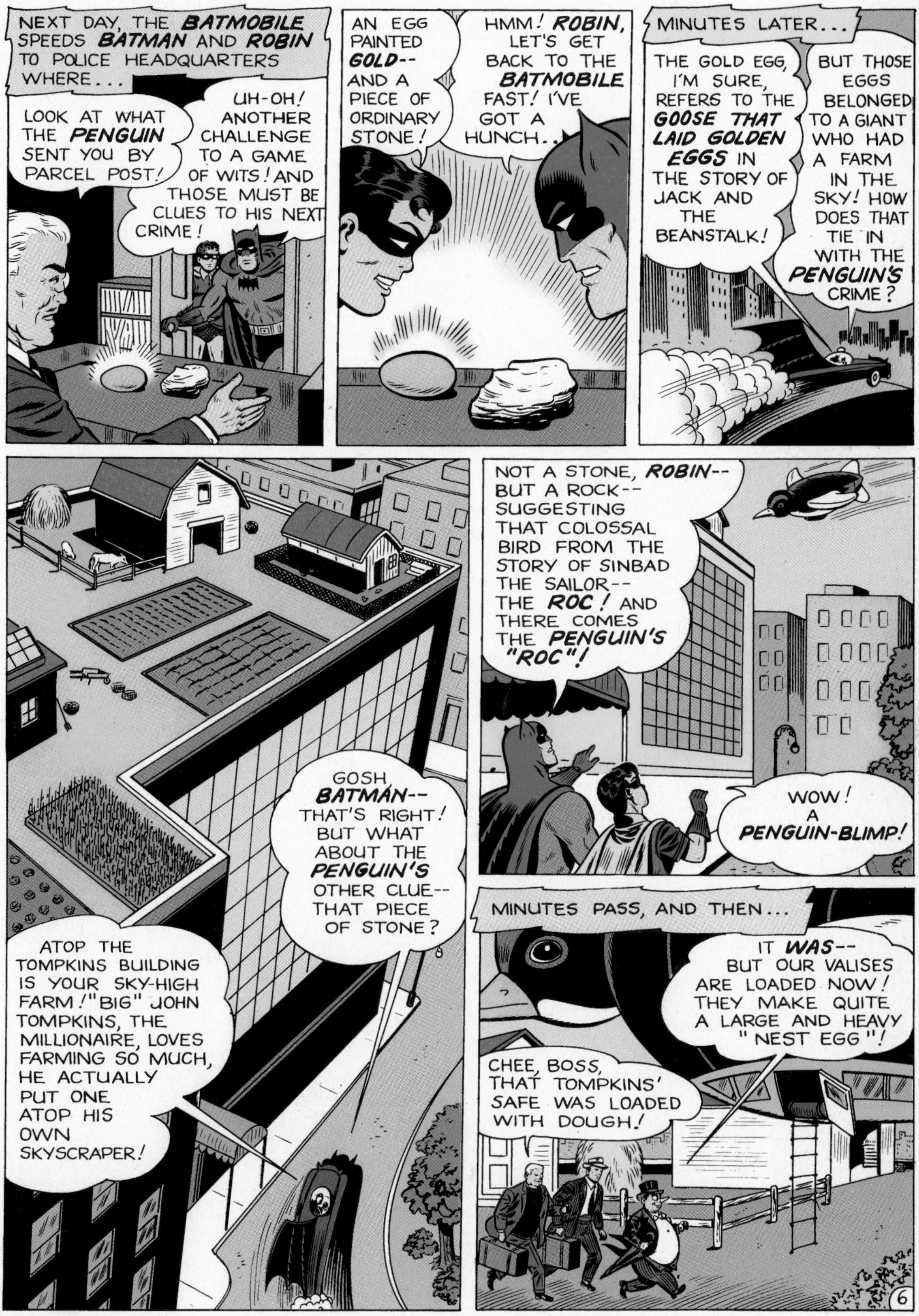
NEXT DAY, THE BATMOBILE SPEEDS BATMAN AND ROBIN TO POLICE HEADQUARTERS WHERE...
LOOK AT WHAT THE PENGUIN SENT YOU BY PARCEL POST!
UH-OH! ANOTHER CHALLENGE TO A GAME OF WITS! AND THOSE MUST BE CLUES TO HIS NEXT CRIME!
AN EGG PAINTED GOLD-- AND A PIECE OF ORDINARY STONE!
HMM! ROBIN, LET'S GET BACK TO THE BATMOBILE FAST! I'VE GOT A HUNCH...
MINUTES LATER...
THE GOLD EGG, I'M SURE, REFERS TO THE GOOSE THAT LAID GOLDEN EGGS IN THE STORY OF JACK AND THE BEANSTALK!
BUT THOSE EGGS BELONGED TO A GIANT WHO HAD A FARM IN THE SKY! HOW DOES THAT TIE IN WITH THE PENGUIN'S CRIME?
ATOP THE TOMPKINS BUILDING IS YOUR SKY-HIGH FARM! "BIG" JOHN TOMPKINS, THE MILLIONAIRE, LOVES FARMING SO MUCH, HE ACTUALLY PUT ONE ATOP HIS OWN SKYSCRAPER!
GOSH, BATMAN-- THAT'S RIGHT! BUT WHAT ABOUT THE PENGUIN'S OTHER CLUE-- THAT PIECE OF STONE?
NOT A STONE, ROBIN-- BUT A ROCK-- SUGGESTING THAT COLOSSAL BIRD FROM THE STORY OF SINBAD THE SAILOR-- THE ROC! AND THERE COMES THE PENGUIN'S "ROC"!
WOW! A PENGUIN-BLIMP!
MINUTES PASS, AND THEN...
CHEE, BOSS, THAT TOMPKINS' SAFE WAS LOADED WITH DOUGH!
IT WAS-- BUT OUR VALISES ARE LOADED NOW! THEY MAKE QUITE A LARGE AND HEAVY "NEST EGG"!
6

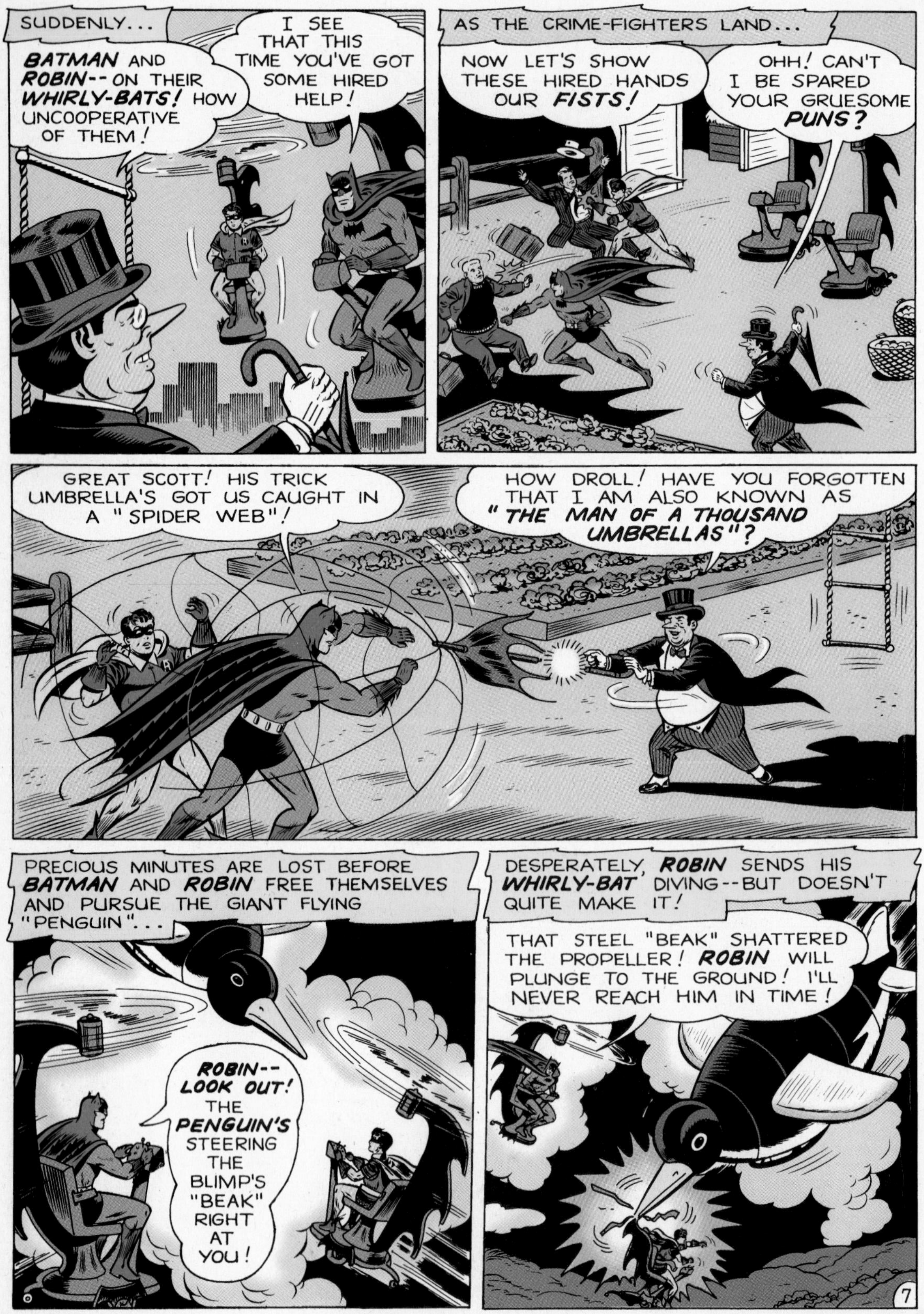
SUDDENLY...
BATMAN AND ROBIN--ON THEIR WHIRLY-BATS! HOW UNCOOPERATIVE OF THEM!
I SEE THAT THIS TIME YOU'VE GOT SOME HIRED HELP!
AS THE CRIME-FIGHTERS LAND...
NOW LET'S SHOW THESE HIRED HANDS OUR FISTS!
OHH! CAN'T I BE SPARED YOUR GRUESOME PUNS?
GREAT SCOTT! HIS TRICK UMBRELLA'S GOT US CAUGHT IN A "SPIDER WEB"!
HOW DROLL! HAVE YOU FORGOTTEN THAT I AM ALSO KNOWN AS "THE MAN OF A THOUSAND UMBRELLAS"?
PRECIOUS MINUTES ARE LOST BEFORE BATMAN AND ROBIN FREE THEMSELVES AND PURSUE THE GIANT FLYING "PENGUIN"...
ROBIN--LOOK OUT! THE PENGUIN'S STEERING THE BLIMP'S "BEAK" RIGHT AT YOU!
DESPERATELY, ROBIN SENDS HIS WHIRLY-BAT DIVING--BUT DOESN'T QUITE MAKE IT!
THAT STEEL "BEAK" SHATTERED THE PROPELLER! ROBIN WILL PLUNGE TO THE GROUND! I'LL NEVER REACH HIM IN TIME!
7

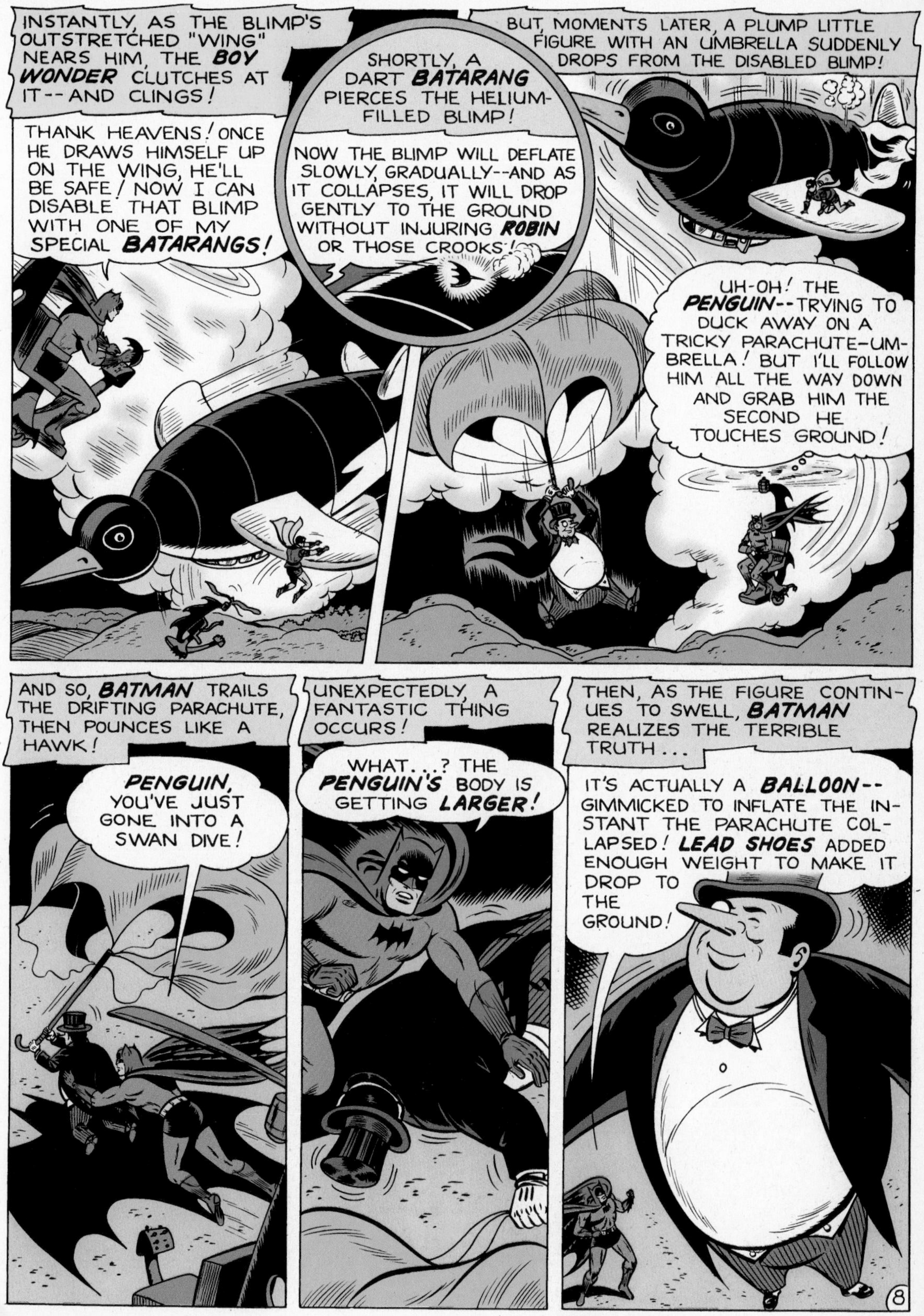

INSTANTLY, AS THE BLIMP'S OUTSTRETCHED "WING" NEARS HIM, THE BOY WONDER CLUTCHES AT IT--AND CLINGS!
THANK HEAVENS! ONCE HE DRAWS HIMSELF UP ON THE WING, HE'LL BE SAFE! NOW I CAN DISABLE THAT BLIMP WITH ONE OF MY SPECIAL BATARANGS!
SHORTLY, A DART BATARANG PIERCES THE HELIUM-FILLED BLIMP!
NOW THE BLIMP WILL DEFLATE SLOWLY, GRADUALLY--AND AS IT COLLAPSES, IT WILL DROP GENTLY TO THE GROUND WITHOUT INJURING ROBIN OR THOSE CROOKS!
BUT, MOMENTS LATER, A PLUMP LITTLE FIGURE WITH AN UMBRELLA SUDDENLY DROPS FROM THE DISABLED BLIMP!
UH-OH! THE PENGUIN--TRYING TO DUCK AWAY ON A TRICKY PARACHUTE-UMBRELLA! BUT I'LL FOLLOW HIM ALL THE WAY DOWN AND GRAB HIM THE SECOND HE TOUCHES GROUND!
AND SO, BATMAN TRAILS THE DRIFTING PARACHUTE, THEN POUNCES LIKE A HAWK!
PENGUIN, YOU'VE JUST GONE INTO A SWAN DIVE!
UNEXPECTEDLY, A FANTASTIC THING OCCURS!
WHAT...? THE PENGUIN'S BODY IS GETTING LARGER!
THEN, AS THE FIGURE CONTINUES TO SWELL, BATMAN REALIZES THE TERRIBLE TRUTH...
IT'S ACTUALLY A BALLOON--GIMMICKED TO INFLATE THE INSTANT THE PARACHUTE COLLAPSED! LEAD SHOES ADDED ENOUGH WEIGHT TO MAKE IT DROP TO THE GROUND!
8

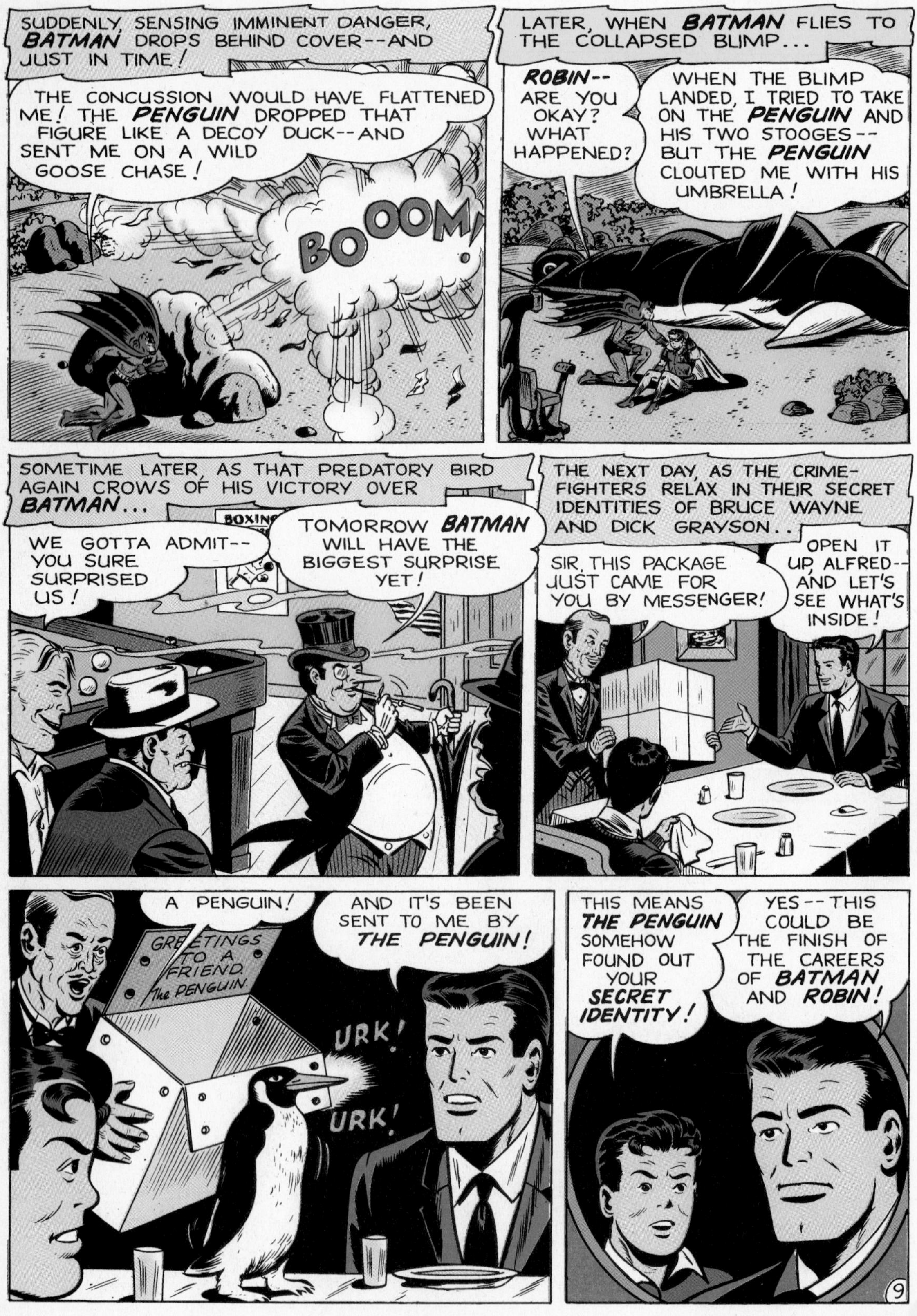
SUDDENLY, SENSING IMMINENT DANGER, BATMAN DROPS BEHIND COVER--AND JUST IN TIME!
THE CONCUSSION WOULD HAVE FLATTENED ME! THE PENGUIN DROPPED THAT FIGURE LIKE A DECOY DUCK--AND SENT ME ON A WILD GOOSE CHASE!
BOOOOM!
LATER, WHEN BATMAN FLIES TO THE COLLAPSED BLIMP...
ROBIN--ARE YOU OKAY? WHAT HAPPENED?
WHEN THE BLIMP LANDED, I TRIED TO TAKE ON THE PENGUIN AND HIS TWO STOOGES--BUT THE PENGUIN CLOUTED ME WITH HIS UMBRELLA!
SOMETIME LATER, AS THAT PREDATORY BIRD AGAIN CROWS OF HIS VICTORY OVER BATMAN...
WE GOTTA ADMIT--YOU SURE SURPRISED US!
TOMORROW BATMAN WILL HAVE THE BIGGEST SURPRISE YET!
THE NEXT DAY, AS THE CRIME-FIGHTERS RELAX IN THEIR SECRET IDENTITIES OF BRUCE WAYNE AND DICK GRAYSON...
SIR, THIS PACKAGE JUST CAME FOR YOU BY MESSENGER!
OPEN IT UP, ALFRED--AND LET'S SEE WHAT'S INSIDE!
A PENGUIN!
AND IT'S BEEN SENT TO ME BY THE PENGUIN!
GREETINGS TO A FRIEND. The PENGUIN.
URK!
URK!
THIS MEANS THE PENGUIN SOMEHOW FOUND OUT YOUR SECRET IDENTITY!
YES--THIS COULD BE THE FINISH OF THE CAREERS OF BATMAN AND ROBIN!
9

BUT LATER, AS *BATMAN* AND *ROBIN* VISIT POLICE HEADQUARTERS...

LOOK AT WHAT *THE PENGUIN* SENT ME!

HE SENT *ME* ONE, TOO!

WH-HAAAT?

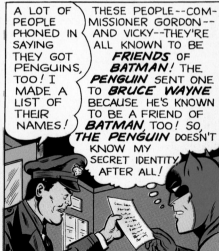

A LOT OF PEOPLE PHONED IN SAYING THEY GOT PENGUINS, TOO! I MADE A LIST OF THEIR NAMES!

THESE PEOPLE--COMMISSIONER GORDON--AND VICKY--THEY'RE ALL KNOWN TO BE *FRIENDS* OF *BATMAN!* THE *PENGUIN* SENT ONE TO *BRUCE WAYNE* BECAUSE HE'S KNOWN TO BE A FRIEND OF *BATMAN*, TOO! SO, *THE PENGUIN* DOESN'T KNOW MY SECRET IDENTITY AFTER ALL!

LATER...

THERE THEY ARE--*TWO DOZEN* PENGUINS THAT WERE SENT TO *BATMAN'S* FRIENDS! WHAT DOES IT MEAN?

A CLUE--TO HIS NEXT CRIME!

AT THAT MOMENT, IN THE MUSEUM OF *THE FRIENDS OF BIRDS SOCIETY,* THE SOCIETY'S SPONSORS ARE HAVING AN ANNIVERSARY CELEBRATION...

GREETINGS, FRIENDS! I NOW GIVE YOU A FITTING BIRTHDAY CAKE AND A FITTING RHYME! "4 AND 20 BLACKBIRDS BAKED IN A PIE; AND WHEN THE PIE WAS OPENED THE BIRDS BEGAN TO SING..."

YOU FORGOT TO COUNT ME! I'M NOT A BLACKBIRD, BUT SOON I EXPECT TO *CROW!*

THE PENGUIN!

NOW THAT THE SLEEPING GAS CARTRIDGE IN MY UMBRELLA-GUN HAS DONE ITS WORK, I'LL TAKE THESE *ORIGINAL* SKETCHES OF BIRDS MADE BY THE FAMOUS *JOHN AUDUBON!* THEY'RE PRICELESS COLLECTOR'S ITEMS!

10

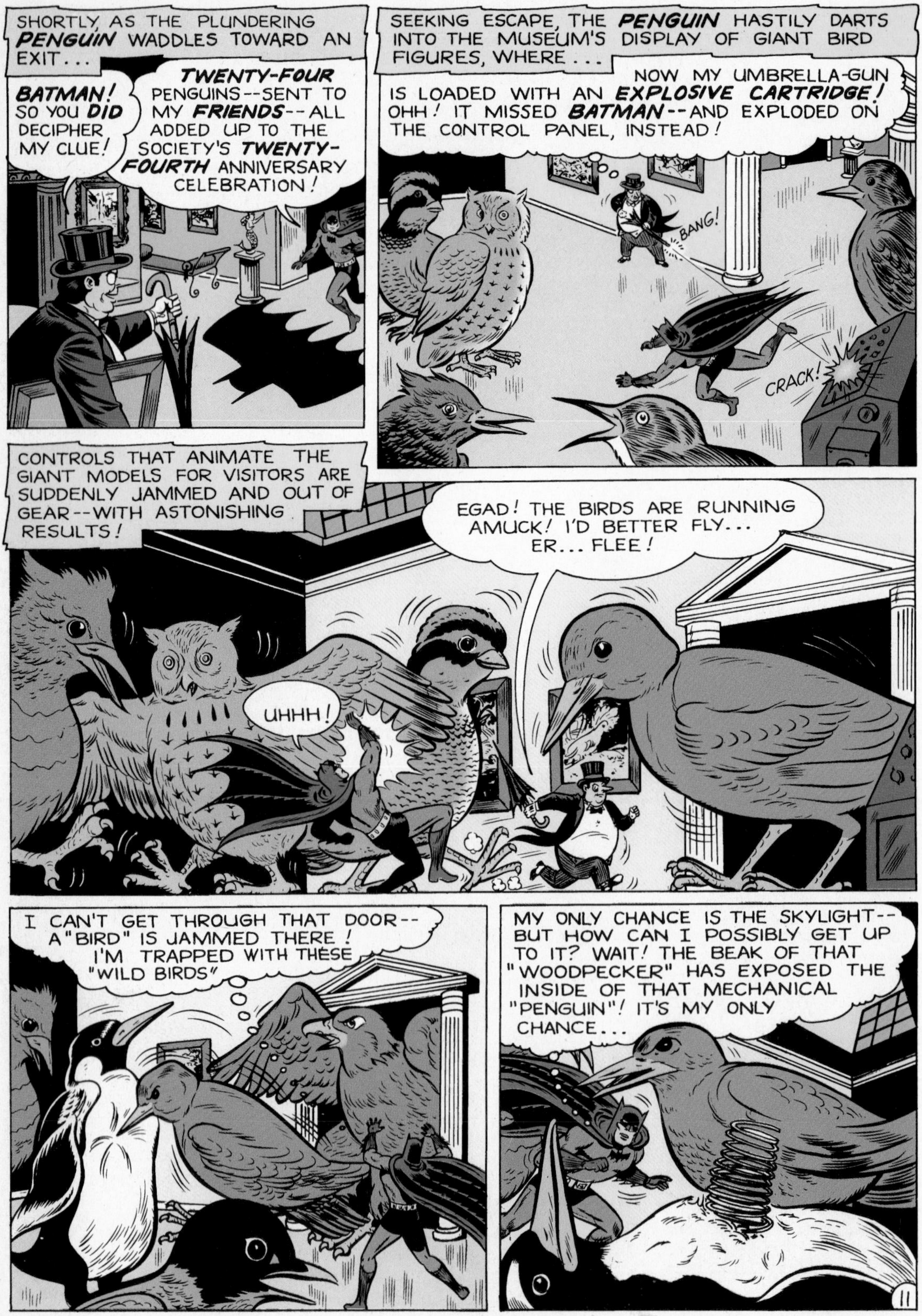
SHORTLY, AS THE PLUNDERING PENGUIN WADDLES TOWARD AN EXIT...
BATMAN! SO YOU DID DECIPHER MY CLUE!
TWENTY-FOUR PENGUINS--SENT TO MY FRIENDS--ALL ADDED UP TO THE SOCIETY'S TWENTY-FOURTH ANNIVERSARY CELEBRATION!
SEEKING ESCAPE, THE PENGUIN HASTILY DARTS INTO THE MUSEUM'S DISPLAY OF GIANT BIRD FIGURES, WHERE ...
NOW MY UMBRELLA-GUN IS LOADED WITH AN EXPLOSIVE CARTRIDGE! OHH! IT MISSED BATMAN--AND EXPLODED ON THE CONTROL PANEL, INSTEAD!
BANG!
CRACK!
CONTROLS THAT ANIMATE THE GIANT MODELS FOR VISITORS ARE SUDDENLY JAMMED AND OUT OF GEAR--WITH ASTONISHING RESULTS!
EGAD! THE BIRDS ARE RUNNING AMUCK! I'D BETTER FLY... ER... FLEE!
UHHH!
I CAN'T GET THROUGH THAT DOOR-- A "BIRD" IS JAMMED THERE! I'M TRAPPED WITH THESE "WILD BIRDS"
MY ONLY CHANCE IS THE SKYLIGHT-- BUT HOW CAN I POSSIBLY GET UP TO IT? WAIT! THE BEAK OF THAT "WOODPECKER" HAS EXPOSED THE INSIDE OF THAT MECHANICAL "PENGUIN"! IT'S MY ONLY CHANCE...
11

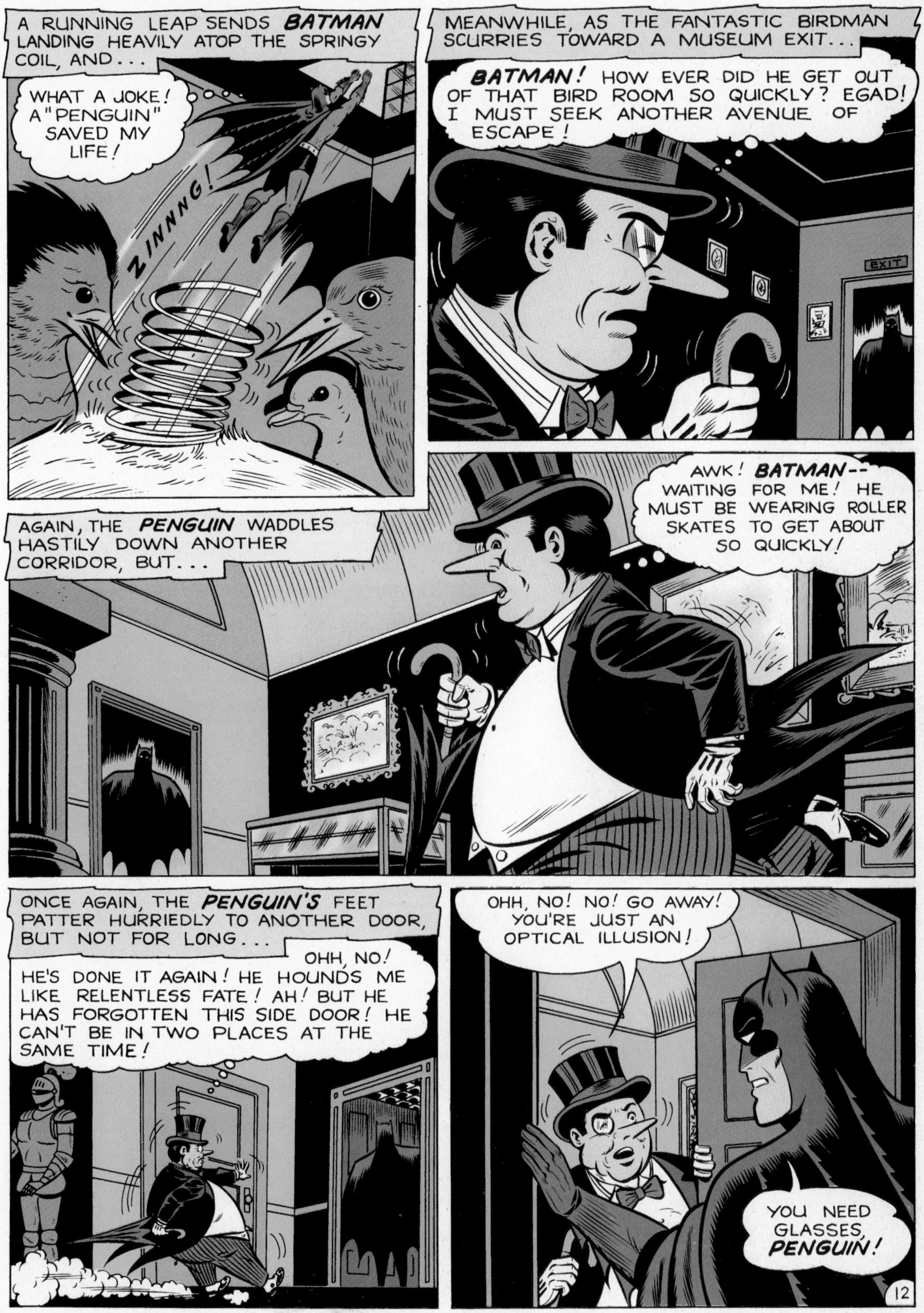
A RUNNING LEAP SENDS BATMAN LANDING HEAVILY ATOP THE SPRINGY COIL, AND...
WHAT A JOKE! A "PENGUIN" SAVED MY LIFE!
ZINNNG!
MEANWHILE, AS THE FANTASTIC BIRDMAN SCURRIES TOWARD A MUSEUM EXIT...
BATMAN! HOW EVER DID HE GET OUT OF THAT BIRD ROOM SO QUICKLY? EGAD! I MUST SEEK ANOTHER AVENUE OF ESCAPE!
EXIT
AGAIN, THE PENGUIN WADDLES HASTILY DOWN ANOTHER CORRIDOR, BUT...
AWK! BATMAN-- WAITING FOR ME! HE MUST BE WEARING ROLLER SKATES TO GET ABOUT SO QUICKLY!
ONCE AGAIN, THE PENGUIN'S FEET PATTER HURRIEDLY TO ANOTHER DOOR, BUT NOT FOR LONG...
OHH, NO! HE'S DONE IT AGAIN! HE HOUNDS ME LIKE RELENTLESS FATE! AH! BUT HE HAS FORGOTTEN THIS SIDE DOOR! HE CAN'T BE IN TWO PLACES AT THE SAME TIME!
OHH, NO! NO! GO AWAY! YOU'RE JUST AN OPTICAL ILLUSION!
YOU NEED GLASSES, PENGUIN!
12

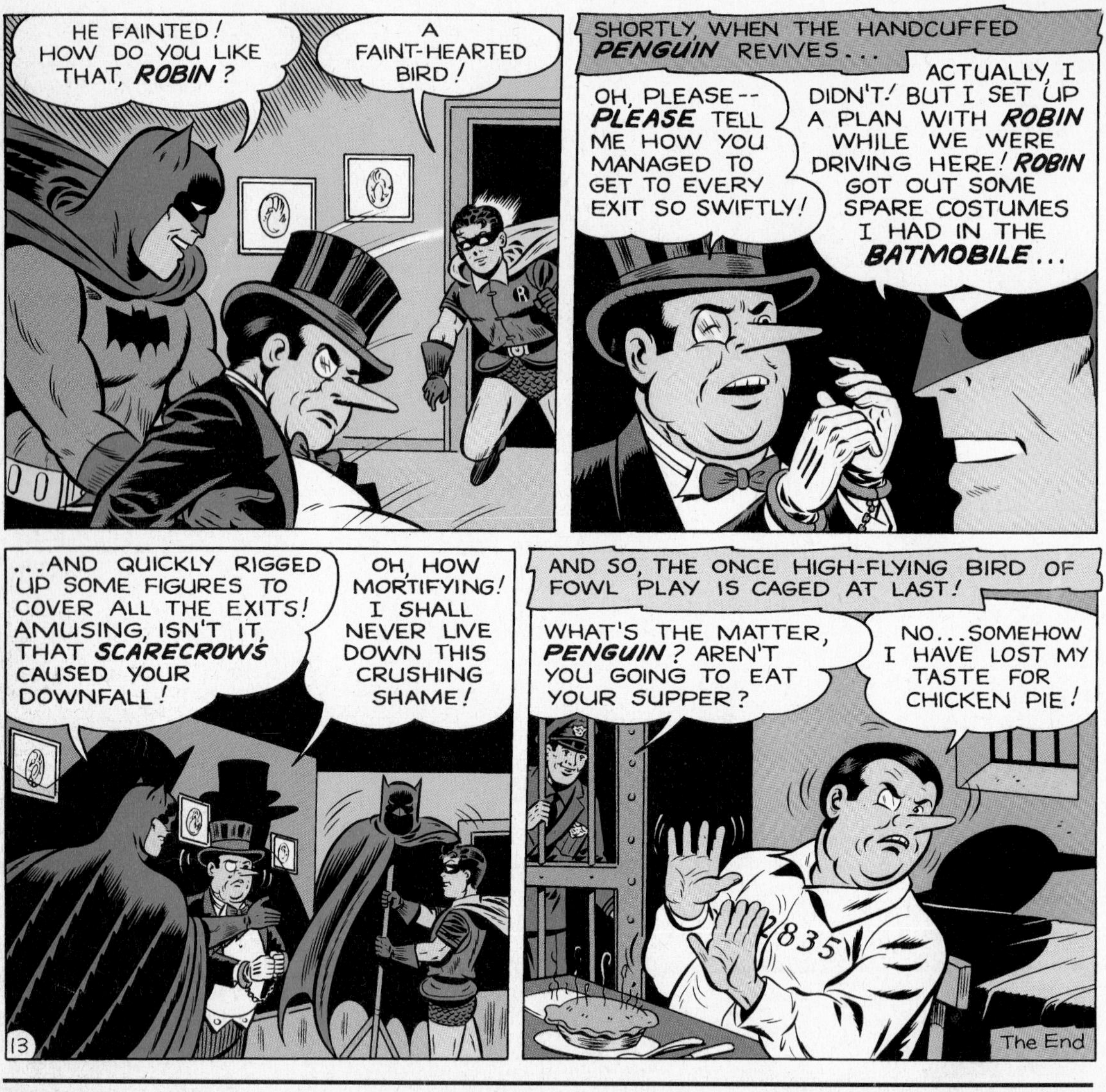
HE FAINTED! HOW DO YOU LIKE THAT, ROBIN?
A FAINT-HEARTED BIRD!
SHORTLY, WHEN THE HANDCUFFED PENGUIN REVIVES...
OH, PLEASE -- PLEASE TELL ME HOW YOU MANAGED TO GET TO EVERY EXIT SO SWIFTLY!
ACTUALLY, I DIDN'T! BUT I SET UP A PLAN WITH ROBIN WHILE WE WERE DRIVING HERE! ROBIN GOT OUT SOME SPARE COSTUMES I HAD IN THE BATMOBILE...
...AND QUICKLY RIGGED UP SOME FIGURES TO COVER ALL THE EXITS! AMUSING, ISN'T IT, THAT SCARECROWS CAUSED YOUR DOWNFALL!
OH, HOW MORTIFYING! I SHALL NEVER LIVE DOWN THIS CRUSHING SHAME!
13
AND SO, THE ONCE HIGH-FLYING BIRD OF FOWL PLAY IS CAGED AT LAST!
WHAT'S THE MATTER, PENGUIN? AREN'T YOU GOING TO EAT YOUR SUPPER?
NO... SOMEHOW I HAVE LOST MY TASTE FOR CHICKEN PIE!
835
The End

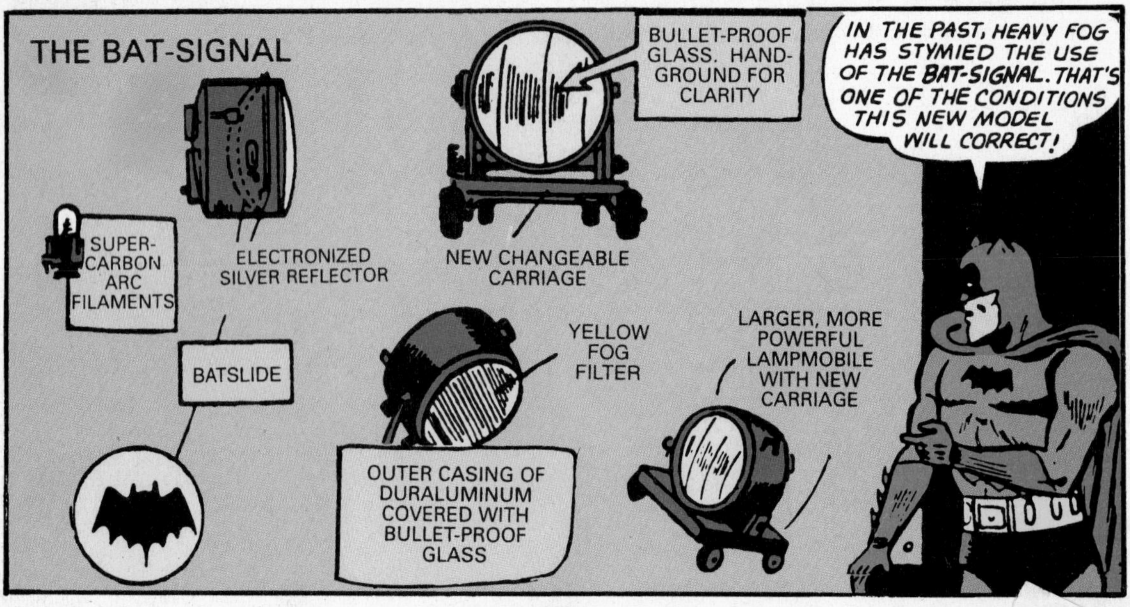
THE BAT-SIGNAL
BULLET-PROOF GLASS. HAND-GROUND FOR CLARITY
IN THE PAST, HEAVY FOG HAS STYMIED THE USE OF THE BAT-SIGNAL. THAT'S ONE OF THE CONDITIONS THIS NEW MODEL WILL CORRECT!
SUPER-CARBON ARC FILAMENTS
ELECTRONIZED SILVER REFLECTOR
NEW CHANGEABLE CARRIAGE
BATSLIDE
YELLOW FOG FILTER
LARGER, MORE POWERFUL LAMPMOBILE WITH NEW CARRIAGE
OUTER CASING OF DURALUMINUM COVERED WITH BULLET-PROOF GLASS

BATMAN'S NEW LOOK

By the mid 1960s, Batman was making his first tentative steps in his evolution from kiddie comic book hero to full-blown super-hero icon. Granted, he was still DC Comics' (then National Periodical Publications) Number Two character, behind Superman. But while tales of super-aliens and secret-identity plots worked well with the science-fiction trappings of the Man of Steel, the same was not true for Batman.

Ironically, editor Julius Schwartz's passion was for science fiction, but he had also been National's most successful editor in reviving and rejuvenating characters from the past, beginning with The Flash in 1956. *Batman* was turned over to Schwartz in 1964 and overnight the aliens were gone—without explanation—as were most of the "Batman Family," including Batwoman, Bat-Girl, Bat-Mite and Ace. Under Schwartz's watch—dubbed the "New Look"—Batman returned to his roots as "The Word's Greatest Detective," a modern-day Sherlock Holmes who solved most of his cases with intelligence and reason, rather than fisticuffs—although this Batman didn't shy away from a well-placed punch or kick when necessary.

Slowly, the emphasis in the strip shifted to telling adventures of Batman the Man. Certainly the "perfect" man, with body and mind honed to impossible perfection. But not a hero with unimaginable powers. No, this hero was a man—a hero that anyone (if you had the desire) could grow up to be.

Granted, there were still fantastic elements to the stories—it seemed that Batman or Robin could pull practically anything from their utility belts. But Schwartz and his writers (most notably Gardner Fox) made sure that the gadgets were steeped in some kind of science.

Television came to change Batman as well in 1966 as the "Batman" television show revolutionized TV and popular culture. A remarkable, multileveled program, "Batman" worked as an adventure series for kids, and a glorious orgy of excess—reflecting the times and culture—for adults. You couldn't go anywhere in 1966 without being bombarded by Batman.

The comics mirrored the show, as editor Schwartz and his crew brought back the super-villains in a hurry and upped the "camp" quotient to the max. For now, the "New Look" was on hold. Batman was on TV!

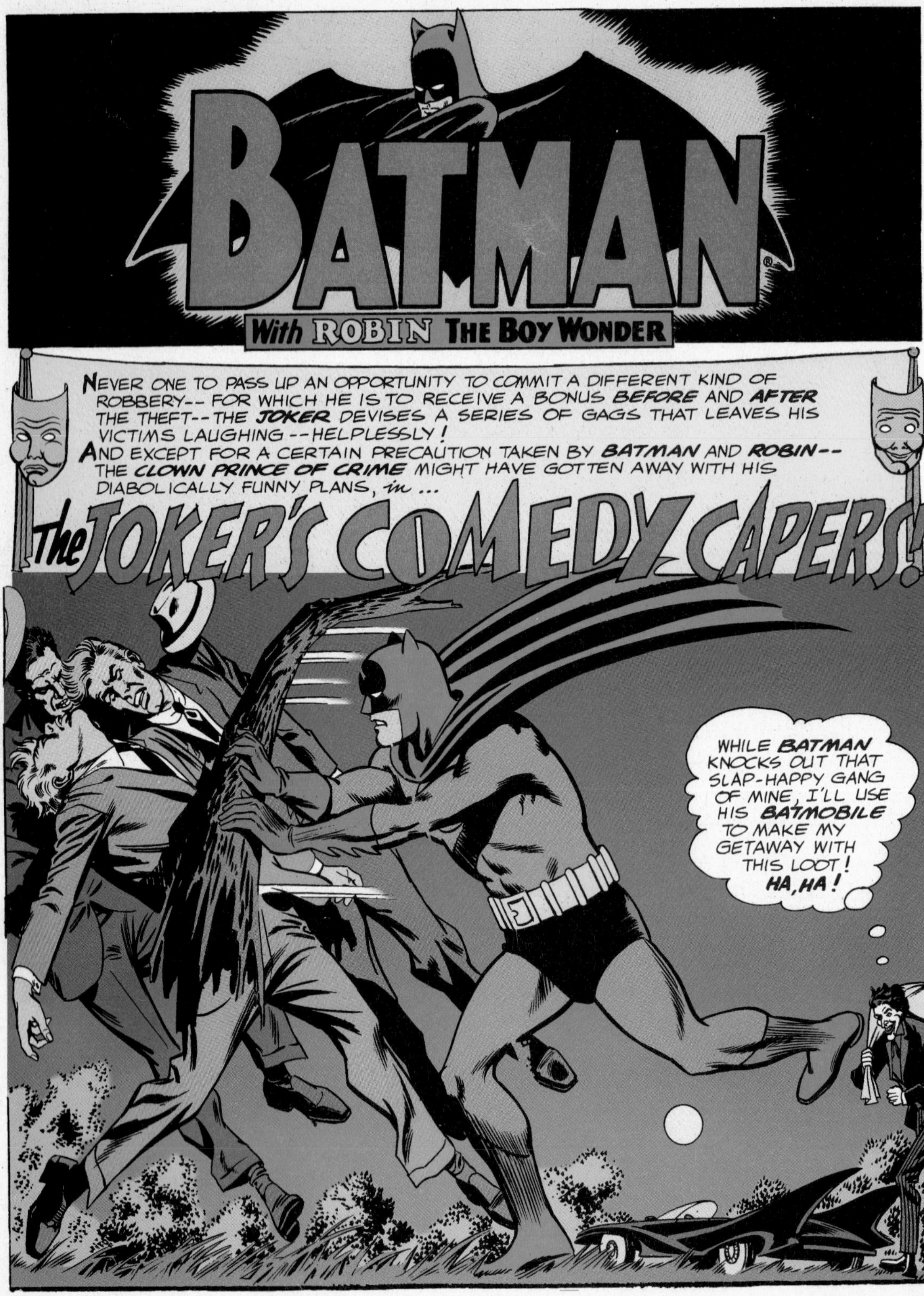
BATMAN
With ROBIN THE BOY WONDER
NEVER ONE TO PASS UP AN OPPORTUNITY TO COMMIT A DIFFERENT KIND OF ROBBERY-- FOR WHICH HE IS TO RECEIVE A BONUS BEFORE AND AFTER THE THEFT--THE JOKER DEVISES A SERIES OF GAGS THAT LEAVES HIS VICTIMS LAUGHING --HELPLESSLY!
AND EXCEPT FOR A CERTAIN PRECAUTION TAKEN BY BATMAN AND ROBIN-- THE CLOWN PRINCE OF CRIME MIGHT HAVE GOTTEN AWAY WITH HIS DIABOLICALLY FUNNY PLANS, in ...
The JOKER'S COMEDY CAPERS!
WHILE BATMAN KNOCKS OUT THAT SLAP-HAPPY GANG OF MINE, I'LL USE HIS BATMOBILE TO MAKE MY GETAWAY WITH THIS LOOT! HA, HA!

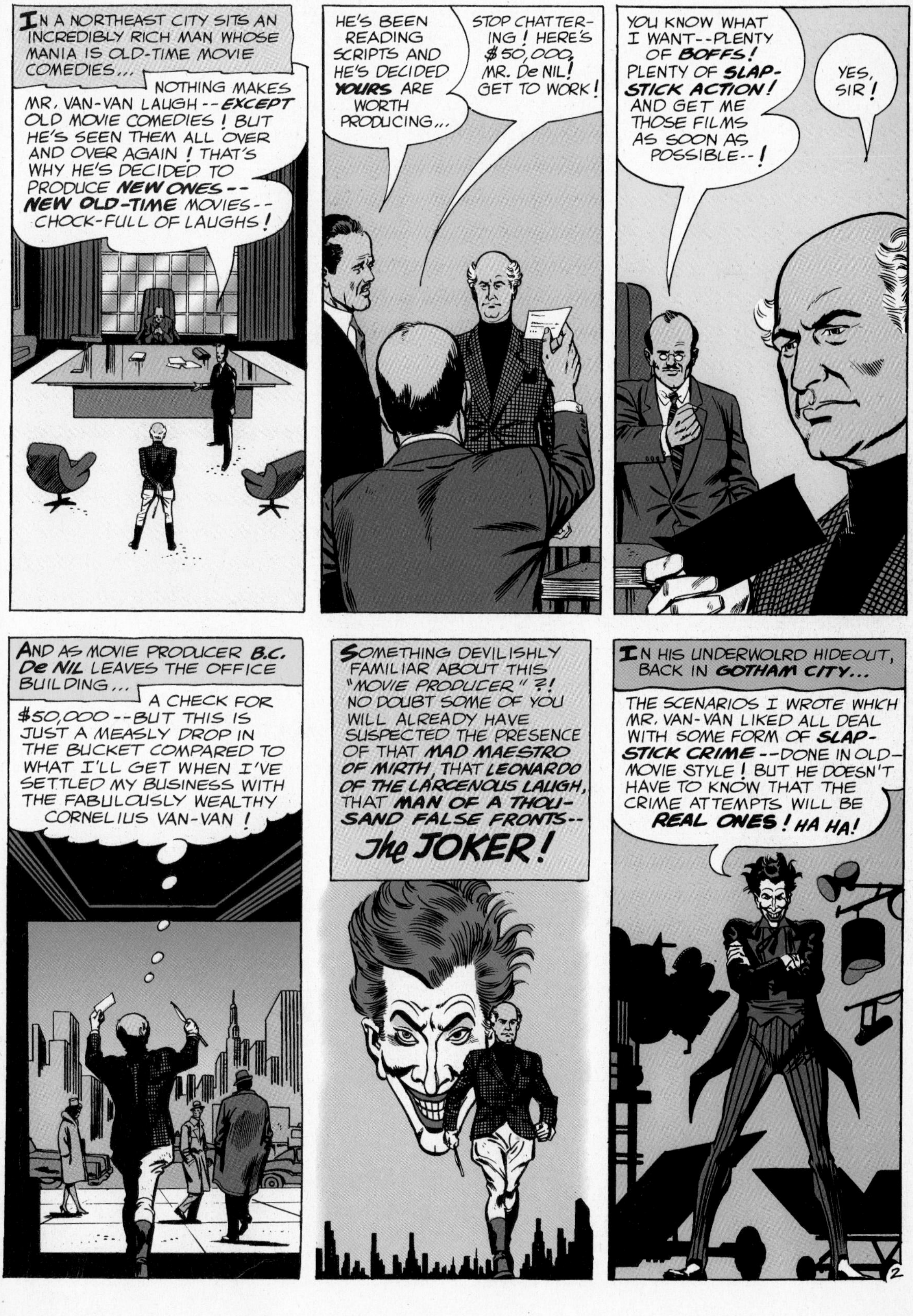
IN A NORTHEAST CITY SITS AN INCREDIBLY RICH MAN WHOSE MANIA IS OLD-TIME MOVIE COMEDIES...
NOTHING MAKES MR. VAN-VAN LAUGH -- EXCEPT OLD MOVIE COMEDIES ! BUT HE'S SEEN THEM ALL OVER AND OVER AGAIN ! THAT'S WHY HE'S DECIDED TO PRODUCE NEW ONES -- NEW OLD-TIME MOVIES -- CHOCK-FULL OF LAUGHS !
HE'S BEEN READING SCRIPTS AND HE'S DECIDED YOURS ARE WORTH PRODUCING...
STOP CHATTERING ! HERE'S $50,000, MR. De NIL ! GET TO WORK !
YOU KNOW WHAT I WANT--PLENTY OF BOFFS ! PLENTY OF SLAPSTICK ACTION ! AND GET ME THOSE FILMS AS SOON AS POSSIBLE-- !
YES, SIR !
AND AS MOVIE PRODUCER B.C. De NIL LEAVES THE OFFICE BUILDING...
A CHECK FOR $50,000 -- BUT THIS IS JUST A MEASLY DROP IN THE BUCKET COMPARED TO WHAT I'LL GET WHEN I'VE SETTLED MY BUSINESS WITH THE FABULOUSLY WEALTHY CORNELIUS VAN-VAN !
SOMETHING DEVILISHLY FAMILIAR ABOUT THIS "MOVIE PRODUCER" ?! NO DOUBT SOME OF YOU WILL ALREADY HAVE SUSPECTED THE PRESENCE OF THAT MAD MAESTRO OF MIRTH, THAT LEONARDO OF THE LARCENOUS LAUGH, THAT MAN OF A THOUSAND FALSE FRONTS -- The JOKER !
IN HIS UNDERWORLD HIDEOUT, BACK IN GOTHAM CITY...
THE SCENARIOS I WROTE WHICH MR. VAN-VAN LIKED ALL DEAL WITH SOME FORM OF SLAPSTICK CRIME -- DONE IN OLD-MOVIE STYLE ! BUT HE DOESN'T HAVE TO KNOW THAT THE CRIME ATTEMPTS WILL BE REAL ONES ! HA HA!
2

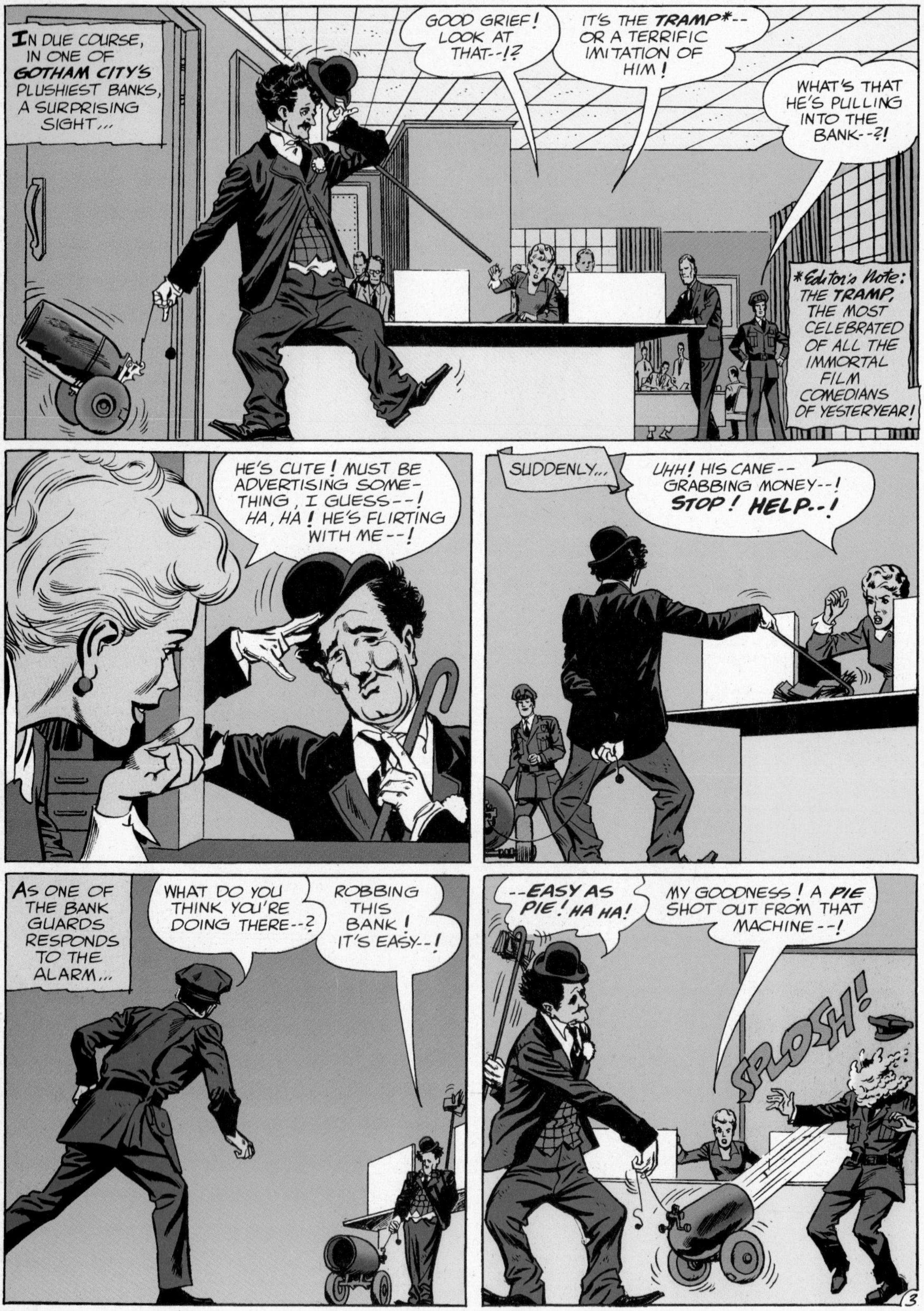
IN DUE COURSE, IN ONE OF GOTHAM CITY'S PLUSHIEST BANKS, A SURPRISING SIGHT...
GOOD GRIEF! LOOK AT THAT--!?
IT'S THE TRAMP*--OR A TERRIFIC IMITATION OF HIM!
WHAT'S THAT HE'S PULLING INTO THE BANK--?!
*Editor's Note: THE TRAMP, THE MOST CELEBRATED OF ALL THE IMMORTAL FILM COMEDIANS OF YESTERYEAR!
HE'S CUTE! MUST BE ADVERTISING SOME-THING, I GUESS--! HA, HA! HE'S FLIRTING WITH ME--!
SUDDENLY...
UHH! HIS CANE--GRABBING MONEY--! STOP! HELP--!
AS ONE OF THE BANK GUARDS RESPONDS TO THE ALARM...
WHAT DO YOU THINK YOU'RE DOING THERE--?
ROBBING THIS BANK! IT'S EASY--!
--EASY AS PIE! HA HA!
MY GOODNESS! A PIE SHOT OUT FROM THAT MACHINE--!
SPLOSH!
3

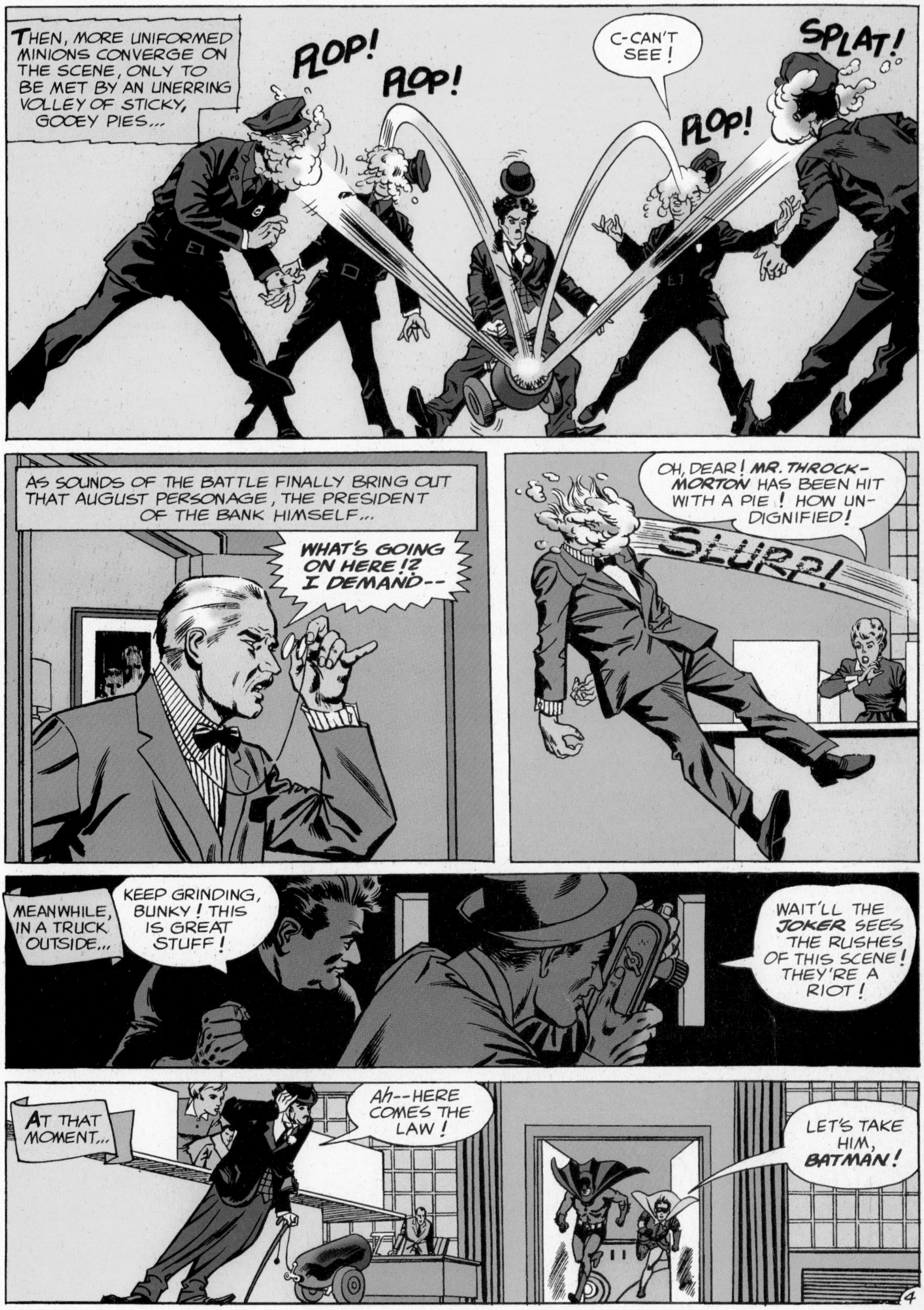

THEN, MORE UNIFORMED MINIONS CONVERGE ON THE SCENE, ONLY TO BE MET BY AN UNERRING VOLLEY OF STICKY, GOOEY PIES...
PLOP!
PLOP!
C-CAN'T SEE!
PLOP!
SPLAT!
AS SOUNDS OF THE BATTLE FINALLY BRING OUT THAT AUGUST PERSONAGE, THE PRESIDENT OF THE BANK HIMSELF...
WHAT'S GOING ON HERE!? I DEMAND--
OH, DEAR! MR. THROCK-MORTON HAS BEEN HIT WITH A PIE! HOW UN-DIGNIFIED!
SLURP!
MEANWHILE, IN A TRUCK OUTSIDE...
KEEP GRINDING, BUNKY! THIS IS GREAT STUFF!
WAIT'LL THE JOKER SEES THE RUSHES OF THIS SCENE! THEY'RE A RIOT!
AT THAT MOMENT...
Ah--HERE COMES THE LAW!
LET'S TAKE HIM, BATMAN!
4

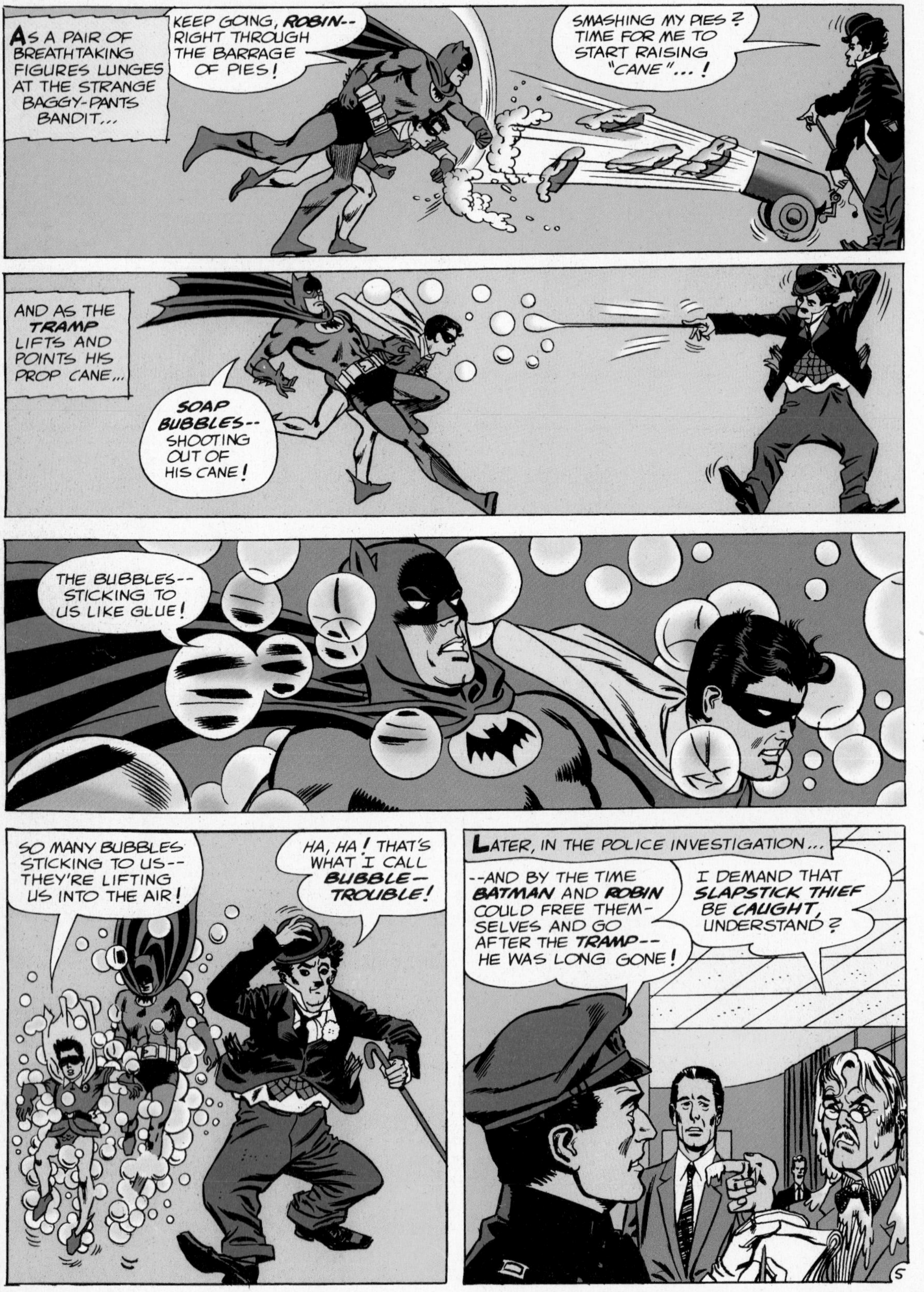
AS A PAIR OF BREATHTAKING FIGURES LUNGES AT THE STRANGE BAGGY-PANTS BANDIT...
KEEP GOING, ROBIN-- RIGHT THROUGH THE BARRAGE OF PIES!
SMASHING MY PIES? TIME FOR ME TO START RAISING "CANE"...!
AND AS THE TRAMP LIFTS AND POINTS HIS PROP CANE...
SOAP BUBBLES-- SHOOTING OUT OF HIS CANE!
THE BUBBLES-- STICKING TO US LIKE GLUE!
SO MANY BUBBLES STICKING TO US-- THEY'RE LIFTING US INTO THE AIR!
HA, HA! THAT'S WHAT I CALL BUBBLE-TROUBLE!
LATER, IN THE POLICE INVESTIGATION...
--AND BY THE TIME BATMAN AND ROBIN COULD FREE THEMSELVES AND GO AFTER THE TRAMP-- HE WAS LONG GONE!
I DEMAND THAT SLAPSTICK THIEF BE CAUGHT, UNDERSTAND?
5

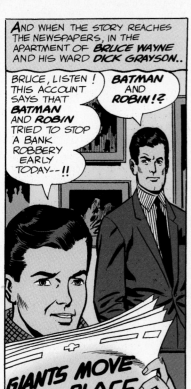

AND WHEN THE STORY REACHES THE NEWSPAPERS, IN THE APARTMENT OF *BRUCE WAYNE* AND HIS WARD *DICK GRAYSON*..

BRUCE, LISTEN! THIS ACCOUNT SAYS THAT *BATMAN* AND *ROBIN* TRIED TO STOP A BANK ROBBERY EARLY TODAY--!!

BATMAN AND *ROBIN*!?

GIANTS MOVE PLACE

SOUNDS TO ME LIKE TWO MEMBERS OF THE GANG *IMPERSONATED US*, DICK-- WE WERE *HERE* ALL THE TIME! BUT THE QUESTION IS-- *WHY* WOULD THEY PULL SUCH A STUNT?

HERE'S A DESCRIPTION OF THE GANG-LEADER...

"...THE THIEF WAS DRESSED UP AS THAT OLD MOVIE COMIC *THE TRAMP*! HE AMUSED THE BANK TELLERS AND AROUSED THEM TO LAUGHTER-- EVEN AS HE *STOLE FROM THEM*!"

Hmm--CRIME AND LAUGHTER! DOESN'T THAT REMIND YOU OF *SOMEONE*--?

IT SURE DOES!

THE JOKER!!

COME ON, DICK! IF *THE JOKER* HAS STARTED AGAIN ON ONE OF HIS NOT-SO-FUNNY CRIME RAMPAGES-- IT'S *NO JOKE*! *BATMAN* AND *ROBIN* HAVE TO STOP HIM!

MOMENTS LATER, IN THE *BAT-CAVE*...

AND I MEAN THE *REAL BATMAN* AND *ROBIN*-- THIS TIME!

I CAN'T WAIT TO DELIVER A *PUNCH LINE* TO STOP THE *JOKER* WITH MY *FIST*!

SOON, A SLEEK VEHICLE PROWLS THE CITY, MANNED BY AN ALERT-EYED DUO...

WE DON'T KNOW WHERE HE'LL STRIKE NEXT! IT COULD BE ANYWHERE--

WE'LL HAVE TO HOPE FOR A BREAK-- USE THE *BATMOBILE* TO KEEP *HUNTING* NIGHT AND DAY!

6

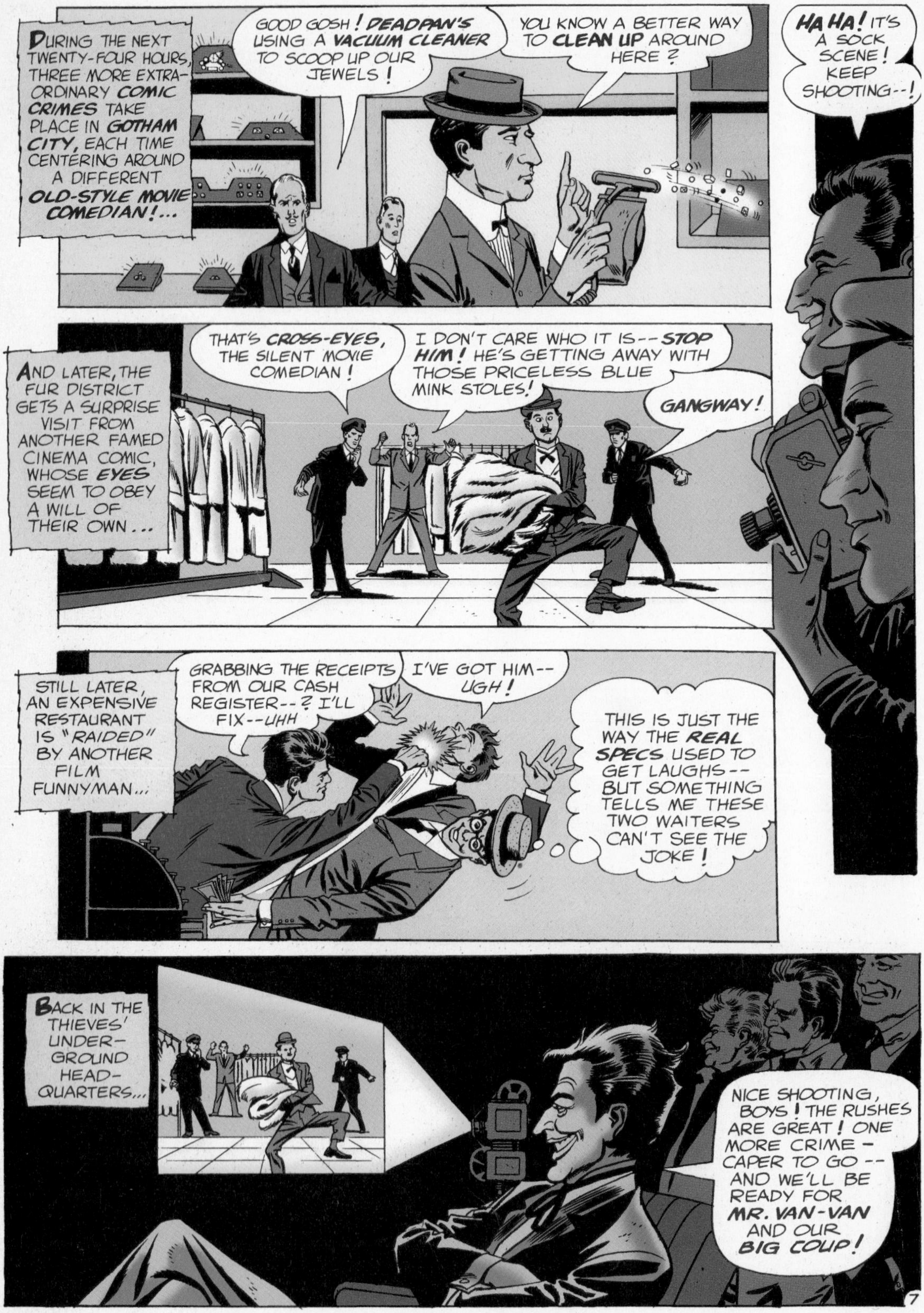
DURING THE NEXT TWENTY-FOUR HOURS, THREE MORE EXTRA-ORDINARY COMIC CRIMES TAKE PLACE IN GOTHAM CITY, EACH TIME CENTERING AROUND A DIFFERENT OLD-STYLE MOVIE COMEDIAN!...
GOOD GOSH! DEADPAN'S USING A VACUUM CLEANER TO SCOOP UP OUR JEWELS!
YOU KNOW A BETTER WAY TO CLEAN UP AROUND HERE?
HA HA! IT'S A SOCK SCENE! KEEP SHOOTING--!
AND LATER, THE FUR DISTRICT GETS A SURPRISE VISIT FROM ANOTHER FAMED CINEMA COMIC, WHOSE EYES SEEM TO OBEY A WILL OF THEIR OWN...
THAT'S CROSS-EYES, THE SILENT MOVIE COMEDIAN!
I DON'T CARE WHO IT IS--STOP HIM! HE'S GETTING AWAY WITH THOSE PRICELESS BLUE MINK STOLES!
GANGWAY!
STILL LATER, AN EXPENSIVE RESTAURANT IS "RAIDED" BY ANOTHER FILM FUNNYMAN...
GRABBING THE RECEIPTS FROM OUR CASH REGISTER--? I'LL FIX--UHH
I'VE GOT HIM--UGH!
THIS IS JUST THE WAY THE REAL SPECS USED TO GET LAUGHS--BUT SOMETHING TELLS ME THESE TWO WAITERS CAN'T SEE THE JOKE!
BACK IN THE THIEVES' UNDER-GROUND HEAD-QUARTERS...
NICE SHOOTING, BOYS! THE RUSHES ARE GREAT! ONE MORE CRIME-CAPER TO GO--AND WE'LL BE READY FOR MR. VAN-VAN AND OUR BIG COUP!
7

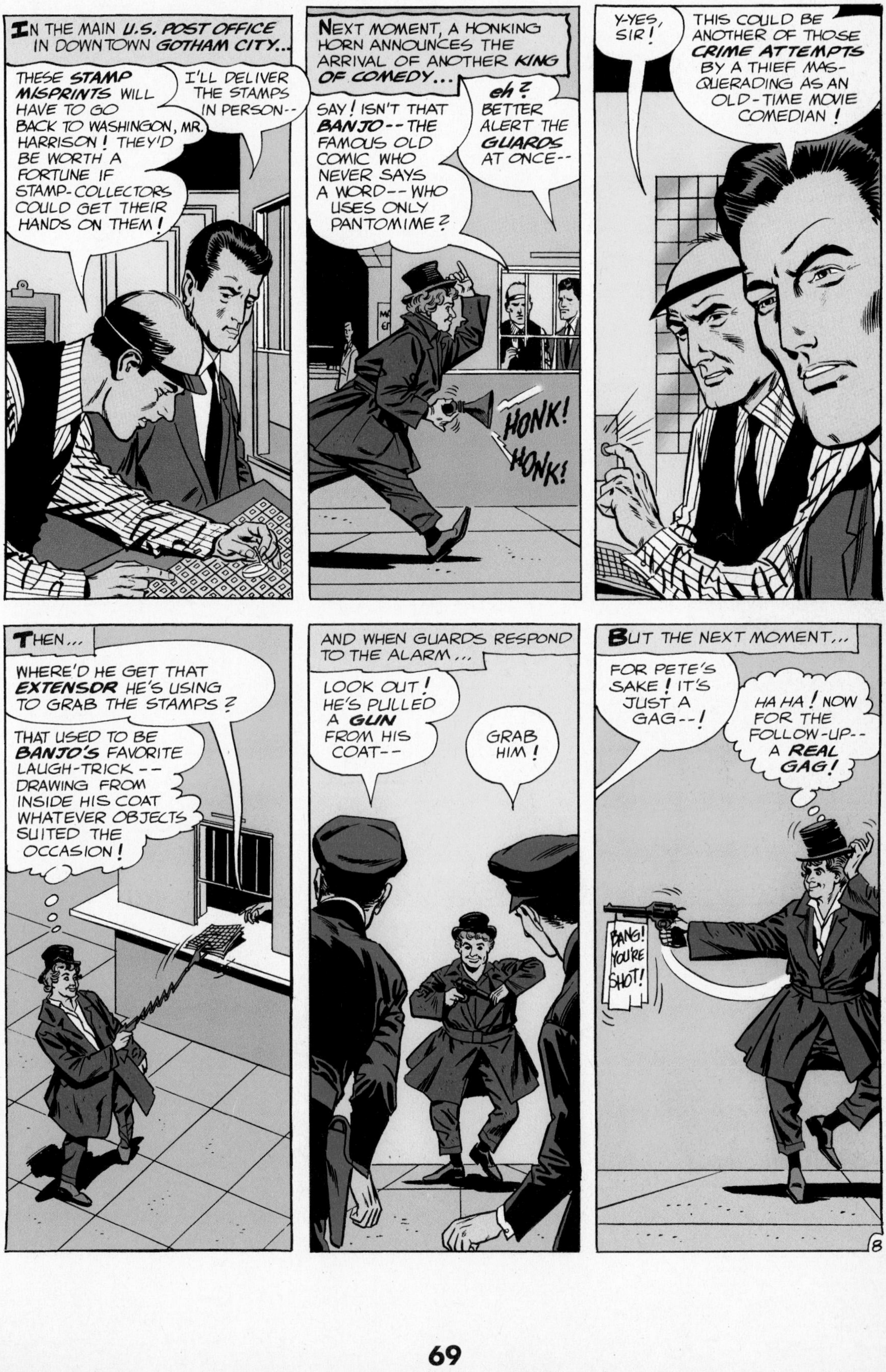
IN THE MAIN U.S. POST OFFICE IN DOWNTOWN GOTHAM CITY...
THESE STAMP MISPRINTS WILL HAVE TO GO BACK TO WASHINGON, MR. HARRISON! THEY'D BE WORTH A FORTUNE IF STAMP-COLLECTORS COULD GET THEIR HANDS ON THEM!
I'LL DELIVER THE STAMPS IN PERSON--
NEXT MOMENT, A HONKING HORN ANNOUNCES THE ARRIVAL OF ANOTHER KING OF COMEDY...
SAY! ISN'T THAT BANJO--THE FAMOUS OLD COMIC WHO NEVER SAYS A WORD--WHO USES ONLY PANTOMIME?
eh? BETTER ALERT THE GUARDS AT ONCE--
HONK! HONK!
Y-YES, SIR!
THIS COULD BE ANOTHER OF THOSE CRIME ATTEMPTS BY A THIEF MASQUERADING AS AN OLD-TIME MOVIE COMEDIAN!
THEN...
WHERE'D HE GET THAT EXTENSOR HE'S USING TO GRAB THE STAMPS?
THAT USED TO BE BANJO'S FAVORITE LAUGH-TRICK -- DRAWING FROM INSIDE HIS COAT WHATEVER OBJECTS SUITED THE OCCASION!
AND WHEN GUARDS RESPOND TO THE ALARM...
LOOK OUT! HE'S PULLED A GUN FROM HIS COAT--
GRAB HIM!
BUT THE NEXT MOMENT...
FOR PETE'S SAKE! IT'S JUST A GAG--!
HA HA! NOW FOR THE FOLLOW-UP-- A REAL GAG!
BANG! YOU'RE SHOT!
8

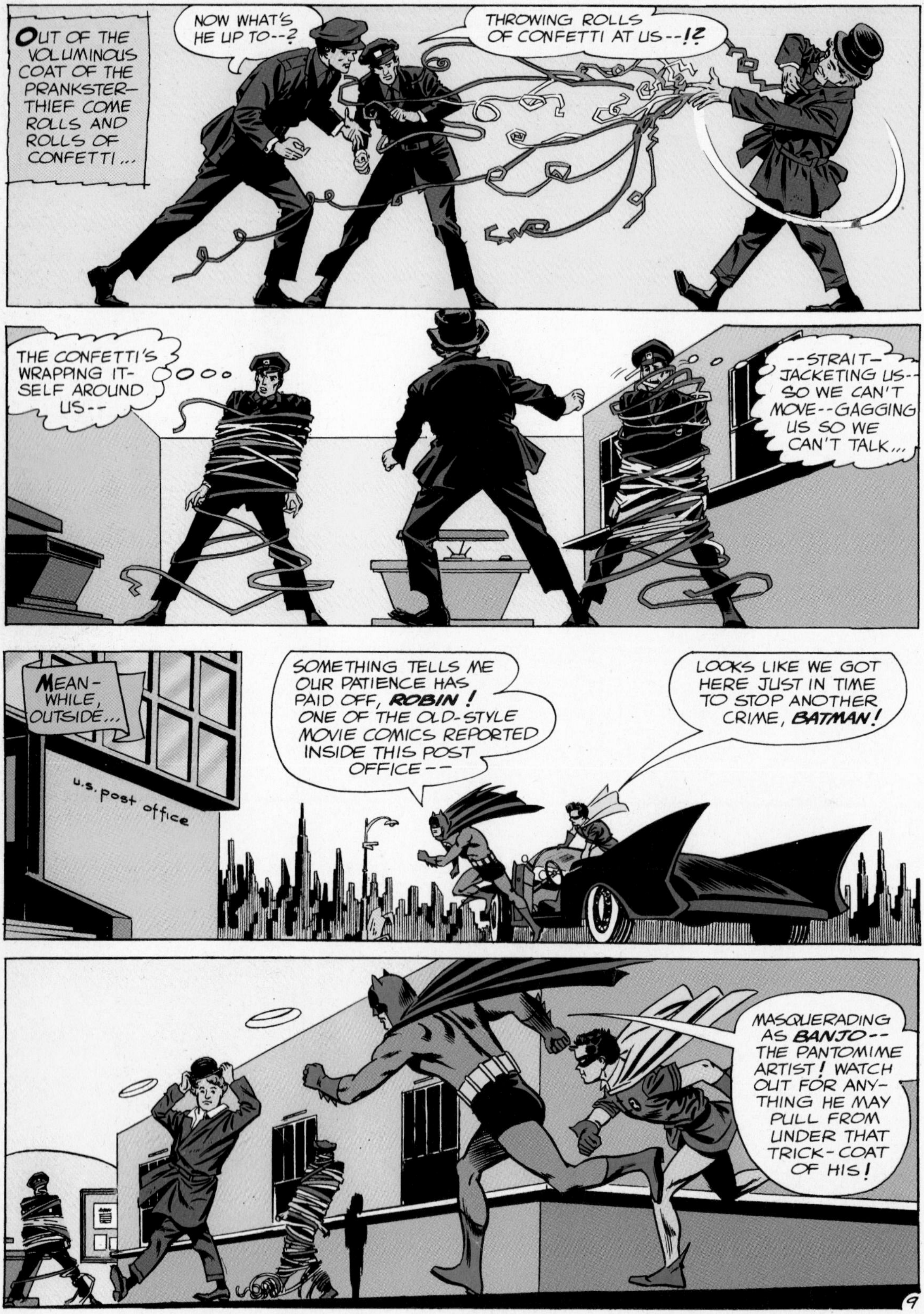
OUT OF THE VOLUMINOUS COAT OF THE PRANKSTER-THIEF COME ROLLS AND ROLLS OF CONFETTI...
NOW WHAT'S HE UP TO--?
THROWING ROLLS OF CONFETTI AT US--!?
THE CONFETTI'S WRAPPING IT-SELF AROUND US--
--STRAIT-JACKETING US--SO WE CAN'T MOVE--GAGGING US SO WE CAN'T TALK...
MEAN-WHILE, OUTSIDE...
u.s. post office
SOMETHING TELLS ME OUR PATIENCE HAS PAID OFF, ROBIN! ONE OF THE OLD-STYLE MOVIE COMICS REPORTED INSIDE THIS POST OFFICE--
LOOKS LIKE WE GOT HERE JUST IN TIME TO STOP ANOTHER CRIME, BATMAN!
MASQUERADING AS BANJO--THE PANTOMIME ARTIST! WATCH OUT FOR ANY-THING HE MAY PULL FROM UNDER THAT TRICK-COAT OF HIS!
9

SO MY OLD FRIENDS *BATMAN* AND *ROBIN* THINK THEY'VE GOT ME, EH?

SPEAKING ALOUD--HE'S STEPPING OUT OF CHARACTER--! AND THAT VOICE--!

THEN SWIFTLY,...

RIPPING OFF HIS WIG! AND UNDERNEATH--*GREEN HAIR*--!

AND NOW FOR THE *UNMASKING*--TO REVEAL--

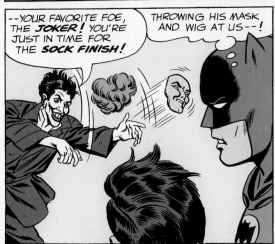

--YOUR FAVORITE FOE, THE *JOKER!* YOU'RE JUST IN TIME FOR THE *SOCK FINISH!*

THROWING HIS MASK AND WIG AT US--!

AS THE SUDDEN MOVE BY THE *MAD MONARCH OF MIRTH* CATCHES THE CRIME CRUSADERS BY SURPRISE...

FUMES--SOME KIND OF *KNOCKOUT GAS*...!

UHH--

LITTLE DIALS WHICH BROKE ON CONTACT! I HAD THEM READY FOR *YOU TWO*--JUST IN CASE!! HA HA HA!

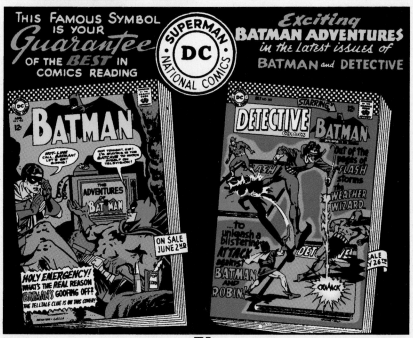

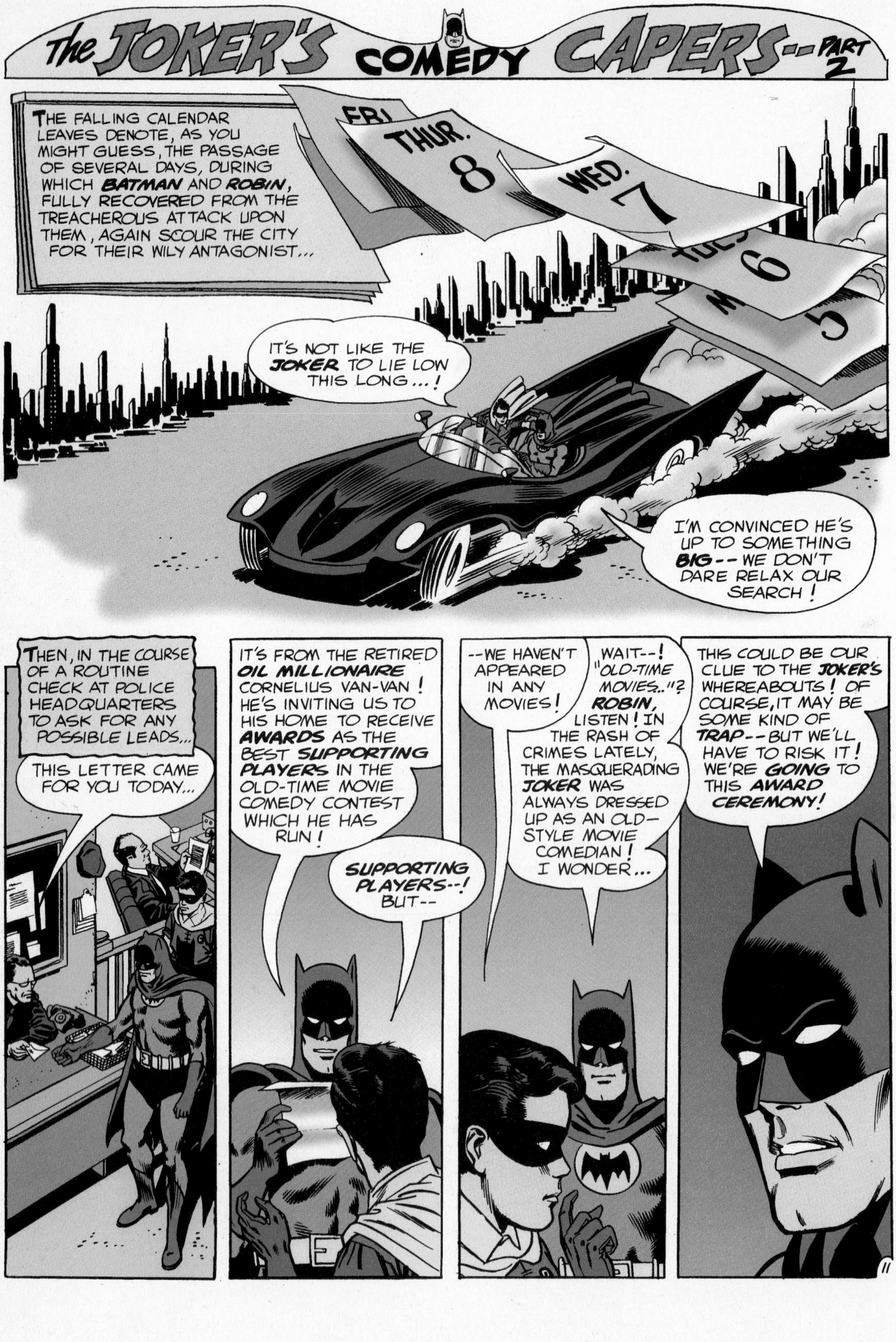
The JOKER'S COMEDY CAPERS--PART 2
THE FALLING CALENDAR LEAVES DENOTE, AS YOU MIGHT GUESS, THE PASSAGE OF SEVERAL DAYS, DURING WHICH BATMAN AND ROBIN, FULLY RECOVERED FROM THE TREACHEROUS ATTACK UPON THEM, AGAIN SCOUR THE CITY FOR THEIR WILY ANTAGONIST...
FRI
THUR. 8
WED. 7
6
M 5
IT'S NOT LIKE THE JOKER TO LIE LOW THIS LONG...!
I'M CONVINCED HE'S UP TO SOMETHING BIG--WE DON'T DARE RELAX OUR SEARCH!
THEN, IN THE COURSE OF A ROUTINE CHECK AT POLICE HEADQUARTERS TO ASK FOR ANY POSSIBLE LEADS...
THIS LETTER CAME FOR YOU TODAY...
IT'S FROM THE RETIRED OIL MILLIONAIRE CORNELIUS VAN-VAN! HE'S INVITING US TO HIS HOME TO RECEIVE AWARDS AS THE BEST SUPPORTING PLAYERS IN THE OLD-TIME MOVIE COMEDY CONTEST WHICH HE HAS RUN!
SUPPORTING PLAYERS--! BUT--
--WE HAVEN'T APPEARED IN ANY MOVIES!
WAIT--! "OLD-TIME MOVIES.."? ROBIN, LISTEN! IN THE RASH OF CRIMES LATELY, THE MASQUERADING JOKER WAS ALWAYS DRESSED UP AS AN OLD-STYLE MOVIE COMEDIAN! I WONDER...
THIS COULD BE OUR CLUE TO THE JOKER'S WHEREABOUTS! OF COURSE, IT MAY BE SOME KIND OF TRAP--BUT WE'LL HAVE TO RISK IT! WE'RE GOING TO THIS AWARD CEREMONY!
11

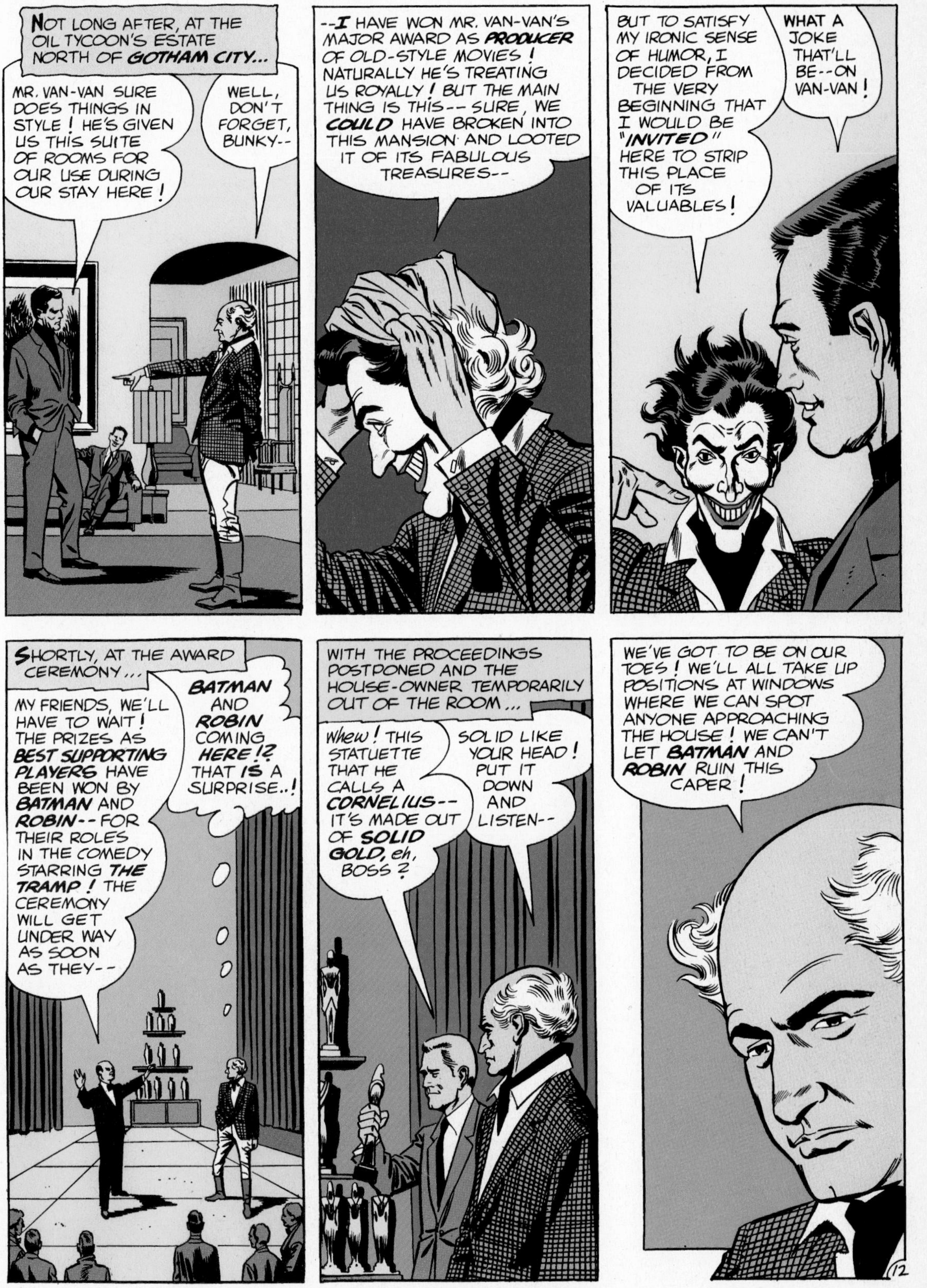
NOT LONG AFTER, AT THE OIL TYCOON'S ESTATE NORTH OF GOTHAM CITY...
MR. VAN-VAN SURE DOES THINGS IN STYLE! HE'S GIVEN US THIS SUITE OF ROOMS FOR OUR USE DURING OUR STAY HERE!
WELL, DON'T FORGET, BUNKY--
--I HAVE WON MR. VAN-VAN'S MAJOR AWARD AS PRODUCER OF OLD-STYLE MOVIES! NATURALLY HE'S TREATING US ROYALLY! BUT THE MAIN THING IS THIS-- SURE, WE COULD HAVE BROKEN INTO THIS MANSION AND LOOTED IT OF ITS FABULOUS TREASURES--
BUT TO SATISFY MY IRONIC SENSE OF HUMOR, I DECIDED FROM THE VERY BEGINNING THAT I WOULD BE "INVITED" HERE TO STRIP THIS PLACE OF ITS VALUABLES!
WHAT A JOKE THAT'LL BE--ON VAN-VAN!
SHORTLY, AT THE AWARD CEREMONY...
MY FRIENDS, WE'LL HAVE TO WAIT! THE PRIZES AS BEST SUPPORTING PLAYERS HAVE BEEN WON BY BATMAN AND ROBIN-- FOR THEIR ROLES IN THE COMEDY STARRING THE TRAMP! THE CEREMONY WILL GET UNDER WAY AS SOON AS THEY--
BATMAN AND ROBIN COMING HERE!? THAT IS A SURPRISE..!
WITH THE PROCEEDINGS POSTPONED AND THE HOUSE-OWNER TEMPORARILY OUT OF THE ROOM...
Whew! THIS STATUETTE THAT HE CALLS A CORNELIUS-- IT'S MADE OUT OF SOLID GOLD, eh, BOSS?
SOLID LIKE YOUR HEAD! PUT IT DOWN AND LISTEN--
WE'VE GOT TO BE ON OUR TOES! WE'LL ALL TAKE UP POSITIONS AT WINDOWS WHERE WE CAN SPOT ANYONE APPROACHING THE HOUSE! WE CAN'T LET BATMAN AND ROBIN RUIN THIS CAPER!
12

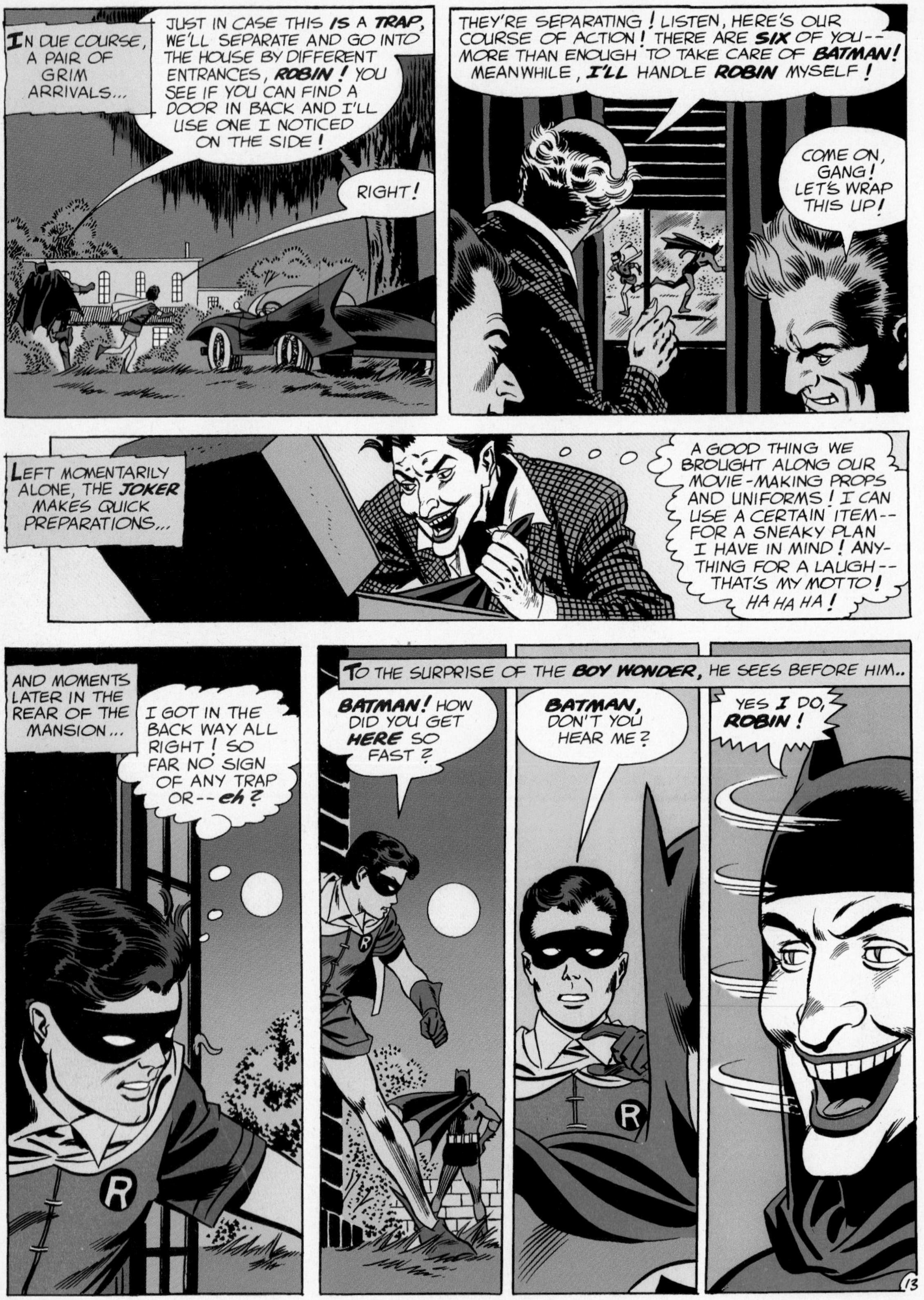
IN DUE COURSE, A PAIR OF GRIM ARRIVALS...
JUST IN CASE THIS IS A TRAP, WE'LL SEPARATE AND GO INTO THE HOUSE BY DIFFERENT ENTRANCES, ROBIN! YOU SEE IF YOU CAN FIND A DOOR IN BACK AND I'LL USE ONE I NOTICED ON THE SIDE!
RIGHT!
THEY'RE SEPARATING! LISTEN, HERE'S OUR COURSE OF ACTION! THERE ARE SIX OF YOU-- MORE THAN ENOUGH TO TAKE CARE OF BATMAN! MEANWHILE, I'LL HANDLE ROBIN MYSELF!
COME ON, GANG! LET'S WRAP THIS UP!
LEFT MOMENTARILY ALONE, THE JOKER MAKES QUICK PREPARATIONS...
A GOOD THING WE BROUGHT ALONG OUR MOVIE-MAKING PROPS AND UNIFORMS! I CAN USE A CERTAIN ITEM-- FOR A SNEAKY PLAN I HAVE IN MIND! ANYTHING FOR A LAUGH-- THAT'S MY MOTTO! HA HA HA!
AND MOMENTS LATER IN THE REAR OF THE MANSION...
I GOT IN THE BACK WAY ALL RIGHT! SO FAR NO SIGN OF ANY TRAP OR--eh?
TO THE SURPRISE OF THE BOY WONDER, HE SEES BEFORE HIM...
BATMAN! HOW DID YOU GET HERE SO FAST?
BATMAN, DON'T YOU HEAR ME?
YES I DO, ROBIN!
13

THEN WITH FIENDISH SWIFTNESS, THE SEMI-DISGUISED *JOKER* USES HIS *"BATROPE"* TO YANK *ROBIN* OFF HIS FEET...

TRICKED--

TRIPPED, YOU MEAN! HA HA!

LEAVING HIS BOY-FOE BOUND AND HELPLESS, THE FAST-MOVING THIEF DOFFS HIS MASQUERADE, AND...

TOO BAD I CAN'T WAIT FOR THE AWARD CEREMONY! BUT THINGS ARE GETTING TOO--er--WARM AROUND HERE! SO I'LL JUST DO MY LOOTING NOW-- AND MAKE MY SOLO GETAWAY!

MEANWHILE, A BATTLE ROYAL IS IN PROGRESS IN THE LANDSCAPED GARDENS OUTSIDE THE MANSION..

GRAB HIM-- UGH!

I DON'T KNOW WHERE THIS GANG THAT'S ATTACKING ME CAME FROM--

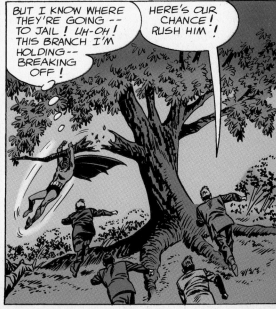

BUT I KNOW WHERE THEY'RE GOING -- TO JAIL! UH-OH! THIS BRANCH I'M HOLDING-- BREAKING OFF!

HERE'S OUR CHANCE! RUSH HIM!

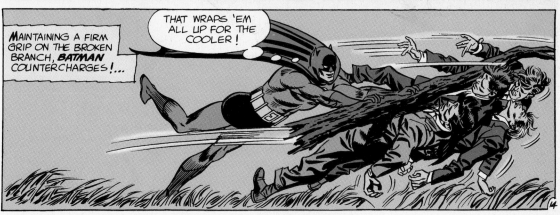

MAINTAINING A FIRM GRIP ON THE BROKEN BRANCH, *BATMAN* COUNTERCHARGES!...

THAT WRAPS 'EM ALL UP FOR THE COOLER!

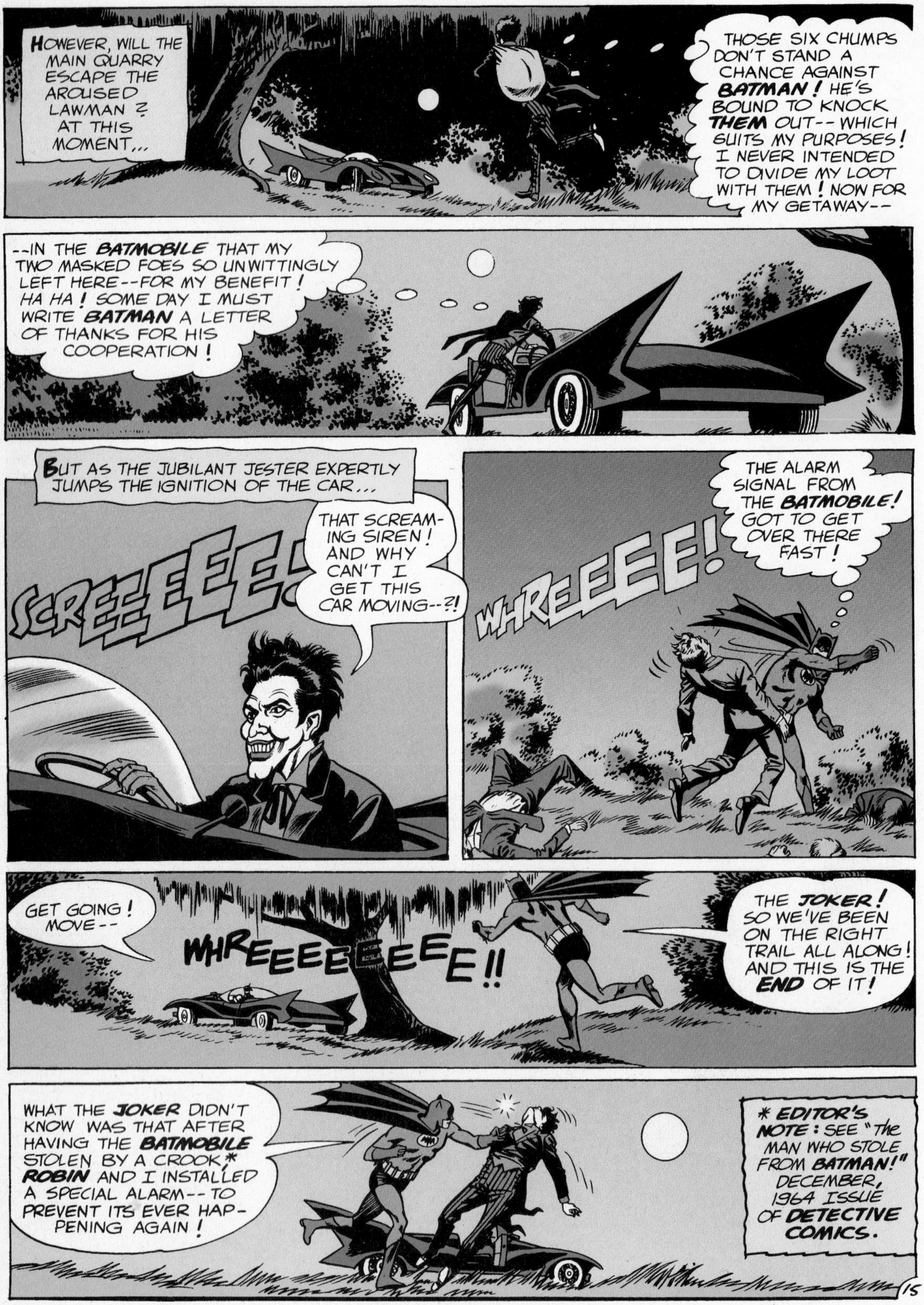
HOWEVER, WILL THE MAIN QUARRY ESCAPE THE AROUSED LAWMAN ? AT THIS MOMENT,...
THOSE SIX CHUMPS DON'T STAND A CHANCE AGAINST BATMAN! HE'S BOUND TO KNOCK THEM OUT--WHICH SUITS MY PURPOSES! I NEVER INTENDED TO DIVIDE MY LOOT WITH THEM! NOW FOR MY GETAWAY--
--IN THE BATMOBILE THAT MY TWO MASKED FOES SO UNWITTINGLY LEFT HERE--FOR MY BENEFIT! HA HA! SOME DAY I MUST WRITE BATMAN A LETTER OF THANKS FOR HIS COOPERATION!
BUT AS THE JUBILANT JESTER EXPERTLY JUMPS THE IGNITION OF THE CAR,...
THAT SCREAMING SIREN! AND WHY CAN'T I GET THIS CAR MOVING--?!
SCREEEEEE
THE ALARM SIGNAL FROM THE BATMOBILE! GOT TO GET OVER THERE FAST!
WHREEEEE!
GET GOING! MOVE--
WHREEEEEEEEE!!
THE JOKER! SO WE'VE BEEN ON THE RIGHT TRAIL ALL ALONG! AND THIS IS THE END OF IT!
WHAT THE JOKER DIDN'T KNOW WAS THAT AFTER HAVING THE BATMOBILE STOLEN BY A CROOK,* ROBIN AND I INSTALLED A SPECIAL ALARM--TO PREVENT ITS EVER HAPPENING AGAIN!
* EDITOR'S NOTE: SEE "The MAN WHO STOLE FROM BATMAN!" DECEMBER, 1964 ISSUE OF DETECTIVE COMICS.
15

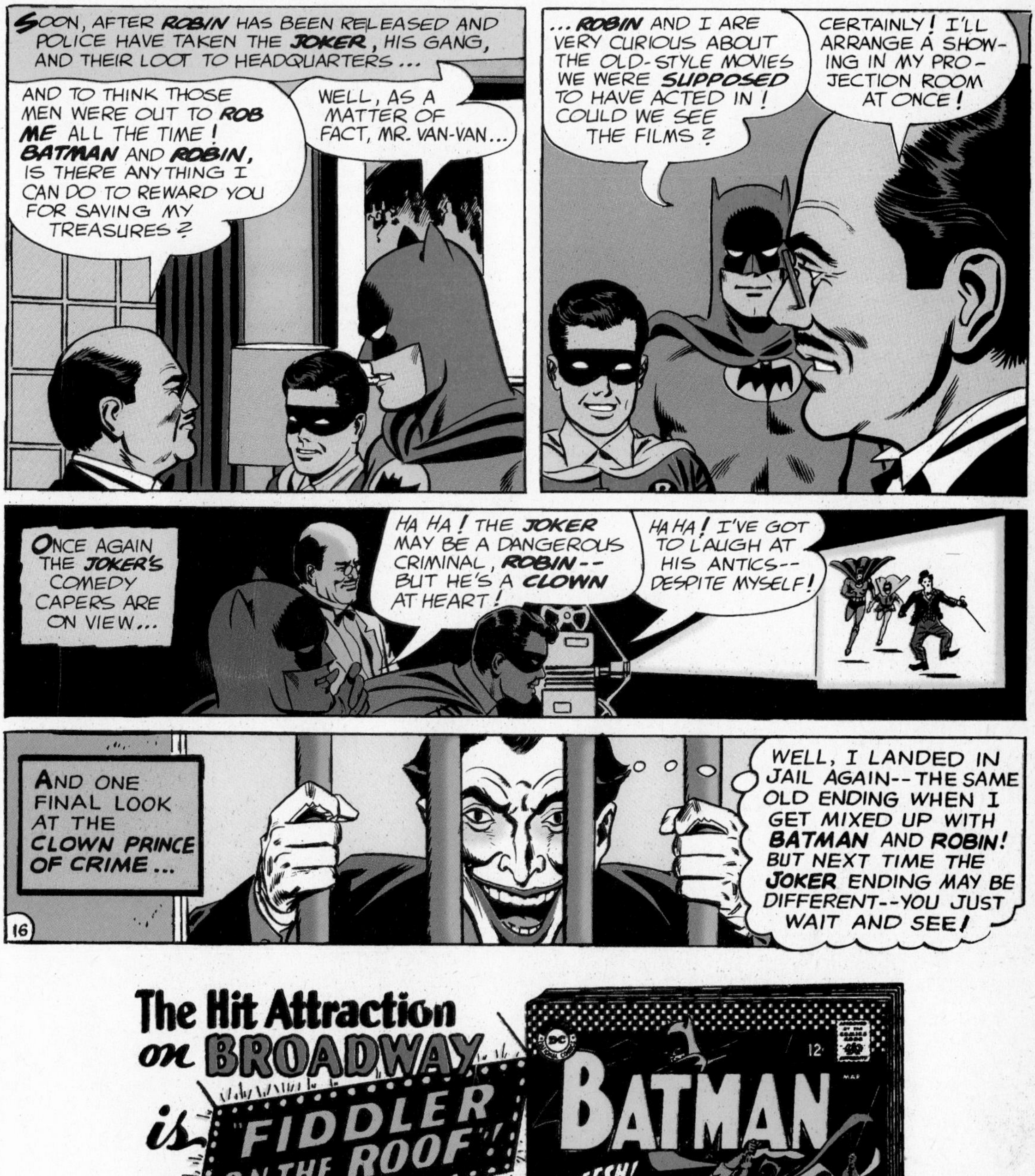
SOON, AFTER ROBIN HAS BEEN RELEASED AND POLICE HAVE TAKEN THE JOKER, HIS GANG, AND THEIR LOOT TO HEADQUARTERS...
AND TO THINK THOSE MEN WERE OUT TO ROB ME ALL THE TIME! BATMAN AND ROBIN, IS THERE ANYTHING I CAN DO TO REWARD YOU FOR SAVING MY TREASURES?
WELL, AS A MATTER OF FACT, MR. VAN-VAN...
...ROBIN AND I ARE VERY CURIOUS ABOUT THE OLD-STYLE MOVIES WE WERE SUPPOSED TO HAVE ACTED IN! COULD WE SEE THE FILMS?
CERTAINLY! I'LL ARRANGE A SHOWING IN MY PROJECTION ROOM AT ONCE!
ONCE AGAIN THE JOKER'S COMEDY CAPERS ARE ON VIEW...
HA HA! THE JOKER MAY BE A DANGEROUS CRIMINAL, ROBIN-- BUT HE'S A CLOWN AT HEART!
HA HA! I'VE GOT TO LAUGH AT HIS ANTICS-- DESPITE MYSELF!
AND ONE FINAL LOOK AT THE CLOWN PRINCE OF CRIME...
WELL, I LANDED IN JAIL AGAIN-- THE SAME OLD ENDING WHEN I GET MIXED UP WITH BATMAN AND ROBIN! BUT NEXT TIME THE JOKER ENDING MAY BE DIFFERENT--YOU JUST WAIT AND SEE!
16

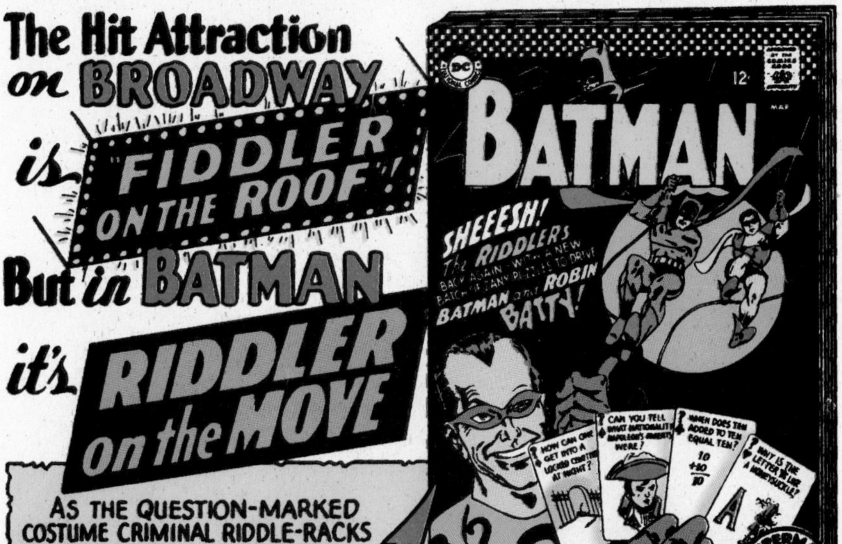
The Hit Attraction on BROADWAY
is "FIDDLER ON THE ROOF"!
But in BATMAN
it's RIDDLER on the MOVE
AS THE QUESTION-MARKED COSTUME CRIMINAL RIDDLE-RACKS BATMAN and ROBIN WITH PUZZLES OF PERIL IN
ON SALE JAN. 20th
BATMAN
12¢
SHEEESH! The RIDDLERS BACK AGAIN WITH A NEW BATCH OF ZANY PUZZLES TO DRIVE BATMAN and ROBIN BATTY!
SUPERMAN DC NATIONAL COMICS

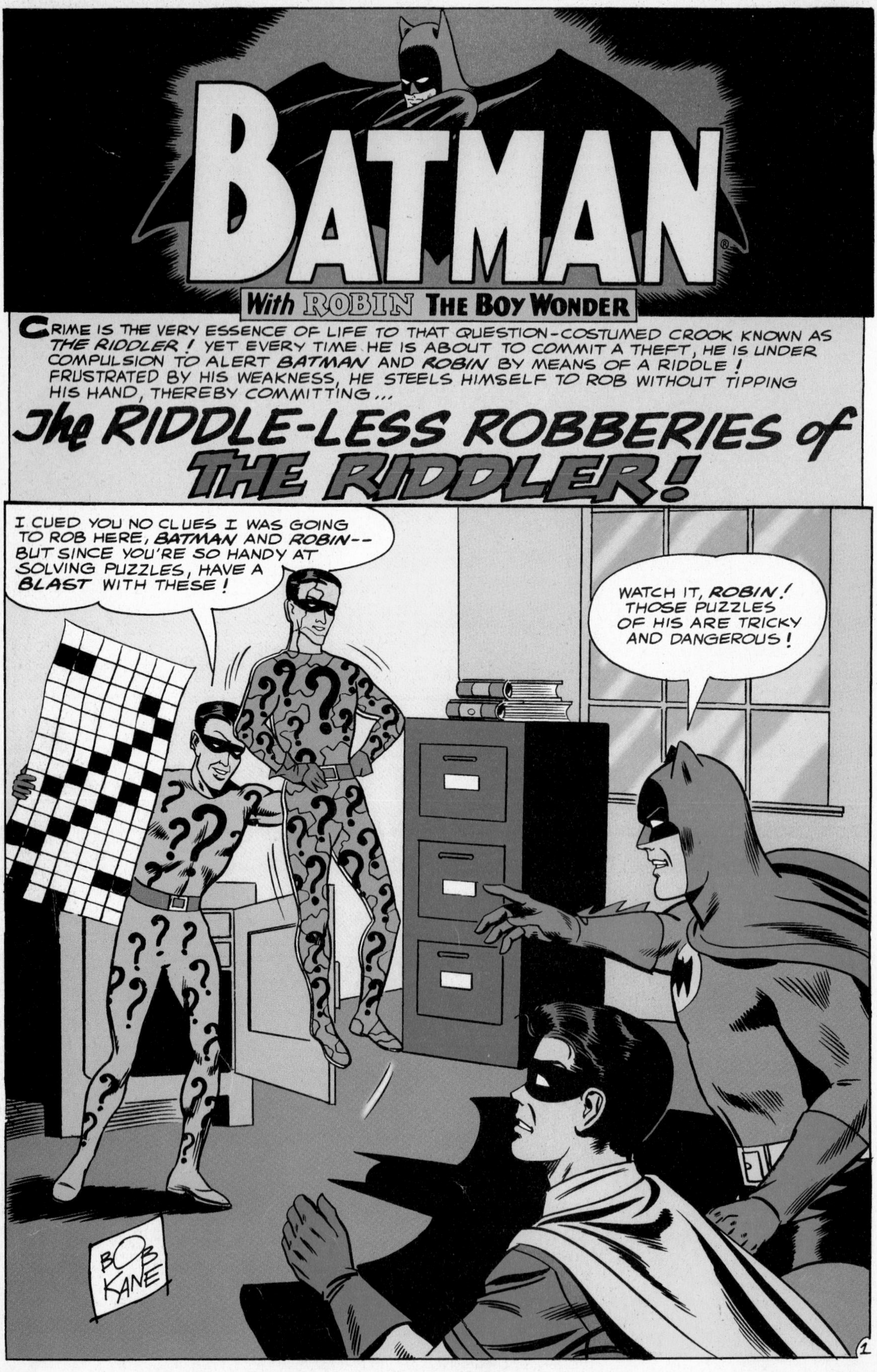
BATMAN
With ROBIN THE BOY WONDER
CRIME IS THE VERY ESSENCE OF LIFE TO THAT QUESTION-COSTUMED CROOK KNOWN AS THE RIDDLER! YET EVERY TIME HE IS ABOUT TO COMMIT A THEFT, HE IS UNDER COMPULSION TO ALERT BATMAN AND ROBIN BY MEANS OF A RIDDLE! FRUSTRATED BY HIS WEAKNESS, HE STEELS HIMSELF TO ROB WITHOUT TIPPING HIS HAND, THEREBY COMMITTING...
The RIDDLE-LESS ROBBERIES of THE RIDDLER!
I CUED YOU NO CLUES I WAS GOING TO ROB HERE, BATMAN AND ROBIN-- BUT SINCE YOU'RE SO HANDY AT SOLVING PUZZLES, HAVE A BLAST WITH THESE!
WATCH IT, ROBIN! THOSE PUZZLES OF HIS ARE TRICKY AND DANGEROUS!
BOB KANE
1

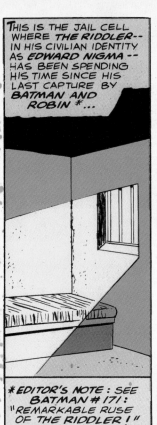

THIS IS THE JAIL CELL WHERE *THE RIDDLER*-- IN HIS CIVILIAN IDENTITY AS *EDWARD NIGMA*-- HAS BEEN SPENDING HIS TIME SINCE HIS LAST CAPTURE BY *BATMAN* AND *ROBIN* *...

*EDITOR'S NOTE: SEE BATMAN #171: "REMARKABLE RUSE OF THE RIDDLER!"

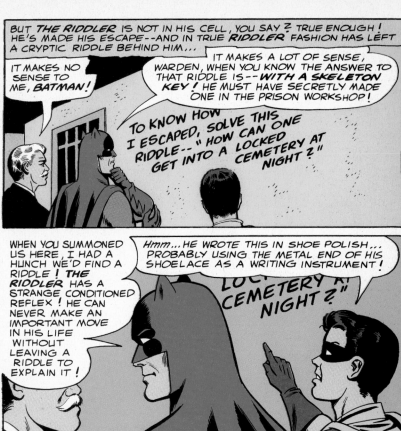

BUT *THE RIDDLER* IS NOT IN HIS CELL, YOU SAY? TRUE ENOUGH! HE'S MADE HIS ESCAPE--AND IN TRUE *RIDDLER* FASHION HAS LEFT A CRYPTIC RIDDLE BEHIND HIM...

IT MAKES NO SENSE TO ME, *BATMAN!*

IT MAKES A LOT OF SENSE, WARDEN, WHEN YOU KNOW THE ANSWER TO THAT RIDDLE IS--*WITH A SKELETON KEY!* HE MUST HAVE SECRETLY MADE ONE IN THE PRISON WORKSHOP!

TO KNOW HOW I ESCAPED, SOLVE THIS RIDDLE--" HOW CAN ONE GET INTO A LOCKED CEMETERY AT NIGHT?"

WHEN YOU SUMMONED US HERE, I HAD A HUNCH WE'D FIND A RIDDLE! *THE RIDDLER* HAS A STRANGE CONDITIONED REFLEX! HE CAN NEVER MAKE AN IMPORTANT MOVE IN HIS LIFE WITHOUT LEAVING A RIDDLE TO EXPLAIN IT!

Hmm...HE WROTE THIS IN SHOE POLISH... PROBABLY USING THE METAL END OF HIS SHOELACE AS A WRITING INSTRUMENT!

...LOC... CEMETERY A... NIGHT?"

AS *BATMAN* AND *ROBIN* LEAVE THE STATE PRISON...

OUR NEXT PROBLEM IS... *WHEN'S* THE *RIDDLER* GOING TO STRIKE-- AND *WHERE?*

THAT'S SOMETHING WE CAN'T ANSWER, *ROBIN*.. NOT UNTIL HE TIPS US OFF WITH ANOTHER RIDDLE!

AND WHAT OF *THE RIDDLER* HIMSELF? IS HE PLANNING TO COMMIT A CRIME? BUT OF COURSE! CRIME IS IN THE VERY AIR HE BREATHES! HOWEVER--THERE *IS* ONE DIFFICULTY...

PAH! EVERY TIME I CONFRONT *BATMAN* WITH A RIDDLE--WHOSE SOLUTION REVEALS WHEN AND WHERE I'M GOING TO COMMIT A CRIME--HE ALWAYS SOLVES IT AND CAPTURES ME!

ONE THING'S SURE! I'VE GOT TO QUIT GIVING OUT RIDDLES-- OR STOP COMMITTING CRIMES! BUT I JUST CAN'T BRING MYSELF TO GIVE UP ROBBERIES! SO-- WHAT DO *I* DO?

2

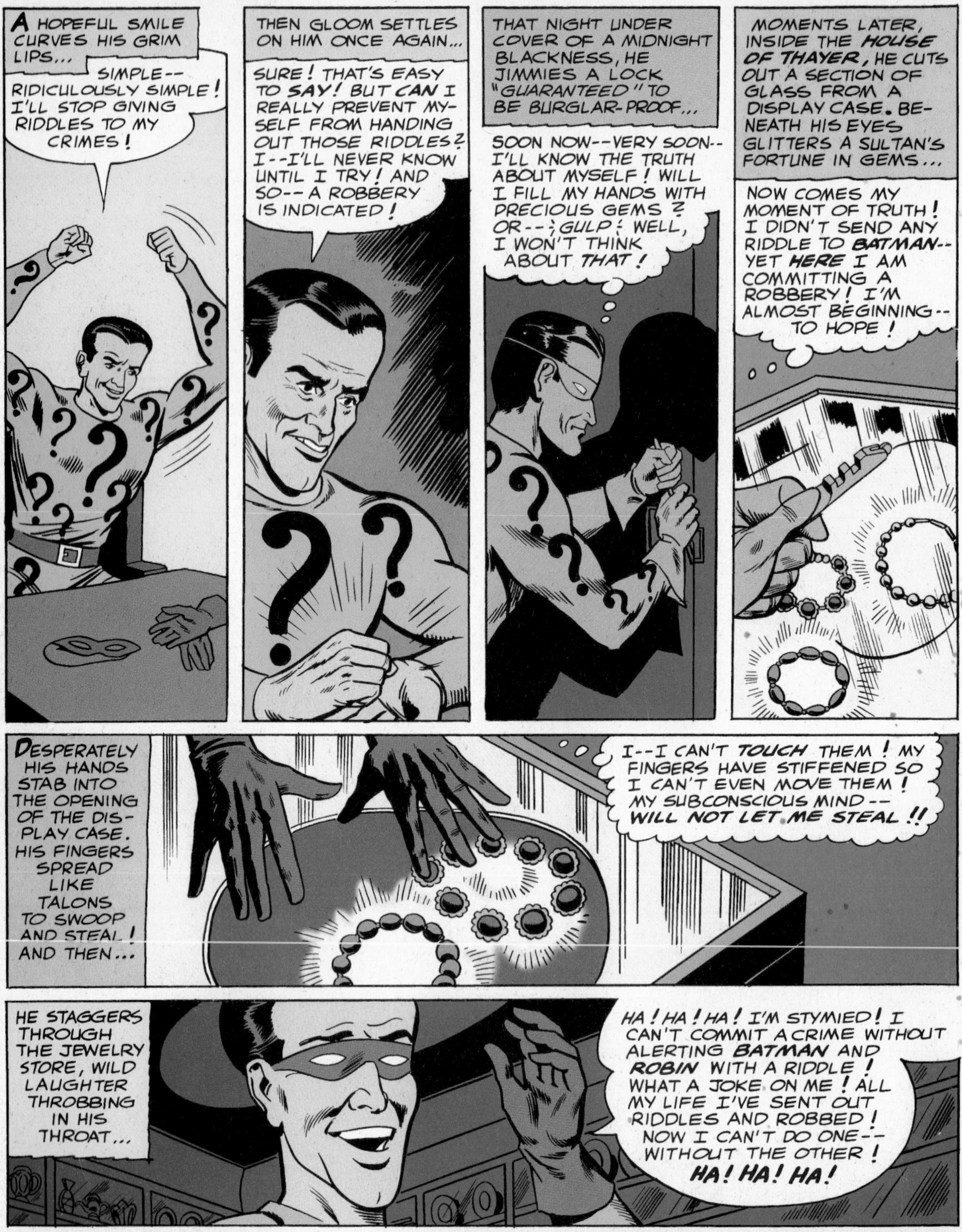
A HOPEFUL SMILE CURVES HIS GRIM LIPS...
SIMPLE-- RIDICULOUSLY SIMPLE! I'LL STOP GIVING RIDDLES TO MY CRIMES!
THEN GLOOM SETTLES ON HIM ONCE AGAIN...
SURE! THAT'S EASY TO SAY! BUT CAN I REALLY PREVENT MYSELF FROM HANDING OUT THOSE RIDDLES? I--I'LL NEVER KNOW UNTIL I TRY! AND SO-- A ROBBERY IS INDICATED!
THAT NIGHT UNDER COVER OF A MIDNIGHT BLACKNESS, HE JIMMIES A LOCK "GUARANTEED" TO BE BURGLAR-PROOF...
SOON NOW--VERY SOON-- I'LL KNOW THE TRUTH ABOUT MYSELF! WILL I FILL MY HANDS WITH PRECIOUS GEMS? OR-- ;GULP; WELL, I WON'T THINK ABOUT THAT!
MOMENTS LATER, INSIDE THE HOUSE OF THAYER, HE CUTS OUT A SECTION OF GLASS FROM A DISPLAY CASE. BENEATH HIS EYES GLITTERS A SULTAN'S FORTUNE IN GEMS...
NOW COMES MY MOMENT OF TRUTH! I DIDN'T SEND ANY RIDDLE TO BATMAN-- YET HERE I AM COMMITTING A ROBBERY! I'M ALMOST BEGINNING-- TO HOPE!
DESPERATELY HIS HANDS STAB INTO THE OPENING OF THE DISPLAY CASE. HIS FINGERS SPREAD LIKE TALONS TO SWOOP AND STEAL! AND THEN...
I--I CAN'T TOUCH THEM! MY FINGERS HAVE STIFFENED SO I CAN'T EVEN MOVE THEM! MY SUBCONSCIOUS MIND-- WILL NOT LET ME STEAL!!
HE STAGGERS THROUGH THE JEWELRY STORE, WILD LAUGHTER THROBBING IN HIS THROAT...
HA! HA! HA! I'M STYMIED! I CAN'T COMMIT A CRIME WITHOUT ALERTING BATMAN AND ROBIN WITH A RIDDLE! WHAT A JOKE ON ME! ALL MY LIFE I'VE SENT OUT RIDDLES AND ROBBED! NOW I CAN'T DO ONE-- WITHOUT THE OTHER! HA! HA! HA!
A HAUNTED LOOK TOUCHES HIS EYES! HE STARES BLINDLY WITH THE SAGGING LOOK OF A BEATEN MAN...
IF I CAN'T ROB--I'M DONE FOR! MY LIFE IS RUINED!
3

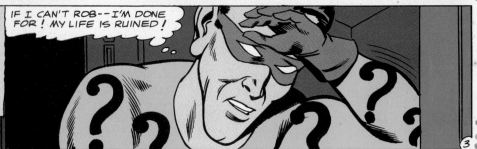

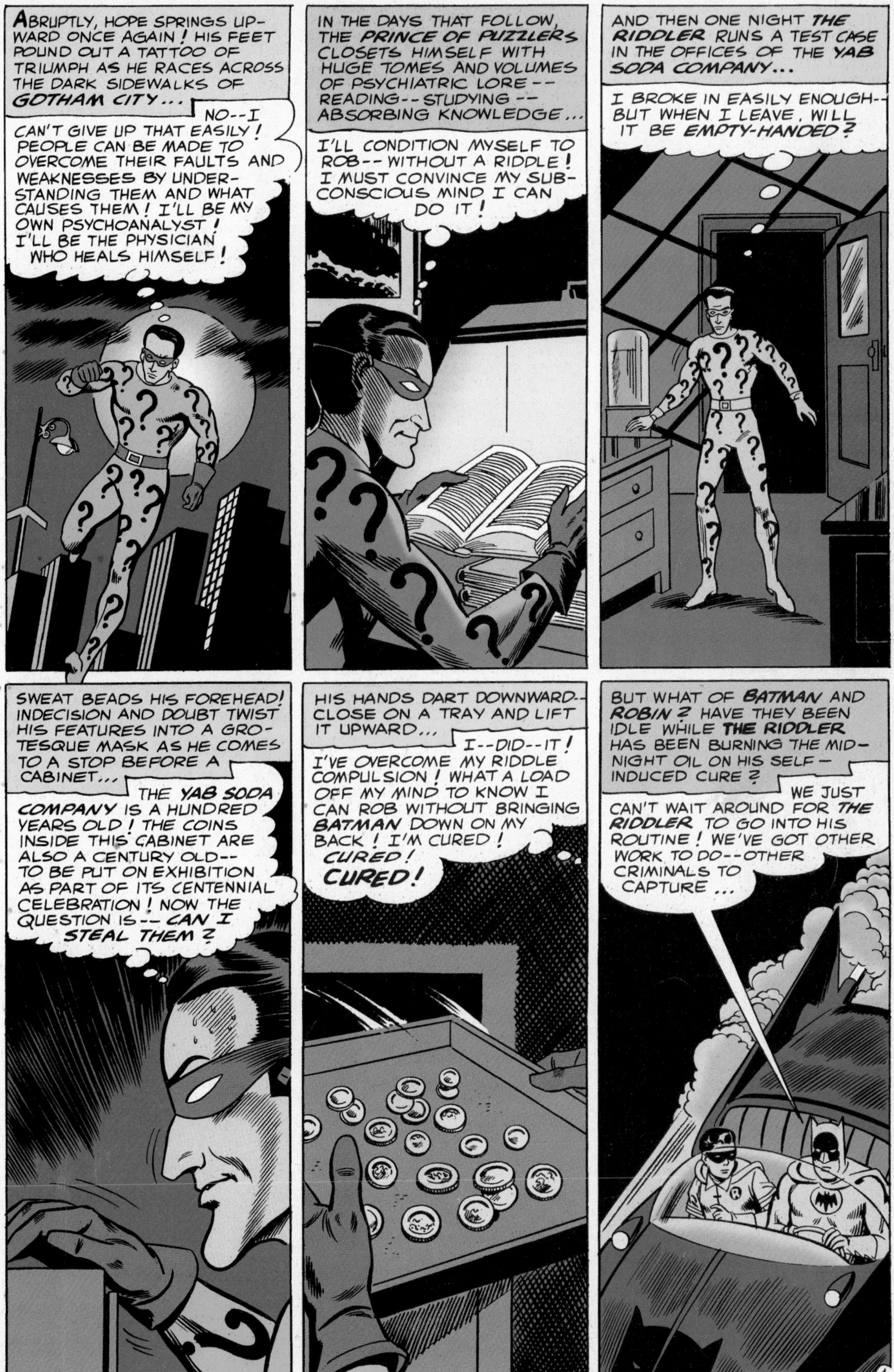
ABRUPTLY, HOPE SPRINGS UPWARD ONCE AGAIN! HIS FEET POUND OUT A TATTOO OF TRIUMPH AS HE RACES ACROSS THE DARK SIDEWALKS OF GOTHAM CITY...
NO--I CAN'T GIVE UP THAT EASILY! PEOPLE CAN BE MADE TO OVERCOME THEIR FAULTS AND WEAKNESSES BY UNDERSTANDING THEM AND WHAT CAUSES THEM! I'LL BE MY OWN PSYCHOANALYST! I'LL BE THE PHYSICIAN WHO HEALS HIMSELF!
IN THE DAYS THAT FOLLOW, THE PRINCE OF PUZZLERS CLOSETS HIMSELF WITH HUGE TOMES AND VOLUMES OF PSYCHIATRIC LORE -- READING--STUDYING -- ABSORBING KNOWLEDGE...
I'LL CONDITION MYSELF TO ROB -- WITHOUT A RIDDLE! I MUST CONVINCE MY SUBCONSCIOUS MIND I CAN DO IT!
AND THEN ONE NIGHT THE RIDDLER RUNS A TEST CASE IN THE OFFICES OF THE YAB SODA COMPANY...
I BROKE IN EASILY ENOUGH-- BUT WHEN I LEAVE, WILL IT BE EMPTY-HANDED?
SWEAT BEADS HIS FOREHEAD! INDECISION AND DOUBT TWIST HIS FEATURES INTO A GROTESQUE MASK AS HE COMES TO A STOP BEFORE A CABINET...
THE YAB SODA COMPANY IS A HUNDRED YEARS OLD! THE COINS INSIDE THIS CABINET ARE ALSO A CENTURY OLD-- TO BE PUT ON EXHIBITION AS PART OF ITS CENTENNIAL CELEBRATION! NOW THE QUESTION IS-- CAN I STEAL THEM?
HIS HANDS DART DOWNWARD-CLOSE ON A TRAY AND LIFT IT UPWARD...
I--DID--IT! I'VE OVERCOME MY RIDDLE COMPULSION! WHAT A LOAD OFF MY MIND TO KNOW I CAN ROB WITHOUT BRINGING BATMAN DOWN ON MY BACK! I'M CURED! CURED! CURED!
BUT WHAT OF BATMAN AND ROBIN? HAVE THEY BEEN IDLE WHILE THE RIDDLER HAS BEEN BURNING THE MIDNIGHT OIL ON HIS SELF-INDUCED CURE?
WE JUST CAN'T WAIT AROUND FOR THE RIDDLER TO GO INTO HIS ROUTINE! WE'VE GOT OTHER WORK TO DO--OTHER CRIMINALS TO CAPTURE...
4

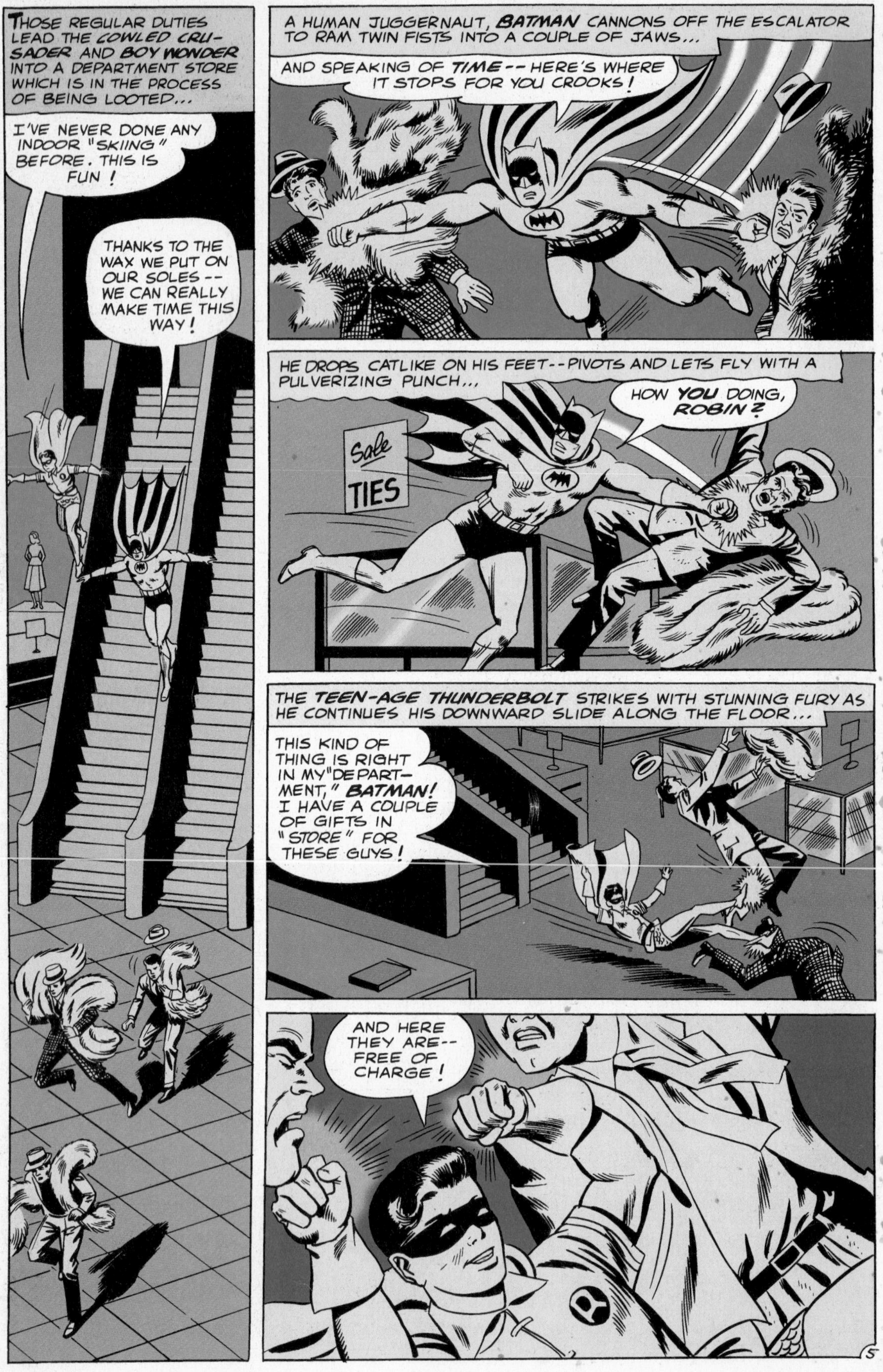
THOSE REGULAR DUTIES LEAD THE COWLED CRUSADER AND BOY WONDER INTO A DEPARTMENT STORE WHICH IS IN THE PROCESS OF BEING LOOTED...
I'VE NEVER DONE ANY INDOOR "SKIING" BEFORE. THIS IS FUN!
THANKS TO THE WAX WE PUT ON OUR SOLES -- WE CAN REALLY MAKE TIME THIS WAY!
A HUMAN JUGGERNAUT, BATMAN CANNONS OFF THE ESCALATOR TO RAM TWIN FISTS INTO A COUPLE OF JAWS...
AND SPEAKING OF TIME -- HERE'S WHERE IT STOPS FOR YOU CROOKS!
HE DROPS CATLIKE ON HIS FEET--PIVOTS AND LETS FLY WITH A PULVERIZING PUNCH...
HOW YOU DOING, ROBIN?
Sale
TIES
THE TEEN-AGE THUNDERBOLT STRIKES WITH STUNNING FURY AS HE CONTINUES HIS DOWNWARD SLIDE ALONG THE FLOOR...
THIS KIND OF THING IS RIGHT IN MY "DEPARTMENT," BATMAN! I HAVE A COUPLE OF GIFTS IN "STORE" FOR THESE GUYS!
AND HERE THEY ARE-- FREE OF CHARGE!
5

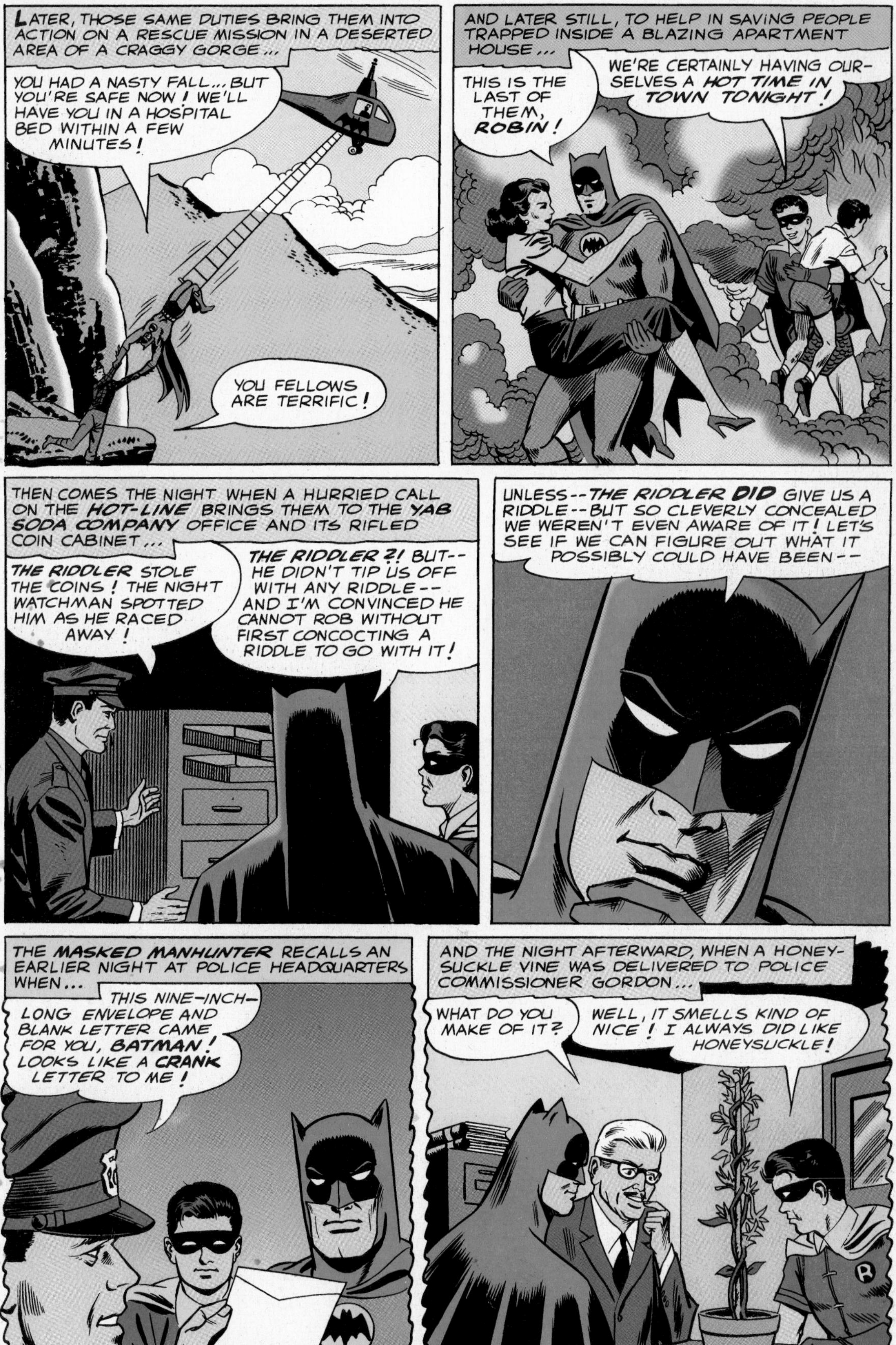
LATER, THOSE SAME DUTIES BRING THEM INTO ACTION ON A RESCUE MISSION IN A DESERTED AREA OF A CRAGGY GORGE...
YOU HAD A NASTY FALL... BUT YOU'RE SAFE NOW! WE'LL HAVE YOU IN A HOSPITAL BED WITHIN A FEW MINUTES!
YOU FELLOWS ARE TERRIFIC!
AND LATER STILL, TO HELP IN SAVING PEOPLE TRAPPED INSIDE A BLAZING APARTMENT HOUSE...
THIS IS THE LAST OF THEM, ROBIN!
WE'RE CERTAINLY HAVING OURSELVES A HOT TIME IN TOWN TONIGHT!
THEN COMES THE NIGHT WHEN A HURRIED CALL ON THE HOT-LINE BRINGS THEM TO THE YAB SODA COMPANY OFFICE AND ITS RIFLED COIN CABINET...
THE RIDDLER STOLE THE COINS! THE NIGHT WATCHMAN SPOTTED HIM AS HE RACED AWAY!
THE RIDDLER?! BUT-- HE DIDN'T TIP US OFF WITH ANY RIDDLE-- AND I'M CONVINCED HE CANNOT ROB WITHOUT FIRST CONCOCTING A RIDDLE TO GO WITH IT!
UNLESS--THE RIDDLER DID GIVE US A RIDDLE--BUT SO CLEVERLY CONCEALED WE WEREN'T EVEN AWARE OF IT! LET'S SEE IF WE CAN FIGURE OUT WHAT IT POSSIBLY COULD HAVE BEEN--
THE MASKED MANHUNTER RECALLS AN EARLIER NIGHT AT POLICE HEADQUARTERS WHEN...
THIS NINE-INCH-LONG ENVELOPE AND BLANK LETTER CAME FOR YOU, BATMAN! LOOKS LIKE A CRANK LETTER TO ME!
AND THE NIGHT AFTERWARD, WHEN A HONEYSUCKLE VINE WAS DELIVERED TO POLICE COMMISSIONER GORDON...
WHAT DO YOU MAKE OF IT?
WELL, IT SMELLS KIND OF NICE! I ALWAYS DID LIKE HONEYSUCKLE!
6

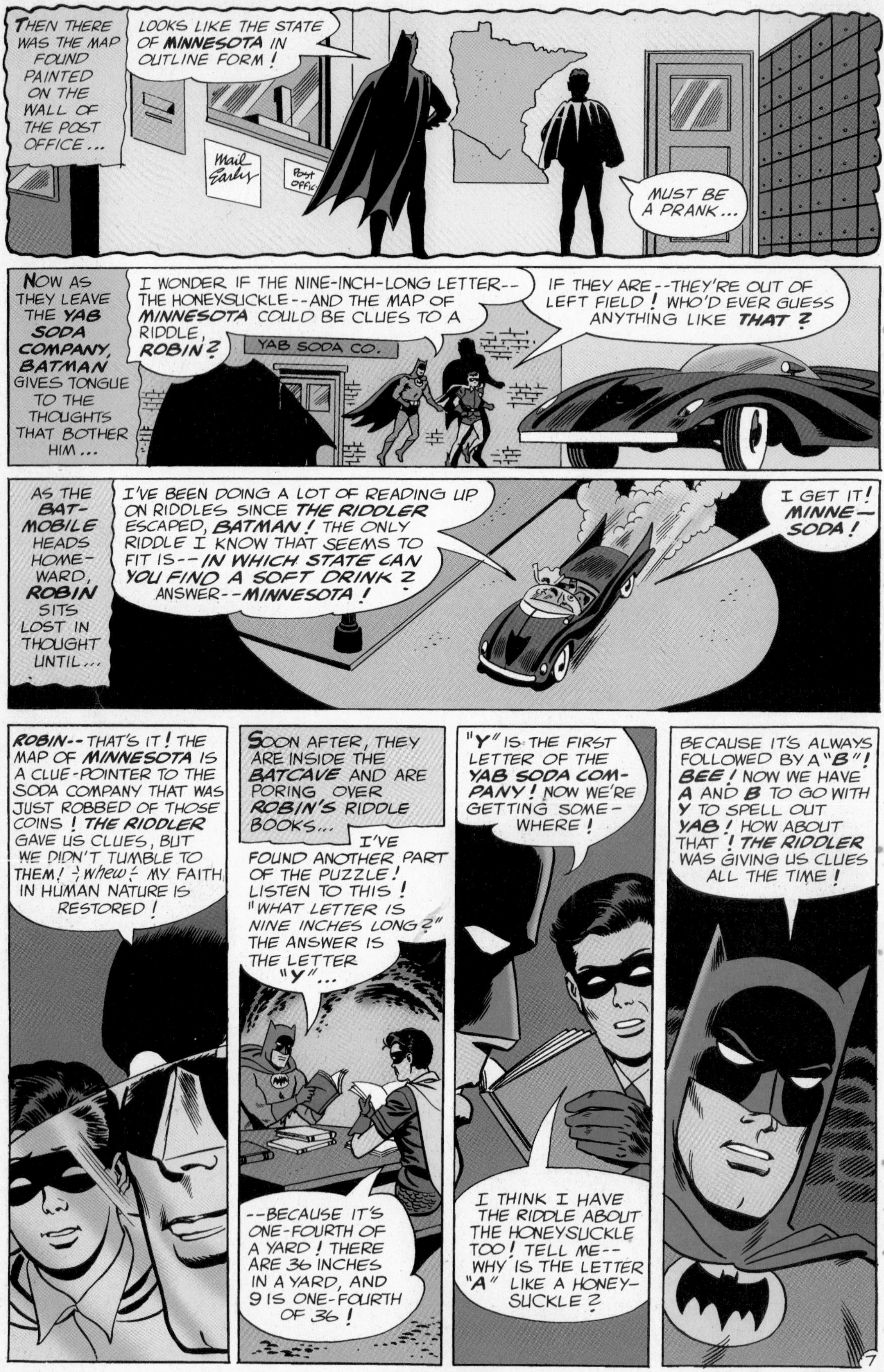
THEN THERE WAS THE MAP FOUND PAINTED ON THE WALL OF THE POST OFFICE...
LOOKS LIKE THE STATE OF MINNESOTA IN OUTLINE FORM!
Mail Early
Post Offic
MUST BE A PRANK...
NOW AS THEY LEAVE THE YAB SODA COMPANY, BATMAN GIVES TONGUE TO THE THOUGHTS THAT BOTHER HIM...
I WONDER IF THE NINE-INCH-LONG LETTER-- THE HONEYSUCKLE--AND THE MAP OF MINNESOTA COULD BE CLUES TO A RIDDLE, ROBIN?
YAB SODA CO.
IF THEY ARE--THEY'RE OUT OF LEFT FIELD! WHO'D EVER GUESS ANYTHING LIKE THAT?
AS THE BAT-MOBILE HEADS HOME-WARD, ROBIN SITS LOST IN THOUGHT UNTIL...
I'VE BEEN DOING A LOT OF READING UP ON RIDDLES SINCE THE RIDDLER ESCAPED, BATMAN! THE ONLY RIDDLE I KNOW THAT SEEMS TO FIT IS--IN WHICH STATE CAN YOU FIND A SOFT DRINK? ANSWER--MINNESOTA!
I GET IT! MINNE-SODA!
ROBIN--THAT'S IT! THE MAP OF MINNESOTA IS A CLUE-POINTER TO THE SODA COMPANY THAT WAS JUST ROBBED OF THOSE COINS! THE RIDDLER GAVE US CLUES, BUT WE DIDN'T TUMBLE TO THEM! -WHEW- MY FAITH IN HUMAN NATURE IS RESTORED!
SOON AFTER, THEY ARE INSIDE THE BATCAVE AND ARE PORING OVER ROBIN'S RIDDLE BOOKS...
I'VE FOUND ANOTHER PART OF THE PUZZLE! LISTEN TO THIS! "WHAT LETTER IS NINE INCHES LONG?" THE ANSWER IS THE LETTER "Y"...
--BECAUSE IT'S ONE-FOURTH OF A YARD! THERE ARE 36 INCHES IN A YARD, AND 9 IS ONE-FOURTH OF 36!
"Y" IS THE FIRST LETTER OF THE YAB SODA COMPANY! NOW WE'RE GETTING SOME-WHERE!
I THINK I HAVE THE RIDDLE ABOUT THE HONEYSUCKLE TOO! TELL ME--WHY IS THE LETTER "A" LIKE A HONEY-SUCKLE?
BECAUSE IT'S ALWAYS FOLLOWED BY A "B"! BEE! NOW WE HAVE A AND B TO GO WITH Y TO SPELL OUT YAB! HOW ABOUT THAT! THE RIDDLER WAS GIVING US CLUES ALL THE TIME!
7

BUT-- IS THE RIDDLER *REALLY* HANDING OUT ANY CLUES? AS WE'VE ALREADY SEEN, HE HAS APPARENTLY CURED HIMSELF OF THIS "COMPULSION"...

YES, SIR-- I'VE KICKED MY HABIT! BUT ALL THE SAME, I BETTER PLAY IT SAFE AND CONTINUE MY PSYCHIATRIC TREATMENTS...

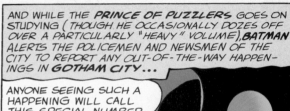

AND WHILE THE *PRINCE OF PUZZLERS* GOES ON STUDYING (THOUGH HE OCCASIONALLY DOZES OFF OVER A PARTICULARLY "HEAVY" VOLUME), *BATMAN* ALERTS THE POLICEMEN AND NEWSMEN OF THE CITY TO REPORT ANY OUT-OF-THE-WAY HAPPENINGS IN *GOTHAM CITY*...

ANYONE SEEING SUCH A HAPPENING WILL CALL THIS SPECIAL NUMBER AT POLICE HEADQUARTERS!

A FEW DAYS LATER, AN ODD FIGURE MAKES HIS APPEARANCE...

CAN ANY OF YOU GOOD PEOPLE TELL ME WHAT NATIONALITY MY PARENTS WERE?

THIS GUY LOOKS AND ACTS LIKE A KOOK-- BUT IT MAY BE JUST WHAT *BATMAN* WANTS TO KNOW ABOUT!

AT A WEDDING, THE DISTRICT ATTORNEY HIMSELF IS ON HAND TO SEE...

A WEDDING PRESENT OF FIFTEEN CENTS TO THE BRIDE--AND A DIME TO THE GROOM...

THIS SEEMS ODD ENOUGH TO CALL *BATMAN* ABOUT!

BATMAN AND *ROBIN* THEMSELVES ARE ON HAND TO WITNESS...

EITHER THAT'S AN ADVERTISING GIMMICK OF SOME KIND--

--OR A RIDDLE! WE'LL TRY AND SOLVE IT LATER!

10 + 10 / 10

CLOSETED WITH THE POLICE COMMISSIONER SOON AFTER, THEY REVIEW THE ODD EVENTS OF THE DAY...

A MAN GIVING TWENTY-FIVE CENTS TO A BRIDE AND GROOM! IT'S *ODD*-- BUT DOES IT MEAN ANYTHING?

HERE IT IS-- ONE OF THOSE "TELLING TIME" RIDDLES! THE TIME THAT THE MAN ACTED OUT WAS-- A *QUARTER* TO TWO!

WE'RE ON THE RIGHT TRACK, *ROBIN*! NOW WHAT ABOUT THE *NAPOLEON* CHARACTER'S QUESTION, "CAN YOU TELL ME WHAT NATIONALITY MY PARENTS WERE?"

COURSE I CAN! GET IT? *CORSICAN*! LET'S GO ON!

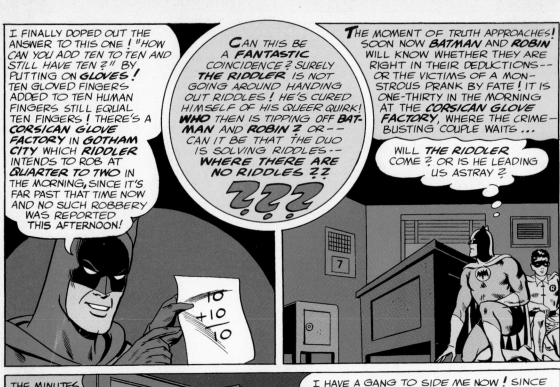

I FINALLY DOPED OUT THE ANSWER TO THIS ONE! "HOW CAN YOU ADD TEN TO TEN AND STILL HAVE TEN?" BY PUTTING ON *GLOVES!* TEN GLOVED FINGERS ADDED TO TEN HUMAN FINGERS STILL EQUAL TEN FINGERS! THERE'S A *CORSICAN GLOVE FACTORY* IN *GOTHAM CITY* WHICH *RIDDLER* INTENDS TO ROB AT *QUARTER TO TWO* IN THE MORNING, SINCE IT'S FAR PAST THAT TIME NOW AND NO SUCH ROBBERY WAS REPORTED THIS AFTERNOON!

CAN THIS BE A *FANTASTIC* COINCIDENCE? SURELY *THE RIDDLER* IS NOT GOING AROUND HANDING OUT RIDDLES! HE'S CURED HIMSELF OF HIS QUEER QUIRK! *WHO* THEN IS TIPPING OFF *BATMAN* AND *ROBIN?* OR-- CAN IT BE THAT THE DUO IS SOLVING RIDDLES-- *WHERE THERE ARE NO RIDDLES??*

THE MOMENT OF TRUTH APPROACHES! SOON NOW *BATMAN* AND *ROBIN* WILL KNOW WHETHER THEY ARE RIGHT IN THEIR DEDUCTIONS-- OR THE VICTIMS OF A MONSTROUS PRANK BY FATE! IT IS ONE-THIRTY IN THE MORNING AT THE *CORSICAN GLOVE FACTORY*, WHERE THE CRIME-BUSTING COUPLE WAITS ...

WILL *THE RIDDLER* COME? OR IS HE LEADING US ASTRAY?

THE MINUTES PASS! AT A QUARTER TO TWO, A DOOR HINGE CREAKS-- AND SHADOWY FIGURES STEAL INTO THE GLOVE COMPANY OFFICE...

I HAVE A GANG TO SIDE ME NOW! SINCE I NO LONGER GIVE OUT RIDDLES TO ALERT *BATMAN*, EVERYBODY WANTS TO GET IN ON THE ACT!

THE LIGHTS SNAP ON! AND--

HIT 'EM HARD, ROBIN!

CLICK!

NO! *NO!* I DON'T BELIEVE IT!

86

STUNG TO DESPERATE ACTION BY THE SURPRISE APPEARANCE OF THE *GOTHAM GANG-BUSTERS,* TWO MOBSTERS FLING FISTS AT *BATMAN...*

WE GOTTA KNOCK HIM OUT--

SOK!

--BEFORE HE KNOCKS US SILLY!

BUT THE *COWLED CRUSADER* IS NOT KNOWN AS THE *"KNOCK-OUT KING"* FOR NOTHING! HE DROPS BEFORE THOSE PUNCHES, ROLLING WITH THEIR FURY...

NOW I HAVE THEM WHERE I WANT THEM!

ON YOUR WAY, FELLAS!

SMAK

SHORT TRIP, WASN'T IT?

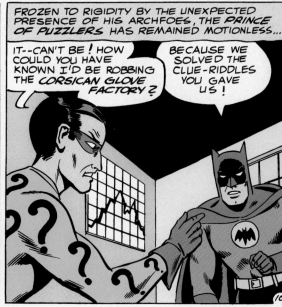

FROZEN TO RIGIDITY BY THE UNEXPECTED PRESENCE OF HIS ARCHFOES, THE *PRINCE OF PUZZLERS* HAS REMAINED MOTIONLESS...

IT--CAN'T BE! HOW COULD YOU HAVE KNOWN I'D BE ROBBING THE *CORSICAN GLOVE FACTORY?*

BECAUSE WE SOLVED THE CLUE-RIDDLES YOU GAVE US!

10

FROM HIS TRICKY UNIFORM *THE RIDDLER* WHIPS OUT A HANDFUL OF JIGSAW PUZZLE PIECES AND...

YOU GUYS HAVE FLIPPED-- I CUED YOU NO CLUES! BUT AS LONG AS YOU'RE SO HANDY AT SOLVING PUZZLES, HAVE A *BLAST* PUTTING THIS JIGSAW TOGETHER!

AS THE CUT-OUTS HIT HIM, *BATMAN* IS BATTERED BY EXPLOSIVE BLASTS...

BAM!

BAM!

BAM!

HAVING KAYOED HIS FOE, ROBIN CHARGES AT *THE RIDDLER*-- ONLY TO BE INTERCEPTED BY A LARGE-SIZED CROSSWORD PUZZLE...

MMPPFFF! GLUPP!!

NOW, NOW, *ROBIN*-- NO *CROSS WORDS*, PLEASE!

AS THAT WHIRLING CLOTH PUZZLE WRAPS AND TWISTS TIGHTLY ABOUT HIM, THE *BOY WONDER* CHANGES HIS ANGLE OF FALL, DELIBERATELY THROWING HIMSELF INTO *BATMAN*...

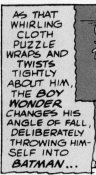

BAM!

BAM!

BAM!

THE RIDDLER'S CROSSING US UP WITH HIS PERILOUS PUZZLES-- BUT I'LL MATCH HIM TRICK FOR TRICK!

POWERED BY *ROBIN'S* SIDE-SWIPE, THE *COWLED CRUSADER* SLAMS THE *PRINCE OF PUZZLERS* INTO THE VERY SAFE HE INTENDED TO ROB...

THAT WILL KEEP HIM KNOCKED OUT LONG ENOUGH TO GIVE US A CHANCE TO OVERCOME HIS PUZZLES!

WHEN THE *MASKED MANHUNTERS* RECOVER...

NOW WHAT'S THIS NONSENSE ABOUT NOT GIVING OUT ANY RIDDLE CLUES? HOW DO YOU THINK WE GOT HERE?

I--I CAN'T IMAGINE! ALL I KNOW IS I DIDN'T GIVE YOU ANY RIDDLES! I'VE TRAINED MYSELF NOT TO!

11

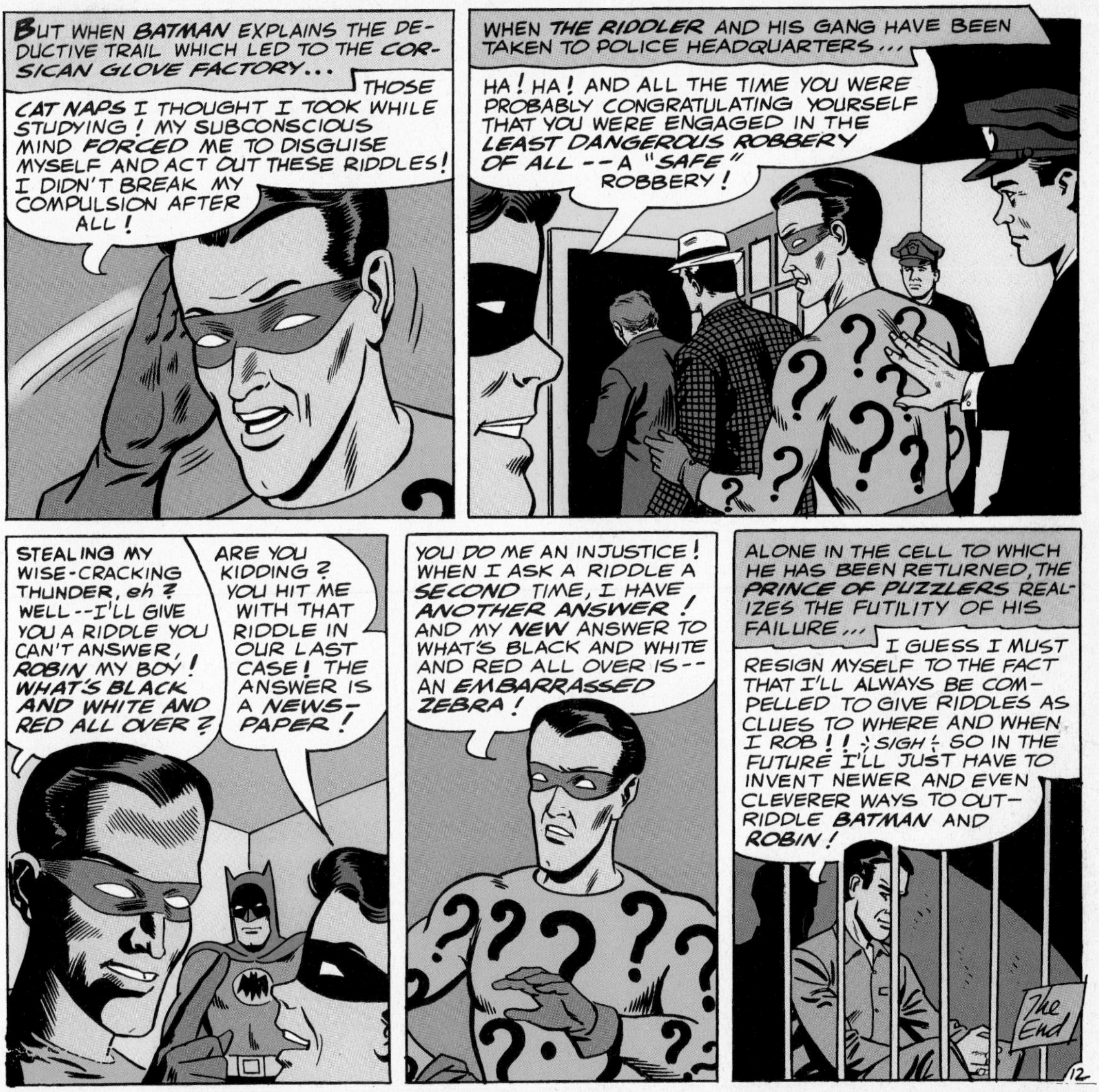
BUT WHEN BATMAN EXPLAINS THE DEDUCTIVE TRAIL WHICH LED TO THE CORSICAN GLOVE FACTORY...
THOSE CAT NAPS I THOUGHT I TOOK WHILE STUDYING! MY SUBCONSCIOUS MIND FORCED ME TO DISGUISE MYSELF AND ACT OUT THESE RIDDLES! I DIDN'T BREAK MY COMPULSION AFTER ALL!
WHEN THE RIDDLER AND HIS GANG HAVE BEEN TAKEN TO POLICE HEADQUARTERS...
HA! HA! AND ALL THE TIME YOU WERE PROBABLY CONGRATULATING YOURSELF THAT YOU WERE ENGAGED IN THE LEAST DANGEROUS ROBBERY OF ALL -- A "SAFE" ROBBERY!
STEALING MY WISE-CRACKING THUNDER, eh? WELL--I'LL GIVE YOU A RIDDLE YOU CAN'T ANSWER, ROBIN MY BOY! WHAT'S BLACK AND WHITE AND RED ALL OVER?
ARE YOU KIDDING? YOU HIT ME WITH THAT RIDDLE IN OUR LAST CASE! THE ANSWER IS A NEWSPAPER!
YOU DO ME AN INJUSTICE! WHEN I ASK A RIDDLE A SECOND TIME, I HAVE ANOTHER ANSWER! AND MY NEW ANSWER TO WHAT'S BLACK AND WHITE AND RED ALL OVER IS-- AN EMBARRASSED ZEBRA!
ALONE IN THE CELL TO WHICH HE HAS BEEN RETURNED, THE PRINCE OF PUZZLERS REALIZES THE FUTILITY OF HIS FAILURE...
I GUESS I MUST RESIGN MYSELF TO THE FACT THAT I'LL ALWAYS BE COMPELLED TO GIVE RIDDLES AS CLUES TO WHERE AND WHEN I ROB!! -SIGH- SO IN THE FUTURE I'LL JUST HAVE TO INVENT NEWER AND EVEN CLEVERER WAYS TO OUT-RIDDLE BATMAN AND ROBIN!
The End
12

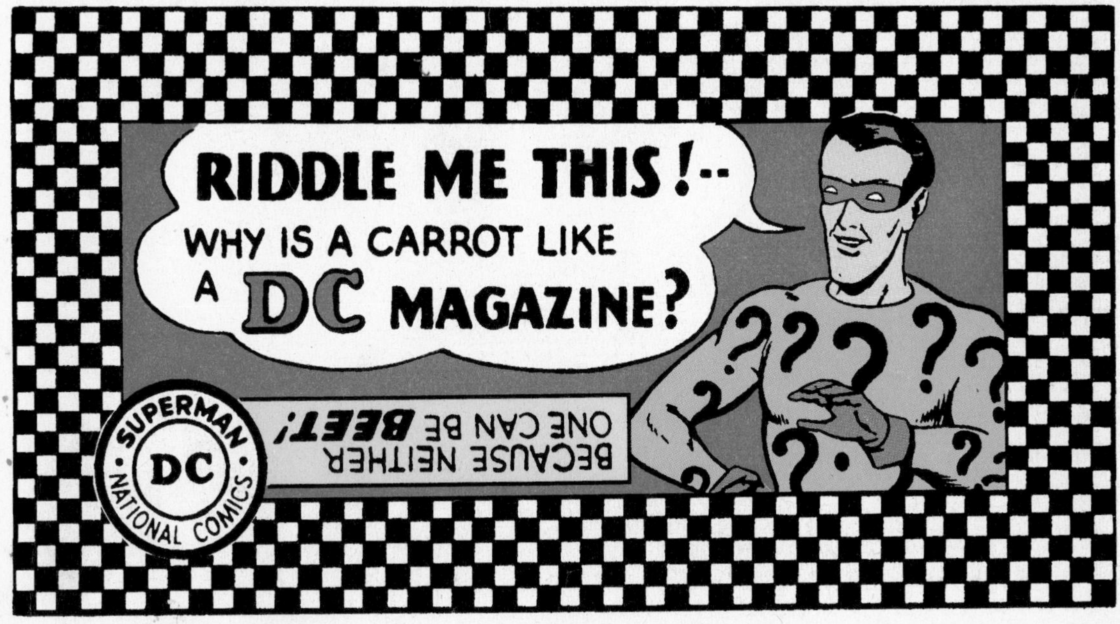
RIDDLE ME THIS!.. WHY IS A CARROT LIKE A DC MAGAZINE?
BECAUSE NEITHER ONE CAN BE BEET!
SUPERMAN DC NATIONAL COMICS

HOW TO DRAW BATMAN

ART by CARMINE INFANTINO

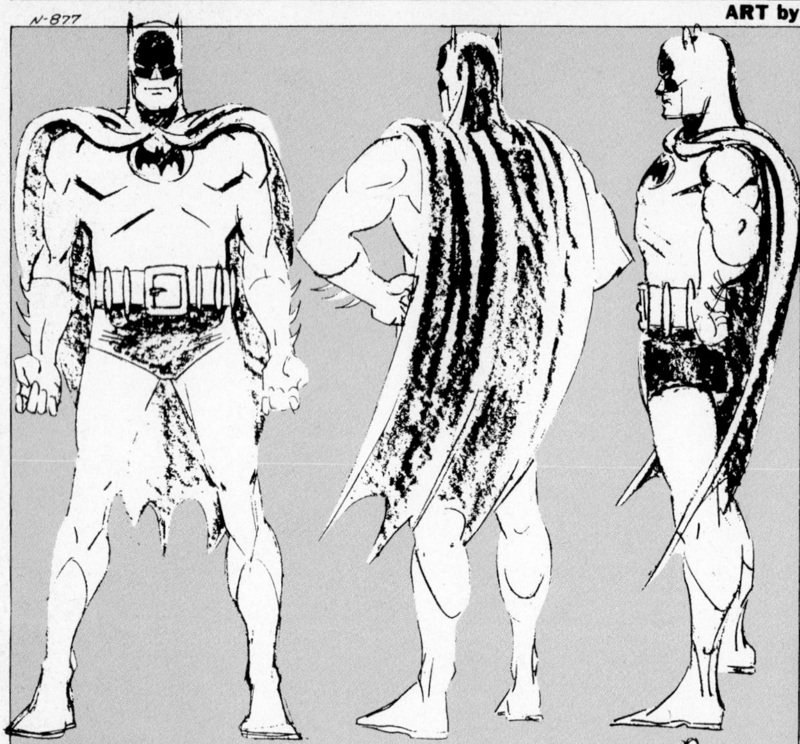
N-877

THESE BASIC PENCIL DRAWINGS SHOW HOW THE ***CAPED CRIME-FIGHTER*** LOOKED FROM THE FRONT, BACK AND SIDE, AS DRAWN BY CARMINE INFANTINO *(NOW PRESIDENT OF NATIONAL PERIODICAL PUBLICATIONS, INC.)* IN SUCH STORIES AS "HATE OF THE HOODED HANGMAN!" NOTE THE BROAD SHOULDERS AND CHEST, AS WELL AS THE MUSCULAR (BUT NOT MUSCLE-BOUND) BUILD.

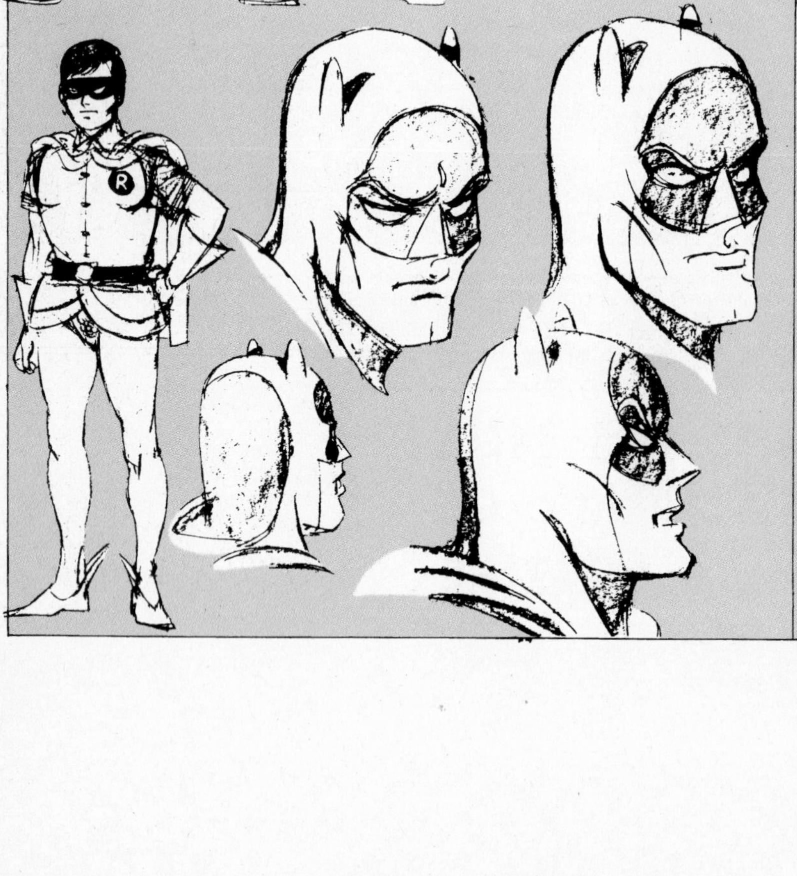

HERE WE SEE ***THE BATMAN'S*** HEAD FROM VARIOUS ANGLES. HIS MOOD IS USUALLY SERIOUS, AND WHEN HE FROWNS, THE EXPRESSION SHOWS ON HIS MASK. AT THE FAR LEFT, WE SEE CARMINE'S PORTRAIT OF ROBIN. BOTH HEROES HAVE CHANGED SLIGHTLY SINCE THESE DRAWINGS WERE DONE, BUT THEY HAVE REMAINED BASICALLY THE SAME SINCE THEY WERE FIRST CREATED, 35 YEARS AGO!

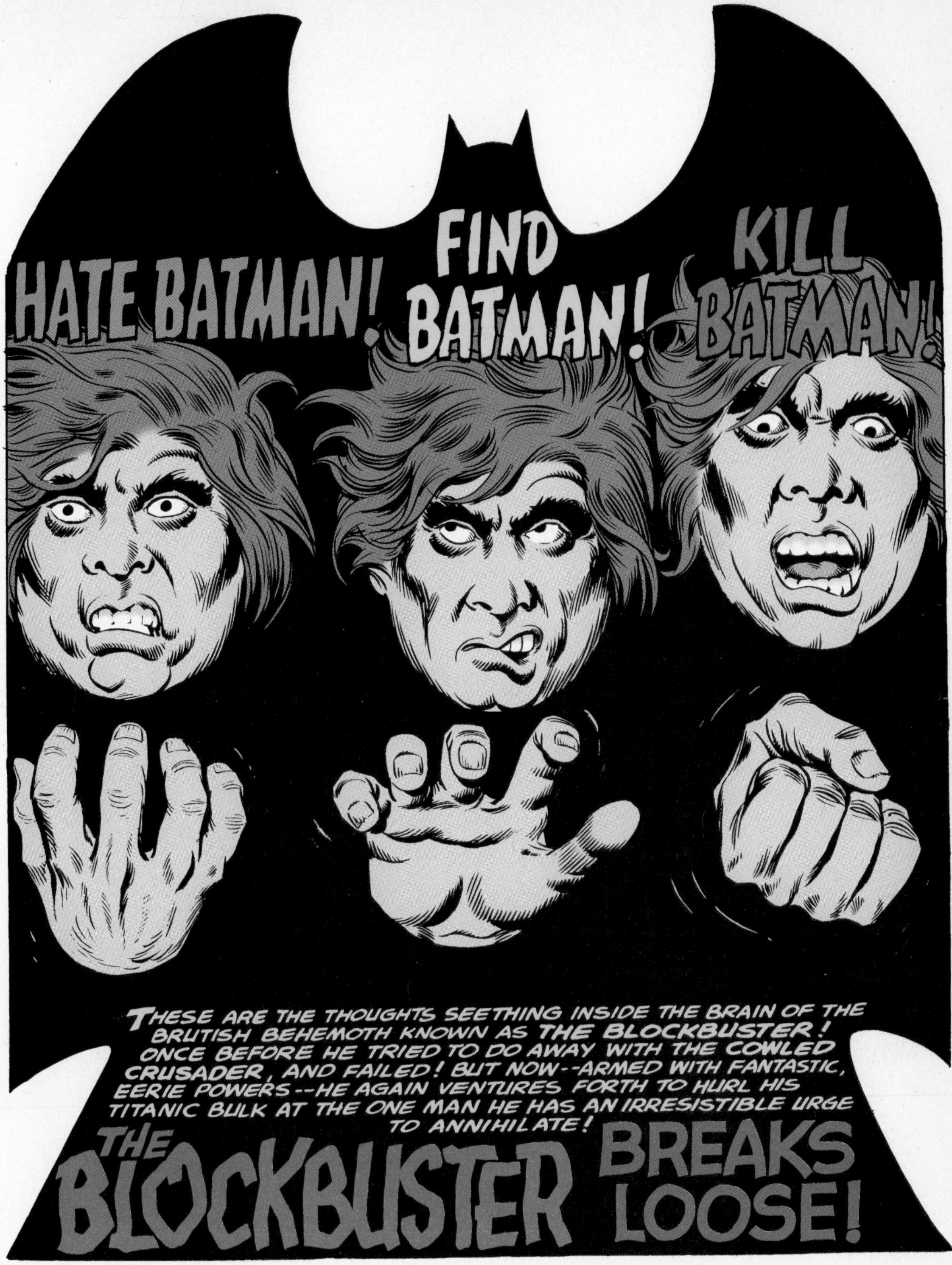
HATE BATMAN!
FIND BATMAN!
KILL BATMAN!
THESE ARE THE THOUGHTS SEETHING INSIDE THE BRAIN OF THE BRUTISH BEHEMOTH KNOWN AS THE BLOCKBUSTER! ONCE BEFORE HE TRIED TO DO AWAY WITH THE COWLED CRUSADER, AND FAILED! BUT NOW--ARMED WITH FANTASTIC, EERIE POWERS--HE AGAIN VENTURES FORTH TO HURL HIS TITANIC BULK AT THE ONE MAN HE HAS AN IRRESISTIBLE URGE TO ANNIHILATE!
THE BLOCKBUSTER BREAKS LOOSE!

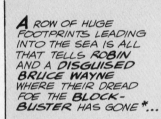

A ROW OF HUGE FOOTPRINTS LEADING INTO THE SEA IS ALL THAT TELLS *ROBIN* AND A *DISGUISED BRUCE WAYNE* WHERE THEIR DREAD FOE THE *BLOCK-BUSTER* HAS GONE *...

* EDITOR'S NOTE: SEE DETECTIVE COMICS # 345: "THE BLOCK-BUSTER INVASION OF GOTHAM CITY"

AS HE STARES DOWN AT THE ENIGMATIC WATERS, BRUCE WAYNE RECALLS HOW HE SAVED *YOUNG MARK DESMOND* FROM A QUICKSAND BOG ON THIS SAME ISLAND, YEARS BEFORE...

JUST RELAX...AND I'LL HAVE YOU OUT IN A JIFFY!

AND LATER--HOW THAT SAME MARK DESMOND, BY TAKING A CERTAIN SERUM OF HIS OWN INVENTION, TRANSFORMED HIS BODY TO GIANT SIZE AND STRENGTH BUT AT THE SAME TIME RETARDED HIS MENTAL DEVELOPMENT UNTIL HE BECAME -- *THE BLOCKBUSTER!*...

CRASH!

NOT EVEN *BATMAN* AND *ROBIN* COULD COPE WITH THE *TITANIC TERROR*...

ONLY HIS BROTHER ROLAND--AND BRUCE WAYNE (BECAUSE HE SAVED HIM FROM THE QUICKSAND BOG)-- COULD KEEP IN CHECK THAT SAVAGE BRUTE...

HE REMEMBERS! HE KNOWS BRUCE WAYNE IS--HIS FRIEND! NOW I CAN HANDLE HIM--

BUT NOW ROLAND DESMOND IS IN JAIL -- AND THE *BLOCKBUSTER* HAS DISAPPEARED...

I WONDER IF WE'LL EVER FIND OUT WHAT HAPPENED TO HIM?

WE CAN'T SPEND OUR LIVES HUNT-ING FOR HIM! WE HAVE OTHER THINGS TO KEEP US BUSY! LET'S GET BACK TO *GOTHAM CITY!*

2

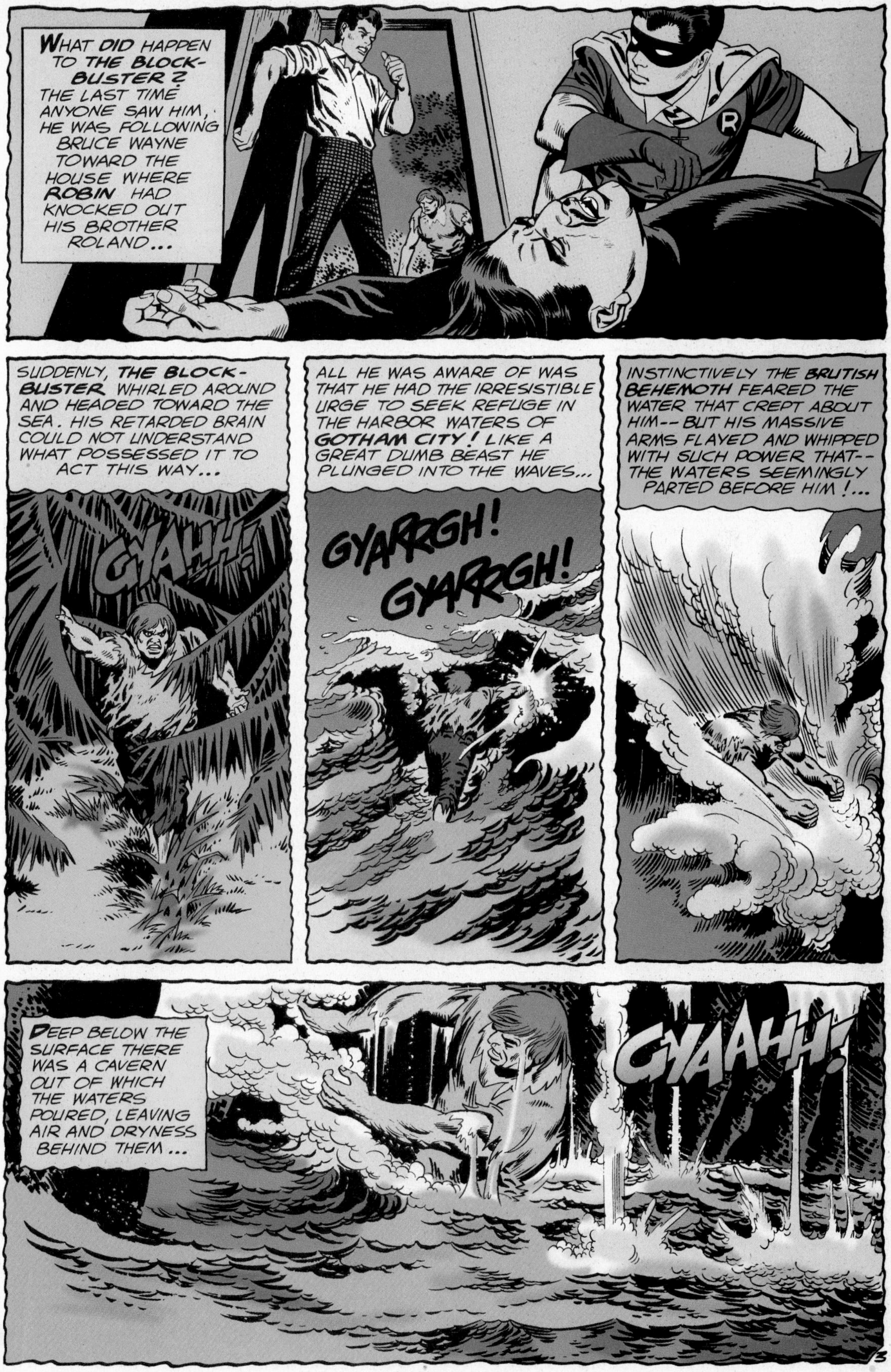

WHAT DID HAPPEN TO THE BLOCK-BUSTER? THE LAST TIME ANYONE SAW HIM, HE WAS FOLLOWING BRUCE WAYNE TOWARD THE HOUSE WHERE ROBIN HAD KNOCKED OUT HIS BROTHER ROLAND...
SUDDENLY, THE BLOCK-BUSTER WHIRLED AROUND AND HEADED TOWARD THE SEA. HIS RETARDED BRAIN COULD NOT UNDERSTAND WHAT POSSESSED IT TO ACT THIS WAY...
GYAHH!
ALL HE WAS AWARE OF WAS THAT HE HAD THE IRRESISTIBLE URGE TO SEEK REFUGE IN THE HARBOR WATERS OF GOTHAM CITY! LIKE A GREAT DUMB BEAST HE PLUNGED INTO THE WAVES...
GYARRGH! GYARRGH!
INSTINCTIVELY THE BRUTISH BEHEMOTH FEARED THE WATER THAT CREPT ABOUT HIM-- BUT HIS MASSIVE ARMS FLAYED AND WHIPPED WITH SUCH POWER THAT-- THE WATERS SEEMINGLY PARTED BEFORE HIM!...
DEEP BELOW THE SURFACE THERE WAS A CAVERN OUT OF WHICH THE WATERS POURED, LEAVING AIR AND DRYNESS BEHIND THEM...
GYAAHH!
3

FOR MONTHS THE *TITANIC TERROR* LIVED IN HIS UNDERSEA CAVE, FINDING FOOD TO EAT AND DRIFT-WOOD WHICH HE CAUSED TO BURN BRIGHTLY...

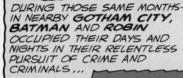

DURING THOSE SAME MONTHS-- IN NEARBY *GOTHAM CITY*, *BATMAN* AND *ROBIN* OCCUPIED THEIR DAYS AND NIGHTS IN THEIR RELENTLESS PURSUIT OF CRIME AND CRIMINALS...

THEY WERE TOO BUSY TO WONDER ABOUT THEIR FORMER FOE...

THEY KNEW ONLY THE DREAD DANGER OF EACH DESPERATE MOMENT!...

BLAM! BLAM!

THEN ONE NIGHT AS THE SHRILL CLAMOR OF A BURGLAR ALARM SUMMONS THE *GOTHAM GANG-BUSTERS* TO DUTY IN A LOCAL DEPARTMENT STORE...

SAFE-CRACKERS TONIGHT-- JAILBIRDS TOMORROW!

BATMAN--*LOOK!* THE FLOOR'S HEAVING UPWARD!

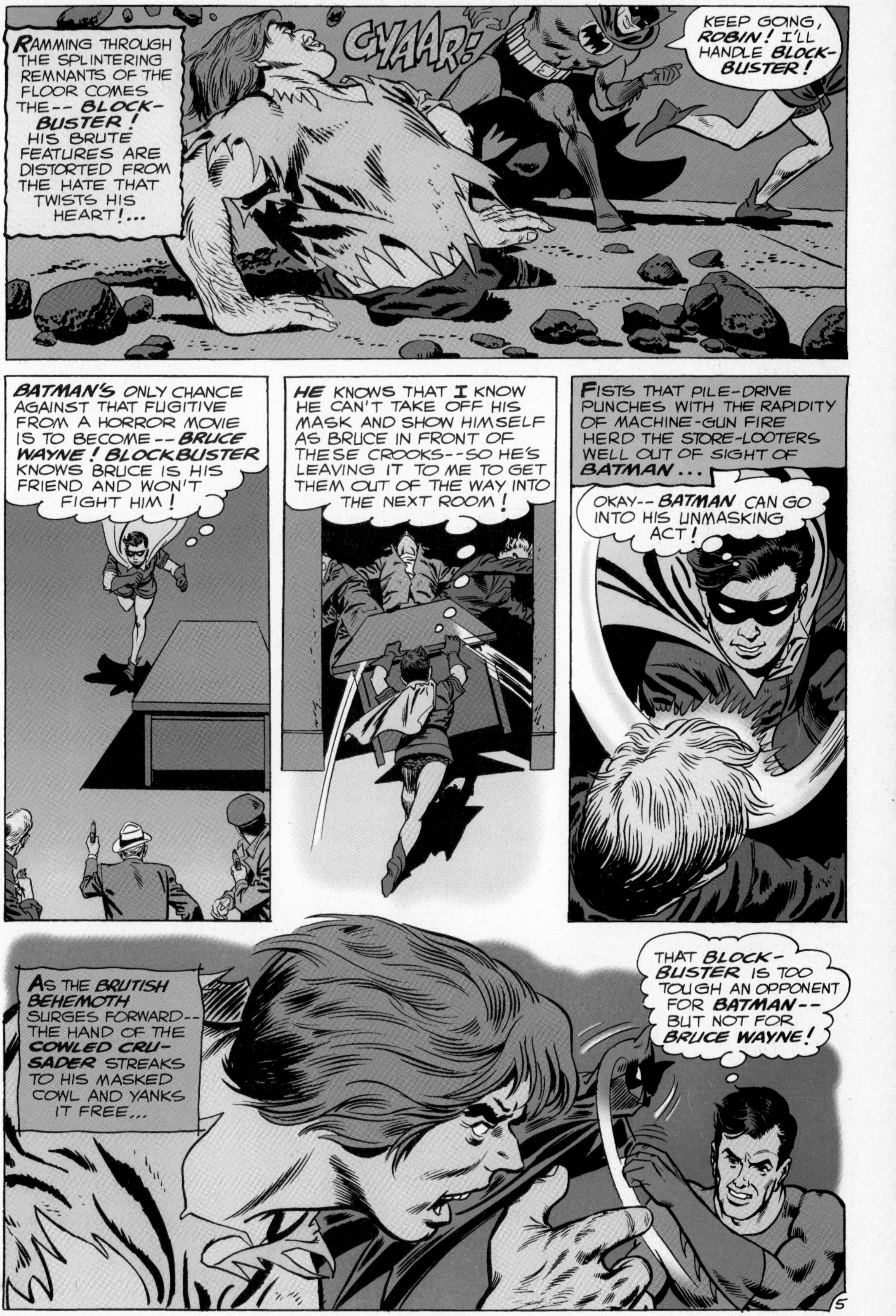
RAMMING THROUGH THE SPLINTERING REMNANTS OF THE FLOOR COMES THE-- BLOCK-BUSTER! HIS BRUTE FEATURES ARE DISTORTED FROM THE HATE THAT TWISTS HIS HEART!...
GYAAR!
KEEP GOING, ROBIN! I'LL HANDLE BLOCK-BUSTER!
BATMAN'S ONLY CHANCE AGAINST THAT FUGITIVE FROM A HORROR MOVIE IS TO BECOME-- BRUCE WAYNE! BLOCKBUSTER KNOWS BRUCE IS HIS FRIEND AND WON'T FIGHT HIM!
HE KNOWS THAT I KNOW HE CAN'T TAKE OFF HIS MASK AND SHOW HIMSELF AS BRUCE IN FRONT OF THESE CROOKS--SO HE'S LEAVING IT TO ME TO GET THEM OUT OF THE WAY INTO THE NEXT ROOM!
FISTS THAT PILE-DRIVE PUNCHES WITH THE RAPIDITY OF MACHINE-GUN FIRE HERD THE STORE-LOOTERS WELL OUT OF SIGHT OF BATMAN...
OKAY-- BATMAN CAN GO INTO HIS UNMASKING ACT!
AS THE BRUTISH BEHEMOTH SURGES FORWARD-- THE HAND OF THE COWLED CRUSADER STREAKS TO HIS MASKED COWL AND YANKS IT FREE...
THAT BLOCK-BUSTER IS TOO TOUGH AN OPPONENT FOR BATMAN-- BUT NOT FOR BRUCE WAYNE!
5

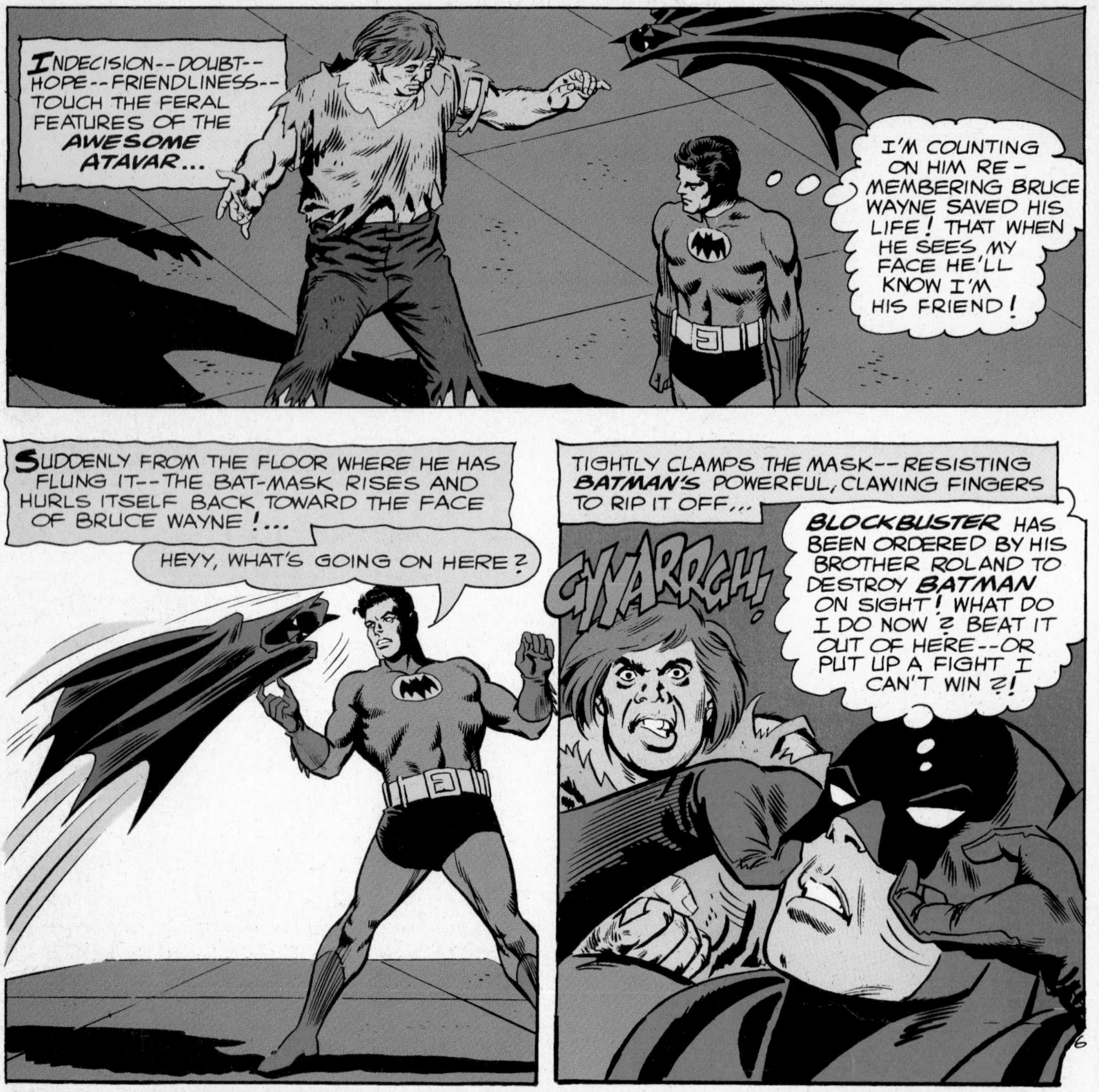
INDECISION--DOUBT--HOPE--FRIENDLINESS--TOUCH THE FERAL FEATURES OF THE AWESOME ATAVAR...
I'M COUNTING ON HIM RE-MEMBERING BRUCE WAYNE SAVED HIS LIFE! THAT WHEN HE SEES MY FACE HE'LL KNOW I'M HIS FRIEND!
SUDDENLY FROM THE FLOOR WHERE HE HAS FLUNG IT--THE BAT-MASK RISES AND HURLS ITSELF BACK TOWARD THE FACE OF BRUCE WAYNE!...
HEYY, WHAT'S GOING ON HERE?
TIGHTLY CLAMPS THE MASK--RESISTING BATMAN'S POWERFUL, CLAWING FINGERS TO RIP IT OFF...
GYARRGH!
BLOCKBUSTER HAS BEEN ORDERED BY HIS BROTHER ROLAND TO DESTROY BATMAN ON SIGHT! WHAT DO I DO NOW? BEAT IT OUT OF HERE--OR PUT UP A FIGHT I CAN'T WIN?!
6

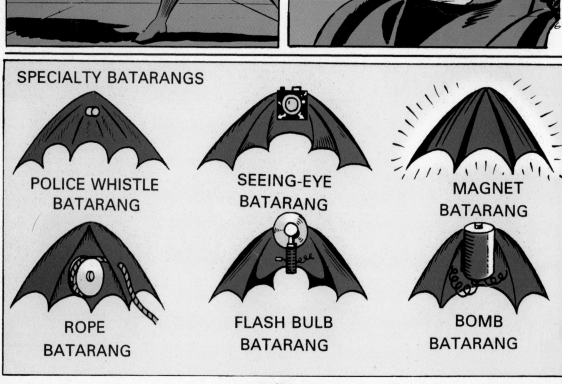

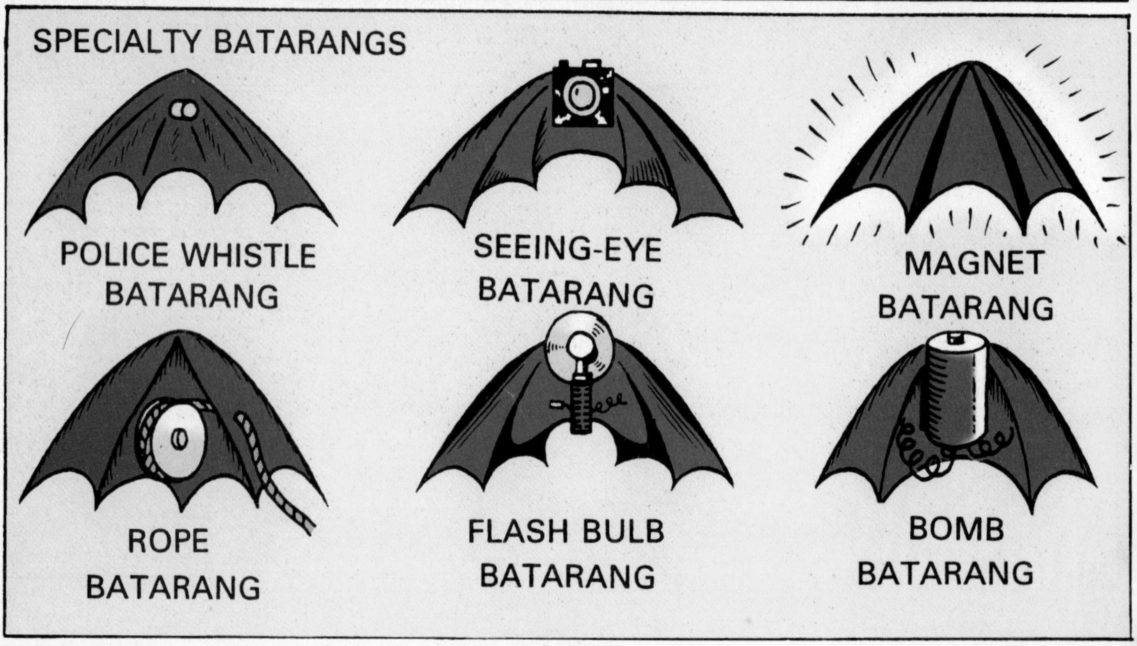
SPECIALTY BATARANGS
POLICE WHISTLE BATARANG
SEEING-EYE BATARANG
MAGNET BATARANG
ROPE BATARANG
FLASH BULB BATARANG
BOMB BATARANG

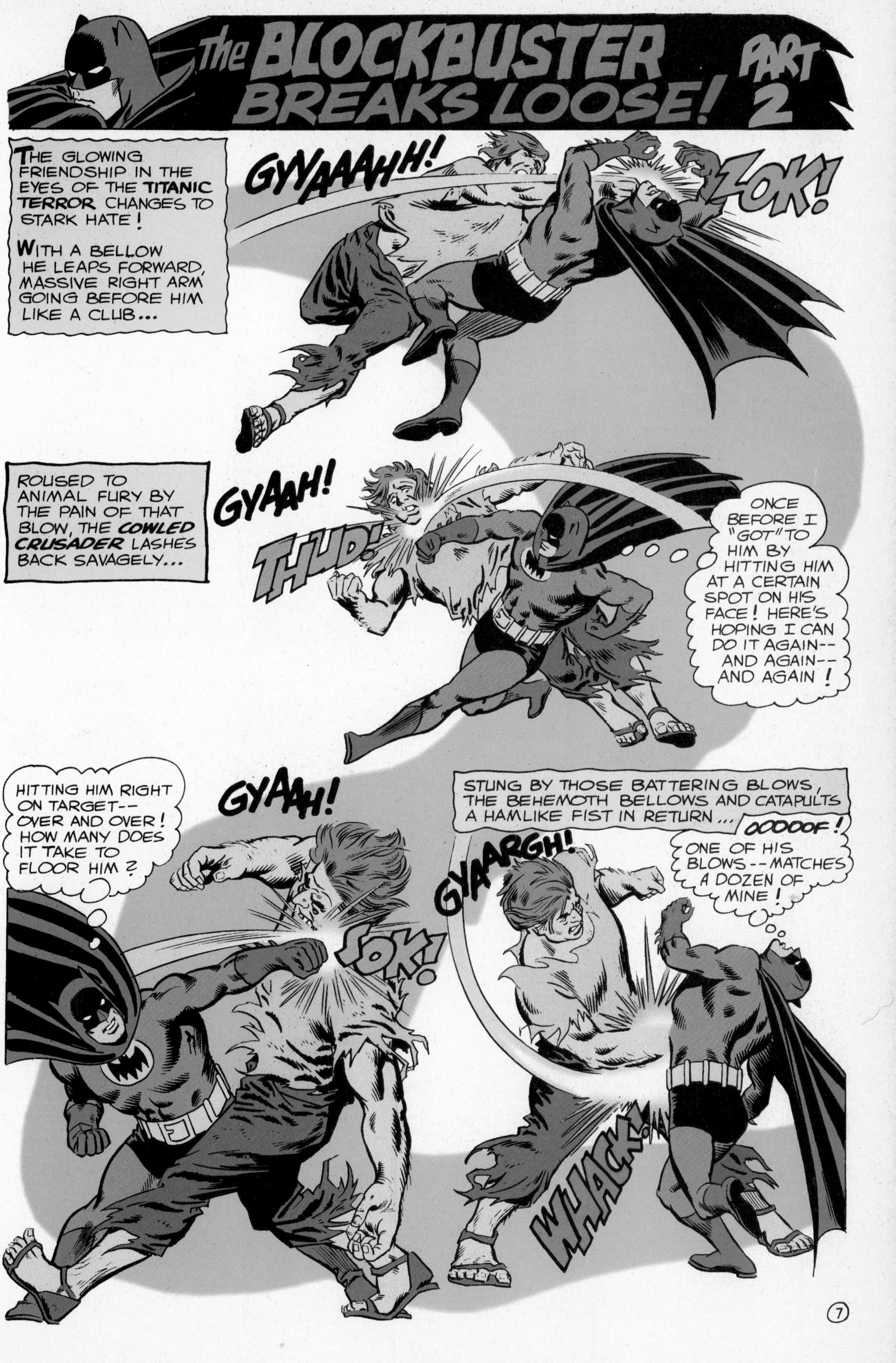
The BLOCKBUSTER BREAKS LOOSE! PART 2
THE GLOWING FRIENDSHIP IN THE EYES OF THE TITANIC TERROR CHANGES TO STARK HATE!
WITH A BELLOW HE LEAPS FORWARD, MASSIVE RIGHT ARM GOING BEFORE HIM LIKE A CLUB...
GYYAAAHH!
ZOK!
ROUSED TO ANIMAL FURY BY THE PAIN OF THAT BLOW, THE COWLED CRUSADER LASHES BACK SAVAGELY...
GYAAH!
THUD!
ONCE BEFORE I "GOT" TO HIM BY HITTING HIM AT A CERTAIN SPOT ON HIS FACE! HERE'S HOPING I CAN DO IT AGAIN-- AND AGAIN-- AND AGAIN!
HITTING HIM RIGHT ON TARGET-- OVER AND OVER! HOW MANY DOES IT TAKE TO FLOOR HIM?
GYAAH!
SOK!
STUNG BY THOSE BATTERING BLOWS, THE BEHEMOTH BELLOWS AND CATAPULTS A HAMLIKE FIST IN RETURN...
GYAARGH!
OOOOOF!
ONE OF HIS BLOWS--MATCHES A DOZEN OF MINE!
WHACK!
7

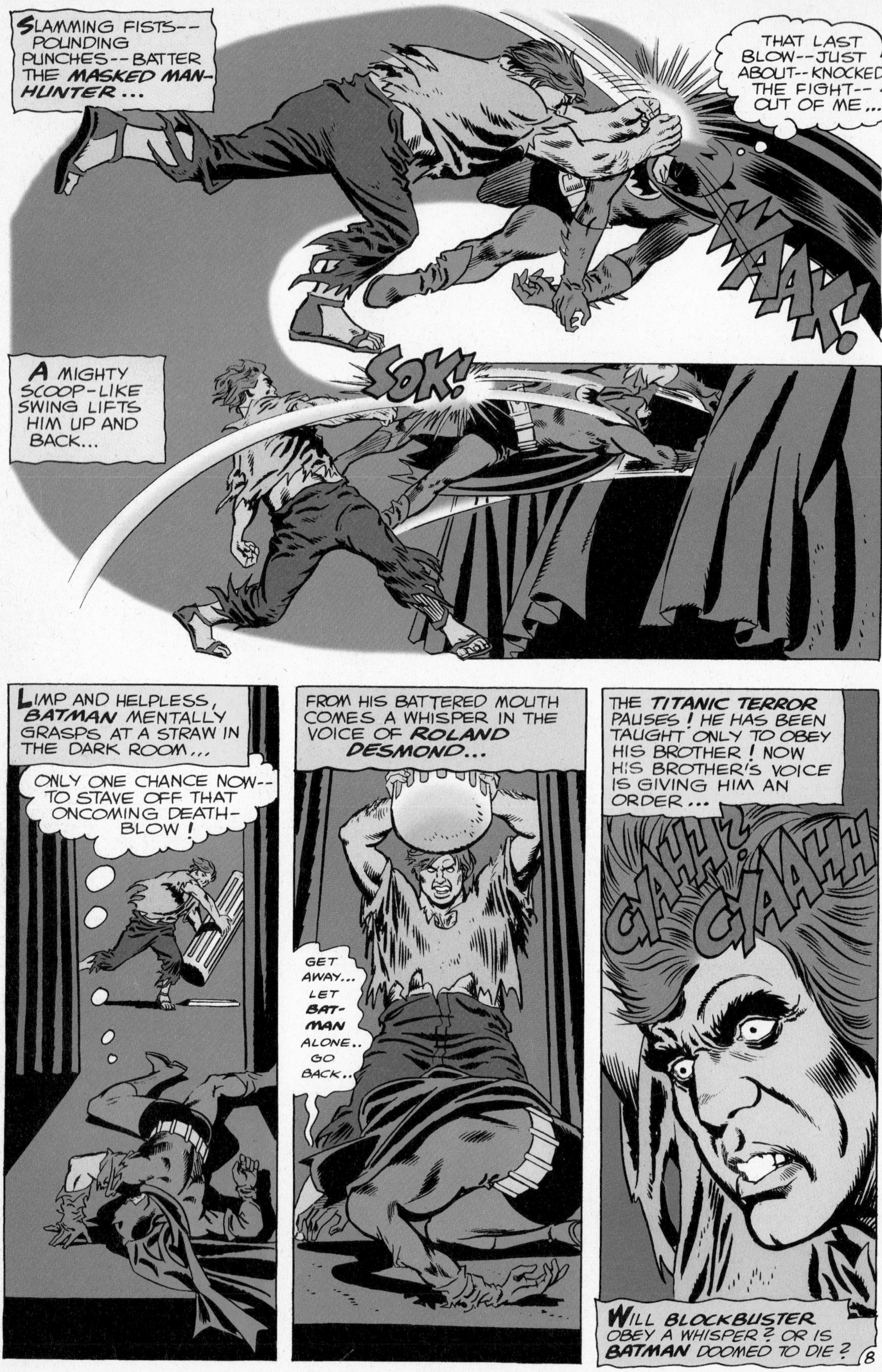

SLAMMING FISTS-- POUNDING PUNCHES--BATTER THE MASKED MAN-HUNTER...
THAT LAST BLOW--JUST ABOUT--KNOCKED THE FIGHT-- OUT OF ME...
WAAK!
A MIGHTY SCOOP-LIKE SWING LIFTS HIM UP AND BACK...
SOK!
LIMP AND HELPLESS, BATMAN MENTALLY GRASPS AT A STRAW IN THE DARK ROOM...
ONLY ONE CHANCE NOW-- TO STAVE OFF THAT ONCOMING DEATH-BLOW!
FROM HIS BATTERED MOUTH COMES A WHISPER IN THE VOICE OF ROLAND DESMOND...
GET AWAY... LET BAT-MAN ALONE.. GO BACK...
THE TITANIC TERROR PAUSES! HE HAS BEEN TAUGHT ONLY TO OBEY HIS BROTHER! NOW HIS BROTHER'S VOICE IS GIVING HIM AN ORDER...
GAHH? GAAHH
WILL BLOCKBUSTER OBEY A WHISPER? OR IS BATMAN DOOMED TO DIE?
8

THEN... GENTLY HE SETS DOWN THAT FEARSOME WEIGHT--TURNS AND SHUFFLES OFF ...

≈GASP≈ IT WORKED! I'M SAFE ...FOR NOW! WONDER HOW...≈PANT≈ ROBIN IS MAKING OUT...?

SHORTLY, STILL IN A DAZE, BUT REVIVED TO SOME DEGREE BY THE FRANTIC TEEN-AGE THUNDER-BOLT, THE MASKED MANHUNTER IS LED TOWARD THE WAITING BATMOBILE ...

I WANTED TO MAKE BLOCK-BUSTER GIVE HIMSELF UP-- BUT MY VOICE GAVE OUT...

EASY, EASY--WE'LL WORK THINGS OUT! THE POLICE HAVE THE THREE CROOKS--SO WE CAN GO HOME NOW!

SOON AFTERWARD IN THE BATCAVE...

THE BLOCK-BUSTER'S MORE DAN-GEROUS THAN EVER! SINCE OUR LAST MEETING, HE'S TAKEN ON FANTASTIC NEW POWERS!

SO IT SEEMS! HOW ELSE CAN WE EXPLAIN AWAY THE MASK LEAP-ING BACK ONTO YOUR FACE-- AND BEING HELD THERE?

WHERE DO WE GO FROM HERE? SINCE YOU CAN'T APPEAR AS BRUCE WAYNE ON ACCOUNT OF THAT ANIMATED MASK-- AND BECAUSE YOU CAN'T GO AROUND HIDING IN DARK PLACES TO IMITATE ROLAND DESMOND'S VOICE--YOU'LL HAVE NO WAY OF CONTROLLING THAT MUSCLE MONSTER!

MAYBE I CAN TURN A DISADVANTAGE INTO AN ADVANTAGE! IF MY MASK WON'T LEAVE ME WHILE THE BLOCK-BUSTER IS AROUND--

I CATCH! YOU'LL USE THE MASK ITSELF TO HELP YOU!

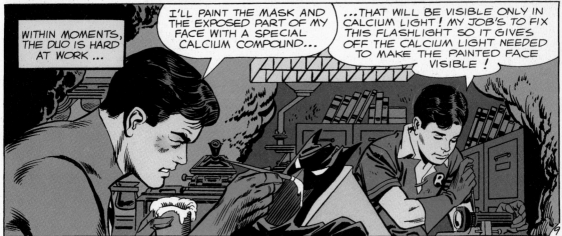

WITHIN MOMENTS, THE DUO IS HARD AT WORK ...

I'LL PAINT THE MASK AND THE EXPOSED PART OF MY FACE WITH A SPECIAL CALCIUM COMPOUND...

...THAT WILL BE VISIBLE ONLY IN CALCIUM LIGHT! MY JOB'S TO FIX THIS FLASHLIGHT SO IT GIVES OFF THE CALCIUM LIGHT NEEDED TO MAKE THE PAINTED FACE VISIBLE!

AFTER SEVERAL HOURS OF PAINSTAKING LABOR...

HOW'D IT TURN OUT, ROBIN?

GREAT! IN THE CALCIUM LIGHT, YOU LOOK *EXACTLY* LIKE ROLAND DESMOND, *BLOCKBUSTER'S* BROTHER!

AND SO -- SAFE-GUARDED AGAINST THE NEXT APPEAR-ANCE BY HIS NEFARIOUS NEMESIS, *BATMAN* TAKES TO HIS NIGHTLY PATROLS...

WE'VE GOT THE SHOW ON THE ROAD AGAIN! ALL WE CAN DO IS WAIT FOR THE STAR PERFORMER TO APPEAR ON STAGE!

FOR NEARLY A WEEK THERE IS NO SIGN OF THE *BLOCK-BUSTER!* THEN ONE NIGHT A *HOT-LINE* CALL FROM POLICE COM-MISSIONER GORDON BRINGS THE *FISTIC FURIES* TO THE CITY ART MUSEUM...

ONE EACH, *ROBIN!*

IT'S NOT OFTEN WE GET EASY ODDS LIKE THIS!

THEN -- CRASHING THROUGH THE VERY WALL COMES *BLOCKBUSTER*..

AH! HIS NIBS IS HERE AGAIN!

TIME TO GO INTO YOUR ACT, *ROBIN!*

CRASH!

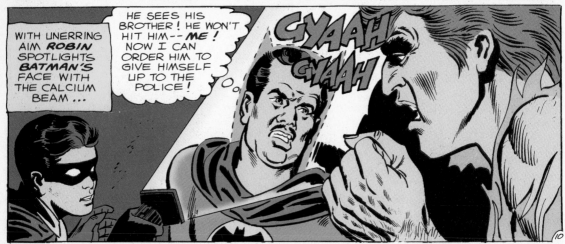

WITH UNERRING AIM *ROBIN* SPOTLIGHTS *BATMAN'S* FACE WITH THE CALCIUM BEAM...

HE SEES HIS BROTHER! HE WON'T HIT HIM -- *ME!* NOW I CAN ORDER HIM TO GIVE HIMSELF UP TO THE POLICE!

GYAAH GYAAH

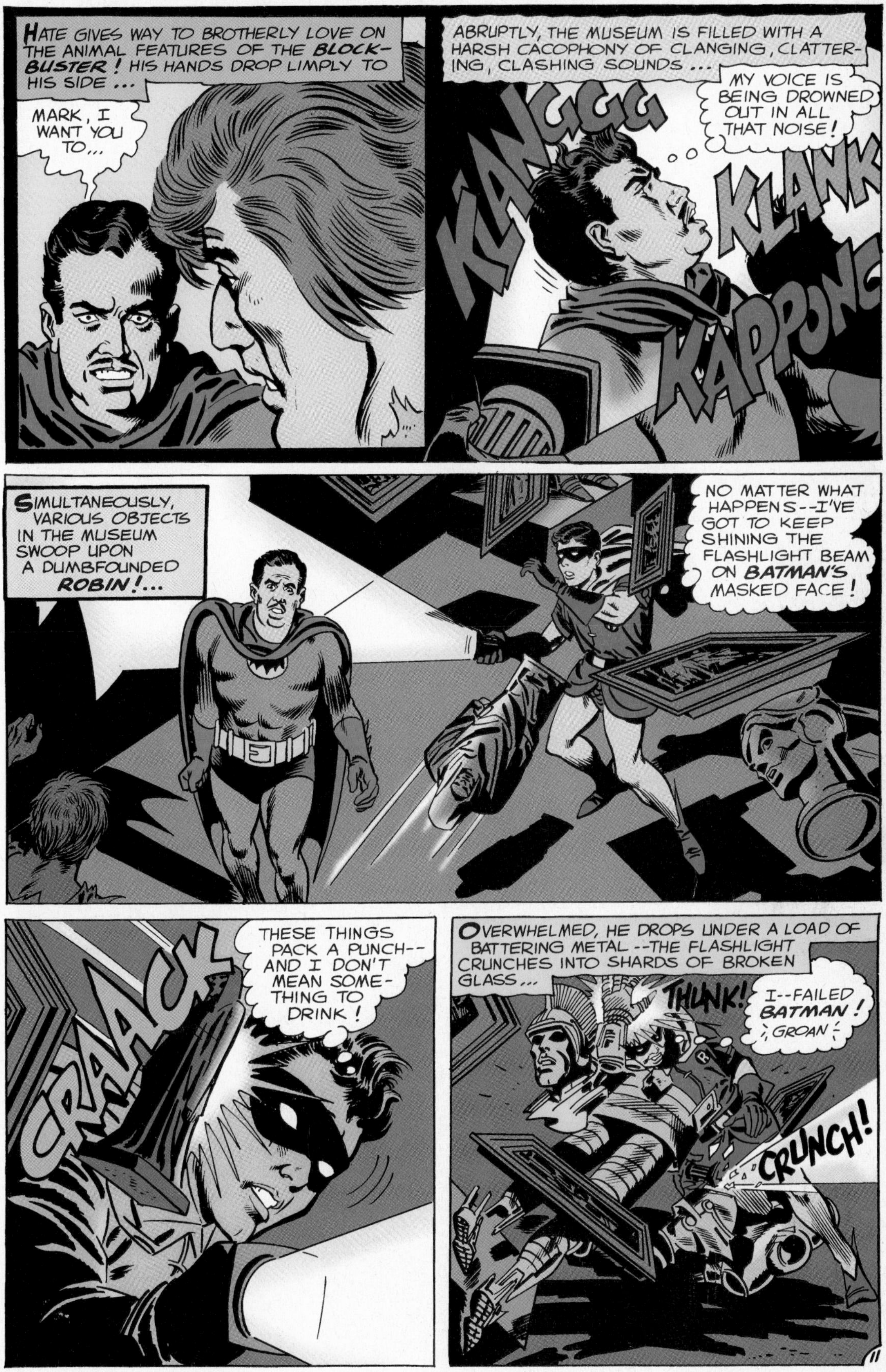
HATE GIVES WAY TO BROTHERLY LOVE ON THE ANIMAL FEATURES OF THE BLOCK-BUSTER! HIS HANDS DROP LIMPLY TO HIS SIDE...
MARK, I WANT YOU TO,...
ABRUPTLY, THE MUSEUM IS FILLED WITH A HARSH CACOPHONY OF CLANGING, CLATTERING, CLASHING SOUNDS...
MY VOICE IS BEING DROWNED OUT IN ALL THAT NOISE!
KLANGGG
KLANK
KAPPONG
SIMULTANEOUSLY, VARIOUS OBJECTS IN THE MUSEUM SWOOP UPON A DUMBFOUNDED ROBIN!...
NO MATTER WHAT HAPPENS--I'VE GOT TO KEEP SHINING THE FLASHLIGHT BEAM ON BATMAN'S MASKED FACE!
CRAACK
THESE THINGS PACK A PUNCH--AND I DON'T MEAN SOMETHING TO DRINK!
OVERWHELMED, HE DROPS UNDER A LOAD OF BATTERING METAL--THE FLASHLIGHT CRUNCHES INTO SHARDS OF BROKEN GLASS...
THUNK!
I--FAILED BATMAN! GROAN
CRUNCH!
11

ONCE AGAIN THE MASKED FEATURES OF **BATMAN** ARE VISIBLE TO **THE BLOCK-BUSTER** ! WITH A ROAR OF FURY HE LETS FLY...

STRUCK SO SUDDENLY-- COULDN'T ROLL WITH THE PUNCH !

GYAAHH!

THUNK

HIS TASK ACCOMPLISHED, **THE BLOCKBUSTER** TURNS AWAY--AS A FIGURE STEPS FROM THE SHADOWS TO THRUST THE INERT FORM OF THE **COWLED CRUSADER** INTO AN EGYPTIAN SARCOPHAGUS..

I'VE RIGGED THIS COFFIN WITH A SPECIAL RADIATION WHICH-- SOON AFTER I SWITCH IT ON-- WILL START TO AGE **BATMAN** YEARS IN MINUTES !

A HAND GRIPS A LEVER, BEGINS TO BRING IT DOWN ...

MY LONG SOUGHT-FOR TRIUMPH OVER **BATMAN** IS AT HAND ! WHILE THE WORLD WONDERS WHERE **BATMAN** HAS DISAPPEARED TO--ONLY I SHALL KNOW HE'S EN-TOMBED IN THIS COFFIN--AS A **MUMMY** !

INSIDE THE SARCOPHAGUS, THE REVIVING **COWLED CRUSADER** FEELS AN AWESOME HEAT THAT MELTS THE CALCIUM COM-POUND PAINTED ON HIS MASK AND FACE ...

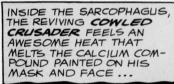

WHERE AM I ? SO HOT IN HERE-- DRIPPING WITH SWEAT...

OUTSIDE THE COFFIN-- HIS FEEBLE MIND CON-FUSED BY DOUBTS (DID HE OVERCOME **BATMAN** OR HIS BROTHER ?) **THE BLOCKBUSTER** RETURNS AND...

GYYAAHH? GYAHHH!!

GET AWAY FROM ME, YOU FOOL ! YOU'VE SERVED YOUR PURPOSE ! I HAVE NO FURTHER USE FOR YOU !

BELLOWING WITH ANGER, THE **BRUTISH BEHEMOTH** LASHES OUT AT THIS NEW ENEMY WHO HAS COME TO LIFE ...

OHHH ! ITS STRENGTH IS SUCH THAT NOT EVEN I CAN STAND UP TO IT ! ONLY **BATMAN** KNOWS HOW TO CONTROL THIS CREATURE--AND WITH **BATMAN** TRAPPED INSIDE THE SARCOPHAGUS, I'M **DOOMED** !

12

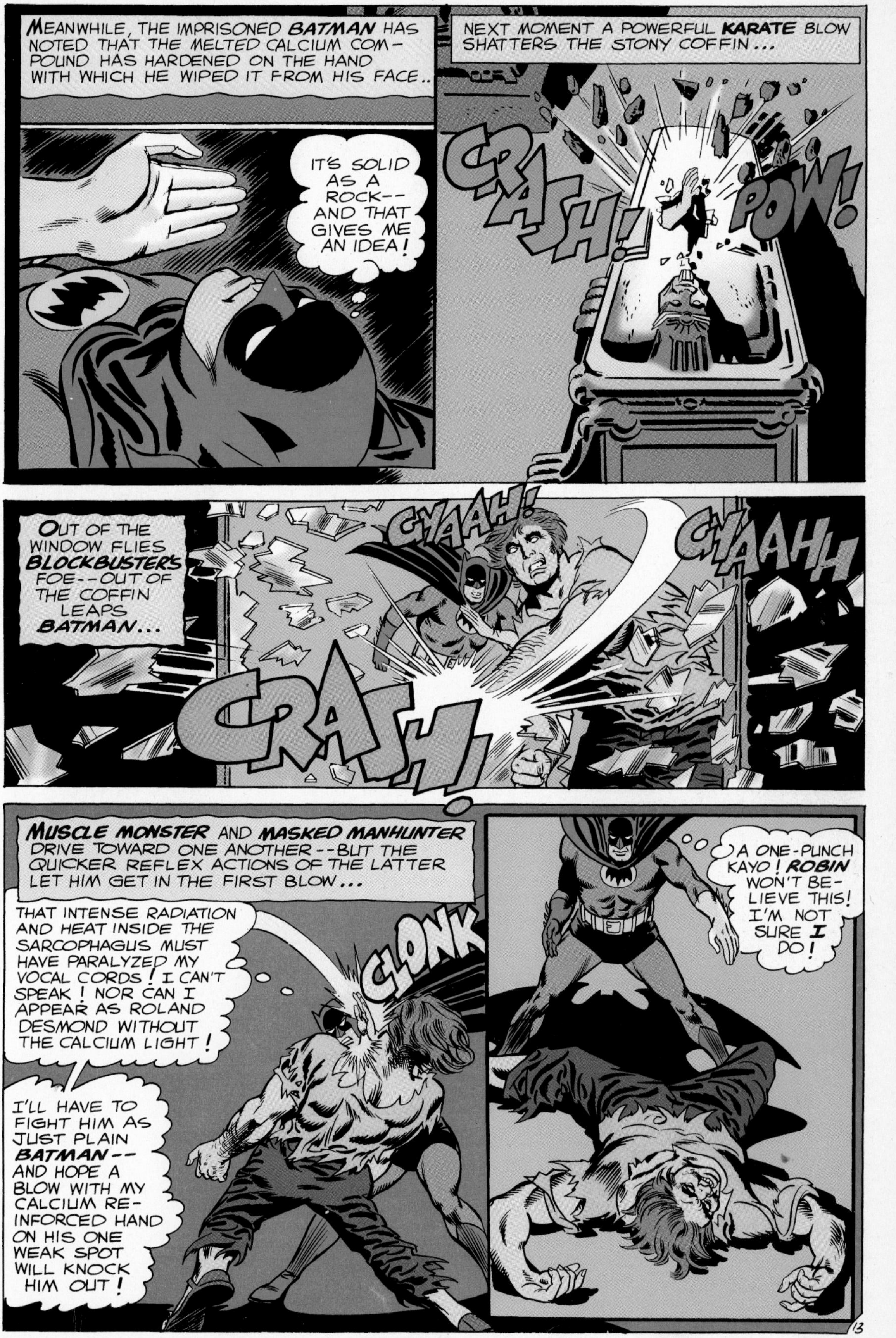
MEANWHILE, THE IMPRISONED BATMAN HAS NOTED THAT THE MELTED CALCIUM COMPOUND HAS HARDENED ON THE HAND WITH WHICH HE WIPED IT FROM HIS FACE..
IT'S SOLID AS A ROCK-- AND THAT GIVES ME AN IDEA!
NEXT MOMENT A POWERFUL KARATE BLOW SHATTERS THE STONY COFFIN...
CRASH!
POW!
OUT OF THE WINDOW FLIES BLOCKBUSTER'S FOE--OUT OF THE COFFIN LEAPS BATMAN...
GYAAH!
GYAAHH
CRASH!
MUSCLE MONSTER AND MASKED MANHUNTER DRIVE TOWARD ONE ANOTHER--BUT THE QUICKER REFLEX ACTIONS OF THE LATTER LET HIM GET IN THE FIRST BLOW...
THAT INTENSE RADIATION AND HEAT INSIDE THE SARCOPHAGUS MUST HAVE PARALYZED MY VOCAL CORDS! I CAN'T SPEAK! NOR CAN I APPEAR AS ROLAND DESMOND WITHOUT THE CALCIUM LIGHT!
I'LL HAVE TO FIGHT HIM AS JUST PLAIN BATMAN-- AND HOPE A BLOW WITH MY CALCIUM REINFORCED HAND ON HIS ONE WEAK SPOT WILL KNOCK HIM OUT!
CLONK
A ONE-PUNCH KAYO! ROBIN WON'T BELIEVE THIS! I'M NOT SURE I DO!
13

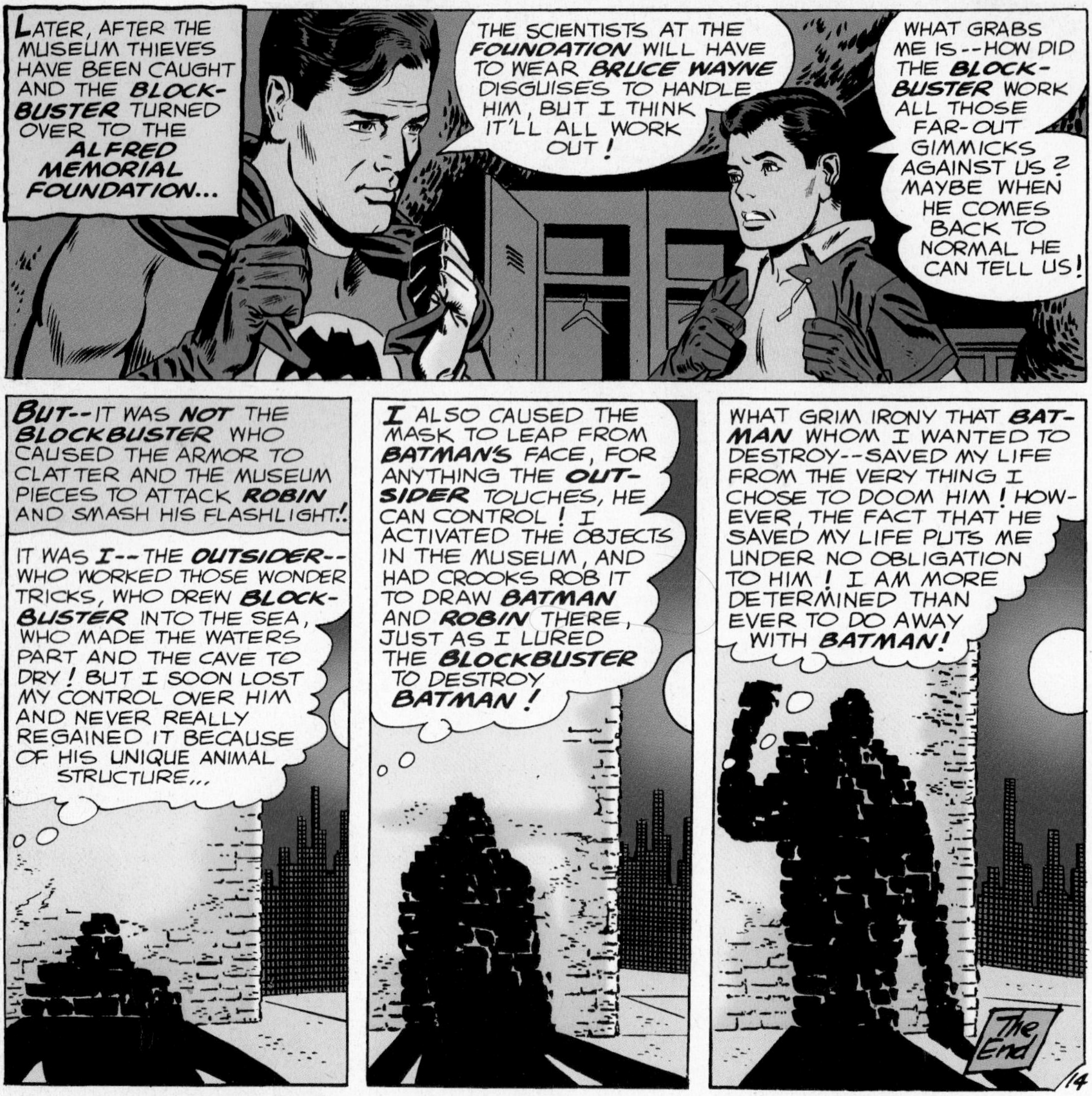
LATER, AFTER THE MUSEUM THIEVES HAVE BEEN CAUGHT AND THE BLOCK-BUSTER TURNED OVER TO THE ALFRED MEMORIAL FOUNDATION...
THE SCIENTISTS AT THE FOUNDATION WILL HAVE TO WEAR BRUCE WAYNE DISGUISES TO HANDLE HIM, BUT I THINK IT'LL ALL WORK OUT!
WHAT GRABS ME IS--HOW DID THE BLOCK-BUSTER WORK ALL THOSE FAR-OUT GIMMICKS AGAINST US? MAYBE WHEN HE COMES BACK TO NORMAL HE CAN TELL US!
BUT--IT WAS NOT THE BLOCKBUSTER WHO CAUSED THE ARMOR TO CLATTER AND THE MUSEUM PIECES TO ATTACK ROBIN AND SMASH HIS FLASHLIGHT!
IT WAS I--THE OUTSIDER--WHO WORKED THOSE WONDER TRICKS, WHO DREW BLOCK-BUSTER INTO THE SEA, WHO MADE THE WATERS PART AND THE CAVE TO DRY! BUT I SOON LOST MY CONTROL OVER HIM AND NEVER REALLY REGAINED IT BECAUSE OF HIS UNIQUE ANIMAL STRUCTURE...
I ALSO CAUSED THE MASK TO LEAP FROM BATMAN'S FACE, FOR ANYTHING THE OUT-SIDER TOUCHES, HE CAN CONTROL! I ACTIVATED THE OBJECTS IN THE MUSEUM, AND HAD CROOKS ROB IT TO DRAW BATMAN AND ROBIN THERE, JUST AS I LURED THE BLOCKBUSTER TO DESTROY BATMAN!
WHAT GRIM IRONY THAT BAT-MAN WHOM I WANTED TO DESTROY--SAVED MY LIFE FROM THE VERY THING I CHOSE TO DOOM HIM! HOW-EVER, THE FACT THAT HE SAVED MY LIFE PUTS ME UNDER NO OBLIGATION TO HIM! I AM MORE DETERMINED THAN EVER TO DO AWAY WITH BATMAN!
The End
14

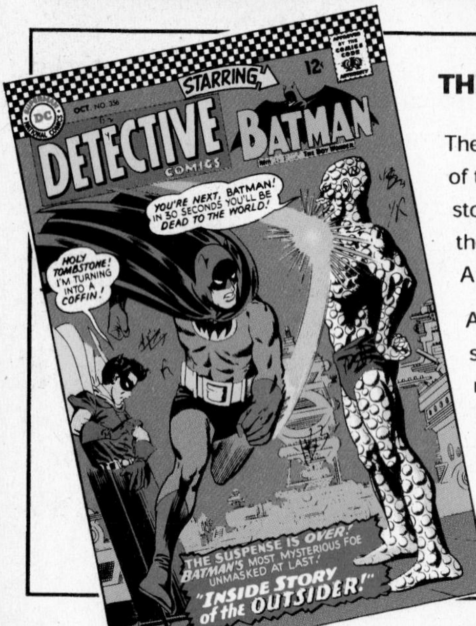
STARRING
12¢
DETECTIVE COMICS
BATMAN
YOU'RE NEXT, BATMAN! IN 30 SECONDS YOU'LL BE DEAD TO THE WORLD!
HOLY TOMBSTONE! I'M TURNING INTO A COFFIN!
THE SUSPENSE IS OVER! BATMAN'S MOST MYSTERIOUS FOE UNMASKED AT LAST!
"INSIDE STORY of the OUTSIDER!"

THE OUTSIDER REVEALED!

The Outsider was a strange villain who manipulated the destinies of the Dynamic Duo from behind the scenes. This series of sporadic stories ended with DETECTIVE COMICS #356 ("Inside Story of the Outsider") when the Outsider was revealed to be Alfred Pennyworth!

Alfred, who had been killed in DETECTIVE COMICS #328 sacrificing himself to save Batman and Robin, was apparently not dead at all. It was revealed that scientific genius Brandon Crawford discovered Alfred's half-alive body and exposed it to a regenerative device that transformed him into The Outsider.

Batman and Robin finally located The Outsider, reversed the process, and Alfred was restored.

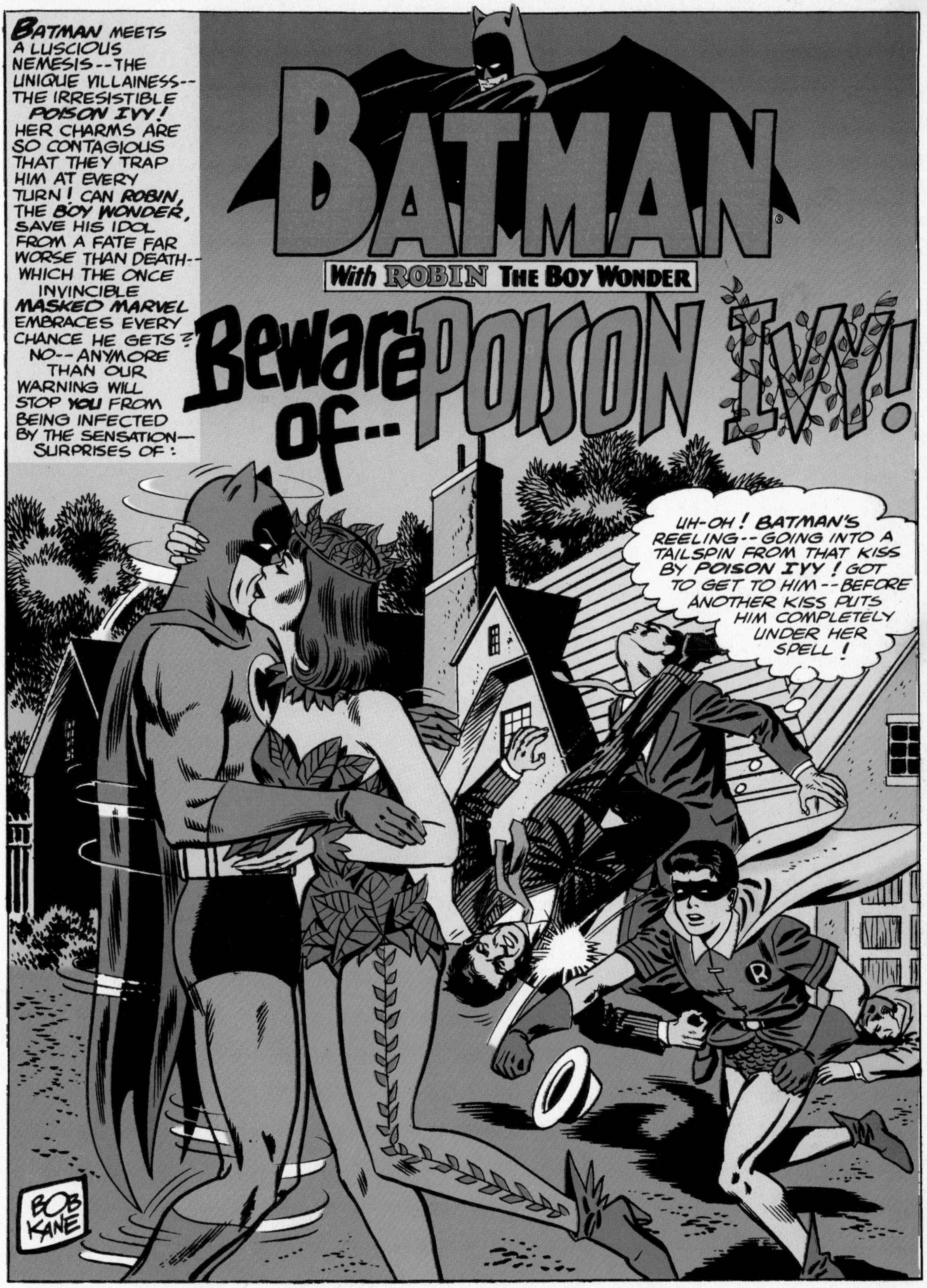
BATMAN MEETS A LUSCIOUS NEMESIS--THE UNIQUE VILLAINESS--THE IRRESISTIBLE POISON IVY! HER CHARMS ARE SO CONTAGIOUS THAT THEY TRAP HIM AT EVERY TURN! CAN ROBIN, THE BOY WONDER, SAVE HIS IDOL FROM A FATE FAR WORSE THAN DEATH--WHICH THE ONCE INVINCIBLE MASKED MARVEL EMBRACES EVERY CHANCE HE GETS? NO--ANYMORE THAN OUR WARNING WILL STOP YOU FROM BEING INFECTED BY THE SENSATION--SURPRISES OF:
BATMAN®
With ROBIN THE BOY WONDER
Beware of.. POISON IVY!
UH-OH! BATMAN'S REELING--GOING INTO A TAILSPIN FROM THAT KISS BY POISON IVY! GOT TO GET TO HIM--BEFORE ANOTHER KISS PUTS HIM COMPLETELY UNDER HER SPELL!
BOB KANE

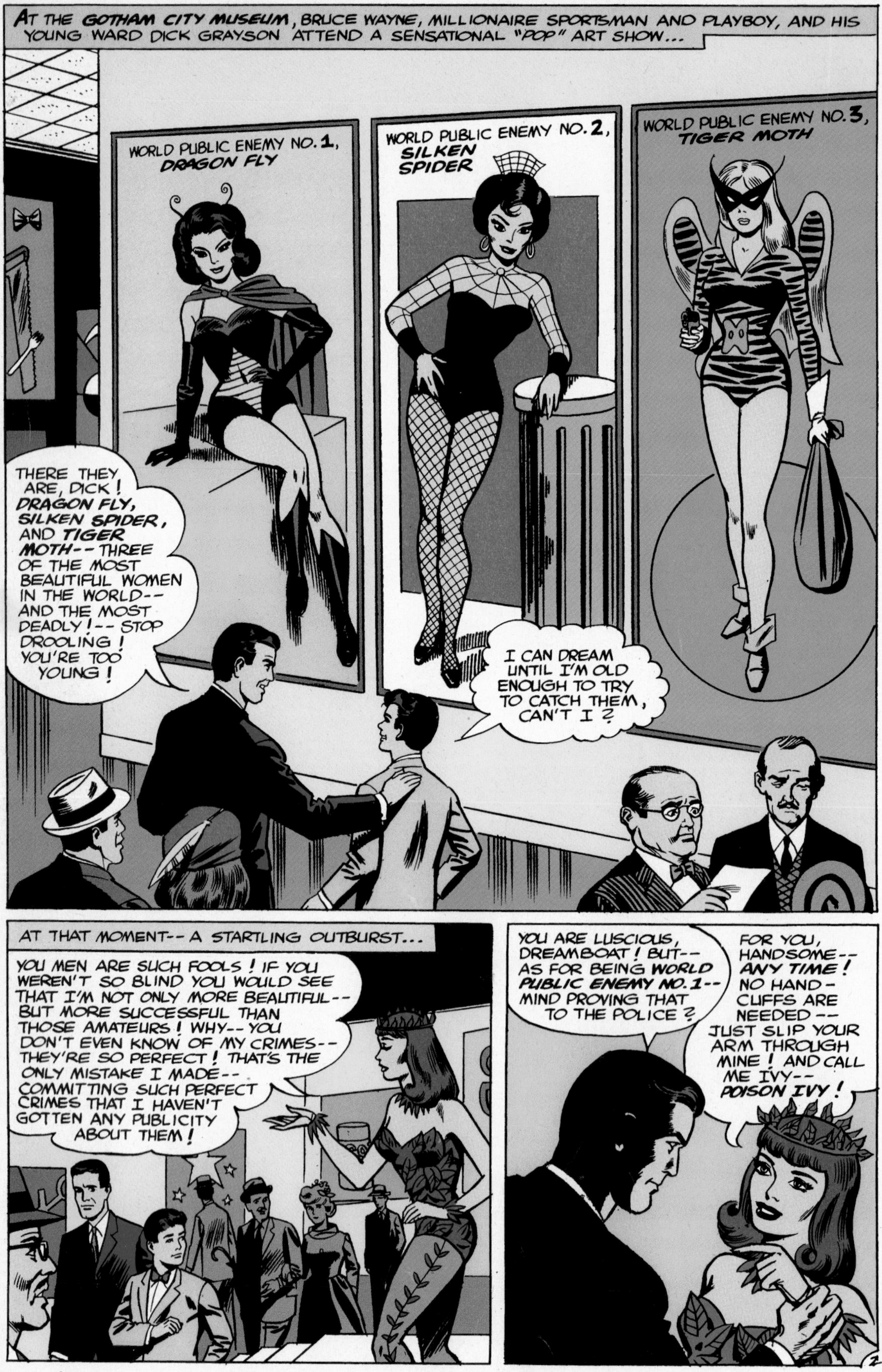

AT THE GOTHAM CITY MUSEUM, BRUCE WAYNE, MILLIONAIRE SPORTSMAN AND PLAYBOY, AND HIS YOUNG WARD DICK GRAYSON ATTEND A SENSATIONAL "POP" ART SHOW...
WORLD PUBLIC ENEMY NO. 1, DRAGON FLY
WORLD PUBLIC ENEMY NO. 2, SILKEN SPIDER
WORLD PUBLIC ENEMY NO. 3, TIGER MOTH
THERE THEY ARE, DICK! DRAGON FLY, SILKEN SPIDER, AND TIGER MOTH-- THREE OF THE MOST BEAUTIFUL WOMEN IN THE WORLD-- AND THE MOST DEADLY!-- STOP DROOLING! YOU'RE TOO YOUNG!
I CAN DREAM UNTIL I'M OLD ENOUGH TO TRY TO CATCH THEM, CAN'T I?
AT THAT MOMENT-- A STARTLING OUTBURST...
YOU MEN ARE SUCH FOOLS! IF YOU WEREN'T SO BLIND YOU WOULD SEE THAT I'M NOT ONLY MORE BEAUTIFUL-- BUT MORE SUCCESSFUL THAN THOSE AMATEURS! WHY-- YOU DON'T EVEN KNOW OF MY CRIMES-- THEY'RE SO PERFECT! THAT'S THE ONLY MISTAKE I MADE-- COMMITTING SUCH PERFECT CRIMES THAT I HAVEN'T GOTTEN ANY PUBLICITY ABOUT THEM!
YOU ARE LUSCIOUS, DREAMBOAT! BUT-- AS FOR BEING WORLD PUBLIC ENEMY NO. 1-- MIND PROVING THAT TO THE POLICE?
FOR YOU, HANDSOME-- ANY TIME! NO HAND-CUFFS ARE NEEDED-- JUST SLIP YOUR ARM THROUGH MINE! AND CALL ME IVY-- POISON IVY!
2

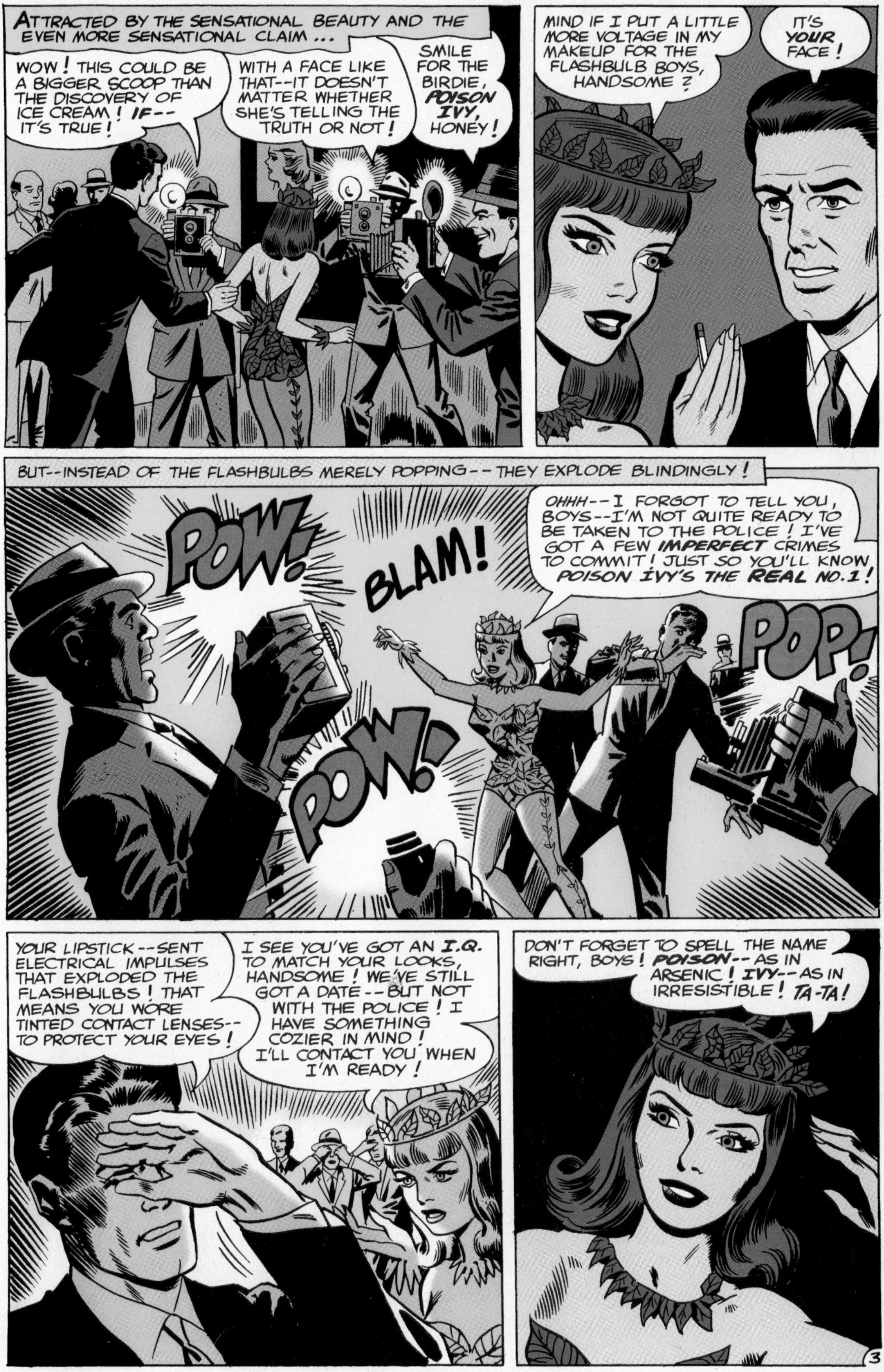
ATTRACTED BY THE SENSATIONAL BEAUTY AND THE EVEN MORE SENSATIONAL CLAIM ...
WOW! THIS COULD BE A BIGGER SCOOP THAN THE DISCOVERY OF ICE CREAM! IF-- IT'S TRUE!
WITH A FACE LIKE THAT--IT DOESN'T MATTER WHETHER SHE'S TELLING THE TRUTH OR NOT!
SMILE FOR THE BIRDIE, POISON IVY, HONEY!
MIND IF I PUT A LITTLE MORE VOLTAGE IN MY MAKEUP FOR THE FLASHBULB BOYS, HANDSOME?
IT'S YOUR FACE!
BUT--INSTEAD OF THE FLASHBULBS MERELY POPPING-- THEY EXPLODE BLINDINGLY!
POW!
BLAM!
OHHH-- I FORGOT TO TELL YOU, BOYS--I'M NOT QUITE READY TO BE TAKEN TO THE POLICE! I'VE GOT A FEW IMPERFECT CRIMES TO COMMIT! JUST SO YOU'LL KNOW POISON IVY'S THE REAL NO.1!
POP!
POW!
YOUR LIPSTICK--SENT ELECTRICAL IMPULSES THAT EXPLODED THE FLASHBULBS! THAT MEANS YOU WORE TINTED CONTACT LENSES-- TO PROTECT YOUR EYES!
I SEE YOU'VE GOT AN I.Q. TO MATCH YOUR LOOKS, HANDSOME! WE'VE STILL GOT A DATE--BUT NOT WITH THE POLICE! I HAVE SOMETHING COZIER IN MIND! I'LL CONTACT YOU WHEN I'M READY!
DON'T FORGET TO SPELL THE NAME RIGHT, BOYS! POISON--AS IN ARSENIC! IVY--AS IN IRRESISTIBLE! TA-TA!
3

IN THE MIDST OF THE TEMPORARILY-BLINDED PEOPLE--HIMSELF UNABLE TO SEE EXCEPT IN THE BLURRIEST MANNER--BRUCE MAKES A DARING CHANGE!

IT'S THE FIRST TIME I'VE EVER CHANGED INTO *BATMAN* IN PUBLIC! BUT NO ONE CAN SEE ME!

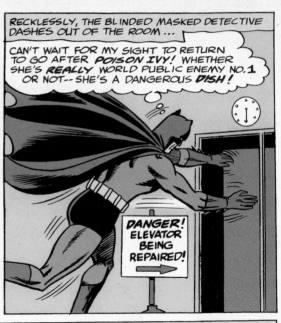

RECKLESSLY, THE BLINDED MASKED DETECTIVE DASHES OUT OF THE ROOM...

CAN'T WAIT FOR MY SIGHT TO RETURN TO GO AFTER *POISON IVY!* WHETHER SHE'S *REALLY* WORLD PUBLIC ENEMY NO. 1 OR NOT-- SHE'S A DANGEROUS *DISH!*

DANGER! ELEVATOR BEING REPAIRED!

IN HIS DARING PURSUIT, THE *ACE ATHLETE* SUDDENLY FINDS HIMSELF HURTLING IN A DEATH DIVE..

WHA--?! I'VE GONE THROUGH AN OPEN DOOR!

THIS FIRST STEP IS A DOOZIE!--I MUST BE IN AN ELEVATOR SHAFT...

MY HANDS ARE BRUSHING ALONG THE CABLES!--IF MY WRISTS DON'T BREAK-- MAYBE I CAN SLOW MYSELF UP...

4

WORKMEN ARE STUNNED TO SEE THE *CAPED CRUSADER* HALT HIS BULLET-LIKE FLIGHT...

NO WONDER THEY CALL HIM *BATMAN!* DID YOU SEE THAT DIVE TO THE OPEN DOOR OF THE LOBBY?

THAT'S MY *CUE* TO GET OFF!

AS THE *MASKED DETECTIVE* IS SPOTTED BY THE SLITHERING SIREN...

BATMAN MUST HAVE BEEN IN THE BUILDING! HE'S OBVIOUSLY ON MY TRAIL! NO MATTER! I'VE ALREADY PREPARED A HUMAN ROADBLOCK FOR ANYONE COMING OUT OF THAT REVOLVING DOOR!

BATMAN IS HURLED BY THE REVOLVING DOOR TOWARD A MENACING MOB...

POISON IVY GAVE US A HUNDRED BUCKS APIECE TO STAY OUT IN THE FRESH AIR! AN' PROMISED US ANOTHER CENTURY NOTE FOR EACH MUG WE STOPPED COMIN' OUT'VE THE MUSEUM! *BATMAN* OUGHTA BE WORTH A COOL *GRAND!*

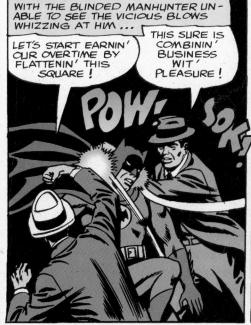

WITH THE BLINDED MANHUNTER UN- ABLE TO SEE THE VICIOUS BLOWS WHIZZING AT HIM...

LET'S START EARNIN' OUR OVERTIME BY FLATTENIN' THIS SQUARE!

THIS SURE IS COMBININ' BUSINESS WIT' PLEASURE!

POW! SOK!

LIKE A BLIND MAN INGENIOUSLY RELYING ON HIS KEEN SENSE OF TOUCH...

I WAS "PATTED" ON BOTH SIDES OF MY JAW! IF THE "SENDERS" ARE STILL IN THE SAME PLACE -- I CAN RETURN THE COMPLIMENT!

POW! SOK!

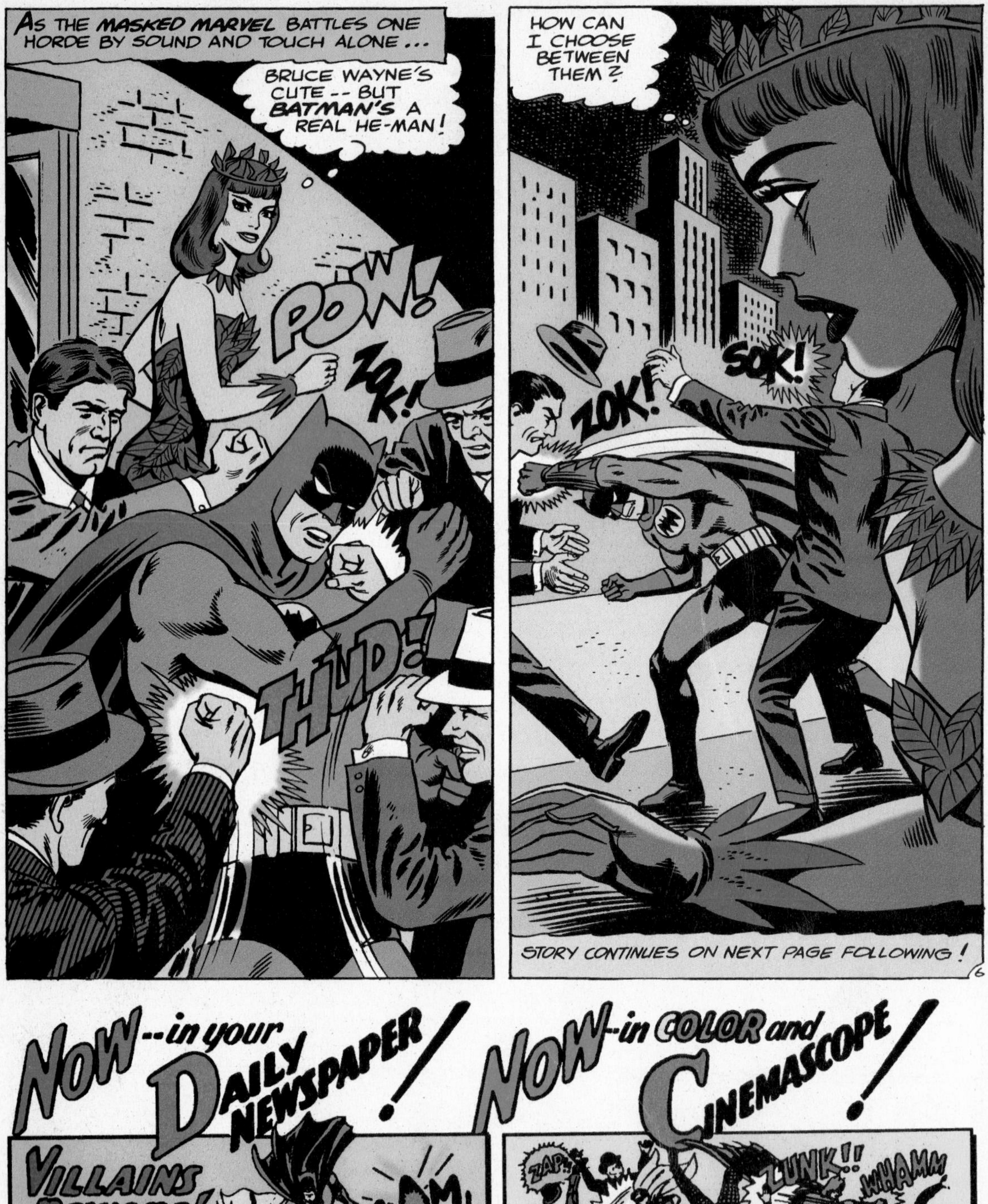
AS THE MASKED MARVEL BATTLES ONE HORDE BY SOUND AND TOUCH ALONE...
BRUCE WAYNE'S CUTE -- BUT BATMAN'S A REAL HE-MAN!
POW!
ZOK!
THUD!
HOW CAN I CHOOSE BETWEEN THEM?
ZOK!
SOK!
STORY CONTINUES ON NEXT PAGE FOLLOWING!
6

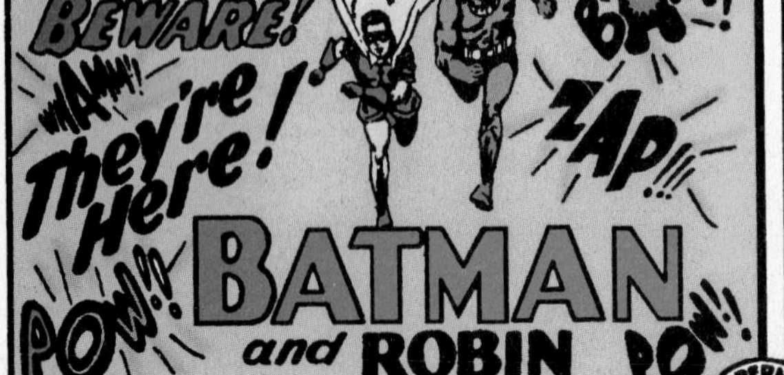
NOW--in your DAILY NEWSPAPER!
VILLAINS BEWARE!
They're Here!
BAM!
ZAP!!!
POW!!
BATMAN
and ROBIN
POW!!
IN THE COMIC PAGES OF MORE THAN
200 NEWSPAPERS FROM COAST TO COAST!
SUPERMAN DC NATIONAL COMICS

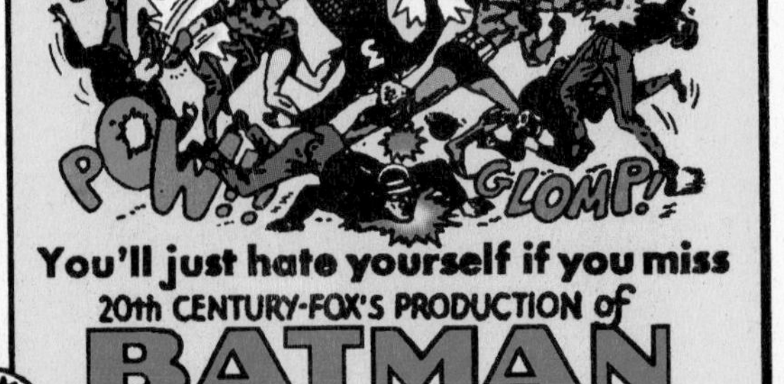
NOW--in COLOR and CINEMASCOPE!
ZAP!!
ZUNK!!
WHAMM
POW!!
GLOMP!
You'll just hate yourself if you miss
20th CENTURY-FOX'S PRODUCTION of
BATMAN
CO-STARRING
The PENGUIN, CATWOMAN and The JOKER!

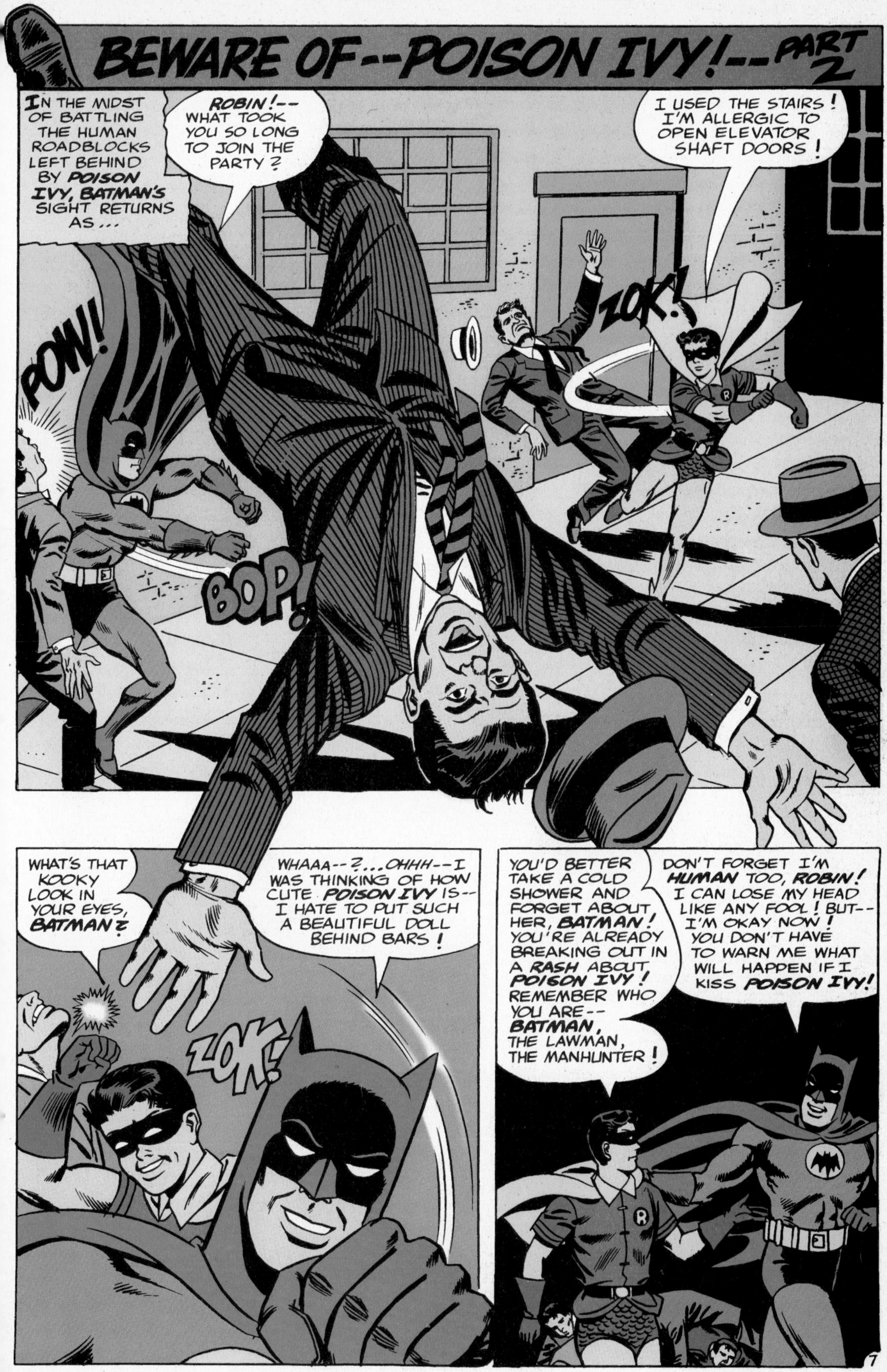
BEWARE OF--POISON IVY!--PART 2
IN THE MIDST OF BATTLING THE HUMAN ROADBLOCKS LEFT BEHIND BY POISON IVY, BATMAN'S SIGHT RETURNS AS...
ROBIN!-- WHAT TOOK YOU SO LONG TO JOIN THE PARTY?
I USED THE STAIRS! I'M ALLERGIC TO OPEN ELEVATOR SHAFT DOORS!
POW!
ZOK!
BOP!
WHAT'S THAT KOOKY LOOK IN YOUR EYES, BATMAN?
WHAAA--?...OHHH--I WAS THINKING OF HOW CUTE POISON IVY IS-- I HATE TO PUT SUCH A BEAUTIFUL DOLL BEHIND BARS!
ZOK!
YOU'D BETTER TAKE A COLD SHOWER AND FORGET ABOUT HER, BATMAN! YOU'RE ALREADY BREAKING OUT IN A RASH ABOUT POISON IVY! REMEMBER WHO YOU ARE-- BATMAN, THE LAWMAN, THE MANHUNTER!
DON'T FORGET I'M HUMAN TOO, ROBIN! I CAN LOSE MY HEAD LIKE ANY FOOL! BUT-- I'M OKAY NOW! YOU DON'T HAVE TO WARN ME WHAT WILL HAPPEN IF I KISS POISON IVY!
7

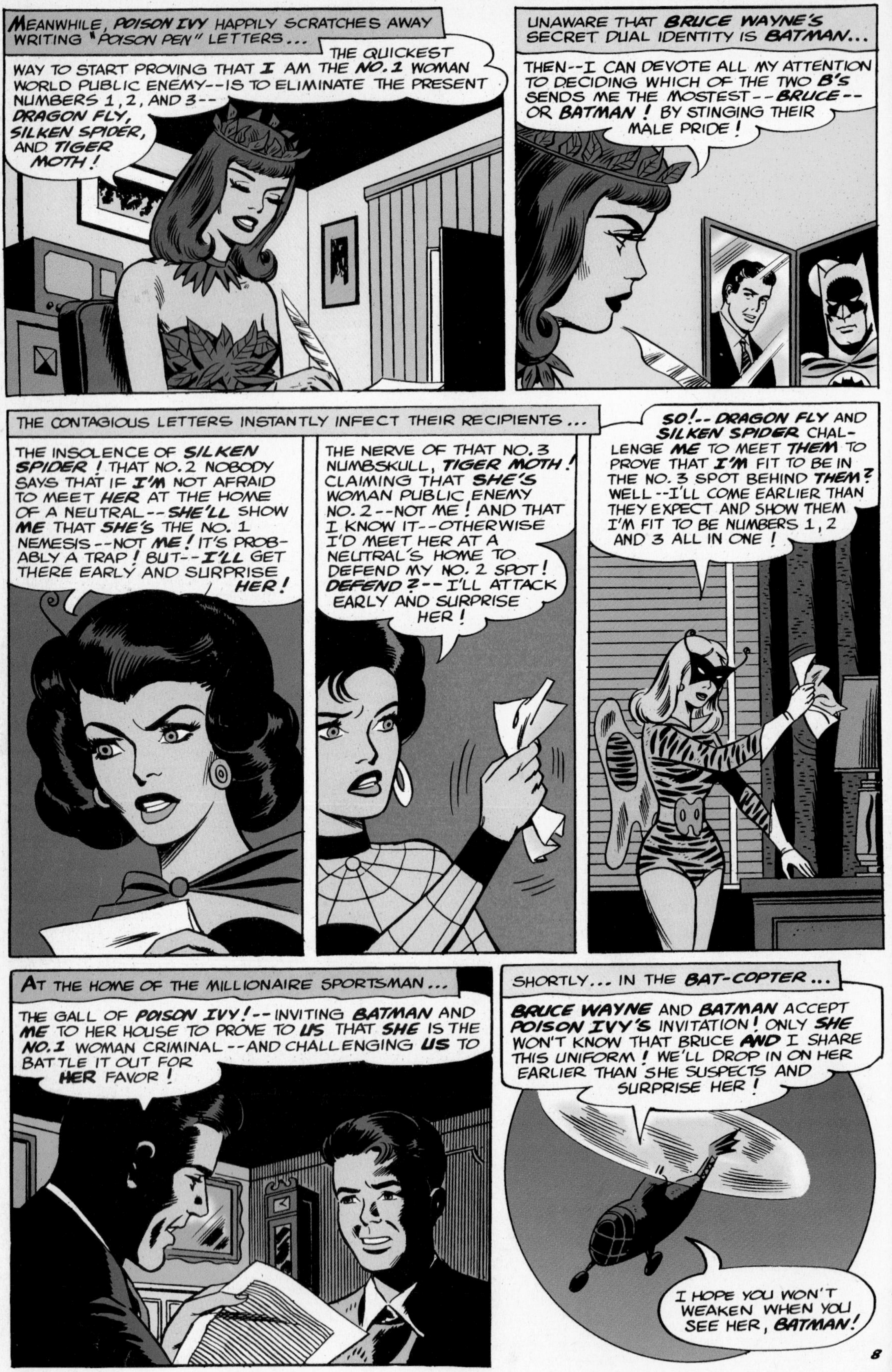
MEANWHILE, POISON IVY HAPPILY SCRATCHES AWAY WRITING "POISON PEN" LETTERS...
THE QUICKEST WAY TO START PROVING THAT I AM THE NO. 1 WOMAN WORLD PUBLIC ENEMY--IS TO ELIMINATE THE PRESENT NUMBERS 1, 2, AND 3--DRAGON FLY, SILKEN SPIDER, AND TIGER MOTH!
UNAWARE THAT BRUCE WAYNE'S SECRET DUAL IDENTITY IS BATMAN...
THEN--I CAN DEVOTE ALL MY ATTENTION TO DECIDING WHICH OF THE TWO B'S SENDS ME THE MOSTEST--BRUCE--OR BATMAN! BY STINGING THEIR MALE PRIDE!
THE CONTAGIOUS LETTERS INSTANTLY INFECT THEIR RECIPIENTS...
THE INSOLENCE OF SILKEN SPIDER! THAT NO. 2 NOBODY SAYS THAT IF I'M NOT AFRAID TO MEET HER AT THE HOME OF A NEUTRAL--SHE'LL SHOW ME THAT SHE'S THE NO. 1 NEMESIS--NOT ME! IT'S PROBABLY A TRAP! BUT--I'LL GET THERE EARLY AND SURPRISE HER!
THE NERVE OF THAT NO. 3 NUMBSKULL, TIGER MOTH! CLAIMING THAT SHE'S WOMAN PUBLIC ENEMY NO. 2--NOT ME! AND THAT I KNOW IT--OTHERWISE I'D MEET HER AT A NEUTRAL'S HOME TO DEFEND MY NO. 2 SPOT! DEFEND?--I'LL ATTACK EARLY AND SURPRISE HER!
SO!--DRAGON FLY AND SILKEN SPIDER CHALLENGE ME TO MEET THEM TO PROVE THAT I'M FIT TO BE IN THE NO. 3 SPOT BEHIND THEM? WELL--I'LL COME EARLIER THAN THEY EXPECT AND SHOW THEM I'M FIT TO BE NUMBERS 1, 2 AND 3 ALL IN ONE!
AT THE HOME OF THE MILLIONAIRE SPORTSMAN...
THE GALL OF POISON IVY!--INVITING BATMAN AND ME TO HER HOUSE TO PROVE TO US THAT SHE IS THE NO. 1 WOMAN CRIMINAL--AND CHALLENGING US TO BATTLE IT OUT FOR HER FAVOR!
SHORTLY... IN THE BAT-COPTER...
BRUCE WAYNE AND BATMAN ACCEPT POISON IVY'S INVITATION! ONLY SHE WON'T KNOW THAT BRUCE AND I SHARE THIS UNIFORM! WE'LL DROP IN ON HER EARLIER THAN SHE SUSPECTS AND SURPRISE HER!
I HOPE YOU WON'T WEAKEN WHEN YOU SEE HER, BATMAN!
8

LEAVING THE UNIQUE *BAT-COPTER* CIRCLING ON AUTOMATIC PILOT, THE DYNAMIC DUO DISCOVERS...

LOOKS LIKE *POISON IVY* SENT OUT A FLOCK OF INVITATIONS! AND EVERYONE SHOWED UP AHEAD OF TIME TO SURPRISE EVERYONE ELSE!

YOU CAN THANK HER FOR COLLECTING SUCH A BIG BAG OF CRIMINALS ALL IN ONE SPOT FOR US! MAYBE THE JUDGE WILL EVEN GIVE HER A FEW YEARS OFF FOR SUCH *"GOOD BEHAVIOR"*!

AT THE SIGHT OF THE DARING DUO...

TRUCE!-- WHILE WE SNAP UP THESE FOOLISH MALE *"INSECTS"* FOR DARING TO INTRUDE ON OUR PRIVATE PARTY!

AGREED!

DITTO!

SWING YOUR LINES, *ROBIN!*

NOW I KNOW WHAT A DUCK IN A SHOOTING GALLERY FEELS LIKE!

ZING!

LIKE HUMAN PENDULUMS, THE *DYNAMIC DUO* SWINGS WITH PILE-DRIVER EFFECT INTO THE RAGING GANGS...

ROBIN--YOU MUST ADMIT THAT *POISON IVY* IS A DOLL FOR HELPING US NET ALL THESE GANGS AT ONE TIME!

SHE'S A DOLL, ALL RIGHT-- ONLY SHE BELONGS IN A DOLLHOUSE WITH BARS! AND I'M HERE TO SEE THAT YOU DON'T FORGET IT!

POW!

BIFF!

SOCK!

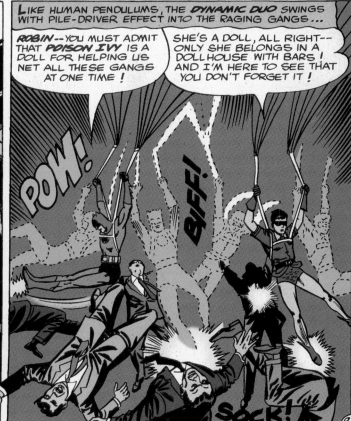

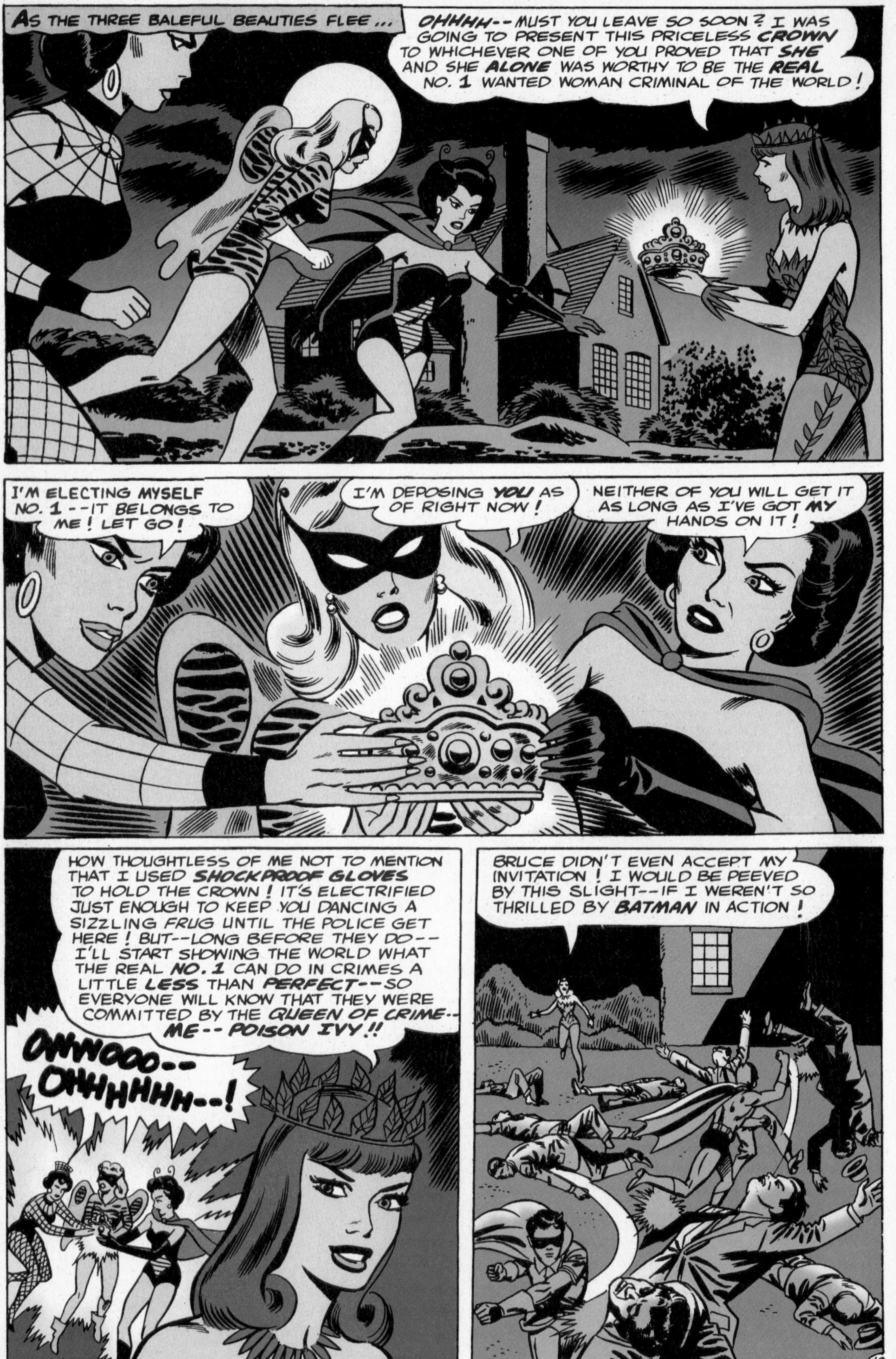
AS THE THREE BALEFUL BEAUTIES FLEE ...
OHHHH--MUST YOU LEAVE SO SOON? I WAS GOING TO PRESENT THIS PRICELESS CROWN TO WHICHEVER ONE OF YOU PROVED THAT SHE AND SHE ALONE WAS WORTHY TO BE THE REAL NO. 1 WANTED WOMAN CRIMINAL OF THE WORLD!
I'M ELECTING MYSELF NO. 1 --IT BELONGS TO ME! LET GO!
I'M DEPOSING YOU AS OF RIGHT NOW!
NEITHER OF YOU WILL GET IT AS LONG AS I'VE GOT MY HANDS ON IT!
HOW THOUGHTLESS OF ME NOT TO MENTION THAT I USED SHOCKPROOF GLOVES TO HOLD THE CROWN! IT'S ELECTRIFIED JUST ENOUGH TO KEEP YOU DANCING A SIZZLING FRUG UNTIL THE POLICE GET HERE! BUT--LONG BEFORE THEY DO--I'LL START SHOWING THE WORLD WHAT THE REAL NO. 1 CAN DO IN CRIMES A LITTLE LESS THAN PERFECT--SO EVERYONE WILL KNOW THAT THEY WERE COMMITTED BY THE QUEEN OF CRIME--ME--POISON IVY!!
OHWOOO--OHHHHHH--!
BRUCE DIDN'T EVEN ACCEPT MY INVITATION! I WOULD BE PEEVED BY THIS SLIGHT--IF I WEREN'T SO THRILLED BY BATMAN IN ACTION!
10

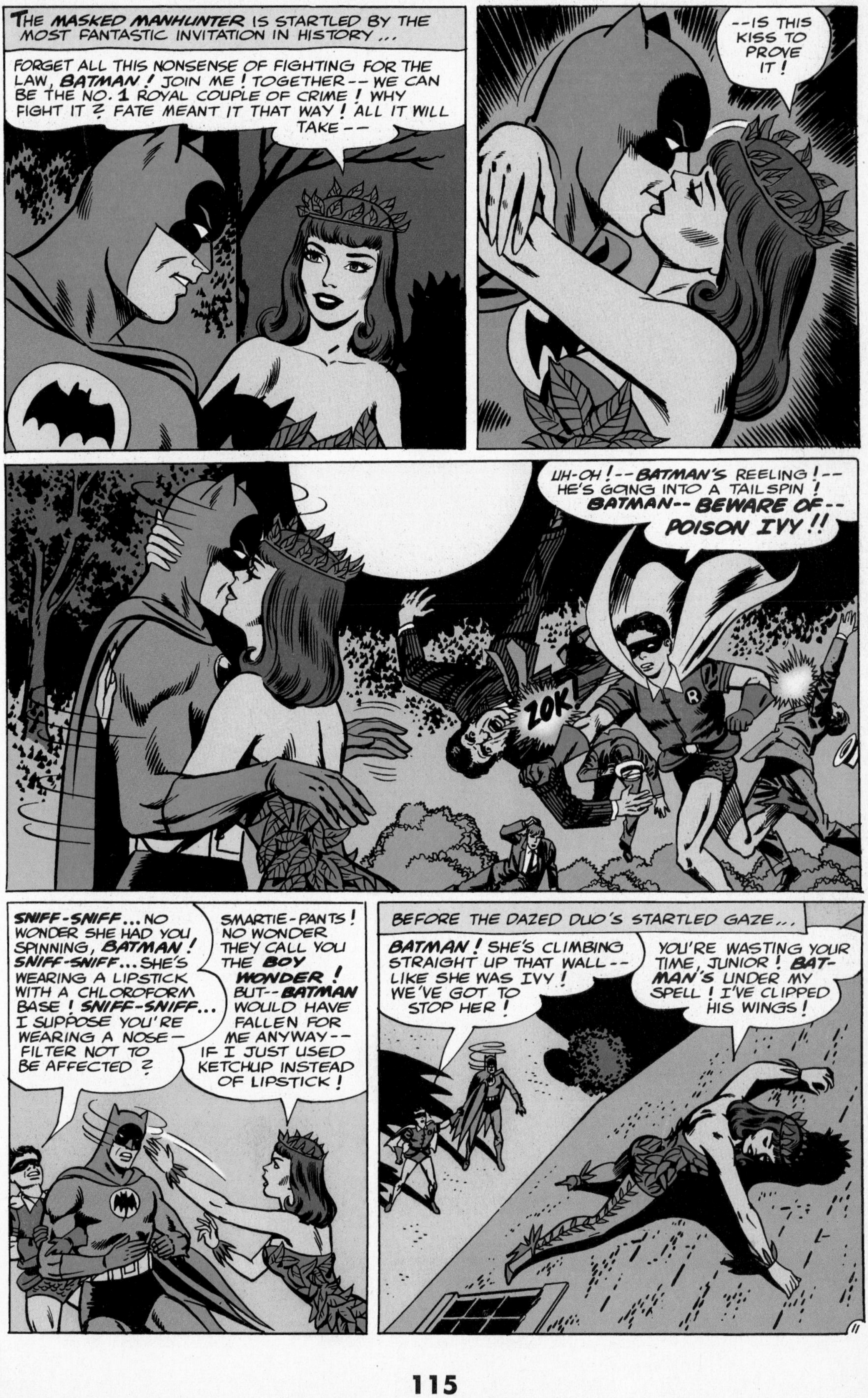
THE MASKED MANHUNTER IS STARTLED BY THE MOST FANTASTIC INVITATION IN HISTORY ...
FORGET ALL THIS NONSENSE OF FIGHTING FOR THE LAW, BATMAN! JOIN ME! TOGETHER -- WE CAN BE THE NO. 1 ROYAL COUPLE OF CRIME! WHY FIGHT IT? FATE MEANT IT THAT WAY! ALL IT WILL TAKE --
--IS THIS KISS TO PROVE IT!
UH-OH! -- BATMAN'S REELING! -- HE'S GOING INTO A TAILSPIN! BATMAN -- BEWARE OF -- POISON IVY!!
ZOK!
SNIFF-SNIFF ... NO WONDER SHE HAD YOU SPINNING, BATMAN! SNIFF-SNIFF ... SHE'S WEARING A LIPSTICK WITH A CHLOROFORM BASE! SNIFF-SNIFF ... I SUPPOSE YOU'RE WEARING A NOSE-FILTER NOT TO BE AFFECTED?
SMARTIE-PANTS! NO WONDER THEY CALL YOU THE BOY WONDER! BUT-- BATMAN WOULD HAVE FALLEN FOR ME ANYWAY -- IF I JUST USED KETCHUP INSTEAD OF LIPSTICK!
BEFORE THE DAZED DUO'S STARTLED GAZE ...
BATMAN! SHE'S CLIMBING STRAIGHT UP THAT WALL -- LIKE SHE WAS IVY! WE'VE GOT TO STOP HER!
YOU'RE WASTING YOUR TIME, JUNIOR! BATMAN'S UNDER MY SPELL! I'VE CLIPPED HIS WINGS!
11

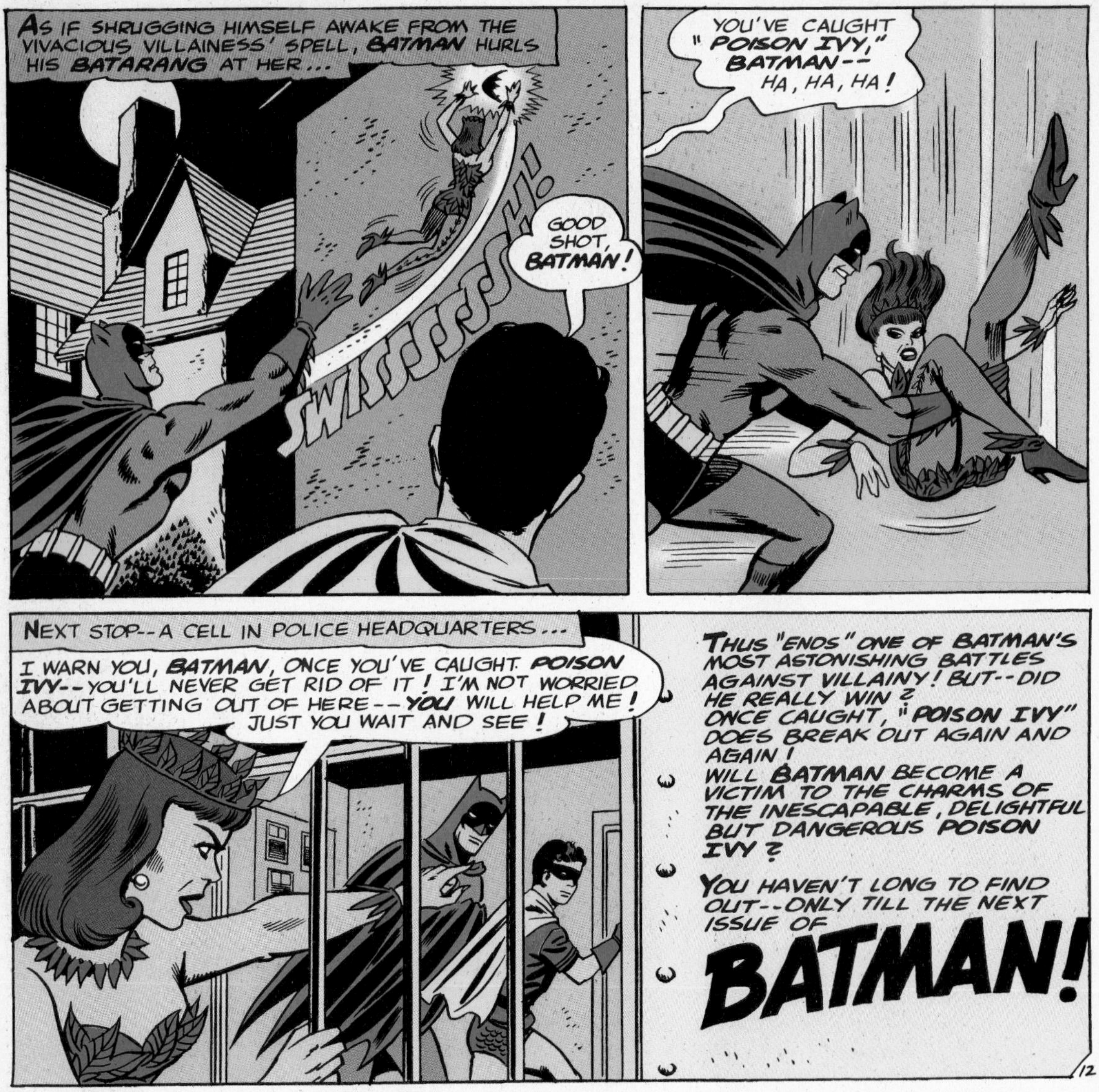

AS IF SHRUGGING HIMSELF AWAKE FROM THE VIVACIOUS VILLAINESS' SPELL, BATMAN HURLS HIS BATARANG AT HER...
SWISSSSSSH!
GOOD SHOT, BATMAN!
YOU'VE CAUGHT "POISON IVY," BATMAN-- HA, HA, HA!
NEXT STOP--A CELL IN POLICE HEADQUARTERS...
I WARN YOU, BATMAN, ONCE YOU'VE CAUGHT POISON IVY--YOU'LL NEVER GET RID OF IT! I'M NOT WORRIED ABOUT GETTING OUT OF HERE--YOU WILL HELP ME! JUST YOU WAIT AND SEE!
THUS "ENDS" ONE OF BATMAN'S MOST ASTONISHING BATTLES AGAINST VILLAINY! BUT--DID HE REALLY WIN? ONCE CAUGHT, "POISON IVY" DOES BREAK OUT AGAIN AND AGAIN! WILL BATMAN BECOME A VICTIM TO THE CHARMS OF THE INESCAPABLE, DELIGHTFUL BUT DANGEROUS POISON IVY?
YOU HAVEN'T LONG TO FIND OUT--ONLY TILL THE NEXT ISSUE OF
BATMAN!
12

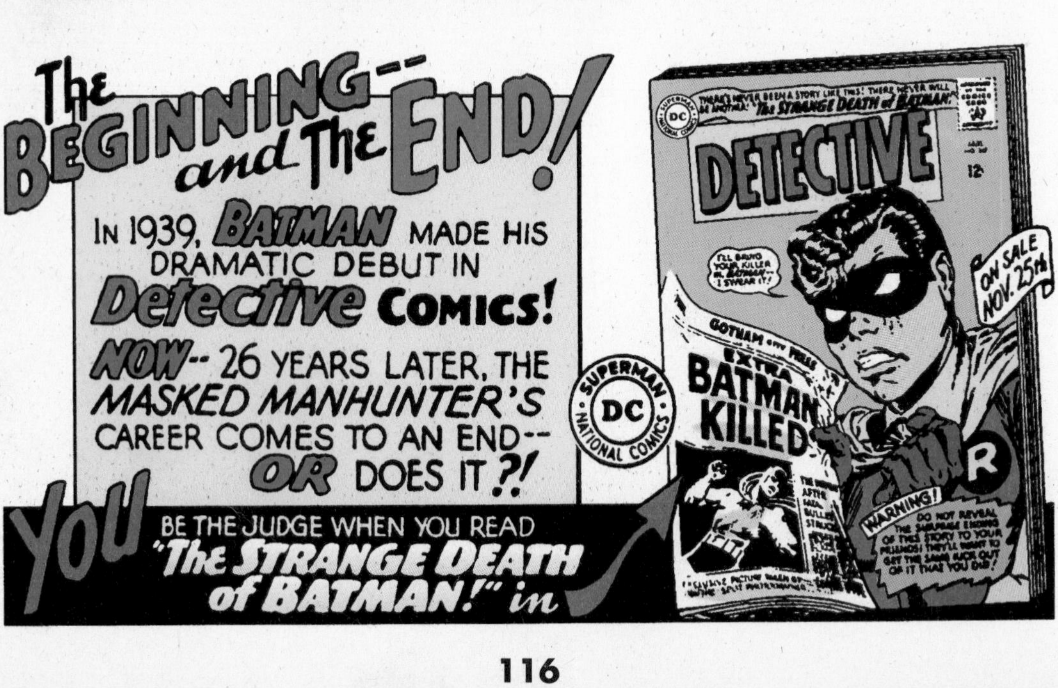

The BEGINNING-- and The END!
IN 1939, BATMAN MADE HIS DRAMATIC DEBUT IN Detective COMICS!
NOW-- 26 YEARS LATER, THE MASKED MANHUNTER'S CAREER COMES TO AN END-- OR DOES IT?!
YOU BE THE JUDGE WHEN YOU READ "The STRANGE DEATH of BATMAN!" in
SUPERMAN DC NATIONAL COMICS
DETECTIVE
12¢
ON SALE NOV. 25th
EXTRA
BATMAN KILLED
WARNING!

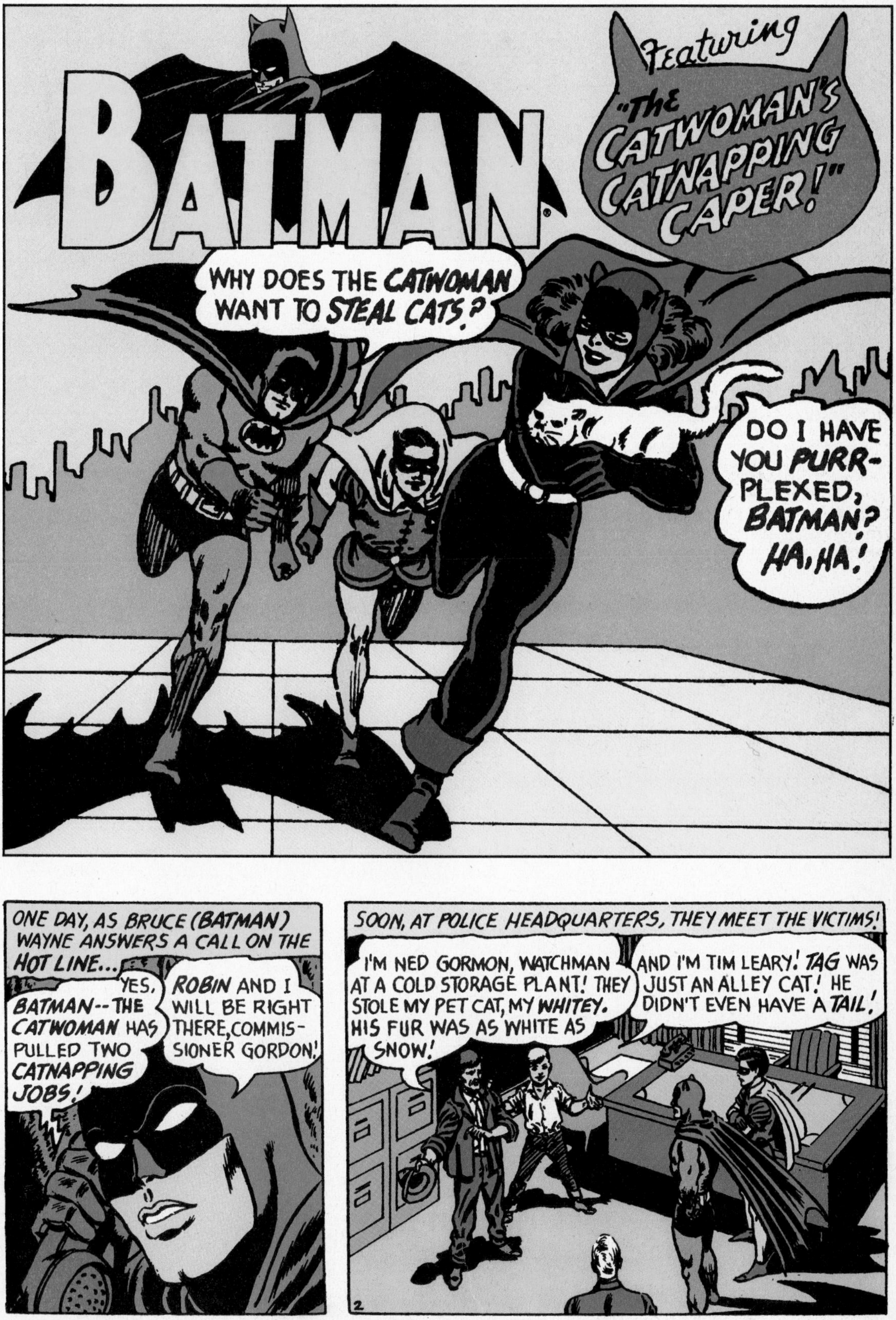
BATMAN
Featuring "The Catwoman's Catnapping Caper!"
WHY DOES THE CATWOMAN WANT TO STEAL CATS?
DO I HAVE YOU PURR-PLEXED, BATMAN? HA, HA!
ONE DAY, AS BRUCE (BATMAN) WAYNE ANSWERS A CALL ON THE HOT LINE...
BATMAN-- THE CATWOMAN HAS PULLED TWO CATNAPPING JOBS!
YES, ROBIN AND I WILL BE RIGHT THERE, COMMISSIONER GORDON!
SOON, AT POLICE HEADQUARTERS, THEY MEET THE VICTIMS!
I'M NED GORMON, WATCHMAN AT A COLD STORAGE PLANT! THEY STOLE MY PET CAT, MY WHITEY. HIS FUR WAS AS WHITE AS SNOW!
AND I'M TIM LEARY! TAG WAS JUST AN ALLEY CAT! HE DIDN'T EVEN HAVE A TAIL!
2

LATER, AS BRUCE AND HIS WARD, DICK GRAYSON, READ THE EVENING PAPER...

GOTHAM NEWS
MUSEUM GETS MUMMY OF CAT
X-RAY REVEALS GEMS IN MUMMY OF PHARAOH'S PET

GEMS-- IN A CAT MUMMY?

RIGHT! THE ANCIENT EGYPTIANS WORSHIPPED CATS AND GAVE THEM ELABORATE FUNERALS! THE CAT-WOMAN WILL BE AFTER THAT LOOT! COME ON!

AND AT THE GOTHAM MUSEUM...

HI, THERE, KITTY! WANT TO MAKE FRIENDS?

SAY, WHY'S HIS TAIL SO STIFF?

¡CHOKE!

GAS! ¡COUGH!

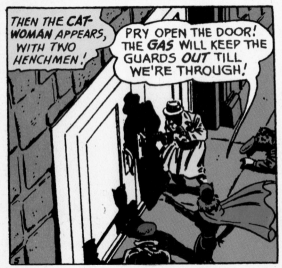

THEN THE CAT-WOMAN APPEARS, WITH TWO HENCHMEN!

PRY OPEN THE DOOR! THE GAS WILL KEEP THE GUARDS OUT TILL WE'RE THROUGH!

MOMENTS LATER...

THIS PHONY TAIL IS REALLY A GAS CYLINDER!

NO WONDER THE CAT-WOMAN WANTED A TAILLESS CAT!

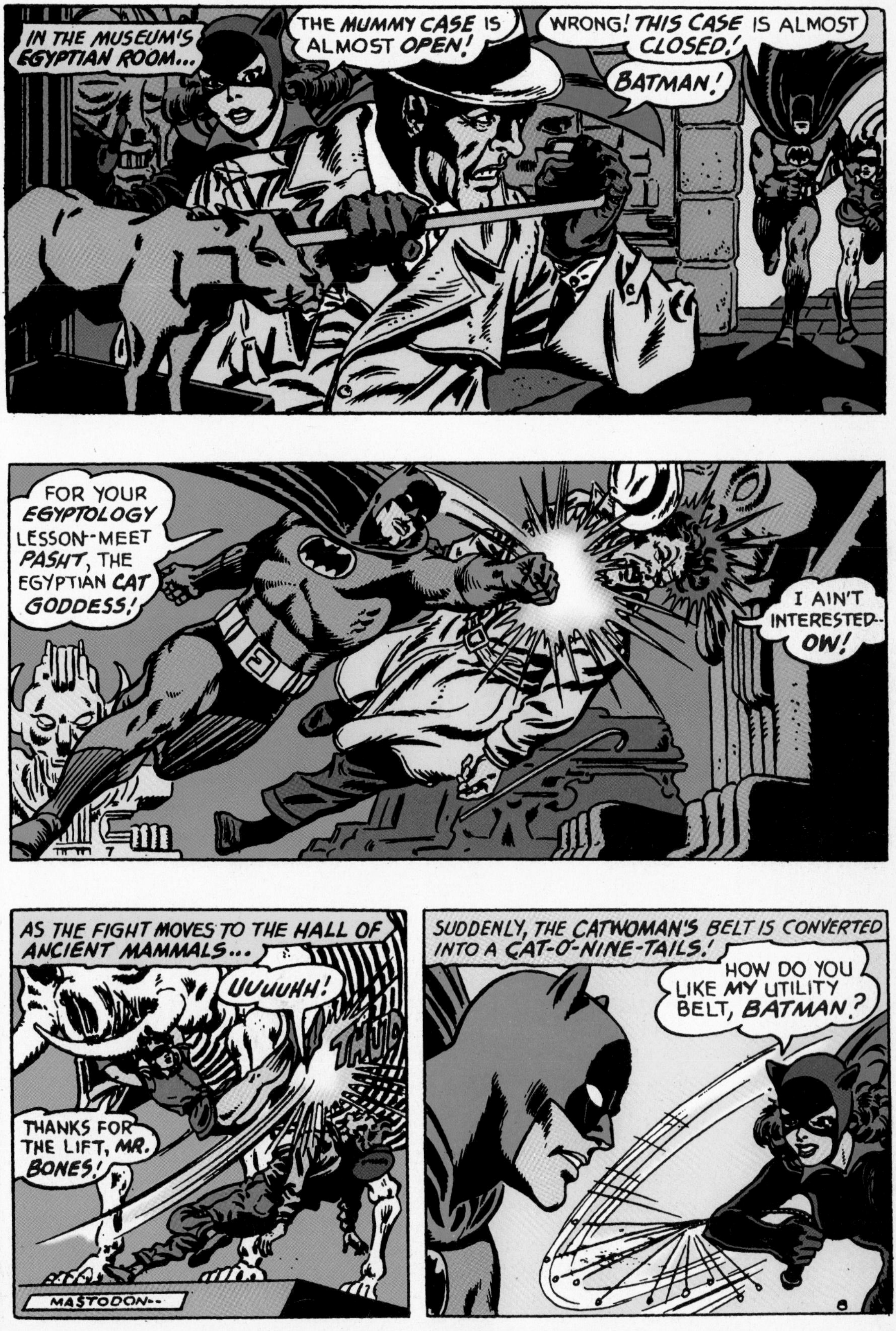
IN THE MUSEUM'S EGYPTIAN ROOM...
THE MUMMY CASE IS ALMOST OPEN!
WRONG! THIS CASE IS ALMOST CLOSED!
BATMAN!
FOR YOUR EGYPTOLOGY LESSON--MEET PASHT, THE EGYPTIAN CAT GODDESS!
I AIN'T INTERESTED-- OW!
AS THE FIGHT MOVES TO THE HALL OF ANCIENT MAMMALS...
UUUUHH!
THANKS FOR THE LIFT, MR. BONES!
MASTODON--
SUDDENLY, THE CATWOMAN'S BELT IS CONVERTED INTO A CAT-O'-NINE-TAILS!
HOW DO YOU LIKE MY UTILITY BELT, BATMAN?

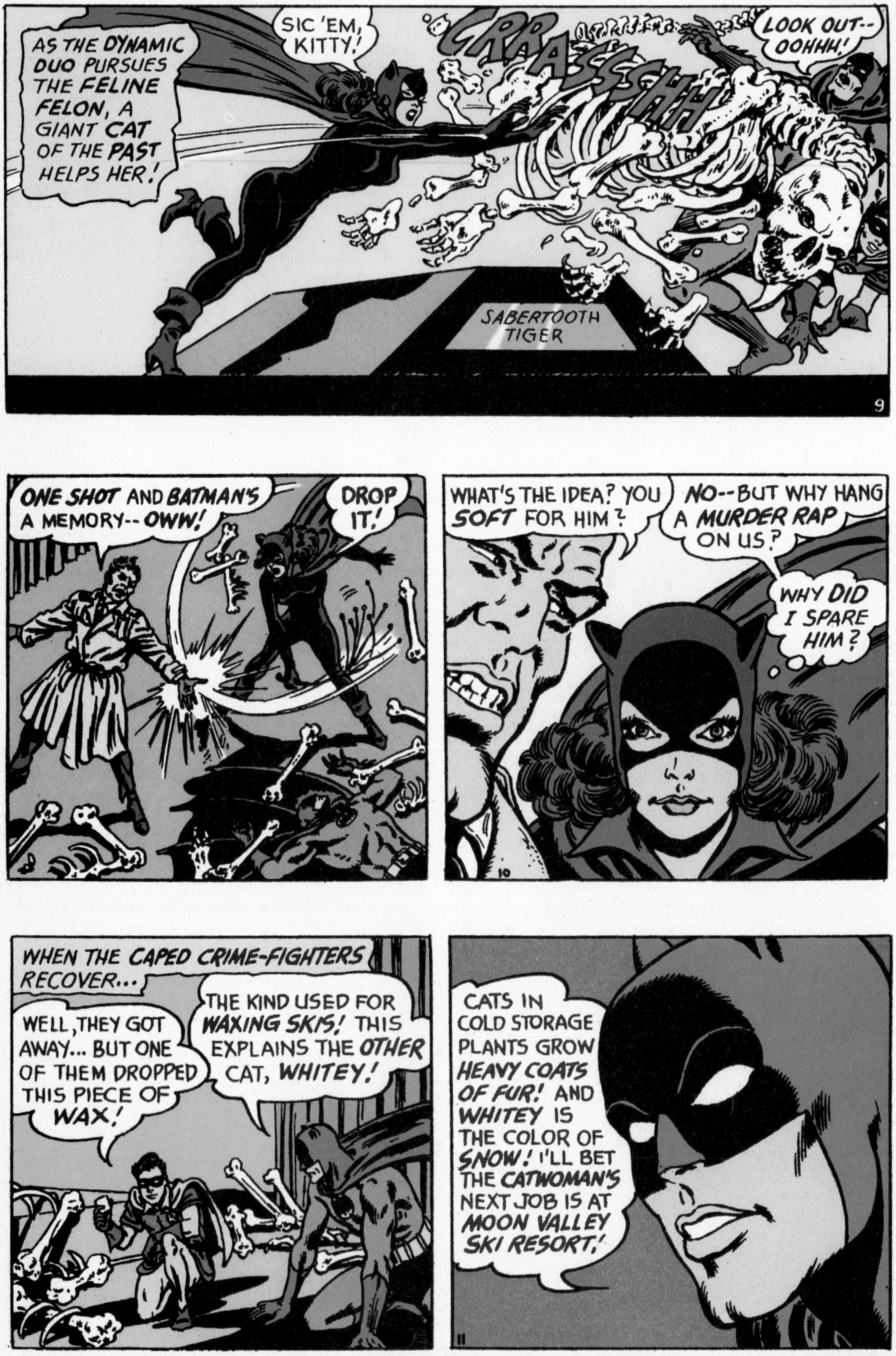
AS THE DYNAMIC DUO PURSUES THE FELINE FELON, A GIANT CAT OF THE PAST HELPS HER!
SIC 'EM, KITTY!
CRRASSSHH
LOOK OUT-- OOHHH!
SABERTOOTH TIGER
ONE SHOT AND BATMAN'S A MEMORY-- OWW!
DROP IT!
WHAT'S THE IDEA? YOU SOFT FOR HIM?
NO--BUT WHY HANG A MURDER RAP ON US?
WHY DID I SPARE HIM?
WHEN THE CAPED CRIME-FIGHTERS RECOVER...
WELL, THEY GOT AWAY... BUT ONE OF THEM DROPPED THIS PIECE OF WAX!
THE KIND USED FOR WAXING SKIS! THIS EXPLAINS THE OTHER CAT, WHITEY!
CATS IN COLD STORAGE PLANTS GROW HEAVY COATS OF FUR! AND WHITEY IS THE COLOR OF SNOW! I'LL BET THE CATWOMAN'S NEXT JOB IS AT MOON VALLEY SKI RESORT!

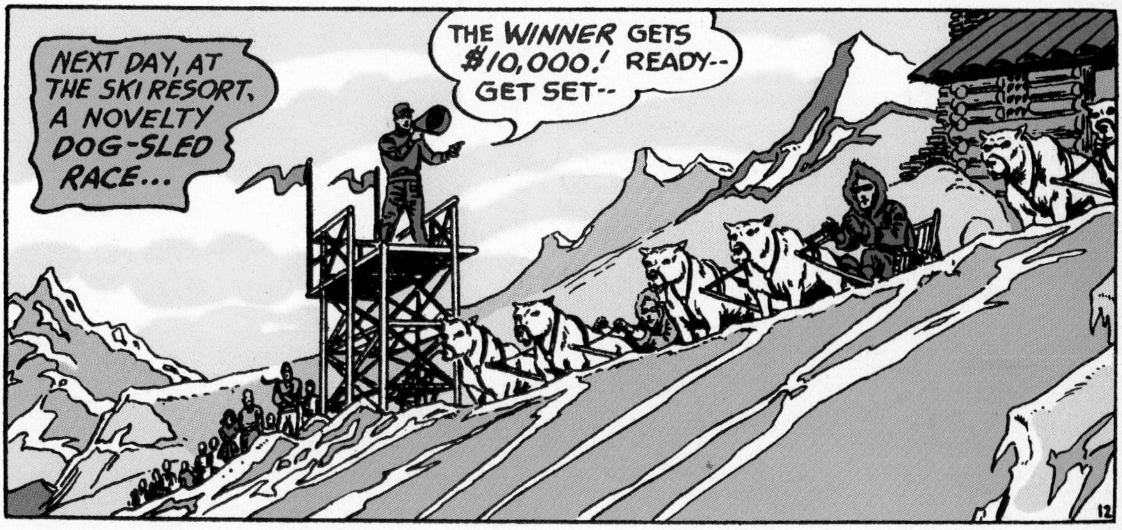
NEXT DAY, AT THE SKI RESORT, A NOVELTY DOG-SLED RACE...
THE WINNER GETS $10,000! READY-- GET SET--
12

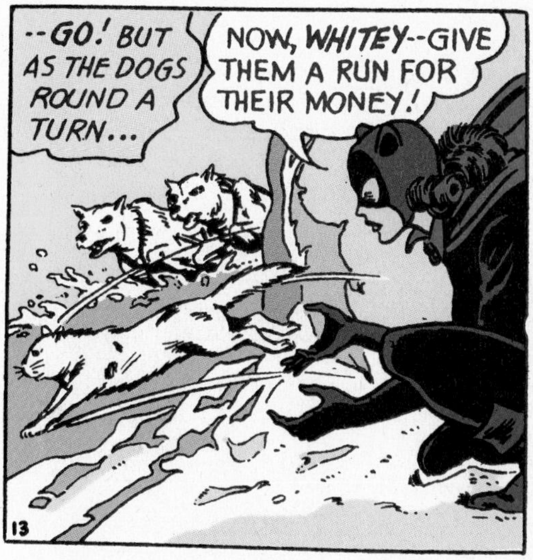
--GO! BUT AS THE DOGS ROUND A TURN...
NOW, WHITEY--GIVE THEM A RUN FOR THEIR MONEY!
13

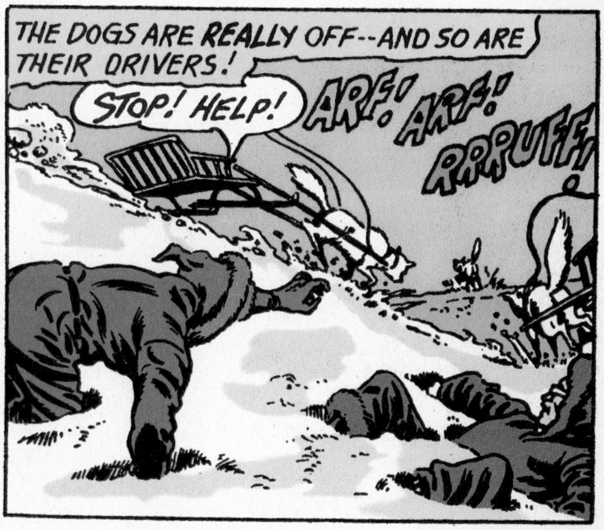
THE DOGS ARE REALLY OFF--AND SO ARE THEIR DRIVERS!
STOP! HELP!
ARF! ARF!
RRRUFF!

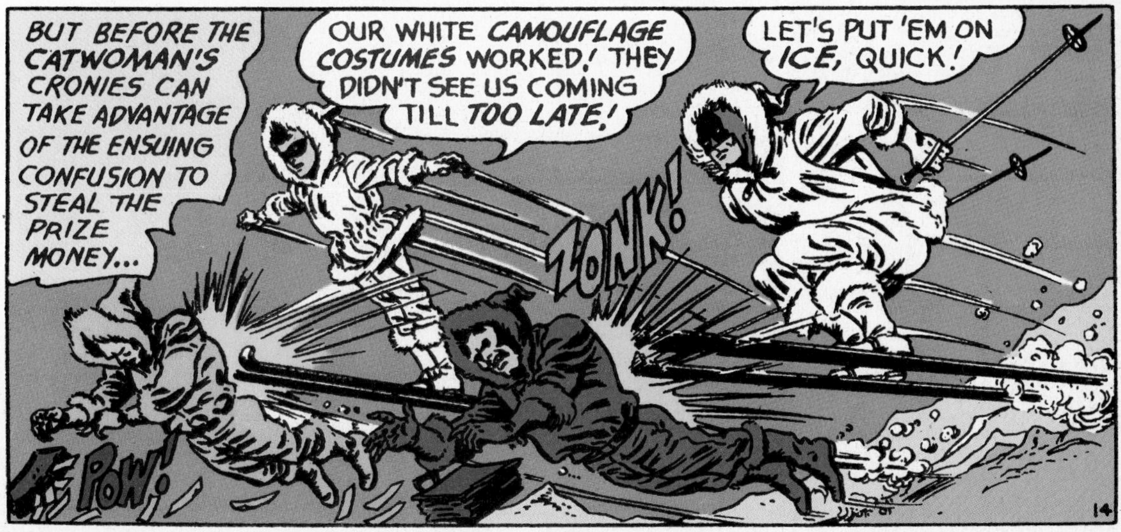
BUT BEFORE THE CATWOMAN'S CRONIES CAN TAKE ADVANTAGE OF THE ENSUING CONFUSION TO STEAL THE PRIZE MONEY...
OUR WHITE CAMOUFLAGE COSTUMES WORKED! THEY DIDN'T SEE US COMING TILL TOO LATE!
LET'S PUT 'EM ON ICE, QUICK!
ZONK!
POW!
14

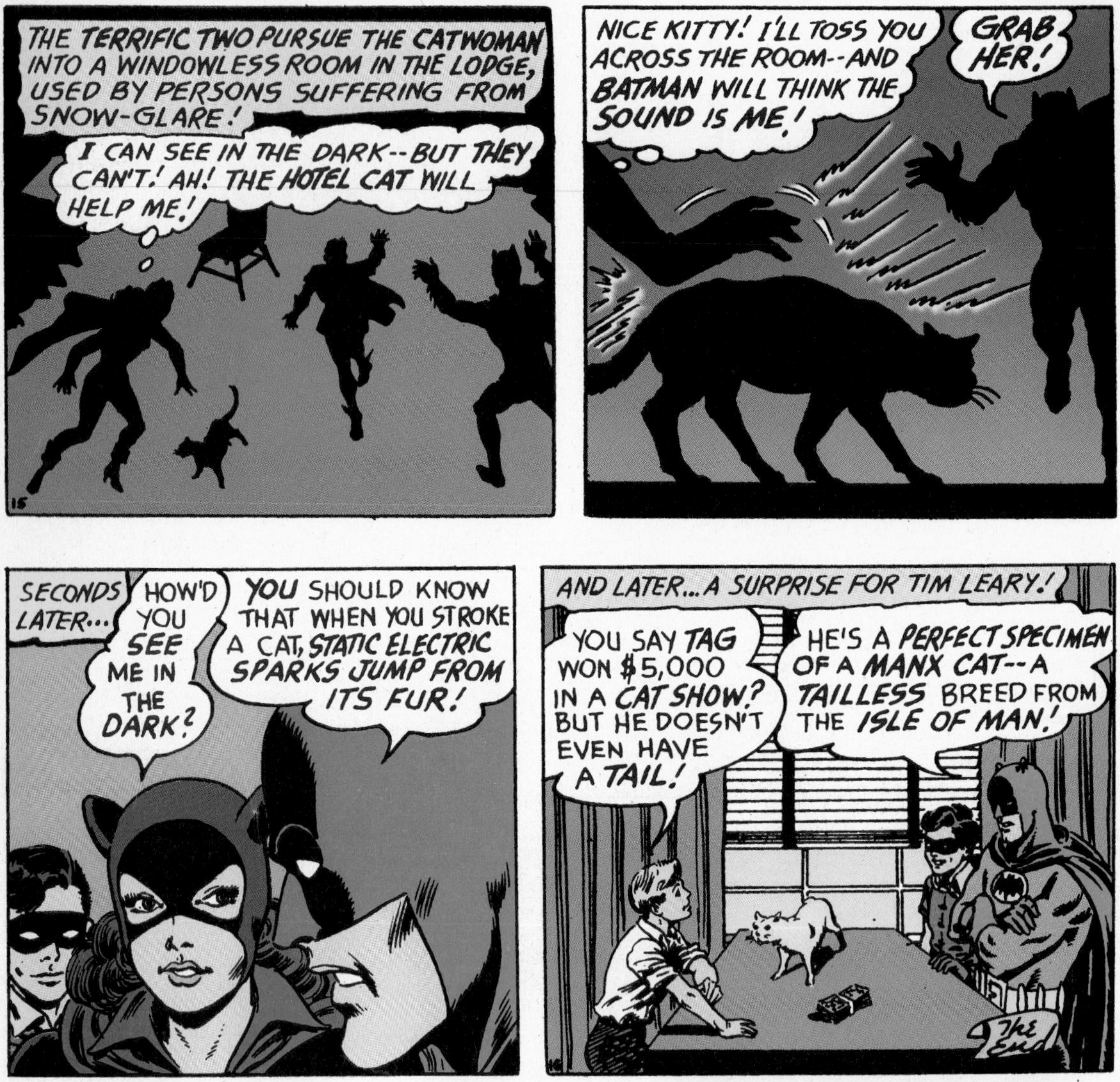
THE TERRIFIC TWO PURSUE THE CATWOMAN INTO A WINDOWLESS ROOM IN THE LODGE, USED BY PERSONS SUFFERING FROM SNOW-GLARE!
I CAN SEE IN THE DARK--BUT THEY CAN'T! AH! THE HOTEL CAT WILL HELP ME!
NICE KITTY! I'LL TOSS YOU ACROSS THE ROOM--AND BATMAN WILL THINK THE SOUND IS ME!
GRAB HER!
SECONDS LATER...
HOW'D YOU SEE ME IN THE DARK?
YOU SHOULD KNOW THAT WHEN YOU STROKE A CAT, STATIC ELECTRIC SPARKS JUMP FROM ITS FUR!
AND LATER... A SURPRISE FOR TIM LEARY!
YOU SAY TAG WON $5,000 IN A CAT SHOW? BUT HE DOESN'T EVEN HAVE A TAIL!
HE'S A PERFECT SPECIMEN OF A MANX CAT--A TAILLESS BREED FROM THE ISLE OF MAN!
The End

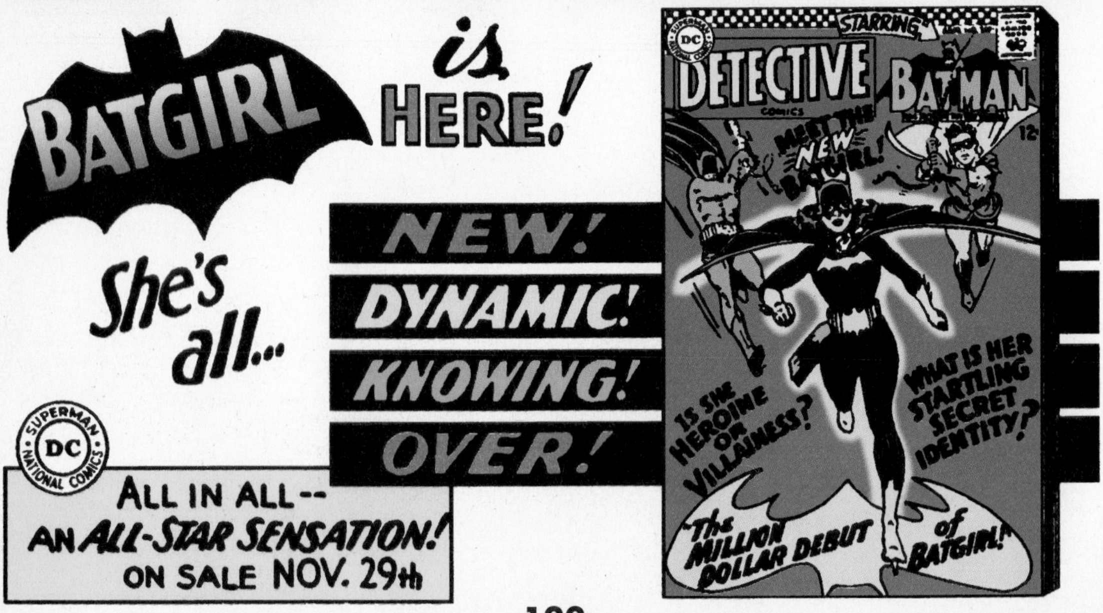
BATGIRL is HERE!
She's all...
NEW!
DYNAMIC!
KNOWING!
OVER!
ALL IN ALL--
AN ALL-STAR SENSATION!
ON SALE NOV. 29th
STARRING
DETECTIVE COMICS
BATMAN
12¢
MEET THE NEW BATGIRL!
IS SHE HEROINE OR VILLAINESS?
WHAT IS HER STARTLING SECRET IDENTITY?
"The MILLION DOLLAR DEBUT of BATGIRL!"

THE BATMOBILE IN THE SIXTIES

It started out as a blue roadster in 1939 and evolved into one of Batman's most often used crime-fighting accessories. Even Batman needed a way to get around Gotham City. Described as a "black thunderbolt on wheels, a swift nemesis to lawbreakers, a mighty machine of justice," it was called the Batmobile.

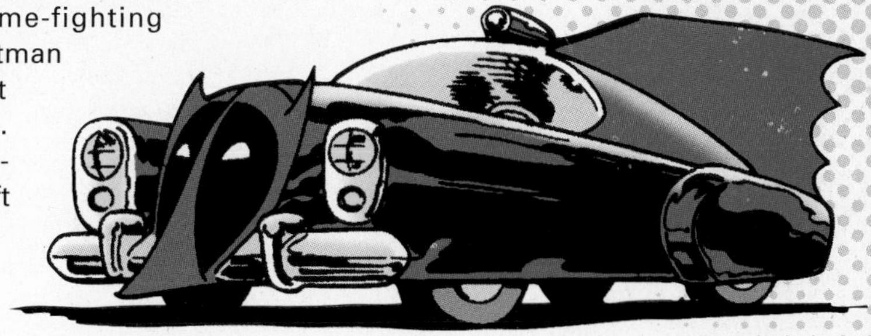

This customized vehicle could reach a speed of 100 miles per hour in 100 feet and stop on a dime. It was ten years ahead of anything else on wheels, according to the Caped Crusader himself. The special crime-fighting devices housed within included a closed-circuit television, a radar screen, a crime lab and a knife-edged steel nose on the bat-head grille, for making short work of any obstacles the car might encounter. This Batmobile was one that Batman and Robin designed to replace the one that had been destroyed in a high-speed auto chase in DETECTIVE COMICS #156.

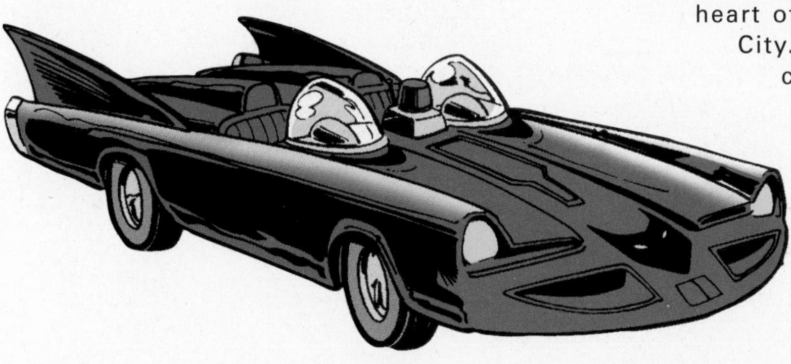

The Batmobile remained unchanged until it was replaced in BATMAN #164 by a smaller, sportier, more maneuverable car.

This Batmobile had the same crime-fighting equipment as its predecessor and more. A hot-line phone to police headquarters, a dashboard button for opening the concealed entrance to the Batcave, and an anti-theft device were just a few of the new options.

In BATMAN #217 Dick Grayson left for college. Bruce Wayne and Alfred closed Wayne Manor and moved into the heart of downtown Gotham City. Batman once again chose to upgrade his transportation, this time to a sleek, turbo-charged sports car. This model featured a remote control device and a one-way mirrored windshield and window devices for creating smoke screens.

Subsequent years brought further changes, but with the exception of the early years of its creation, the sixties remain the Batmobile's most radical decade of evolution.

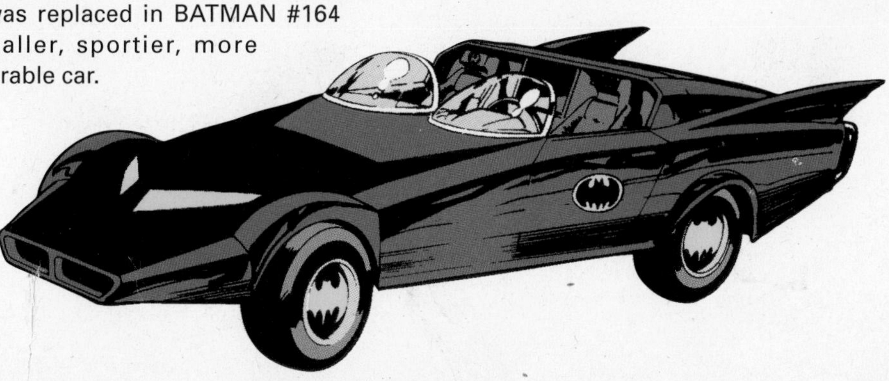

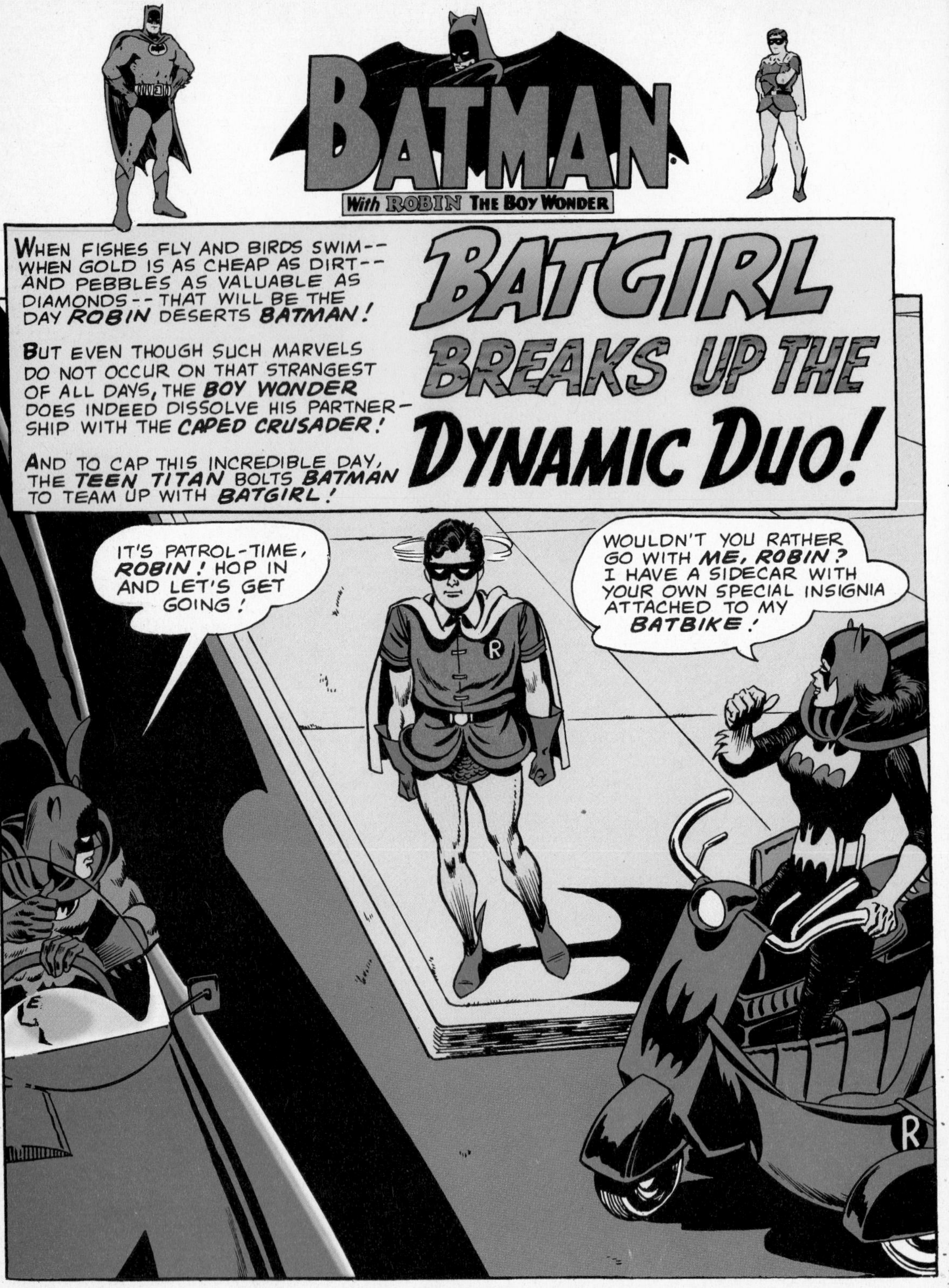
BATMAN
With ROBIN THE BOY WONDER
WHEN FISHES FLY AND BIRDS SWIM-- WHEN GOLD IS AS CHEAP AS DIRT-- AND PEBBLES AS VALUABLE AS DIAMONDS--THAT WILL BE THE DAY ROBIN DESERTS BATMAN!
BUT EVEN THOUGH SUCH MARVELS DO NOT OCCUR ON THAT STRANGEST OF ALL DAYS, THE BOY WONDER DOES INDEED DISSOLVE HIS PARTNERSHIP WITH THE CAPED CRUSADER!
AND TO CAP THIS INCREDIBLE DAY, THE TEEN TITAN BOLTS BATMAN TO TEAM UP WITH BATGIRL!
BATGIRL BREAKS UP THE DYNAMIC DUO!
IT'S PATROL-TIME, ROBIN! HOP IN AND LET'S GET GOING!
WOULDN'T YOU RATHER GO WITH ME, ROBIN? I HAVE A SIDECAR WITH YOUR OWN SPECIAL INSIGNIA ATTACHED TO MY BATBIKE!

ONE NIGHT ON A STRETCH OF COUNTRY ROAD OUTSIDE *GOTHAM CITY* A MOTORCYCLIST WAITS BEHIND A BILLBOARD...

HERE COMES A SPEEDING CAR NOW!

THE CLEANER SOAP

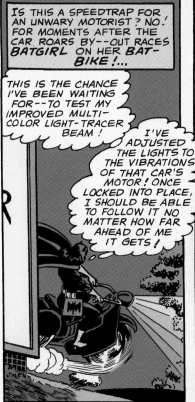

IS THIS A SPEEDTRAP FOR AN UNWARY MOTORIST? NO! FOR MOMENTS AFTER THE CAR ROARS BY--OUT RACES *BATGIRL* ON HER *BAT-BIKE!*...

THIS IS THE CHANCE I'VE BEEN WAITING FOR--TO TEST MY IMPROVED MULTI-COLOR LIGHT-TRACER BEAM!

I'VE ADJUSTED THE LIGHTS TO THE VIBRATIONS OF THAT CAR'S MOTOR! ONCE LOCKED INTO PLACE, I SHOULD BE ABLE TO FOLLOW IT NO MATTER HOW FAR AHEAD OF ME IT GETS!

SUDDENLY, THE *BAT-BIKE* BRAKES TO AN ALMOST INSTANT STOP AS...

STOP! HELP! SOME CROOKS JUST SHOVED ME OUT OF THEIR CAR!

WHY--IT'S *BATGIRL!* GET AFTER THEM-- THEY JUST ROBBED THE *GOTHAM GOTHIC ARTS MUSEUM!*

I'M ONE OF THE GUARDS--AND THEY GRABBED ME AS A HOSTAGE TO INSURE THEIR GETAWAY! SOON AS THEY GOT IN THE CLEAR, THEY LET ME GO!

BUT NEVER MIND ME! I'M ALL RIGHT! JUST GO GET THOSE CROOKS, *BATGIRL!*

PICKING UP THE THIEVES' TRAIL, *BATGIRL* ROCKETS INTO THE AREA KNOWN AS *MISTY SWAMP*...

THEY CROSSED OVER THAT BRIDGE UP AHEAD!

I MUST BE CLOSING IN ON THEM! MY LIGHT-BEAMS ARE INCREASING IN INTENSITY!

BUT WHEN THE MOTORBIKE SPEEDS ACROSS THE CRUDE WOODEN BRIDGE...

OHHH!

THE BRIDGE IS-- SINKING! THE WATER SLOWING ME DOWN...

I--MAY--NOT-- BE--ABLE--TO-- MAKE--IT--TO THE--OTHER--SIDE!

2

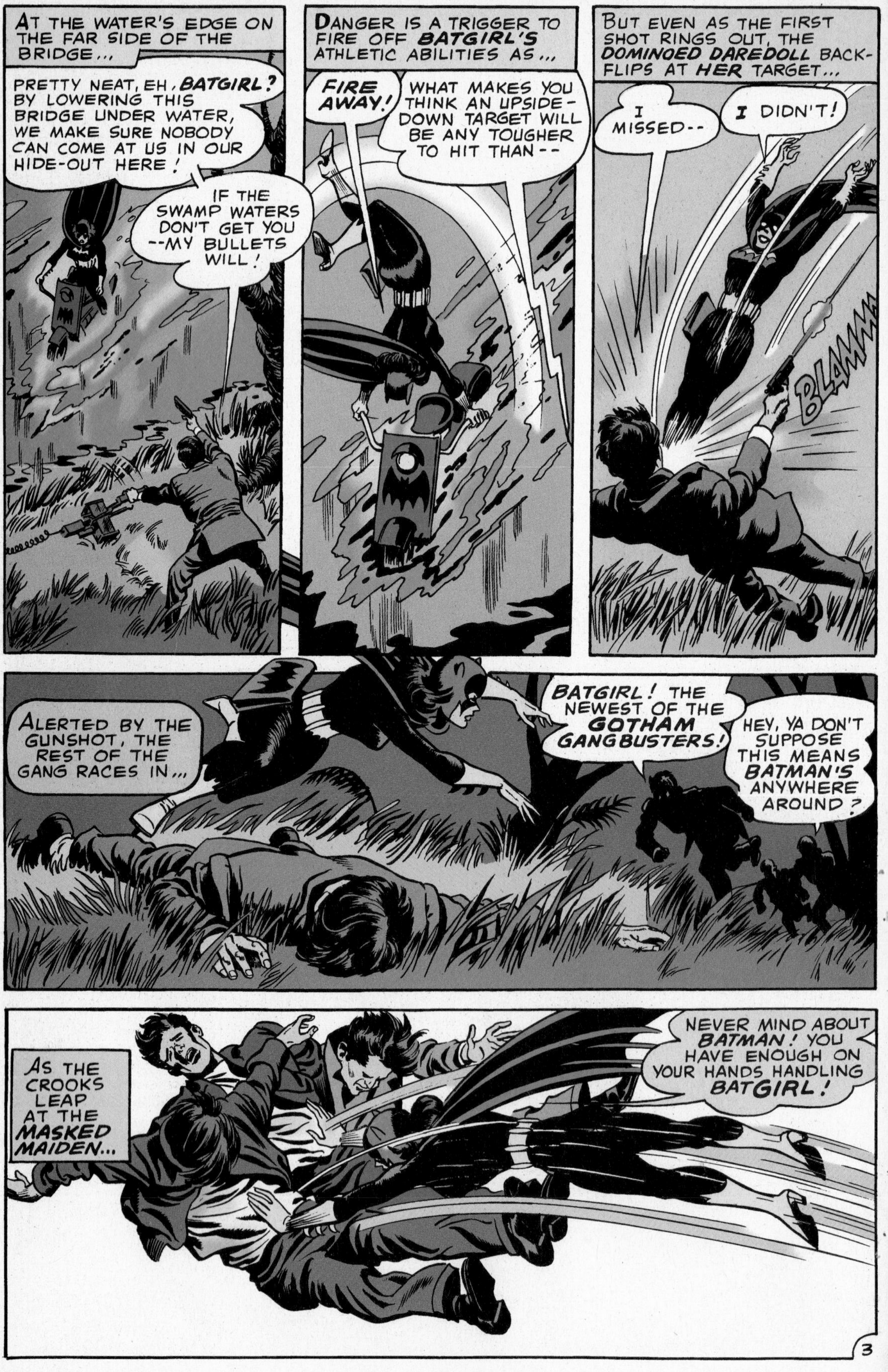
AT THE WATER'S EDGE ON THE FAR SIDE OF THE BRIDGE...
PRETTY NEAT, EH, BATGIRL? BY LOWERING THIS BRIDGE UNDER WATER, WE MAKE SURE NOBODY CAN COME AT US IN OUR HIDE-OUT HERE!
IF THE SWAMP WATERS DON'T GET YOU --MY BULLETS WILL!
DANGER IS A TRIGGER TO FIRE OFF BATGIRL'S ATHLETIC ABILITIES AS...
FIRE AWAY!
WHAT MAKES YOU THINK AN UPSIDE-DOWN TARGET WILL BE ANY TOUGHER TO HIT THAN--
BUT EVEN AS THE FIRST SHOT RINGS OUT, THE DOMINOED DAREDOLL BACK-FLIPS AT HER TARGET...
I MISSED--
I DIDN'T!
BLAMMM
ALERTED BY THE GUNSHOT, THE REST OF THE GANG RACES IN...
BATGIRL! THE NEWEST OF THE GOTHAM GANGBUSTERS!
HEY, YA DON'T SUPPOSE THIS MEANS BATMAN'S ANYWHERE AROUND?
AS THE CROOKS LEAP AT THE MASKED MAIDEN...
NEVER MIND ABOUT BATMAN! YOU HAVE ENOUGH ON YOUR HANDS HANDLING BATGIRL!
3

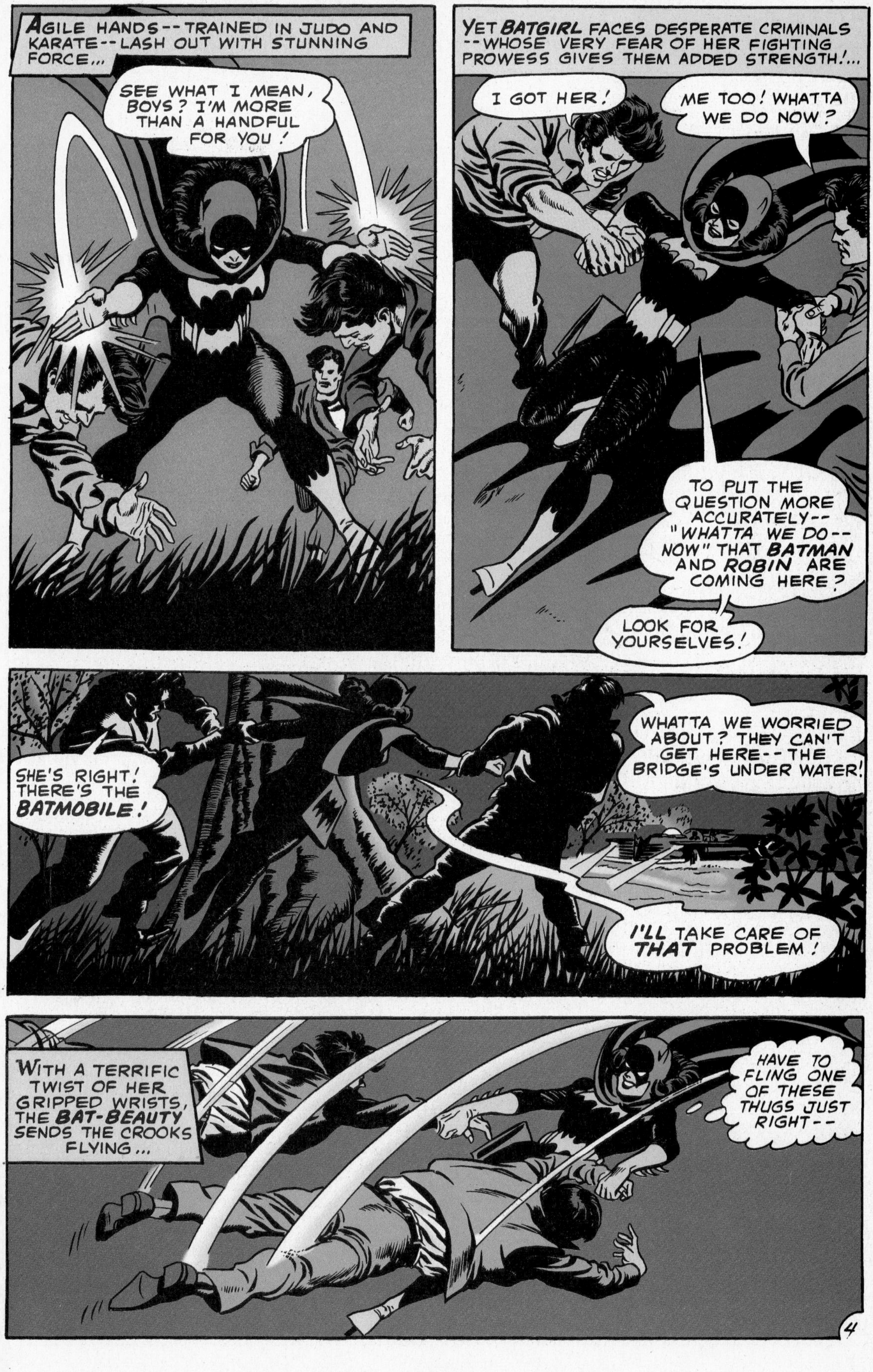
AGILE HANDS--TRAINED IN JUDO AND KARATE--LASH OUT WITH STUNNING FORCE...
SEE WHAT I MEAN, BOYS? I'M MORE THAN A HANDFUL FOR YOU!
YET BATGIRL FACES DESPERATE CRIMINALS --WHOSE VERY FEAR OF HER FIGHTING PROWESS GIVES THEM ADDED STRENGTH!...
I GOT HER!
ME TOO! WHATTA WE DO NOW?
TO PUT THE QUESTION MORE ACCURATELY-- "WHATTA WE DO--NOW" THAT BATMAN AND ROBIN ARE COMING HERE?
LOOK FOR YOURSELVES!
SHE'S RIGHT! THERE'S THE BATMOBILE!
WHATTA WE WORRIED ABOUT? THEY CAN'T GET HERE--THE BRIDGE'S UNDER WATER!
I'LL TAKE CARE OF THAT PROBLEM!
WITH A TERRIFIC TWIST OF HER GRIPPED WRISTS, THE BAT-BEAUTY SENDS THE CROOKS FLYING...
HAVE TO FLING ONE OF THESE THUGS JUST RIGHT--
4

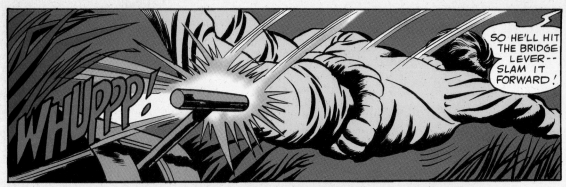

WHUPPP!

SO HE'LL HIT THE BRIDGE LEVER-- SLAM IT FORWARD!

AND MOMENTS LATER THE BRIDGE RISES-- ENABLING THE *BATMOBILE* TO SPEED ACROSS IT...

NICE GOING, *BATGIRL!*

YOU CAN RELAX NOW--WHILE *WE* TAKE OVER!

A RAPID-FIRE *DYNAMIC DUO* ONSLAUGHT-- WITH *BATMAN* DISPOSING OF THE FINAL CROOK...

SPLAASH!

BUT AS THE SOFT MUD OF THE SWAMP ISLAND GIVES WAY BEFORE THE HEAVILY MUSCLED BODY OF THE *CAPED CRUSADER*...

MY FOOT SLIPPED--

I'M TAKING A HEADER INTO THE SWAMP WATERS!

READY HANDS ARE EXTENDED TO THE FLOUNDERING CRIME-FIGHTER...

GRAB HOLD, *BATMAN!* WE'LL HAVE YOU OUT OF THERE IN A JIFFY!

BRRR... THIS WATER'S NOT THAT COLD! WHY AM I SHIVERING?

5

AND IN ANSWER TO MUTUAL QUESTIONS ON WHAT BROUGHT EACH OF THEM TO THIS PLACE...

...AND SO THE TESTING OF MY *MULTICOLOR TRACKER BEAM* LED ME ONTO THE TRAIL OF THESE CROOKS AND THEIR *SWAMPLAND HIDEAWAY!*

...WHILE OUR INVESTIGATION OF A SUDDEN, MYSTERIOUS INTERFERENCE WITH OUR *BATMOBILE'S* ELECTRONIC DEVICE LED *US* HERE!

BATMAN'S CHILLS --FOLLOWED BY THAT *MUSTARD COMPLEXION* ON HIS FACE! IS IT POSSIBLE--?

IT'S CLEAR NOW THAT YOUR NEW TRACKER BEAM CAUSED THE INTERFERENCE! YOU'LL HAVE TO MAKE AN ADJUSTMENT IN IT...

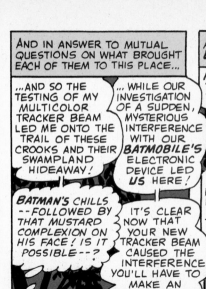

AS THE *MASKED MANHUNTER BATCUFFS* THE CRIMINALS...

ROBIN, I'M AFRAID THERE'S SOMETHING WRONG WITH *BATMAN!*

SOMETHING WRONG...? BUT *WHAT?*

CAN'T TELL YOU NOW--BUT LET ME KNOW WHAT ROUTE YOU'RE SCHEDULED TO TAKE TOMORROW NIGHT IN THE *BATMOBILE* SO I CAN TRAIL YOU!

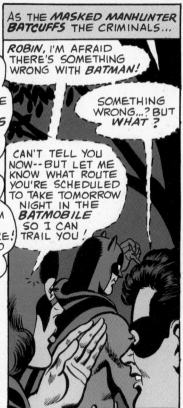

SSSSH! HERE HE COMES!

ALL RIGHT, YOU TWO-- BREAK IT UP! LET'S GET GOING!

WONDER WHAT THEY WERE GABBING ABOUT?

NEXT DAY, HEAD LIBRARIAN BARBARA *(BATGIRL)* GORDON, PH. D., IS HARD AT WORK IN THE MEDICAL RESEARCH DIVISION OF THE *GOTHAM CITY LIBRARY...*

WHAT I BELIEVE HAPPENED TO *BATMAN* IS TOO IMPORTANT TO RELY ON MY PHOTOGRAPHIC MEMORY...

YES-- THE INITIAL SYMPTOMS ARE THE SAME-- CHILLS AND MUSTARD-COLOR COMPLEXION-- WHICH QUICKLY DISAPPEAR!

BATMAN'S COMING DOWN WITH A TYPE OF *SWAMP FEVER!*

RIGHT NOW HE'S GOING THROUGH AN INCUBATION PERIOD OF FROM ONE TO SEVEN DAYS--WHEN NOT EVEN A DOCTOR CAN HELP HIM! WHEN HE GETS THE FULL FEVER, HE'S GOING TO *COLLAPSE!*

IF HE SHOULD COLLAPSE DURING THE DAY, THERE'S NO SERIOUS PROBLEM! BUT -- IF IT HAPPENS AT *NIGHT*, WHEN HE'S FIGHTING CROOKS -- HE'LL BE UNABLE TO DEFEND HIMSELF AND -- OH! I HATE TO THINK WHAT WILL HAPPEN TO HIM!

IT'S UP TO *ME* TO BE *BATMAN'S* SECRET *"GUARDIAN ANGEL"* -- SO THERE GO MY DATE-NIGHTS FOR THE NEXT SEVEN DAYS!

6

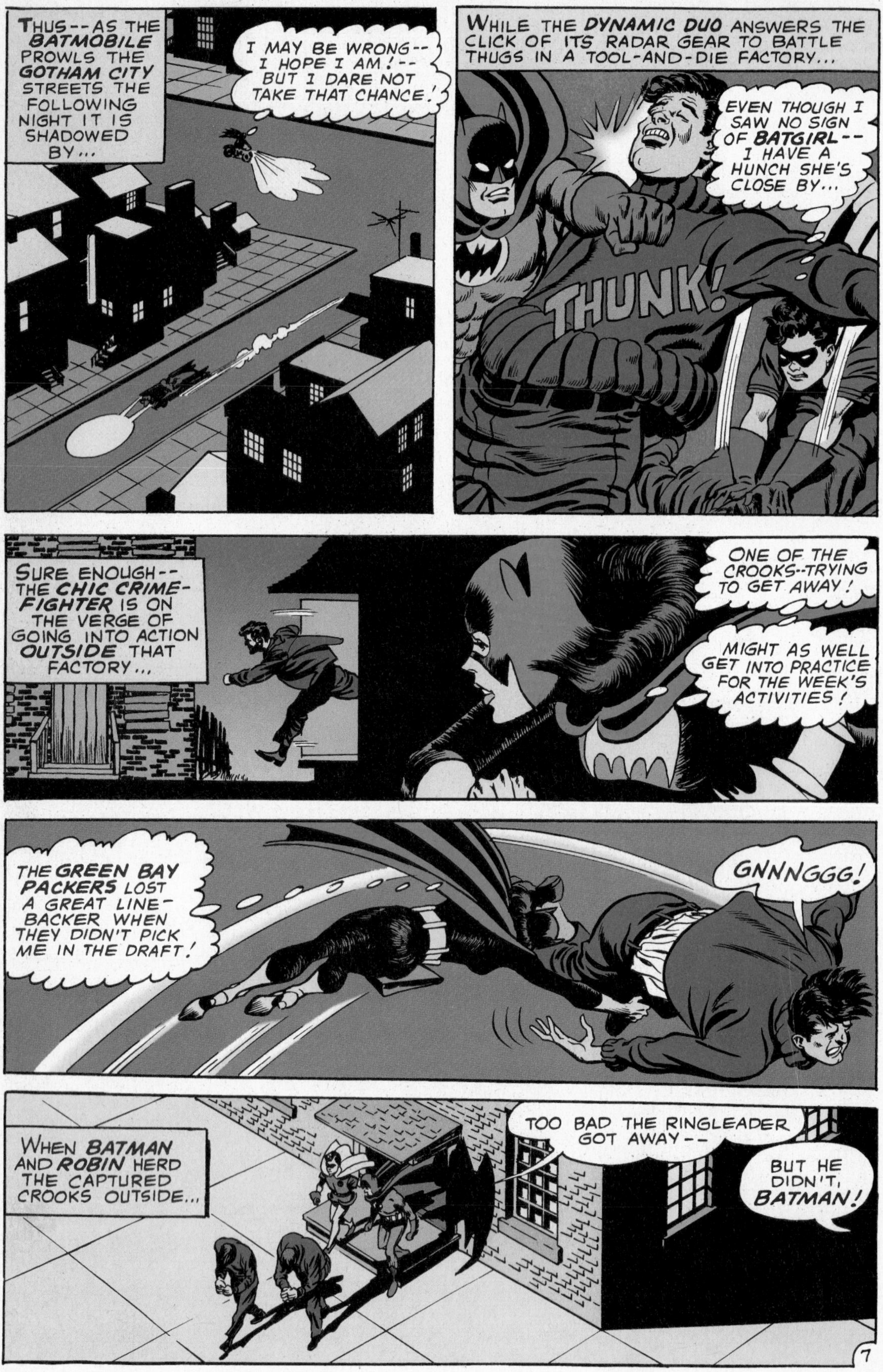

THUS--AS THE BATMOBILE PROWLS THE GOTHAM CITY STREETS THE FOLLOWING NIGHT IT IS SHADOWED BY...
I MAY BE WRONG-- I HOPE I AM!-- BUT I DARE NOT TAKE THAT CHANCE!
WHILE THE DYNAMIC DUO ANSWERS THE CLICK OF ITS RADAR GEAR TO BATTLE THUGS IN A TOOL-AND-DIE FACTORY...
EVEN THOUGH I SAW NO SIGN OF BATGIRL-- I HAVE A HUNCH SHE'S CLOSE BY...
THUNK!
SURE ENOUGH-- THE CHIC CRIME-FIGHTER IS ON THE VERGE OF GOING INTO ACTION OUTSIDE THAT FACTORY...
ONE OF THE CROOKS--TRYING TO GET AWAY!
MIGHT AS WELL GET INTO PRACTICE FOR THE WEEK'S ACTIVITIES!
THE GREEN BAY PACKERS LOST A GREAT LINE-BACKER WHEN THEY DIDN'T PICK ME IN THE DRAFT!
GNNNGGG!
WHEN BATMAN AND ROBIN HERD THE CAPTURED CROOKS OUTSIDE...
TOO BAD THE RINGLEADER GOT AWAY--
BUT HE DIDN'T, BATMAN!
7

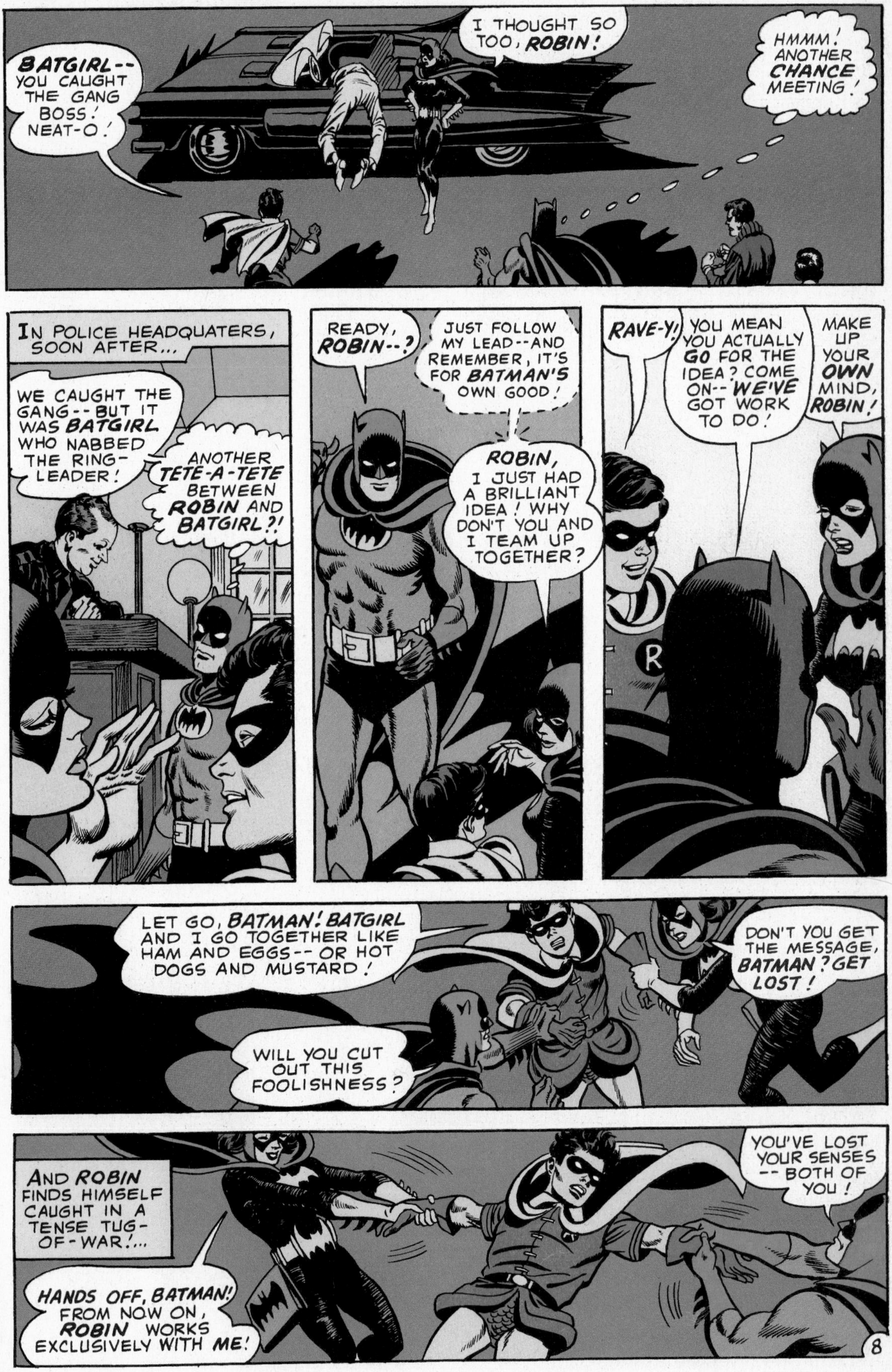
BATGIRL-- YOU CAUGHT THE GANG BOSS! NEAT-O!
I THOUGHT SO TOO, ROBIN!
HMMM! ANOTHER CHANCE MEETING!
IN POLICE HEADQUATERS, SOON AFTER...
WE CAUGHT THE GANG--BUT IT WAS BATGIRL WHO NABBED THE RING-LEADER!
ANOTHER TETE-A-TETE BETWEEN ROBIN AND BATGIRL?!
READY, ROBIN--?
JUST FOLLOW MY LEAD--AND REMEMBER, IT'S FOR BATMAN'S OWN GOOD!
ROBIN, I JUST HAD A BRILLIANT IDEA! WHY DON'T YOU AND I TEAM UP TOGETHER?
RAVE-Y!
YOU MEAN YOU ACTUALLY GO FOR THE IDEA? COME ON--WE'VE GOT WORK TO DO!
MAKE UP YOUR OWN MIND, ROBIN!
LET GO, BATMAN! BATGIRL AND I GO TOGETHER LIKE HAM AND EGGS--OR HOT DOGS AND MUSTARD!
DON'T YOU GET THE MESSAGE, BATMAN? GET LOST!
WILL YOU CUT OUT THIS FOOLISHNESS?
AND ROBIN FINDS HIMSELF CAUGHT IN A TENSE TUG-OF-WAR!...
YOU'VE LOST YOUR SENSES--BOTH OF YOU!
HANDS OFF, BATMAN! FROM NOW ON, ROBIN WORKS EXCLUSIVELY WITH ME!
8

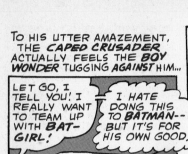

To his utter amazement, the *Caped Crusader* actually feels the *Boy Wonder* tugging against him...

LET GO, I TELL YOU! I REALLY WANT TO TEAM UP WITH *BAT-GIRL!*

I HATE DOING THIS TO *BATMAN*-- BUT IT'S FOR HIS OWN GOOD!

ALL RIGHT--IF THAT'S THE WAY YOU WANT IT...

YOU WON'T BE SORRY, *ROBIN!*

WE'LL START OUR TEAM-UP TOMORROW NIGHT--AT EIGHT O'CLOCK!

DON'T TELL ME *ROBIN'S* GOING TO HAVE HER PICK HIM UP AT THE *BAT-CAVE?* BESIDES, HOW'S SHE EXPECT TO DRIVE HIM AROUND ON THAT MOTOR-BIKE BUILT FOR *ONE?*

TELL YOU WHAT, *ROBIN!* LET'S MEET RIGHT HERE AT POLICE HEAD-QUARTERS!

WHAT-EVER YOU SAY, *BAT-GIRL!* I'LL BE HERE...

I'LL BE HERE TOO-- IF ONLY TO SEE HOW *BATGIRL* PLANS TO GO ABOUT IT!

In a strained silence--with *Batgirl* on her motorbike secretly shadowing them along the city streets-- the *Dynamic Duo* completes its uneventful last patrol ...

HOW COULD *ROBIN* DO THIS TO ME? WHAT'S HE THINKING OF--EXCHANGING *ME* FOR *BATGIRL?*

UNLESS...

LOOKS LIKE *BATMAN* IS TAKING IT HARD! BUT IT WOULDN'T DO ANY GOOD TO TELL HIM THE REAL REASON BEHIND THIS!

HE WOULDN'T QUIT AND TAKE IT EASY THE REST OF THE WEEK! RATHER THAN "LIE DOWN" ON THE JOB, HE'D KEEP ON GOING --NO MATTER WHAT DANGERS WERE IN STORE FOR HIM!

ROBIN'S GOT A *CRUSH* ON *BATGIRL!* SURE, *THAT'S* THE ANSWER!

I'LL JUST HAVE TO WAIT UNTIL HE'S OVER IT!

THE FOLLOWING EVENING...

ALMOST READY FOR OUR PATROLS, BRUCE! HOW'S ABOUT DROPPING ME OFF AT POLICE HEADQUARTERS IN THE *BATMOBILE?*

DICK MAY HAVE LOST HIS SENSES -- BUT NOT HIS *NERVE!*

BUT I'LL SHOW HIM I'M A GOOD SPORT-- AS WELL AS A GOOD LOSER!

CRIME WAVE IN GOTHAM

9

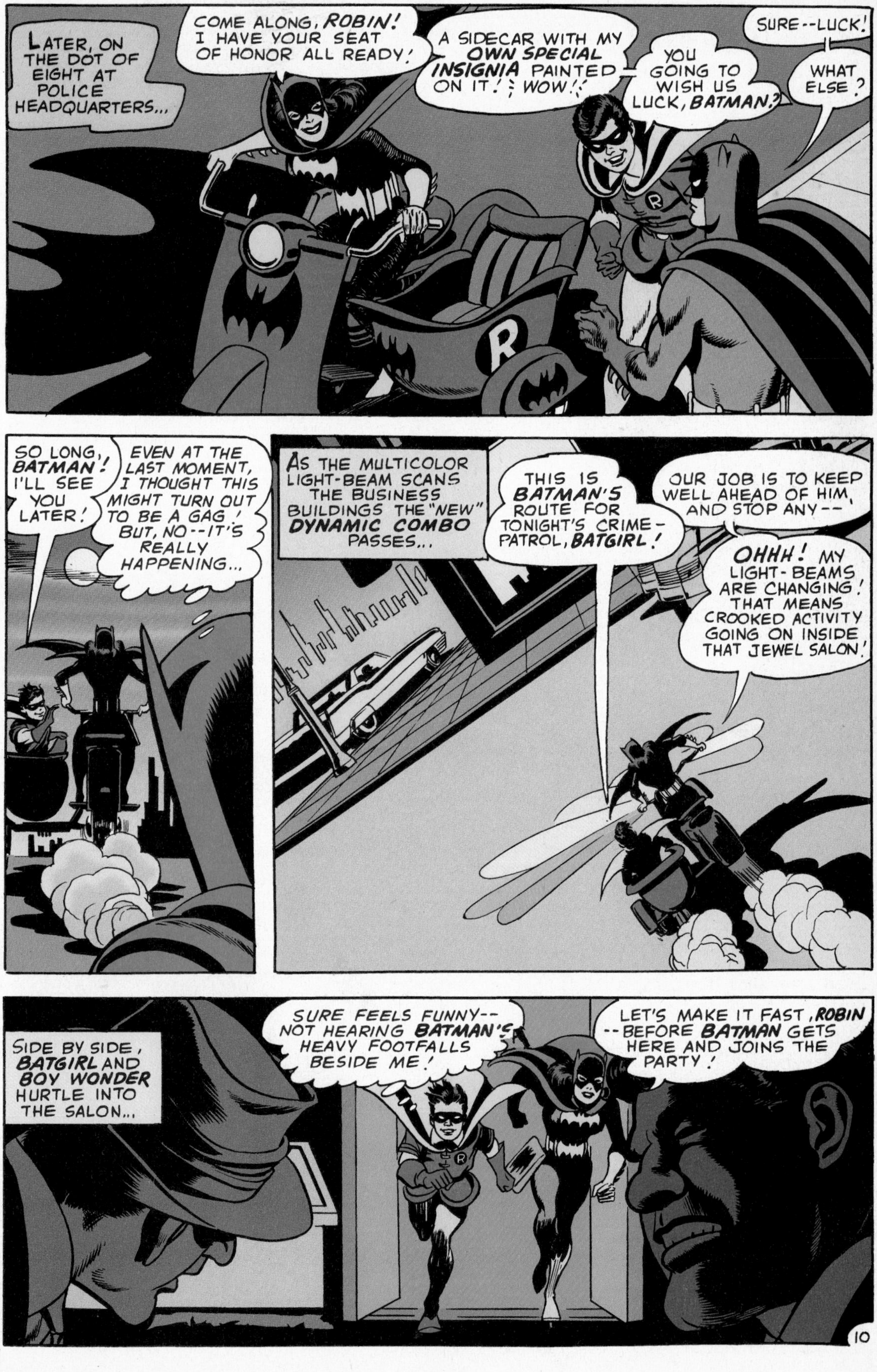
LATER, ON THE DOT OF EIGHT AT POLICE HEADQUARTERS...
COME ALONG, ROBIN! I HAVE YOUR SEAT OF HONOR ALL READY!
A SIDECAR WITH MY OWN SPECIAL INSIGNIA PAINTED ON IT! -- WOW!
YOU GOING TO WISH US LUCK, BATMAN?
SURE--LUCK!
WHAT ELSE?
SO LONG, BATMAN! I'LL SEE YOU LATER!
EVEN AT THE LAST MOMENT, I THOUGHT THIS MIGHT TURN OUT TO BE A GAG! BUT, NO--IT'S REALLY HAPPENING...
AS THE MULTICOLOR LIGHT-BEAM SCANS THE BUSINESS BUILDINGS THE "NEW" DYNAMIC COMBO PASSES...
THIS IS BATMAN'S ROUTE FOR TONIGHT'S CRIME-PATROL, BATGIRL!
OUR JOB IS TO KEEP WELL AHEAD OF HIM, AND STOP ANY--
OHHH! MY LIGHT-BEAMS ARE CHANGING! THAT MEANS CROOKED ACTIVITY GOING ON INSIDE THAT JEWEL SALON!
SIDE BY SIDE, BATGIRL AND BOY WONDER HURTLE INTO THE SALON...
SURE FEELS FUNNY--NOT HEARING BATMAN'S HEAVY FOOTFALLS BESIDE ME!
LET'S MAKE IT FAST, ROBIN--BEFORE BATMAN GETS HERE AND JOINS THE PARTY!
10

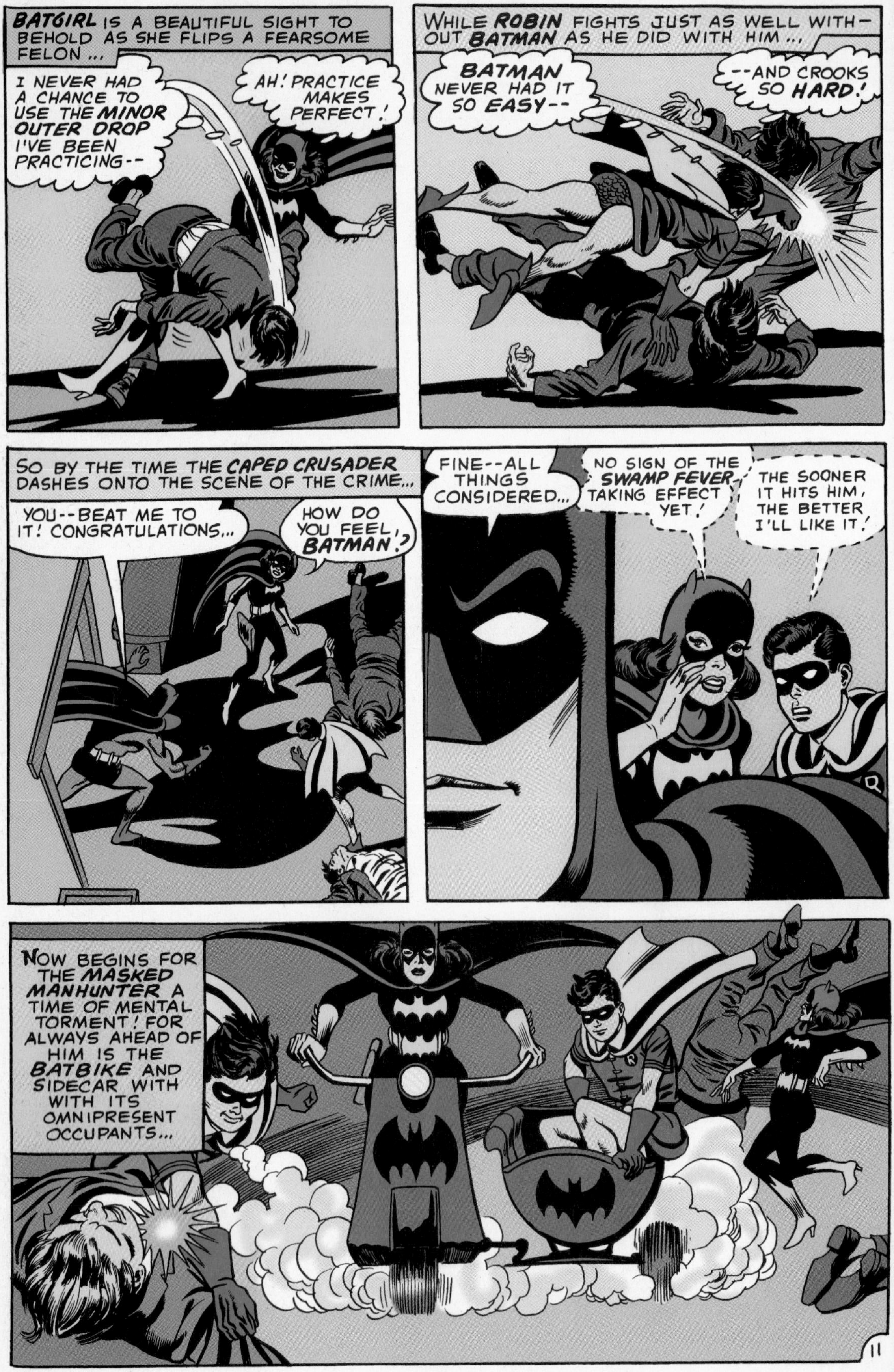
BATGIRL IS A BEAUTIFUL SIGHT TO BEHOLD AS SHE FLIPS A FEARSOME FELON ...
I NEVER HAD A CHANCE TO USE THE MINOR OUTER DROP I'VE BEEN PRACTICING--
AH! PRACTICE MAKES PERFECT!
WHILE ROBIN FIGHTS JUST AS WELL WITH-OUT BATMAN AS HE DID WITH HIM ...
BATMAN NEVER HAD IT SO EASY--
--AND CROOKS SO HARD!
SO BY THE TIME THE CAPED CRUSADER DASHES ONTO THE SCENE OF THE CRIME...
YOU--BEAT ME TO IT! CONGRATULATIONS...
HOW DO YOU FEEL, BATMAN?
FINE--ALL THINGS CONSIDERED...
NO SIGN OF THE SWAMP FEVER TAKING EFFECT YET!
THE SOONER IT HITS HIM, THE BETTER I'LL LIKE IT!
NOW BEGINS FOR THE MASKED MANHUNTER A TIME OF MENTAL TORMENT! FOR ALWAYS AHEAD OF HIM IS THE BATBIKE AND SIDECAR WITH WITH ITS OMNIPRESENT OCCUPANTS...
11

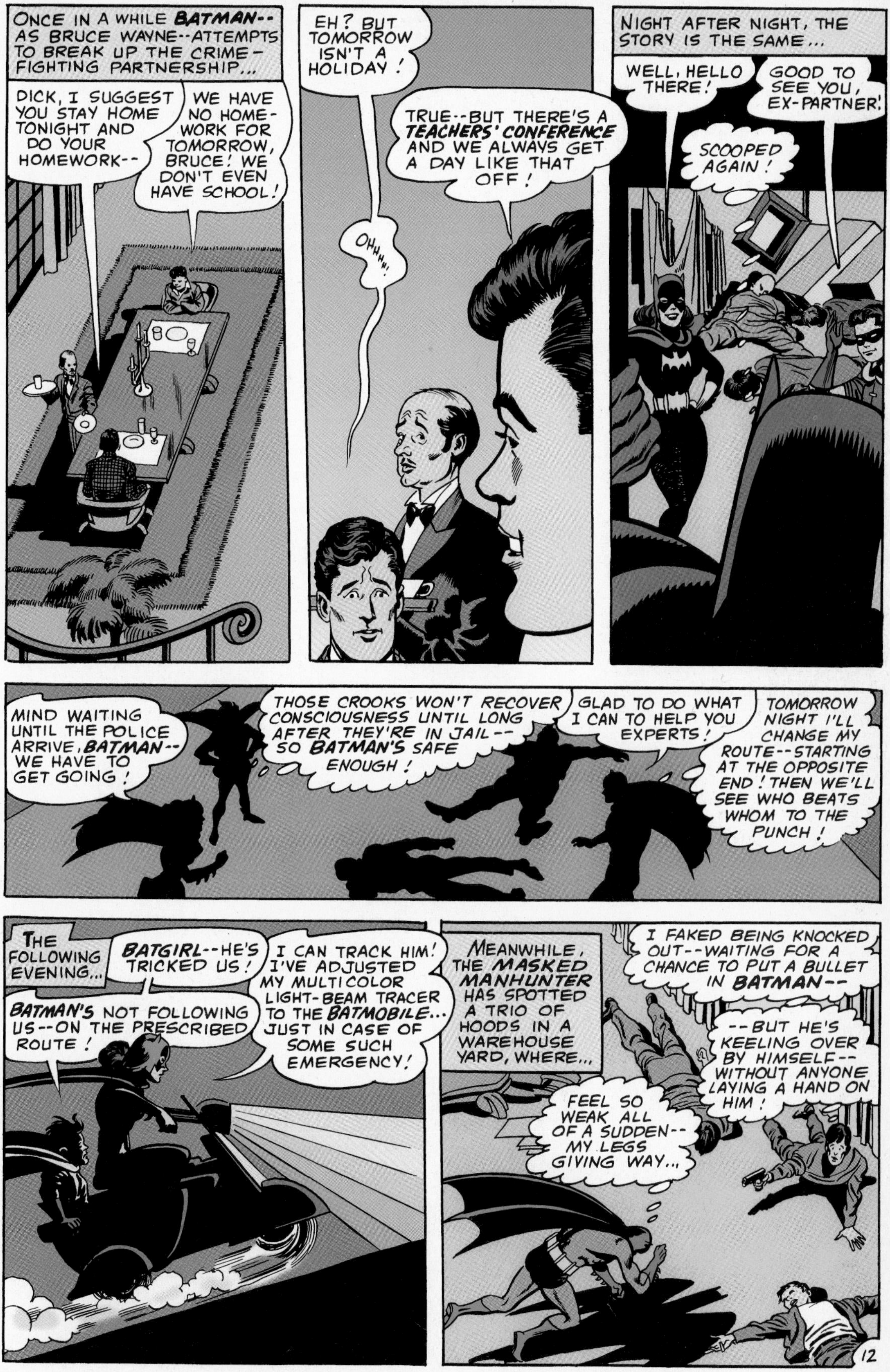

ONCE IN A WHILE BATMAN-- AS BRUCE WAYNE--ATTEMPTS TO BREAK UP THE CRIME-FIGHTING PARTNERSHIP...
DICK, I SUGGEST YOU STAY HOME TONIGHT AND DO YOUR HOMEWORK--
WE HAVE NO HOME-WORK FOR TOMORROW, BRUCE! WE DON'T EVEN HAVE SCHOOL!
EH? BUT TOMORROW ISN'T A HOLIDAY!
TRUE--BUT THERE'S A TEACHERS' CONFERENCE AND WE ALWAYS GET A DAY LIKE THAT OFF!
OHHHH!
NIGHT AFTER NIGHT, THE STORY IS THE SAME...
WELL, HELLO THERE!
GOOD TO SEE YOU, EX-PARTNER!
SCOOPED AGAIN!
MIND WAITING UNTIL THE POLICE ARRIVE, BATMAN-- WE HAVE TO GET GOING!
THOSE CROOKS WON'T RECOVER CONSCIOUSNESS UNTIL LONG AFTER THEY'RE IN JAIL-- SO BATMAN'S SAFE ENOUGH!
GLAD TO DO WHAT I CAN TO HELP YOU EXPERTS!
TOMORROW NIGHT I'LL CHANGE MY ROUTE--STARTING AT THE OPPOSITE END! THEN WE'LL SEE WHO BEATS WHOM TO THE PUNCH!
THE FOLLOWING EVENING...
BATGIRL--HE'S TRICKED US!
BATMAN'S NOT FOLLOWING US--ON THE PRESCRIBED ROUTE!
I CAN TRACK HIM! I'VE ADJUSTED MY MULTICOLOR LIGHT-BEAM TRACER TO THE BATMOBILE... JUST IN CASE OF SOME SUCH EMERGENCY!
MEANWHILE, THE MASKED MANHUNTER HAS SPOTTED A TRIO OF HOODS IN A WAREHOUSE YARD, WHERE...
I FAKED BEING KNOCKED OUT--WAITING FOR A CHANCE TO PUT A BULLET IN BATMAN--
--BUT HE'S KEELING OVER BY HIMSELF--WITHOUT ANYONE LAYING A HAND ON HIM!
FEEL SO WEAK ALL OF A SUDDEN-- MY LEGS GIVING WAY...
12

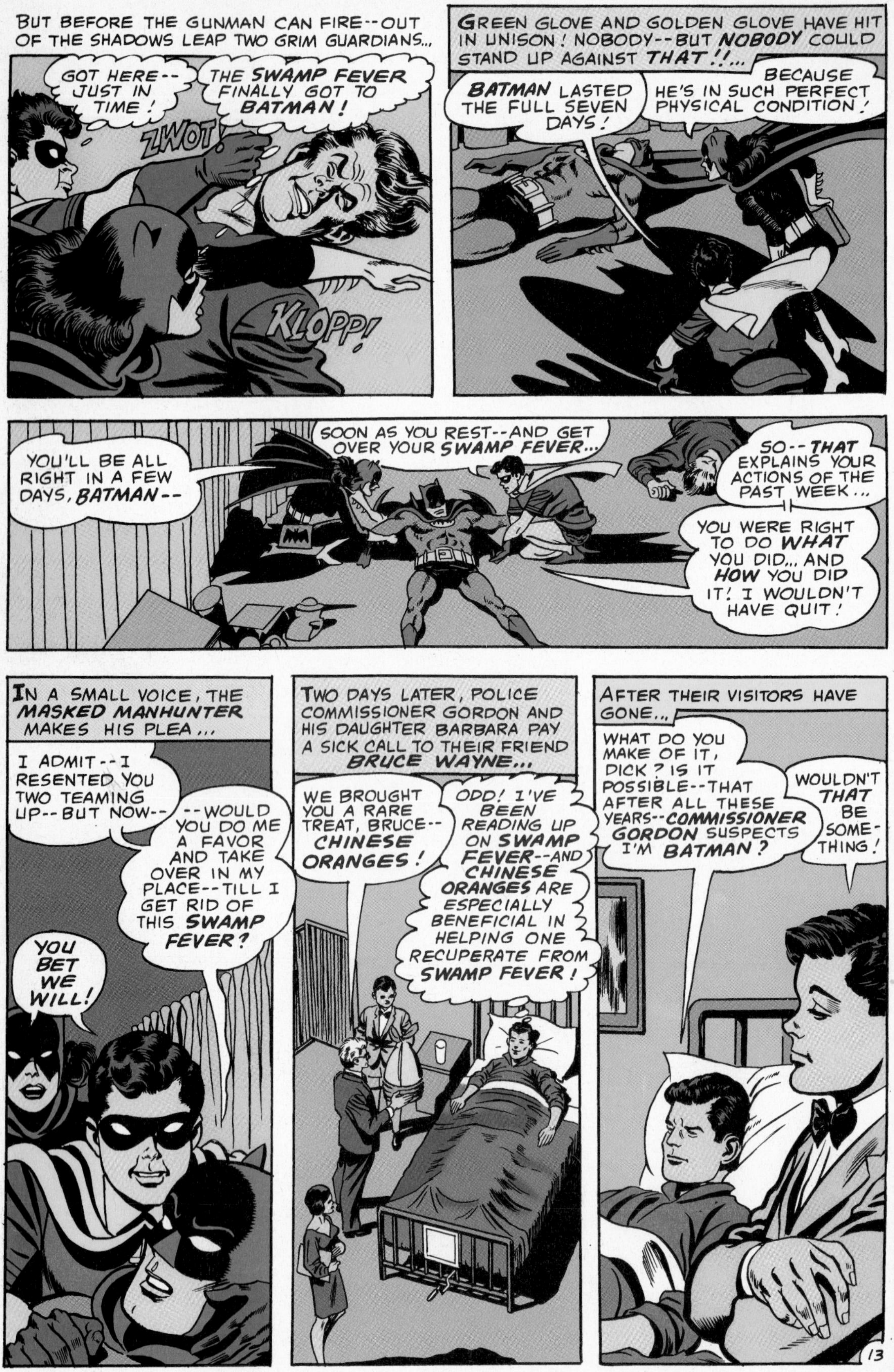

BUT BEFORE THE GUNMAN CAN FIRE--OUT OF THE SHADOWS LEAP TWO GRIM GUARDIANS...
GOT HERE--JUST IN TIME!
THE SWAMP FEVER FINALLY GOT TO BATMAN!
ZWOT!
KLOPP!
GREEN GLOVE AND GOLDEN GLOVE HAVE HIT IN UNISON! NOBODY--BUT NOBODY COULD STAND UP AGAINST THAT!!...
BATMAN LASTED THE FULL SEVEN DAYS!
BECAUSE HE'S IN SUCH PERFECT PHYSICAL CONDITION!
YOU'LL BE ALL RIGHT IN A FEW DAYS, BATMAN--
SOON AS YOU REST--AND GET OVER YOUR SWAMP FEVER...
SO--THAT EXPLAINS YOUR ACTIONS OF THE PAST WEEK...
YOU WERE RIGHT TO DO WHAT YOU DID... AND HOW YOU DID IT! I WOULDN'T HAVE QUIT!
IN A SMALL VOICE, THE MASKED MANHUNTER MAKES HIS PLEA...
I ADMIT--I RESENTED YOU TWO TEAMING UP--BUT NOW--
--WOULD YOU DO ME A FAVOR AND TAKE OVER IN MY PLACE--TILL I GET RID OF THIS SWAMP FEVER?
YOU BET WE WILL!
TWO DAYS LATER, POLICE COMMISSIONER GORDON AND HIS DAUGHTER BARBARA PAY A SICK CALL TO THEIR FRIEND BRUCE WAYNE...
WE BROUGHT YOU A RARE TREAT, BRUCE--CHINESE ORANGES!
ODD! I'VE BEEN READING UP ON SWAMP FEVER--AND CHINESE ORANGES ARE ESPECIALLY BENEFICIAL IN HELPING ONE RECUPERATE FROM SWAMP FEVER!
AFTER THEIR VISITORS HAVE GONE...
WHAT DO YOU MAKE OF IT, DICK? IS IT POSSIBLE--THAT AFTER ALL THESE YEARS--COMMISSIONER GORDON SUSPECTS I'M BATMAN?
WOULDN'T THAT BE SOME-THING!
13

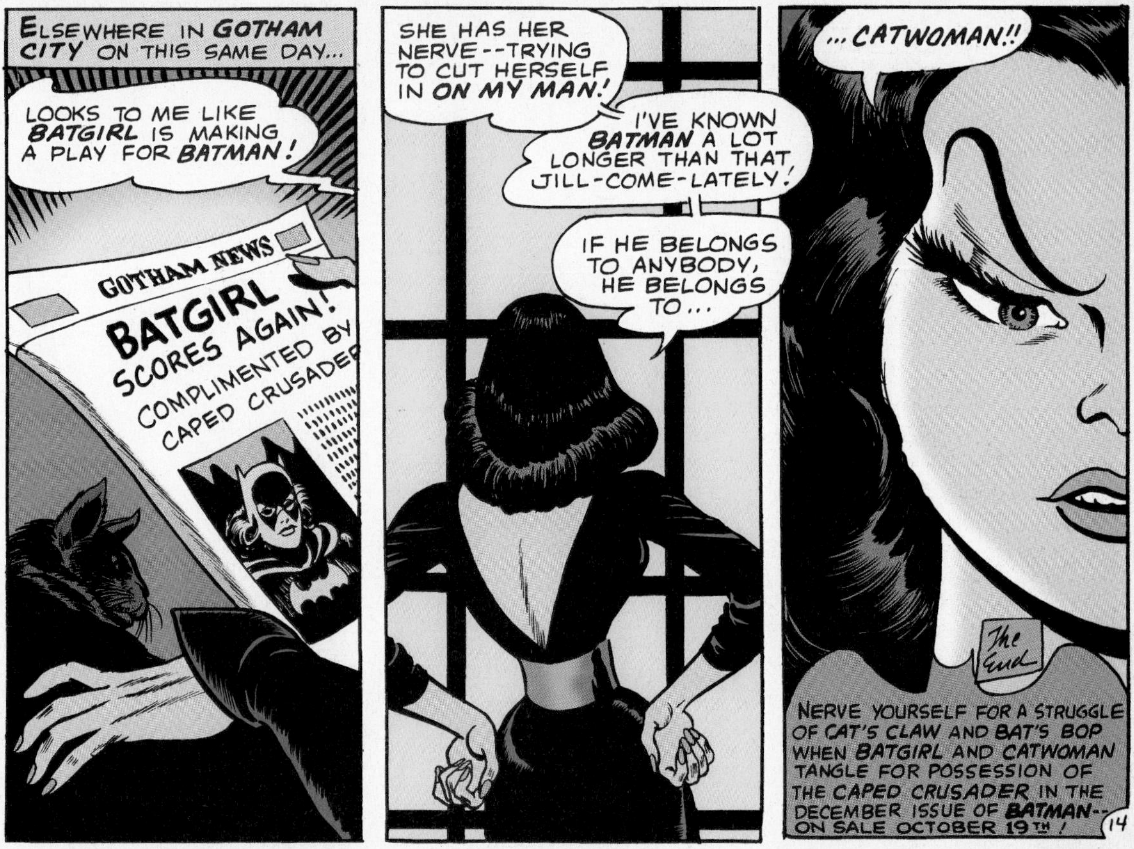
ELSEWHERE IN GOTHAM CITY ON THIS SAME DAY...
LOOKS TO ME LIKE BATGIRL IS MAKING A PLAY FOR BATMAN!
GOTHAM NEWS
BATGIRL SCORES AGAIN! COMPLIMENTED BY CAPED CRUSADE
SHE HAS HER NERVE--TRYING TO CUT HERSELF IN ON MY MAN!
I'VE KNOWN BATMAN A LOT LONGER THAN THAT JILL-COME-LATELY!
IF HE BELONGS TO ANYBODY, HE BELONGS TO...
...CATWOMAN!!
The End
NERVE YOURSELF FOR A STRUGGLE OF CAT'S CLAW AND BAT'S BOP WHEN BATGIRL AND CATWOMAN TANGLE FOR POSSESSION OF THE CAPED CRUSADER IN THE DECEMBER ISSUE OF BATMAN--ON SALE OCTOBER 19TH!
14

BARBARA GORDON'S TRANFORMATION TO BATGIRL!

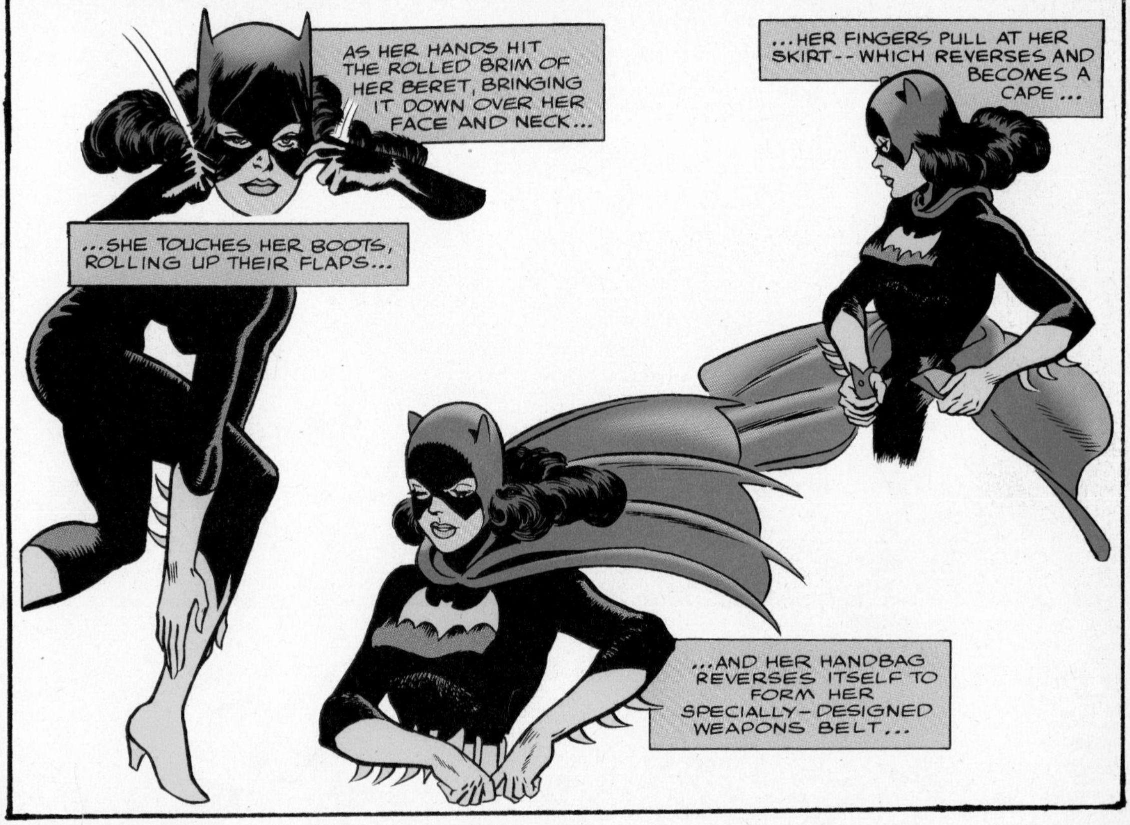
AS HER HANDS HIT THE ROLLED BRIM OF HER BERET, BRINGING IT DOWN OVER HER FACE AND NECK...
...HER FINGERS PULL AT HER SKIRT--WHICH REVERSES AND BECOMES A CAPE...
...SHE TOUCHES HER BOOTS, ROLLING UP THEIR FLAPS...
...AND HER HANDBAG REVERSES ITSELF TO FORM HER SPECIALLY-DESIGNED WEAPONS BELT...

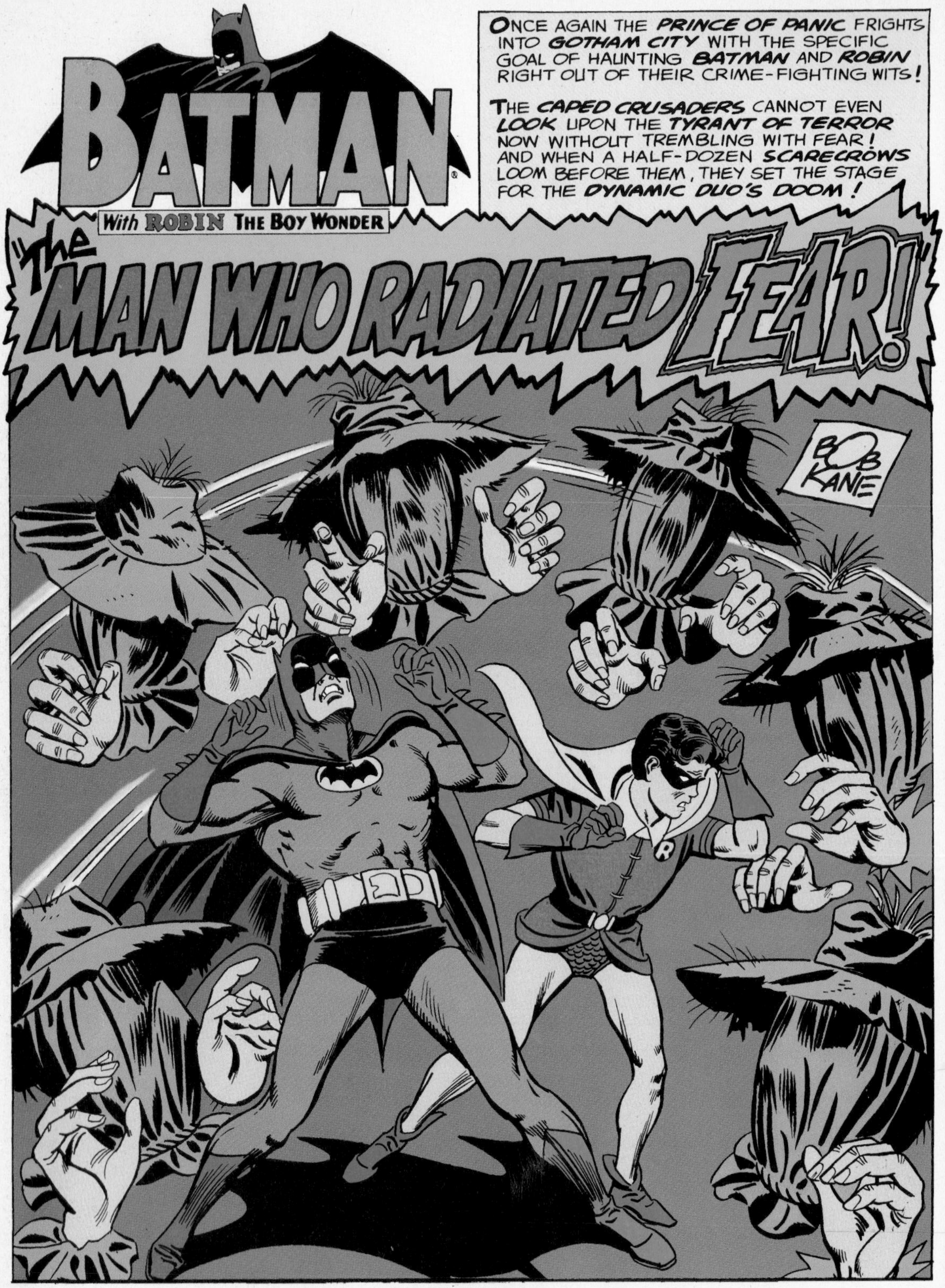
BATMAN
With ROBIN THE BOY WONDER
ONCE AGAIN THE PRINCE OF PANIC FRIGHTS INTO GOTHAM CITY WITH THE SPECIFIC GOAL OF HAUNTING BATMAN AND ROBIN RIGHT OUT OF THEIR CRIME-FIGHTING WITS!
THE CAPED CRUSADERS CANNOT EVEN LOOK UPON THE TYRANT OF TERROR NOW WITHOUT TREMBLING WITH FEAR! AND WHEN A HALF-DOZEN SCARECROWS LOOM BEFORE THEM, THEY SET THE STAGE FOR THE DYNAMIC DUO'S DOOM!
"The MAN WHO RADIATED FEAR!"
BOB KANE

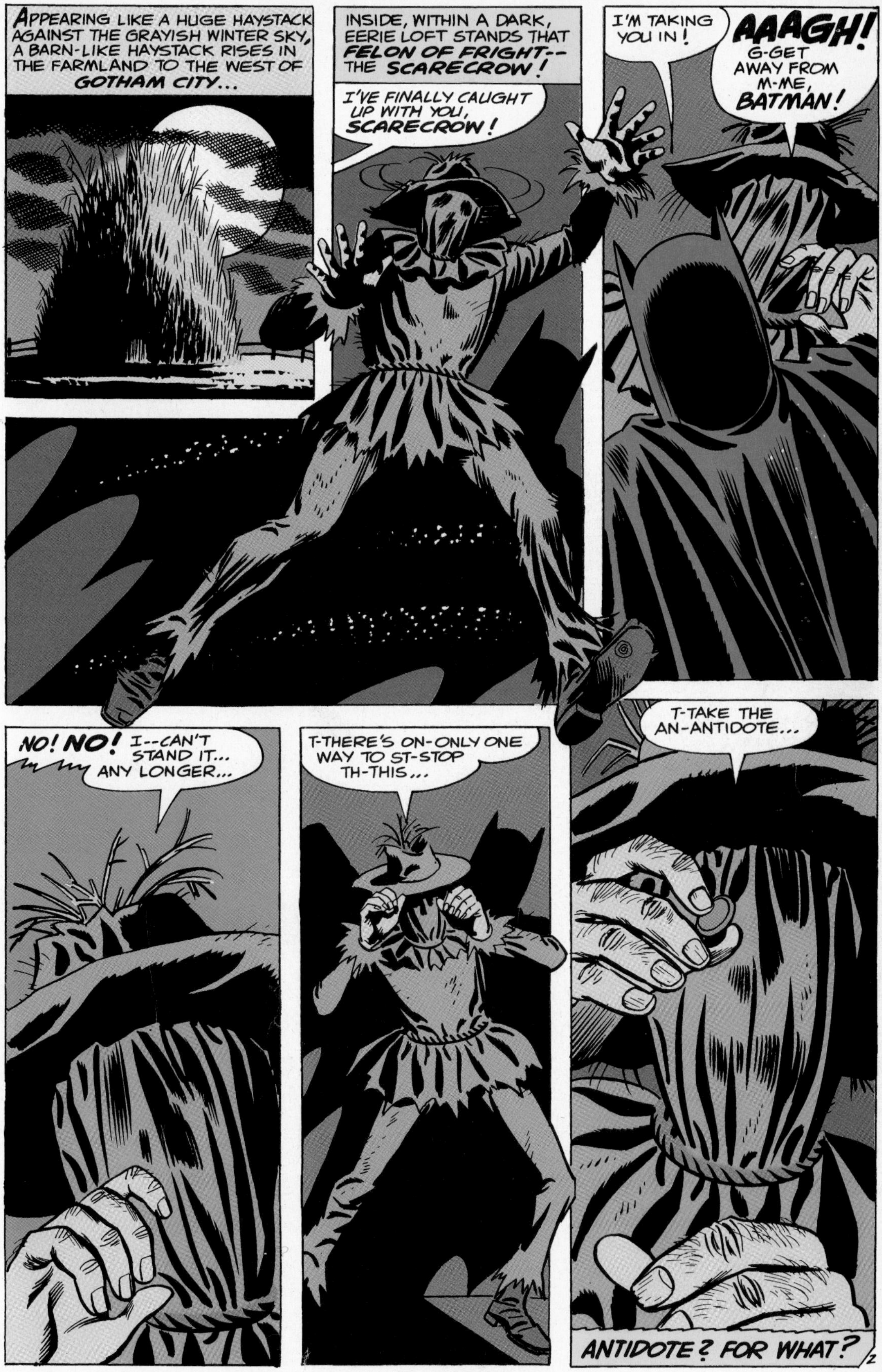
APPEARING LIKE A HUGE HAYSTACK AGAINST THE GRAYISH WINTER SKY, A BARN-LIKE HAYSTACK RISES IN THE FARMLAND TO THE WEST OF GOTHAM CITY...
INSIDE, WITHIN A DARK, EERIE LOFT STANDS THAT FELON OF FRIGHT-- THE SCARECROW!
I'VE FINALLY CAUGHT UP WITH YOU, SCARECROW!
I'M TAKING YOU IN!
AAAGH! G-GET AWAY FROM M-ME, BATMAN!
NO! NO! I--CAN'T STAND IT... ANY LONGER...
T-THERE'S ON-ONLY ONE WAY TO ST-STOP TH-THIS...
T-TAKE THE AN-ANTIDOTE...
ANTIDOTE? FOR WHAT?
2

HA HA HA! I OUTSCARED THE SCARECROW!

YOU PUT ON A GREAT BAT-ACT, LARRY! THE EXPERIMENT WAS A SUCCESS!

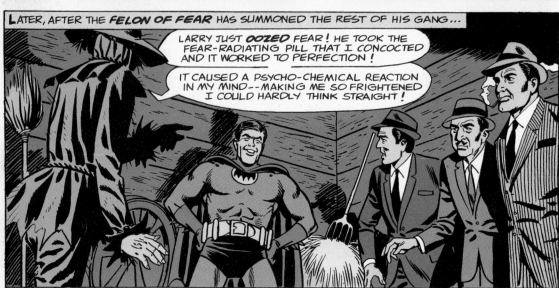

LATER, AFTER THE FELON OF FEAR HAS SUMMONED THE REST OF HIS GANG...

LARRY JUST OOZED FEAR! HE TOOK THE FEAR-RADIATING PILL THAT I CONCOCTED AND IT WORKED TO PERFECTION!

IT CAUSED A PSYCHO-CHEMICAL REACTION IN MY MIND--MAKING ME SO FRIGHTENED I COULD HARDLY THINK STRAIGHT!

NOW I HAVE THE PERFECT WAY TO SCARE BATMAN RIGHT OUT OF HIS CRIME-FIGHTING WITS! HA HA HA!

SOME NIGHTS LATER, ON THE WORLD-FAMOUS GOTHAM JEWELRY ROW...

THIS WAITING IS GETTING TO ME, SCARECROW! WE'VE BEEN ROOTED TO THIS SPOT FOR FOUR NIGHTS NOW AND BATMAN STILL HASN'T SHOWN UP!

PATIENCE, MR. RAYBOURNE, PATIENCE! HE WILL COME EVENTUALLY!

AH-- LISTEN NOW!

PLACES, EVERYONE! OUR LOOKOUT HAS SPOTTED HIM COMING THIS WAY!

HELP! THE JEWELRY STORE'S BEIN' ROBBED!

LOOKS LIKE WE ARRIVED JUST AT THE RIGHT TIME, BATMAN!

3

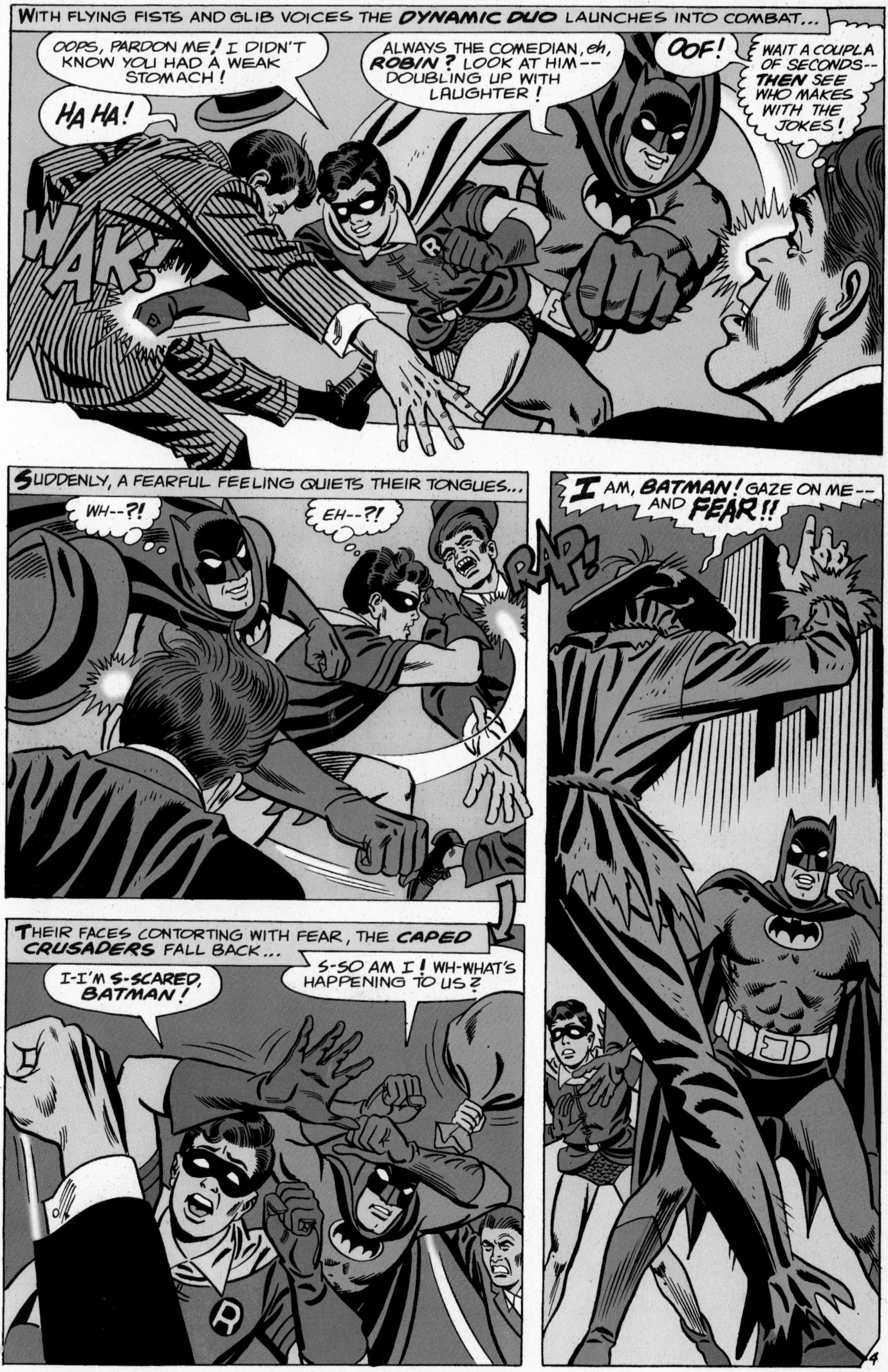
WITH FLYING FISTS AND GLIB VOICES THE DYNAMIC DUO LAUNCHES INTO COMBAT...
OOPS, PARDON ME! I DIDN'T KNOW YOU HAD A WEAK STOMACH!
HA HA!
ALWAYS THE COMEDIAN, eh, ROBIN? LOOK AT HIM-- DOUBLING UP WITH LAUGHTER!
OOF!
WAIT A COUPLA OF SECONDS-- THEN SEE WHO MAKES WITH THE JOKES!
WAK!
SUDDENLY, A FEARFUL FEELING QUIETS THEIR TONGUES...
WH--?!
EH--?!
RAP!
I AM, BATMAN! GAZE ON ME-- AND FEAR!!
THEIR FACES CONTORTING WITH FEAR, THE CAPED CRUSADERS FALL BACK...
I-I'M S-SCARED, BATMAN!
S-SO AM I! WH-WHAT'S HAPPENING TO US?
4

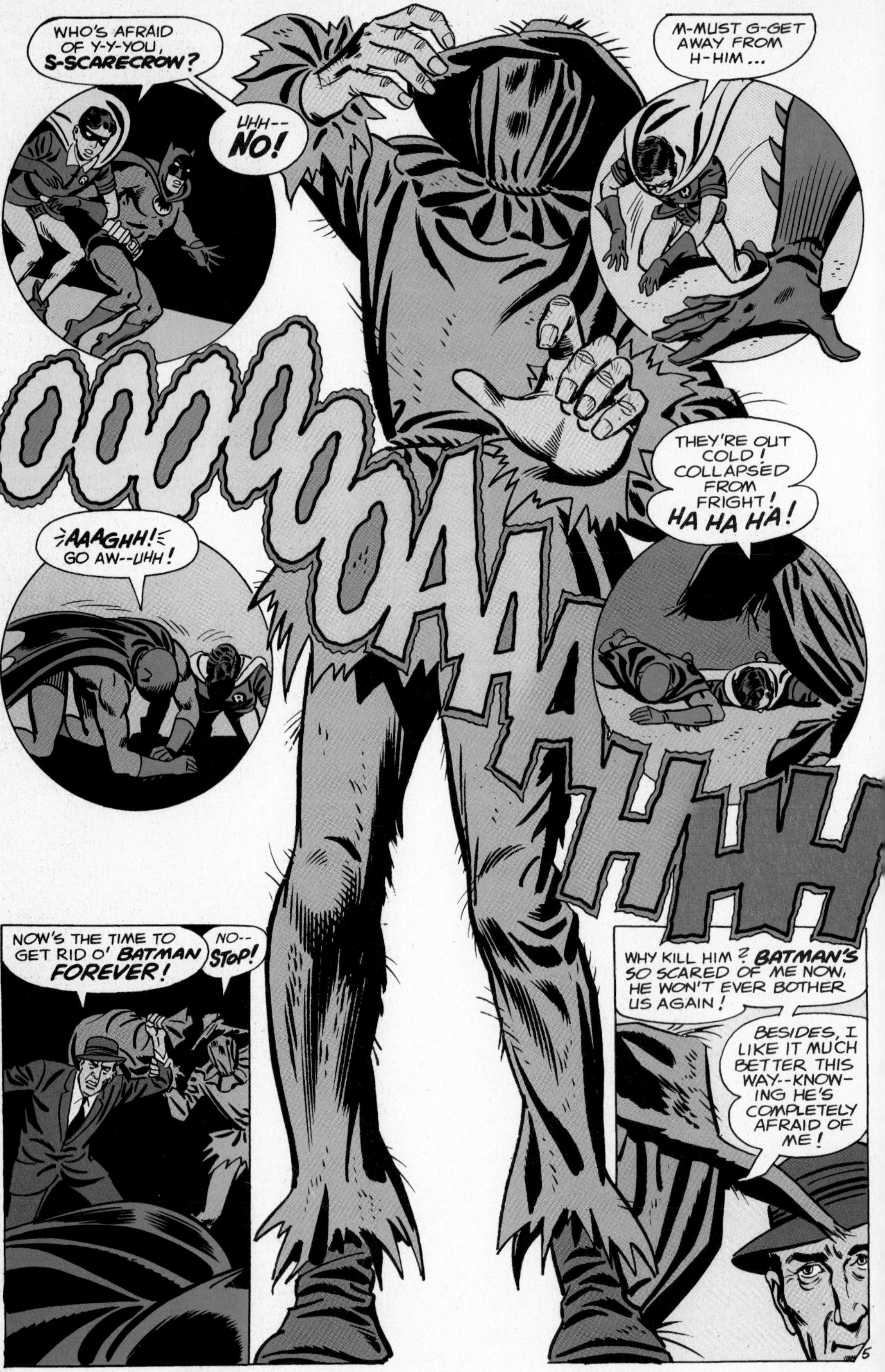
WHO'S AFRAID OF Y-Y-YOU, S-SCARECROW?
UHH-- NO!
M-MUST G-GET AWAY FROM H-HIM...
OOOOOOAAAHHHH
THEY'RE OUT COLD! COLLAPSED FROM FRIGHT! HA HA HA!
AAAGHH! GO AW--UHH!
NOW'S THE TIME TO GET RID O' BATMAN FOREVER!
NO-- STOP!
WHY KILL HIM? BATMAN'S SO SCARED OF ME NOW, HE WON'T EVER BOTHER US AGAIN!
BESIDES, I LIKE IT MUCH BETTER THIS WAY--KNOWING HE'S COMPLETELY AFRAID OF ME!
5

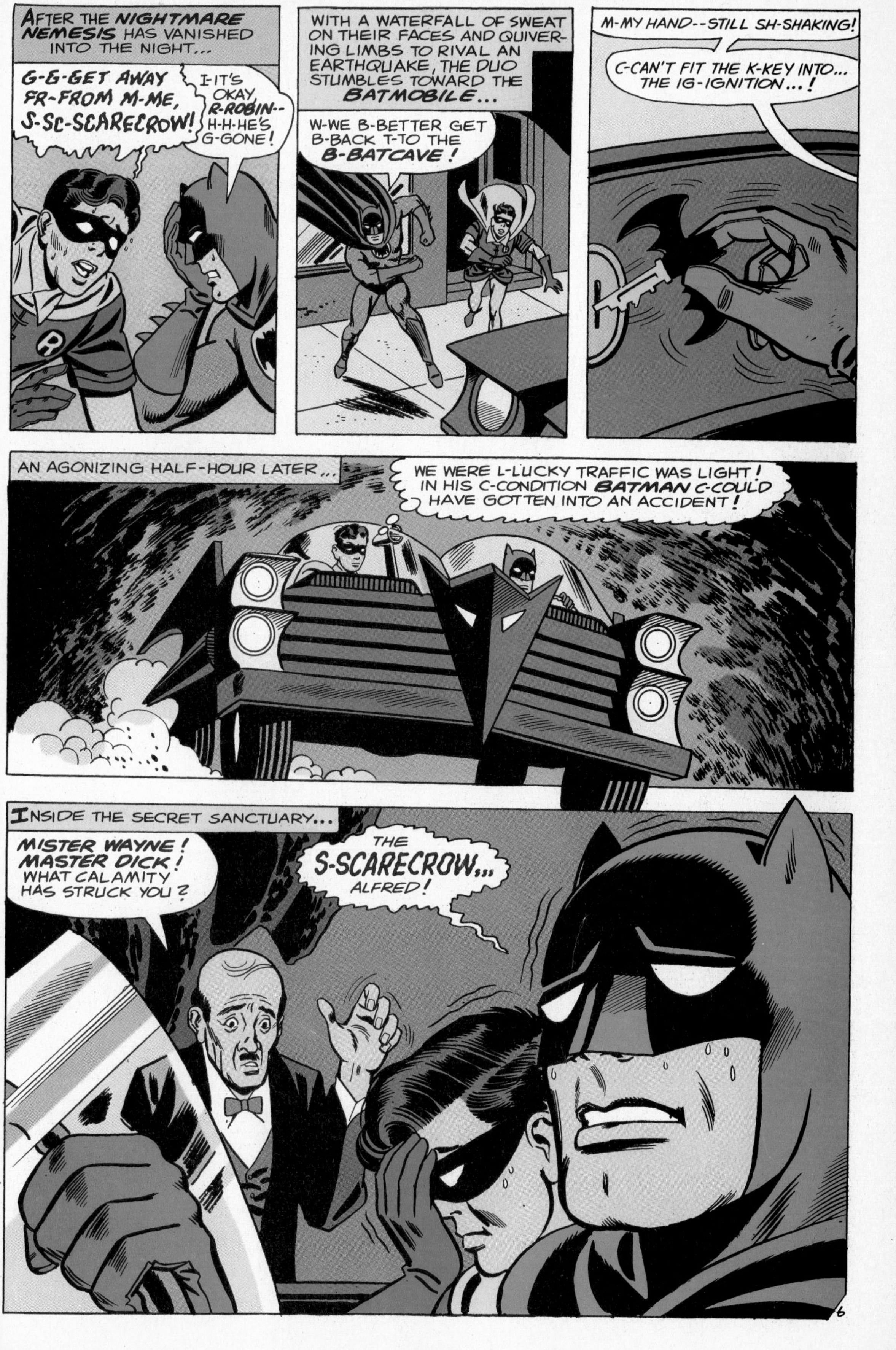
AFTER THE NIGHTMARE NEMESIS HAS VANISHED INTO THE NIGHT...
G-G-GET AWAY FR-FROM M-ME, S-SC-SCARECROW!
I-IT'S OKAY, R-ROBIN-- H-H-HE'S G-GONE!
WITH A WATERFALL OF SWEAT ON THEIR FACES AND QUIVERING LIMBS TO RIVAL AN EARTHQUAKE, THE DUO STUMBLES TOWARD THE BATMOBILE...
W-WE B-BETTER GET B-BACK T-TO THE B-BATCAVE!
M-MY HAND--STILL SH-SHAKING!
C-CAN'T FIT THE K-KEY INTO... THE IG-IGNITION...!
AN AGONIZING HALF-HOUR LATER...
WE WERE L-LUCKY TRAFFIC WAS LIGHT! IN HIS C-CONDITION BATMAN C-COULD HAVE GOTTEN INTO AN ACCIDENT!
INSIDE THE SECRET SANCTUARY...
MISTER WAYNE! MASTER DICK! WHAT CALAMITY HAS STRUCK YOU?
THE S-SCARECROW... ALFRED!
6

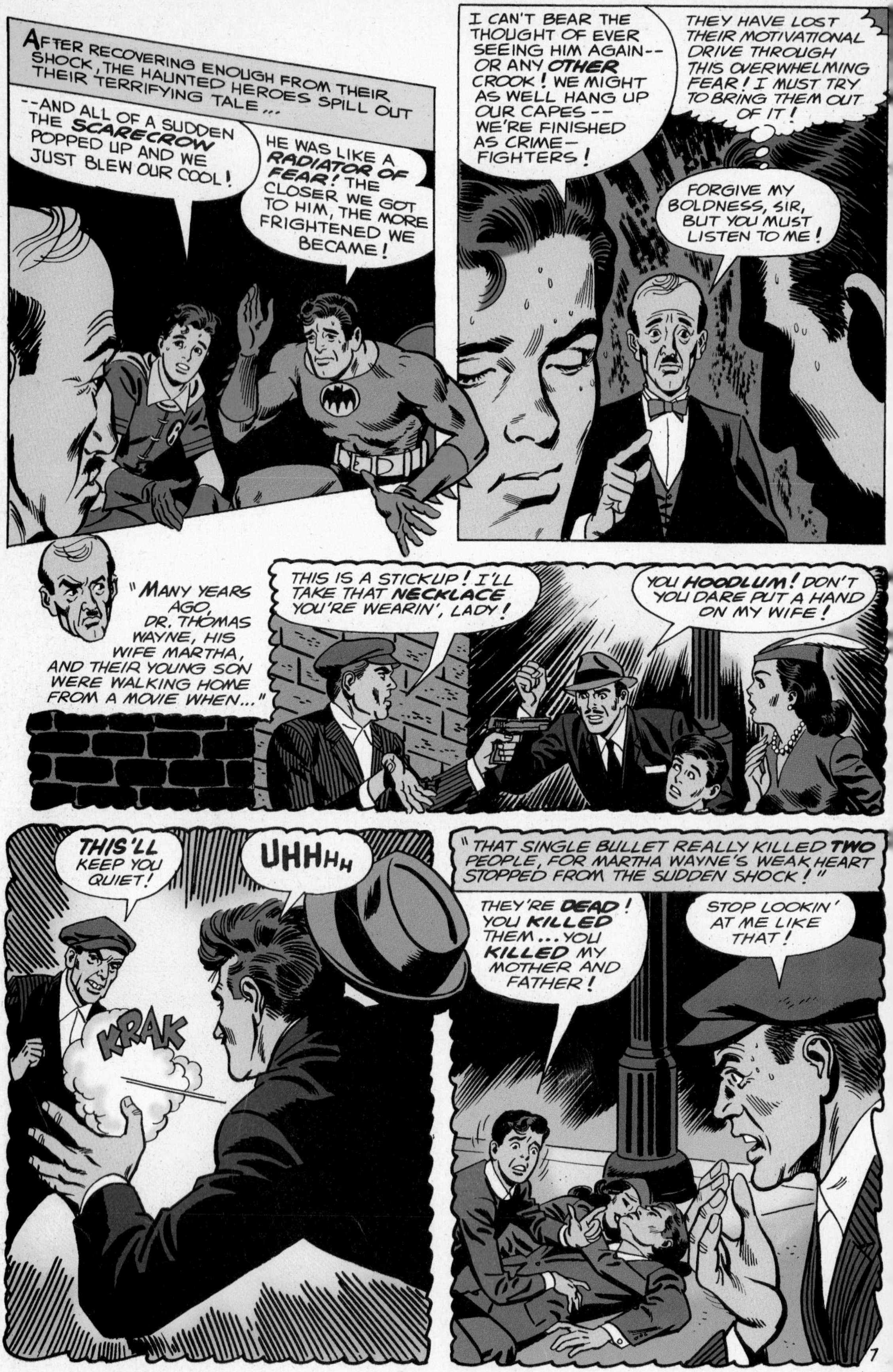
AFTER RECOVERING ENOUGH FROM THEIR SHOCK, THE HAUNTED HEROES SPILL OUT THEIR TERRIFYING TALE...
--AND ALL OF A SUDDEN THE SCARECROW POPPED UP AND WE JUST BLEW OUR COOL!
HE WAS LIKE A RADIATOR OF FEAR! THE CLOSER WE GOT TO HIM, THE MORE FRIGHTENED WE BECAME!
I CAN'T BEAR THE THOUGHT OF EVER SEEING HIM AGAIN--OR ANY OTHER CROOK! WE MIGHT AS WELL HANG UP OUR CAPES--WE'RE FINISHED AS CRIME-FIGHTERS!
THEY HAVE LOST THEIR MOTIVATIONAL DRIVE THROUGH THIS OVERWHELMING FEAR! I MUST TRY TO BRING THEM OUT OF IT!
FORGIVE MY BOLDNESS, SIR, BUT YOU MUST LISTEN TO ME!
"MANY YEARS AGO, DR. THOMAS WAYNE, HIS WIFE MARTHA, AND THEIR YOUNG SON WERE WALKING HOME FROM A MOVIE WHEN..."
THIS IS A STICKUP! I'LL TAKE THAT NECKLACE YOU'RE WEARIN', LADY!
YOU HOODLUM! DON'T YOU DARE PUT A HAND ON MY WIFE!
THIS'LL KEEP YOU QUIET!
UHHHH
KRAK
"THAT SINGLE BULLET REALLY KILLED TWO PEOPLE, FOR MARTHA WAYNE'S WEAK HEART STOPPED FROM THE SUDDEN SHOCK!"
THEY'RE DEAD! YOU KILLED THEM... YOU KILLED MY MOTHER AND FATHER!
STOP LOOKIN' AT ME LIKE THAT!
7

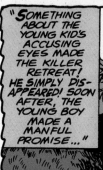

"SOMETHING ABOUT THE YOUNG KID'S ACCUSING EYES MADE THE KILLER RETREAT! HE SIMPLY DISAPPEARED! SOON AFTER, THE YOUNG BOY MADE A MANFUL PROMISE..."

I SWEAR I'LL DEDICATE MY LIFE AND INHERITANCE TO BRINGING YOUR KILLER TO JUSTICE... AND FIGHTING **ALL** CRIMINALS! I **SWEAR** IT!

WAYNE
THOMAS   MARTHA

"THE YEARS PASSED AS THE BOY PREPARED FOR HIS CHOSEN CAREER!"

"HE MASTERED SCIENTIFIC CRIMINAL INVESTIGATION."

"HE TRAINED HIS BODY TO SUCH PHYSICAL AND ATHLETIC PERFECTION THAT HE COULD PERFORM ANY DAREDEVIL FEAT..."

"THEN ONE DAY HE WAS READY FOR HIS NEW ROLE!"

CRIMINALS ARE A SUPERSTITIOUS, COWARDLY LOT, SO I MUST WEAR A DISGUISE THAT WILL STRIKE TERROR IN THEIR HEARTS! I MUST BE A CREATURE OF THE NIGHT, LIKE A... A...

"AND, AS IF IN ANSWER, A WINGED CREATURE FLEW IN THROUGH THE OPEN WINDOW!"

A **BAT**! THAT'S IT! IT'S LIKE AN **OMEN**! I SHALL BECOME A **BAT**!

"THUS WAS BORN THIS WEIRD FIGURE OF THE SHADOWS...THIS DARK AVENGER OF EVIL-- **BATMAN**!"

SOMEDAY I'LL FIND THE KILLER OF MY PARENTS... **SOME** DAY...

8

145

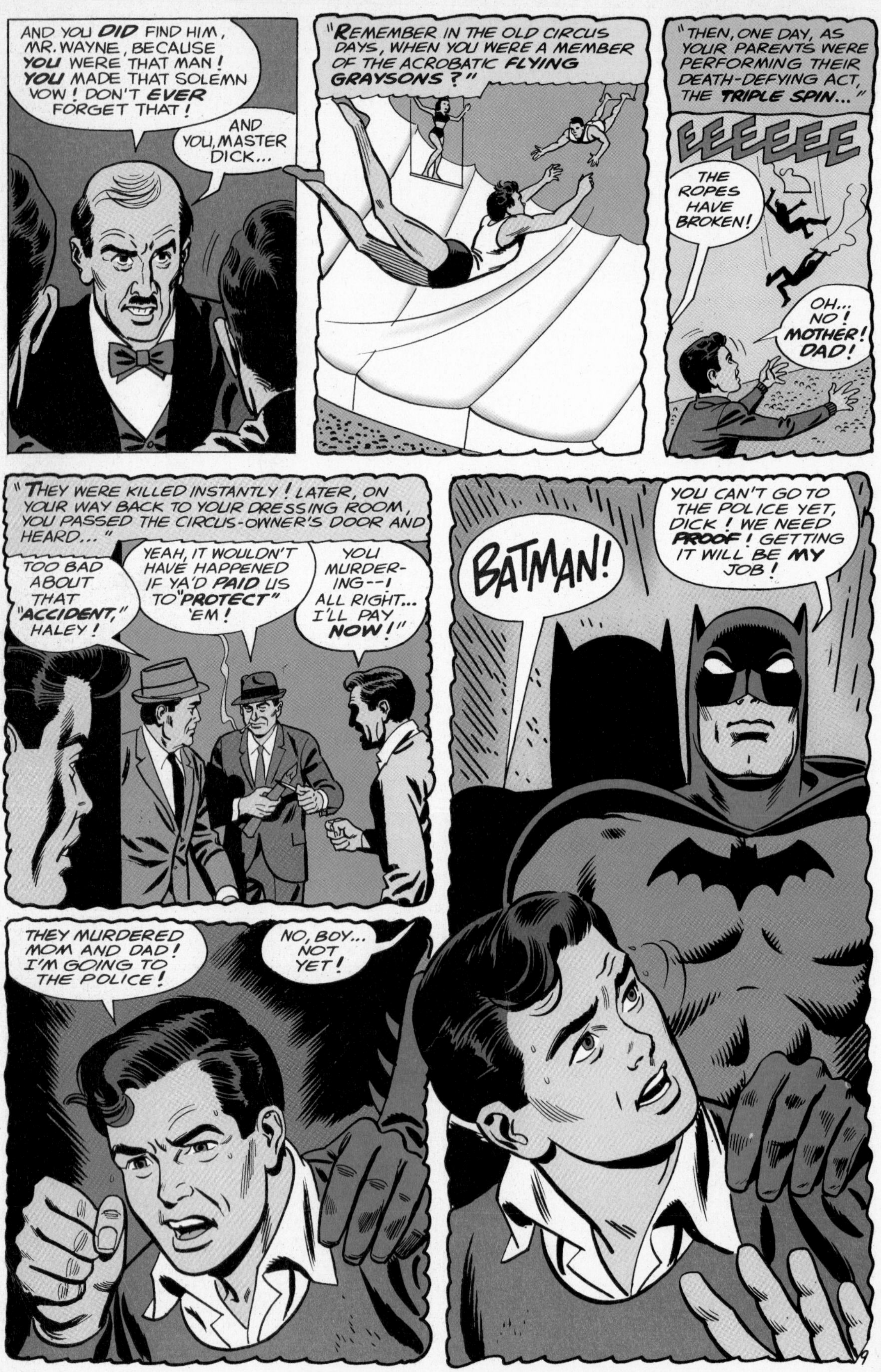

AND YOU DID FIND HIM, MR. WAYNE, BECAUSE YOU WERE THAT MAN! YOU MADE THAT SOLEMN VOW! DON'T EVER FORGET THAT!
AND YOU, MASTER DICK...
"REMEMBER IN THE OLD CIRCUS DAYS, WHEN YOU WERE A MEMBER OF THE ACROBATIC FLYING GRAYSONS?"
"THEN, ONE DAY, AS YOUR PARENTS WERE PERFORMING THEIR DEATH-DEFYING ACT, THE TRIPLE SPIN..."
EEEEEEE
THE ROPES HAVE BROKEN!
OH... NO! MOTHER! DAD!
"THEY WERE KILLED INSTANTLY! LATER, ON YOUR WAY BACK TO YOUR DRESSING ROOM, YOU PASSED THE CIRCUS-OWNER'S DOOR AND HEARD..."
TOO BAD ABOUT THAT "ACCIDENT," HALEY!
YEAH, IT WOULDN'T HAVE HAPPENED IF YA'D PAID US TO "PROTECT" 'EM!
YOU MURDERING--! ALL RIGHT... I'LL PAY NOW!"
THEY MURDERED MOM AND DAD! I'M GOING TO THE POLICE!
NO, BOY... NOT YET!
BATMAN!
YOU CAN'T GO TO THE POLICE YET, DICK! WE NEED PROOF! GETTING IT WILL BE MY JOB!
9

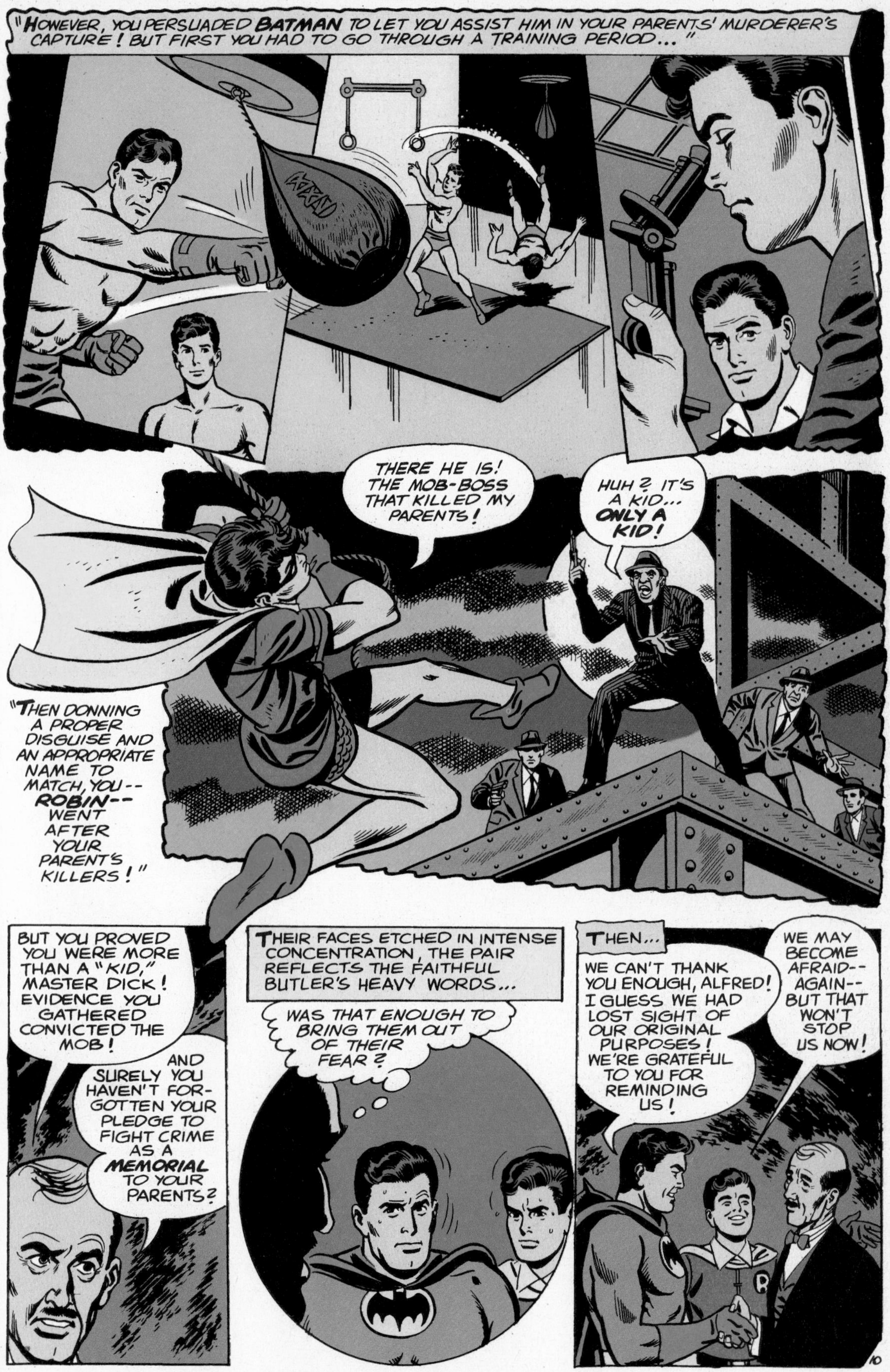
"HOWEVER, YOU PERSUADED BATMAN TO LET YOU ASSIST HIM IN YOUR PARENTS' MURDERER'S CAPTURE! BUT FIRST YOU HAD TO GO THROUGH A TRAINING PERIOD..."
THERE HE IS! THE MOB-BOSS THAT KILLED MY PARENTS!
HUH? IT'S A KID... ONLY A KID!
"THEN DONNING A PROPER DISGUISE AND AN APPROPRIATE NAME TO MATCH, YOU-- ROBIN-- WENT AFTER YOUR PARENT'S KILLERS!"
BUT YOU PROVED YOU WERE MORE THAN A "KID," MASTER DICK! EVIDENCE YOU GATHERED CONVICTED THE MOB!
AND SURELY YOU HAVEN'T FOR-GOTTEN YOUR PLEDGE TO FIGHT CRIME AS A MEMORIAL TO YOUR PARENTS?
THEIR FACES ETCHED IN INTENSE CONCENTRATION, THE PAIR REFLECTS THE FAITHFUL BUTLER'S HEAVY WORDS...
WAS THAT ENOUGH TO BRING THEM OUT OF THEIR FEAR?
THEN...
WE CAN'T THANK YOU ENOUGH, ALFRED! I GUESS WE HAD LOST SIGHT OF OUR ORIGINAL PURPOSES! WE'RE GRATEFUL TO YOU FOR REMINDING US!
WE MAY BECOME AFRAID-- AGAIN-- BUT THAT WON'T STOP US NOW!
10

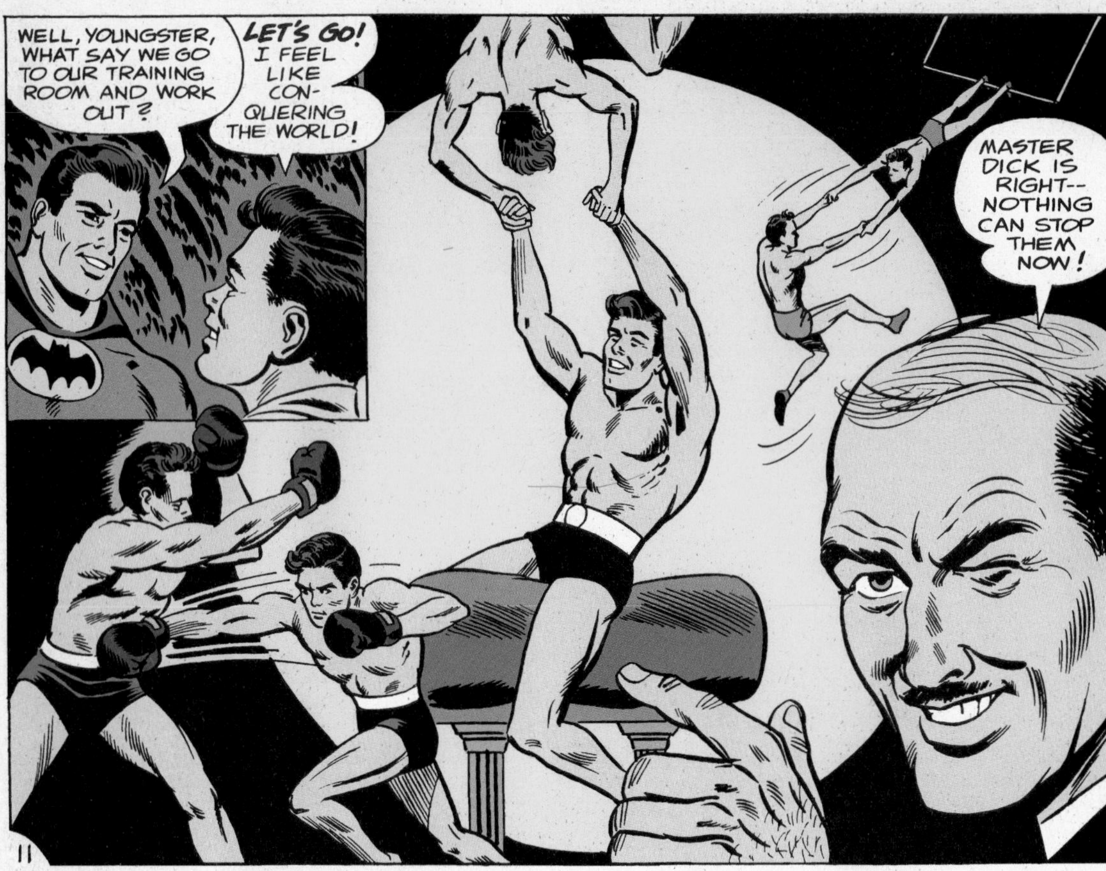
WELL, YOUNGSTER, WHAT SAY WE GO TO OUR TRAINING ROOM AND WORK OUT?
LET'S GO! I FEEL LIKE CON-QUERING THE WORLD!
MASTER DICK IS RIGHT-- NOTHING CAN STOP THEM NOW!

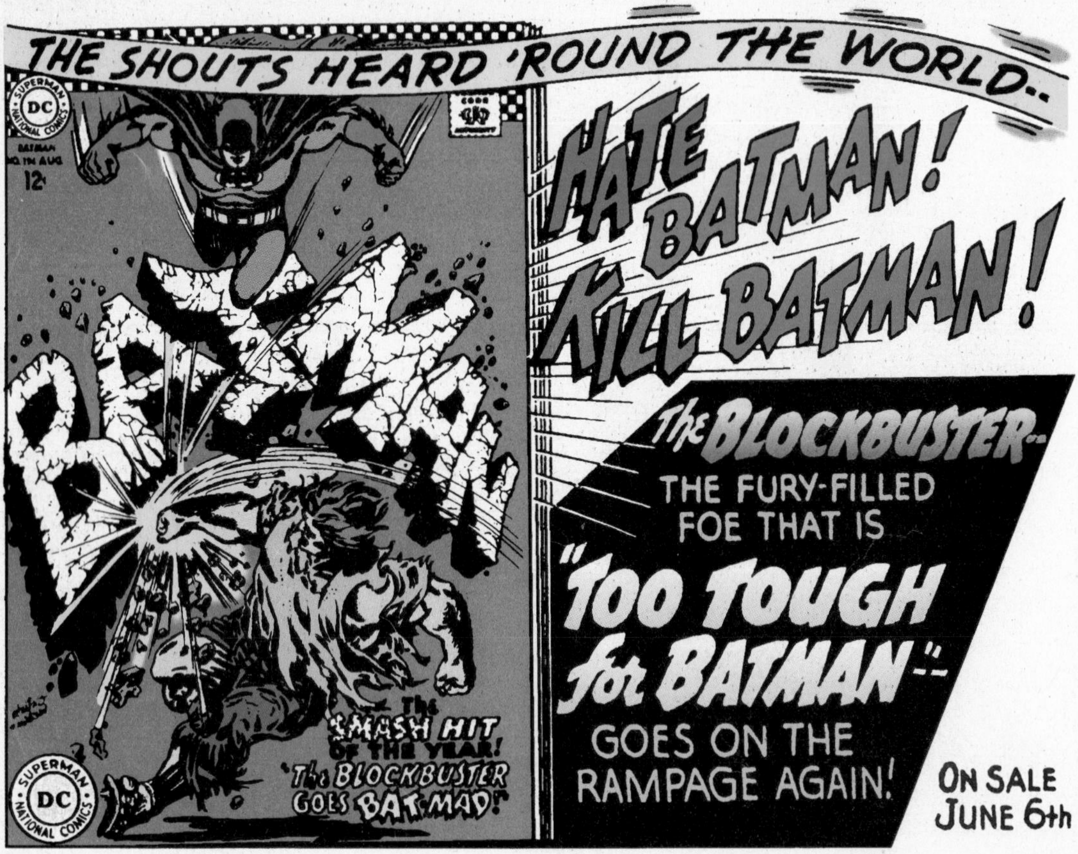
THE SHOUTS HEARD 'ROUND THE WORLD..
The SMASH HIT OF THE YEAR!
The BLOCKBUSTER GOES BAT-MAD!
HATE BATMAN!
KILL BATMAN!
The BLOCKBUSTER--
THE FURY-FILLED FOE THAT IS
"TOO TOUGH for BATMAN"--
GOES ON THE RAMPAGE AGAIN!
ON SALE JUNE 6th

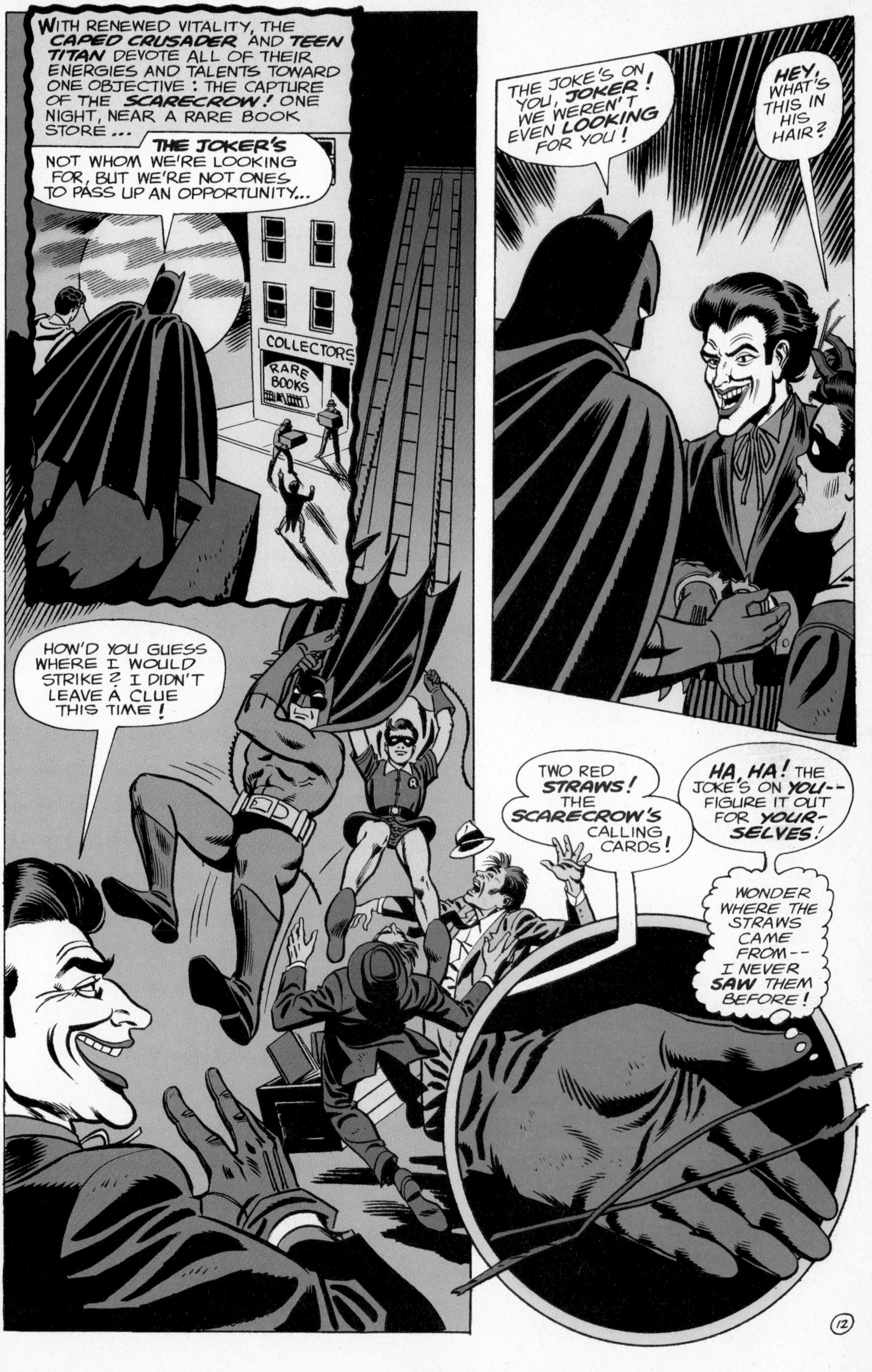

WITH RENEWED VITALITY, THE CAPED CRUSADER AND TEEN TITAN DEVOTE ALL OF THEIR ENERGIES AND TALENTS TOWARD ONE OBJECTIVE : THE CAPTURE OF THE SCARECROW! ONE NIGHT, NEAR A RARE BOOK STORE...
THE JOKER'S NOT WHOM WE'RE LOOKING FOR, BUT WE'RE NOT ONES TO PASS UP AN OPPORTUNITY...
COLLECTORS
RARE BOOKS
HOW'D YOU GUESS WHERE I WOULD STRIKE? I DIDN'T LEAVE A CLUE THIS TIME!
THE JOKE'S ON YOU, JOKER! WE WEREN'T EVEN LOOKING FOR YOU!
HEY, WHAT'S THIS IN HIS HAIR?
TWO RED STRAWS! THE SCARECROW'S CALLING CARDS!
HA, HA! THE JOKE'S ON YOU-- FIGURE IT OUT FOR YOURSELVES!
WONDER WHERE THE STRAWS CAME FROM-- I NEVER SAW THEM BEFORE!
12

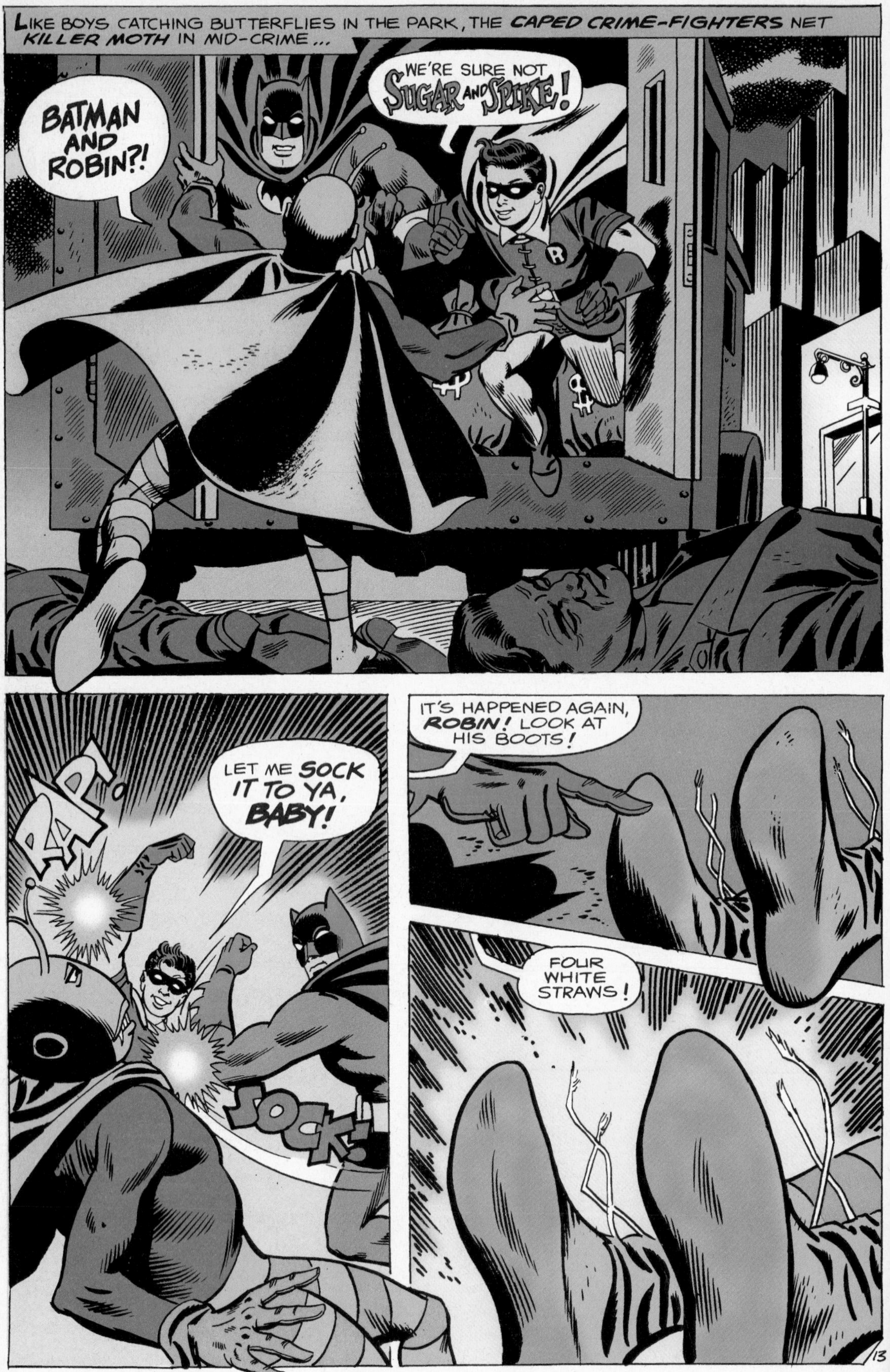
LIKE BOYS CATCHING BUTTERFLIES IN THE PARK, THE CAPED CRIME-FIGHTERS NET KILLER MOTH IN MID-CRIME...
BATMAN AND ROBIN?!
WE'RE SURE NOT SUGAR AND SPIKE!
RAP!
LET ME SOCK IT TO YA, BABY!
SOCK!
IT'S HAPPENED AGAIN, ROBIN! LOOK AT HIS BOOTS!
FOUR WHITE STRAWS!
13

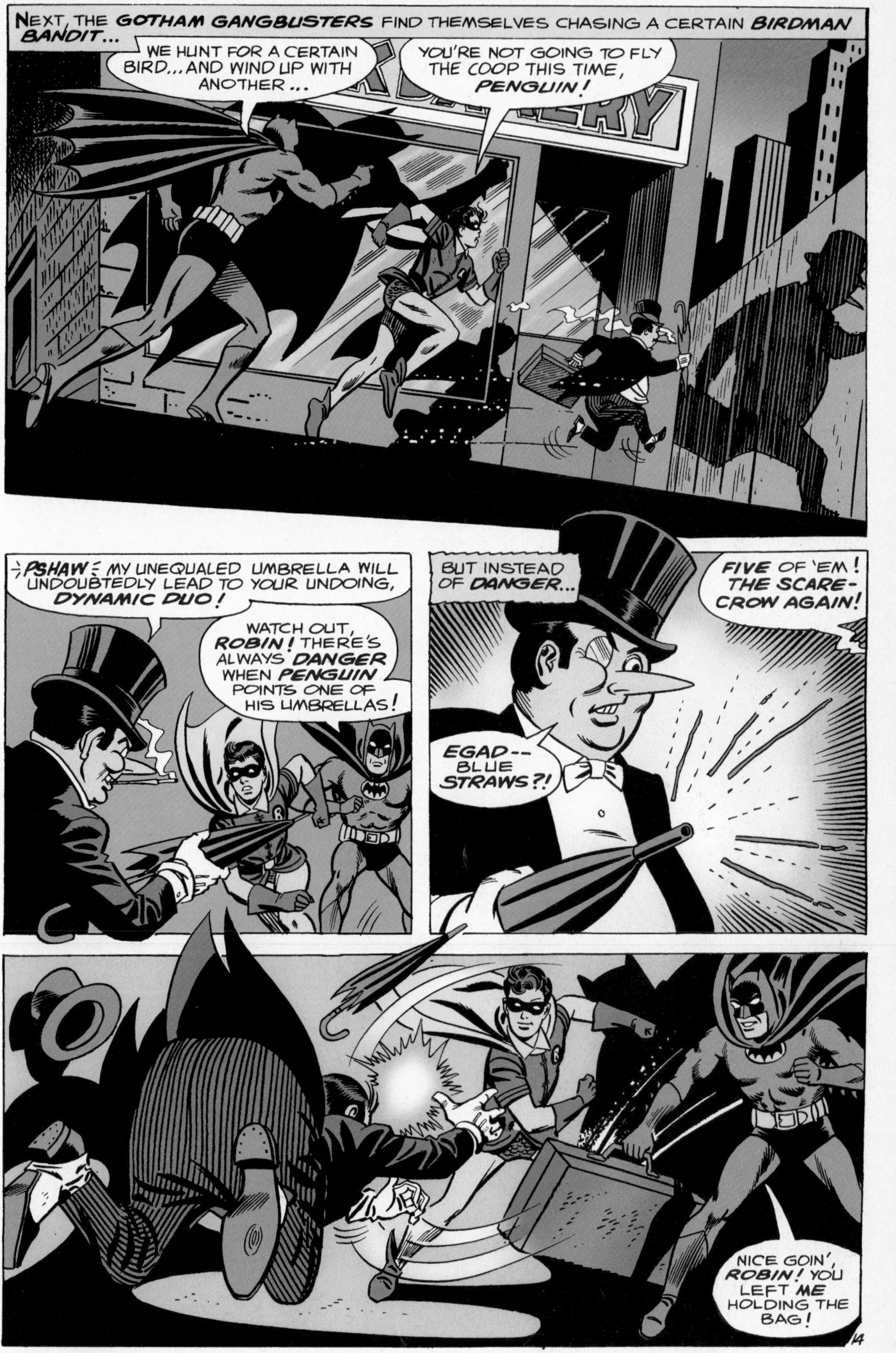
NEXT, THE GOTHAM GANGBUSTERS FIND THEMSELVES CHASING A CERTAIN BIRDMAN BANDIT...
WE HUNT FOR A CERTAIN BIRD... AND WIND UP WITH ANOTHER...
YOU'RE NOT GOING TO FLY THE COOP THIS TIME, PENGUIN!
PSHAW! MY UNEQUALED UMBRELLA WILL UNDOUBTEDLY LEAD TO YOUR UNDOING, DYNAMIC DUO!
WATCH OUT, ROBIN! THERE'S ALWAYS DANGER WHEN PENGUIN POINTS ONE OF HIS UMBRELLAS!
BUT INSTEAD OF DANGER...
FIVE OF 'EM! THE SCARE-CROW AGAIN!
EGAD-- BLUE STRAWS?!
NICE GOIN', ROBIN! YOU LEFT ME HOLDING THE BAG!
14

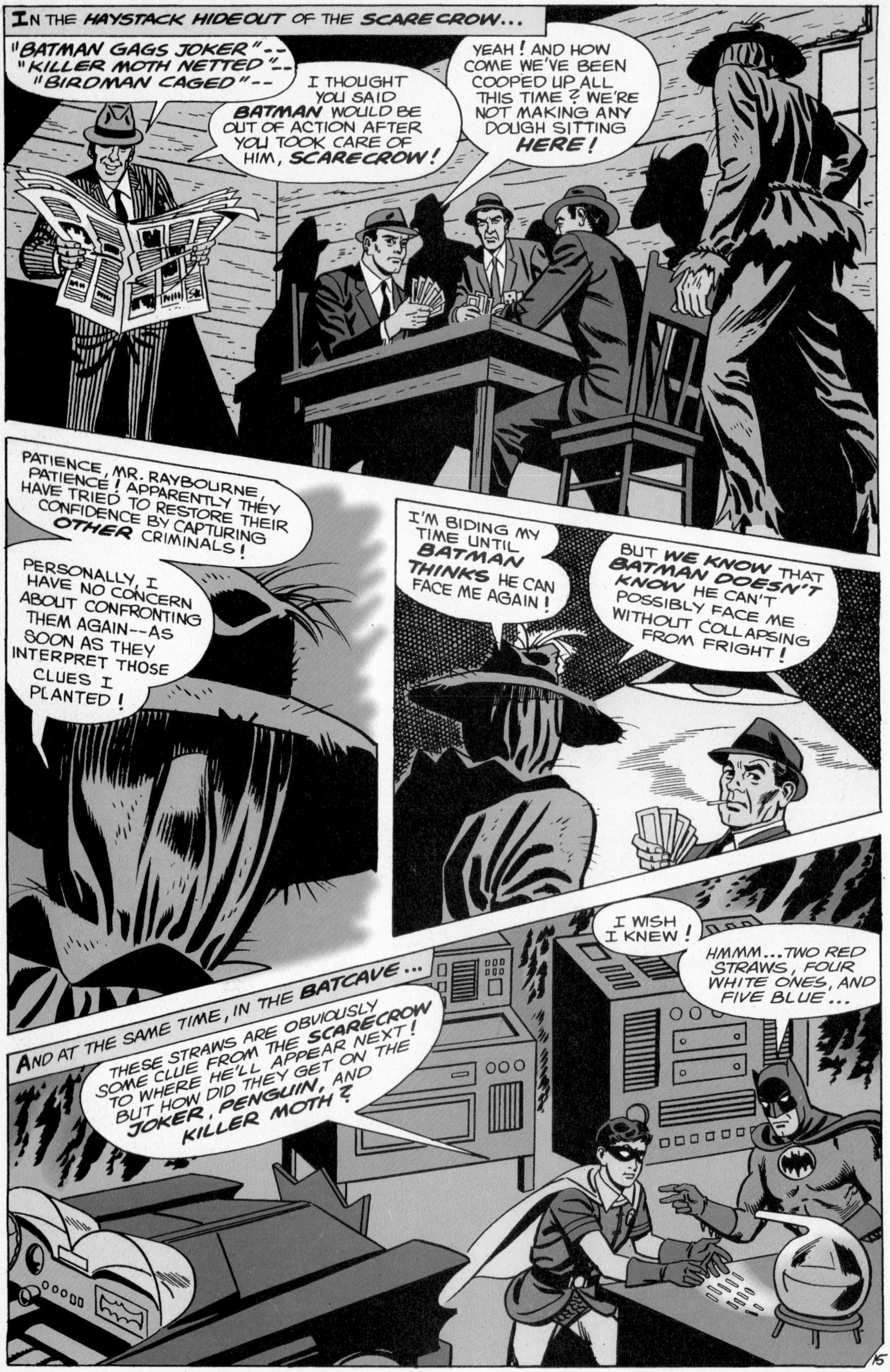
IN THE HAYSTACK HIDEOUT OF THE SCARECROW...
"BATMAN GAGS JOKER"-- "KILLER MOTH NETTED"-- "BIRDMAN CAGED"--
I THOUGHT YOU SAID BATMAN WOULD BE OUT OF ACTION AFTER YOU TOOK CARE OF HIM, SCARECROW!
YEAH! AND HOW COME WE'VE BEEN COOPED UP ALL THIS TIME? WE'RE NOT MAKING ANY DOUGH SITTING HERE!
PATIENCE, MR. RAYBOURNE, PATIENCE! APPARENTLY THEY HAVE TRIED TO RESTORE THEIR CONFIDENCE BY CAPTURING OTHER CRIMINALS!
PERSONALLY, I HAVE NO CONCERN ABOUT CONFRONTING THEM AGAIN--AS SOON AS THEY INTERPRET THOSE CLUES I PLANTED!
I'M BIDING MY TIME UNTIL BATMAN THINKS HE CAN FACE ME AGAIN!
BUT WE KNOW THAT BATMAN DOESN'T KNOW HE CAN'T POSSIBLY FACE ME WITHOUT COLLAPSING FROM FRIGHT!
AND AT THE SAME TIME, IN THE BATCAVE...
THESE STRAWS ARE OBVIOUSLY SOME CLUE FROM THE SCARECROW TO WHERE HE'LL APPEAR NEXT! BUT HOW DID THEY GET ON THE JOKER, PENGUIN, AND KILLER MOTH?
I WISH I KNEW!
HMMM...TWO RED STRAWS, FOUR WHITE ONES, AND FIVE BLUE...
15

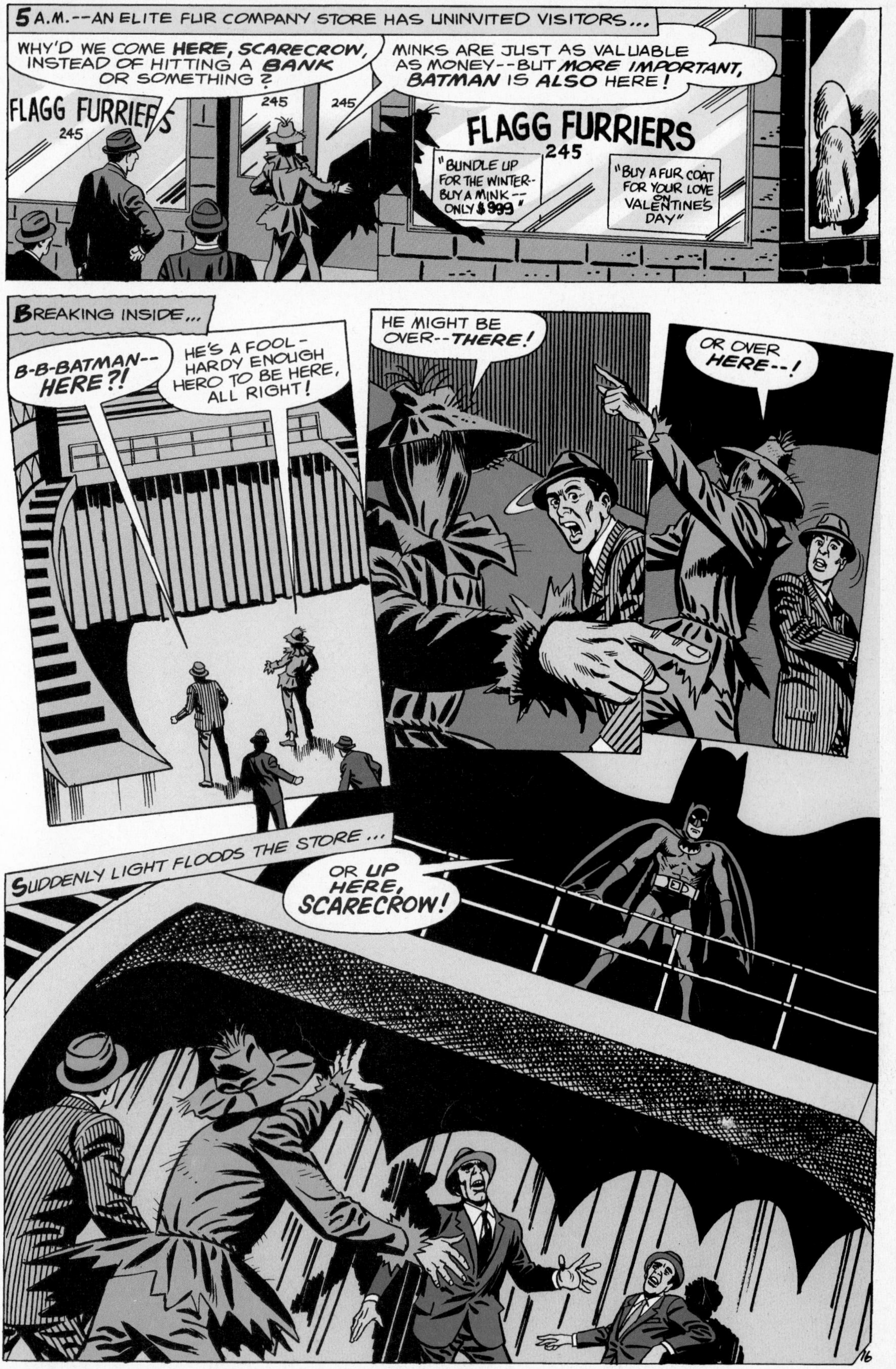

5 A.M.--AN ELITE FUR COMPANY STORE HAS UNINVITED VISITORS...
WHY'D WE COME HERE, SCARECROW, INSTEAD OF HITTING A BANK OR SOMETHING?
MINKS ARE JUST AS VALUABLE AS MONEY--BUT MORE IMPORTANT, BATMAN IS ALSO HERE!
FLAGG FURRIERS
245
"BUNDLE UP FOR THE WINTER-- BUY A MINK -- ONLY $999"
"BUY A FUR COAT FOR YOUR LOVE ON VALENTINE'S DAY"
BREAKING INSIDE...
B-B-BATMAN-- HERE?!
HE'S A FOOL-HARDY ENOUGH HERO TO BE HERE, ALL RIGHT!
HE MIGHT BE OVER--THERE!
OR OVER HERE--!
SUDDENLY LIGHT FLOODS THE STORE...
OR UP HERE, SCARECROW!
16

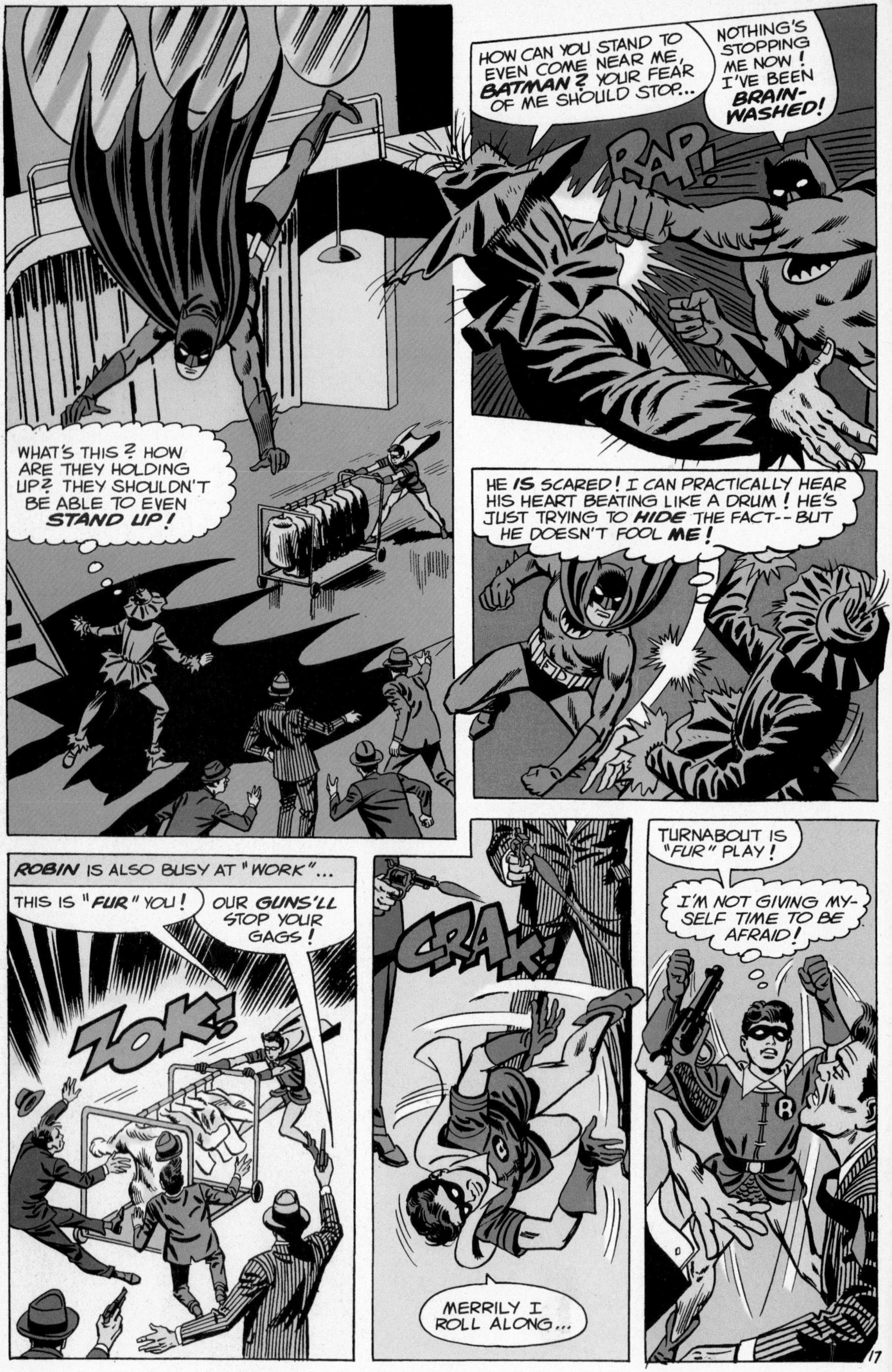
WHAT'S THIS? HOW ARE THEY HOLDING UP? THEY SHOULDN'T BE ABLE TO EVEN STAND UP!
HOW CAN YOU STAND TO EVEN COME NEAR ME, BATMAN? YOUR FEAR OF ME SHOULD STOP...
NOTHING'S STOPPING ME NOW! I'VE BEEN BRAIN-WASHED!
RAP!
HE IS SCARED! I CAN PRACTICALLY HEAR HIS HEART BEATING LIKE A DRUM! HE'S JUST TRYING TO HIDE THE FACT-- BUT HE DOESN'T FOOL ME!
ROBIN IS ALSO BUSY AT "WORK"...
THIS IS "FUR" YOU!
OUR GUNS'LL STOP YOUR GAGS!
ZOK!
CRAK!
MERRILY I ROLL ALONG...
TURNABOUT IS "FUR" PLAY!
I'M NOT GIVING MY-SELF TIME TO BE AFRAID!
17

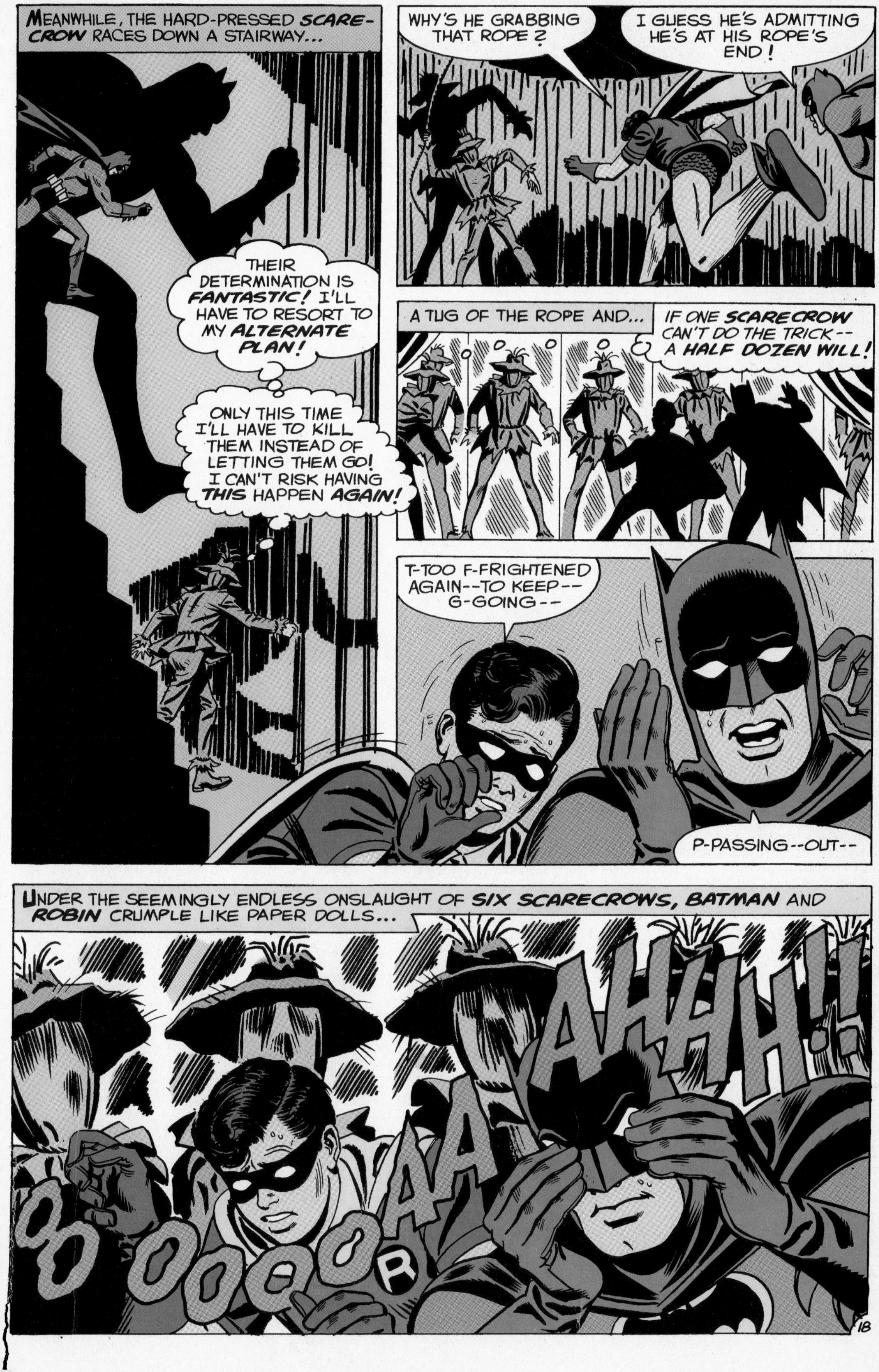
MEANWHILE, THE HARD-PRESSED SCARECROW RACES DOWN A STAIRWAY...
THEIR DETERMINATION IS FANTASTIC! I'LL HAVE TO RESORT TO MY ALTERNATE PLAN!
ONLY THIS TIME I'LL HAVE TO KILL THEM INSTEAD OF LETTING THEM GO! I CAN'T RISK HAVING THIS HAPPEN AGAIN!
WHY'S HE GRABBING THAT ROPE?
I GUESS HE'S ADMITTING HE'S AT HIS ROPE'S END!
A TUG OF THE ROPE AND...
IF ONE SCARECROW CAN'T DO THE TRICK-- A HALF DOZEN WILL!
T-TOO F-FRIGHTENED AGAIN--TO KEEP-- G-GOING--
P-PASSING--OUT--
UNDER THE SEEMINGLY ENDLESS ONSLAUGHT OF SIX SCARECROWS, BATMAN AND ROBIN CRUMPLE LIKE PAPER DOLLS...
AHHH!!
AA
OOOOOOR
18

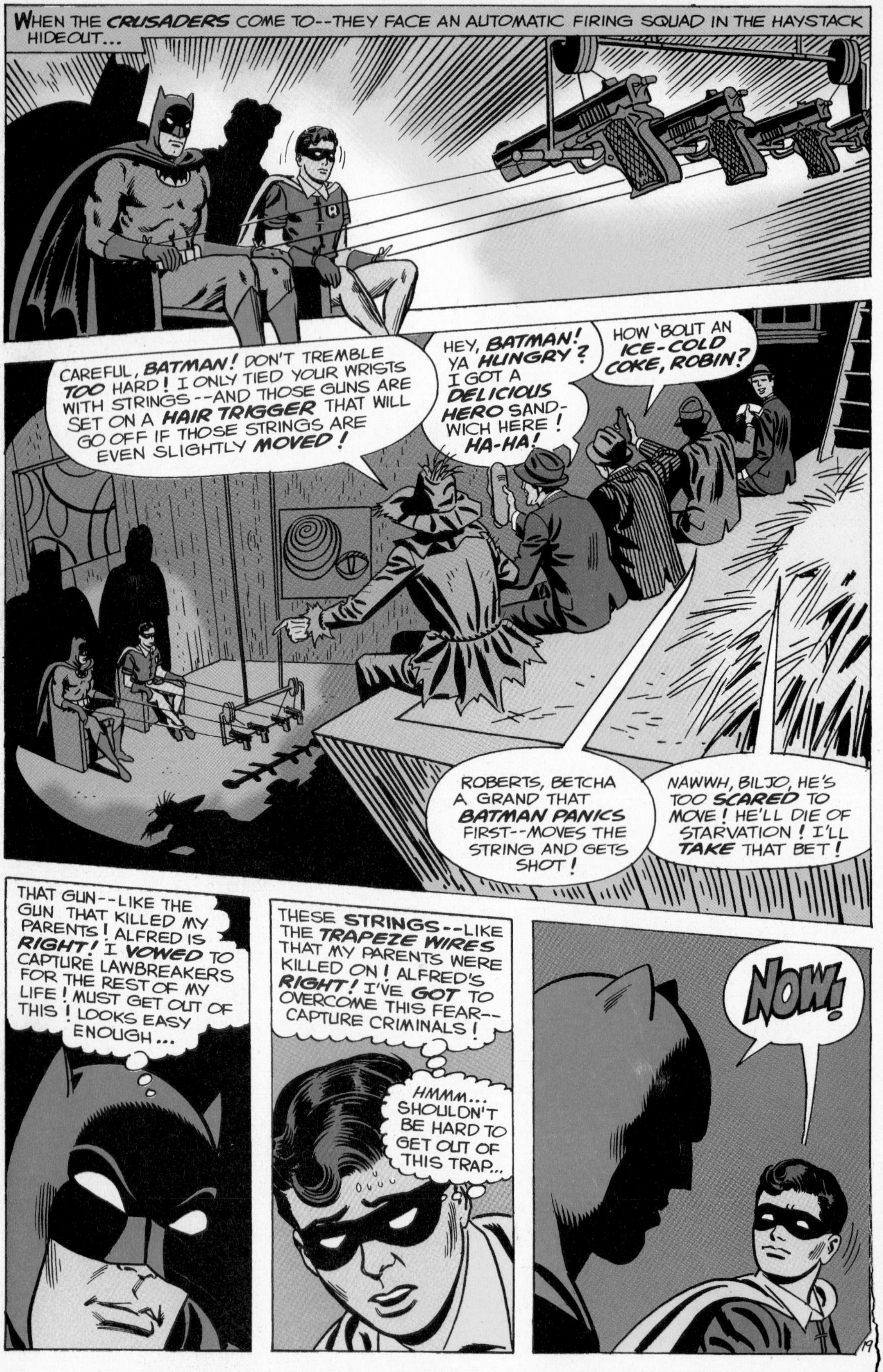
WHEN THE CRUSADERS COME TO--THEY FACE AN AUTOMATIC FIRING SQUAD IN THE HAYSTACK HIDEOUT...
CAREFUL, BATMAN! DON'T TREMBLE TOO HARD! I ONLY TIED YOUR WRISTS WITH STRINGS--AND THOSE GUNS ARE SET ON A HAIR TRIGGER THAT WILL GO OFF IF THOSE STRINGS ARE EVEN SLIGHTLY MOVED!
HEY, BATMAN! YA HUNGRY? I GOT A DELICIOUS HERO SAND-WICH HERE! HA-HA!
HOW 'BOUT AN ICE-COLD COKE, ROBIN?
ROBERTS, BETCHA A GRAND THAT BATMAN PANICS FIRST--MOVES THE STRING AND GETS SHOT!
NAWWH, BILJO, HE'S TOO SCARED TO MOVE! HE'LL DIE OF STARVATION! I'LL TAKE THAT BET!
THAT GUN--LIKE THE GUN THAT KILLED MY PARENTS! ALFRED IS RIGHT! I VOWED TO CAPTURE LAWBREAKERS FOR THE REST OF MY LIFE! MUST GET OUT OF THIS! LOOKS EASY ENOUGH...
THESE STRINGS--LIKE THE TRAPEZE WIRES THAT MY PARENTS WERE KILLED ON! ALFRED'S RIGHT! I'VE GOT TO OVERCOME THIS FEAR--CAPTURE CRIMINALS!
HMMM... SHOULDN'T BE HARD TO GET OUT OF THIS TRAP...
NOW!
19

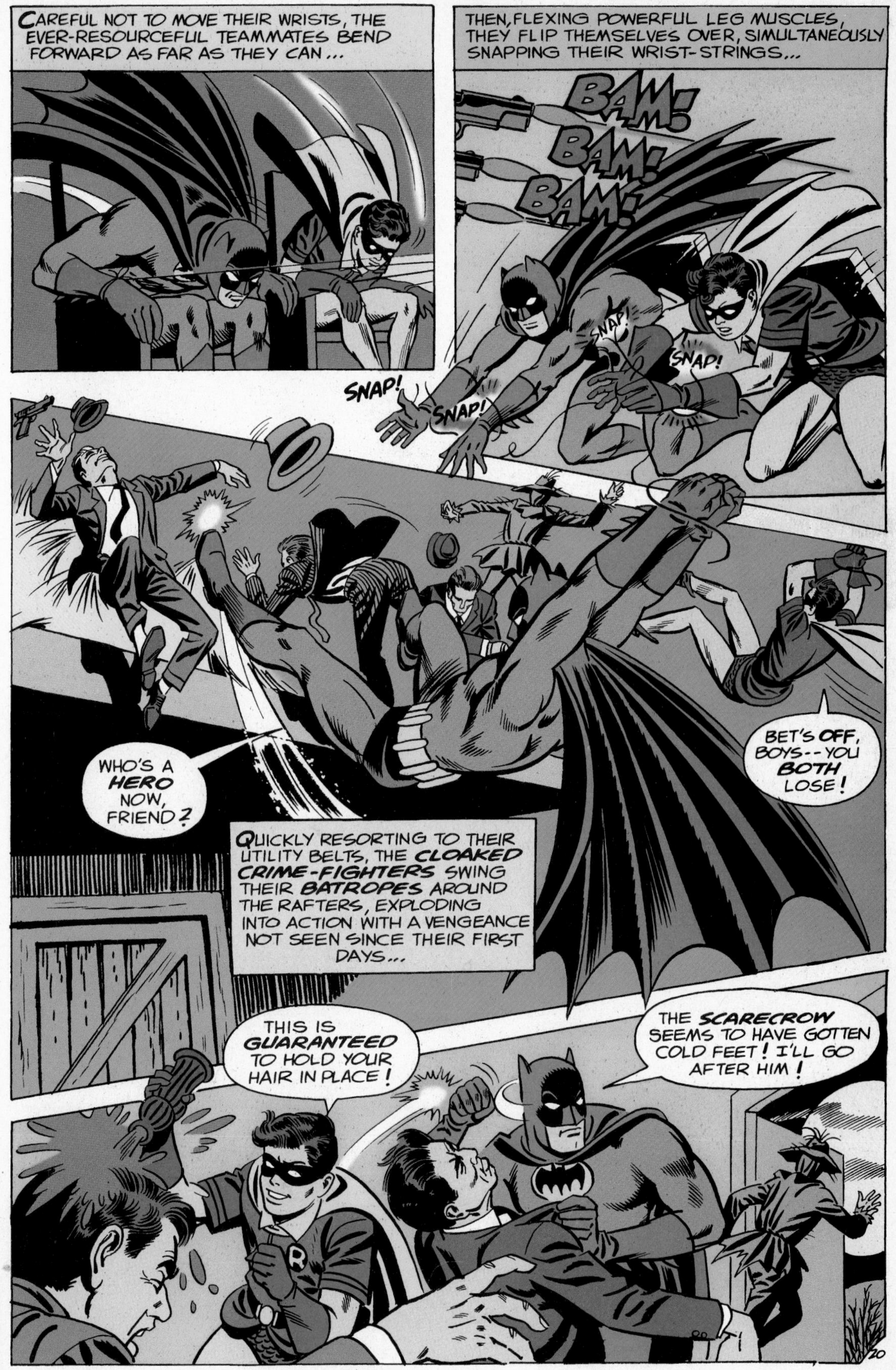
CAREFUL NOT TO MOVE THEIR WRISTS, THE EVER-RESOURCEFUL TEAMMATES BEND FORWARD AS FAR AS THEY CAN...
THEN, FLEXING POWERFUL LEG MUSCLES, THEY FLIP THEMSELVES OVER, SIMULTANEOUSLY SNAPPING THEIR WRIST-STRINGS...
BAM! BAM! BAM!
SNAP!
SNAP!
SNAP!
SNAP!
WHO'S A HERO NOW, FRIEND?
BET'S OFF, BOYS--YOU BOTH LOSE!
QUICKLY RESORTING TO THEIR UTILITY BELTS, THE CLOAKED CRIME-FIGHTERS SWING THEIR BATROPES AROUND THE RAFTERS, EXPLODING INTO ACTION WITH A VENGEANCE NOT SEEN SINCE THEIR FIRST DAYS...
THIS IS GUARANTEED TO HOLD YOUR HAIR IN PLACE!
THE SCARECROW SEEMS TO HAVE GOTTEN COLD FEET! I'LL GO AFTER HIM!
20

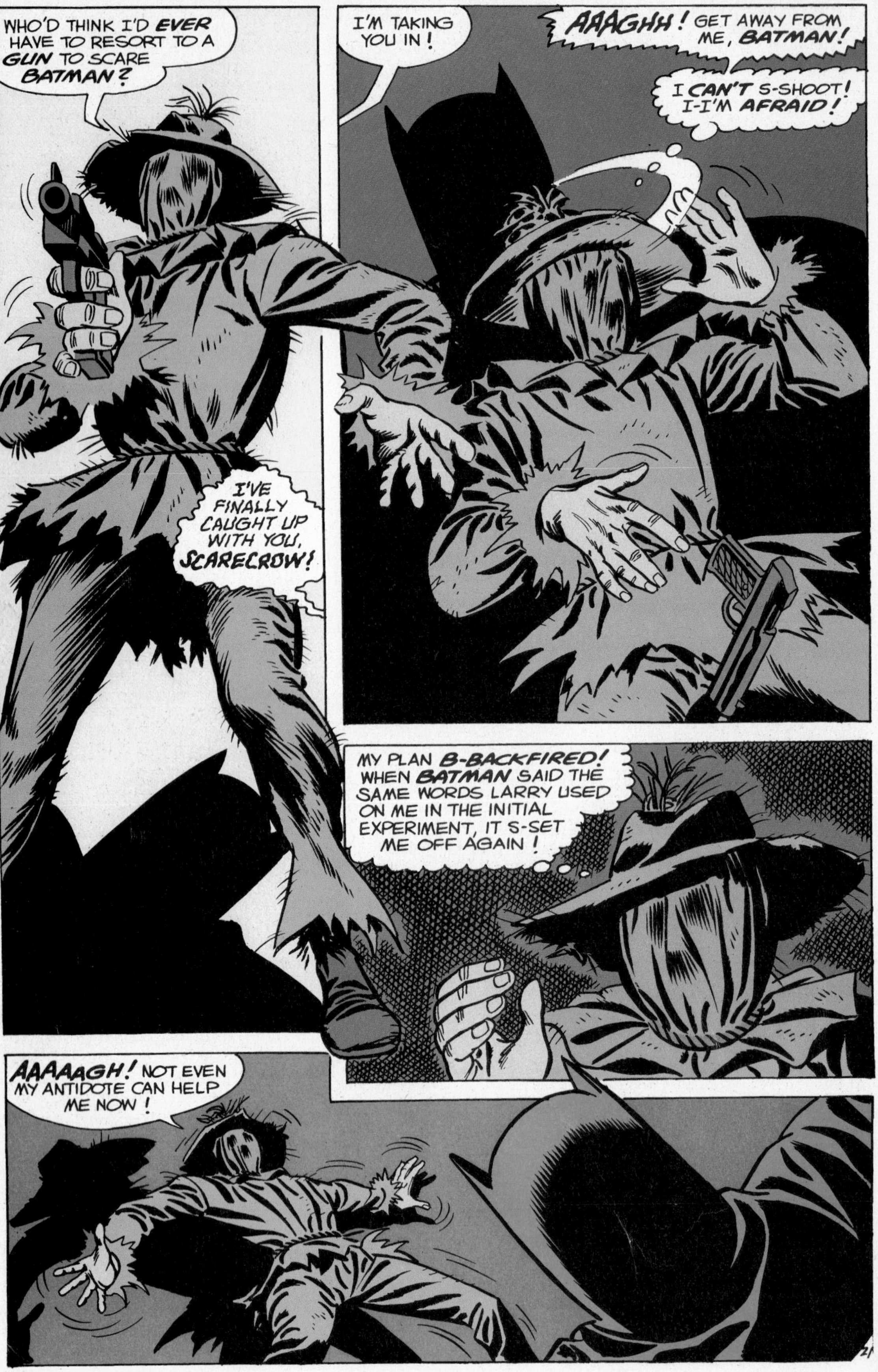
WHO'D THINK I'D EVER HAVE TO RESORT TO A GUN TO SCARE BATMAN?
I'VE FINALLY CAUGHT UP WITH YOU, SCARECROW!
I'M TAKING YOU IN!
AAAGHH! GET AWAY FROM ME, BATMAN!
I CAN'T S-SHOOT! I-I'M AFRAID!
MY PLAN B-BACKFIRED! WHEN BATMAN SAID THE SAME WORDS LARRY USED ON ME IN THE INITIAL EXPERIMENT, IT S-SET ME OFF AGAIN!
AAAAAGH! NOT EVEN MY ANTIDOTE CAN HELP ME NOW!
21

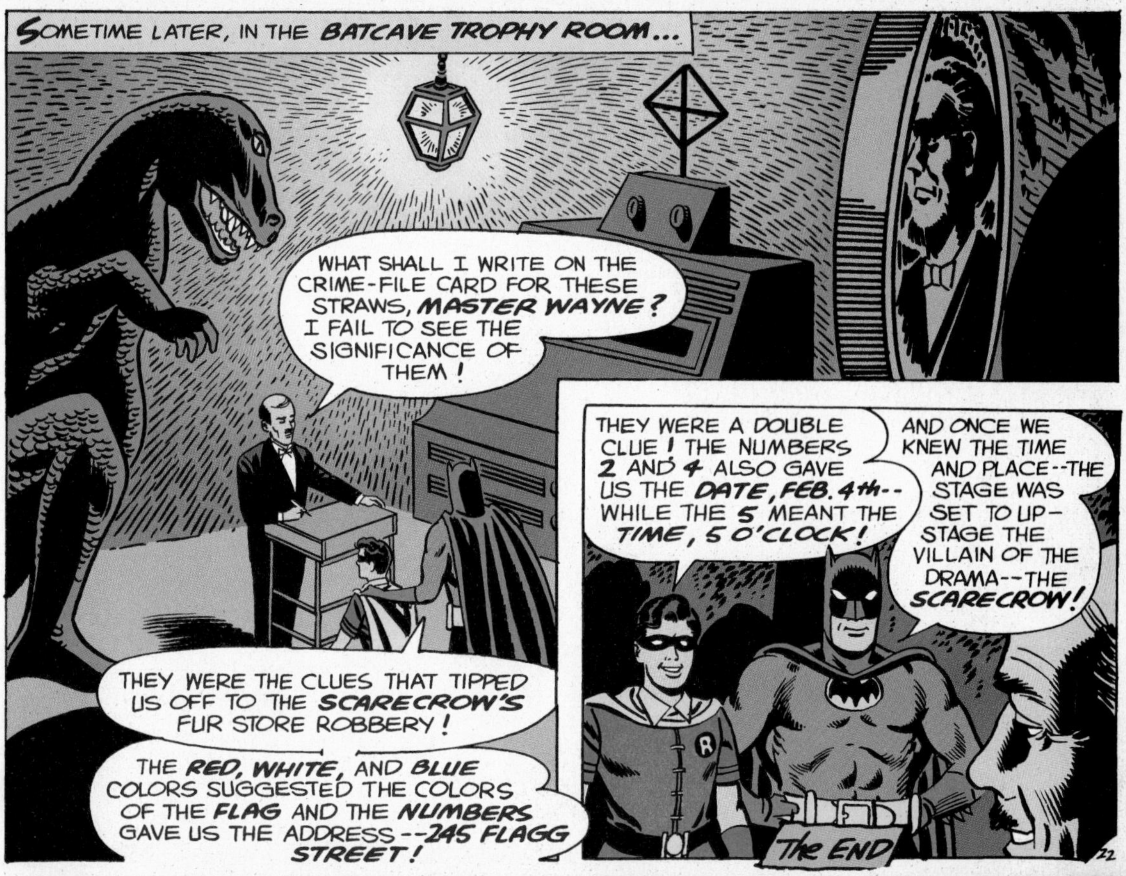
SOMETIME LATER, IN THE BATCAVE TROPHY ROOM...
WHAT SHALL I WRITE ON THE CRIME-FILE CARD FOR THESE STRAWS, MASTER WAYNE? I FAIL TO SEE THE SIGNIFICANCE OF THEM!
THEY WERE THE CLUES THAT TIPPED US OFF TO THE SCARECROW'S FUR STORE ROBBERY!
THE RED, WHITE, AND BLUE COLORS SUGGESTED THE COLORS OF THE FLAG AND THE NUMBERS GAVE US THE ADDRESS--245 FLAGG STREET!
THEY WERE A DOUBLE CLUE! THE NUMBERS 2 AND 4 ALSO GAVE US THE DATE, FEB. 4th--WHILE THE 5 MEANT THE TIME, 5 O'CLOCK!
AND ONCE WE KNEW THE TIME AND PLACE--THE STAGE WAS SET TO UP-STAGE THE VILLAIN OF THE DRAMA--THE SCARECROW!
The END
22

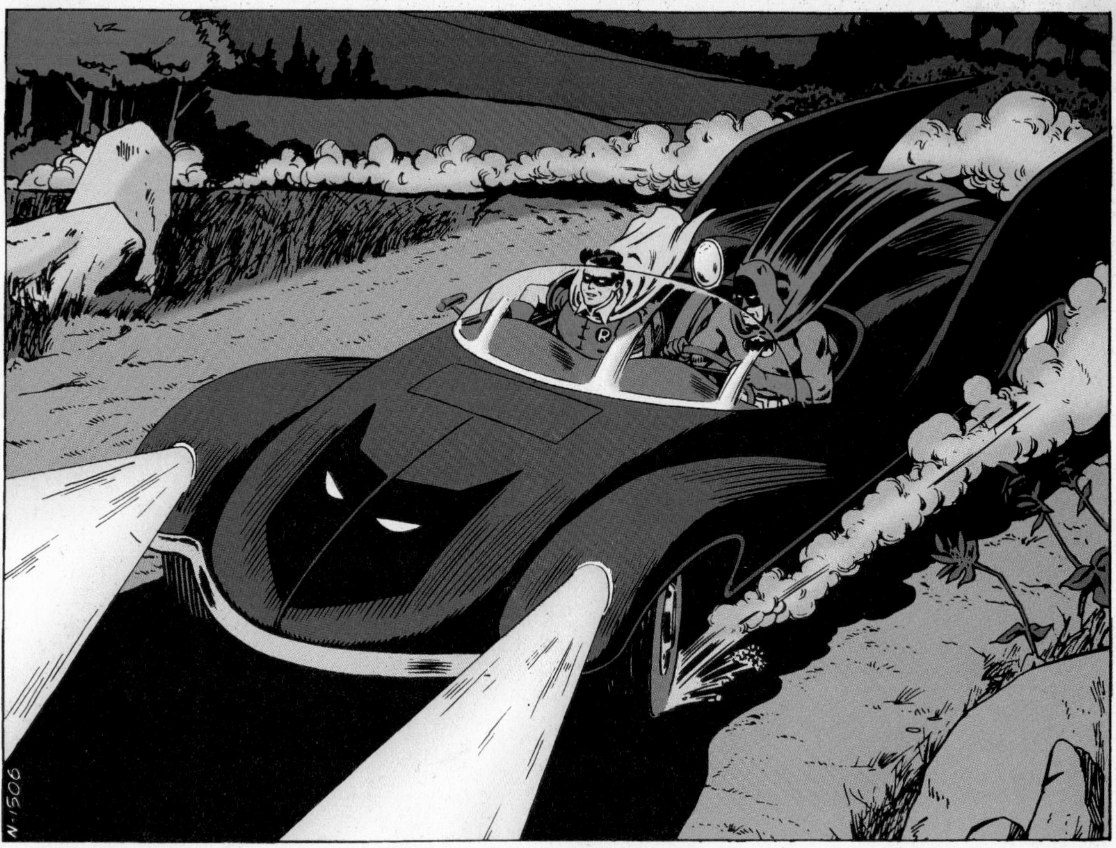

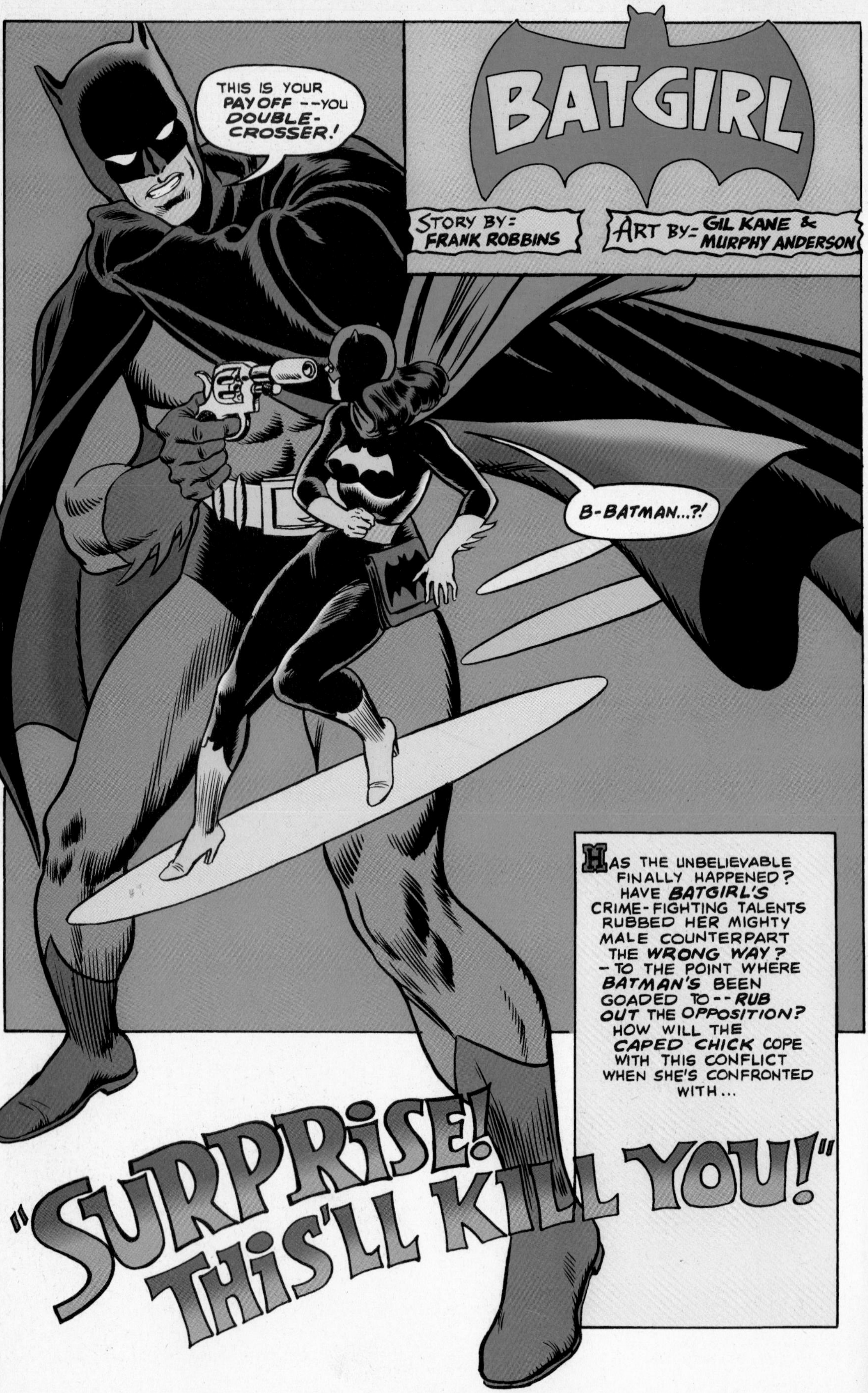
BATGIRL
STORY BY: FRANK ROBBINS
ART BY: GIL KANE & MURPHY ANDERSON
THIS IS YOUR PAYOFF --YOU DOUBLE-CROSSER!
B-BATMAN...?!
HAS THE UNBELIEVABLE FINALLY HAPPENED? HAVE BATGIRL'S CRIME-FIGHTING TALENTS RUBBED HER MIGHTY MALE COUNTERPART THE WRONG WAY? - TO THE POINT WHERE BATMAN'S BEEN GOADED TO--RUB OUT THE OPPOSITION? HOW WILL THE CAPED CHICK COPE WITH THIS CONFLICT WHEN SHE'S CONFRONTED WITH...
"SURPRISE! THIS'LL KILL YOU!"

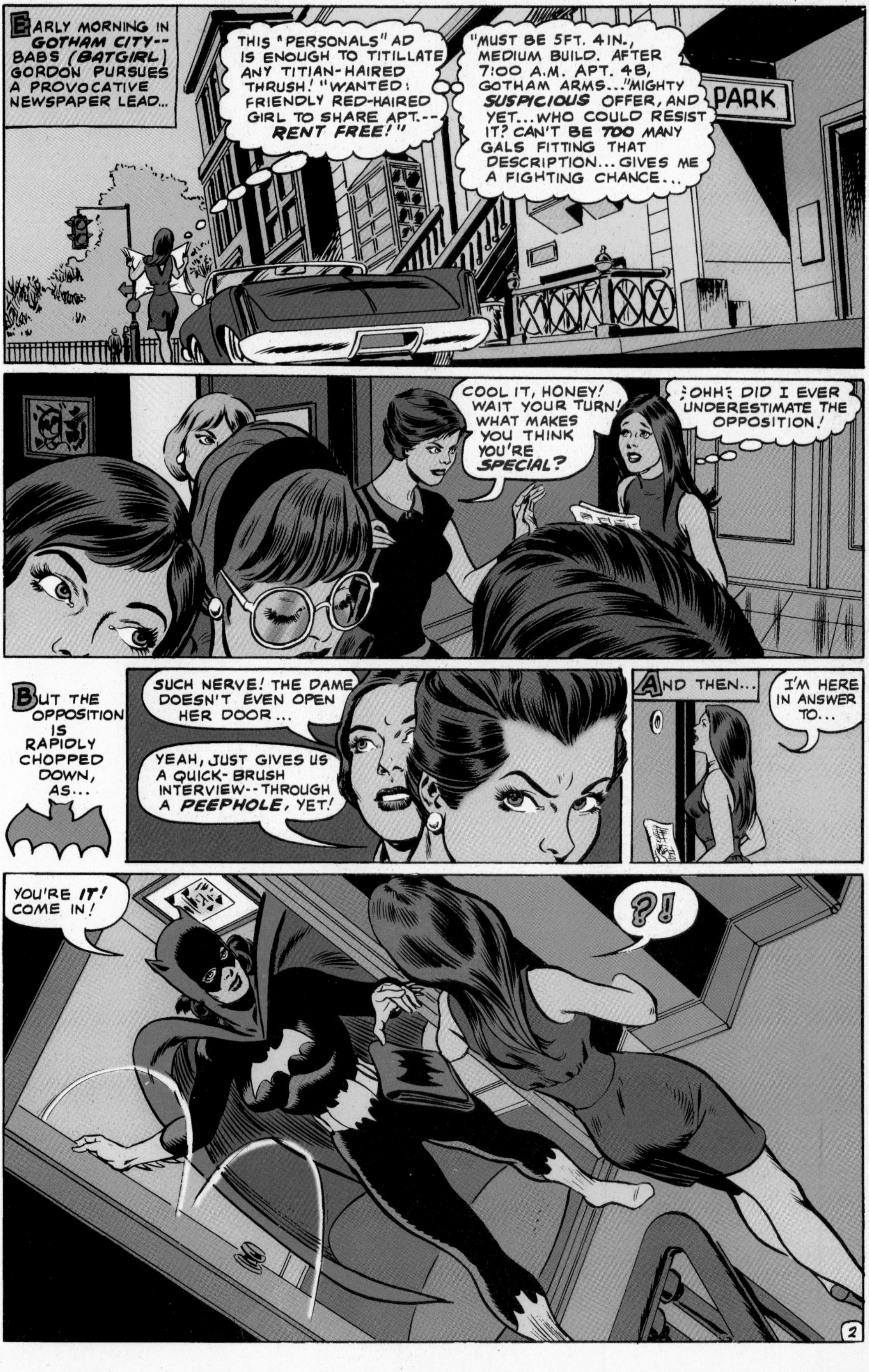
EARLY MORNING IN GOTHAM CITY-- BABS (BATGIRL) GORDON PURSUES A PROVOCATIVE NEWSPAPER LEAD...
THIS "PERSONALS" AD IS ENOUGH TO TITILLATE ANY TITIAN-HAIRED THRUSH! "WANTED: FRIENDLY RED-HAIRED GIRL TO SHARE APT.-- RENT FREE!"
"MUST BE 5FT. 4IN., MEDIUM BUILD. AFTER 7:00 A.M. APT. 4B, GOTHAM ARMS..." MIGHTY SUSPICIOUS OFFER, AND YET... WHO COULD RESIST IT? CAN'T BE TOO MANY GALS FITTING THAT DESCRIPTION... GIVES ME A FIGHTING CHANCE...
PARK
COOL IT, HONEY! WAIT YOUR TURN! WHAT MAKES YOU THINK YOU'RE SPECIAL?
OHH! DID I EVER UNDERESTIMATE THE OPPOSITION!
BUT THE OPPOSITION IS RAPIDLY CHOPPED DOWN, AS...
SUCH NERVE! THE DAME DOESN'T EVEN OPEN HER DOOR...
YEAH, JUST GIVES US A QUICK-BRUSH INTERVIEW--THROUGH A PEEPHOLE, YET!
AND THEN...
I'M HERE IN ANSWER TO...
YOU'RE IT! COME IN!
?!
2

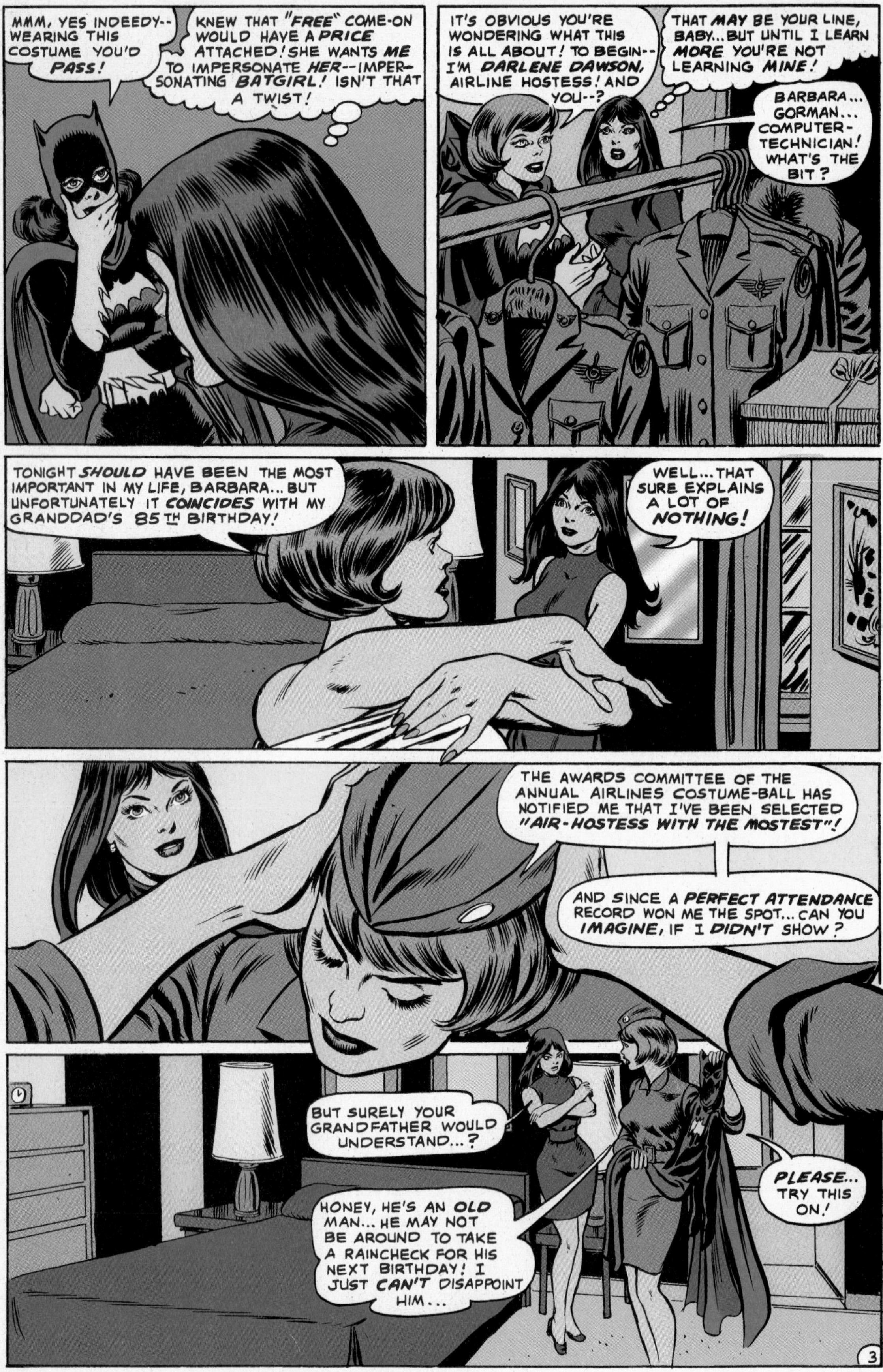

MMM, YES INDEEDY--WEARING THIS COSTUME YOU'D PASS!
KNEW THAT "FREE" COME-ON WOULD HAVE A PRICE ATTACHED! SHE WANTS ME TO IMPERSONATE HER--IMPERSONATING BATGIRL! ISN'T THAT A TWIST!
IT'S OBVIOUS YOU'RE WONDERING WHAT THIS IS ALL ABOUT! TO BEGIN--I'M DARLENE DAWSON, AIRLINE HOSTESS! AND YOU--?
THAT MAY BE YOUR LINE, BABY... BUT UNTIL I LEARN MORE YOU'RE NOT LEARNING MINE!
BARBARA... GORMAN... COMPUTER-TECHNICIAN! WHAT'S THE BIT?
TONIGHT SHOULD HAVE BEEN THE MOST IMPORTANT IN MY LIFE, BARBARA... BUT UNFORTUNATELY IT COINCIDES WITH MY GRANDDAD'S 85TH BIRTHDAY!
WELL... THAT SURE EXPLAINS A LOT OF NOTHING!
THE AWARDS COMMITTEE OF THE ANNUAL AIRLINES COSTUME-BALL HAS NOTIFIED ME THAT I'VE BEEN SELECTED "AIR-HOSTESS WITH THE MOSTEST"!
AND SINCE A PERFECT ATTENDANCE RECORD WON ME THE SPOT... CAN YOU IMAGINE, IF I DIDN'T SHOW?
BUT SURELY YOUR GRANDFATHER WOULD UNDERSTAND...?
HONEY, HE'S AN OLD MAN... HE MAY NOT BE AROUND TO TAKE A RAINCHECK FOR HIS NEXT BIRTHDAY! I JUST CAN'T DISAPPOINT HIM...
PLEASE... TRY THIS ON!
3

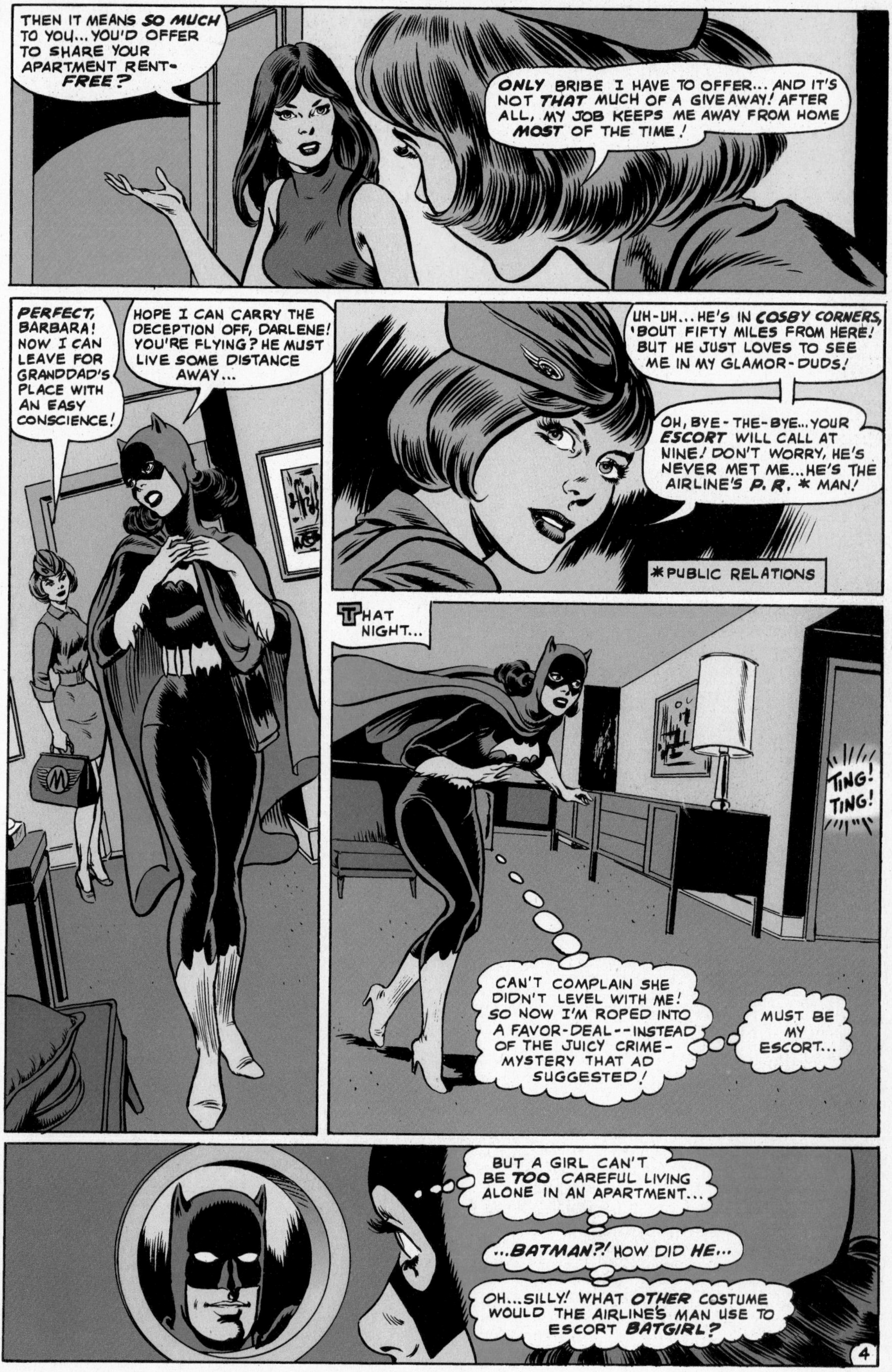
THEN IT MEANS SO MUCH TO YOU... YOU'D OFFER TO SHARE YOUR APARTMENT RENT-FREE?
ONLY BRIBE I HAVE TO OFFER... AND IT'S NOT THAT MUCH OF A GIVEAWAY! AFTER ALL, MY JOB KEEPS ME AWAY FROM HOME MOST OF THE TIME!
PERFECT, BARBARA! NOW I CAN LEAVE FOR GRANDDAD'S PLACE WITH AN EASY CONSCIENCE!
HOPE I CAN CARRY THE DECEPTION OFF, DARLENE! YOU'RE FLYING? HE MUST LIVE SOME DISTANCE AWAY...
UH-UH... HE'S IN COSBY CORNERS, 'BOUT FIFTY MILES FROM HERE! BUT HE JUST LOVES TO SEE ME IN MY GLAMOR-DUDS!
OH, BYE-THE-BYE... YOUR ESCORT WILL CALL AT NINE! DON'T WORRY, HE'S NEVER MET ME... HE'S THE AIRLINE'S P.R. * MAN!
* PUBLIC RELATIONS
THAT NIGHT...
TING! TING!
CAN'T COMPLAIN SHE DIDN'T LEVEL WITH ME! SO NOW I'M ROPED INTO A FAVOR-DEAL--INSTEAD OF THE JUICY CRIME-MYSTERY THAT AD SUGGESTED!
MUST BE MY ESCORT...
BUT A GIRL CAN'T BE TOO CAREFUL LIVING ALONE IN AN APARTMENT...
...BATMAN?! HOW DID HE...
OH...SILLY! WHAT OTHER COSTUME WOULD THE AIRLINE'S MAN USE TO ESCORT BATGIRL?
4

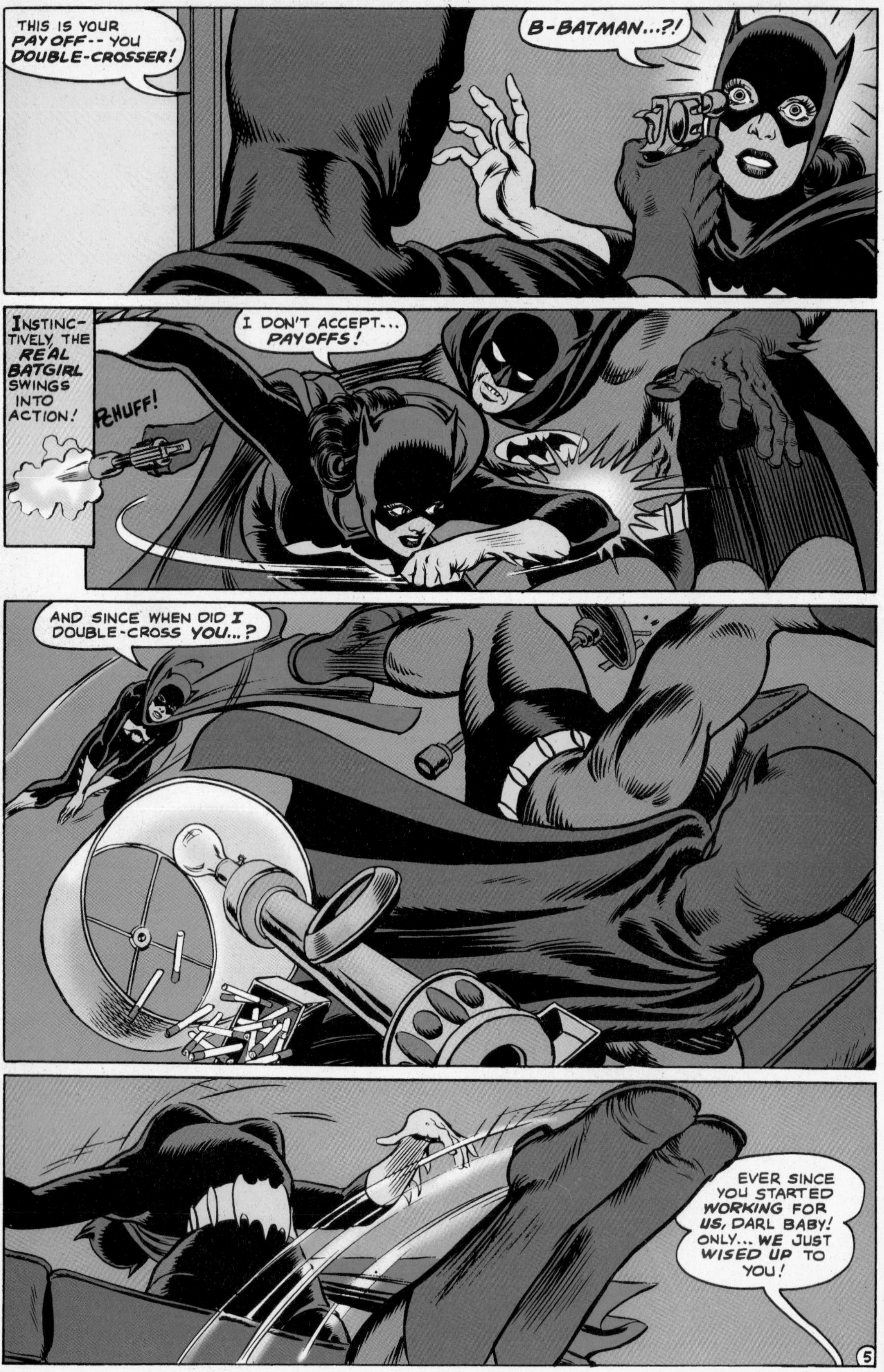
THIS IS YOUR PAYOFF -- YOU DOUBLE-CROSSER!
B-BATMAN...?!
INSTINCTIVELY, THE REAL BATGIRL SWINGS INTO ACTION!
I DON'T ACCEPT... PAYOFFS!
CHUFF!
AND SINCE WHEN DID I DOUBLE-CROSS YOU...?
EVER SINCE YOU STARTED WORKING FOR US, DARL BABY! ONLY... WE JUST WISED UP TO YOU!
5

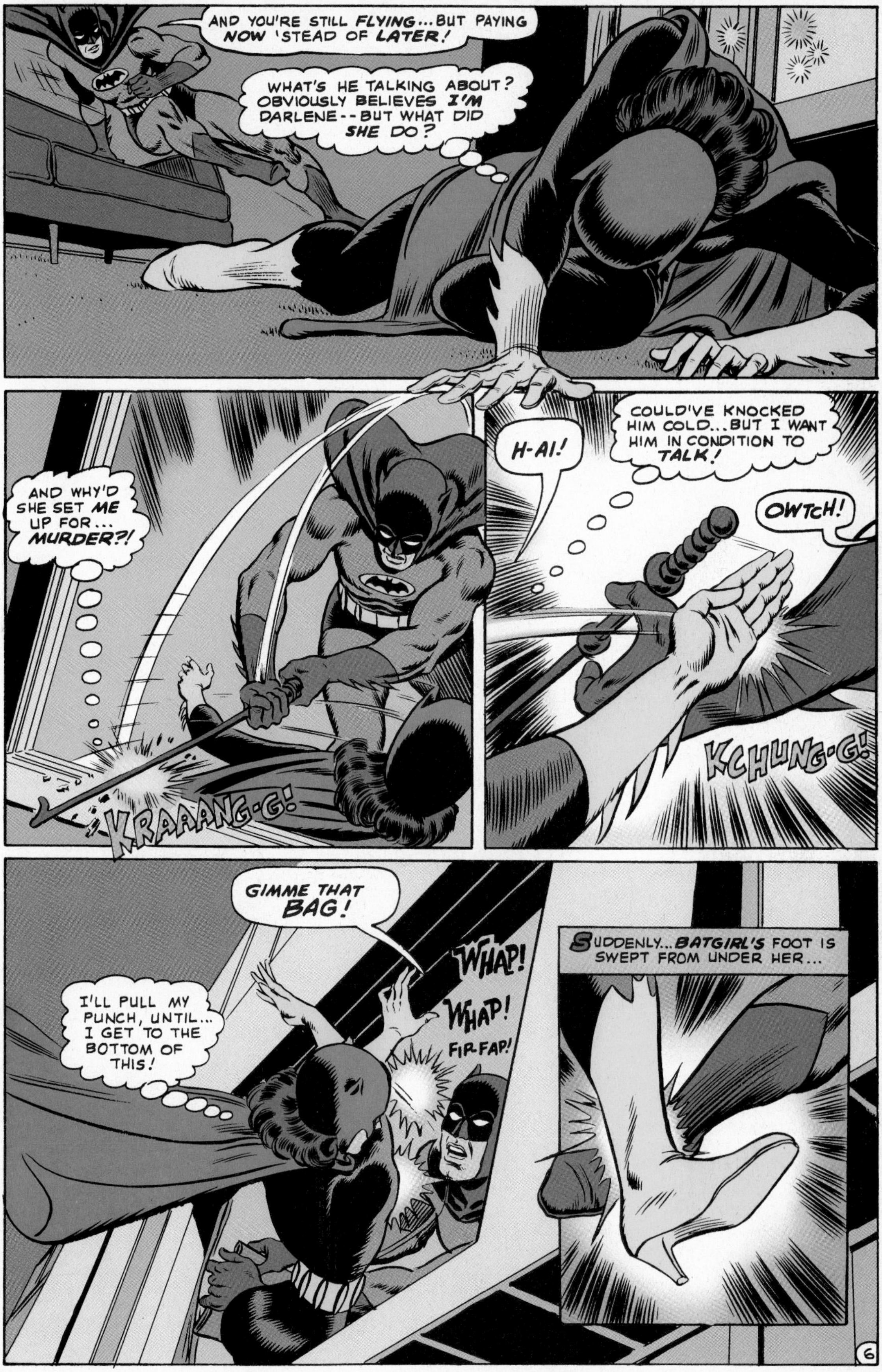
AND YOU'RE STILL FLYING... BUT PAYING NOW 'STEAD OF LATER!
WHAT'S HE TALKING ABOUT? OBVIOUSLY BELIEVES I'M DARLENE--BUT WHAT DID SHE DO?
AND WHY'D SHE SET ME UP FOR... MURDER?!
KRAAANG-G!
H-AI!
COULD'VE KNOCKED HIM COLD...BUT I WANT HIM IN CONDITION TO TALK!
OWTCH!
KCHUNG-G!
GIMME THAT BAG!
I'LL PULL MY PUNCH, UNTIL... I GET TO THE BOTTOM OF THIS!
WHAP!
WHAP!
FIP-FAP!
SUDDENLY...BATGIRL'S FOOT IS SWEPT FROM UNDER HER...
6

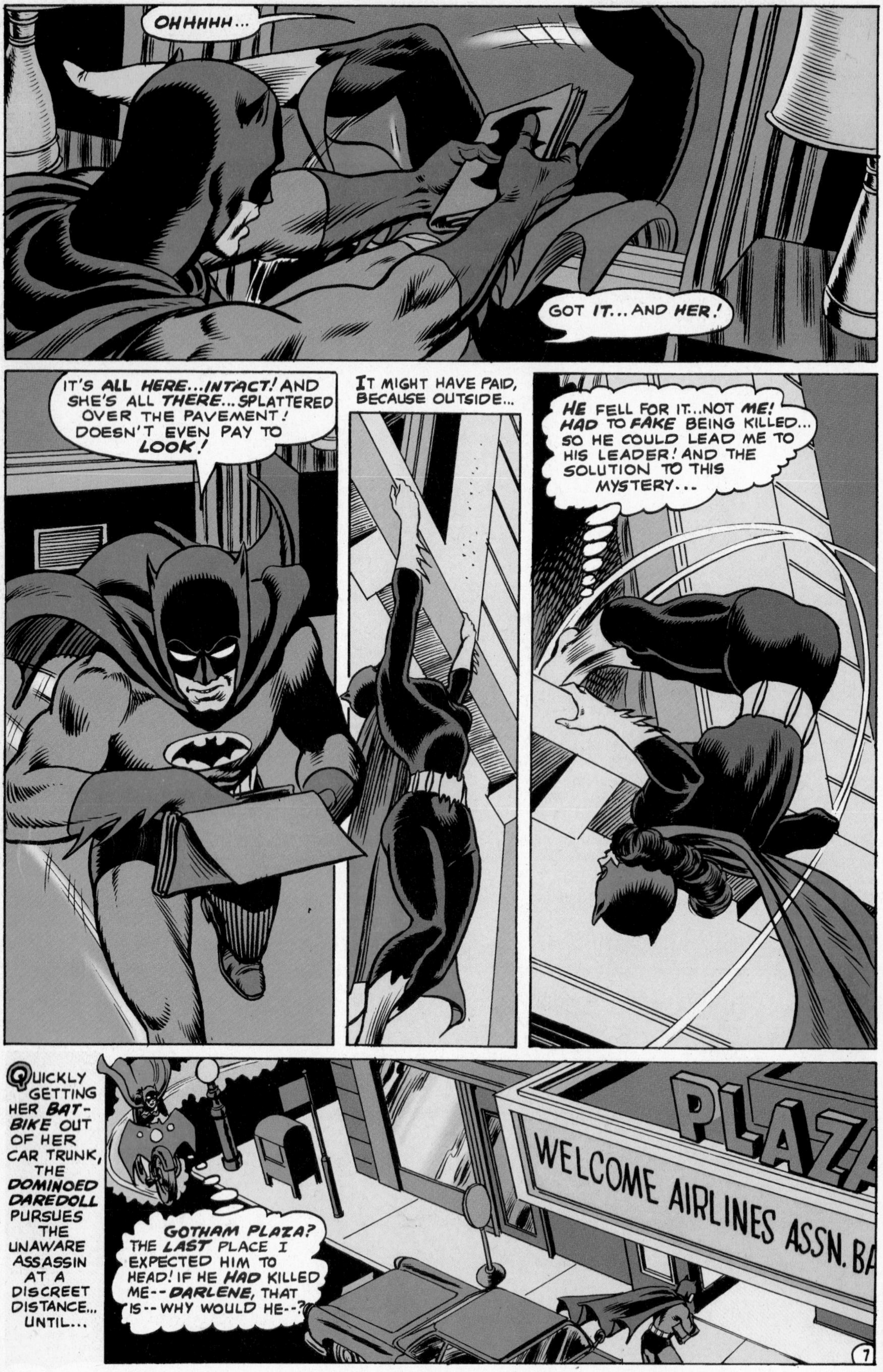
OHHHHH...
GOT IT... AND HER!
IT'S ALL HERE...INTACT! AND SHE'S ALL THERE...SPLATTERED OVER THE PAVEMENT! DOESN'T EVEN PAY TO LOOK!
IT MIGHT HAVE PAID, BECAUSE OUTSIDE...
HE FELL FOR IT...NOT ME! HAD TO FAKE BEING KILLED... SO HE COULD LEAD ME TO HIS LEADER! AND THE SOLUTION TO THIS MYSTERY...
QUICKLY GETTING HER BAT-BIKE OUT OF HER CAR TRUNK, THE DOMINOED DAREDOLL PURSUES THE UNAWARE ASSASSIN AT A DISCREET DISTANCE... UNTIL...
PLAZA
WELCOME AIRLINES ASSN. BA
GOTHAM PLAZA? THE LAST PLACE I EXPECTED HIM TO HEAD! IF HE HAD KILLED ME--DARLENE, THAT IS--WHY WOULD HE--?
7

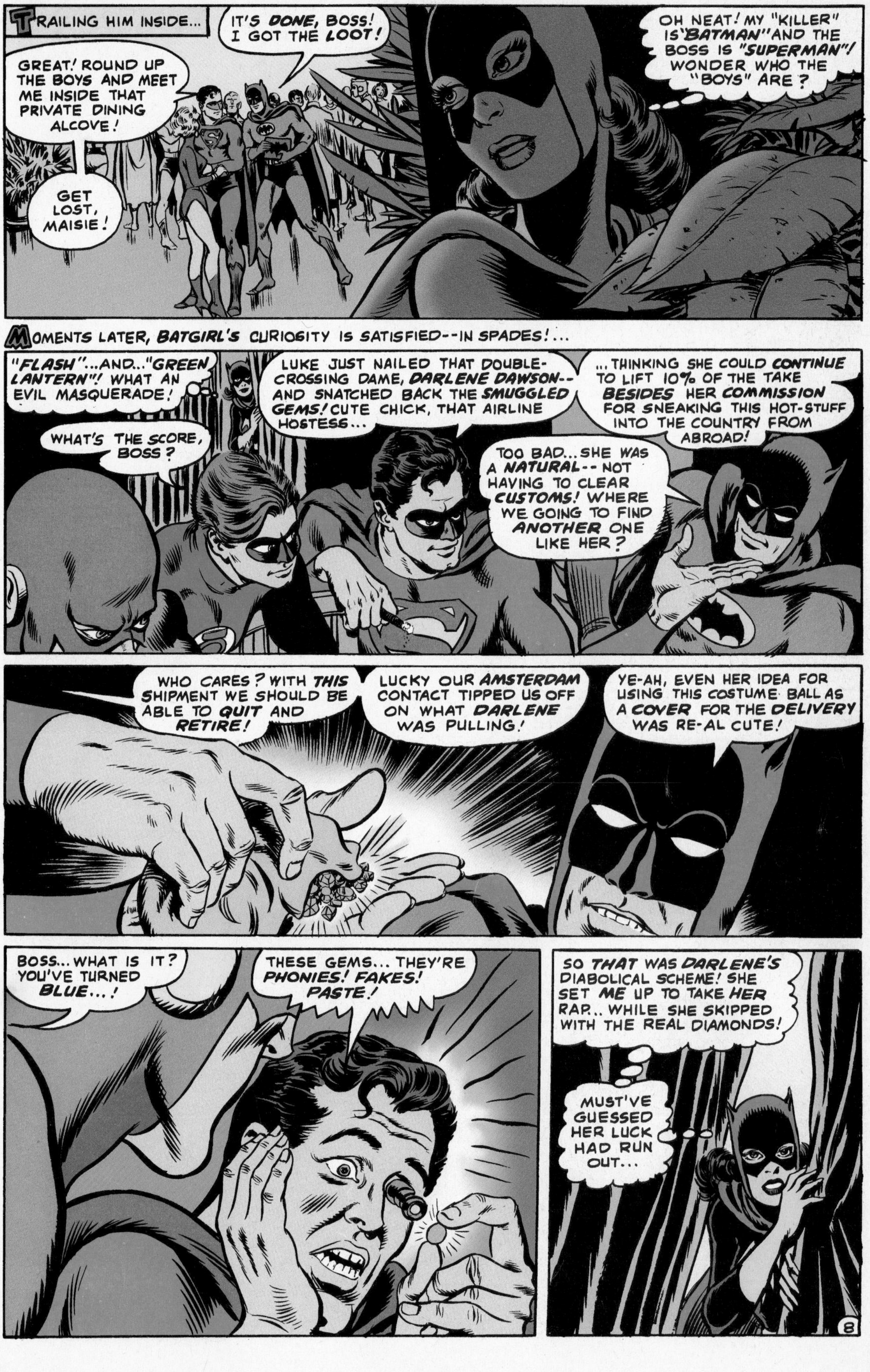
TRAILING HIM INSIDE...
IT'S DONE, BOSS! I GOT THE LOOT!
GREAT! ROUND UP THE BOYS AND MEET ME INSIDE THAT PRIVATE DINING ALCOVE!
GET LOST, MAISIE!
OH NEAT! MY "KILLER" IS "BATMAN" AND THE BOSS IS "SUPERMAN"! WONDER WHO THE "BOYS" ARE?
MOMENTS LATER, BATGIRL'S CURIOSITY IS SATISFIED--IN SPADES!...
"FLASH"...AND..."GREEN LANTERN"! WHAT AN EVIL MASQUERADE!
WHAT'S THE SCORE, BOSS?
LUKE JUST NAILED THAT DOUBLE-CROSSING DAME, DARLENE DAWSON--AND SNATCHED BACK THE SMUGGLED GEMS! CUTE CHICK, THAT AIRLINE HOSTESS...
...THINKING SHE COULD CONTINUE TO LIFT 10% OF THE TAKE BESIDES HER COMMISSION FOR SNEAKING THIS HOT-STUFF INTO THE COUNTRY FROM ABROAD!
TOO BAD...SHE WAS A NATURAL--NOT HAVING TO CLEAR CUSTOMS! WHERE WE GOING TO FIND ANOTHER ONE LIKE HER?
WHO CARES? WITH THIS SHIPMENT WE SHOULD BE ABLE TO QUIT AND RETIRE!
LUCKY OUR AMSTERDAM CONTACT TIPPED US OFF ON WHAT DARLENE WAS PULLING!
YE-AH, EVEN HER IDEA FOR USING THIS COSTUME BALL AS A COVER FOR THE DELIVERY WAS RE-AL CUTE!
BOSS... WHAT IS IT? YOU'VE TURNED BLUE...!
THESE GEMS... THEY'RE PHONIES! FAKES! PASTE!
SO THAT WAS DARLENE'S DIABOLICAL SCHEME! SHE SET ME UP TO TAKE HER RAP... WHILE SHE SKIPPED WITH THE REAL DIAMONDS!
MUST'VE GUESSED HER LUCK HAD RUN OUT...
8

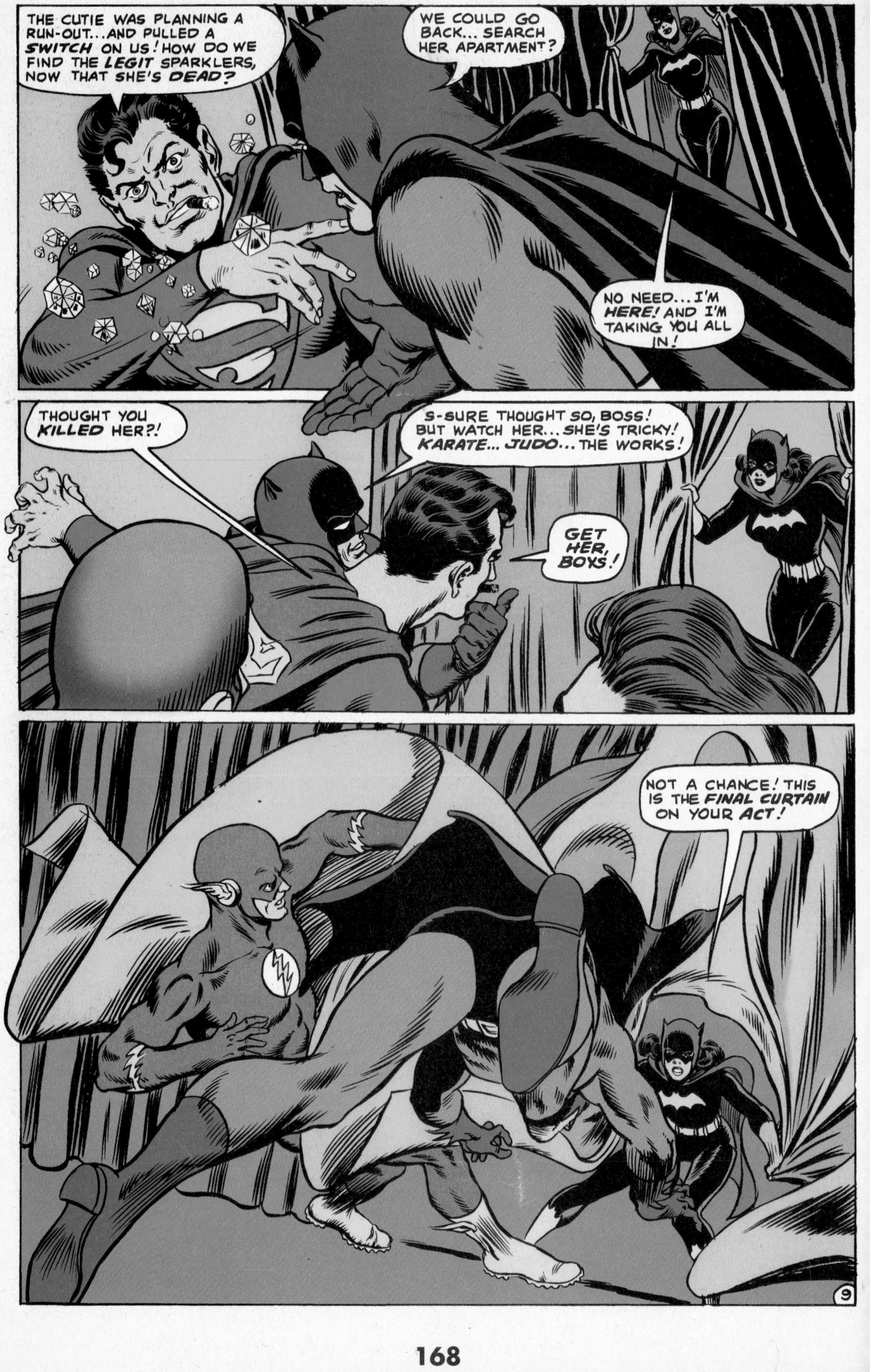
THE CUTIE WAS PLANNING A RUN-OUT...AND PULLED A SWITCH ON US! HOW DO WE FIND THE LEGIT SPARKLERS, NOW THAT SHE'S DEAD?
WE COULD GO BACK... SEARCH HER APARTMENT?
NO NEED... I'M HERE! AND I'M TAKING YOU ALL IN!
THOUGHT YOU KILLED HER?!
S-SURE THOUGHT SO, BOSS! BUT WATCH HER... SHE'S TRICKY! KARATE... JUDO... THE WORKS!
GET HER, BOYS!
NOT A CHANCE! THIS IS THE FINAL CURTAIN ON YOUR ACT!
9

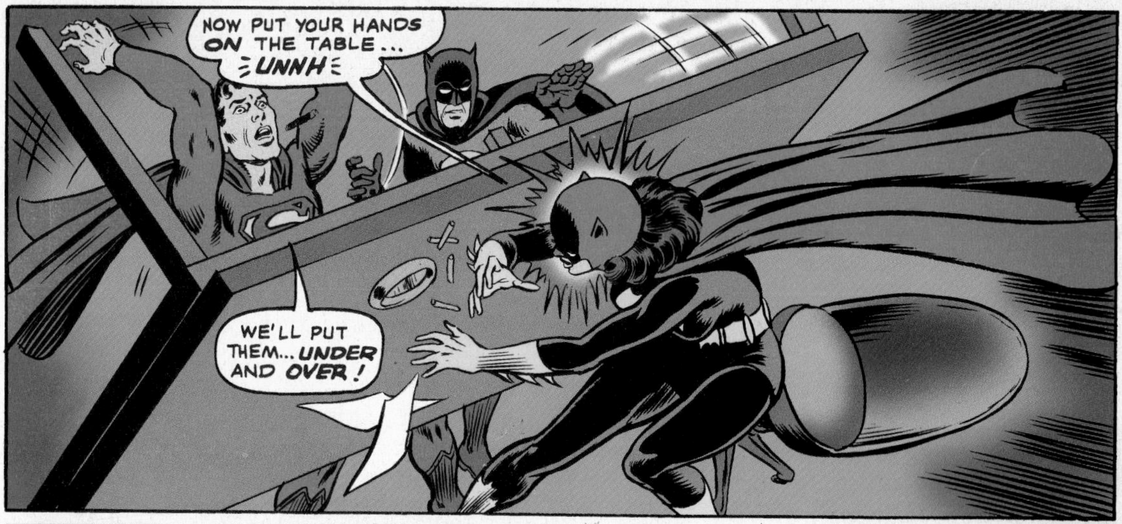
NOW PUT YOUR HANDS ON THE TABLE... UNNH
WE'LL PUT THEM... UNDER AND OVER!

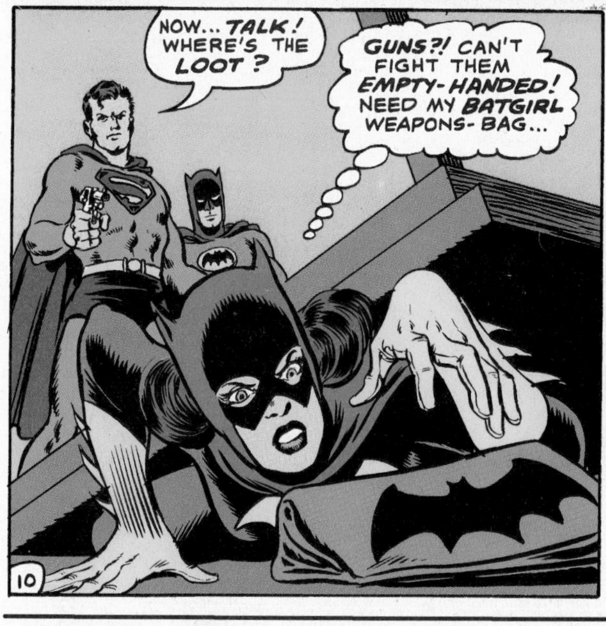
NOW... TALK! WHERE'S THE LOOT?
GUNS?! CAN'T FIGHT THEM EMPTY-HANDED! NEED MY BATGIRL WEAPONS-BAG...
10

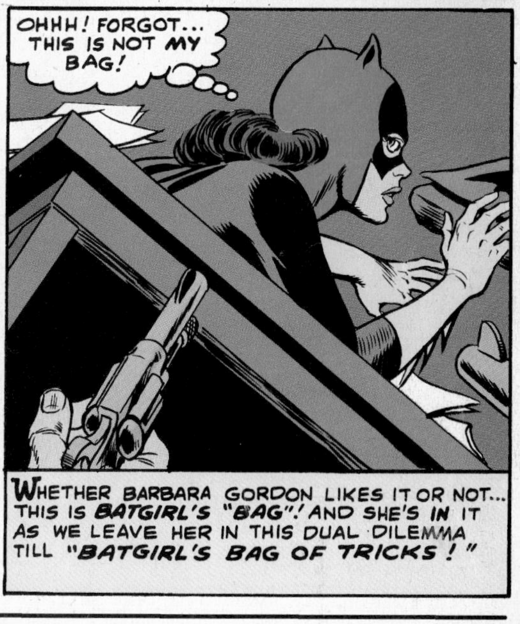
OHHH! FORGOT... THIS IS NOT MY BAG!
WHETHER BARBARA GORDON LIKES IT OR NOT... THIS IS BATGIRL'S "BAG"! AND SHE'S IN IT AS WE LEAVE HER IN THIS DUAL DILEMMA TILL "BATGIRL'S BAG OF TRICKS!"

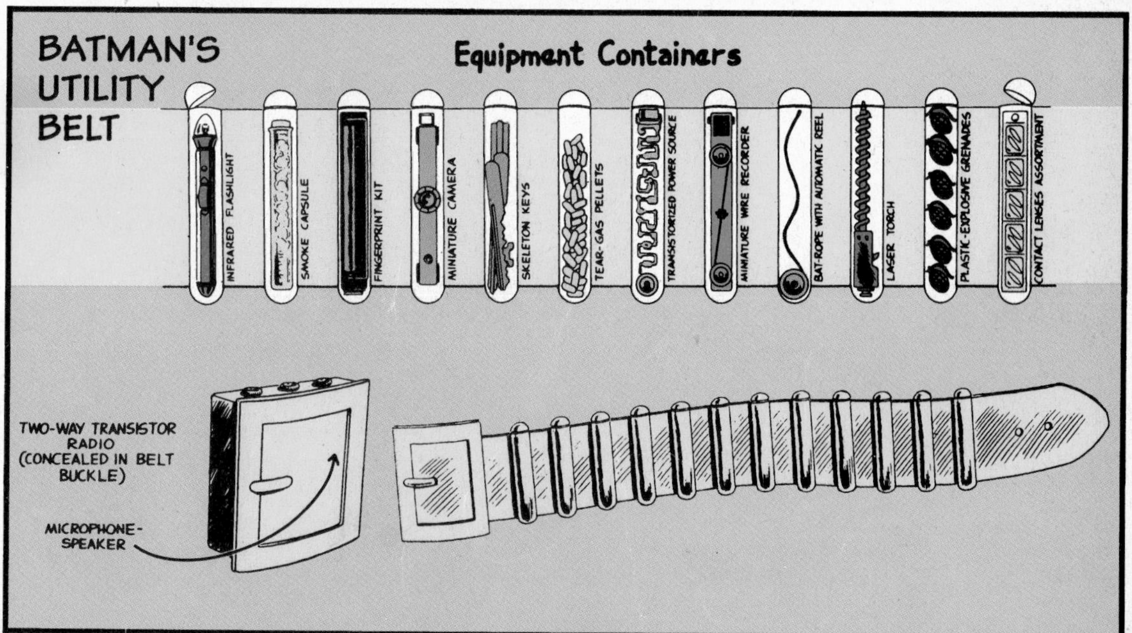
BATMAN'S UTILITY BELT
Equipment Containers
INFRARED FLASHLIGHT
SMOKE CAPSULE
FINGERPRINT KIT
MINIATURE CAMERA
SKELETON KEYS
TEAR-GAS PELLETS
TRANSISTORIZED POWER SOURCE
MINIATURE WIRE RECORDER
BAT-ROPE WITH AUTOMATIC REEL
LASER TORCH
PLASTIC-EXPLOSIVE GRENADES
CONTACT LENSES ASSORTMENT
TWO-WAY TRANSISTOR RADIO (CONCEALED IN BELT BUCKLE)
MICROPHONE-SPEAKER

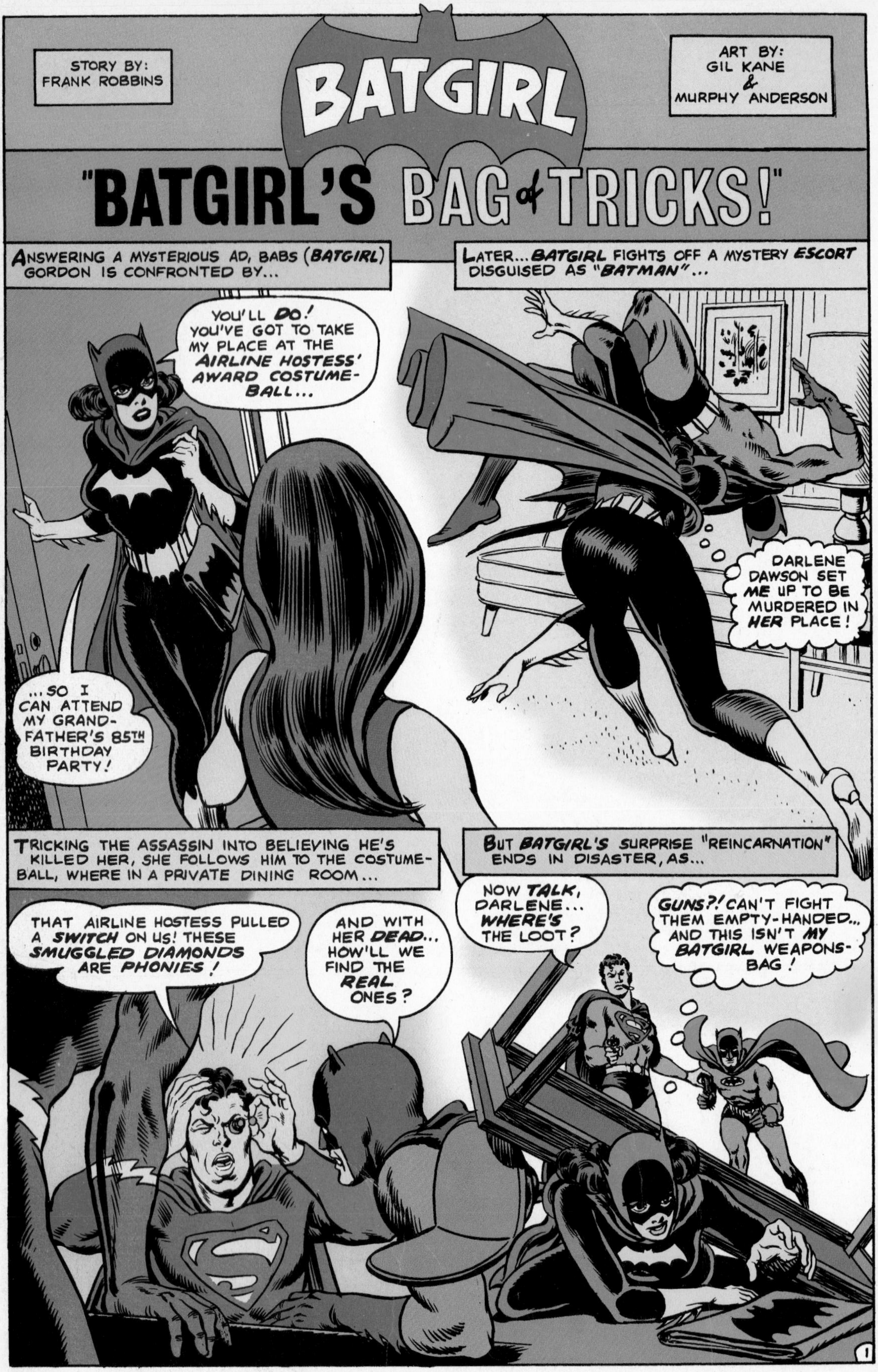
STORY BY: FRANK ROBBINS
BATGIRL
ART BY: GIL KANE & MURPHY ANDERSON
"BATGIRL'S BAG of TRICKS!"
ANSWERING A MYSTERIOUS AD, BABS (BATGIRL) GORDON IS CONFRONTED BY...
YOU'LL DO! YOU'VE GOT TO TAKE MY PLACE AT THE AIRLINE HOSTESS' AWARD COSTUME-BALL...
...SO I CAN ATTEND MY GRAND-FATHER'S 85TH BIRTHDAY PARTY!
LATER... BATGIRL FIGHTS OFF A MYSTERY ESCORT DISGUISED AS "BATMAN"...
DARLENE DAWSON SET ME UP TO BE MURDERED IN HER PLACE!
TRICKING THE ASSASSIN INTO BELIEVING HE'S KILLED HER, SHE FOLLOWS HIM TO THE COSTUME-BALL, WHERE IN A PRIVATE DINING ROOM...
THAT AIRLINE HOSTESS PULLED A SWITCH ON US! THESE SMUGGLED DIAMONDS ARE PHONIES!
AND WITH HER DEAD... HOW'LL WE FIND THE REAL ONES?
BUT BATGIRL'S SURPRISE "REINCARNATION" ENDS IN DISASTER, AS...
NOW TALK, DARLENE... WHERE'S THE LOOT?
GUNS?! CAN'T FIGHT THEM EMPTY-HANDED... AND THIS ISN'T MY BATGIRL WEAPONS-BAG!
1

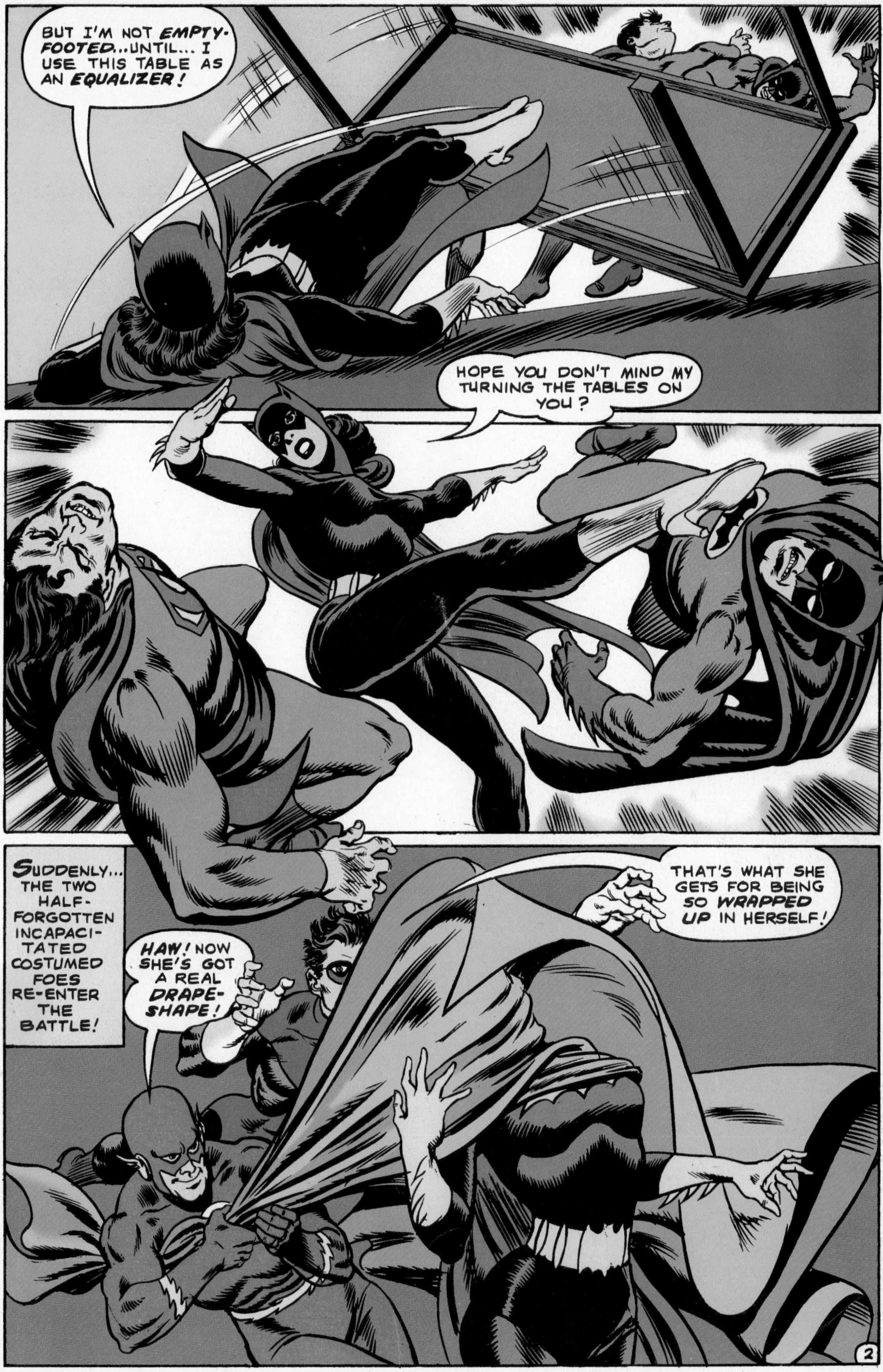

BUT I'M NOT EMPTY-FOOTED...UNTIL... I USE THIS TABLE AS AN EQUALIZER!
HOPE YOU DON'T MIND MY TURNING THE TABLES ON YOU?
SUDDENLY... THE TWO HALF-FORGOTTEN INCAPACITATED COSTUMED FOES RE-ENTER THE BATTLE!
THAT'S WHAT SHE GETS FOR BEING SO WRAPPED UP IN HERSELF!
HAW! NOW SHE'S GOT A REAL DRAPE-SHAPE!
2

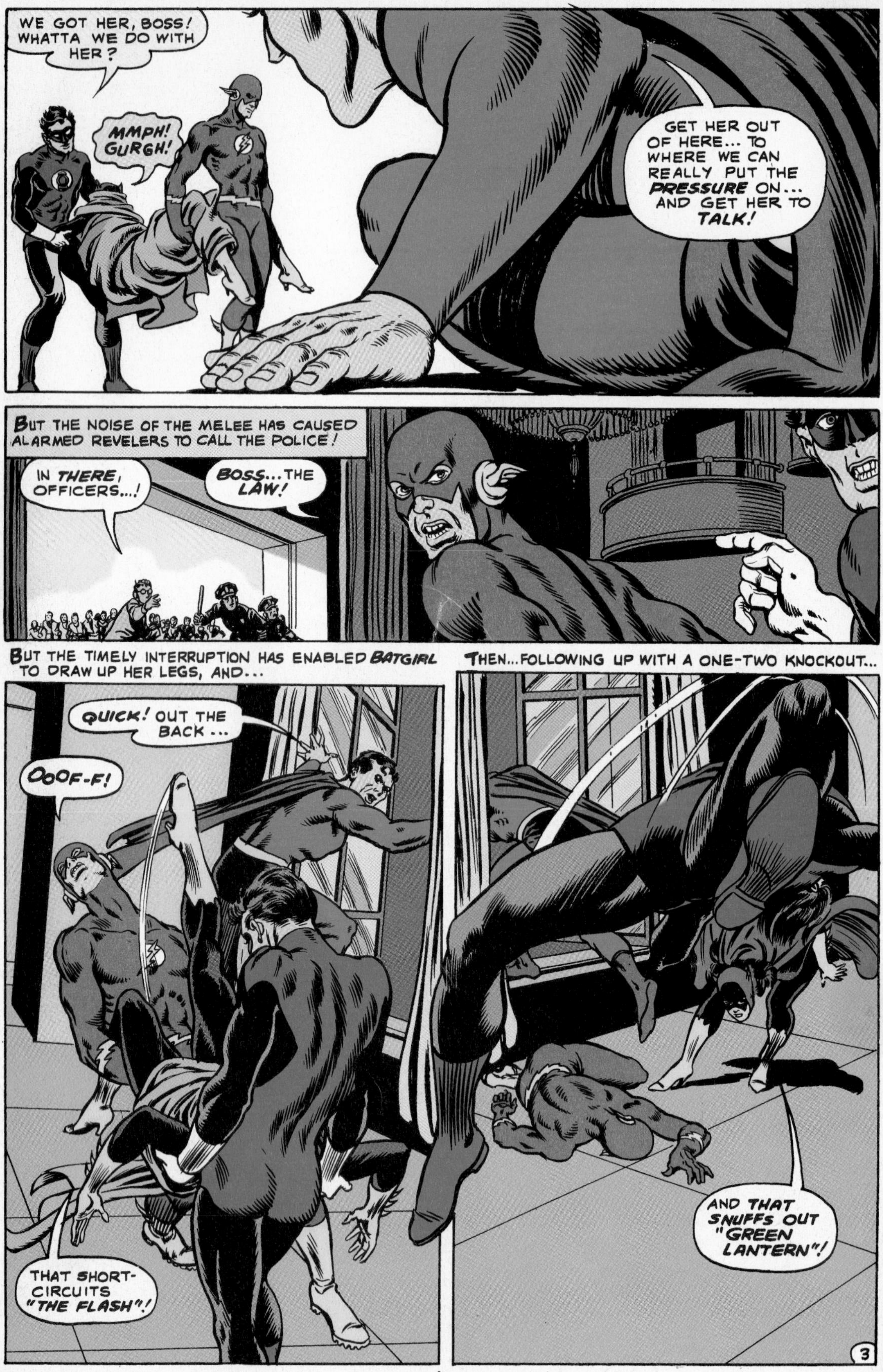
WE GOT HER, BOSS! WHATTA WE DO WITH HER?
MMPH! GURGH!
GET HER OUT OF HERE... TO WHERE WE CAN REALLY PUT THE PRESSURE ON... AND GET HER TO TALK!
BUT THE NOISE OF THE MELEE HAS CAUSED ALARMED REVELERS TO CALL THE POLICE!
IN THERE, OFFICERS...!
BOSS... THE LAW!
BUT THE TIMELY INTERRUPTION HAS ENABLED BATGIRL TO DRAW UP HER LEGS, AND...
QUICK! OUT THE BACK...
OOOF-F!
THAT SHORT-CIRCUITS "THE FLASH"!
THEN...FOLLOWING UP WITH A ONE-TWO KNOCKOUT...
AND THAT SNUFFS OUT "GREEN LANTERN"!
3

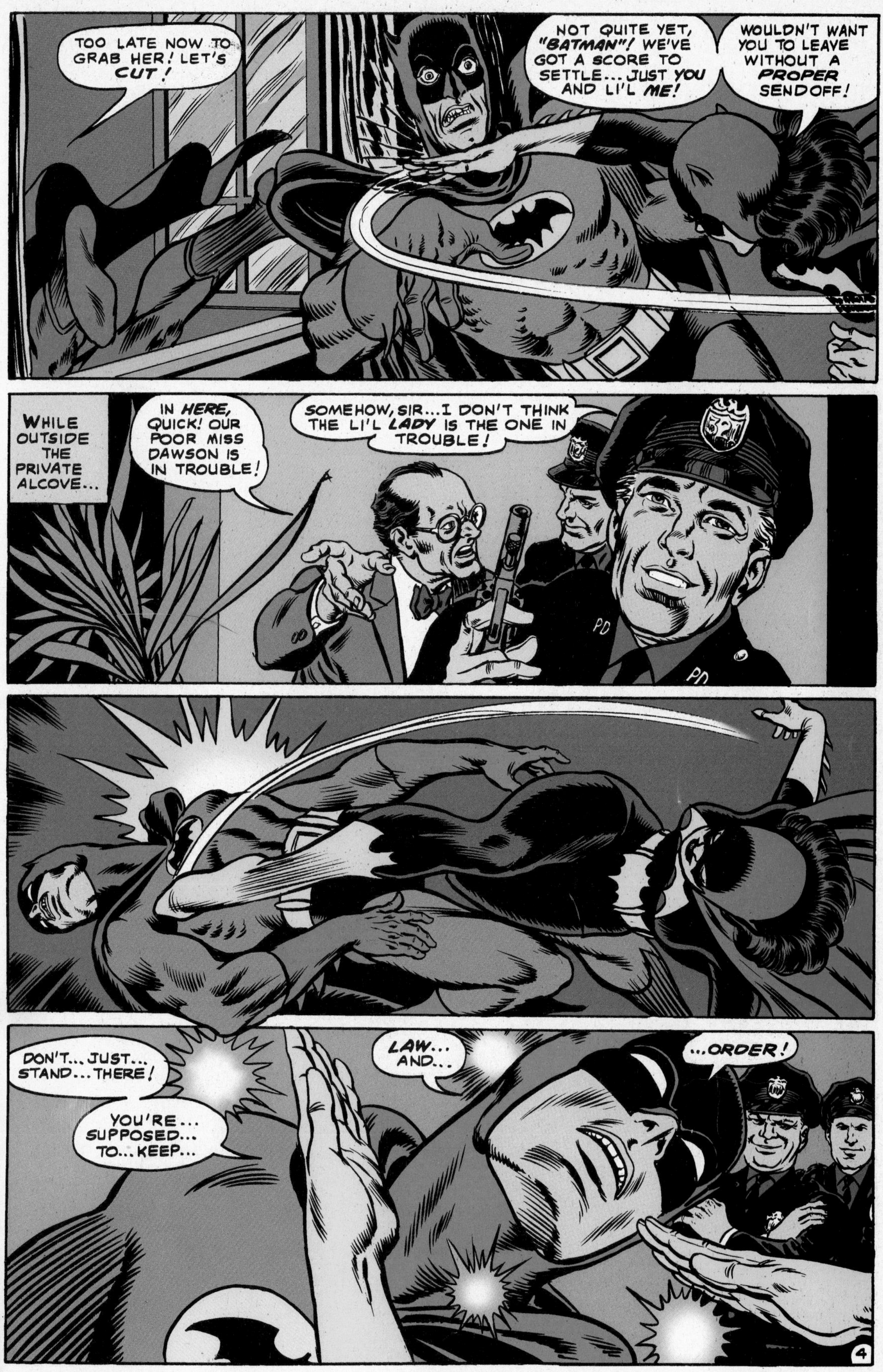
TOO LATE NOW TO GRAB HER! LET'S CUT!
NOT QUITE YET, "BATMAN"! WE'VE GOT A SCORE TO SETTLE... JUST YOU AND LI'L ME!
WOULDN'T WANT YOU TO LEAVE WITHOUT A PROPER SENDOFF!
WHILE OUTSIDE THE PRIVATE ALCOVE...
IN HERE, QUICK! OUR POOR MISS DAWSON IS IN TROUBLE!
SOMEHOW, SIR... I DON'T THINK THE LI'L LADY IS THE ONE IN TROUBLE!
DON'T... JUST... STAND... THERE!
YOU'RE... SUPPOSED... TO... KEEP...
LAW... AND...
...ORDER!
4

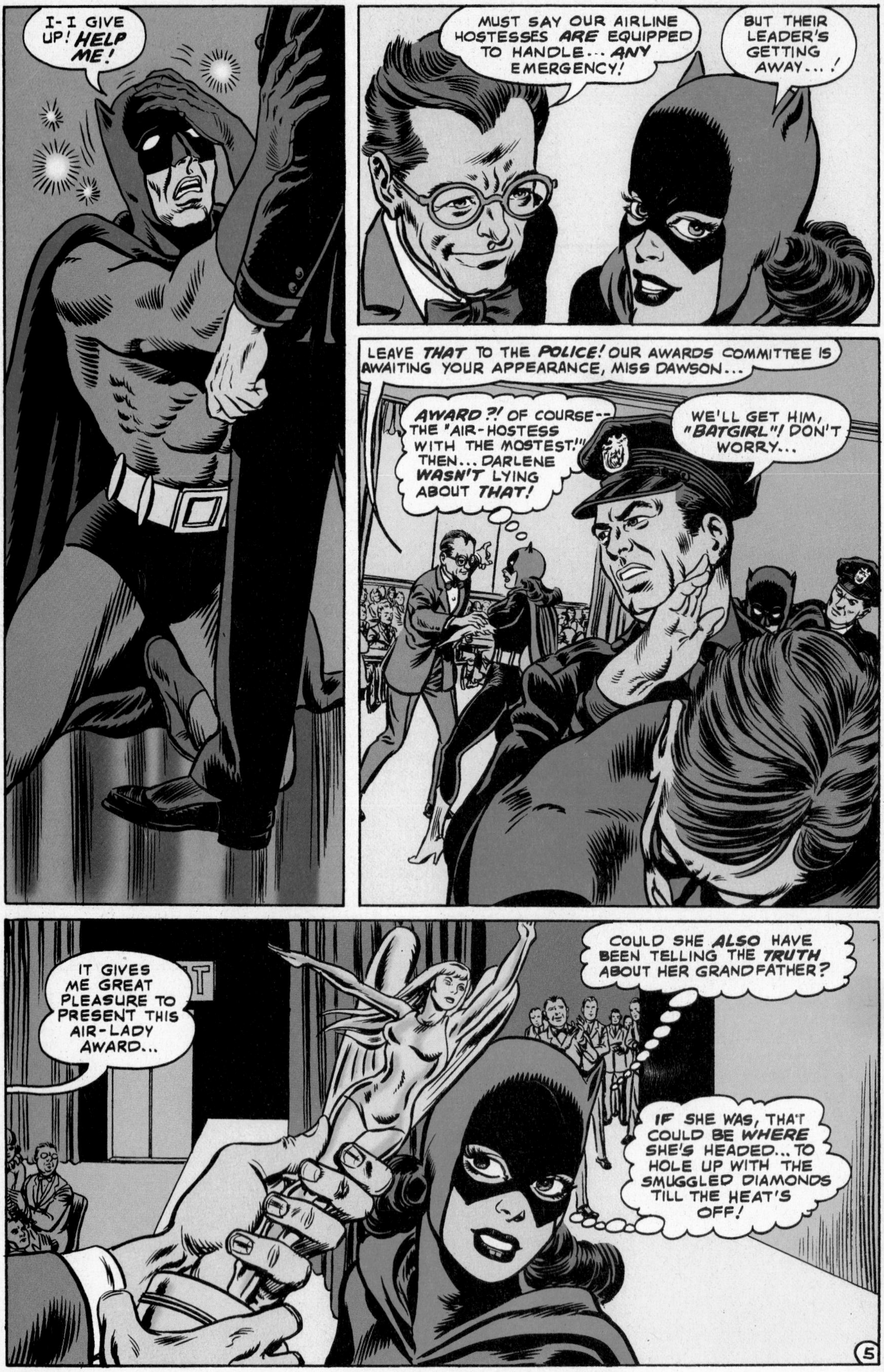
I- I GIVE UP! HELP ME!
MUST SAY OUR AIRLINE HOSTESSES ARE EQUIPPED TO HANDLE... ANY EMERGENCY!
BUT THEIR LEADER'S GETTING AWAY...!
LEAVE THAT TO THE POLICE! OUR AWARDS COMMITTEE IS AWAITING YOUR APPEARANCE, MISS DAWSON...
AWARD?! OF COURSE-- THE "AIR-HOSTESS WITH THE MOSTEST!" THEN... DARLENE WASN'T LYING ABOUT THAT!
WE'LL GET HIM, "BATGIRL"! DON'T WORRY...
IT GIVES ME GREAT PLEASURE TO PRESENT THIS AIR-LADY AWARD...
COULD SHE ALSO HAVE BEEN TELLING THE TRUTH ABOUT HER GRANDFATHER?
IF SHE WAS, THAT COULD BE WHERE SHE'S HEADED... TO HOLE UP WITH THE SMUGGLED DIAMONDS TILL THE HEAT'S OFF!
5

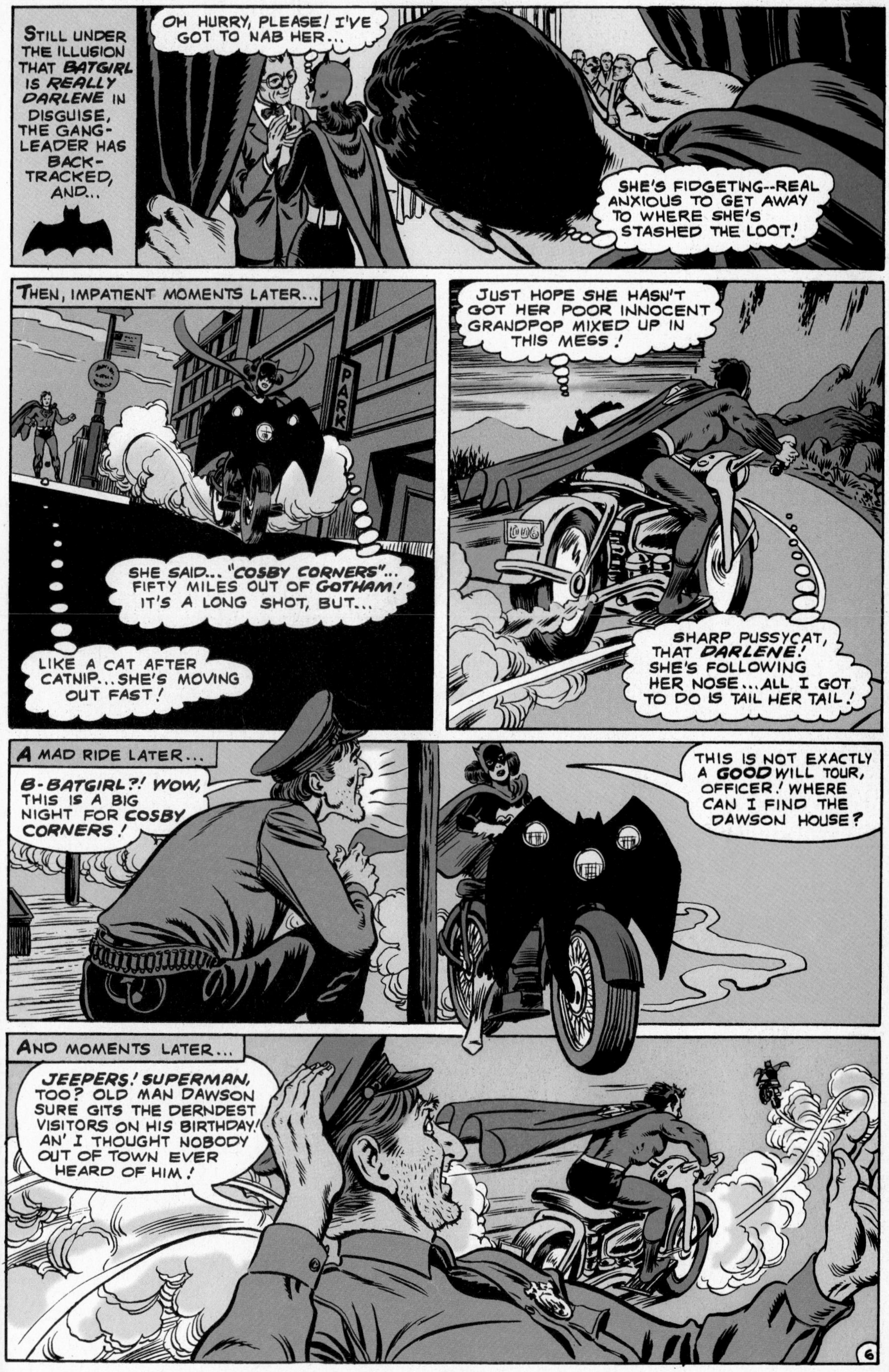
STILL UNDER THE ILLUSION THAT BATGIRL IS REALLY DARLENE IN DISGUISE, THE GANG-LEADER HAS BACK-TRACKED, AND...
OH HURRY, PLEASE! I'VE GOT TO NAB HER...
SHE'S FIDGETING--REAL ANXIOUS TO GET AWAY TO WHERE SHE'S STASHED THE LOOT!
THEN, IMPATIENT MOMENTS LATER...
PARK
SHE SAID... "COSBY CORNERS"... FIFTY MILES OUT OF GOTHAM! IT'S A LONG SHOT, BUT...
LIKE A CAT AFTER CATNIP...SHE'S MOVING OUT FAST!
JUST HOPE SHE HASN'T GOT HER POOR INNOCENT GRANDPOP MIXED UP IN THIS MESS!
SHARP PUSSYCAT, THAT DARLENE! SHE'S FOLLOWING HER NOSE...ALL I GOT TO DO IS TAIL HER TAIL!
A MAD RIDE LATER...
B-BATGIRL?! WOW, THIS IS A BIG NIGHT FOR COSBY CORNERS!
THIS IS NOT EXACTLY A GOOD WILL TOUR, OFFICER! WHERE CAN I FIND THE DAWSON HOUSE?
AND MOMENTS LATER...
JEEPERS! SUPERMAN, TOO? OLD MAN DAWSON SURE GITS THE DERNDEST VISITORS ON HIS BIRTHDAY! AN' I THOUGHT NOBODY OUT OF TOWN EVER HEARD OF HIM!
6

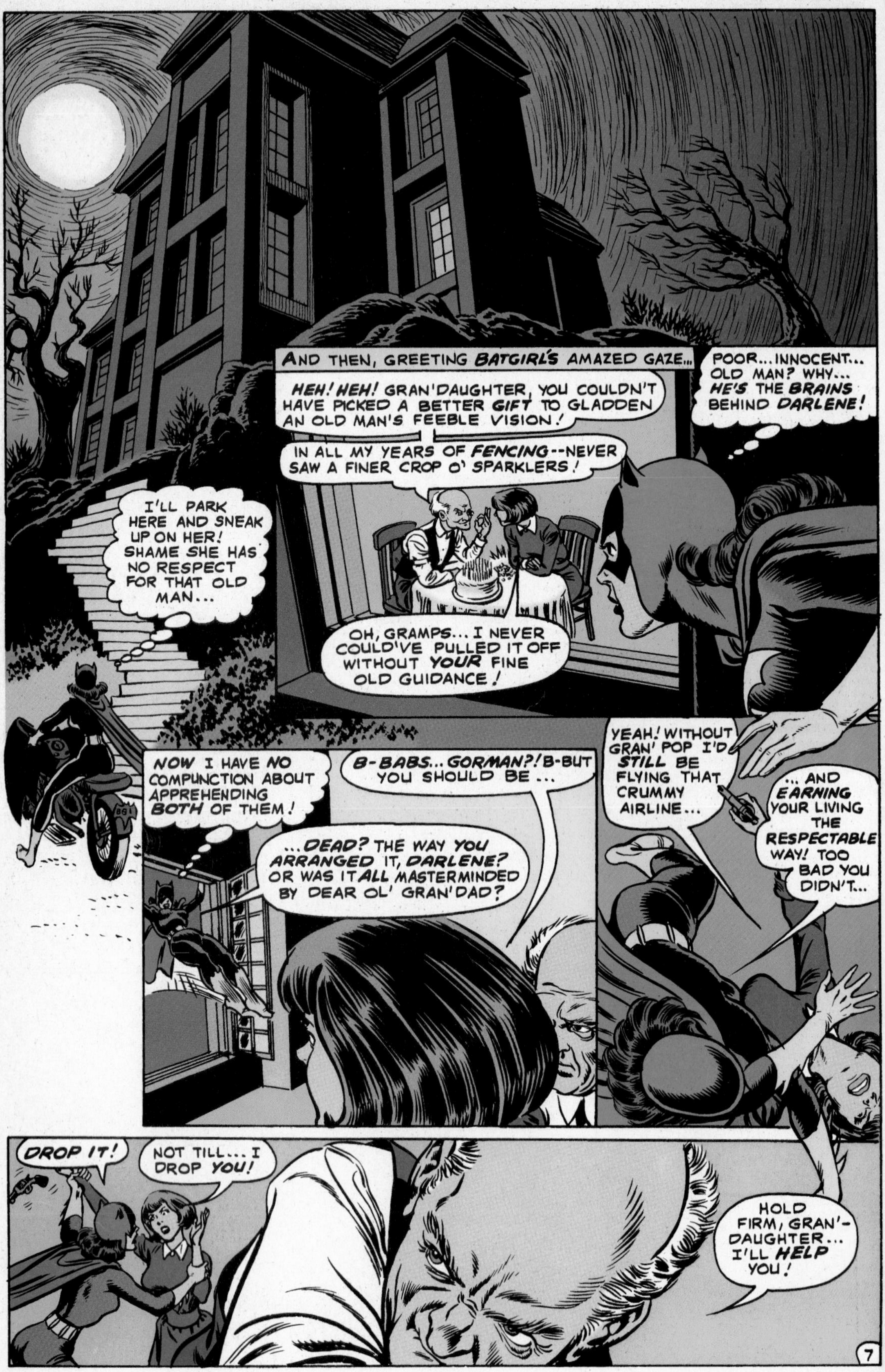
AND THEN, GREETING BATGIRL'S AMAZED GAZE...
HEH! HEH! GRAN'DAUGHTER, YOU COULDN'T HAVE PICKED A BETTER GIFT TO GLADDEN AN OLD MAN'S FEEBLE VISION!
IN ALL MY YEARS OF FENCING--NEVER SAW A FINER CROP O' SPARKLERS!
POOR... INNOCENT... OLD MAN? WHY... HE'S THE BRAINS BEHIND DARLENE!
I'LL PARK HERE AND SNEAK UP ON HER! SHAME SHE HAS NO RESPECT FOR THAT OLD MAN...
OH, GRAMPS... I NEVER COULD'VE PULLED IT OFF WITHOUT YOUR FINE OLD GUIDANCE!
NOW I HAVE NO COMPUNCTION ABOUT APPREHENDING BOTH OF THEM!
B-BABS... GORMAN?! B-BUT YOU SHOULD BE...
...DEAD? THE WAY YOU ARRANGED IT, DARLENE? OR WAS IT ALL MASTERMINDED BY DEAR OL' GRAN'DAD?
YEAH! WITHOUT GRAN' POP I'D STILL BE FLYING THAT CRUMMY AIRLINE...
... AND EARNING YOUR LIVING THE RESPECTABLE WAY! TOO BAD YOU DIDN'T...
DROP IT!
NOT TILL... I DROP YOU!
HOLD FIRM, GRAN'-DAUGHTER... I'LL HELP YOU!
7

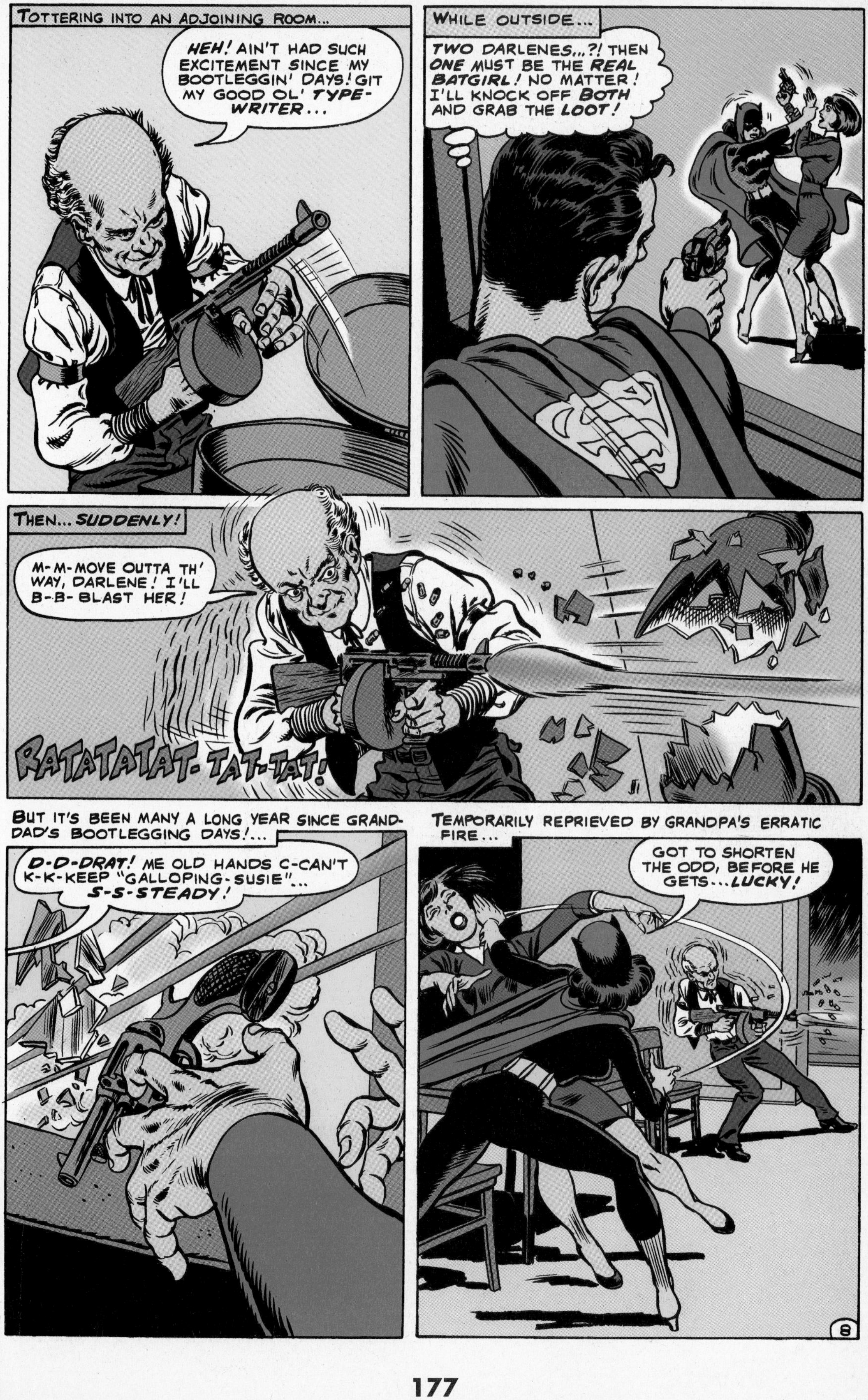
TOTTERING INTO AN ADJOINING ROOM...
HEH! AIN'T HAD SUCH EXCITEMENT SINCE MY BOOTLEGGIN' DAYS! GIT MY GOOD OL' TYPE-WRITER...
WHILE OUTSIDE...
TWO DARLENES...?! THEN ONE MUST BE THE REAL BATGIRL! NO MATTER! I'LL KNOCK OFF BOTH AND GRAB THE LOOT!
THEN... SUDDENLY!
M-M-MOVE OUTTA TH' WAY, DARLENE! I'LL B-B-BLAST HER!
RATATATAT-TAT-TAT!
BUT IT'S BEEN MANY A LONG YEAR SINCE GRAND-DAD'S BOOTLEGGING DAYS!...
D-D-DRAT! ME OLD HANDS C-CAN'T K-K-KEEP "GALLOPING-SUSIE"... S-S-STEADY!
TEMPORARILY REPRIEVED BY GRANDPA'S ERRATIC FIRE...
GOT TO SHORTEN THE ODD, BEFORE HE GETS...LUCKY!
8

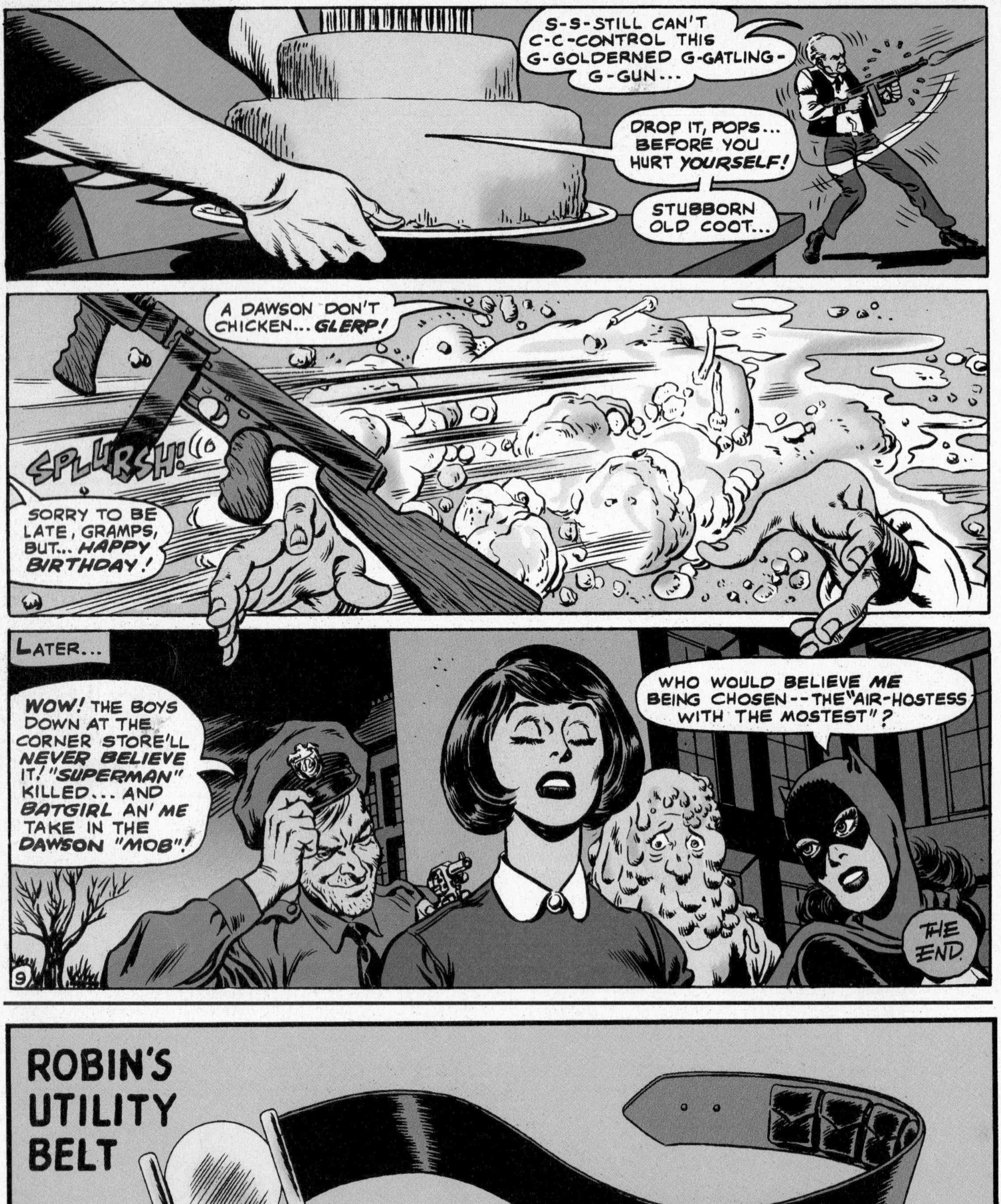
S-S-STILL CAN'T C-C-CONTROL THIS G-GOLDERNED G-GATLING-G-GUN...
DROP IT, POPS... BEFORE YOU HURT YOURSELF!
STUBBORN OLD COOT...
A DAWSON DON'T CHICKEN... GLERP!
SPLURSH!
SORRY TO BE LATE, GRAMPS, BUT... HAPPY BIRTHDAY!
LATER...
WOW! THE BOYS DOWN AT THE CORNER STORE'LL NEVER BELIEVE IT! "SUPERMAN" KILLED... AND BATGIRL AN' ME TAKE IN THE DAWSON "MOB"!
WHO WOULD BELIEVE ME BEING CHOSEN--THE "AIR-HOSTESS WITH THE MOSTEST"?
THE END.

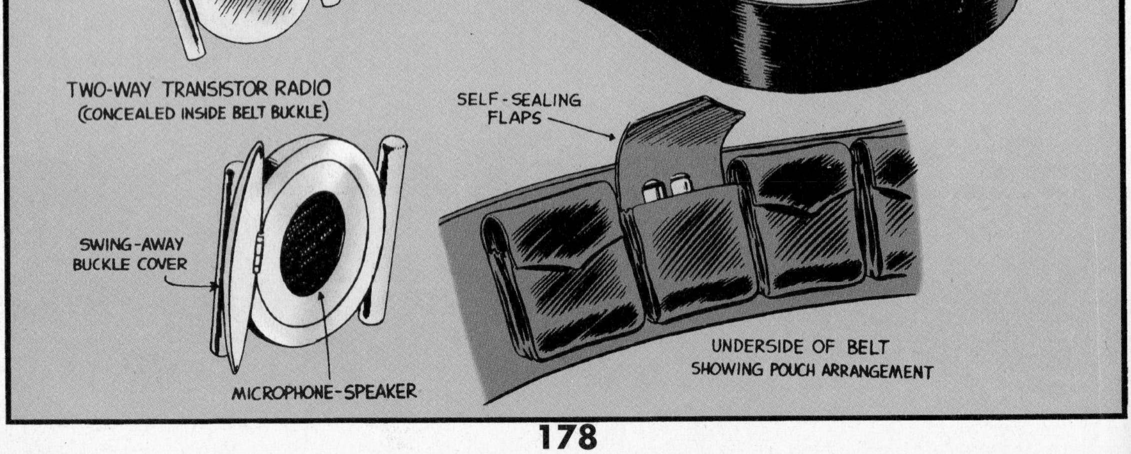
ROBIN'S UTILITY BELT
TWO-WAY TRANSISTOR RADIO (CONCEALED INSIDE BELT BUCKLE)
SELF-SEALING FLAPS
SWING-AWAY BUCKLE COVER
MICROPHONE-SPEAKER
UNDERSIDE OF BELT SHOWING POUCH ARRANGEMENT

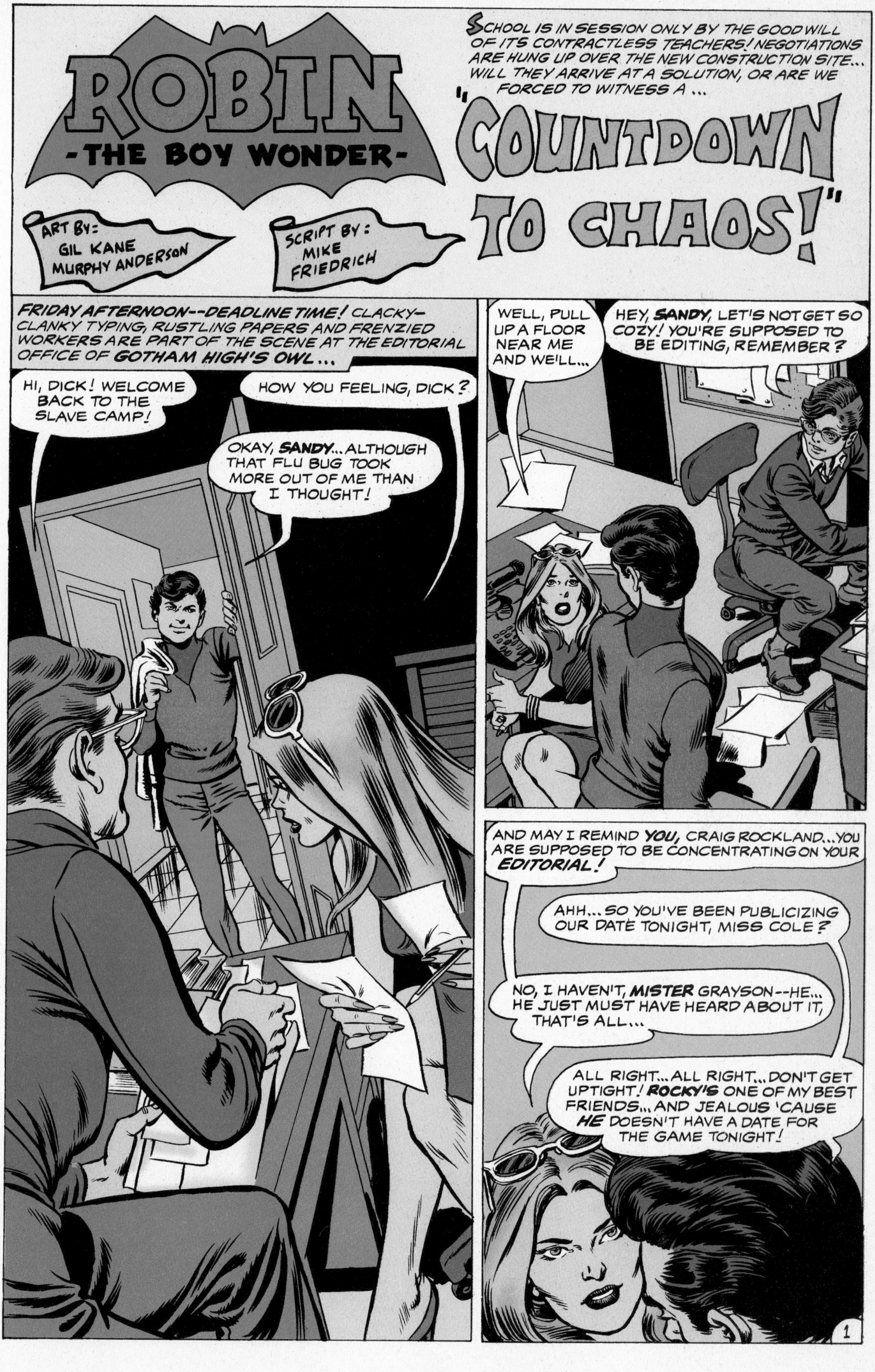
ROBIN
-THE BOY WONDER-
SCHOOL IS IN SESSION ONLY BY THE GOOD WILL OF ITS CONTRACTLESS TEACHERS! NEGOTIATIONS ARE HUNG UP OVER THE NEW CONSTRUCTION SITE... WILL THEY ARRIVE AT A SOLUTION, OR ARE WE FORCED TO WITNESS A ...
"COUNTDOWN TO CHAOS!"
ART BY: GIL KANE MURPHY ANDERSON
SCRIPT BY: MIKE FRIEDRICH
FRIDAY AFTERNOON--DEADLINE TIME! CLACKY-CLANKY TYPING, RUSTLING PAPERS AND FRENZIED WORKERS ARE PART OF THE SCENE AT THE EDITORIAL OFFICE OF GOTHAM HIGH'S OWL...
HI, DICK! WELCOME BACK TO THE SLAVE CAMP!
HOW YOU FEELING, DICK?
OKAY, SANDY... ALTHOUGH THAT FLU BUG TOOK MORE OUT OF ME THAN I THOUGHT!
WELL, PULL UP A FLOOR NEAR ME AND WE'LL...
HEY, SANDY, LET'S NOT GET SO COZY! YOU'RE SUPPOSED TO BE EDITING, REMEMBER?
AND MAY I REMIND YOU, CRAIG ROCKLAND... YOU ARE SUPPOSED TO BE CONCENTRATING ON YOUR EDITORIAL!
AHH... SO YOU'VE BEEN PUBLICIZING OUR DATE TONIGHT, MISS COLE?
NO, I HAVEN'T, MISTER GRAYSON--HE... HE JUST MUST HAVE HEARD ABOUT IT, THAT'S ALL...
ALL RIGHT... ALL RIGHT... DON'T GET UPTIGHT! ROCKY'S ONE OF MY BEST FRIENDS... AND JEALOUS 'CAUSE HE DOESN'T HAVE A DATE FOR THE GAME TONIGHT!
1

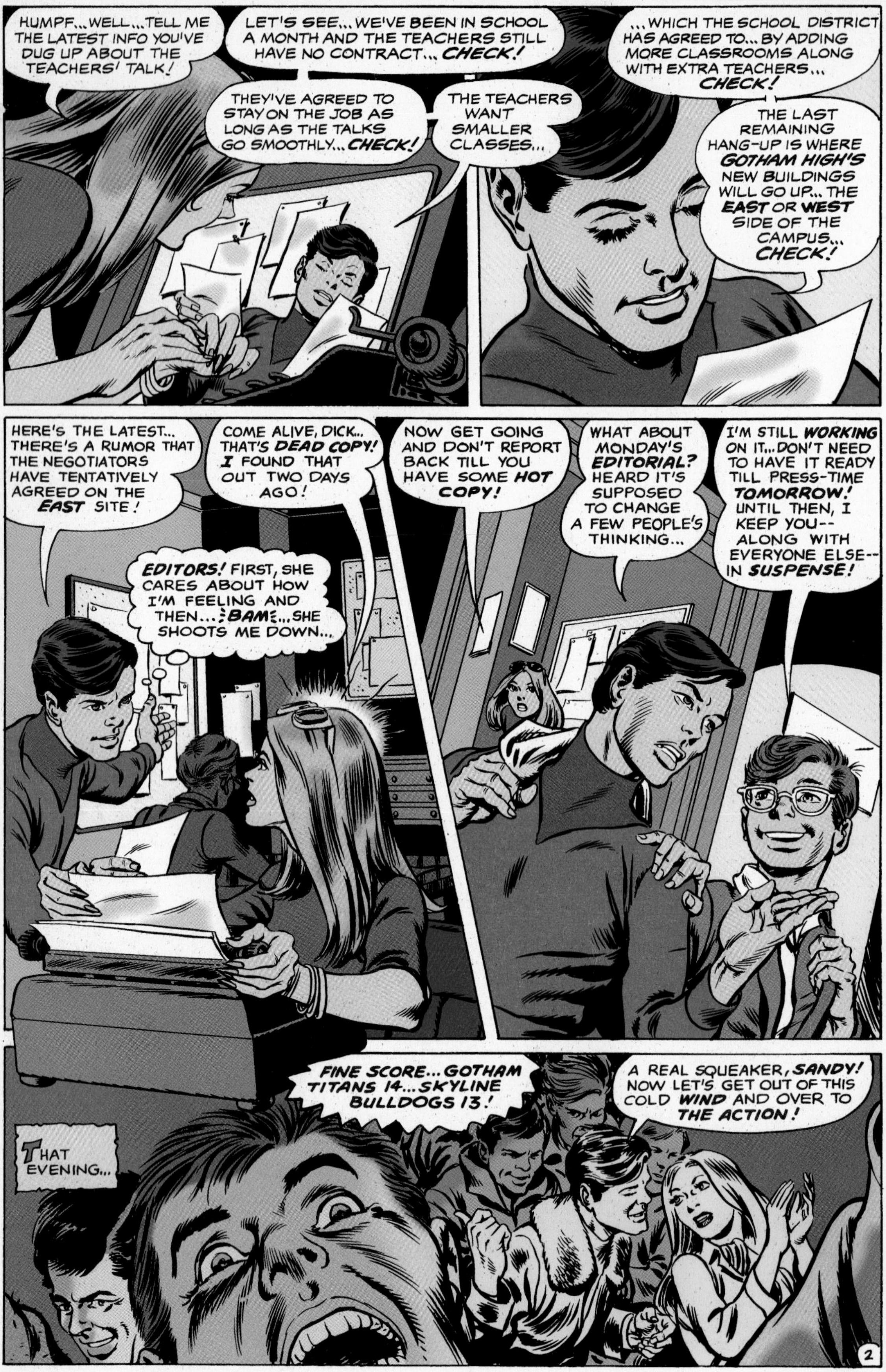
HUMPF... WELL... TELL ME THE LATEST INFO YOU'VE DUG UP ABOUT THE TEACHERS' TALK!
LET'S SEE... WE'VE BEEN IN SCHOOL A MONTH AND THE TEACHERS STILL HAVE NO CONTRACT... CHECK!
THEY'VE AGREED TO STAY ON THE JOB AS LONG AS THE TALKS GO SMOOTHLY... CHECK!
THE TEACHERS WANT SMALLER CLASSES...
...WHICH THE SCHOOL DISTRICT HAS AGREED TO... BY ADDING MORE CLASSROOMS ALONG WITH EXTRA TEACHERS... CHECK!
THE LAST REMAINING HANG-UP IS WHERE GOTHAM HIGH'S NEW BUILDINGS WILL GO UP... THE EAST OR WEST SIDE OF THE CAMPUS... CHECK!
HERE'S THE LATEST... THERE'S A RUMOR THAT THE NEGOTIATORS HAVE TENTATIVELY AGREED ON THE EAST SITE!
COME ALIVE, DICK... THAT'S DEAD COPY! I FOUND THAT OUT TWO DAYS AGO!
EDITORS! FIRST, SHE CARES ABOUT HOW I'M FEELING AND THEN... BAM... SHE SHOOTS ME DOWN...
NOW GET GOING AND DON'T REPORT BACK TILL YOU HAVE SOME HOT COPY!
WHAT ABOUT MONDAY'S EDITORIAL? HEARD IT'S SUPPOSED TO CHANGE A FEW PEOPLE'S THINKING...
I'M STILL WORKING ON IT... DON'T NEED TO HAVE IT READY TILL PRESS-TIME TOMORROW! UNTIL THEN, I KEEP YOU-- ALONG WITH EVERYONE ELSE-- IN SUSPENSE!
THAT EVENING...
FINE SCORE... GOTHAM TITANS 14... SKYLINE BULLDOGS 13!
A REAL SQUEAKER, SANDY! NOW LET'S GET OUT OF THIS COLD WIND AND OVER TO THE ACTION!
2

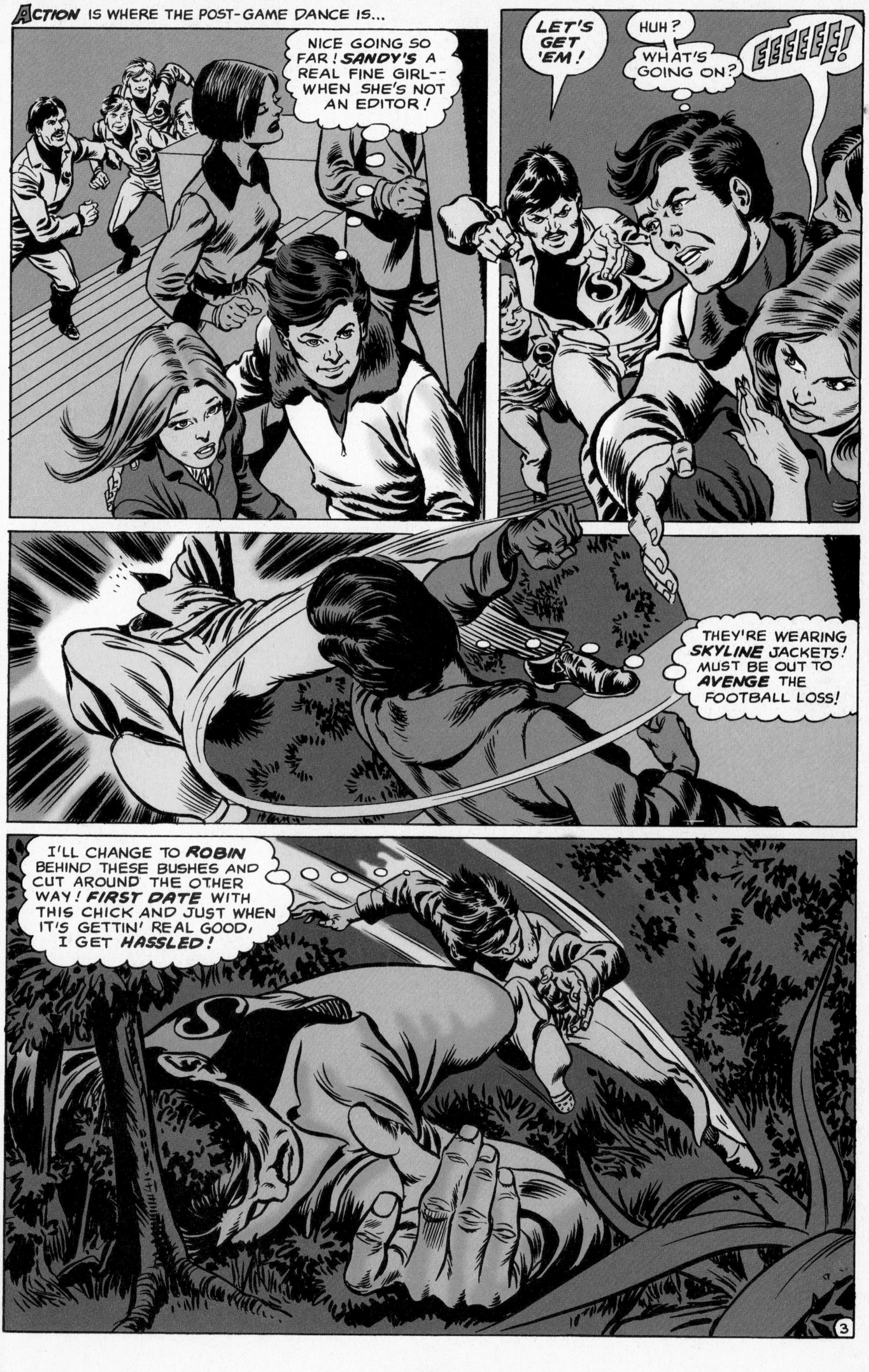
ACTION IS WHERE THE POST-GAME DANCE IS...
NICE GOING SO FAR! SANDY'S A REAL FINE GIRL-- WHEN SHE'S NOT AN EDITOR!
LET'S GET 'EM!
HUH?
WHAT'S GOING ON?
EEEEEE!
THEY'RE WEARING SKYLINE JACKETS! MUST BE OUT TO AVENGE THE FOOTBALL LOSS!
I'LL CHANGE TO ROBIN BEHIND THESE BUSHES AND CUT AROUND THE OTHER WAY! FIRST DATE WITH THIS CHICK AND JUST WHEN IT'S GETTIN' REAL GOOD, I GET HASSLED!
3

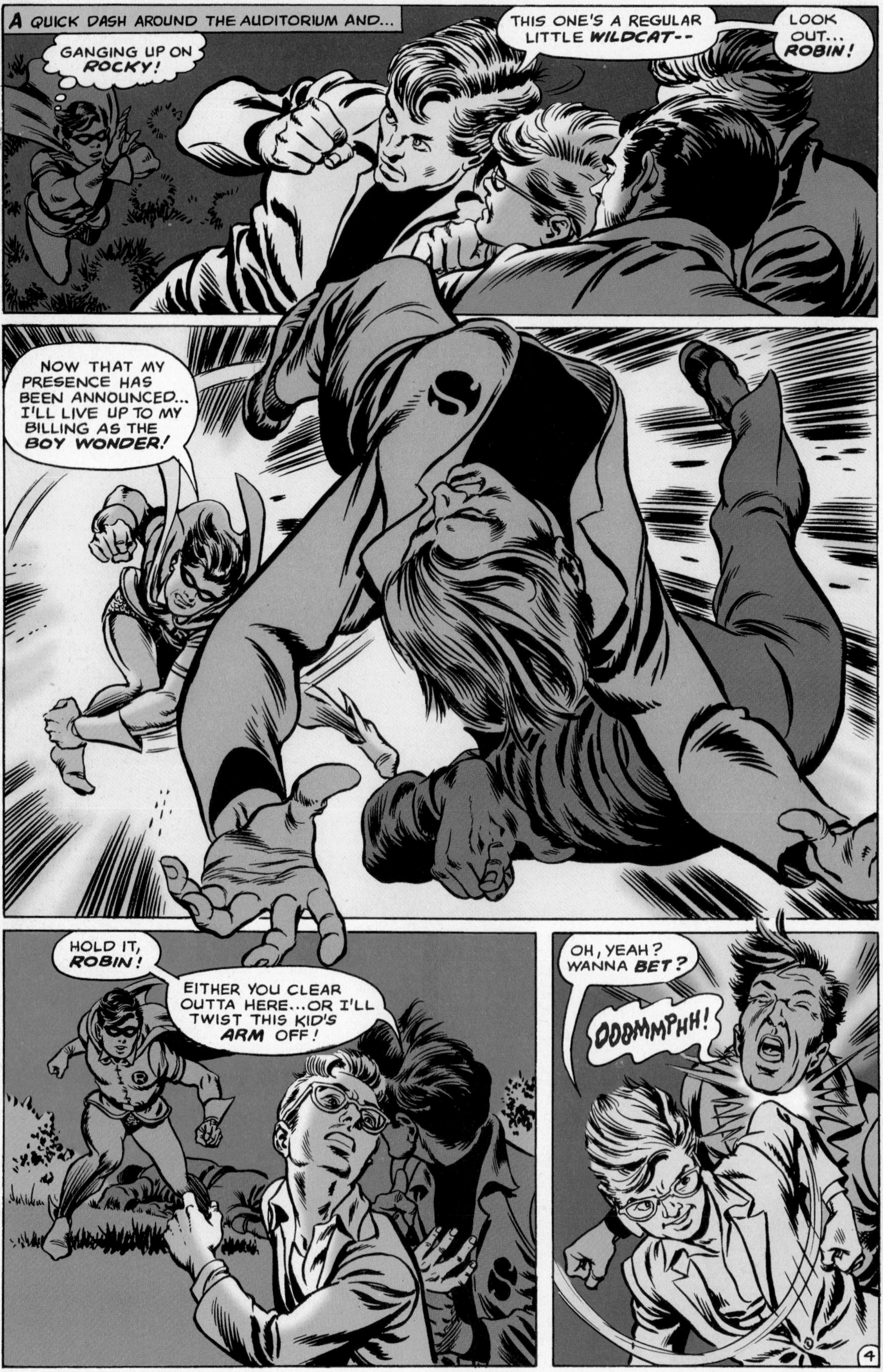
A QUICK DASH AROUND THE AUDITORIUM AND...
GANGING UP ON ROCKY!
THIS ONE'S A REGULAR LITTLE WILDCAT--
LOOK OUT... ROBIN!
NOW THAT MY PRESENCE HAS BEEN ANNOUNCED... I'LL LIVE UP TO MY BILLING AS THE BOY WONDER!
HOLD IT, ROBIN!
EITHER YOU CLEAR OUTTA HERE...OR I'LL TWIST THIS KID'S ARM OFF!
OH, YEAH? WANNA BET?
OOOMMPHH!
4

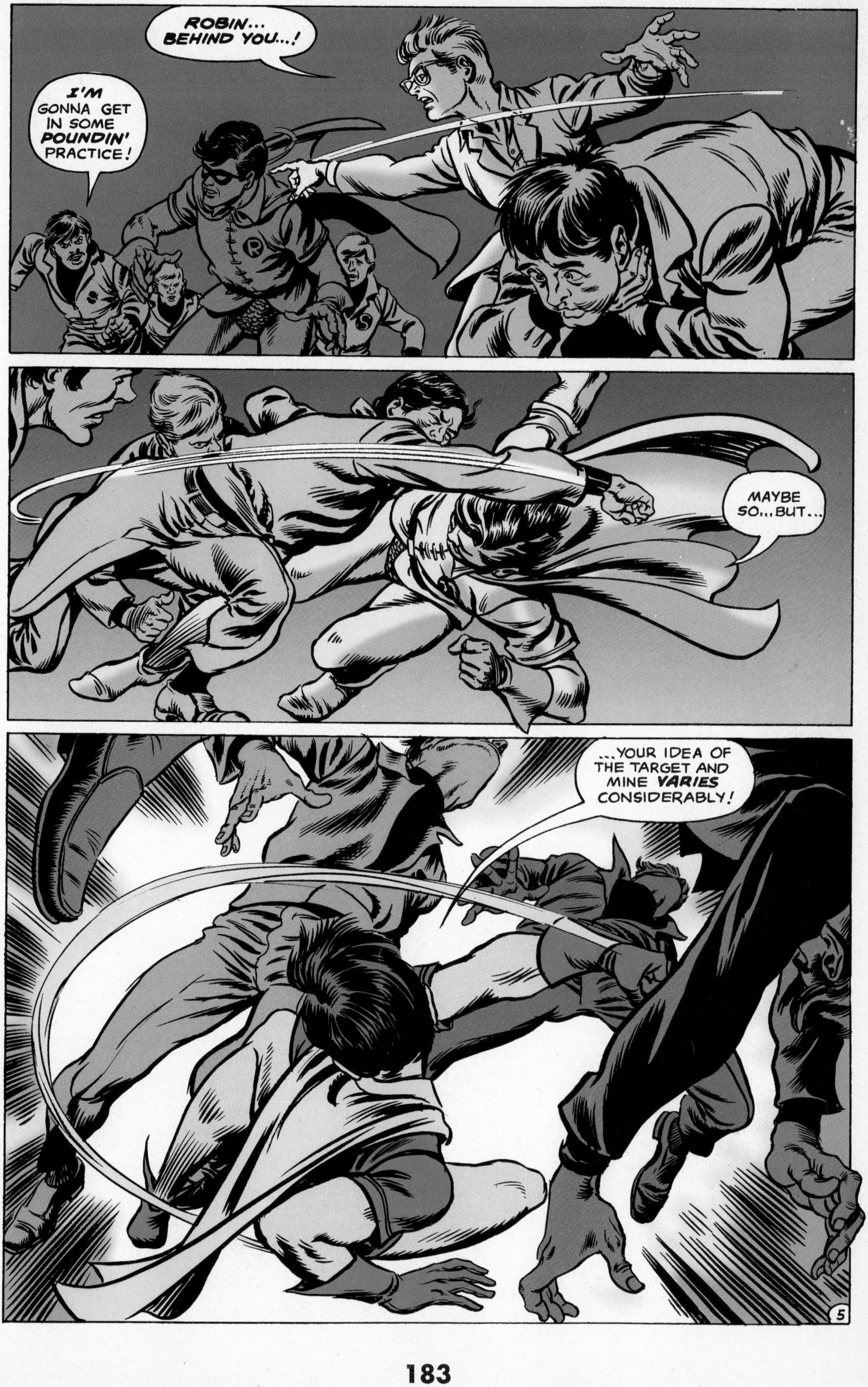
ROBIN... BEHIND YOU...!
I'M GONNA GET IN SOME POUNDIN' PRACTICE!
MAYBE SO... BUT...
...YOUR IDEA OF THE TARGET AND MINE VARIES CONSIDERABLY!
5

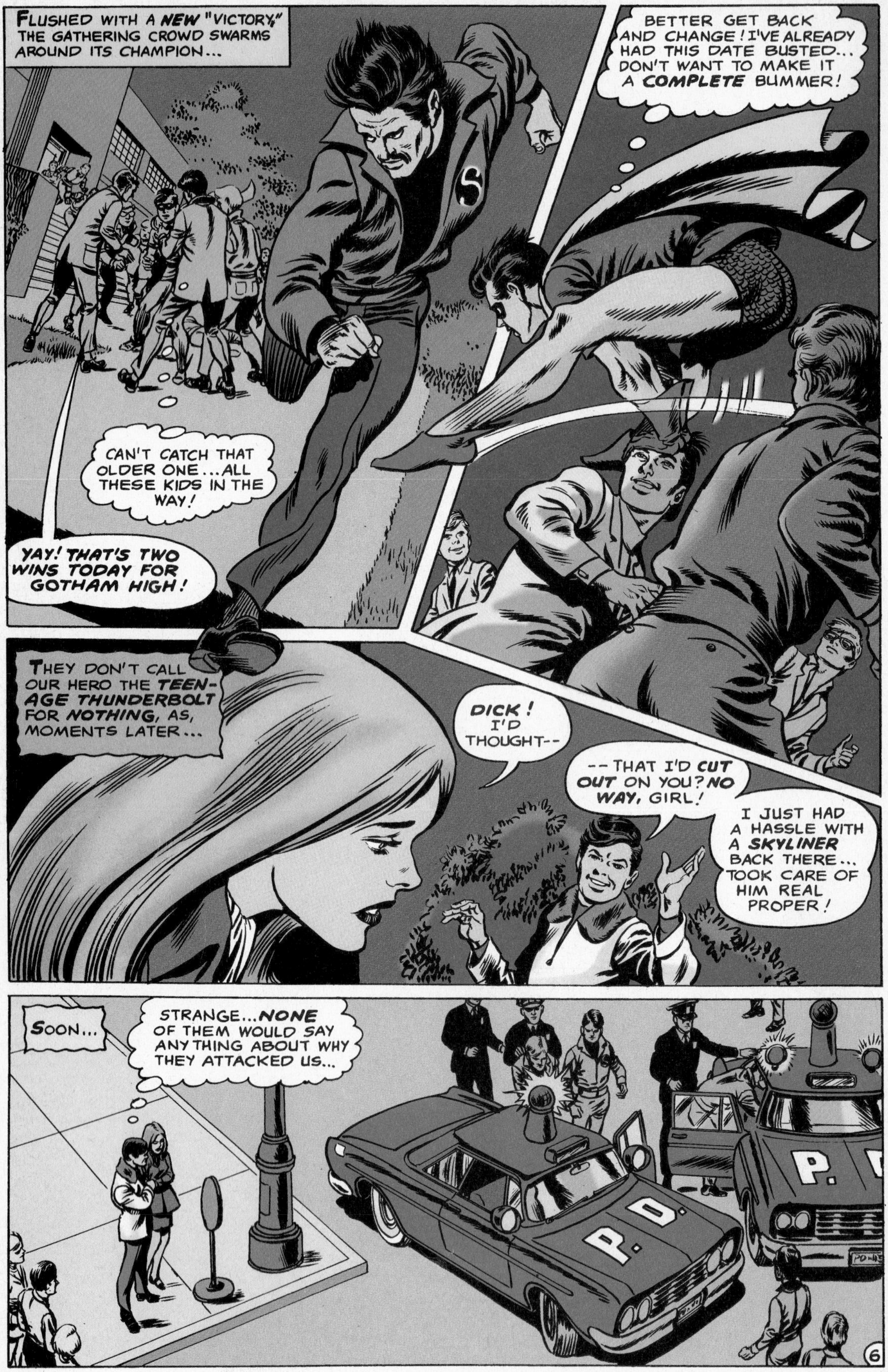
FLUSHED WITH A NEW "VICTORY," THE GATHERING CROWD SWARMS AROUND ITS CHAMPION...
BETTER GET BACK AND CHANGE! I'VE ALREADY HAD THIS DATE BUSTED... DON'T WANT TO MAKE IT A COMPLETE BUMMER!
CAN'T CATCH THAT OLDER ONE...ALL THESE KIDS IN THE WAY!
YAY! THAT'S TWO WINS TODAY FOR GOTHAM HIGH!
THEY DON'T CALL OUR HERO THE TEEN-AGE THUNDERBOLT FOR NOTHING, AS, MOMENTS LATER...
DICK! I'D THOUGHT--
--THAT I'D CUT OUT ON YOU? NO WAY, GIRL!
I JUST HAD A HASSLE WITH A SKYLINER BACK THERE... TOOK CARE OF HIM REAL PROPER!
SOON...
STRANGE...NONE OF THEM WOULD SAY ANYTHING ABOUT WHY THEY ATTACKED US...
P.D.
6

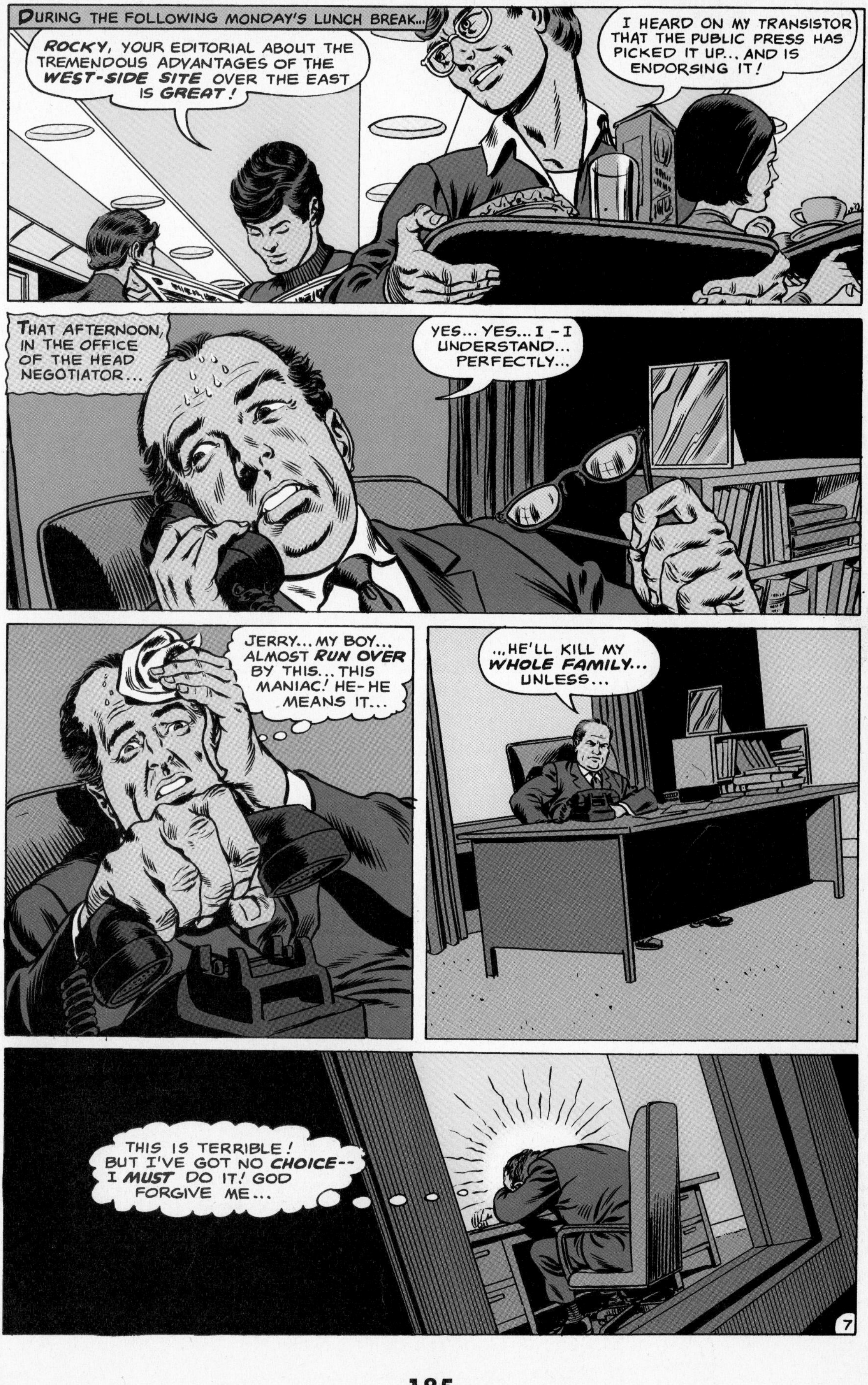
DURING THE FOLLOWING MONDAY'S LUNCH BREAK...
ROCKY, YOUR EDITORIAL ABOUT THE TREMENDOUS ADVANTAGES OF THE WEST-SIDE SITE OVER THE EAST IS GREAT!
I HEARD ON MY TRANSISTOR THAT THE PUBLIC PRESS HAS PICKED IT UP... AND IS ENDORSING IT!
THAT AFTERNOON, IN THE OFFICE OF THE HEAD NEGOTIATOR...
YES... YES... I - I UNDERSTAND... PERFECTLY...
JERRY... MY BOY... ALMOST RUN OVER BY THIS... THIS MANIAC! HE- HE MEANS IT...
...HE'LL KILL MY WHOLE FAMILY... UNLESS...
THIS IS TERRIBLE! BUT I'VE GOT NO CHOICE-- I MUST DO IT! GOD FORGIVE ME...
7

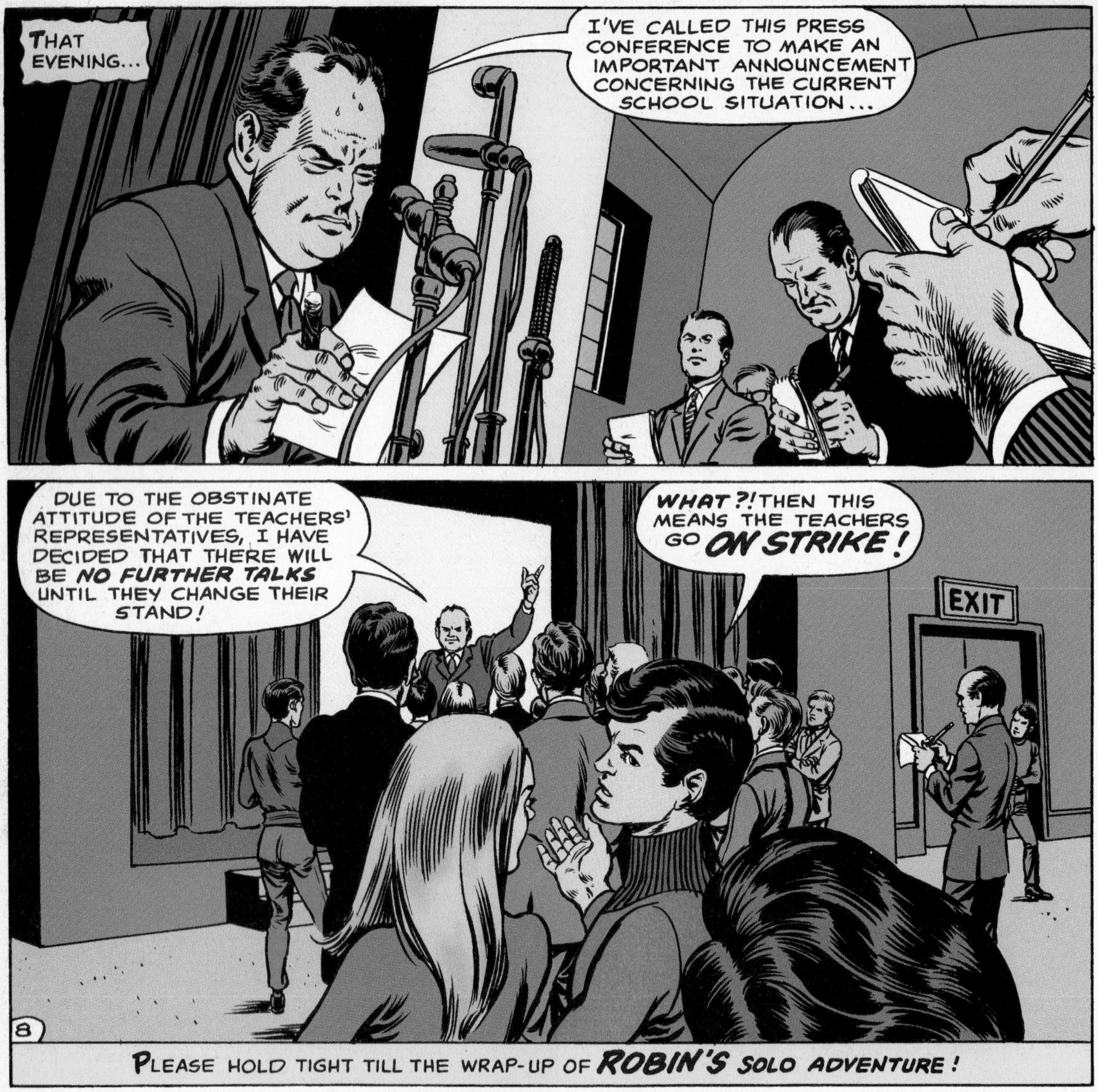
THAT EVENING...
I'VE CALLED THIS PRESS CONFERENCE TO MAKE AN IMPORTANT ANNOUNCEMENT CONCERNING THE CURRENT SCHOOL SITUATION...
DUE TO THE OBSTINATE ATTITUDE OF THE TEACHERS' REPRESENTATIVES, I HAVE DECIDED THAT THERE WILL BE NO FURTHER TALKS UNTIL THEY CHANGE THEIR STAND!
WHAT?! THEN THIS MEANS THE TEACHERS GO ON STRIKE!
EXIT
8
PLEASE HOLD TIGHT TILL THE WRAP-UP OF ROBIN'S SOLO ADVENTURE!

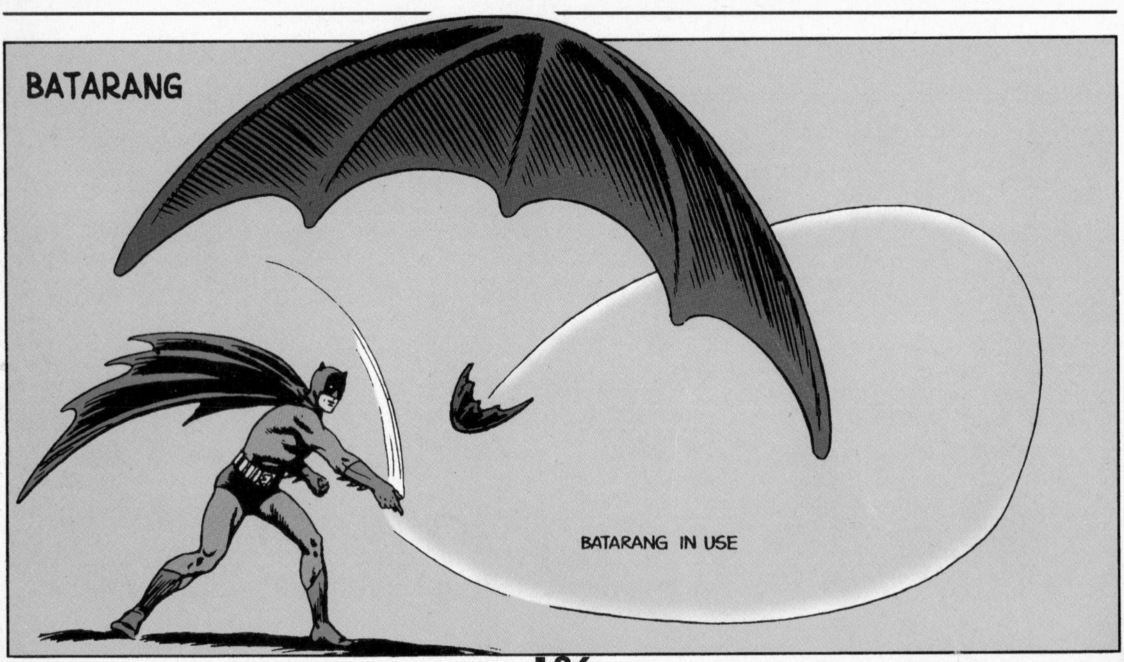
BATARANG
BATARANG IN USE

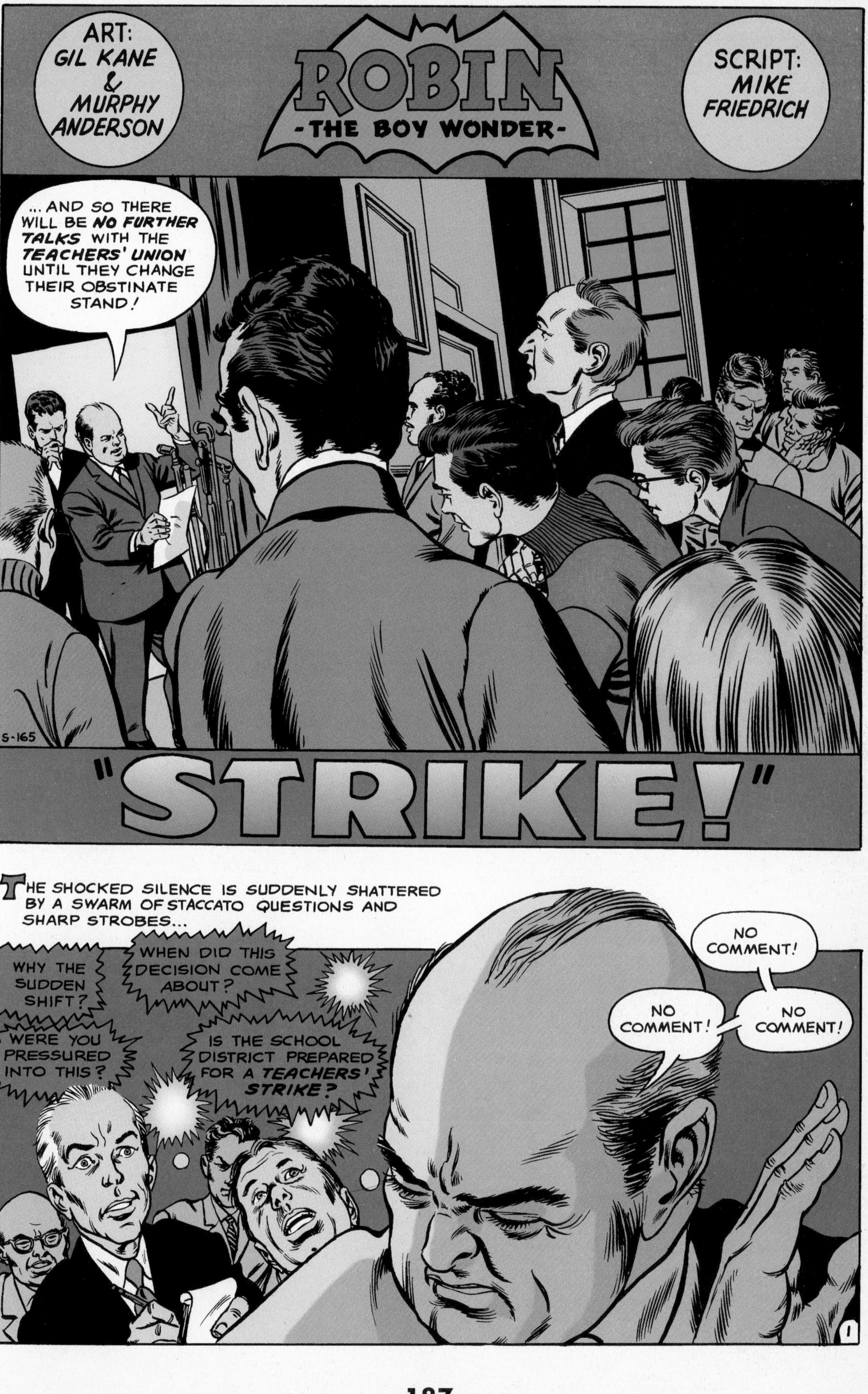
ART:
GIL KANE & MURPHY ANDERSON
ROBIN
-THE BOY WONDER-
SCRIPT:
MIKE FRIEDRICH
...AND SO THERE WILL BE NO FURTHER TALKS WITH THE TEACHERS' UNION UNTIL THEY CHANGE THEIR OBSTINATE STAND!
S-165
"STRIKE!"
THE SHOCKED SILENCE IS SUDDENLY SHATTERED BY A SWARM OF STACCATO QUESTIONS AND SHARP STROBES...
WHY THE SUDDEN SHIFT?
WHEN DID THIS DECISION COME ABOUT?
WERE YOU PRESSURED INTO THIS?
IS THE SCHOOL DISTRICT PREPARED FOR A TEACHERS' STRIKE?
NO COMMENT!
NO COMMENT!
NO COMMENT!
1

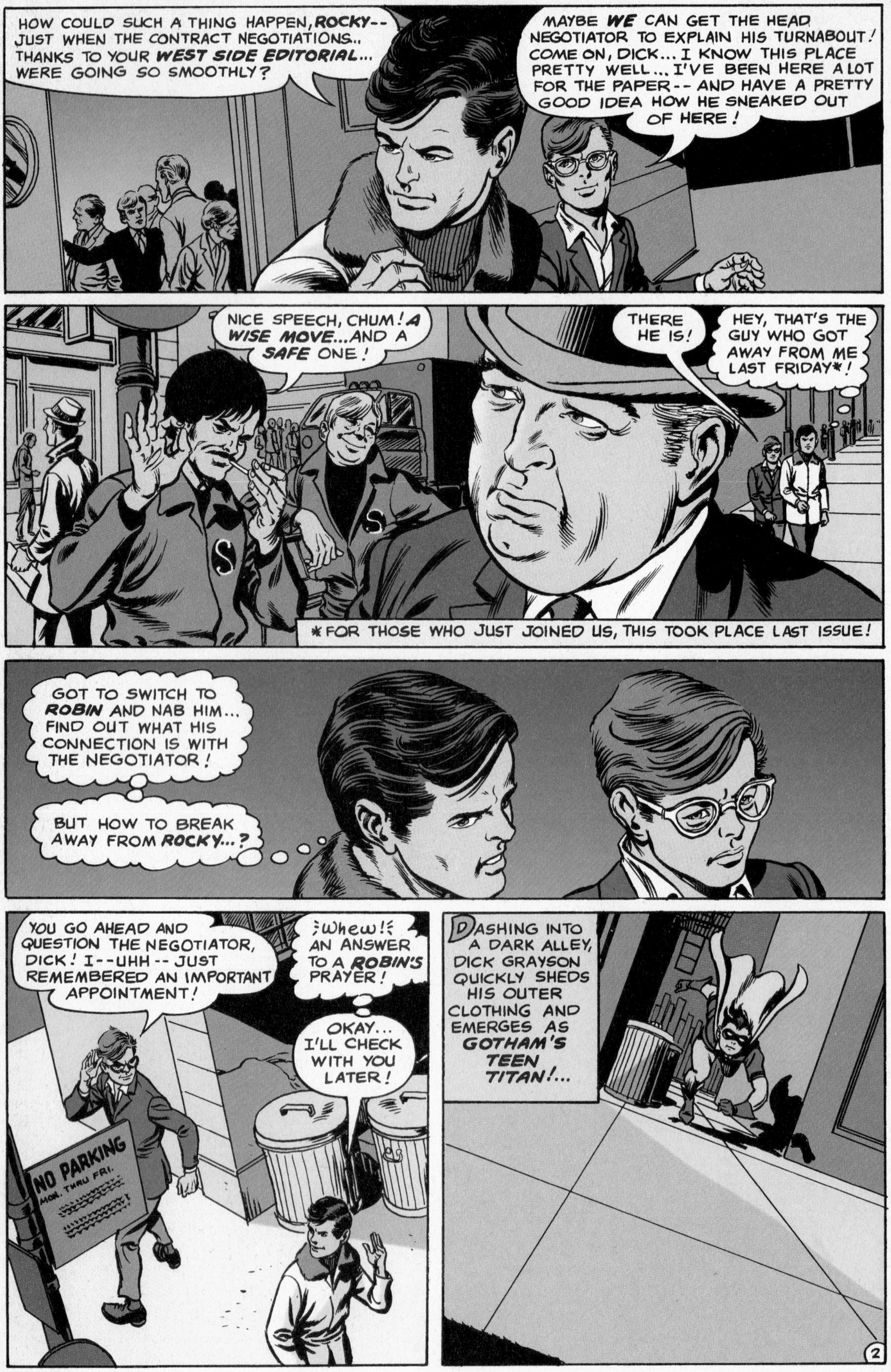
HOW COULD SUCH A THING HAPPEN, ROCKY-- JUST WHEN THE CONTRACT NEGOTIATIONS.. THANKS TO YOUR WEST SIDE EDITORIAL... WERE GOING SO SMOOTHLY?
MAYBE WE CAN GET THE HEAD NEGOTIATOR TO EXPLAIN HIS TURNABOUT! COME ON, DICK... I KNOW THIS PLACE PRETTY WELL... I'VE BEEN HERE A LOT FOR THE PAPER-- AND HAVE A PRETTY GOOD IDEA HOW HE SNEAKED OUT OF HERE!
NICE SPEECH, CHUM! A WISE MOVE...AND A SAFE ONE!
THERE HE IS!
HEY, THAT'S THE GUY WHO GOT AWAY FROM ME LAST FRIDAY*!
*FOR THOSE WHO JUST JOINED US, THIS TOOK PLACE LAST ISSUE!
GOT TO SWITCH TO ROBIN AND NAB HIM... FIND OUT WHAT HIS CONNECTION IS WITH THE NEGOTIATOR!
BUT HOW TO BREAK AWAY FROM ROCKY...?
YOU GO AHEAD AND QUESTION THE NEGOTIATOR, DICK! I--UHH -- JUST REMEMBERED AN IMPORTANT APPOINTMENT!
Whew! AN ANSWER TO A ROBIN'S PRAYER!
OKAY... I'LL CHECK WITH YOU LATER!
NO PARKING
MON. THRU FRI.
DASHING INTO A DARK ALLEY, DICK GRAYSON QUICKLY SHEDS HIS OUTER CLOTHING AND EMERGES AS GOTHAM'S TEEN TITAN!...
2

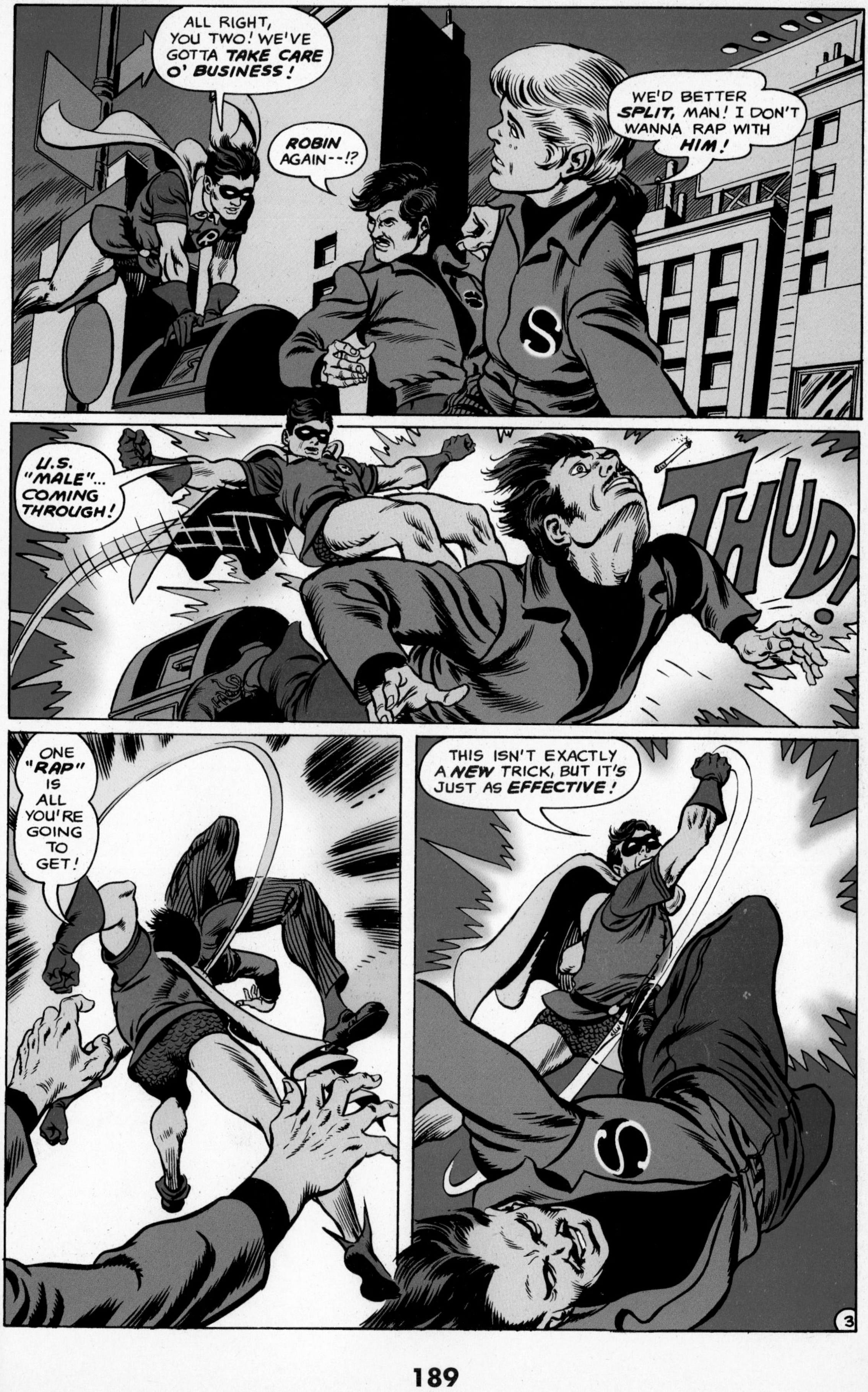

ALL RIGHT, YOU TWO! WE'VE GOTTA TAKE CARE O' BUSINESS!
ROBIN AGAIN--!?
WE'D BETTER SPLIT, MAN! I DON'T WANNA RAP WITH HIM!
U.S. "MALE"... COMING THROUGH!
THUD!
ONE "RAP" IS ALL YOU'RE GOING TO GET!
THIS ISN'T EXACTLY A NEW TRICK, BUT IT'S JUST AS EFFECTIVE!
3

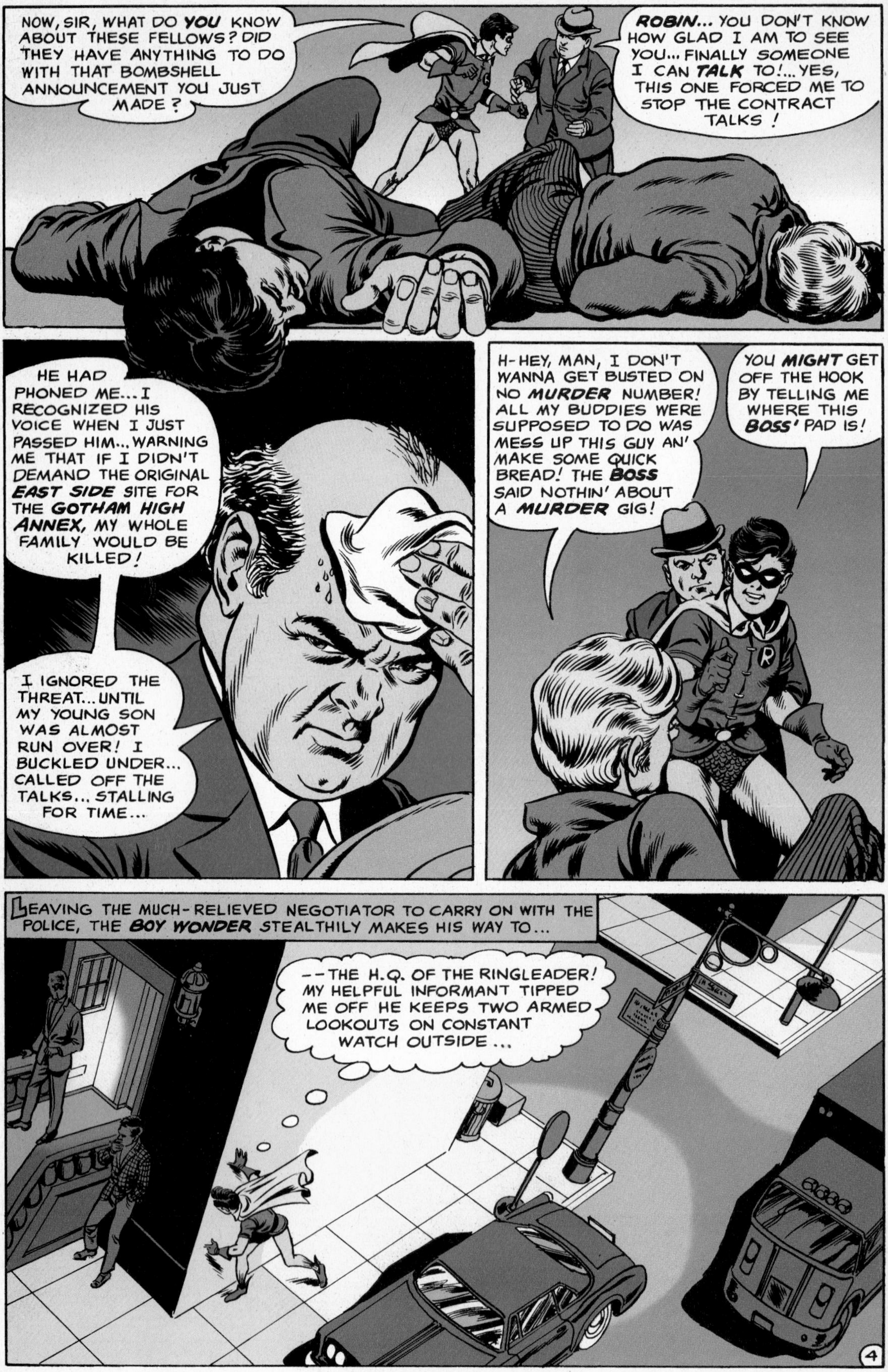
NOW, SIR, WHAT DO YOU KNOW ABOUT THESE FELLOWS? DID THEY HAVE ANYTHING TO DO WITH THAT BOMBSHELL ANNOUNCEMENT YOU JUST MADE?
ROBIN... YOU DON'T KNOW HOW GLAD I AM TO SEE YOU... FINALLY SOMEONE I CAN TALK TO!... YES, THIS ONE FORCED ME TO STOP THE CONTRACT TALKS!
HE HAD PHONED ME... I RECOGNIZED HIS VOICE WHEN I JUST PASSED HIM... WARNING ME THAT IF I DIDN'T DEMAND THE ORIGINAL EAST SIDE SITE FOR THE GOTHAM HIGH ANNEX, MY WHOLE FAMILY WOULD BE KILLED!
I IGNORED THE THREAT... UNTIL MY YOUNG SON WAS ALMOST RUN OVER! I BUCKLED UNDER... CALLED OFF THE TALKS... STALLING FOR TIME...
H-HEY, MAN, I DON'T WANNA GET BUSTED ON NO MURDER NUMBER! ALL MY BUDDIES WERE SUPPOSED TO DO WAS MESS UP THIS GUY AN' MAKE SOME QUICK BREAD! THE BOSS SAID NOTHIN' ABOUT A MURDER GIG!
YOU MIGHT GET OFF THE HOOK BY TELLING ME WHERE THIS BOSS' PAD IS!
LEAVING THE MUCH-RELIEVED NEGOTIATOR TO CARRY ON WITH THE POLICE, THE BOY WONDER STEALTHILY MAKES HIS WAY TO...
--THE H.Q. OF THE RINGLEADER! MY HELPFUL INFORMANT TIPPED ME OFF HE KEEPS TWO ARMED LOOKOUTS ON CONSTANT WATCH OUTSIDE...
4

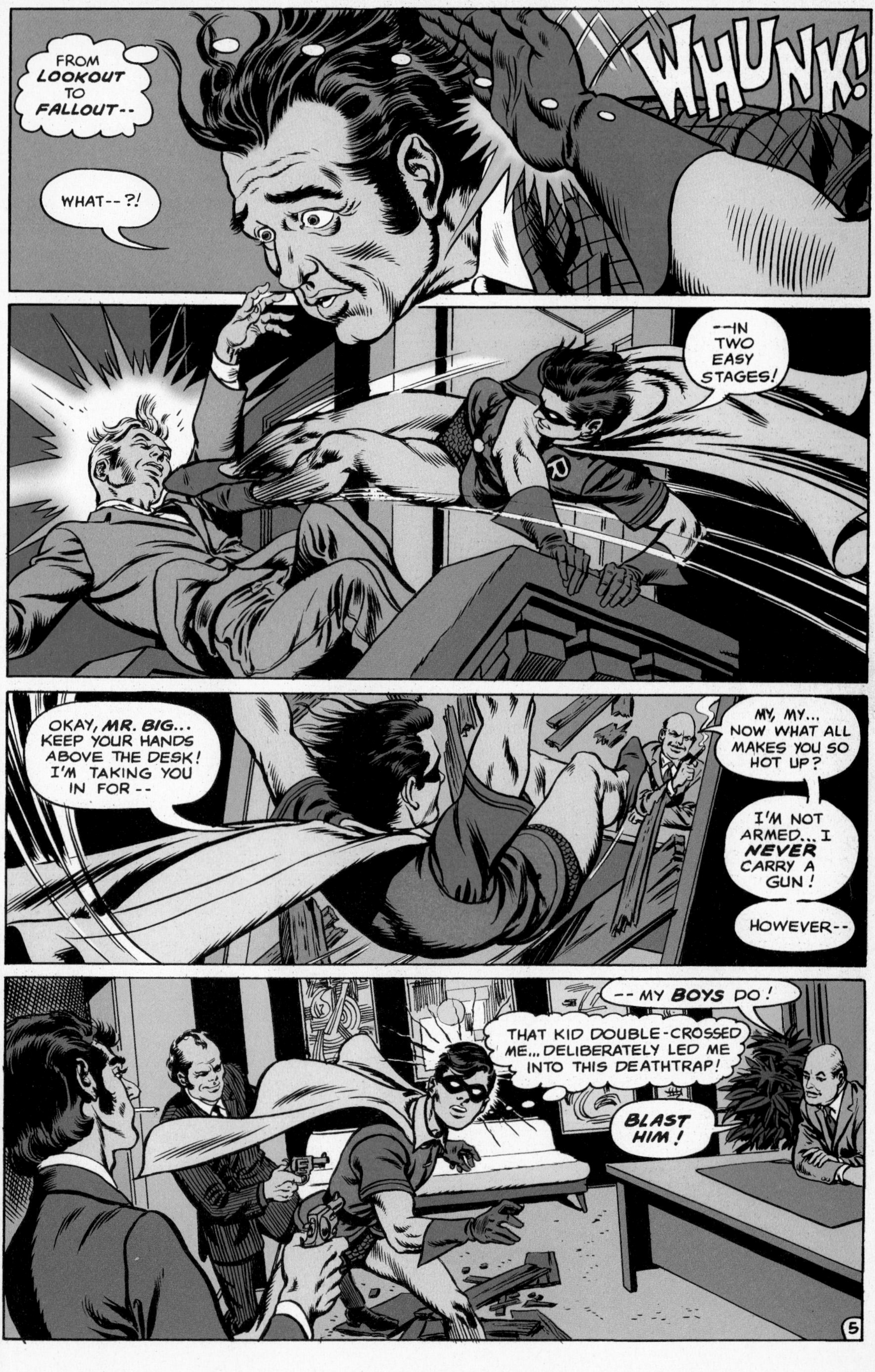
FROM LOOKOUT TO FALLOUT--
WHUNK!
WHAT--?!
--IN TWO EASY STAGES!
OKAY, MR. BIG... KEEP YOUR HANDS ABOVE THE DESK! I'M TAKING YOU IN FOR--
MY, MY... NOW WHAT ALL MAKES YOU SO HOT UP?
I'M NOT ARMED... I NEVER CARRY A GUN!
HOWEVER--
--MY BOYS DO!
THAT KID DOUBLE-CROSSED ME... DELIBERATELY LED ME INTO THIS DEATHTRAP!
BLAST HIM!
5

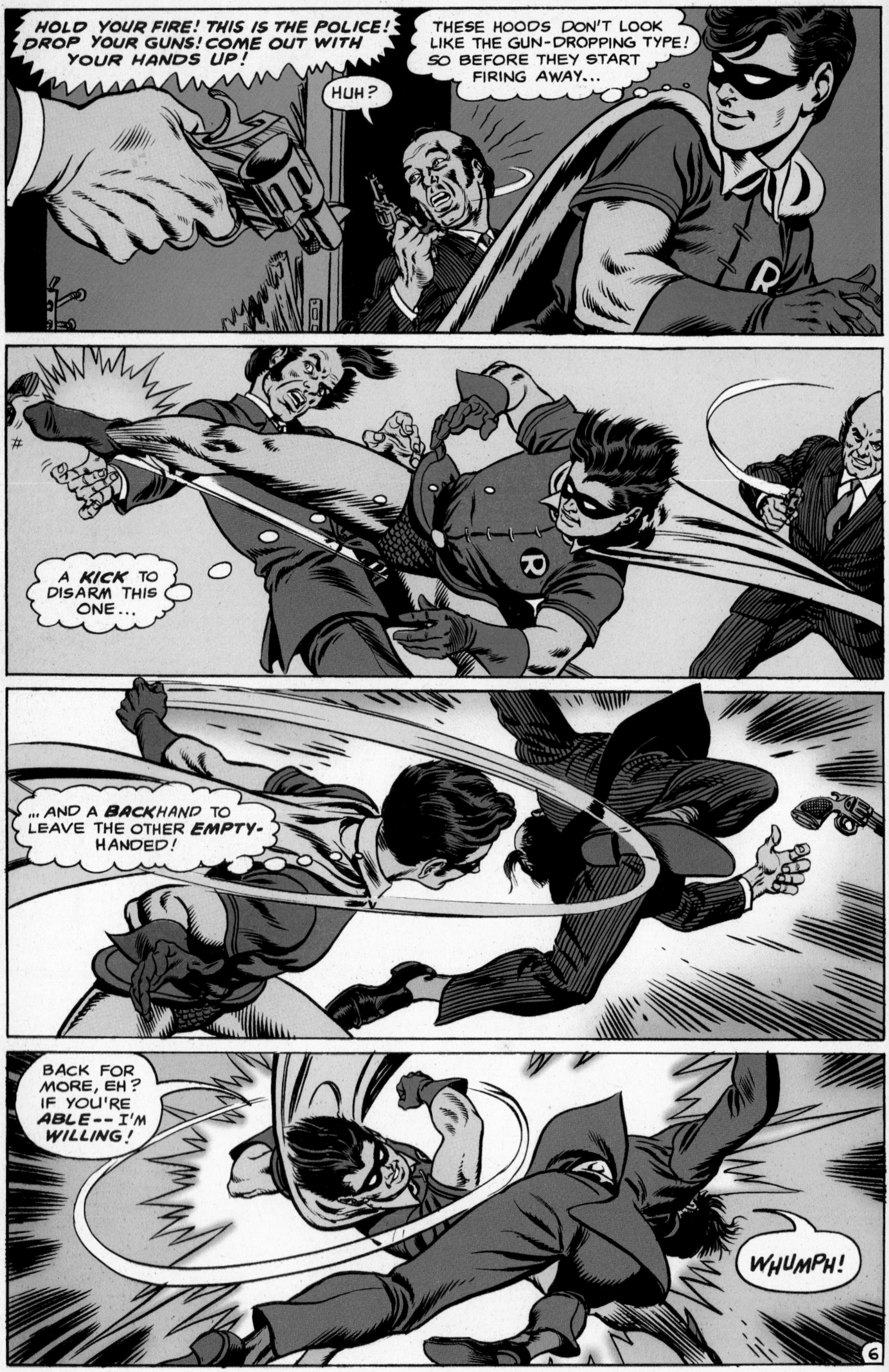
HOLD YOUR FIRE! THIS IS THE POLICE! DROP YOUR GUNS! COME OUT WITH YOUR HANDS UP!
HUH?
THESE HOODS DON'T LOOK LIKE THE GUN-DROPPING TYPE! SO BEFORE THEY START FIRING AWAY...
A KICK TO DISARM THIS ONE...
...AND A BACKHAND TO LEAVE THE OTHER EMPTY-HANDED!
BACK FOR MORE, EH? IF YOU'RE ABLE-- I'M WILLING!
WHUMPH!
6

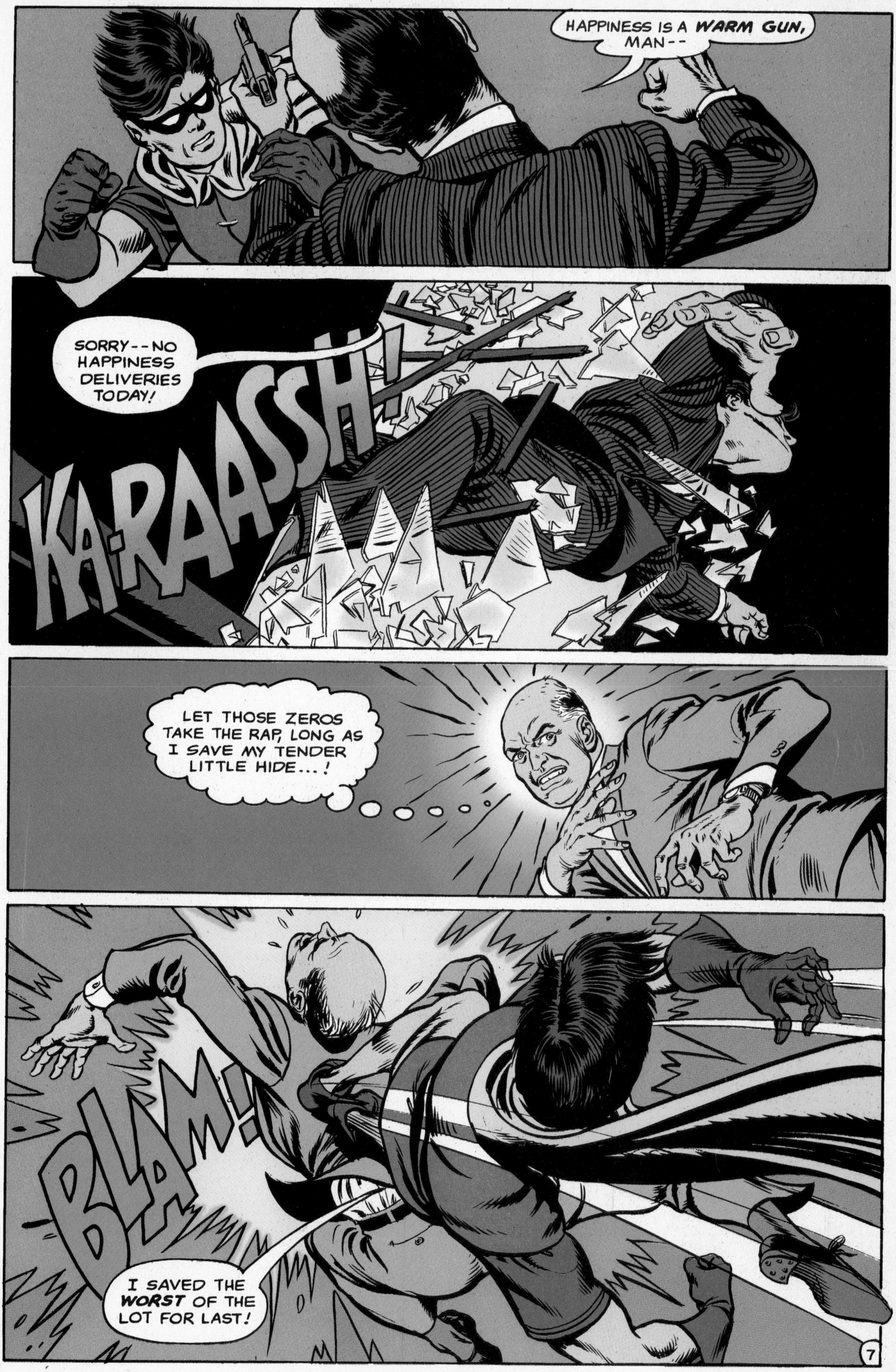
HAPPINESS IS A **WARM GUN**, MAN--
SORRY--NO HAPPINESS DELIVERIES TODAY!
KA-RAASSH!
LET THOSE ZEROS TAKE THE RAP, LONG AS I SAVE MY TENDER LITTLE HIDE...!
BLAM!
I SAVED THE **WORST** OF THE LOT FOR LAST!
7

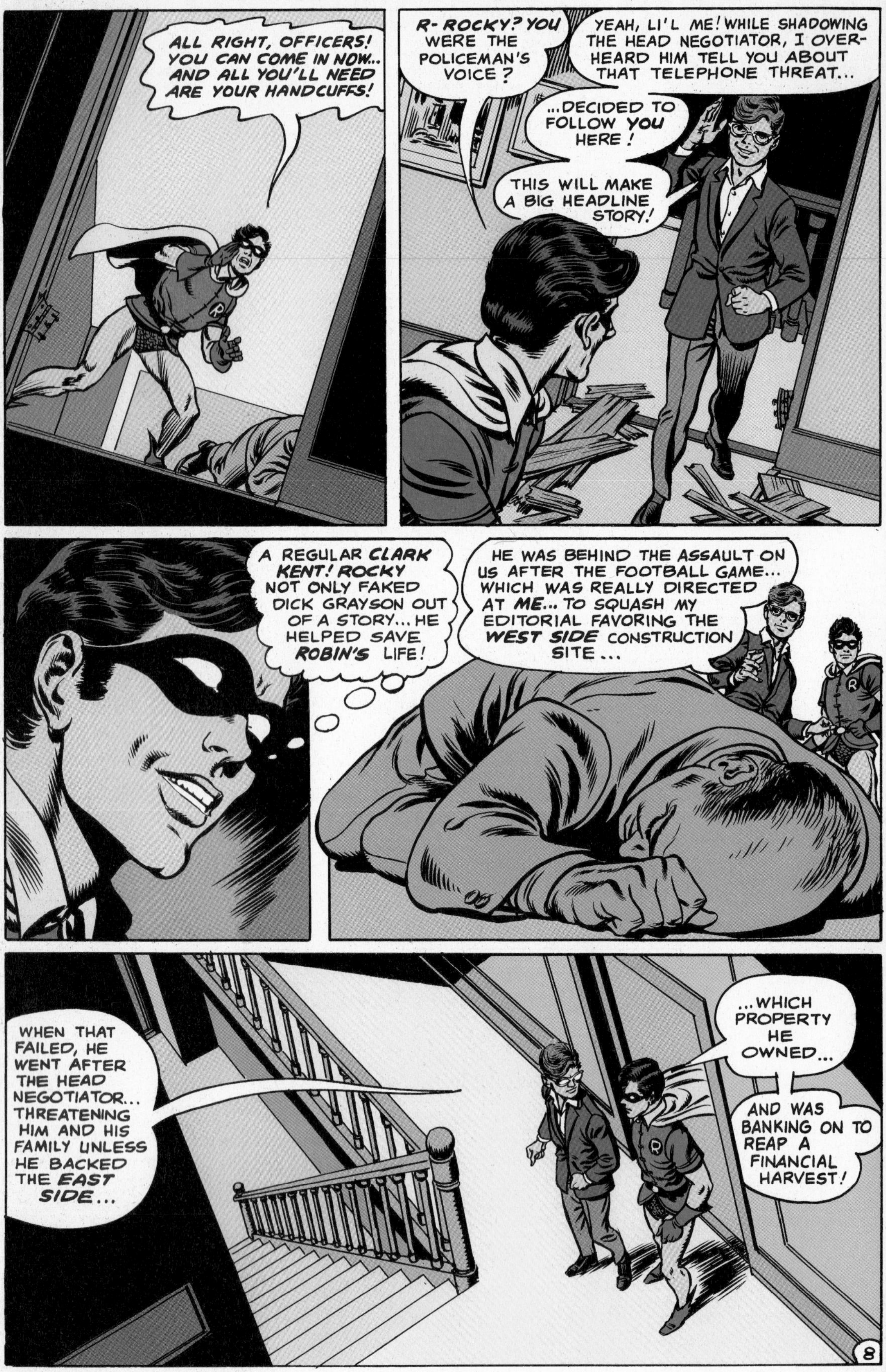
ALL RIGHT, OFFICERS! YOU CAN COME IN NOW... AND ALL YOU'LL NEED ARE YOUR HANDCUFFS!
R-ROCKY? YOU WERE THE POLICEMAN'S VOICE?
YEAH, LI'L ME! WHILE SHADOWING THE HEAD NEGOTIATOR, I OVERHEARD HIM TELL YOU ABOUT THAT TELEPHONE THREAT...
...DECIDED TO FOLLOW YOU HERE!
THIS WILL MAKE A BIG HEADLINE STORY!
A REGULAR CLARK KENT! ROCKY NOT ONLY FAKED DICK GRAYSON OUT OF A STORY... HE HELPED SAVE ROBIN'S LIFE!
HE WAS BEHIND THE ASSAULT ON US AFTER THE FOOTBALL GAME... WHICH WAS REALLY DIRECTED AT ME... TO SQUASH MY EDITORIAL FAVORING THE WEST SIDE CONSTRUCTION SITE...
WHEN THAT FAILED, HE WENT AFTER THE HEAD NEGOTIATOR... THREATENING HIM AND HIS FAMILY UNLESS HE BACKED THE EAST SIDE...
...WHICH PROPERTY HE OWNED...
AND WAS BANKING ON TO REAP A FINANCIAL HARVEST!
8

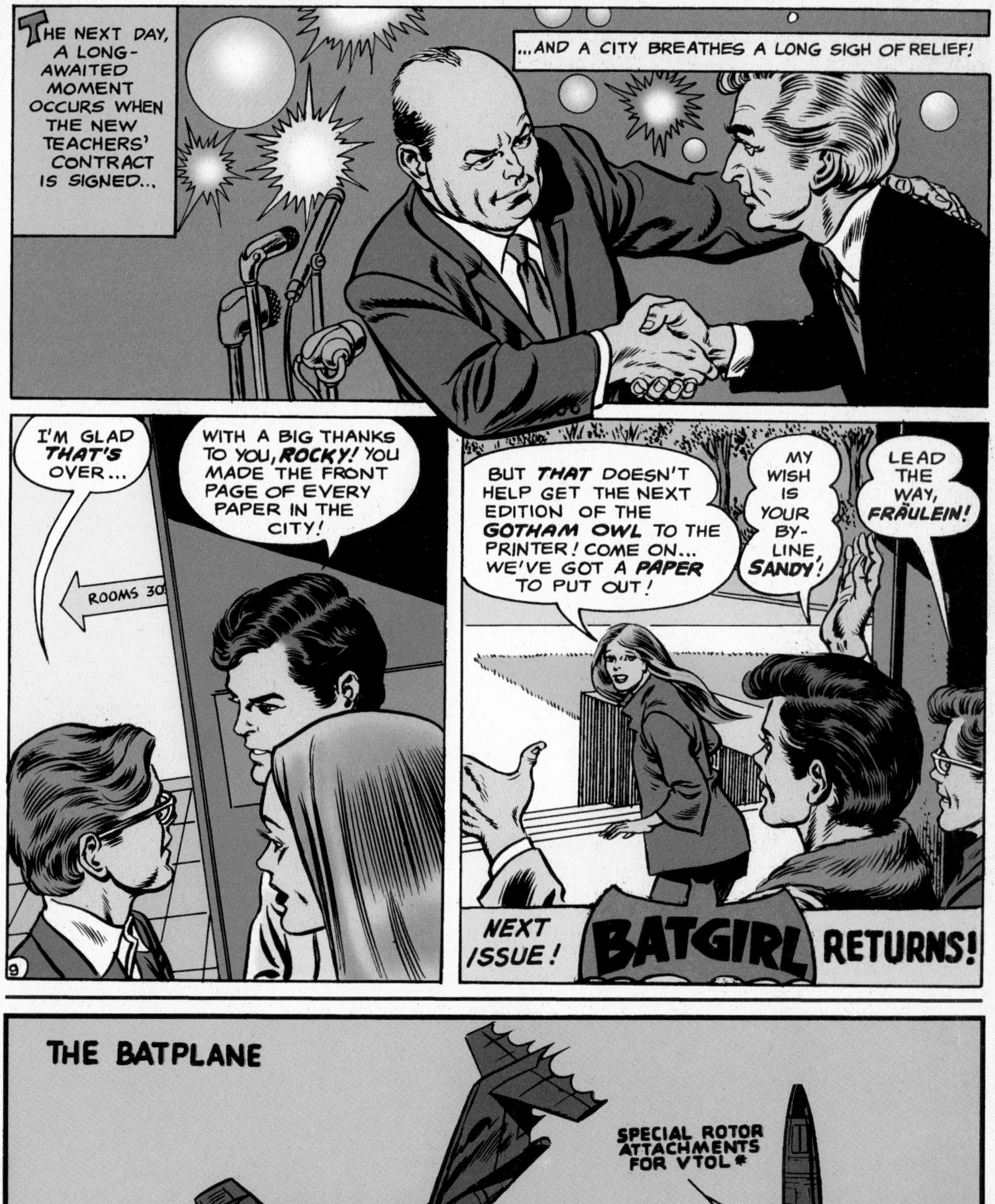
THE NEXT DAY, A LONG-AWAITED MOMENT OCCURS WHEN THE NEW TEACHERS' CONTRACT IS SIGNED...
...AND A CITY BREATHES A LONG SIGH OF RELIEF!
I'M GLAD THAT'S OVER...
WITH A BIG THANKS TO YOU, ROCKY! YOU MADE THE FRONT PAGE OF EVERY PAPER IN THE CITY!
ROOMS 30
BUT THAT DOESN'T HELP GET THE NEXT EDITION OF THE GOTHAM OWL TO THE PRINTER! COME ON... WE'VE GOT A PAPER TO PUT OUT!
MY WISH IS YOUR BY-LINE, SANDY!
LEAD THE WAY, FRÄULEIN!
NEXT ISSUE! BATGIRL RETURNS!
9

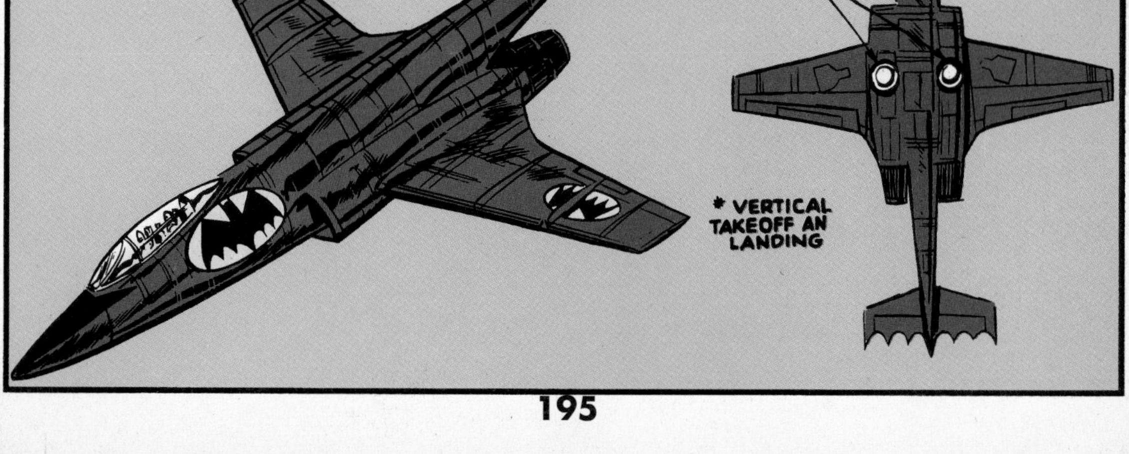
THE BATPLANE
SPECIAL ROTOR ATTACHMENTS FOR VTOL*
* VERTICAL TAKEOFF AN LANDING

RETURN TO THE DARK KNIGHT

The "Batman" TV show ended in 1968 and so did its influence on the comic books—the intent of the "New Look" was resumed. The stories again became more serious, and many of the super-villains (at least the more colorful and outrageous ones) were set aside.

Batman's foes tended to be small-time gangsters, crooked politicians and murderers during this period, but something had indeed changed. Batman was now encountering more of the "hot-button" topics of the times, albeit in subtle ways. Women's Liberation became an issue when the new Batgirl was introduced in 1967. Batman had to learn — slowly, at first—to deal with her as an individual and an equal, rather than the appendage that the earlier incarnations of Bat-females were. And his longtime partner, Robin the Boy Wonder, had finally grown up, something the Batman finally had to acknowledge in 1969 when Dick Grayson entered college in "One Bullet Too Many" (BATMAN #217).

This was a shocking move at the time—Batman and Robin had fought together as a team for almost 30 years. But the more astute readers realized that this was a natural evolution and tacit evidence that comic books had started to grow up along with them.

Part of the reason for this was that many of the longtime writers and artists were leaving the series, and younger writers—more in touch with current events and pop culture—were coming to comics. There was a taste of what was to come as young artist Neal Adams began drawing occasional covers for BATMAN and DETECTIVE COMICS in 1969. The following year would see the celebrated collaboration between Adams and a new journalist-turned-comics-writer, Dennis O'Neil. O'Neil's "street-level" view of The Batman and Adams's gritty, realistic portrayal led to Frank Miller's nightmarish treatment of the Dark Knight in 1986. The Batman would never be the same.

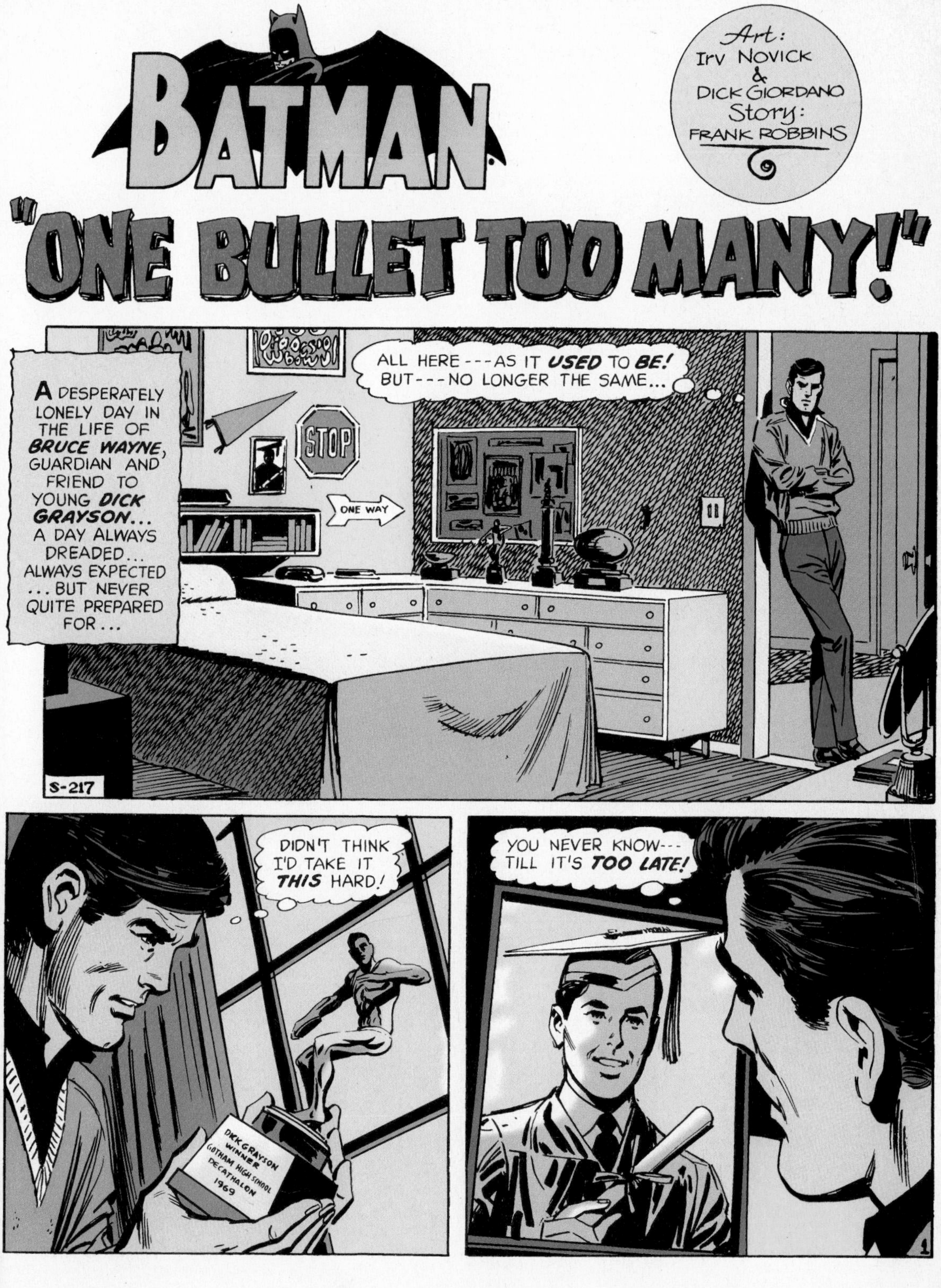
BATMAN
"ONE BULLET TOO MANY!"
Art: Irv Novick & Dick Giordano
Story: Frank Robbins
A DESPERATELY LONELY DAY IN THE LIFE OF BRUCE WAYNE, GUARDIAN AND FRIEND TO YOUNG DICK GRAYSON... A DAY ALWAYS DREADED... ALWAYS EXPECTED ... BUT NEVER QUITE PREPARED FOR...
ALL HERE---AS IT USED TO BE! BUT---NO LONGER THE SAME...
STOP
ONE WAY
S-217
DIDN'T THINK I'D TAKE IT THIS HARD!
DICK GRAYSON WINNER GOTHAM HIGH SCHOOL DECATHALON 1969
YOU NEVER KNOW--- TILL IT'S TOO LATE!

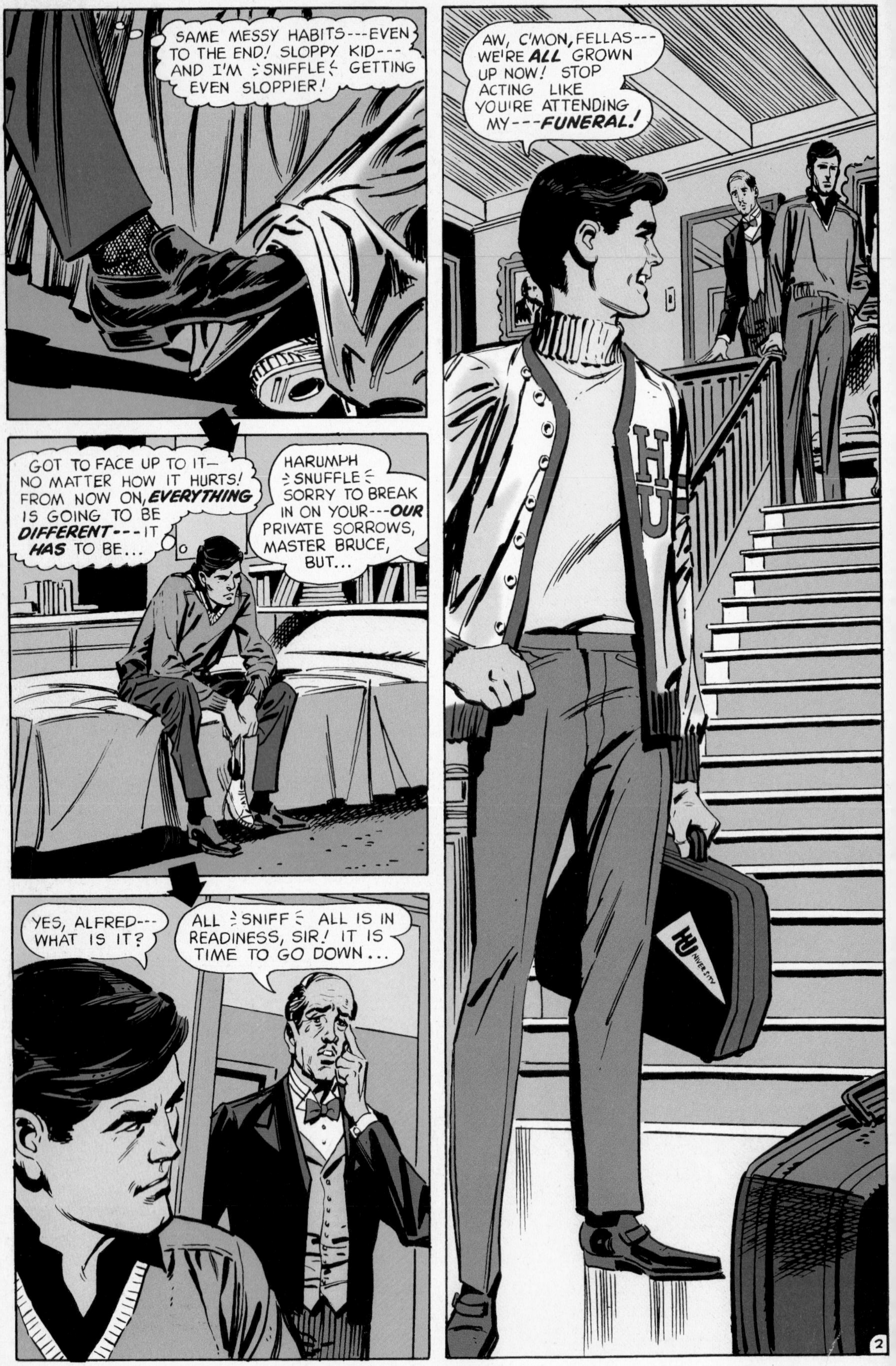
SAME MESSY HABITS---EVEN TO THE END! SLOPPY KID--- AND I'M ⸗SNIFFLE⸗ GETTING EVEN SLOPPIER!
GOT TO FACE UP TO IT— NO MATTER HOW IT HURTS! FROM NOW ON, EVERYTHING IS GOING TO BE DIFFERENT---IT HAS TO BE...
HARUMPH ⸗SNUFFLE⸗ SORRY TO BREAK IN ON YOUR---OUR PRIVATE SORROWS, MASTER BRUCE, BUT...
YES, ALFRED--- WHAT IS IT?
ALL ⸗SNIFF⸗ ALL IS IN READINESS, SIR! IT IS TIME TO GO DOWN...
AW, C'MON, FELLAS--- WE'RE ALL GROWN UP NOW! STOP ACTING LIKE YOU'RE ATTENDING MY---FUNERAL!
2

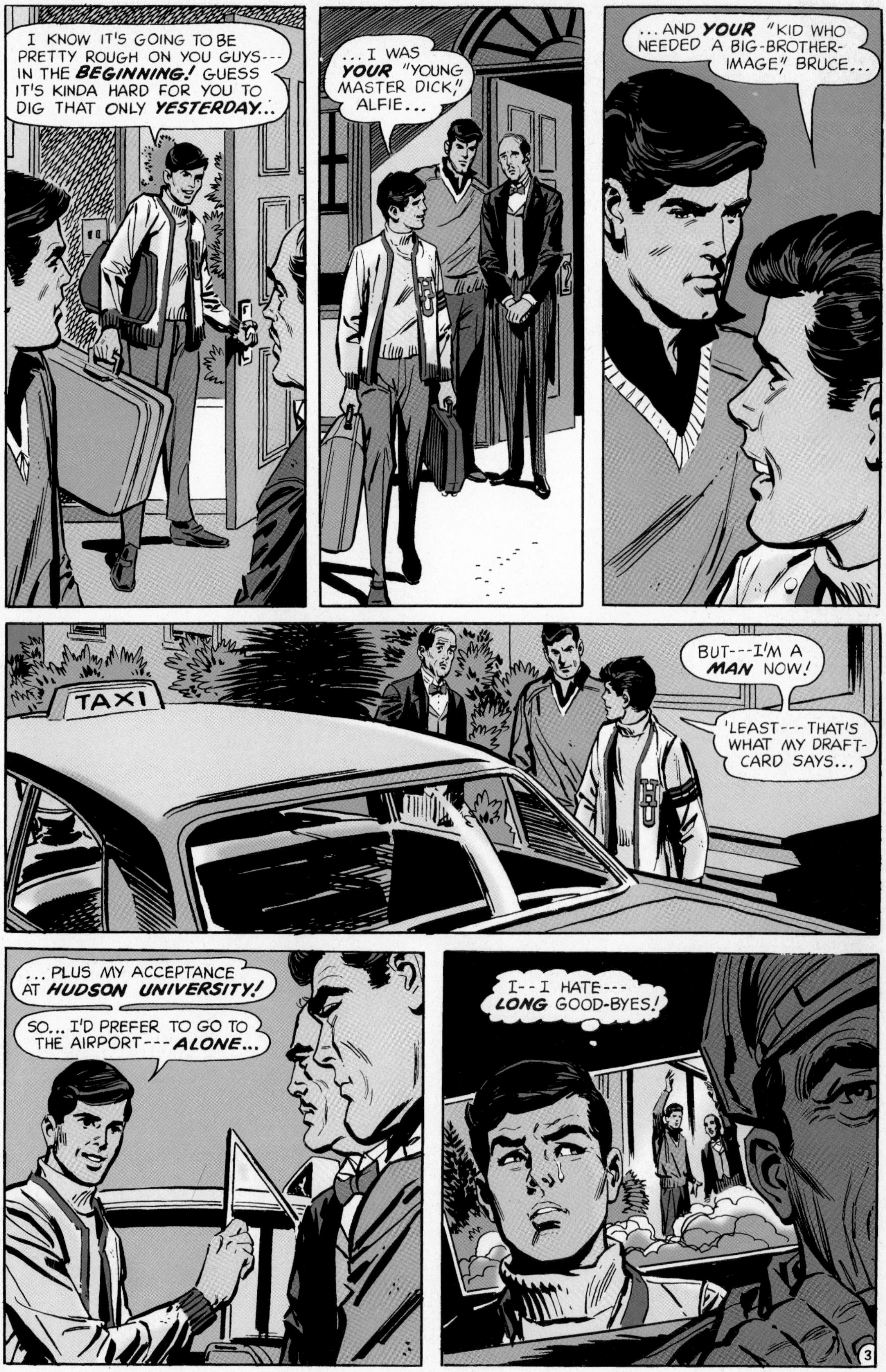
I KNOW IT'S GOING TO BE PRETTY ROUGH ON YOU GUYS--- IN THE BEGINNING! GUESS IT'S KINDA HARD FOR YOU TO DIG THAT ONLY YESTERDAY...
...I WAS YOUR "YOUNG MASTER DICK," ALFIE...
...AND YOUR "KID WHO NEEDED A BIG-BROTHER-IMAGE," BRUCE...
TAXI
BUT---I'M A MAN NOW!
'LEAST---THAT'S WHAT MY DRAFT-CARD SAYS...
...PLUS MY ACCEPTANCE AT HUDSON UNIVERSITY!
SO...I'D PREFER TO GO TO THE AIRPORT---ALONE...
I--I HATE--- LONG GOOD-BYES!
3

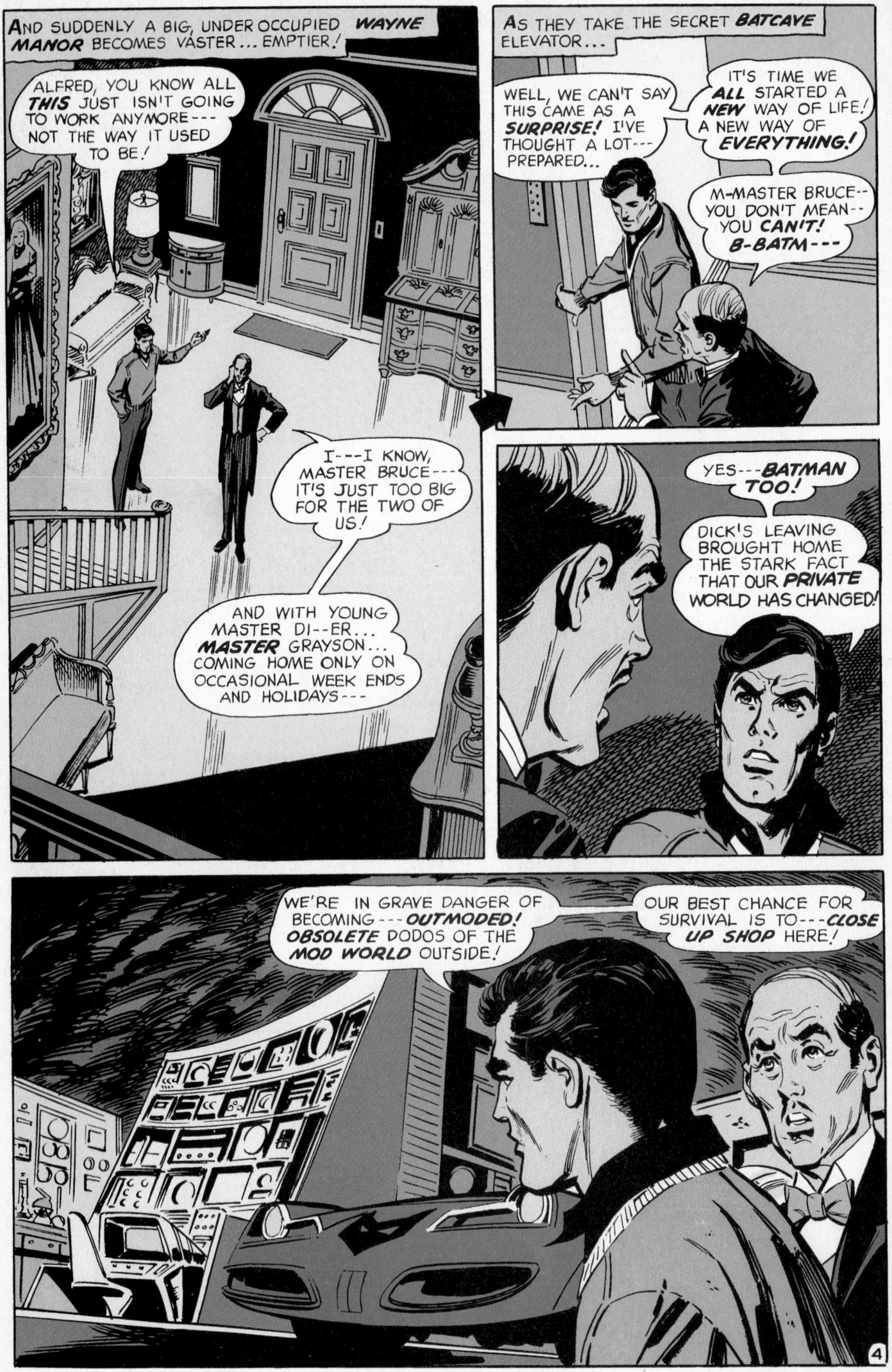
AND SUDDENLY A BIG, UNDER OCCUPIED WAYNE MANOR BECOMES VASTER... EMPTIER!
ALFRED, YOU KNOW ALL THIS JUST ISN'T GOING TO WORK ANYMORE--- NOT THE WAY IT USED TO BE!
I---I KNOW, MASTER BRUCE--- IT'S JUST TOO BIG FOR THE TWO OF US!
AND WITH YOUNG MASTER DI--ER... MASTER GRAYSON... COMING HOME ONLY ON OCCASIONAL WEEK ENDS AND HOLIDAYS---
AS THEY TAKE THE SECRET BATCAVE ELEVATOR...
WELL, WE CAN'T SAY THIS CAME AS A SURPRISE! I'VE THOUGHT A LOT--- PREPARED...
IT'S TIME WE ALL STARTED A NEW WAY OF LIFE! A NEW WAY OF EVERYTHING!
M-MASTER BRUCE-- YOU DON'T MEAN-- YOU CAN'T! B-BATM---
YES---BATMAN TOO!
DICK'S LEAVING BROUGHT HOME THE STARK FACT THAT OUR PRIVATE WORLD HAS CHANGED!
WE'RE IN GRAVE DANGER OF BECOMING---OUTMODED! OBSOLETE DODOS OF THE MOD WORLD OUTSIDE!
OUR BEST CHANCE FOR SURVIVAL IS TO---CLOSE UP SHOP HERE!
4

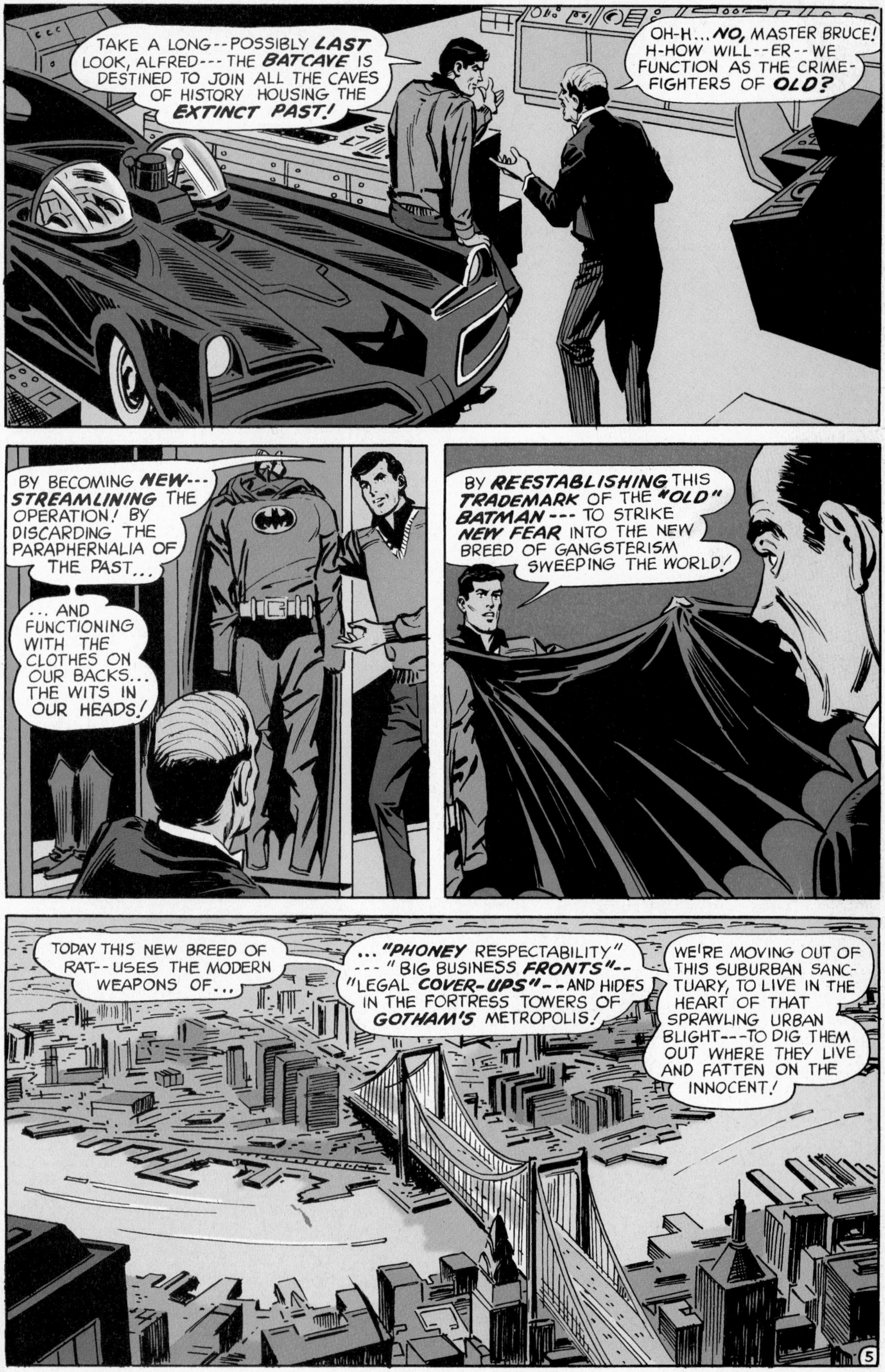
TAKE A LONG--POSSIBLY LAST LOOK, ALFRED--- THE BATCAVE IS DESTINED TO JOIN ALL THE CAVES OF HISTORY HOUSING THE EXTINCT PAST!
OH-H... NO, MASTER BRUCE! H-HOW WILL--ER--WE FUNCTION AS THE CRIME-FIGHTERS OF OLD?
BY BECOMING NEW--- STREAMLINING THE OPERATION! BY DISCARDING THE PARAPHERNALIA OF THE PAST...
... AND FUNCTIONING WITH THE CLOTHES ON OUR BACKS... THE WITS IN OUR HEADS!
BY REESTABLISHING THIS TRADEMARK OF THE "OLD" BATMAN--- TO STRIKE NEW FEAR INTO THE NEW BREED OF GANGSTERISM SWEEPING THE WORLD!
TODAY THIS NEW BREED OF RAT--USES THE MODERN WEAPONS OF...
... "PHONEY RESPECTABILITY" --- "BIG BUSINESS FRONTS"-- "LEGAL COVER-UPS"--AND HIDES IN THE FORTRESS TOWERS OF GOTHAM'S METROPOLIS!
WE'RE MOVING OUT OF THIS SUBURBAN SANCTUARY, TO LIVE IN THE HEART OF THAT SPRAWLING URBAN BLIGHT---TO DIG THEM OUT WHERE THEY LIVE AND FATTEN ON THE INNOCENT!
5

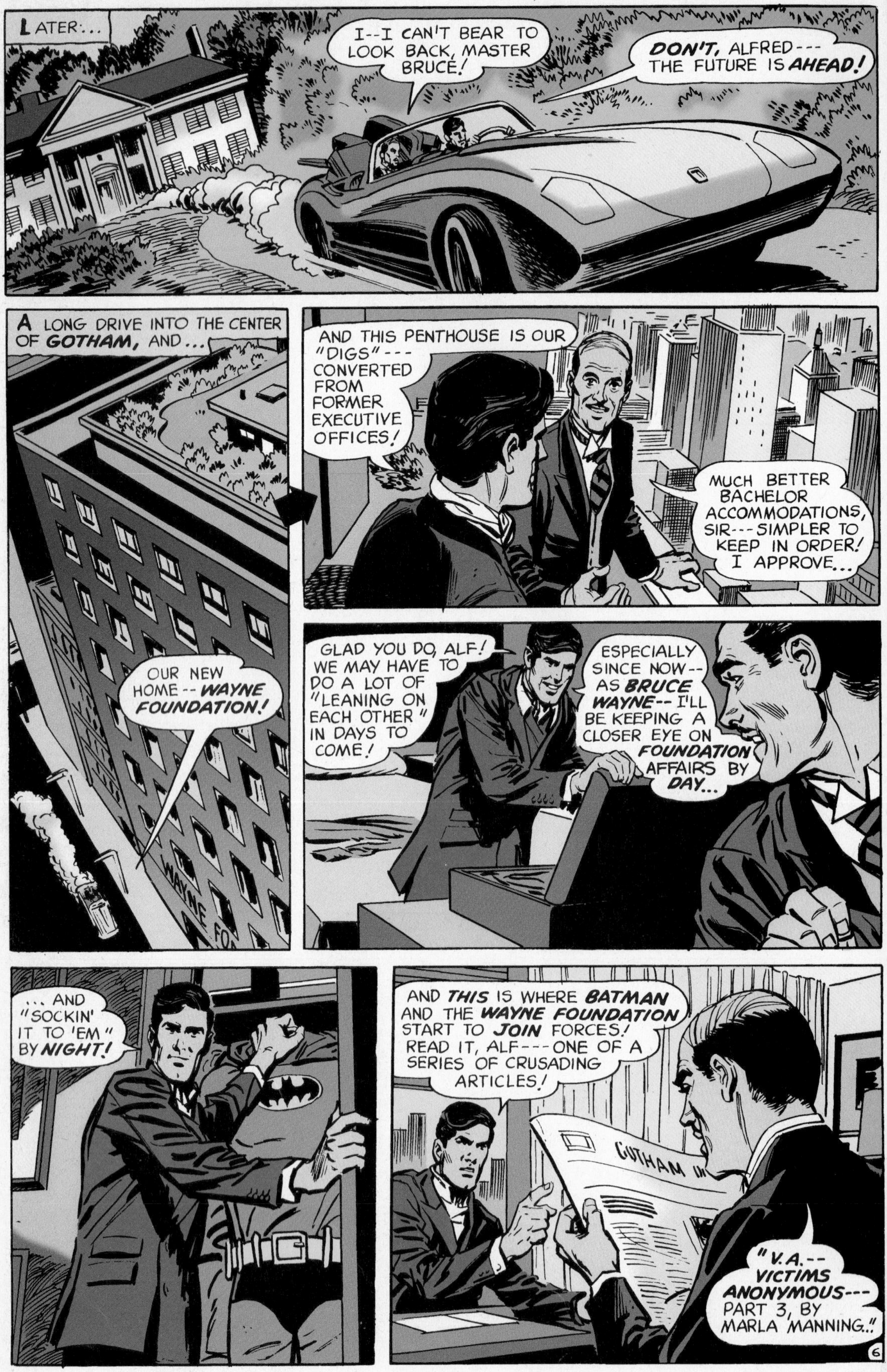
LATER...
I--I CAN'T BEAR TO LOOK BACK, MASTER BRUCE!
DON'T, ALFRED--- THE FUTURE IS AHEAD!
A LONG DRIVE INTO THE CENTER OF GOTHAM, AND...
OUR NEW HOME--WAYNE FOUNDATION!
WAYNE FO
AND THIS PENTHOUSE IS OUR "DIGS"--- CONVERTED FROM FORMER EXECUTIVE OFFICES!
MUCH BETTER BACHELOR ACCOMMODATIONS, SIR---SIMPLER TO KEEP IN ORDER! I APPROVE...
GLAD YOU DO, ALF! WE MAY HAVE TO DO A LOT OF "LEANING ON EACH OTHER" IN DAYS TO COME!
ESPECIALLY SINCE NOW--AS BRUCE WAYNE--I'LL BE KEEPING A CLOSER EYE ON FOUNDATION AFFAIRS BY DAY...
...AND "SOCKIN' IT TO 'EM" BY NIGHT!
AND THIS IS WHERE BATMAN AND THE WAYNE FOUNDATION START TO JOIN FORCES! READ IT, ALF---ONE OF A SERIES OF CRUSADING ARTICLES!
GOTHAM IN
"V.A.--VICTIMS ANONYMOUS--- PART 3, BY MARLA MANNING."
6

"...LATEST VICTIM IN THE UNSUNG CASE HISTORY OF INNOCENTS IN THE WAR AGAINST CRIME--- *DR. SUSAN FIELDING*, PEDIATRICIAN..."

"...AND WIFE OF *DR. JONAH FIELDING*, SLAIN LAST WEEK WHILE TREATING AN UNKNOWN GUNSHOT PATIENT! IN THIS UNSOLVED TRAGEDY..."

"UNSOLVED"--- THE CRIMINAL *UNPUNISHED!* THINK OF IT, ALF...

...HOW MANY UNDERWORLD KILLINGS--MAIMINGS ---IN THIS VAST CITY LEAVE A TRAIL OF INNOCENT VICTIMS OF THE *"VICTIM"!* WIVES-- MOTHERS--CHILDREN...

...MANY LEFT WITH-OUT ANY MEANS OF SUPPORT! IT'S THE GREAT *UNPUBLICIZED TRAGEDY* OF OUR TIME!

WE SUFFER GREAT PAIN OVER *TRUE* JUSTICE --- *"RIGHTS OF THE INDIVIDUAL"* --- *"INNOCENT UNTIL PROVEN GUILTY"*...

...ALL FOR THE *ACCUSED* PARTIES! BUT WHAT ABOUT THE *"PROVEN"* INNOCENT-- THE *VICTIMS?*

INNOCENT VICTIMS SUCH AS *DICK* AND *I* WERE-- WHEN *OUR* PARENTS WERE BRUTALLY SLAIN! THEIR *DEATHS* WERE THE *BIRTHS* OF--- *BATMAN* AND *ROBIN!*

WE WERE IN THE FORTUNATE POSITION TO CLAIM JUSTICE FOR *OURSELVES* --- BUT WHAT OF THE LESS FORTUNATE?

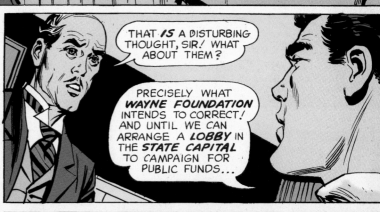

THAT *IS* A DISTURBING THOUGHT, SIR! WHAT ABOUT THEM?

PRECISELY WHAT *WAYNE FOUNDATION* INTENDS TO CORRECT! AND UNTIL WE CAN ARRANGE A *LOBBY* IN THE *STATE CAPITAL* TO CAMPAIGN FOR PUBLIC FUNDS...

...WE'RE SETTING UP A *SPECIAL ASSISTANCE PROGRAM* HERE TO AID THESE PEOPLE!

WORTHY IDEA, SIR! WHILE THESE POOR VICTIMS ARE FORGOTTEN BY THE PUBLIC--- TO *US* THEY'RE *VERY IMPOR-TANT PEOPLE!* V.I.P.'S, YOU MIGHT SAY!

7

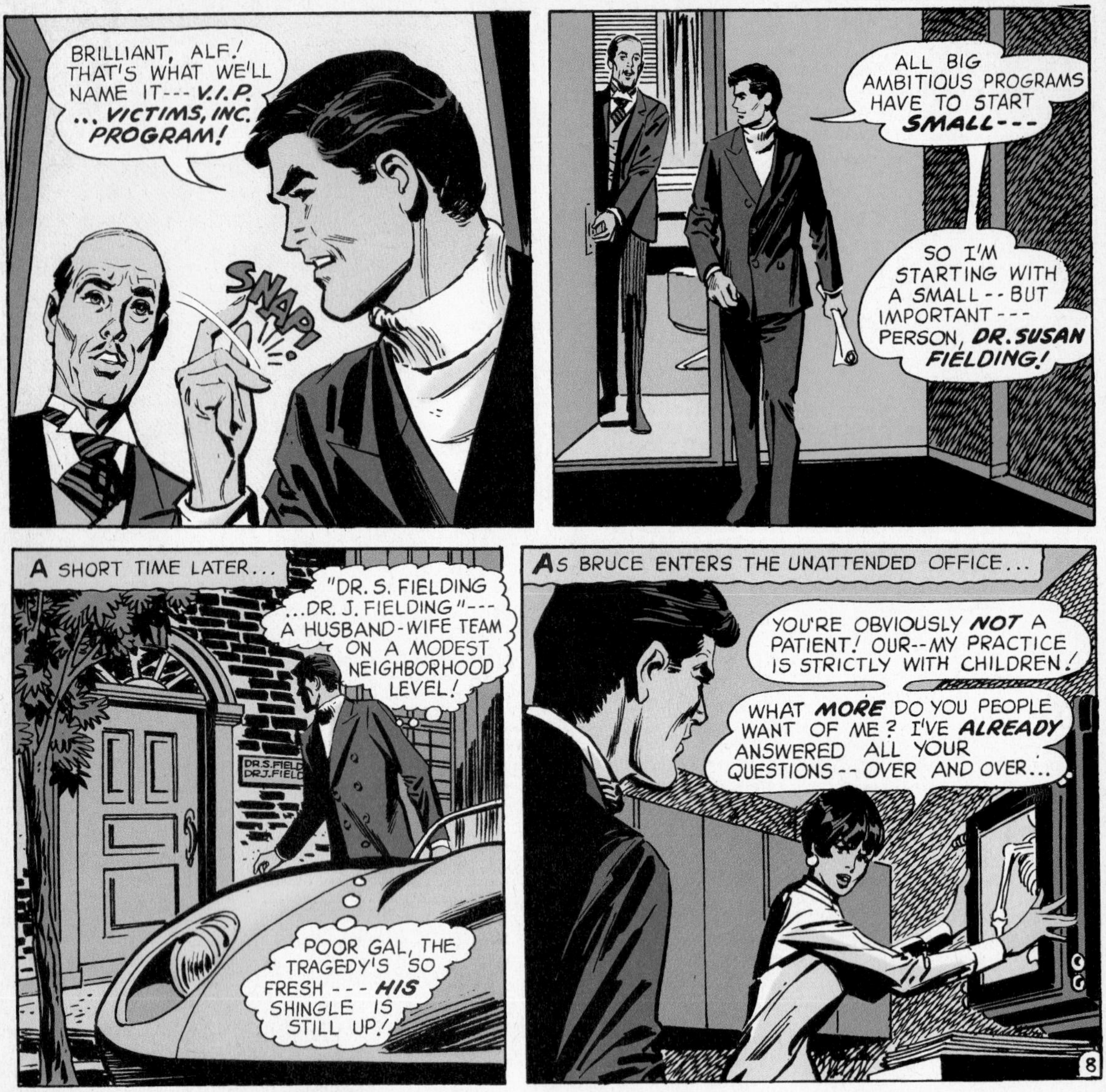
BRILLIANT, ALF! THAT'S WHAT WE'LL NAME IT--- V.I.P. ...VICTIMS, INC. PROGRAM!
SNAP!
ALL BIG AMBITIOUS PROGRAMS HAVE TO START SMALL---
SO I'M STARTING WITH A SMALL--BUT IMPORTANT--- PERSON, DR. SUSAN FIELDING!
A SHORT TIME LATER...
"DR. S. FIELDING ...DR. J. FIELDING"--- A HUSBAND-WIFE TEAM ON A MODEST NEIGHBORHOOD LEVEL!
POOR GAL, THE TRAGEDY'S SO FRESH --- HIS SHINGLE IS STILL UP!
AS BRUCE ENTERS THE UNATTENDED OFFICE...
YOU'RE OBVIOUSLY NOT A PATIENT! OUR--MY PRACTICE IS STRICTLY WITH CHILDREN!
WHAT MORE DO YOU PEOPLE WANT OF ME? I'VE ALREADY ANSWERED ALL YOUR QUESTIONS -- OVER AND OVER...
8

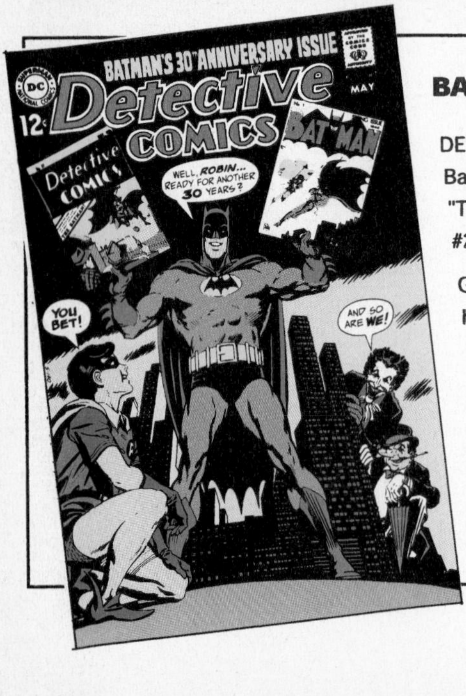
BATMAN'S 30TH ANNIVERSARY ISSUE
12¢
Detective Comics
MAY
WELL, ROBIN... READY FOR ANOTHER 30 YEARS?
YOU BET!
AND SO ARE WE!

BATMAN TURNS THIRTY!

DETECTIVE COMICS #387 was the thirtieth anniversary issue for Batman. In recognition of this landmark, Batman's first adventure, "The Case of the Chemical Syndicate" from DETECTIVE COMICS #27, would be retold and updated.

Given a modern twist, this version also included Robin, who had not yet been created at the telling of the original tale.

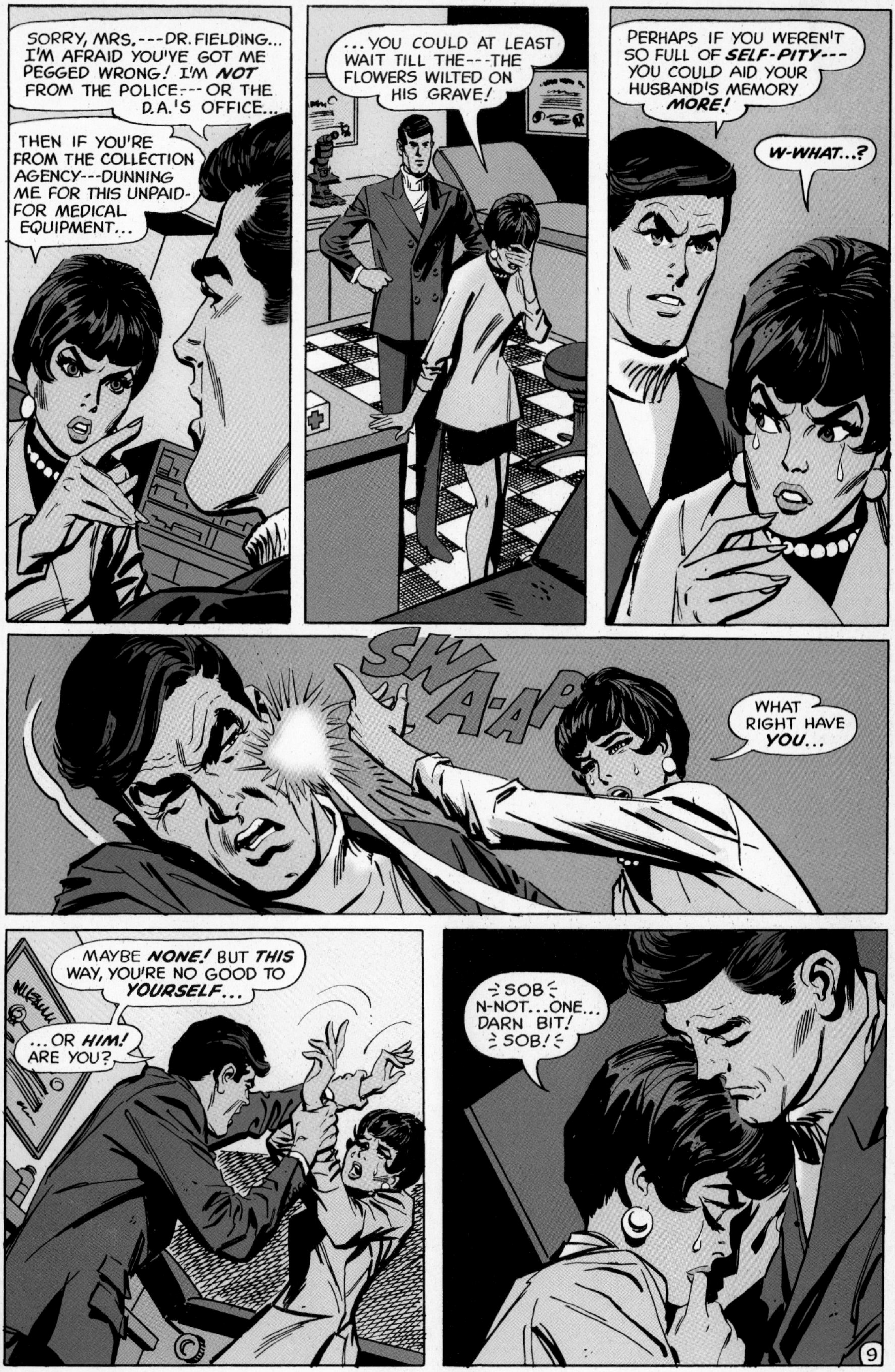
SORRY, MRS.---DR. FIELDING... I'M AFRAID YOU'VE GOT ME PEGGED WRONG! I'M NOT FROM THE POLICE---OR THE D.A.'S OFFICE...
THEN IF YOU'RE FROM THE COLLECTION AGENCY---DUNNING ME FOR THIS UNPAID-FOR MEDICAL EQUIPMENT...
...YOU COULD AT LEAST WAIT TILL THE---THE FLOWERS WILTED ON HIS GRAVE!
PERHAPS IF YOU WEREN'T SO FULL OF SELF-PITY---YOU COULD AID YOUR HUSBAND'S MEMORY MORE!
W-WHAT...?
SWA-AP
WHAT RIGHT HAVE YOU...
MAYBE NONE! BUT THIS WAY, YOU'RE NO GOOD TO YOURSELF...
...OR HIM! ARE YOU?
SOB N-NOT...ONE... DARN BIT! SOB!
9

I---I SHOULDN'T ⸳SOB⸳ BE DOING THIS! I ⸳SOB⸳ DON'T EVEN *KNOW* YOU!

I COULD BE A *FRIEND*-- IF YOU'LL *LET* ME!

⸳SNIFF⸳ THANKS! WHO... WHO ARE YOU?

BRUCE WAYNE --HEAD OF *WAYNE FOUNDATION!* WE WANT TO AID PEOPLE LIKE YOU--- VICTIMS OF INJUSTICE...

I DON'T NEED YOUR *CHARITY!* AND WITH ALL YOUR WEALTH --YOU CAN'T BRING JONAH BACK!

BUT *YOU* HAVE A FUTURE AHEAD OF YOU, *SERVING* MANKIND---*IF* YOU WANT TO FACE IT!

WE'RE NOT "*DO-GOODERS*" --- WE WANT TO *HELP!*

JUST BEFORE, YOU INDICATED THAT YOU'RE IN *DEBT!* BOTH OF YOU HAD BEEN OPERATING ON A SHOESTRING, I GATHER?

WE WORKED OUR WAY THROUGH MEDICAL SCHOOL, WHERE WE MET-- SET UP JOINT- PRACTICE HERE WHEN WE MARRIED...

...SCRIMPING FOR OUR NEXT TEN YEARS TOGETHER TO BUY PROPER EQUIPMENT...TO TEND TO OUR LITTLE PATIENTS' NEEDS, *PROPERLY!* BUT *NOW...*

NOW THE CREDITORS WON'T PUT *SENTIMENT* BEFORE *CASH,* EH?

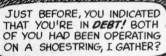

DR. J. FIELDING
DR. S. FIELDING

SO SUPPOSE *WAYNE FOUNDATION* EXTENDS YOU AN INDEFINITE-PERIOD *LOAN* WITH *NO* INTEREST CHARGES? *THAT* WOULDN'T BE CHARITY---

BUT IT WOULD MAKE YOU AWFUL DARN --- FOOLS, I GUESS!

BUT, YES ---*YES!* I ACCEPT YOUR OFFER!

10

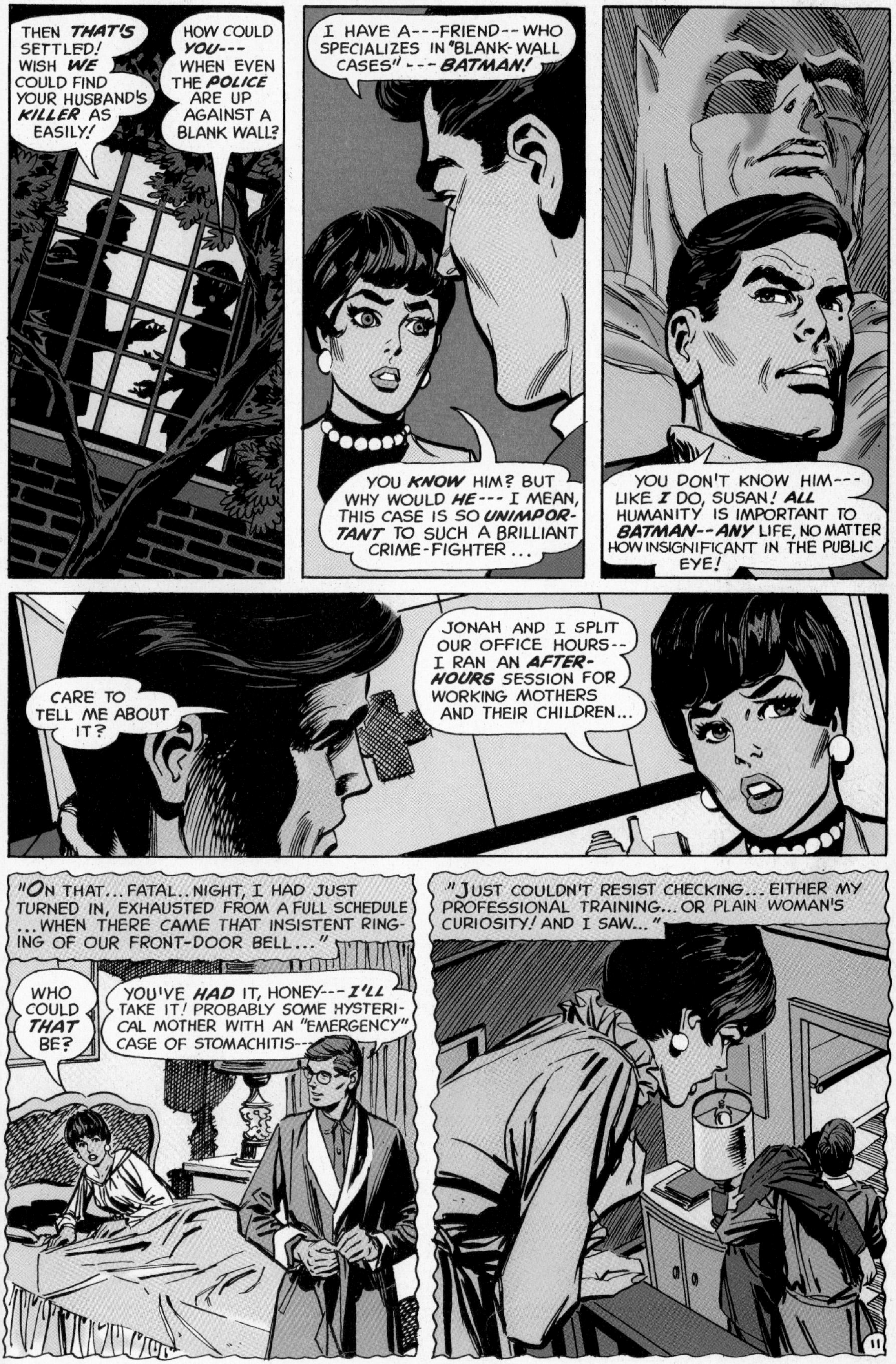

THEN THAT'S SETTLED! WISH WE COULD FIND YOUR HUSBAND'S KILLER AS EASILY!
HOW COULD YOU--- WHEN EVEN THE POLICE ARE UP AGAINST A BLANK WALL?
I HAVE A---FRIEND--WHO SPECIALIZES IN "BLANK-WALL CASES" ---BATMAN!
YOU KNOW HIM? BUT WHY WOULD HE--- I MEAN, THIS CASE IS SO UNIMPORTANT TO SUCH A BRILLIANT CRIME-FIGHTER...
YOU DON'T KNOW HIM--- LIKE I DO, SUSAN! ALL HUMANITY IS IMPORTANT TO BATMAN--ANY LIFE, NO MATTER HOW INSIGNIFICANT IN THE PUBLIC EYE!
CARE TO TELL ME ABOUT IT?
JONAH AND I SPLIT OUR OFFICE HOURS-- I RAN AN AFTER-HOURS SESSION FOR WORKING MOTHERS AND THEIR CHILDREN...
"ON THAT...FATAL...NIGHT, I HAD JUST TURNED IN, EXHAUSTED FROM A FULL SCHEDULE ...WHEN THERE CAME THAT INSISTENT RINGING OF OUR FRONT-DOOR BELL..."
WHO COULD THAT BE?
YOU'VE HAD IT, HONEY---I'LL TAKE IT! PROBABLY SOME HYSTERICAL MOTHER WITH AN "EMERGENCY" CASE OF STOMACHITIS--
"JUST COULDN'T RESIST CHECKING... EITHER MY PROFESSIONAL TRAINING...OR PLAIN WOMAN'S CURIOSITY! AND I SAW..."
11

SAW *WHAT*, SUSAN?

A BIG MAN--OBVIOUSLY IN *TROUBLE!* A TRAIL OF BLOOD-- MY HUSBAND HELPING HIM IN! COULDN'T SEE HIS *FACE*...

WAS HE *LIMPING?* HOLDING HIS LEG?

NOT THAT I NOTICED!

HMM--THE PAPER SAID THE *KILLER* WAS A *GUNSHOT* VICTIM--- AND SINCE EVERY DOCTOR *HAS* TO REPORT SUCH CASES TO THE POLICE...

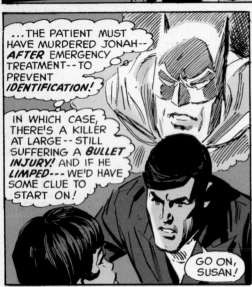

...THE PATIENT MUST HAVE MURDERED JONAH-- *AFTER* EMERGENCY TREATMENT--TO PREVENT *IDENTIFICATION!*

IN WHICH CASE, THERE'S A KILLER AT LARGE-- STILL SUFFERING A *BULLET INJURY!* AND IF HE *LIMPED---* WE'D HAVE SOME CLUE TO START ON!

GO ON, SUSAN!

"*I* WAS BACK IN BED, FITFULLY TRYING TO SLEEP... *WHEN IT CAME!* TWO HORRIBLE *GUN-BLASTS* DOWNSTAIRS... A DOOR SLAMMING! FEARFULLY, I RAN DOWN AND..."

I-- I DIDN'T HAVE TO BE A DOCTOR TO-- *KNOW!* HE'D DIED--- *INSTANTLY!*

EASY, GAL! I KNOW HOW PAINFUL IT STILL IS...

AND THE--PATIENT?

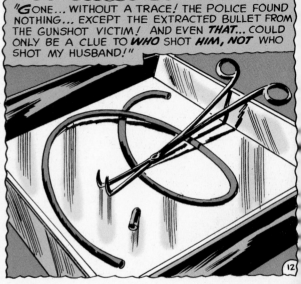

"*G*ONE... WITHOUT A TRACE! THE POLICE FOUND NOTHING... EXCEPT THE EXTRACTED BULLET FROM THE GUNSHOT VICTIM! AND EVEN *THAT*... COULD ONLY BE A CLUE TO *WHO* SHOT *HIM, NOT* WHO SHOT MY HUSBAND!"

12

SO YOU SEE, BRUCE-- HOW FRUITLESS IT ALL IS! THAT BULLET ---THE *ONLY* CLUE--DOESN'T TELL US *WHO* SHOT *JONAH!*

EXCEPT THAT THE KILLER HAD TO LEAVE AS HE CAME-- *WOUNDED!*

ANY WAY OF KNOWING --- HOW *BADLY* HE WAS SHOT? THE POLICE MAY BE LOOKING FOR A MAN ---*ALREADY DEAD!*

THERE WAS THAT *TOURNIQUET!*..

INDICATING HE WAS SHOT IN AN *EXTREMITY* --ARM OR LEG!

AND SINCE HE WASN'T *LIMPING* WHEN HE CAME IN--- WE'RE LOOKING FOR A KILLER WITH HIS *ARM* IN A *SLING!*

BUT--GO LOOK FOR AN UNKNOWN MAN WITH A SLING --AMONG EIGHT-MILLION FACELESS PEOPLE! WOULDN'T CHECK INTO A HOSPITAL--- PROBABLY HOLED UP SOMEWHERE NURSING HIS ARM, *ALONE!*

THINK OF SOMETHING, BRUCE?

THINK I BETTER TURN THIS INFO OVER TO *BATMAN*-- IT'S ABOVE *MY* HEAD! I'LL KEEP IN TOUCH, SUSAN!

PLEASE DO, BRUCE! I'M SO GRATEFUL-- FOR EVERYTHING!

MINUTES LATER, AT THE SOUND OF A DOOR OPENING...

W-WHO'S THERE?

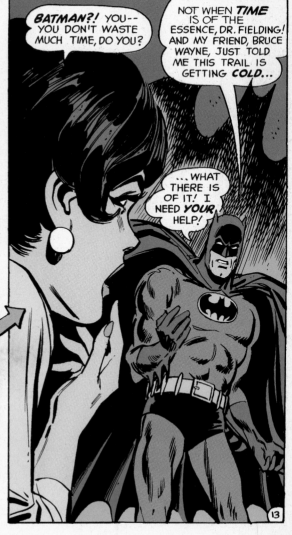

BATMAN?! YOU-- YOU DON'T WASTE MUCH TIME, DO YOU?

NOT WHEN *TIME* IS OF THE ESSENCE, DR. FIELDING! AND MY FRIEND, BRUCE WAYNE, JUST TOLD ME THIS TRAIL IS GETTING *COLD...*

...WHAT THERE IS OF IT! I NEED *YOUR* HELP!

13

YOU AND BRUCE MAKE QUITE A *TEAM, BATMAN!* I NEED *HIS* HELP---AND *YOU* NEED *MINE!*

WHAT COULD I POSSIBLY DO?

DECOY YOUR HUSBAND'S KILLER--- BACK *HERE!*

W-WHAT...? IS THAT THE "HELP" YOU NEED--- MY *LIFE?*

LET'S LEVEL-- AND GET IT STRAIGHT! WITHOUT *YOU*-- I AND THE ENTIRE POLICE FORCE--DON'T STAND A CHANCE...

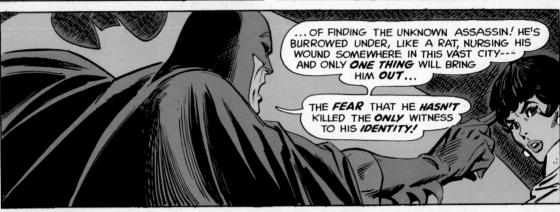

...OF FINDING THE UNKNOWN ASSASSIN! HE'S BURROWED UNDER, LIKE A RAT, NURSING HIS WOUND SOMEWHERE IN THIS VAST CITY--- AND ONLY *ONE THING* WILL BRING HIM *OUT...*

THE *FEAR* THAT HE *HASN'T* KILLED THE *ONLY* WITNESS TO HIS *IDENTITY!*

B-BUT HE ⸮SOB⸮ *DID!* ONLY *JONAH* COULD'VE...

BUT *HE* DOESN'T KNOW THAT! SUPPOSE... HE GOT THE IDEA THAT *YOU* ALSO SAW HIS FACE...

...AND SOONER OR LATER, WHEN YOU GOT OVER YOUR TERROR--YOU'D *DESCRIBE* HIM TO THE POLICE?

HE'D COME *HERE*-- AND DO TO *ME* WHAT HE DID TO ⸮SOB⸮

PRECISELY! BUT IF I STAKE- OUT AND *WAIT* FOR HIM...

I REALIZE THERE'S SOME SMALL *RISK* INVOLVED, BUT---IF YOU *TRUST* ME?

IT--IT'S NOT *FAIR* TO LET *JONAH'S* DEATH GO-- *UNPUNISHED!*

14

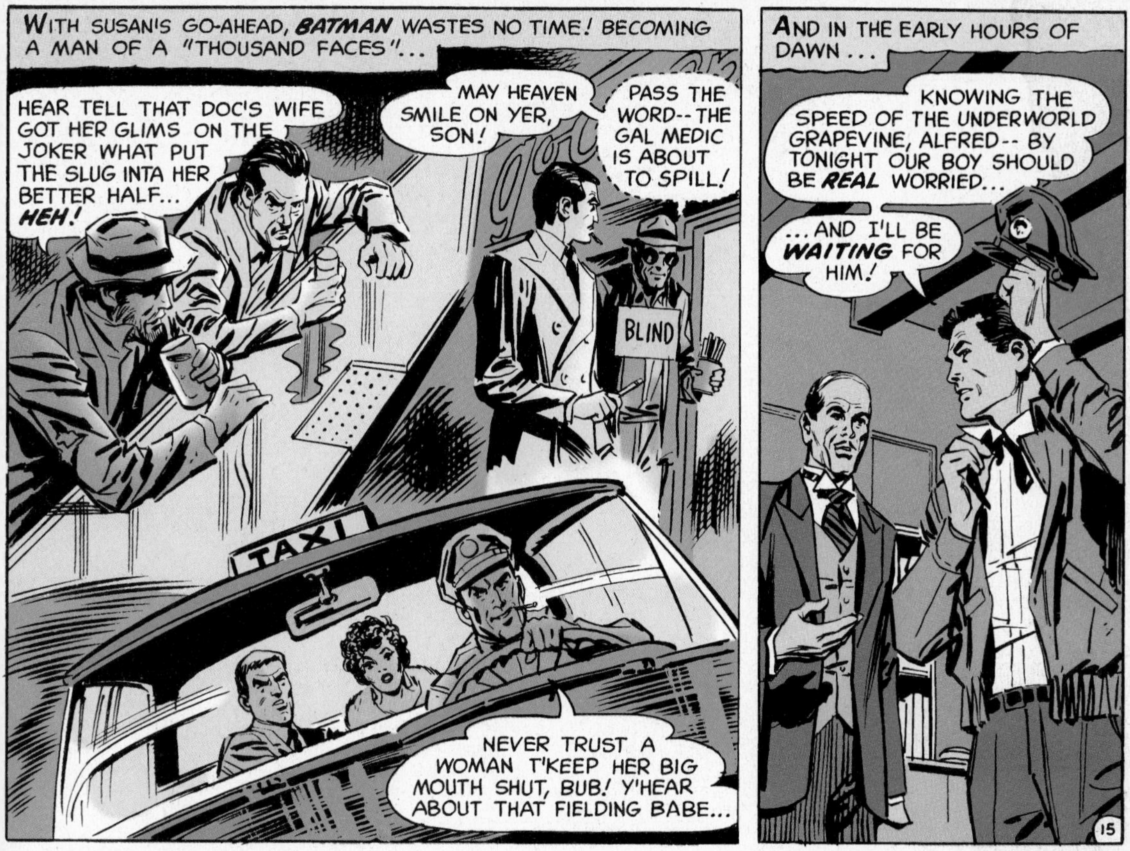
WITH SUSAN'S GO-AHEAD, BATMAN WASTES NO TIME! BECOMING A MAN OF A "THOUSAND FACES"...
HEAR TELL THAT DOC'S WIFE GOT HER GLIMS ON THE JOKER WHAT PUT THE SLUG INTA HER BETTER HALF... HEH!
MAY HEAVEN SMILE ON YER, SON!
PASS THE WORD--THE GAL MEDIC IS ABOUT TO SPILL!
BLIND
TAXI
NEVER TRUST A WOMAN T'KEEP HER BIG MOUTH SHUT, BUB! Y'HEAR ABOUT THAT FIELDING BABE...
AND IN THE EARLY HOURS OF DAWN...
KNOWING THE SPEED OF THE UNDERWORLD GRAPEVINE, ALFRED-- BY TONIGHT OUR BOY SHOULD BE REAL WORRIED...
...AND I'LL BE WAITING FOR HIM!
15

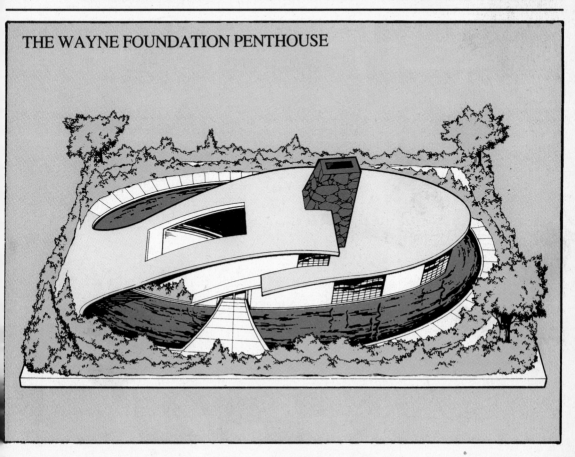

THE WAYNE FOUNDATION PENTHOUSE

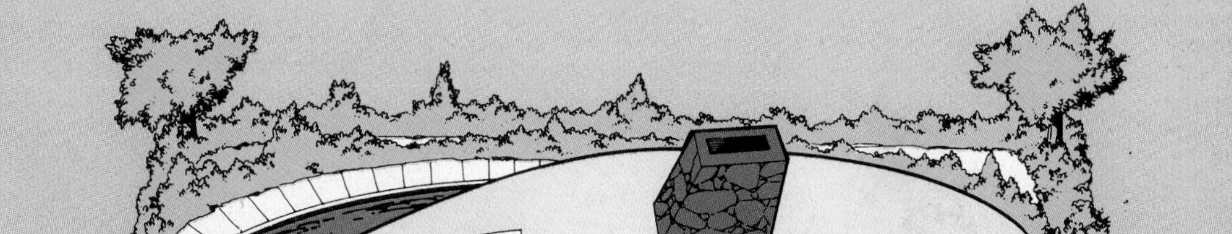

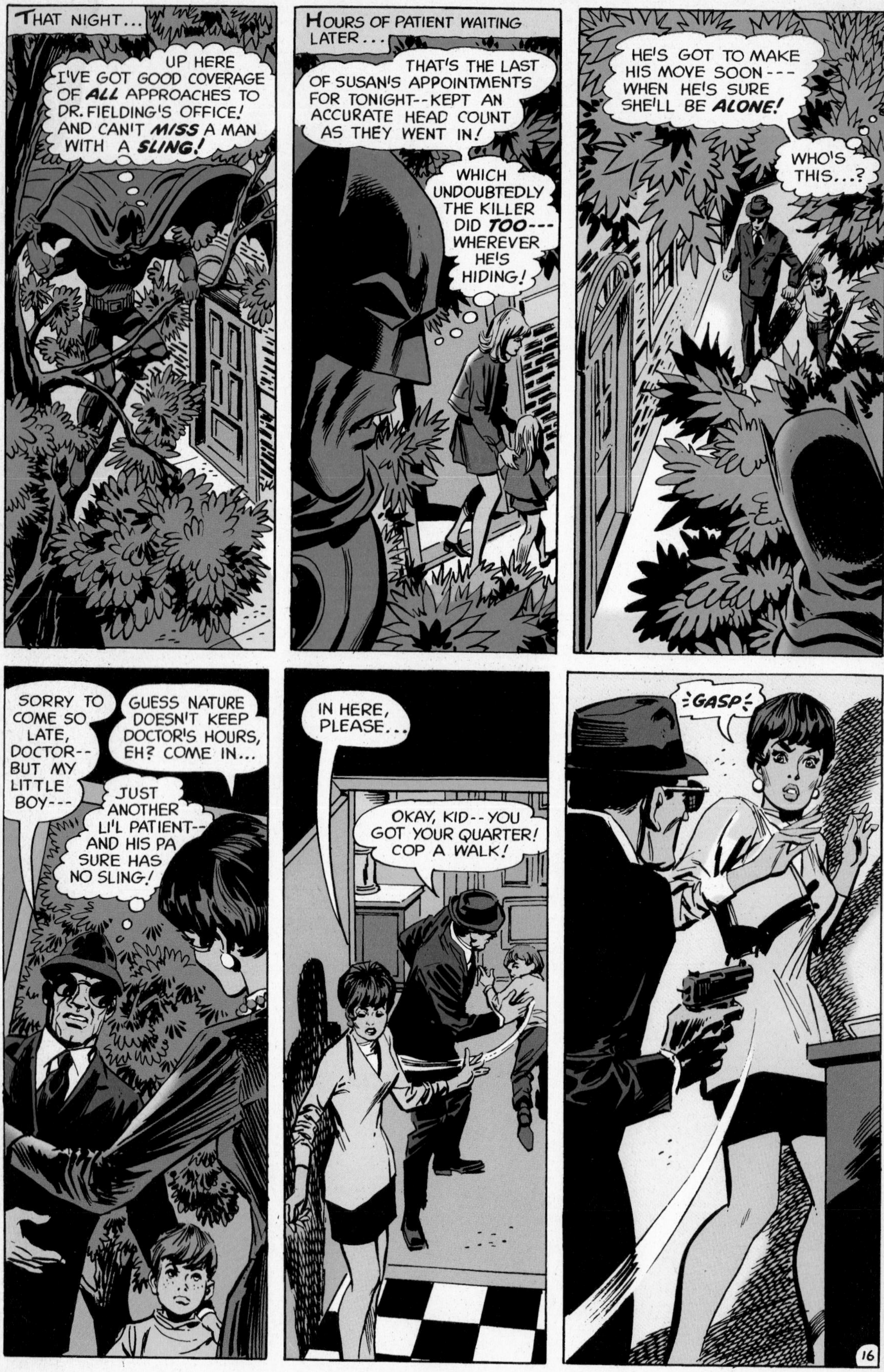
THAT NIGHT...
UP HERE I'VE GOT GOOD COVERAGE OF ALL APPROACHES TO DR. FIELDING'S OFFICE! AND CAN'T MISS A MAN WITH A SLING!
HOURS OF PATIENT WAITING LATER...
THAT'S THE LAST OF SUSAN'S APPOINTMENTS FOR TONIGHT--KEPT AN ACCURATE HEAD COUNT AS THEY WENT IN!
WHICH UNDOUBTEDLY THE KILLER DID TOO--- WHEREVER HE'S HIDING!
HE'S GOT TO MAKE HIS MOVE SOON--- WHEN HE'S SURE SHE'LL BE ALONE!
WHO'S THIS...?
SORRY TO COME SO LATE, DOCTOR-- BUT MY LITTLE BOY---
GUESS NATURE DOESN'T KEEP DOCTOR'S HOURS, EH? COME IN...
JUST ANOTHER LI'L PATIENT-- AND HIS PA SURE HAS NO SLING!
IN HERE, PLEASE...
OKAY, KID--YOU GOT YOUR QUARTER! COP A WALK!
GASP
16

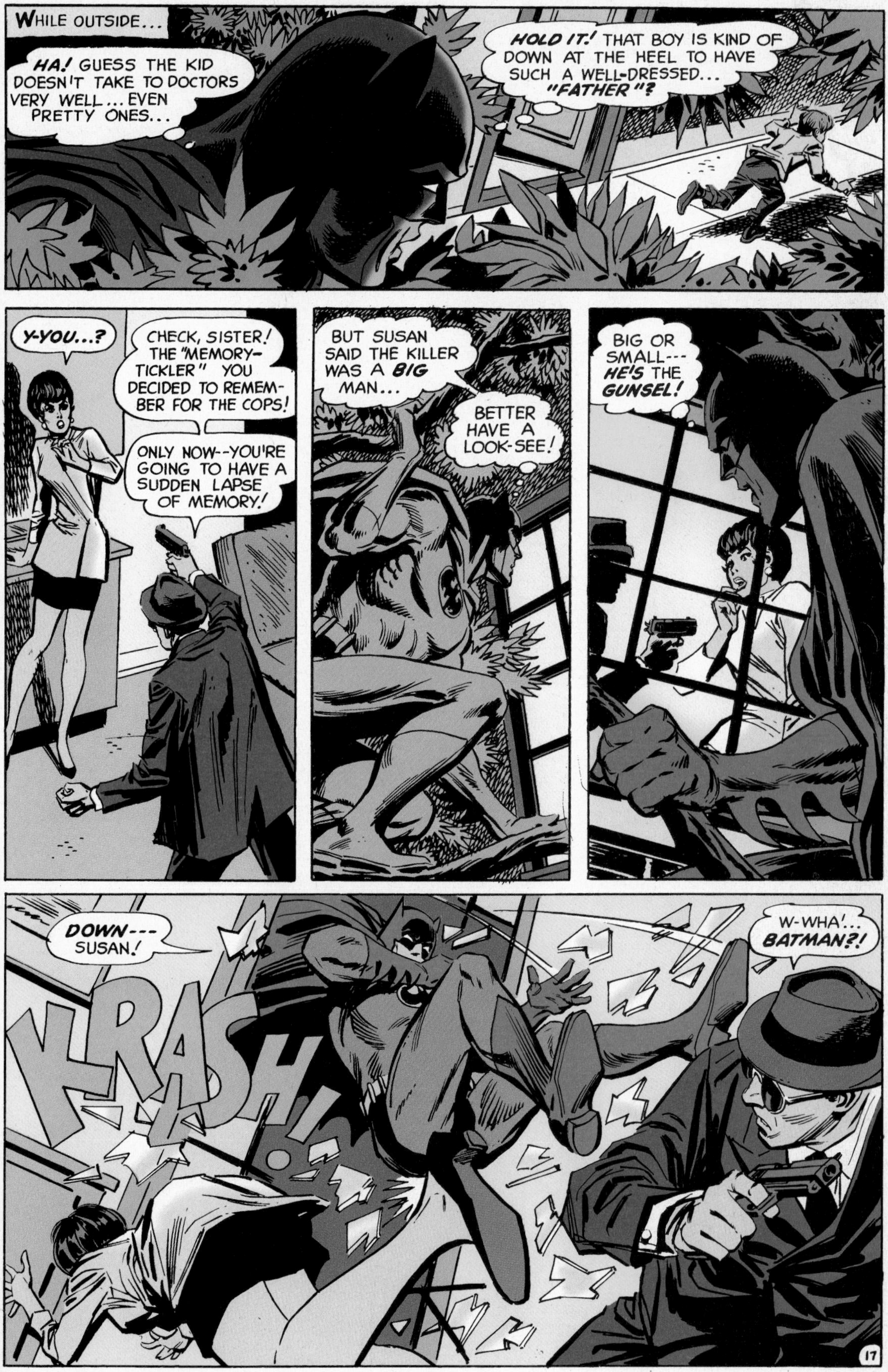
WHILE OUTSIDE...
HA! GUESS THE KID DOESN'T TAKE TO DOCTORS VERY WELL... EVEN PRETTY ONES...
HOLD IT! THAT BOY IS KIND OF DOWN AT THE HEEL TO HAVE SUCH A WELL-DRESSED... "FATHER"?
Y-YOU...?
CHECK, SISTER! THE "MEMORY-TICKLER" YOU DECIDED TO REMEMBER FOR THE COPS!
ONLY NOW--YOU'RE GOING TO HAVE A SUDDEN LAPSE OF MEMORY!
BUT SUSAN SAID THE KILLER WAS A BIG MAN...
BETTER HAVE A LOOK-SEE!
BIG OR SMALL--- HE'S THE GUNSEL!
DOWN--- SUSAN!
KRASH!
W-WHA!... BATMAN?!
17

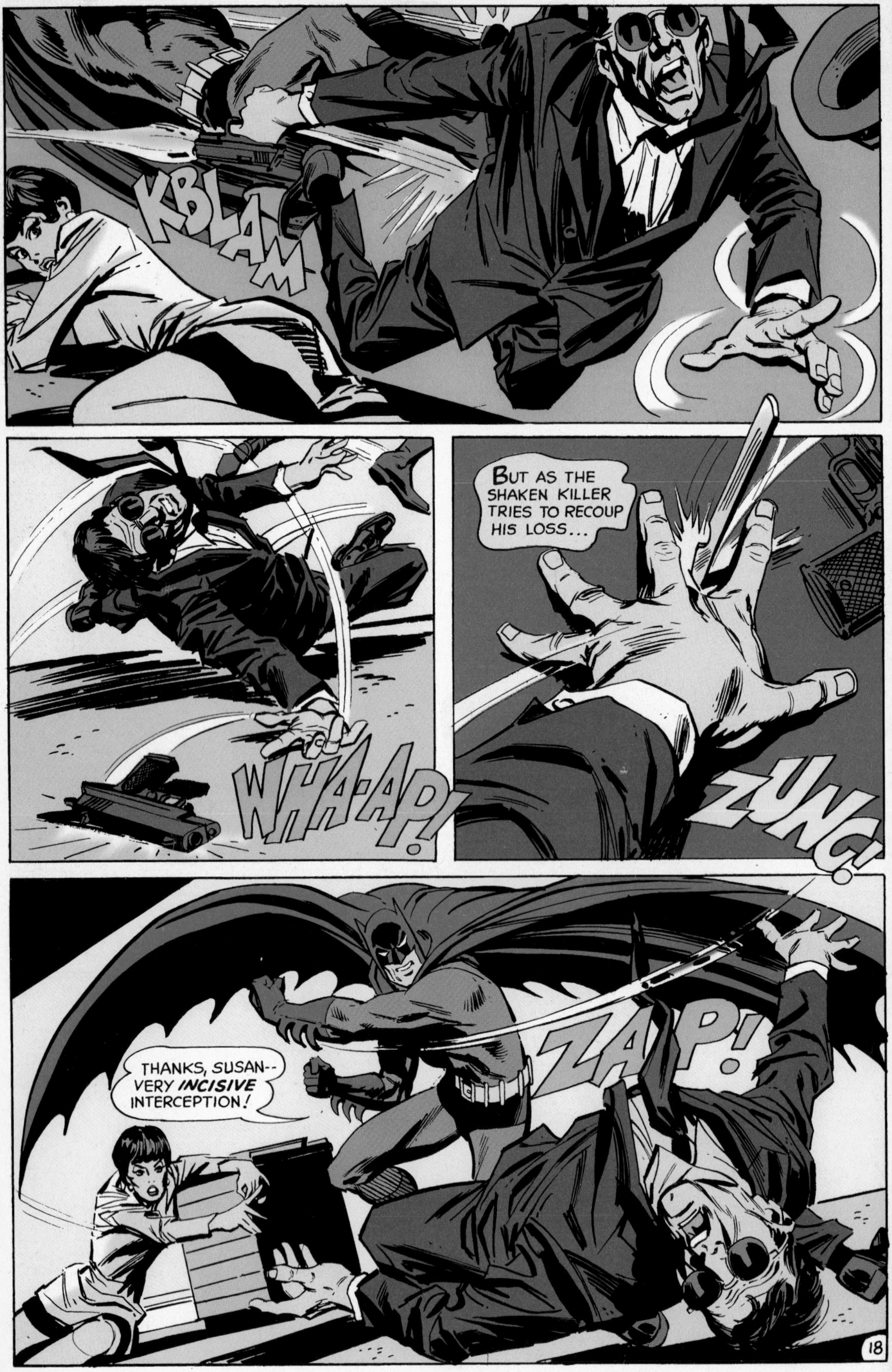
KBLAM
WHA-AP!
BUT AS THE SHAKEN KILLER TRIES TO RECOUP HIS LOSS...
ZUNG!
ZAP!
THANKS, SUSAN-- VERY *INCISIVE* INTERCEPTION!
18

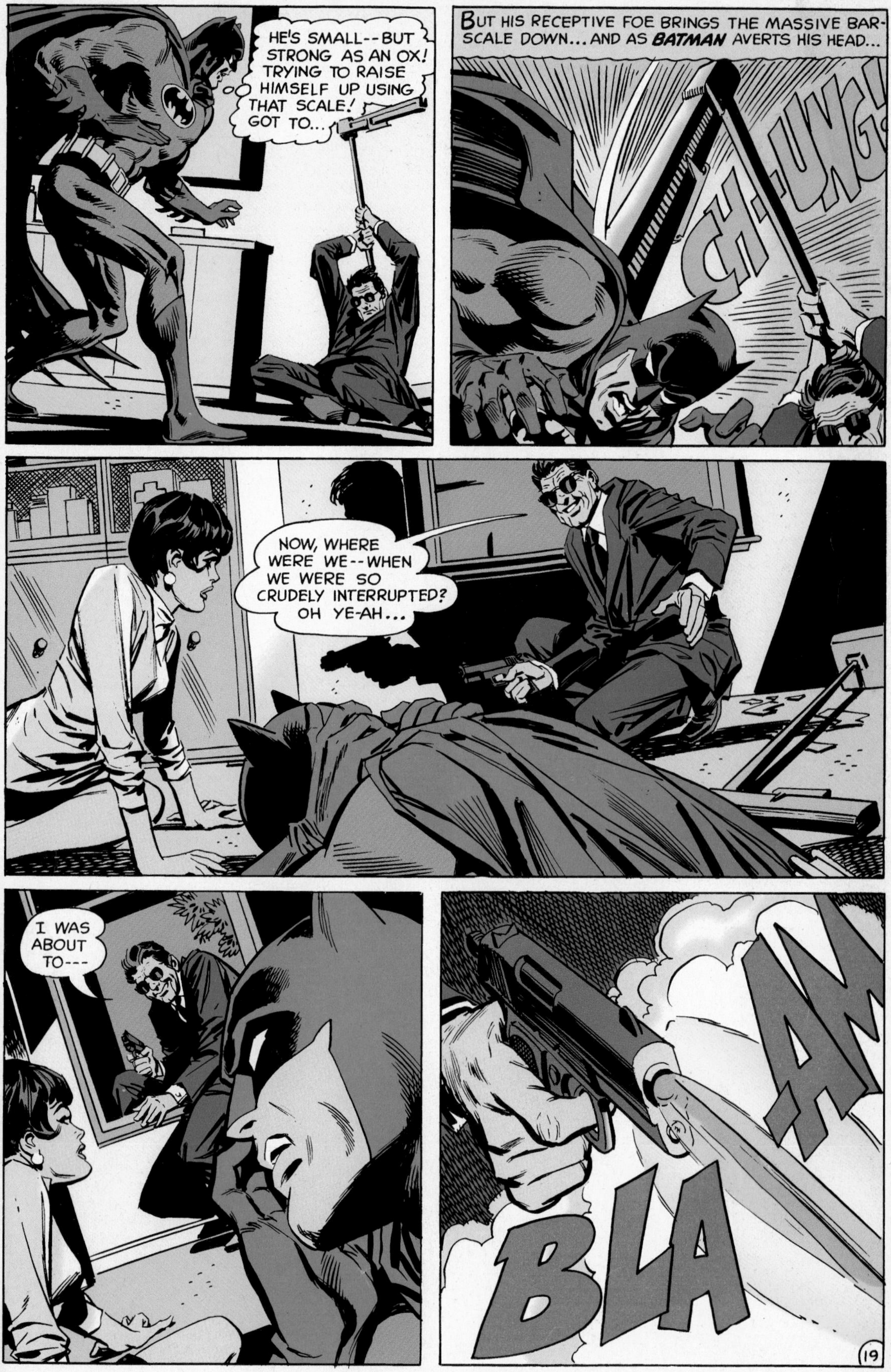
HE'S SMALL--BUT STRONG AS AN OX! TRYING TO RAISE HIMSELF UP USING THAT SCALE! GOT TO...
BUT HIS RECEPTIVE FOE BRINGS THE MASSIVE BAR-SCALE DOWN... AND AS BATMAN AVERTS HIS HEAD...
CH-LUNG!
NOW, WHERE WERE WE--WHEN WE WERE SO CRUDELY INTERRUPTED? OH YE-AH...
I WAS ABOUT TO---
BLAAM
19

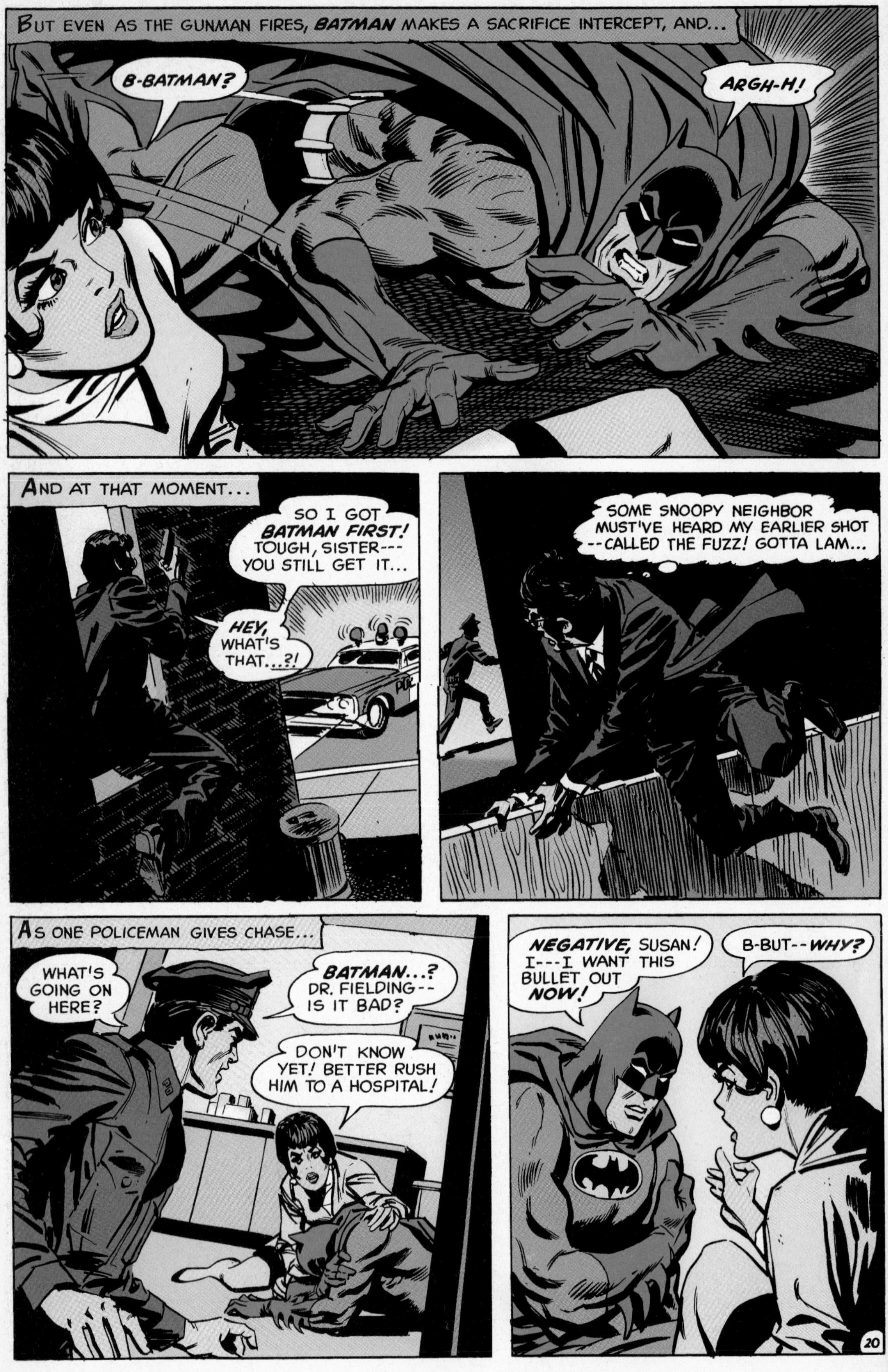

BUT EVEN AS THE GUNMAN FIRES, BATMAN MAKES A SACRIFICE INTERCEPT, AND...
B-BATMAN?
ARGH-H!
AND AT THAT MOMENT...
SO I GOT BATMAN FIRST! TOUGH, SISTER--- YOU STILL GET IT...
HEY, WHAT'S THAT...?!
SOME SNOOPY NEIGHBOR MUST'VE HEARD MY EARLIER SHOT --CALLED THE FUZZ! GOTTA LAM...
AS ONE POLICEMAN GIVES CHASE...
WHAT'S GOING ON HERE?
BATMAN...? DR. FIELDING-- IS IT BAD?
DON'T KNOW YET! BETTER RUSH HIM TO A HOSPITAL!
NEGATIVE, SUSAN! I---I WANT THIS BULLET OUT NOW!
B-BUT--WHY?
20

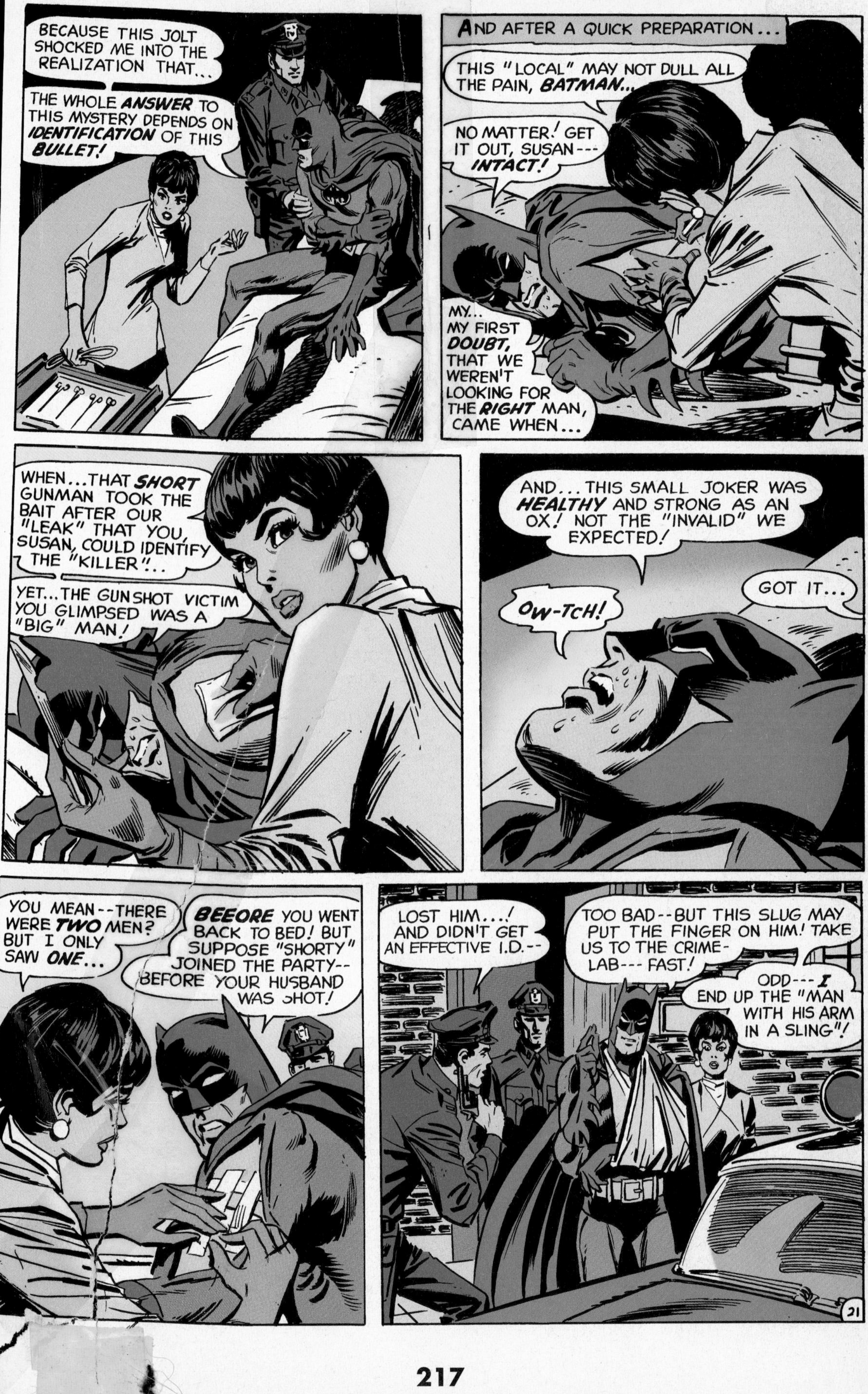
BECAUSE THIS JOLT SHOCKED ME INTO THE REALIZATION THAT...
THE WHOLE ANSWER TO THIS MYSTERY DEPENDS ON IDENTIFICATION OF THIS BULLET!
AND AFTER A QUICK PREPARATION...
THIS "LOCAL" MAY NOT DULL ALL THE PAIN, BATMAN...
NO MATTER! GET IT OUT, SUSAN--- INTACT!
MY... MY FIRST DOUBT, THAT WE WEREN'T LOOKING FOR THE RIGHT MAN, CAME WHEN...
WHEN...THAT SHORT GUNMAN TOOK THE BAIT AFTER OUR "LEAK" THAT YOU, SUSAN, COULD IDENTIFY THE "KILLER"...
YET...THE GUNSHOT VICTIM YOU GLIMPSED WAS A "BIG" MAN!
AND...THIS SMALL JOKER WAS HEALTHY AND STRONG AS AN OX! NOT THE "INVALID" WE EXPECTED!
GOT IT...
OW-TCH!
YOU MEAN--THERE WERE TWO MEN? BUT I ONLY SAW ONE...
BEEORE YOU WENT BACK TO BED! BUT SUPPOSE "SHORTY" JOINED THE PARTY-- BEFORE YOUR HUSBAND WAS SHOT!
LOST HIM....! AND DIDN'T GET AN EFFECTIVE I.D.--
TOO BAD--BUT THIS SLUG MAY PUT THE FINGER ON HIM! TAKE US TO THE CRIME-LAB--- FAST!
ODD--- I END UP THE "MAN WITH HIS ARM IN A SLING"!
21

LATER, AT POLICE H.Q....

YEP---THEY *MATCH!* THE ONE FROM YOUR ARM, *BATMAN*-- AND THE ONE WE TOOK FROM DR. FIELDING'S BODY!

ONE SLUG-- BUT SUSAN HEARD *TWO* SHOTS! NOW IT ALL FALLS INTO PLACE!

GIVE ME A COMPARISON-CHECK ON THE *THIRD* BULLET! THE ONE JONAH FIELDING EXTRACTED FROM HIS GUN-SHOT "VICTIM"!

BUT WHERE DOES *THAT* FIGURE IN? *CAN'T* BE THE SAME AS THESE TWO!

A GUY DOESN'T SHOOT *HIMSELF* ON PURPOSE BEFORE GOING TO A DOC..?

PRECISELY!

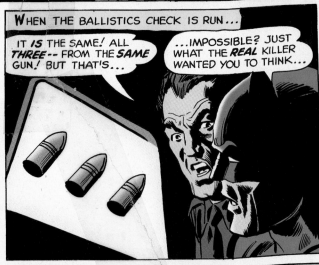

WHEN THE BALLISTICS CHECK IS RUN...

IT *IS* THE SAME! ALL *THREE*-- FROM THE *SAME* GUN! BUT THAT'S...

...IMPOSSIBLE? JUST WHAT THE *REAL* KILLER WANTED YOU TO THINK...

SO YOU'D ALL GO ON A WILD-GOOSE CHASE, HUNTING *ONE* MAN WITH HIS ARM IN A SLING! THE GUN SHOT *VICTIM*...

...WHO MAY BE AT THE *BOTTOM* OF THE *RIVER*, WHILE "SHORTY" ROAMS *FREE!*

SURE... SURE! "HOP" MILLER-- AND "STUB" SARTEL! AND BIG "HOP" HASN'T BEEN SEEN AROUND LATELY!

THE WAY I SEE IT-- *TWO* THUGS HAD A FALLING OUT! "SHORTY" SHOOTS HIS PARTNER-- BUT NOT GOOD ENOUGH-- HE GETS AWAY! "SHORTY" FOLLOWS-- CATCHES HIM IN THE DOC'S OFFICE...

...AND BLASTS THEM *BOTH!* CARRIES OFF HIS EX-BUDDY-- AND DISPOSES OF HIM!

NOW WHAT "TEAM" FITS THAT VAGUE DESCRIPTION?

SO-- DRAG THE RIVER-- AND GET OUT AN ALL-POINTS ALERT FOR "STUB"! AND YOU'VE CLOSED THE CASE OF... "ONE BULLET TOO MANY"!

22

218

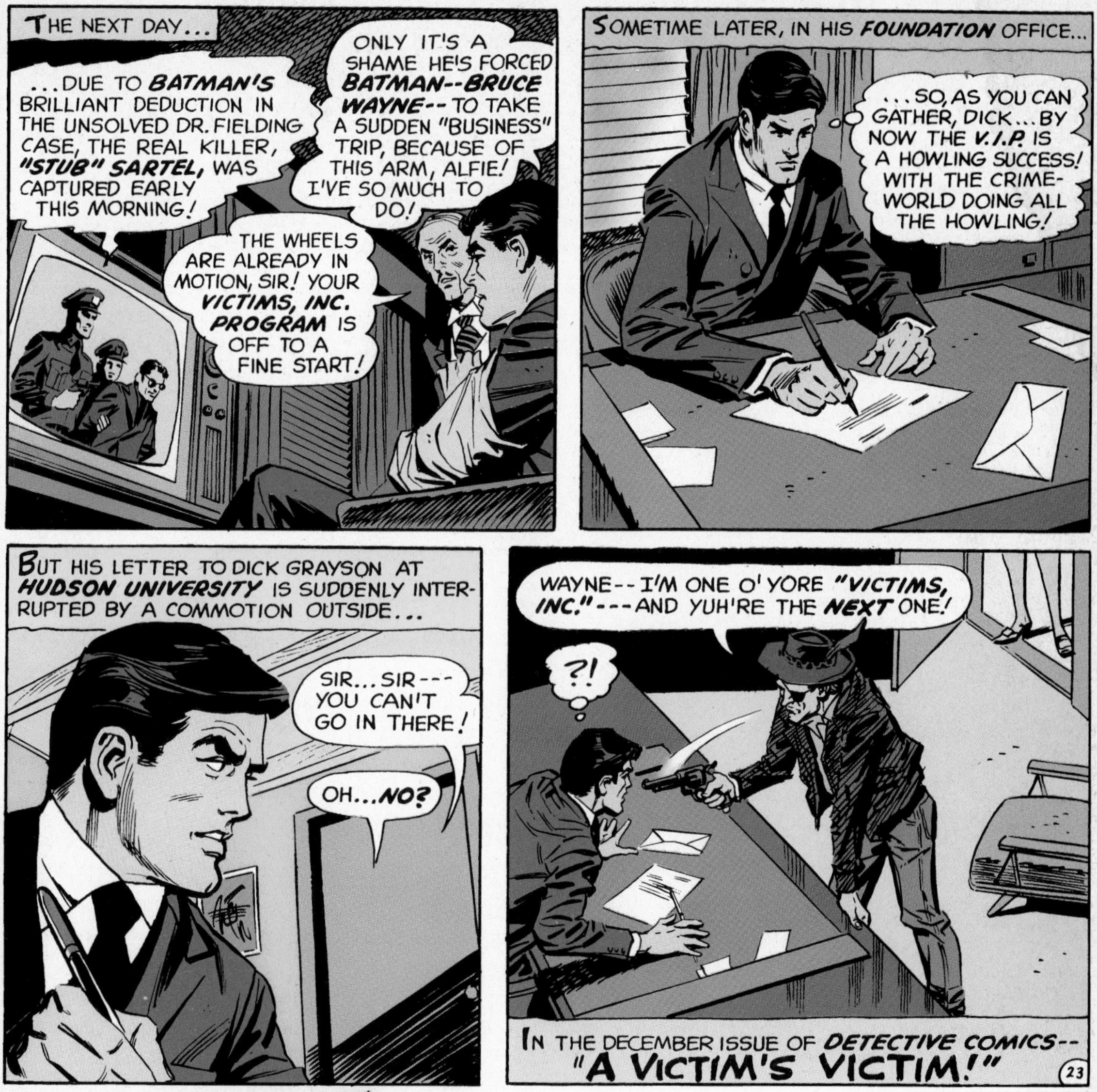
THE NEXT DAY...
...DUE TO BATMAN'S BRILLIANT DEDUCTION IN THE UNSOLVED DR. FIELDING CASE, THE REAL KILLER, "STUB" SARTEL, WAS CAPTURED EARLY THIS MORNING!
ONLY IT'S A SHAME HE'S FORCED BATMAN--BRUCE WAYNE--TO TAKE A SUDDEN "BUSINESS" TRIP, BECAUSE OF THIS ARM, ALFIE! I'VE SO MUCH TO DO!
THE WHEELS ARE ALREADY IN MOTION, SIR! YOUR VICTIMS, INC. PROGRAM IS OFF TO A FINE START!
SOMETIME LATER, IN HIS FOUNDATION OFFICE...
...SO, AS YOU CAN GATHER, DICK...BY NOW THE V.I.P. IS A HOWLING SUCCESS! WITH THE CRIME-WORLD DOING ALL THE HOWLING!
BUT HIS LETTER TO DICK GRAYSON AT HUDSON UNIVERSITY IS SUDDENLY INTERRUPTED BY A COMMOTION OUTSIDE...
SIR... SIR--- YOU CAN'T GO IN THERE!
OH...NO?
WAYNE--I'M ONE O' YORE "VICTIMS, INC."---AND YUH'RE THE NEXT ONE!
?!
IN THE DECEMBER ISSUE OF DETECTIVE COMICS--
"A VICTIM'S VICTIM!"
23

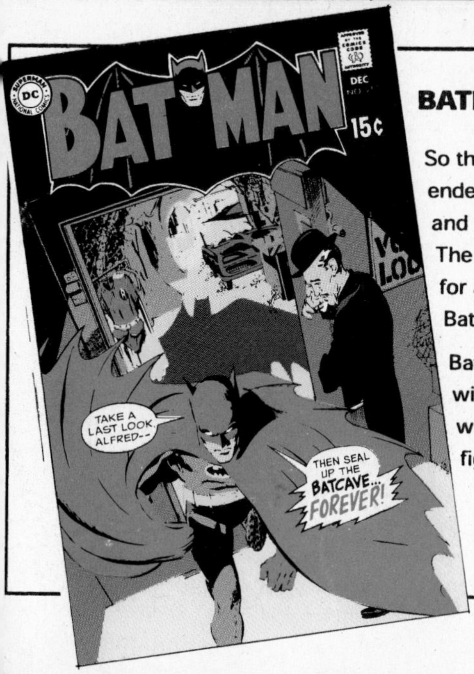
BATMAN
DEC
15¢
TAKE A LAST LOOK, ALFRED--
THEN SEAL UP THE BATCAVE... FOREVER!

BATMAN GOES SOLO

So the decade that had already shown much change for Batman ended with the most radical changes of all. Batman, Robin and Batgirl, who had acted as a team, were now solo acts. The vehicles, gadgets and Batcave were gone. The villains, for a while, were less spectacular, more common gangsters. Batman was back on the streets an equalizer for the underdog.

Batman was now on an avenging path that remains consistent with the one he is set upon to this day. The young man who witnessed his parents' murder once more became the shadowy figure of the night.

CONTRIBUTORS

MURPHY ANDERSON

Murphy Anderson entered comics in 1944 drawing features for Fiction House and, after a tour with the Navy, worked for a variety of publishers. In 1947, he took over drawing the *Buck Rogers* syndicated newspaper strip. Anderson began his long association with DC in 1950, drawing countless super-hero and science-fiction features, including *Captain Comet*, *The Atomic Knights*, *Hawkman*, and *The Spectre*. In addition to pencilling, Anderson was one of comics' best and most versatile inkers, with numerous credits on such strips as *Adam Strange*, *The Atom*, *Superman*, and, of course, *Batman*. His most famous collaborations were with pencillers Carmine Infantino and Gil Kane. Anderson has also produced instructional comic books for the U.S. Army and headed a publisher's support service company that provided color separations and typesetting for the comics industry.

E. NELSON BRIDWELL

E. Nelson Bridwell went from being one of comics' earliest fans in the 1950s to a position as assistant to editor Mort Weisinger in 1965. Renowned for his encyclopedic knowledge of comics history, Bridwell was soon serving as DC's unofficial "continuity cop" during an era when editors and writers were only just beginning to tie together DC's more than quarter century of history. In addition to his editorial duties, Bridwell was also a prolific writer whose credits included a run on the *Batman* syndicated newspaper strip, SHAZAM!, THE INFERIOR FIVE, THE SECRET SIX, SUPER FRIENDS, and many stories for the *Superman* and *Batman* families of titles. Bridwell continued writing and editing for DC until his death in 1987.

JOHN BROOME

In addition to his work on *Batman*, John Broome scripted the majority of the Silver Age *Flash* stories, beginning with the second tale in SHOWCASE #4, the character's first appearance, and continuing on the title until 1970. Prior to *Flash*, Broome had accumulated a lively résumé of comic-book credits, including *Captain Marvel* and the rest of the Marvel Family, the Golden Age *Green Lantern*, *The Justice Society of America*, *Captain Comet*, the Silver Age revival of *Green Lantern*, the *Atomic Knights*, *Star Hawkins*, *Rex the Wonder Dog*, *Detective Chimp*, and a variety of science-fiction tales. Broome retired from comics in the 1970s and currently teaches English in Japan.

BILL FINGER

Bill Finger was one of the true innovative talents and legendary figures of the comics industry. He collaborated with Bob Kane on the development of *Batman* and scripted the first two episodes of the Dark Knight's appearances in DETECTIVE COMICS. Finger went on to write features for many publishers, including *Plastic Man* (for Quality Comics), *Green Lantern*, *Wildcat*, *Vigilante*, *Johnny Quick*, *Superman*, *Superboy*, *Blackhawk*, *Tomahawk*, *Robin*, *Challengers of the Unknown*, *Batman* (in the comics and in the syndicated newspaper strip), as well as *Captain America* and *All Winners Comics* (for Timely). Finger also wrote for radio and television, contributing scripts to "Mark Trail," "77 Sunset Strip," "The Roaring Twenties," "Hawaiian Eye," and, naturally enough, two episodes of the "Batman" TV program in 1966. He also wrote television commercials and one feature film, the 1969 cult film *The Green Slime*. Bill Finger was still writing for DC Comics at the time of his death in 1974.

GARDNER FOX

As much as any writer, Gardner Fox helped create the tone and feel of the *Batman* stories of the 1960s. Fox was an attorney who began his prolific and innovative second career as a writer in the late 1930s on *Batman* and went on to create such Golden Age classics as the original *Flash*, *Hawkman*, *Starman*, *Doctor Fate*, and *The Justice Society of America*. His influence extended throughout the 1950s and 1960s when, until his retirement from DC Comics in 1968, he created and/or wrote such memorable features as *The Justice League of America*, *Adam Strange*, *The Atom*, *Hawkman*, and, of course, *Batman*, all under the auspices of legendary comics editor Julius Schwartz. Until his death in 1986, Gardner Fox continued writing comics and novels. He published over 100 books in numerous genres, some under the pseudonyms of Jefferson Cooper and Bart Sommers, as well as many fantasy novels under his own name.

MIKE FRIEDRICH

Writer Mike Friedrich was one of the first wave of new comic book creators to enter the field in the 1960s. He scripted numerous features for such companies as DC and Marvel and, in the 1970s, helped launch the self-publishing comics industry with his "ground level" black and white comic, STAR*REACH, which featured the talents of many of the most influential young creators of the day. In later years, Friedrich turned his talents from the creative end of comics and became one of the first agents in the field. Today, his Star*Reach agency represents a long roster of talent, both established and upcoming.

JOE GIELLA

Inker Joe Giella began his career in the 1940s as an inker for Hillman Publications and Timely Comics, the company that was to become Marvel years later. Giella first worked for DC Comics in 1951 and, in the 1960s, his style of embellishment became associated with some of the company's greatest heroes, including Batman (over the work of penciller Sheldon Moldoff), The Flash (with artist Carmine Infantino), and The Atom (with penciller Gil Kane). Giella, who also pencilled and inked a run of the *Batman* syndicated newspaper strip during the 1960s, retired from comics in the early 1980s.

DICK GIORDANO

Dick Giordano was part of the creative team that, more than any other, helped change the face of comic books in the late 1960s and early 1970s. Along with writer Dennis O'Neil and penciller Neal Adams,

Dick helped bring Batman back to his roots as a dark, brooding "creature of the night," and brought relevance to comics in the pages of GREEN LANTERN/GREEN ARROW. Giordano began his career as an artist for Charlton Comics in 1952 and became the company's editor-in-chief in 1965. In that capacity, he revamped their line by adding an emphasis on such "Action Heroes" as The Question, Captain Atom, and The Blue Beetle. In 1967, Dick came over to DC for a three-year stint as editor, bringing with him many of the talents who would help shape the industry of the day, including Dennis O'Neil, Jim Aparo, and Steve Skeates. Winner of numerous industry awards, Giordano later returned to DC, rising to the position of Vice President-Executive Editor before "retiring" in 1993 to once again pursue a full-time career as penciller and inker.

SID GREENE

Artist Sid Greene got his start in comics in 1941 and was soon drawing features for such publishing houses as Timely and Novelty. Greene came to DC in 1955, where he did the bulk of his work throughout the 1960s and 1970s, pencilling and/or inking a wide variety of genre stories and such features as *Star Rovers*, *Johnny Peril*, *The Atom*, *Elongated Man*, *Hawkman*, *The Justice League of America*, *The Flash*, *Hourman*, and, of course, *Batman*. His credits for Marvel Comics from the late 1970s include KA-ZAR and S.H.I.E.L.D.

CARMINE INFANTINO

The man most closely associated with the "New Look" Batman, Carmine Infantino began working in comics in the mid-1940s as the artist on such features as *Green Lantern*, *Black Canary*, *Ghost Patrol*, and the Golden Age *Flash*. Infantino's unique style continued to grace a variety of superhero, supernatural, and Western features throughout the 1950s until he was tapped to pencil the 1956 revival of *The Flash*. He also provided the art for other strips, including *Elongated Man* and *Adam Strange*. Infantino became DC's editorial director in 1967 and, later, publisher before returning to freelancing in 1976. Since that time he has pencilled and inked numerous features, including the *Batman* newspaper strip, *Green Lantern Corps*, and *Danger Trail*.

GIL KANE

Gil Kane is recognized as one of the most influential artists in comic books, with a string of credits at DC, Marvel and other companies that includes *Batman*, *Superman*, *Green Lantern*, *The Atom*, *The Flash*, WARLOCK, CONAN, T.H.U.N.D.E.R. AGENTS and many others. In the late 1950s and early 1960s, he was the artist tapped to relaunch both *Green Lantern* and *The Atom*, and, during the '60s, he was responsible for the first mass-market comic books, including the magazine HIS NAME IS SAVAGE and the illustrated paperback novel *Blackmark*. His work continues to appear to this day in THE LIFE STORY OF THE FLASH and numerous other DC projects. The *Batgirl* stories reprinted in this volume represent some of his most memorable work on the Batman of the 1960s.

ROBERT KANIGHER

Robert Kanigher has long been recognized as one of the most prolific and innovative writers and editors in the comic-book field. Since the 1940s, Kanigher has written and/or created more characters than nearly anyone, including Batman, Black Canary, Captain Marvel, Flash, Sgt. Rock, The Haunted Tank, Wonder Woman, Lois Lane, and innumerable war, horror, and romance scripts. Kanigher scripted Flash's origin story in SHOWCASE #4, contributing several more tales to subsequent SHOWCASE appearances, before finally returning to the character for an extended run as regular writer on THE FLASH in 1970.

SHELDON MOLDOFF

Sheldon Moldoff, who began his career at DC Comics in 1938, came to prominence in comics in the early 1940s with his work on the *Hawkman* feature in FLASH COMICS under the signature "Shelly." Moldoff's early style, reminiscent of the work of Alex Raymond and Hal Foster, was distinctive in its own right, earning him work on a variety of adventure and humor features for DC and other publishers throughout the 1940s and 1950s. In 1943, Moldoff began what was to be a 25-year association with the *Batman* feature in both BATMAN and DETECTIVE COMICS, and his style as both penciller and inker was so dominant he served to define the look and style of the *Batman* feature for the duration of his run. Moldoff left comics in the late 1960s to work on animation storyboards for such cartoon series as *Courageous Cat & Minute Mouse* and *Cool McCool*.

IRV NOVICK

Irv Novick began his comic-book career at the dawn of the Golden Age, and among his earliest work was the first appearance of *The Shield* in 1940 for MLJ Magazines, later Archie Comics. Novick was also the artist on *Steel Sterling* and other features for MLJ and numerous other publishers. He later came to work for DC Comics, working on stories for the war anthologies and features, including *Captain Storm*, and, later, on super-hero titles. During the 1960s, Novick's work was featured in BATMAN and DETECTIVE COMICS. He was later to have a long run as penciller on THE FLASH.

CHARLES PARIS

Inker Charles Paris began his career inking Mort Meskin on the *Johnny Quick* and *Vigilante* features for DC in the 1940s, but he is best known for his work on *Batman*, a feature he inked from 1947 through 1964 over such pencillers as Jack Burnley, Fred Ray, Sheldon Moldoff, and Dick Sprang. After *Batman* (including many of the *Batman* Sunday newspaper strips of the 1940s), Paris went on to ink other DC features, including *Metamorpho*, many issues of THE BRAVE AND THE BOLD, including the first appearance of the Teen Titans. Paris retired from comics in 1968 to travel and paint.

FRANK ROBBINS

Frank Robbins was an internationally recognized comics creator who began his career in 1939 on the *Scorchy Smith* comic strip. In 1944, he created the long-running syndicated newspaper strip *Johnny Hazzard*. Robbins came to comic books in 1968, doing the bulk of his work for DC as a writer, contributing hundreds of stories to such titles as BATMAN, SUPERBOY, THE SHADOW, and THE UNKNOWN SOLDIER. In addition to writing, he also drew many *Batman* and *Unknown Soldier* stories. Robbins has also contributed illustrations to such publications as *Life*, *Look*, and

The Saturday Evening Post and had paintings exhibited at many museums, including the Whitney and the Metropolitan.

DICK SPRANG

Dick Sprang was one of the first artists hired by DC to draw Batman in the early 1940s when the demand for stories outstripped the ability of Dark Knight creator Bob Kane's studio to produce material. Sprang's dynamic, energetic style was unique among all the Batman "ghost" artists, and his 25-year run on the *Batman* titles (with regular forays into the pages of WORLD'S FINEST COMICS) helped define the look of the character throughout the 1950s. Sprang retired from comics freelancing in 1961 and currently lives in Arizona where, in between creating giant-sized, full-color, painted reproductions of his famous *Batman* covers from the 1940s and 1950s, he contributes the occasional illustration or cover to DC.

CHIC STONE

Inker Chic Stone's credits date back to the 1950s and the American Comics Group. His work gained recognition in the pages of the Marvel comics of the early 1960s when it appeared over such pencillers as Jack Kirby and Don Heck. Stone was also an accomplished penciller, his work appearing in issues of many Marvel comics, as well as at DC on *Batman*.

THE QUEST FOR JUSTICE CONTINUES IN THESE BOOKS FROM DC:

FOR READERS OF ALL AGES

THE BATMAN ADVENTURES
Puckett/Pasko/Templeton/
Rader/Burchett

BATMAN:
THE DARK KNIGHT ADVENTURES
Kelley Puckett/Mike Parobeck/
Rick Burchett

GRAPHIC NOVELS

BATMAN:
ARKHAM ASYLUM
Suggested for mature readers
Grant Morrison/Dave McKean

BATMAN:
THE KILLING JOKE
Suggested for mature readers
Alan Moore/Brian Bolland/John Higgins

COLLECTIONS

THE KNIGHTFALL Trilogy

BATMAN: KNIGHTFALL Part 1:
Broken Bat
Various writers and artists

BATMAN: KNIGHTFALL Part 2:
Who Rules the Night
Various writers and artists

BATMAN: KNIGHTSEND
Various writers and artists

BATMAN: YEAR ONE
Frank Miller/David Mazzucchelli

BATMAN:
A DEATH IN THE FAMILY
Jim Starlin/Jim Aparo/Mike DeCarlo

BATMAN:
A LONELY PLACE OF DYING
Marv Wolfman/George Pérez/various

BATMAN BLACK AND WHITE
Various writers and artists

BATMAN:
COLLECTED LEGENDS OF THE DARK KNIGHT
Robinson/Moore/Grant/Sale/Russell/O'Neil

BATMAN: CONTAGION
Various writers and artists

BATMAN:
THE DARK KNIGHT RETURNS
10TH ANNIVERSARY EDITION
Frank Miller/Lynn Varley/Klaus Janson

BATMAN:
DARK LEGENDS
Various writers and artists

BATMAN: FACES
Matt Wagner

BATMAN:
FEATURING TWO-FACE AND THE RIDDLER
Various writers and artists

BATMAN:
FOUR OF A KIND
Various writers and artists

BATMAN: GOTHIC
Grant Morrison/Klaus Janson

BATMAN:
HAUNTED KNIGHT
Jeph Loeb/Tim Sale

BATMAN:
THE LAST ARKHAM
Alan Grant/Norm Breyfogle

BATMAN: LEGACY
Various writers and artists

BATMAN: MAN-BAT
Jaime Delano/John Bolton

BATMAN: OTHER REALMS
Mark Kneece/Bo Hampton/Scott Hampton

BATMAN: PRODIGAL
Various writers and artists

BATMAN:
SWORD OF AZRAEL
Dennis O'Neil/Joe Quesada/Kevin Nowlan

BATMAN:
TALES OF THE DEMON
Dennis O'Neil/Neal Adams/various

BATMAN:
THE MOVIES
Dennis O'Neil/various artists

BATMAN:
THRILLKILLER
Howard Chaykin/Dan Brereton

BATMAN: VENOM
Dennis O'Neil/Trevor Von Eeden/various

BATMAN VS. PREDATOR:
THE COLLECTED EDITION
Dave Gibbons/Andy Kubert/Adam Kubert

BATMAN VS. PREDATOR II:
BLOODMATCH
Doug Moench/Paul Gulacy/Terry Austin

BATMAN VS. PREDATOR III:
BLOOD TIES
Chuck Dixon/Rodolfo Damaggio/
Robert Campanella

THE GREATEST BATMAN STORIES
EVER TOLD Vol. 1
Various writers and artists

THE GREATEST JOKER STORIES
EVER TOLD
Various writers and artists

CATWOMAN:
THE CATFILE
Chuck Dixon/Jim Balent/Bob Smith

NIGHTWING:
TIES THAT BIND
Dennis O'Neil/Alan Grant/various artists

NIGHTWING:
A KNIGHT IN BLÜDHAVEN
Chuck Dixon/Scott McDaniel/Karl Story

ROBIN:
A HERO REBORN
Chuck Dixon/Tom Lyle/Bob Smith

ARCHIVE EDITIONS

BATMAN ARCHIVES Vol. 1
(Batman's adventures from
DETECTIVE COMICS 27-50)
Bob Kane/Bill Finger/various

BATMAN ARCHIVES Vol. 2
(Batman's adventures from
DETECTIVE COMICS 51-70)
Bob Kane/Bill Finger/various

BATMAN ARCHIVES Vol. 3
(Batman's adventures from
DETECTIVE COMICS 71-86)
Bob Kane/Bill Finger/various

BATMAN ARCHIVES Vol. 4
(Batman's adventures from
DETECTIVE COMICS 87-102)
Bob Kane/Bill Finger/Dick Sprang/
Various

BATMAN:
THE DARK KNIGHT ARCHIVES Vol. 2
(BATMAN 5-8)
Bob Kane/Bill Finger/various

For the nearest comics shop carry-

ing collected editions and monthly

titles from DC Comics,

call 1-888-COMIC BOOK.

BM9811